Google Analytics
Breakthrough

Google Analytics Breakthrough

From Zero to Business Impact

Feras Alhlou,
Shiraz Asif, and Eric Fettman

WILEY

Published by John Wiley & Sons, Inc., Hoboken, New Jersey.
Published simultaneously in Canada.

For general information on our other products and services or for technical support, please contact our
Customer Care Department within the United States at (800) 762-2974, outside the United States at (317)
572-3993 or fax (317) 572-4002.

Wiley publishes in a variety of print and electronic formats and by print-on-demand. Some material
included with standard print versions of this book may not be included in e-books or in print-on-demand.
If this book refers to media such as a CD or DVD that is not included in the version you purchased, you may
download this material at http://booksupport.wiley.com. For more information about Wiley products, visit
www.wiley.com.

ISBN 9781119144014 (Hardcover)
ISBN 9781119231707 (ePDF)
ISBN 9781119231691 (ePub)

Printed in the United States of America

10 9 8 7 6 5 4 3 2 1

In Memory of Shiraz Asif

When we embarked on *Google Analytics Breakthrough,* we could never have imagined that Shiraz would no longer be with us for the book's publication. He became ill with the flu and later pneumonia in February 2016, and after battling for several weeks in the ICU, he passed away on the morning of Friday, March 18th. Shiraz is survived by his parents, siblings, in-laws, loving wife and four young children.

Those who knew Shiraz personally and professionally understand that he was among the hardest-working colleagues, most generous mentors, and most thoughtful friends. He was always a catalyst for development and change, and his thirst for knowledge benefitted everyone around him.

Shiraz, we miss you and will always remember you. May your honorable character, kindheartedness, and open spirit inspire us all to embrace each day in gratitude for the gift of life.

Feras Alhlou, Eric Fettman, and the entire E-Nor family

Contents

Foreword

I t seems a little crazy that I'm about to recommend that you pay serious attention to data and the power of analytics by buying this book. Simply because what has been hyped more over the last decade than data? Nothing.

We had the promise of being able to collect all the data about everyone. Web servers were practically switched on with data spewing out. Then we went into the hype cycle of data warehouses and then analytics tools and then the Earth was hypnotized by the mesmerizing power of Big Data. Nothing was safe; everything was going to be cured!

And yet precious little has changed.

It is ironic that we live in the most data-rich environment in mankind's evolution, yet we are barely any smarter than we were when none of this existed 20 years ago.

So what's the problem? And why hype this book?

A part of it is a generational divide in how executives made decisions (experience first, data second—ideally optional). This is changing with time (sadly, the Earth moves, we all get old, we retire, move to a golden retirement home in Florida!).

A part of it was our initial approach of taking all the data we could get our hands on and then puking it like crazy (as if the shower of reports and metrics by themselves could make people smarter). Having failed at changing anything beyond local maxima, I feel that people are ready to stop all the data puking.

A part of it was a lack of a holistic understanding of what's possible, and the ability to create a winning strategy where the objective was not to nuclear bomb the world into changing overnight, but rather have a step-by-step approach customized to your amazing and unique business.

These last two reasons are why I'm so excited about Feras, Shiraz, and Eric's book. They take a soup-to-nuts approach to helping you understand the entire landscape of possibilities (from implementation to data collection to data processing to data analysis to deliver insights). They hold your hand and lead you step-by-baby-step in helping you understand each amazing element of a successful analytics strategy (covering tag management, audience segmentation, dashboards, and experimentation). In each chapter there is a simple way to figure out exactly where you are today, and then create the next few steps required to go from good to great.

There is almost nothing that's missing from the book that you'll need to create an effective analytics and optimization strategy that drives online and offline business profit. The only ingredient that you'll have to bring, is a deeper understanding of your business strategy (be BFFs with your boss's boss's boss) and a hunger to get better every day.

Data awaits. Carpe diem!

Avinash Kaushik

Author: *Web Analytics 2.0, Web Analytics: An Hour a Day*

Digital Marketing Evangelist: Google

Acknowledgments

The journey of writing *Google Analytics Breakthrough* started long before we signed the agreement with the publisher. The idea had been brewing in our minds for years.

For more than 12 years in our analytics consulting work at E-Nor, we've had the good fortune of working with some incredibly smart people—marketers, analysts, and executives from some of the most recognized brands in the world. It's very fulfilling when, during our discussions, we see that spark in their eyes when they "get" analytics and have the "aha!" moment. To "get" analytics involves asking great, sometimes difficult questions and then challenging yourself to find the answers. We are sincerely grateful to our clients and training participants for encouraging, nudging, and requiring us (sometimes in that order!) to push the envelope—both for the Google Analytics product and for ourselves—to positively impact their organizations.

We also owe a debt of gratitude to industry veterans and "founders" who helped foster a family atmosphere and shape a cooperative and collaborative analytics community. We especially want to recognize Avinash Kaushik for evangelizing analytics to the non-converted, Jim Sterne for being the one and only analytics godfather, Eric Peterson for writing one of the very first books on demystifying analytics, and Brian Clifton, whose books provided much of the technical foundation that we still leverage many years later. We'd also like to recognize the high-cardinality list (data-geek joke) of acquaintances and friends within the industry for being giants whose shoulders we're able to stand on. You have and will continue to inspire us.

A special thank you to the Digital Analytics Association (DAA) community, volunteers, and dedicated staff for all of your countless hours dedicated toward advancing our industry. Of course, we also want to thank our competitors and "frenemies." You all know who you are, and we still read your blogs and learn from you!

We wanted this book to include tips and advice from the trenches, so we sought out thought leaders and top practitioners to add more color and a diversity of perspective and experience to the book. Thank you to all the guest contributors for their invaluable input.

We also thank the team at our partner Google, namely the Google Analytics and Google Tag Manager teams. From the technical and marketing leadership to product managers, to Analytics 360 partner managers, sales, and support, to every Googler who has contributed to making GA the amazing product it is today. Few products benefit companies on such a large scale and in such an irreplaceable way. Keep on innovating!

Special thanks go to the Wiley team: Sheck Cho, who helped us refine our vision for the book, Pete Gaughan and Connor O'Brien for their expert guidance and editorial insight, Michael Henton for easing so much detail into the cover design, and Vincent Nordhaus for getting us to the finish line.

We also want to humbly thank our families, loved ones, and friends who have supported us at every step. Ghaidaa and Amina, your sacrifices and support have been invaluable to us as a company, and especially as individuals. We love you and thank you all.

Last, but definitely not least, we literally couldn't have completed this project without the amazing "E-Norians." The culture of teamwork, collaboration, learning, respect, and support that we are fortunate to work in easily makes E-Nor the best company on the planet to work for.

A high-five and thank you to our E-Nor family:

- **John H.** - You were right all along: we are lucky that you deal with us.
- **Allaedin** - You're the heartbeat of E-Nor.
- **Joel** - We don't know what is in the Portland water supply (in those uncovered water reservoirs), but keep drinking, baby. Oh, and bring back the 'stache.
- **Tracy** - You keep us informed and always bring us back to the big picture.
- **Tara** - The mile-high city produced some mile-high talent.
- **Mike** - The Warriors keep beating the Rockets. Wish you would embrace it instead of fighting it, but we still love you.
- **Patrick** - Unassuming demeanor + incisive mind = great combination.
- **Awwad** - Every company needs a gem: you're ours.
- **Madel** - Not sure what happened in Thailand, but keep it up. :)
- **Nabil** - Our traffic cop: nothing gets by you.
- **Nesreen** - Thank you for keeping us on task and on time!
- **Morsi** - CampaignAlyzer is the next BIG thing; couldn't have done it without you.
- **Hazem** - Kind, sincere, and reliable. We wish we could clone you.
- **Bilal** - BHS (Bald-Headed Syndrome) or not, your guidance, humor, and insight are invaluable.
- **Abdullah** - You are a rockstar. Next time, share the Porsche.
- **Bashar** - Thank you for pioneering our efforts in the new MENA frontiers.
- **Pat** - Everything is super-sized in Texas, and so is your support and help.
- **Tina** - Too many things to include in one line. You are a rock.
- **Sri** - Content is king, but you'll rule it in 2016 and beyond.
- **John A.** - Our very own Ferrari. How's the beach, buddy? :)
- **Farid** - You can sing and dance, and you have nice hair. You are awesome—no joke.

Of course a very, very special thank-you to **Asmaa** for her dedication and creativity in supporting us with the graphic design and illustrations for the book, and for putting up with our crazy schedule and last-minute requests.

With gratitude,

Feras, Shiraz, and Eric

About the Author(s)

Feras Alhlou Feras Alhlou is co-founder and Principal Consultant of E-Nor (founded in 2003). Feras is passionate about improving his clients' ROI. He has built an industry-thought leader organization supporting the evolving analytics and marketing intelligence needs of some of the world's most recognized brands.

He led his organization to achieve multiple certifications, including Analytics 360 Reseller, Google Cloud Platform, Tableau, Optimizely, Crimson Hexagon, and others.

A Certified Web Analyst and co-chair of the Digital Analytics Association's San Francisco chapter, Feras is also a blogger and a speaker who is quoted in national and international media outlets.

Feras received a Master of Science in Engineering Management from the University of South Florida and a Bachelor of Science in Electrical Engineering from the University of Tulsa. He's married with three children, enjoys skiing, listening to audiobooks, volunteering, and practicing aikido, in which he has earned a second-degree black belt.

Shiraz Asif Shiraz Asif is co-founder and VP of Analytics of E-Nor. Shiraz has an unwavering passion for project success and customer satisfaction. He lives by the motto "Knowledge Talks. Wisdom Listens."

Shiraz has extensive background in the areas of solutions architecture and Web/mobile analytics, specializing in advanced analytics implementations, report creation and automation, and integrated data analysis.

As the VP of Analytics, Shiraz has managed complex analytics implementations for governmental agencies and Fortune 500 companies, overseeing the end-to-end process ranging from defining key performance metrics to identifying actionable insights, through to reporting delivery and automation.

Eric Fettman Drawing upon a wide range of development and marketing experience, Eric positions analytics within a real-world business and technical framework as Director of Training at E-Nor.

At googleanalyticstest.com, which Eric developed, participants have completed more than 100,000 tests. The site has been widely recognized as a leading resource for Google Analytics Individual Qualification (GAIQ) preparation and practical Google Analytics skills training.

Eric has earned certification as a Java Programmer, as well ISO 9000 quality management internal auditor qualification, which strengthened his commitment to customer focus and continuous business performance improvement. He holds a BA with High Honors from Harvard University.

As an educator and a lifelong learner, Eric empowers his students to strive, grow, and excel in all endeavors.

About the Contributors

Anas Abbar is a seasoned executive with over 20 years work experience across multinationals and regional companies; his role is to execute on a vision that transforms ideas to products. Anas is the CEO and co-founder of 7awi.com, a leading online media publisher in MENA with top properties in Lifestyle and Entertainment, Autos, and Classifieds. Diverse career roles at Microsoft and Yahoo! in North America, Europe, the Middle East, and emerging markets have provided hands-on experience, refining his skills in strategies, product development and marketing, business development, and public sector roles. Anas is a believer in building smart teams that build products and solutions.

Simo Ahava (senior data advocate at Reaktor) is a recognized expert on customizing Web analytics and tag management solutions to improve the entire "life cycle" of data collection, processing, and reporting. His main areas of expertise lie with Google Analytics and Google Tag Manager, and Google has appointed him as a Google Developer Expert in these fields. He is especially interested in the interface between marketing and development, and his main focus is on increasing awareness, skills, and critical thinking around data.

Hannah Alvarez leads the content marketing team at UserTesting, the world's fastest and most advanced user experience research platform. Her team creates content that helps designers and marketers build amazing products, sites, and campaigns. With a background in nonprofit development, she's passionate about creating experiences that help people, and she's on a mission to eliminate bad UX from the face of the planet.

Duff Anderson is a visionary in digital Voice of the Customer research with over 20+ years' experience. Duff is SVP and co-founder at iPerceptions, a leading digital customer research company that is evolving digital analytics, enriching marketing technologies, and improving the customer experience for over 1,200 brands across 80 countries.

Tim Ash is the author of the bestselling book *Landing Page Optimization* (Sybex, 2012) and CEO of SiteTuners. He has developed successful Web-based initiatives for companies like Google, Expedia, eHarmony, Facebook, American Express, Canon, Nestle, Symantec, and Intuit. Tim is a highly regarded keynote speaker and presenter at industry conferences worldwide. He is the founder and chairperson of Conversion Conference and a frequent contributor to print and online publications.

Meta S. Brown is president of A4A Brown, Inc., a boutique consulting firm focused on promoting effective communication between management and technical professionals. She is author of *Data Mining for Dummies,* and creator of the Storytelling for Data Analysts and Storytelling for Tech workshops.

Jon Burns leads a lean and mean Web team at a leading semiconductor company in San Jose, developing and executing compelling Web experiences that all start with the data. Starting out a few short years ago with almost no insightful data, he has laid a foundation and built up the internal discipline over time by partnering closely with the business stakeholders, marketers, and analytics experts. It all started with the first step.

Brian Clifton, PhD, is a measurement strategist, advisor, and renowned practitioner of performance optimization using Google Analytics. Recognized internationally as a Google Analytics expert, his best-selling books have been translated many times and are used by students and professionals worldwide. As Google's first head of Web Analytics for Europe (2005–2008), Brian built the pan-European team of product specialists. A legacy of his work is the online learning center for the Google Analytics Individual Qualification (GAIQ). Brian is a guest lecturer at University College London (MSc, "Web Economics"), Copenhagen University, and at the Stockholm School of Economics.

June Dershewitz has spent her career driving analytics strategies for major businesses. She is currently the head of Data Governance & Analytics at Twitch, the world's leading video platform and community for gamers (a subsidiary of Amazon). A key aspect of her role is to ensure that data is collected, understood, and used effectively throughout the company. Previously, she was the director of Digital Analytics at Apollo Education Group, where she created an end-to-end view of digital customer behavior and enabled advanced marketing attribution. Prior to that she was a member of the leadership team at Semphonic, a prominent analytics consultancy (now part of Ernst & Young). As a long-standing advocate of the analytics community, June was an original co-founder of Web Analytics Wednesdays; she's also a Director Emeritus of the Digital Analytics Association.

Andrew Duffle, director FP&A, Analytics & Optimization, APMEX, is a data science advocate who encourages new and innovative data-driven applications to enhance Ecommerce companies' competitive advantage. His core focus revolves around implementing sustainable big data programs that enhance customers' experience and meet the objectives of the business. He has a financial foundation but a career full of data science; he is a devoted Google Analytics user and BigQuery champion.

Smita Dugar is a consumer insights professional and leads digital and marketing analytics initiatives at TiVo. She is responsible for mobile app analytics, site analytics, and optimization for TiVo's digital properties. She is passionate about consumer experience and the use of data in making business decisions. In previous roles, she has managed market research at Netflix and worked in market research companies with consulting clients like Microsoft, IBM, HP, and Procter & Gamble.

Bryan and Jeffrey Eisenberg are the co-founders of training company BuyerLegends .com. Bryan Eisenberg is also co-founder and Chairman Emeritus of the Digital Analytics Association and co-author of *Always Be Testing* (Sybex, 2008). Together, Bryan and Jeffrey co-authored *Waiting for Your Cat to Bark?* (Thomas Nelson, 2006) and *Call to Action* (Thomas Nelson, 2006), both *Wall Street Journal* and *New York Times* best-selling books. Their latest book is *Buyer Legends: The Executive Storyteller's Guide* (CreateSpace Independent Publishing Platform, 2015). Since 1998 they have trained and advised companies like HP, Google, GE Healthcare, Overstock, NBC Universal, Orvis, and Edmunds to implement accountable digital marketing strategies emphasizing optimization of revenue conversion rates for engagements, leads, subscriptions, and sales.

Jeff Feng is a product manager at Tableau Software, working to transform the way that people visualize data from cloud, big data, and relational data sources. Prior to Tableau, Jeff was a management consultant at McKinsey & Co., where he advised Fortune 500 high-tech companies on their business and technology strategy, and a program manager at Apple, where he helped with the launch of the iPhone 4. Jeff holds an MBA from the MIT Sloan School of Management and an MS and a BS in electrical engineering from the University of Illinois at Urbana-Champaign.

Eric Goldsmith is a data scientist for TED Conferences. He helps with the collection and interpretation of data to inform and support business decisions and strategic direction. His career began with a computer science degree from The Ohio State University and includes time in the online and Internet space with CompuServe, AOL, and UUNET, with some stops along the way with telecom and commercial network providers. As a lifelong learner, Eric is constantly evolving and growing. His deep interest and expertise is in data analytics and visualization, but he has also spent portions of his career in areas of performance engineering and software development.

Chris Goward is the person companies like Google, Electronic Arts, eBay, Magento, and 1-800-Flowers call on for great marketing optimization results. He founded WiderFunnel with the belief that marketing agencies should prove their value. He is the brain behind the LIFT Model and WiderFunnel System, conversion optimization strategies that consistently lift results for leading companies. He wrote the book *You Should Test That!* (Sybex, 2013), which redefined conversion optimization, and has spoken at over 200 conferences and events globally, showing how to create dramatic business improvements. You can read his blog at WiderFunnel.com/blog.

Stéphane Hamel is a seasoned consultant and distinguished thought leader in the field of digital analytics. Named Most Influential Industry Contributor by the Digital Analytics Association, he has made significant contributions to the industry, including creating the Digital Analytics Maturity Model and the Web Analytics Solution Profiler (WASP) quality assurance tool. He is frequently called on to speak at events around the world and is an often-quoted media contributor on the topic of digital intelligence and analysis. Stéphane holds advisory positions for several organizations and holds an MBA specializing in eBusiness.

Alex Harris is a conversion rate optimization manager with over 15 years experience with Ecommerce, lead generation, and UX. Alex is also a best-selling author of two books on Ecommerce optimization, and host of the Marketing Optimization Video Podcast.

Bobby Hewitt is the president and founder of Creative Thirst, the conversion rate optimization agency that focuses exclusively on increasing revenue and average order value for companies selling direct-to-consumer health products and natural health supplements. He has over 15 years experience in Web design and Internet marketing and holds a bachelor's degree in Marketing from Rutgers University. He is also certified in Online Testing, Value Proposition Development, and Landing Page Optimization, and a Certified Funnel Optimization Expert, Visual Website Optimizer certified partner, and winner of the Jim Novo Award of Academic Excellence for Web Analytics from The University of British Columbia and the Digital Marketing Association.

Avinash Kaushik is the digital marketing evangelist for Google and the co-founder of Market Motive Inc. Through his blog, Occam's Razor, and his best-selling books, *Web Analytics: An Hour a Day* (Sybex, 2007) and *Web Analytics 2.0* (Sybex, 2009), Avinash has become recognized as an authoritative voice on how executive teams can leverage digital platforms and data to out-innovate their competitors and achieve superior financial results. He has received rave reviews for bringing his energetic, inspiring, and practical insights to companies like P&G, Dell, Time Warner, Chase Bank, Hyatt, Porsche, and IBM. Avinash has delivered keynotes at a variety of global conferences, including Search Engine Strategies, Ad-Tech, Monaco Media Forum, iCitizen, JMP Innovators' Summit, The Art of Marketing, and Web 2.0.

Vanessa Sabino transforms data into marketing insights. She started her career as a system analyst in 2000, and in 2010 she jumped at the opportunity to start working with Digital Analytics, which brought together her educational background in business, applied mathematics, and computer science. She gained experience from top Internet companies in Brazil before moving to Canada, where she is now a data analysis lead for Shopify, helping make commerce better for everyone.

Krista Seiden is an experienced leader in the digital analytics industry and a frequent speaker at industry events. She has driven analytics and optimization practices at companies such as Adobe, the Apollo Group, and Google. Currently, she is an analytics advocate for Google, where she is responsible for educating and advocating for analytics and optimization best practices, as well as running the Analytics 360 training program. As an active member of the digital analytics community, she also co-chairs the San Francisco chapter of the Digital Analytics Association (DAA). Krista was the winner of the 2014 DAA Rising Star Award and the 2015 DAA Practitioner of the Year Award. She holds a BA in economics and political science from the University of California–Berkeley and a marketing certification from the Wharton Business School.

Irv Shapiro is responsible for overall business strategy and corporate leadership as the CEO of DialogTech, an Inc. 500 high-growth company in the Voice-Based Marketing Automation space. Prior to forming DialogTech in 2005, Irv founded Metamor Technologies in 1985, a two-time Inc. 500 company, and grew Metamor to over 500 employees. Following the sale of Metamor to CORESTAFF in 1997, Irv participated in 10 acquisitions, directed the growth of Metamor to $52 million in sales, and helped create a $250 million consulting services group. In 1999, Irv founded the online education platform Edventions, which was later sold to Edison Schools in 2001. Irv has been inducted into the Chicago Area Entrepreneurship Hall of Fame, and in 2011 was a Gold Winner in the Best of Biz Awards as Executive of the Year. Irv earned a BS in computer science from Washington University in St. Louis.

Matt Stannard is an innovator, excited by API releases and new technologies. He strongly believes that innovation allows different thinking and valuable peer and client insights. Matt's interest in data and technology began early; he started programming from the day he sat down at his first computer. This interest led him to study computer science, reading modules on intelligent Internet commerce, advanced artificial intelligence, and advanced neural networks. During and after university Matt was employed in the development team of multi-national insurance brokers, Willis, where he worked on platform proof of concepts as well as Willis's intra, extram and Internet sites. He later joined a direct marketing company working with data on behalf of Oxfam, the Guardian, and a number of UK local authorities. In his role at 4Ps, Matt is a digital director and responsible for maintaining the company's position at the cutting edge of technology. His key goal is to see clients maximize profit from their data. Matt works with clients such as Selfridges, The White Company, Audi, Storage King, Jamie Oliver, Lindt, WGSN, White & Case, and the White Company to ensure they're at the forefront of analytics and tracking.

James Standen is the founder of nModal Solutions, and the creator of the Analytics Canvas framework. James has over 20 years experience with data, including advanced process control, artificial intelligence, data warehousing, and business intelligence and digital marketing analytics. He is an active member of the Google Analytics trusted tester group, and Analytics Canvas has been a leading integration tool for Google Analytics and Analytics 360 since 2010.

Jim Sterne is an international consultant who focuses on measuring the value of creating and strengthening customer relationships. Sterne has written eight books on interactive marketing, is the founding president and current board chair of the Digital Analytics Association and produces the eMetrics Summits and the Media Analytics Summits.

Dan Stone is the lead product manager for user-centric analysis and audience marketing at Google Analytics. Prior to joining Google, Dan's experience ranged from venture-funded consumer technology startups, where he led product and user acquisition, to working with top 100 companies in the telecommunications, media, and technology industries, leading advanced analytics, sentiment analysis, and marketing optimization. Dan holds a BS in management science from MIT.

Mike Telem is VP of product marketing, real-time personalization at Marketo, the leader in digital marketing software and solutions. Mike has extensive experience in digital marketing, especially in the areas of Web personalization and account-based marketing. Previously the co-founder of Insightera (acquired by Marketo in 2014), he drove marketing and sales operations as well as global business initiatives. Before co-founding Insightera, Mike served as a business development manager in the RAD-Bynet group.

Holger Tempel is founder of the German company webalytics GmbH. He has acted as a consultant and trainer since 1991 in the business fields of IT and Web analytics. In 2005 he became one of the first 14 worldwide Google Partners and therefore is one of the leading knowledge carriers for Google Analytics and digital analytics in general. He is also the co-founder and member of the board of the Digital Analytics Association Germany e.V. and the person in charge of developing the certification track to becoming a future digital analyst. Due to data privacy issues in the European area he gained high-level expertise on how to make Google Analytics in European Countries data privacy compliant.

Introduction

WHY THIS BOOK?

Many very useful Google Analytics (GA) resources are readily accessible online: Google Analytics Academy, the Google Analytics and Google Tag Manager Solutions Guides, and a broad range of GA-focused blogs, e-books, and tutorials—including those that we produce ourselves—that steadily enrich the conversation and provide real value for learning. Why, then, did we go the extra step and take on the significant task to write a Google Analytics book? Much more importantly, why should you invest your time and energy to read it?

Consolidated Resource for Learning Effectiveness   With millions of GA installations worldwide, the fact remains that only a small percentage of organizations are using GA to anywhere near its full power.

We've worked with hundreds of clients, from start-ups to the Fortune 25, and we've seen the ongoing struggle of marketers to achieve a complete GA implementation for their websites and mobile apps, master the specialized reporting capabilities, optimize their channel attribution, integrate GA data with other data sources, and move from data to insight to performance improvement. The objective of this book is to provide a consolidated and focused learning experience that guides you from potential confusion and frustration to solid understanding and confident action, starting with the core nuts-and-bolts competencies and building to more advanced and future-facing strategies and techniques.

Not the Encyclopedia of Google Analytics   While comprehensive in scope, this book is not designed as a full reference of every GA feature—the Google help articles are there to serve this purpose. Furthermore, much of the GA reporting functionality becomes intuitive as soon as you begin navigating through the reports, so it would not be the best use of space or time to explain what's easy and obvious.

A Focus on What's Difficult and Most Important   To contrast with the previous point, the book does thoroughly cover the fundamentals of measurement strategy, implementation, and reporting, and goes on to focus on the topics that normally present the most challenges and/or typically generate the greatest insight and actionability. We have also endeavored to call out potential sticking points, gotchas, and pitfalls along the way, and especially to warn you where real danger lurks.

Framework for Conversion Optimization, Marketing ROI, and Competitive Advantage   The book is conceived, above all, to help you improve your own key performance indicators (KPIs), such as Ecommerce transactions, lead submissions, or content engagement. With detailed discussions about conversion tracking, including goal and Enhanced Ecommerce funnels, you'll learn how to identify the website or mobile app elements that are helping or hurting your conversion success.

It's not enough, however, to track conversion rates. You must have clean traffic attribution to understand where your success and return on investment (ROI) are coming from, so we devote in-depth discussions to attribution reporting—campaign tracking in particular—and go beyond last-click attribution to identify which traffic sources are providing conversion support prior to the session in which the goal completion or Ecommerce transaction occurs.

When you begin to understand what really is and is not working, analytics has become your long-term competitive advantage. And the time to gain that understanding is in periods of stability; emergency analytics ramp-ups do not usually solve mysteries or relieve crises.

Contributions from Industry Luminaries and Leading Analytics and Optimization Practitioners   We sought out input from world-recognized experts, members of the GA team itself, and practitioners who are doing amazing things in analytics and optimization each day. Their contributions add immeasurably to the learning experience and provide a range and depth of insight and technique that are rarely found within a single resource.

Graphical Format   Since the book is not an encyclopedia, it's not written or designed like one. The many annotated screen shots, color diagrams, and special callouts are included to make the discussions more approachable and, overall, to provide a more interesting and impactful learning experience.

Technical Deep Dives   The previous paragraph notwithstanding, we do not shy away from the technical details where they are needed. Following the advice of Albert Einstein, we've aimed to make everything as simple as possible, but no simpler. Whether for the event tracking through the Google Tag Manager data layer, the formula for Google page value calculation, or the coding required for Enhanced Ecommerce, we go deep into the concepts and procedures that you need for successful implementation and advanced skill in reporting and analysis.

User Focus, Qualitative Inputs, and Testing   Taking a broader perspective on optimization, we learn techniques for designing and evaluating for user experience, including survey tools, A/B testing, and their integrations into GA.

Specialized Techniques and Advanced Integrations   As the chapters progress, the book discusses many specialized techniques, such as remarketing audience configuration and phone tracking setup, and introduces advanced integrations with CRM, data extraction and visualization tools, and marketing automation.

Your Role as Communicator and Change Agent   Analysis tends to have little organizational impact without clear and effective communication. Throughout the book, we offer insights on streamlined presentation of Google Analytics reporting to clients and internal stakeholders as well as communication and collaboration between the marketing and IT departments for implementation initiatives.

Key Takeaways and Actions   Each chapter concludes with "Key Takeaways" and "Actions and Exercises," so you can review the main points of the chapter and immediately try out the techniques and begin planning broader, longer-term objectives.

Foundation for Ongoing Learning and Achievement   Google is on a fast-paced innovation path. With no doubt, Google Analytics will introduce new capabilities between the time we finished writing and publication date, but the concepts, techniques, and best practices will still be very applicable and will empower you to continue exploring, learning, and taking advantage of the tool's new capabilities. Additionally, the implementation and reporting checklists available and the resource recommendations maintained at `http://www.e-nor.com/gabook` will help keep you up to date.

Even very experienced GA users constantly refine their existing techniques and learn new approaches. This book is designed to build the foundation from which your own analytics skills can evolve and deepen with each measurement challenge and each feature update.

The Benefits of Analytics and Optimization   We've seen first-hand the remarkable improvements that Google Analytics can generate, but these are possible only with a sound implementation, the right reporting know-how, and a long-term commitment to optimization of user experience, marketing ROI, and conversion performance. The book is designed to provide the technical building blocks and inspire the initiative and dedication necessary for ongoing improvement.

WHO SHOULD READ THIS BOOK?

This book is written with the premise that within an organization, Google Analytics should be "owned" by Marketing or a dedicated Analytics/Business Intelligence team rather than by IT. That said, IT support is critical, as many of the Google Analytics implementation steps require close developer involvement.

Thus, while many of the discussions are intended primarily for a marketer or analyst, many others are geared more toward the technical team, or toward the marketer or analyst who needs to understand how data gets into GA and articulate code-level implementation requirements to the technical team. To facilitate this communication, even the more technical discussions are broken down into manageable, understandable steps and concepts.

Product managers, designers, user experience (UX) specialists, content writers, and individuals in various roles at advertising and design agencies can also use this book to learn how GA and the optimization mind-set can help them gain data-driven insights and improve their results.

If you're approaching GA from a data science or broader business intelligence role, the later chapters on data integration and visualization should be particularly relevant.

The book can also serve as an introduction to GA capabilities for managers and executives. With the callouts, guest contributions, illustrations, and key takeaways throughout, the book can provide a good overview of GA, even if the more detailed and technical discussions are skipped.

Regardless of your role, if you're new to GA or have been using GA for some time but have yet to attain the level of proficiency that you want and need, the book can, in fact, provide the blueprint for your own GA breakthrough, taking you beyond the default gaps and usage toward mastery and real effectiveness. If you're already fairly adept with GA, the book will provide a solid review of best practices and surely many new tips and perspectives.

As a related note, the book was not written with the Google Analytics Individual Qualification (GAIQ) in mind, but if you read the book and apply the learning, you should be well equipped to take and pass the exam.

CHAPTER SUMMARY

Chapter 2: Google Analytics Reporting Overview   Before our discussion of measurement strategy and GA implementation in the following chapters, this chapter provides an overview of the Audience and Behavior reports as well as a thorough walk-through of the functionalities that will enable you to take full advantage of the GA reporting interface.

Chapter 3: Measurement Strategy   This chapter discusses measurement strategy as the foundation for your analytics program. We assess your current analytics implementations and evaluate the need for more specialized tracking and reporting. Also reviewed are process and communication challenges, analytics ownership within the enterprise, and a sample measurement plan.

Chapter 4: Account Creation and Tracking Code Installation   Here, we go back to the first steps in GA account creation and map the account/property/view hierarchy. We access the GA tracking code and demonstrate the range of data that is recorded with each pageview hit. We also consider tracking for templated websites and standalone pages.

Chapter 5: Google Tag Manager   After installing the native tracking code in the previous chapter, we switch (for the rest of the book) to a better way for deploying the GA tracking code: Google Tag Manager (GTM). This chapter reviews the advantages of GTM over native deployment and emphasizes three main GTM concepts: container, tags, and triggers.

Chapter 6: Events, Virtual Pageviews, Social Actions, and Errors   As perhaps the biggest gap in a default GA website implementation, user actions that do not cause a page load are not recorded. We address this gap with events and virtual pageview tracking to capture video plays, page scrolls, and multiscreen AJAX processes. We also learn about social tracking and error tracking and take advantage of the GTM data layer.

Chapter 7: Acquisition Reports   Google Analytics does the best job it can in determining where your website traffic comes from, but it needs a great deal of help from you, in the form of campaign parameters, to correctly attribute traffic from email, social, and banner campaigns. We also discuss paid and organic search engine traffic and review Google Search Console as an important complement to GA.

Chapter 8: Goal and Ecommerce Tracking   To populate the Conversions reports, you must tell GA what constitutes a successful session. In this chapter, we walk through goal and funnel setup, clarify the Conversion Rate and Abandonment Rate metrics, and configure Ecommerce and Enhanced Ecommerce tracking to record transactions with product category, tax, and funnels from impression through conversion.

Chapter 9: View Settings, View Filters, and Access Rights   In this chapter, we apply view settings and filters to the raw GA data to remove internal traffic, consolidate URL variations, configure site search tracking, and create specific data subsets based on subdirectory, device, traffic source, or geography. We also review the four types of user permissions and consider governance principles.

Chapter 10: Segments   For much of the analysis we need to perform, aggregation can hide significant data points and hinder insight. In this chapter, we break down our data with segments that map to different audience constituencies and amplify trends, and we define behavioral segments that correlate behaviors such as a page or video view to conversion outcomes.

Chapter 11: Dashboards, Custom Reports, and Intelligence Alerts   Here, we review the easy and flexible dashboard functionality in GA and also cover the automated emailing option for dashboards and reports. We also configure custom reports for more focused analysis and communication, and we set up intelligence alerts to send out proactive notifications for metric fluctuations.

Chapter 12: Implementation Customizations   In this chapter, we configure custom dimensions, custom metrics, and content groupings that allow GA reporting to more closely reflect our own organizations, taxonomies, and end-user experiences. We also set up cross-domain tracking and roll-up for management and executive reporting, and we learn how to track logged-in users across devices.

Chapter 13: Mobile App Measurement   This chapter focuses specifically on app tracking through the Android and iOS software development kits (SDKs) and through Google Tag Manager. We also review campaign tracking for clickthroughs to Google Play and the App Store, and measure app open rate after download. Best practices for GA mobile app account structure are also outlined.

Chapter 14: Google Analytics Integrations—The Power of Together   This chapter reviews the rich AdWords reporting available to you in GA as an advertiser and also discusses AdSense metrics for you as a publisher. We also examine the powerful capability of GA remarketing audiences and consider GA integrations with email and social media platforms.

Chapter 15: Integrating Google Analytics with CRM Data   Here, we step through two approaches to get website source data into customer relationship management (CRM) systems: directly through hidden fields on the lead form, or through importing GA data into the CRM against a common key. This integration will allow us to calculate cost per qualified lead and long-term value for different marketing channels.

Chapter 16: Advanced Reporting and Visualization with Third-Party Tools   Furthering our data integration discussions, this chapter discusses the integration of GA data with other data sources and interactive visualizations in Tableau. We also explore automated export from Google Analytics 360 to BigQuery storage and the role of Analytics Canvas and ShufflePoint as middleware for data extraction and transformation.

Chapter 17: Data Import and Measurement Protocol   This chapter discusses two additional ways to record data into GA: import of content, campaign, and marketing cost data through the admin panel or the GA Management API, and the Measurement Protocol, which allows you send hits to GA from any programmed and networked environment.

Chapter 18: Analytics 360   To address the needs of enterprise installations, Analytics 360 (formerly called GA Premium) offers greatly increased data limits, data freshness, and custom dimensions. This chapter discusses these features as well as unsampled data export, custom funnels, DoubleClick integration, and also service-level agreements and support.

GET STARTED

Now that we have charted the learning objectives and outlined the chapter content, it's time to get started. Take the necessary time, stay focused, try everything out yourself, don't forget to enjoy the learning process, and always keep the end in mind: understanding, mastery, real-world results, and a foundation for ongoing learning and success.

If you need access to a test account, or if you have questions or feedback along the way, don't hesitate to reach out to us at GAbook@e-nor.com.

GUEST SPOT   **The Three Masters of Analytics**

Jim Sterne

Jim Sterne is the founding president and current board chair of the Digital Analytics Association.

You can't please everybody, but there are three masters whom you need to serve if you are to succeed at analytics:

➤ Whoever Pays the Bills
➤ The Customer
➤ Your Intellectual Curiosity

Validating the Raw Material

For each of these masters, trustworthy data is the cornerstone. *Blindly consuming any analytics tool without a deep understanding of the provenance of the underlying data—or of the inherent gaps in a default implementation—is a surefire way to run right into a brick wall.*

All data is collected in a certain way, cleaned in a certain way, sampled in a certain way, and munged together just so before you ever see the output. It is your underlying responsibility to know where the data comes from and how it's been manipulated before you can get comfortable with others seeing "results." Others in your organization will assume you have this well in hand, and the first time it's discovered that the reports are bad because the data was not validated will be the last time the Three Masters of Analytics will trust you with its interpretation—most importantly, the person with their hands on the purse strings.

Whoever Pays the Bills   Your boss, the VP, the board, the client, the committee; whoever is responsible for funding your technology and human resources must feel they are getting their money's worth.

If they want reports about "hits," then, by golly, you will give them Hits Reports. If they want to know how many uniques there are every month, that's your job. Like it or not. If they have a strong opinion about a specific attribution model, then for good or ill, that will be your top priority.

Make very sure that you have very clear definitions that everybody understands. What do *they* mean by hits, uniques, and attribution? After that, then you can bring in more and more information about things that will actually move the business forward.

continues

continued

Eventually, you will find colleagues who understand what you are trying to accomplish, and they will become more interested in getting information that will actually be useful to making business decisions.

The Customer   In order to sell more stuff, get more readers, grow your fan base, or convert public opinion, your message must reach those people and persuade them to take appropriate action. Whatever your boss wants or the company prizes, "the customer" is your target audience or user.

Customer satisfaction and usability come into the picture here. Testing, optimizing conversion, and monitoring social interaction are all on your plate. While the reporting goes on apace, your analysis must serve those who are connecting with your customer base and give them the immediate information they need to do their jobs.

Your Intellectual Curiosity   Last, but far from least, is your own innate curiosity. Call it data mining, data diving, or data interrogation, your highest purpose is to derive insights previously hidden. "Gee, that's funny ... I wonder," says Isaac Asimov, is more important than knowledge.

Yes, you must put your back into validating the raw material. Yes, you must crank out those reports whether you believe in them or not. Yes, you must support the ongoing A/B split testing teams and landing page optimizers. But if you don't come up with the occasional bright idea or bring some obscure yet actionable observation to the attention of the powers that be, you can be replaced.

Finding tasty tidbits in the data stream is also the only way you can maintain your own interest in the whole process. It's the fun part. It's also what makes the difference between a data plumber and an analyst. The plumber spends an entire career collecting, managing, and reporting on data. The analyst makes it a point to understand the goals of the organization well enough to go fathoming the depths of the data for relevant nuggets. Knowing which goals are the most valuable makes the process exciting. The analyst wonders what other treasures might be hidden in the stream, awaiting discovery.

Whoever pays the bills will keep you supplied with technology and human resources. Happy customers give the budget controller the means to do so. Only you can maintain your interest and draw valuable insights from the data.

I saw the angel in the marble and carved until I set him free.

–Michelangelo

2

Google Analytics Reporting Overview: User Characteristics and Behavior

Before we begin strategizing in Chapter 3, "Measurement Strategy," and dive into implementation in Chapter 4, "Account Creation and Tracking Code Installation," and Chapter 5, "Google Tag Manager," this chapter will review the wide range of reports and reporting functionality provided in the Google Analytics UI (user interface).

In this chapter and throughout the book, some of the discussions become quite detailed and technical. If there are any specific points that are not immediately clear, we recommend that you make a note (mentally, digitally, or in ink) and then continue with your reading and exploration in the Google Analytics (GA) UI. Many of the concepts and functionalities that may be challenging at first will become clearer and easier as you proceed with your learning and your work in GA each day.

If you're just starting out with GA, it might also be useful to review an online GA glossary (such as E-Nor's "Google Analytics Visual Glossary" at `https://www.e-nor.com/blog/google-analytics/google-analytics-visual-glossary`).

> ### .Note
>
> ## Access to a Test Account
>
> As you read through the chapters in this book, we urge you to view actual Google Analytics reports for a website (or app) that you or your organization manages. You'll need only Read & Analyze rights to access the Reporting section and to use a range of interesting features, such as segments and custom reports. Chapter 9, "View Settings, View Filters, and Access Rights," discusses access rights in detail.
>
> If you're not in a position to obtain access to any GA data, contact us at GAbook@e-nor.com.

GOOGLE ANALYTICS REPORTING: USER CHARACTERISTICS AND BEHAVIOR

Once you implement GA on your website, the reporting will provide two basic types of data:

- User characteristics (location, traffic source, technology)
- User behavior

In the remainder of the chapter, we discuss each of the sections in the left navigation panel of the GA reporting tab. Interestingly, the four main report groupings appear not at the top of the left navigation panel in the Reporting section, but at the bottom, as shown in Figure 2.1, so that's where we'll start.

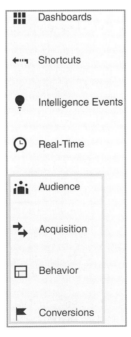

FIGURE 2.1 The four main reporting sections appear at the bottom of the left navigation panel.

Note

Quick Tip: Hide and Display the Left Navigation

If you need some additional horizontal space for your GA reports, toggle the left navigation menu by clicking the small triangle icon at the top right of the menu, or type M on your keyboard.

Audience Reports

The Audience reports break your users down by different characteristics, including geography, technology, and behaviors such as return visits.

While we can broadly think of the audience reports as describing *who* visits your site, don't look for any personally identifiable information (PII) such as name or email address in GA: it's not recorded by default, and the terms of service forbid any collection of any user PII, even as part of the page URL (which can occur if a form containing a name or email address field is configured as a post action rather than a get action). In Chapter 4, "Account Creation and Tracking Code Installation," Brian Clifton details the steps you can take in your implementation to avoid PII collection.

Next, we discuss several reports within the Audience section.

Audience Overview Report

Let's review some of the Audience Overview report metrics, as shown in Figure 2.2.

Sessions	Users	Pageviews	Pages / Sessions
2,481,729	1,611,020	10,901,838	4.39

Avg. Session Duration	Bounce Rate	% New Sessions	
00:03:13	41.71%	49.74%	

FIGURE 2.2 Metrics in the Audience Overview.

Terminology

Sparklines

The small horizontal trendlines below the metrics in the Overview reports as in Figure 2.2 are called *sparklines*. You can click the sparklines to display the corresponding metric as the main over-time graph.

Sessions and Users

A session is defined as a period of user activity not interrupted by more than 30 minutes. Let's use the classic phone call interruption example:

1. Deborah views a page on your website.
2. Deborah receives a phone call that lasts 29 minutes.
3. Deborah views another page on your website.

Deborah would increment both the session and user count only by one, since the second pageview occurred within the 30-minute session timeout. As another example:

1. Igor views a page on your website.
2. Igor receives a phone call that lasts 31 minutes.
3. Igor views another page on your website.

Igor would increment the session count by two, since the second pageview occurred after the 30-minute session timeout. The user count, however, would have incremented by one only, since the _ga cookie that the tracking code initially stored in Igor's browser would allow GA to recognize Igor as the same returning user. In app tracking, the device ID identifies the same user, and session calculation is also based by default on the 30-minute timeout.

These scenarios are quite straightforward. Let's consider the metrics calculation for the following sequence as well:

1. Vincent accesses a long article page on your website.
2. For 40 minutes, Vincent scrolls, reads, expands spoilers and clicks tabs to reveal additional information, and watches an embedded video.
3. Vincent views another page on your website.

By default, the metrics for Vincent would be the same as Igor's. As we discuss in Chapter 4, "Account Creation and Tracking Code Installation," the basic GA tracking code sends data to the GA servers only when the page loads. If, however, you tracked Vincent's on-page actions as events or virtual pageviews as outlined in Chapter 6, "Events, Virtual Pageviews, Social Actions, and Errors," each action would refresh the session timeout for 30 minutes, and Victor would increment sessions and users by one only.

Overall, since a single user can generate many sessions, session count will be higher than user count.

As a note, sessions also increment at midnight according to the time zone setting of your GA view; that is, if a user accesses one page at 11:59 PM and then another page at 12:01 AM, GA will record two sessions. A session thus remains confined to a single day.

Terminology

Sessions and Users versus Visits and Unique Visitors

We may recall that, until somewhat recently, the terms *visits* and *unique visitors* appeared in GA instead of *sessions* and *users*. This terminology change probably occurred because each physical visit can actually generate multiple sessions (as the scenario with Igor illustrates), so *session* more accurately describes the metric that's displayed.

Unique visitors likely changed to *users* because a single individual can appear as multiple users in GA for a variety of reasons: different browsers, different devices, incognito sessions, or cookie deletion. The _ga cookie is the key to identifying the same user, and in fact allows GA to bundle multiple pageviews (and other hit types, such as events) into the same session. Dependency on the _ga cookie is discussed further in Chapter 4, "Account Creation and Tracking Code Installation."

The *Cross-Device Tracking* session in Chapter 12, "Implementation Customizations," also discusses how Google Analytics can recognize the same logged-in user across different devices: *users* is somewhat more suitable than *unique visitors* in the context of mobile apps.

As an editorial note, we use *session* and *visit* fairly synonymously throughout the book, as we do with *user* and *visitor*.

As discussed in Chapter 12, "Implementation Customizations," you can opt to change the session timeout, but the 30-minute default is left in place as routine practice.

By default, hits that occur with less than 30 minutes of interruption are considered to be part of the same session, as shown in Figure 2.3. After 30 minutes or more, the next hits are considered to be part of the new session but are attributed to the same user as long as the _ga cookie is present in the browser.

Bounce Rate

The definition of a bounce is a bit more subtle than we may first believe. Routine definitions that you may hear for *bounce* are a *single-page visit* or *"somebody comes to your website and leaves without doing anything."* The second definition more closely reflects what a bounce should mean: no *interactions* after the first pageview, whether that second interaction would be another pageview or any of the many actions that we can record as events or virtual pageviews, such as Vincent's interactions on the long article page.

Since pageviews, events, and virtual pageviews are all types of hits, and since we also discussed why *session* is a somewhat more accurate term than *visit*, let's propose a better, more technical definition for bounce, as demonstrated in Figure 2.4: *a single-hit session.* (As a somewhat rare exception, a noninteraction event, which we discuss in Chapter 6, does not affect bounce rate.) We further examine *hit* as a concept in Chapter 4 and throughout the book.

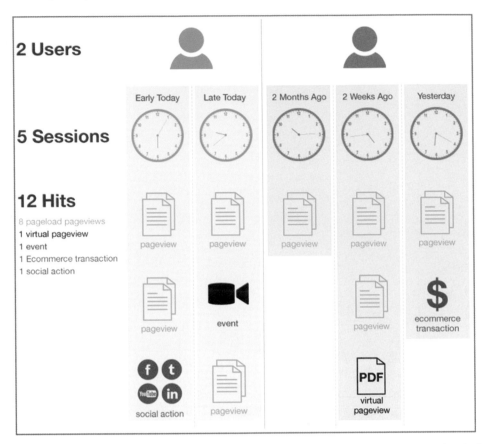

FIGURE 2.3 The _ga cookie allows Google Analytics to associate multiple hits with a single session and multiple sessions with a single user.

Pages/Session and Average Session Duration

We can refer to Pages/Session (or Screens/Session for a mobile app property) and Session Duration as *engagement* metrics, since they indicate an overall level of engagement with your website or app.

The definition of Pages/Session is clear, but Average Session Duration is not as straightforward as it seems. Since GA calculates time based on the differences in the timestamps of the pageviews (or any other hit type) that are sent, the user engagement after the last hit is never calculated. Let's consider the following scenario:

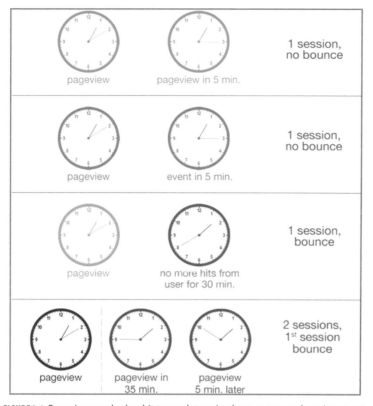

FIGURE 2.4 Pageviews and other hit types determine bounce rate and session count.

1:00:00—Beatriz accesses a page on your website.

1:01:00—Beatriz accesses another page on your website.

1:06:30—Beatriz exits the website after reading the second page for 5 minutes and 30 seconds.

Surprising as it may seem, GA would, by default, calculate a duration of only 00:01:00 for Beatriz's session. If Beatriz had only spent one minute on the first page and had not accessed a second page, the session duration would have been recorded as 00:00:00. Without another timestamp for a new hit following a given page, GA has no way to calculate how long Beatriz spent on that page. If you were tracking page scrolling as discussed in Chapter 6, each scroll event would have its own timestamp, so GA could calculate the duration for Beatriz's session much closer to the actual 00:06:30 that she spent engaged with your website.

> **Note**
>
> ## Are High Average Session Duration and Pages (or Screens) per Session Positive Indicators?
>
> For several of the metrics in GA, context is extremely important. If you have a website or mobile app that is primarily informational and not designed to drive one specific action—and especially if you're monetizing through ad display—Average Session Duration and Pages or Screens/Session would be positive indicators of engagement, and you'd want to see these metrics increasing over time.
>
> For an Ecommerce or lead generation website (or app), or even for a website or app that's designed to provide customer support, Average Session Duration and Pages or Screens/Session are ambiguous. An increase in these metrics could represent greater engagement, but they might also indicate confusion and frustration on the part of your users.
>
> This ambiguity helps to illustrate the critical need for goal and/or Ecommerce tracking. In the case of an Ecommerce website, increased Session Duration and increased Ecommerce Conversion Rate and Revenue would seem to indicate, logically, that your users are more positively engaged with your experience, while increased Session Duration and decreased Ecommerce metrics as shown in Figure 2.5 would tell the opposite story (unless your phone or offline conversions are increasing—we discuss these scenarios in the book as well).
>
> If you configure a goal for your support app that corresponds to a user's "mark this issue as resolved" action, an increased Session Duration and increased Conversion Rate for that goal would be seem to be a positive indicator overall, while decreased Session Duration and increased conversion rate would be ideal.
>
> In any case, if you do observe a negative trend, you can begin further analysis, as described below, to determine which pages users are spending the most time on and from which pages they're exiting most frequently.
>
>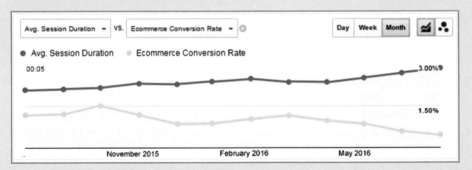
>
> **FIGURE 2.5** By displaying two metrics on the main over-time graph in one of the GA reports, we see Ecommerce Conversion Rate trending down, which may clarify the upward trend in Session Duration as a negative user experience.

New versus Returning Report

The New versus Returning report (Figure 2.6) breaks down the number of sessions attributed to new users and returning users. Two fundamental aspects of this report are potentially a bit confusing:

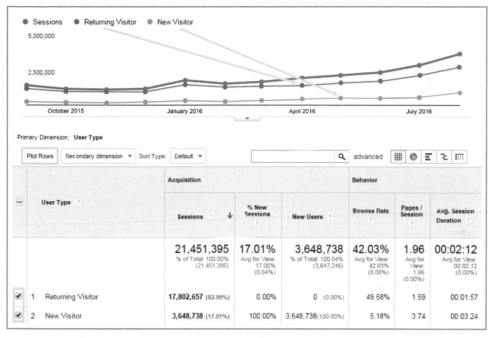

FIGURE 2.6 With the date selection set to the past 12 months and rows plotted, we can see growth in sessions from both new and returning visitors.

- The same user can appear as both User Types within the same time period, if a new session was followed by one or more returning sessions.
- A user is considered returning even if the previous visit occurred before the start of the date selection.

Also keep in mind that because of cookie deletion and the other factors mentioned previously as preventing GA from identifying a returning user, the new visitors will undoubtedly be overreported relative to actual site usage, and returning visitors will always be underreported. This discrepancy does not manifest in the New versus Returning report within a GA mobile app property, since GA can reliably identify returning users by device ID in this case.

An increase in both returning and new visitors over time would be positive indicators.

Location Report

In the Location report, you can display metrics based on the following geographical divisions:

- Continent
- Subcontinent
- Country

- Region
- Metro (United States only; corresponds to Nielsen Designated Market Area [DMA])
- City

Region can mean different things in different countries. As a few examples, region corresponds to state in India, Brazil, and the United States, province in Canada, and department in France. In the United Kingdom, region is recorded as England, Scotland, Wales, or Northern Ireland.

Location information is not recorded directly but is instead derived from user IP address. Because a user's IP address depends on the Internet service provider (ISP) and sometimes indicates a location that differs significantly from the user's physical location, it's advisable to consider the more granular geographical data in GA—especially city—as more directional than completely literal.

The IP address itself doesn't appear in the reports. As Holger Tempel explains in Chapter 12, you may need to "anonymize" IP addresses in GA if you're operating within the European Union.

> ### Note
>
> ## Optimization Opportunities from the Location Reports
> The location reports can provide many insights. A high level of existing traffic and conversions from a specific geographic area could influence your decisions on marketing, sales, live events, and even brick-and-mortar initiatives.
>
> If you're running an offline campaign such as a print ad in a regional publication or a billboard, you can monitor any increased traffic (and conversions) from that region. (As discussed in Chapter 7, you can use campaign parameters to closely track print and QR redirects.)

Technology and Mobile Reports

In the Technology and Mobile reports, you can break down your data by the following dimensions, among others:

- Browser and Browser Version
- Operating System (OS)
- Screen Resolution

The Technology and Mobile reports can help you identify and understand:

- **Design optimization opportunities.** For example, let's say that 25% of your traffic is using a mobile device (*mobile* essentially meaning *smartphone* in GA), but the conversion rate for your main goal is only 0.5% on mobile versus 1.5% on desktop. By implementing or improving your responsive Web design or your mobile-redirected Web pages, you could increase conversion rate—or perhaps drive toward a different type of conversion (such as clicking to dial your call center) that might be more suitable to mobile.

- **Marketing optimization opportunities.** For instance, you can allocate more of your AdWords spend to desktop until you improve your tablet conversion rate.
- **Browsers and operating system underperformance.** If bounce rate is high or conversion rate is particularly low on a specific browser or OS, there are likely specific usability issues that manifest in these environments.
- **Device profiles to accommodate.** What is the widest you can or should go in your next design? How many different screen resolutions must you accommodate?
- **Devices you need to test on.** On which devices are your visitors accessing your website or mobile app? Make sure to test any design or development changes accordingly.

Warning   !

Don't test on your preferred platform only.

Make sure to test design and development changes on all devices, operating systems, browsers, browser versions, and screen resolutions that your visitors are currently using to access your website or mobile app. If you're partial to Chrome on Mac but significant numbers of your visitors are using Internet Explorer on Windows, you could potentially miss usability issues that can undermine your conversion optimization efforts.

By the same token, if only a negligible number of your users are still on IE7, you don't necessarily need to spend much time testing and optimizing for that browser.

As a note, device emulators (including those available within the browser) are useful as a proxy for testing on different device types and screen resolutions, but physical devices are more reliable for testing important design updates.

Demographics Reports and Interests Reports

The Demographics reports and the Interests reports are not populated by default. As one of the steps outlined in Chapter 12 for enabling the Demographics and Interests reports, the GA Terms of Service require us to revise our privacy policy, since the data in these reports originate not from our own website or app. Instead, the Demographics and Interests data is communicated to GA via the third-party DoubleClick cookie for Web traffic and anonymous identifiers for mobile apps. This data is derived from three sources:

- age and gender drop-downs within forms on websites that participate in the DoubleClick ad network
- interest inferences, also from websites in DoubleClick network
- data that users have entered into their Google Plus profiles

Within GA, the Demographics and Interests data is reported in aggregate only, and as the Demographics Overview and Interests Overview reports indicate, GA is able to record this data for only a portion of your audience—typically just 50%–60% of your traffic. Because the data is partial and compiled in different ways with varying accuracy, we're advised to interpret these reports directionally rather than literally.

If, for instance, you notice a higher proportion of visitors in the 45–54 age band than you expected, you might consider testing different messaging, imagery, or even offerings. As is discussed in Chapter 14, "Google Analytics Integrations—The Power of Together," one interesting use of the Demographics and Interests reports is to map the best-performing groups on your website (in terms of goal and Ecommerce conversion) to display and retargeting campaigns on the Google Display Network through AdWords. Since AdWords uses the same Demographics and Interests classifications as GA, it seems to make sense to advertise to the groups that are already demonstrating the highest conversion rates, regardless of how those groups are actually defined.

Note

Does Google Have Your Own Demographics and Interests Data Right?

Sign into Google and go to `http://www.google.com/ads/preferences` to see your age, gender, and interests according to Google. (If you see a wide range of interests, don't be surprised.)

Acquisition Reports

Understanding what's driving your website visits is essential for effective analytics, but, by default, the Acquisition reports are plagued with inaccuracies and are not specific enough to provide clear insight. GA is not to blame: it does the best job it can with the acquisition information that it has access to. Chapter 7, "Acquisition Reports," examines traffic channels in detail and provides the steps that you'll need to take to help GA report traffic sources with the necessary accuracy and specificity.

Behavior Reports

The Behavior reports provide the *what* of GA: what users did on your website or in your app. For a website, there are two basic types of behavior data:

- *Pageviews,* which occur when a user loads a page in the browser and which are recorded by the default tracking code.
- *Events* (or virtual pageviews), which correspond to all user interactions—as in the Vincent example earlier in this chapter—and which you must explicitly configure as explained in Chapter 6.

For apps, the two basic types of behavior data are *screen views* and events, but screen views overall may constitute a somewhat smaller proportion of the behavior data for mobile apps than pageviews do for websites, since screen loading is not quite as fundamental or frequent in the design of apps as page loading is for websites. In other words, users tend to do more on a single app screen than a single Web page. The exception would be an actual *Web app* that's designed for rich user interaction with minimal page loads—in this case, your GA Web property might also end up with more event data than pageview data (based on your implementation).

Below we discuss the reports and metrics in the Behavior > Site Content section for a Web property.

Pages

Referred to as *All Pages* in the left navigation panel and as just *Pages* in the report title, this central behavior report in GA, shown in Figure 2.7, corresponds most directly to the data that is recorded each time that page loads and the GA tracking code executes. As we learn in Chapter 6, any virtual pageviews that we configure will be listed within the Pages report and anywhere else that physical pageviews appear.

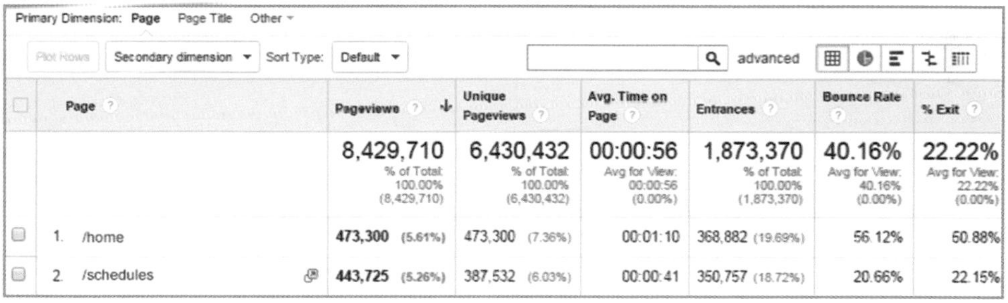

	Page ?	Pageviews ? ↓	Unique Pageviews ?	Avg. Time on Page ?	Entrances ?	Bounce Rate ?	% Exit ?
		8,429,710 % of Total: 100.00% (8,429,710)	6,430,432 % of Total: 100.00% (6,430,432)	00:00:56 Avg for View: 00:00:56 (0.00%)	1,873,370 % of Total: 100.00% (1,873,370)	40.16% Avg for View: 40.16% (0.00%)	22.22% Avg for View: 22.22% (0.00%)
☐ 1.	/home	473,300 (5.61%)	473,300 (7.36%)	00:01:10	368,882 (19.69%)	56.12%	50.88%
☐ 2.	/schedules	443,725 (5.26%)	387,532 (6.03%)	00:00:41	350,757 (18.72%)	20.66%	22.15%

Primary Dimension: **Page** Page Title Other ▾

Plot Rows Secondary dimension ▾ Sort Type: Default ▾   🔍 advanced ▦ ◕ ☰ ⇄ ▥

FIGURE 2.7 Metrics in the All Pages report.

In the left column of this report, Page appears as the primary dimension. (We discuss dimensions and metrics in greater detail later in this chapter.) By default, Page corresponds to the portion of the URL after the domain (and without any GA campaign parameters).

Terminology

Page = Request URI

In GA, the Page dimension corresponds to the portion of the URL after the domain, and without any GA campaign parameters that may have appeared in the URL when the page was accessed. For instance, if a user accessed your page with the following URL:

```
http://www.mysite.com/article.jsp?id=439&utm_source=twitter&utm_
medium=social-paid&utm_campaign=20160715-summer-highlights
```

the Page dimension would be populated as:

```
/article.jsp?id=439
```

In other GA contexts—particularly within view filter configuration, which we discuss in Chapter 9—Page is called *Request URI* (uniform resource identifier). You can think of *Page* and *Request URI* synonymously.

Below, we discuss several of the metrics that appear in the Pages report. Note that you can see pageviews and the other metrics:

- By page.
- By directory (in the Content Drilldown report).
- By Content Group (if you have implemented Content Groups as described in Chapter 12).
- For the entire website, or for a subset of website data after segmentation as described in Chapter 7, or filtering as described in Chapter 9.

Pageviews

The Pageviews metric indicates how many times the Google Analytics tracking code executed on that page. It's the most essential metric in the Site Content reports.

Unique Pageviews (and Unique Screen Views)

The Unique Pageviews metric is actually a session count: the number of sessions during which a page was viewed at least one time. For some analysis purposes, the number of times that a page is viewed during a session is not considered as important as the fact that the user was exposed to the page at least once during the session. When we learn about behavioral segments in Chapter 7 and about goal funnels and Page Value in Chapter 9, we'll see that the concept of at least one pageview per session (or per user) is more relevant than total pageviews.

Terminology

Pageviews versus Unique Pageviews

The Pageview and Unique Pageview metrics seem like they could have been named the opposite way, with Unique Pageviews indicating the total number of times a page was viewed. You can keep these definitions straight by thinking of Pageviews as total pageviews of a page and Unique Pageviews as sessions with at least one pageview of a page.

Average Time on Page (and Average Time on Screen)

As we saw in the previous example with Beatriz, GA has no way to calculate the amount of time that a user was still engaged with your website or app after the last hit is sent. This limitation affects Average Session Duration in the Audience reports and Average Time on Page in the Site Content reports differently.

Let's consider another example:

- Your blog receives 1,000 visits in a given time period.
- In 999 visits, the visitors read the blog post and went to another website, closed the browser, or otherwise did not access another page (or generate any events) within the 30-minute session timeout.

- In one visit, the visitor spent 5 minutes on the first page and then accessed the second page.

  In this case, the Average Session Duration would be calculated as follows:

  ```
  00:05:00 total recorded session duration / 1000 sessions =
  0.3 seconds
  ```

  Average Time on Page for that page, however, would be calculated as follows:

  ```
  00:05:00 total recorded time for that page / 1 instance
  in which GA was able to calculate the time for that page =
  00:05:00
  ```

As we see, the total session count is always used as the denominator for Average Session Duration, so for a site that may experience many single-page sessions (with no additional event hits), Average Session Duration can appear very low. Average Time on Page, on the other hand, is based only on the number of instances (one or more within a session) in which another pageview followed and GA was therefore able to calculate time on page. (A subsequent virtual pageview would also allow GA to calculate time on page, but an event would not, even though virtual pageviews and events both pertain to Average Session Duration.)

Note

Consider Trends and Comparisons More than Absolute Values

We've examined the inherent technical difficulties in fully calculating the time metrics, but we should also consider the several practical factors that can also influence the time metrics:

- ➤ A user is distracted within the session, as in the earlier example of the 29-minute phone call.
- ➤ A user opens a different tab.
- ➤ A mobile user (on your website or in your app) is multitasking and accessing pages and screens sporadically.

These factors can certainly affect many metrics in GA, such as Bounce Rate and Sessions, but they impact Average Session Duration and Average Time on Page the most drastically—in many cases, inflating these metrics to implausibly long durations.

The recommendation is therefore to interpret the time metrics through trends and comparisons rather than as literal values. If, for instance, GA shows a 00:01:00 Average Time on Page for your hammers page and 00:02:00 for your drills page, and both pages have a similar design, length, and call to action, it's safe to say that users are spending about twice as long on the drills page. Similarly, if your news app is showing a 00:03:00 Average Session Duration this July versus 00:02:30 for the same time period in the previous year, you can feel confident and happy that engagement has increased in the past year.

The same advice can apply to all metrics in GA: there can be some variation in accuracy for any given metric, and a single metric at a single point in time is not always as meaningful for insight and optimization as comparison with other metrics and time periods.

Entrances, Bounce Rate, and Percent Exit

The Entrances metric indicates the number of times that a page was the first that a user accessed in a session, and, in most cases, corresponds exactly to the Sessions metric listed in the Landing Pages report (which will be shown in Figure 2.11). Bounce, as illustrated earlier in Figure 2.4, indicates a single-hit session; thus, in the Pages and Landing Pages reports, Bounce Rate indicates the percentage of instances in which the page served as the first page in a session and was not followed by another pageview (or other hit type).

As a note, the Landing Pages report is not limited to pages that you've designated as landing pages for your marketing campaigns; any page on which a site entrance occurs will appear in the Landing Pages report.

Percent Exit (also referred to as *Exit Rate*) and Bounce Rate have different meanings. A bounce occurs only in a single-hit session, whereas an exit must occur in each session. It's also important to remember that a user does not need to actively "exit" a website or an app for an exit to occur: the exit page or exit screen is defined only as the last page or screen that is accessed during a session. Even if a user accesses another page or screen after a session timeout without accessing another website or app and without closing the browser or the app, the last page or screen viewed before the session timeout will be considered the exit page or screen for the previous session.

Note

Is an Exit Always a Bad Thing?

Since each session must have an exit page, an exit is not a bad thing if it occurs after a successful session, which is normally indicated through a goal completion (based on a specific page or an engagement threshold) or an Ecommerce transaction. A high Percent Exit, as indicated in the Pages or Exit Pages report, would be a negative indicator for any page intended as part of a multistep process, such as a payment page on an Ecommerce site. On a page that indicates the completion of a goal or an Ecommerce transaction, Percent Exit is a more neutral indicator. (From an optimization standpoint, however, a thank-you page offers a prime opportunity to offer additional products, services, or information sign-ups to the user who has just completed one type of conversion and could therefore be inclined to complete another.)

Page Value

Though not shown in Figure 2.7, the Page Value metric also appears in the Pages report. As discussed in Chapter 8, Page Value can help you identify the pages that were not necessarily designed as part of your conversion path (such as an About Us page) but that are nonetheless supporting conversion (and to which you should therefore consider directing more of your traffic).

Page Title

In the Pages report, Page Title appears as an alternate primary dimension that you can select for your report. As a rule, Page Title is not used much in GA for the basic reason that Page Titles can be duplicated on Web pages, whereas URLs (and the Page/Request URI dimensions) are, by definition, unique. We will, however, consider the potential role of Page Title in error tracking, as described in Chapter 6.

Note

Bonus Tip: Review Page Titles in GA for SEO Opportunities

Following the procedures described below, you can add Page Title as a secondary dimension in the Pages report and filter Page Title for (not set). If you see many instances of (not set) in pages that do not reside behind a login and should therefore be accessible to the search engines, you can email the report to your search engine optimization (SEO) team so they can address this significant on-page SEO problem.

Duplicated titles for multiple pages might also indicate a hindrance for SEO, but if the pages vary only by a query parameter, the problem may instead be due to URL fragmentation for the same page content, which the search engines may be able to address on their own, but which you must resolve yourself in GA with the Exclude URL Query Parameter view setting as explained in Chapter 9.

Navigation Summary

The Navigation Summary appears as a tab within the Pages report rather than in the left navigation. The Navigation Summary differs from most other GA reports in that it focuses on a single page at a time. More specifically, it shows how many times the selected page served as the entrance (i.e., landing) page and the exit page, and also the number of times that other pages were accessed before and after the page.

The Navigation Summary can be helpful to identify unexpected flows through your website and take optimization steps accordingly. For instance, the Navigation Summary for a jewelry Ecommerce site in Figure 2.8 shows that the top page after /deals is /jewelry, which does not align with your intention to guide users from the /deals page to the /purchase page primarily. When you inspect the /deals page, you notice the Purchase button is not visible without scrolling, so you quickly work with your designer to move the Purchase button further up in the page as a more prominent call to action. (Or you set up a test, as we discuss in Appendix A.)

Previous Page Path		Pageviews	% Pageviews
/jewelry		20,215	18.23%
/watches		2,353	2.12%
/quality-assurance-money-back-guarantee		2,264	2.04%

Next Page Path		Pageviews	% Pageviews
/jewelry		4,238	3.83%
/purchase		4,087	3.69%
/free-next-day-shipping-orders-exceeding-200-dollars		3,015	2.73%

FIGURE 2.8 The Navigation Summary in the Pages report shows how users are navigating to and from the selected page.

Note that you can also apply Content Grouping to the Navigation Summary to display how users are moving between page types or content categories. (Content Grouping is discussed in Chapter 12.)

GUEST SPOT | **Three Tips to Improve Your Mobile Navigation**

Tim Ash

Tim Ash is the CEO of the strategic conversion rate optimization agency SiteTuners, author of the bestselling books on Landing Page Optimization, and the founder and chair of the international Conversion Conference.

Mobile experience is hard to get right.

Even if you have the know-how to redirect traffic to m.website or mobile.website, or even if you have implemented responsive, certain usability principles are just drastically different for smartphones compared to desktops and laptops.

Here are a few ways you can improve the user experience for your mobile visitors.

1. **Don't list your primary navigation options on every screen.** Instead, have the menu display when the user clicks a control (like a three-bar hamburger menu).
2. **Organize your navigation elements.** In Google Analytics, apply the built-in Mobile Traffic segment to your Behavior and Conversions reports to identify the current top interactions for mobile users, and then display the most commonly accessed topics or product areas on your hamburger menu—don't rely on default sorting.
3. **Use big hotspots for navigation.** When visitors do tap on menu launchers, you basically have the license to use the entire mobile device screen, as you can see in the screen shot below. You need to utilize this fully—fingers are not very precise instruments, so making the hotspots larger can have a dramatic impact on reducing user errors.

Once a user taps the menu launcher, use as much of the screen as you need, and display big hotspots.

Behavior Flow Reports

The Behavior Flow report is comparable to the Navigation Summary but shows multiple flows rather than focusing on a single page. In addition to pageviews, the Behavior Flow also allows you to display events within the flows.

Within the Behavior Flow, a node (shown in green in Figure 2.9) can represent a single page or multiple pages that GA has grouped algorithmically, usually based on similar request URI. You can also highlight traffic through a single node in the Behavior Flow, and you can also drill down to display flow though that node only. The Users Flow report within the Audience section of the left navigation is very similar to Behavior Flow, but it does not provide the option to display events or apply a Content Grouping.

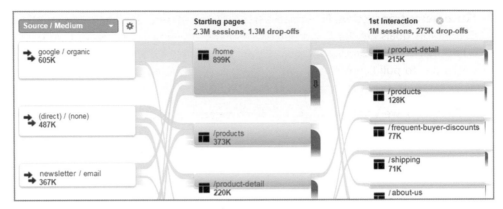

FIGURE 2.9 The Behavior Flow report can help you identify drop-off points at several stages in user navigation through your website.

As a note, the Behavior and Users Flow can be (overly) challenging to interpret at a granular level, so you don't necessarily need to devote a great deal of attention to these reports if you're just starting out with GA, but you can always refer to them to get some sense of overall traffic patterns and to quickly identify unexpected drop-off points at different stages in your processes, and you can also use them in coordination with the Navigation Summary to identify navigation issues.

As mentioned earlier, within the Behavior Flow report, you can also apply any Content Grouping that you have configured in the view and thereby see flow between men's clothes, women's clothes, and children's clothes on a clothing website or between sports, international, and local interest on a news website, as two examples. (Content Grouping is discussed in Chapter 12, "Implementation Customizations.")

Also note that Behavior Flow is available in a GA mobile app view, while Navigation Summary is not.

Conversions Reports

By default, the Conversions reports are not populated at all, but this should in no way suggest lesser importance. The Conversions reports are critical for measuring success, but you must tell GA what success means to you before GA can tell you how many of your sessions are successful.

In GA, a conversion represents one of two things:

- **Goal completion.** This usually corresponds to a pageview of a thank-you or confirmation page, but can also be based on an event that you have configured (such as completion of a video) or a specific engagement threshold (in terms of pageviews/ screen views per session or session duration).

- **Ecommerce transaction.** Ecommerce transactions are not calculated from existing GA data as goals are; for Ecommerce or Enhanced Ecommerce, you must provide additional product, promotion, and transaction details. You typically work with your developer to pull Ecommerce data from the back end and write to the data layer, where the data becomes accessible to the GA tags in Google Tag Manager.

In Chapter 8, we learn about goal and Ecommerce configuration and reporting in detail.

GUEST SPOT   **Google Analytics as a Growth Engine**

Anas Abbar

Anas Abbar is the CEO and cofounder of 7awi.com

A New Digital Experience in the Middle East

The political turmoil in early 2010 impacted all aspects of life in the Middle East. With no doubt, it has been a major contributor to the exponential growth of connectivity and digital communication in the region that has become the umbilical cord interconnecting Arabic-speaking communities globally, freely enabling a once censored or muffled voice of debate in an uncensored conversation, and lifting the region's mysteriousness to the Western world.

By mid-2012, in a small coffee shop in Seattle, Washington, the agreement of digitizing one of the largest traditional Arabic language publisher assets was sealed. The domain www.7awi.com (pronounced HAWI) was registered. After several weeks of market research and analysis, the product portfolio was identified, the road map and priorities, the personas, the technology stack, and the unique differentiators—most importantly, an innovative, interactive user experience—were defined and set to enable 7awi to stand out from the rest of the crowd in the Middle East.

Understanding Content Consumption

7awi's first priority was to launch an innovative digital media product based on the popular *Layalina* monthly magazine. Developing the media platforms for layalina.com was only the first step. Immediately, it was realized that success is hinged on how well we could understand our audiences' consumption of our content, user experience, product interactivity, and, most importantly, content relevance by time, day, and country. Understanding the data proved to be our competitive advantage and quickly became the utmost priority. Hardly a decision was made without having supporting data. On a daily basis the engineering, product, and editorial teams sat with eyes glued to GA to help understand what was causing a spike in readership and what was not.

Leveraging Google Trends

One of the key learnings from the early days was to use the standalone Google Trends tool to analyze what people were searching for on Google, and to then create corresponding content on our website. The result was an exponential growth in terms of inbound traffic from social media (Facebook, Google+, Twitter, Instagram).

continues

continued

Morocco Breakthrough: Basic but Critical Data from the Locations Report

While general lifestyle content may have been relevant throughout the Middle East/North Africa region, the need to have specific and local content was critical to the growth of each individual market and to attracting top-paying local advertisers.

Our biggest breakthrough came when we noticed an unexpectedly high volume of traffic from Morocco, which prompted us to start covering stories of a local Moroccan celebrity. Within weeks, we became the number-one celebrity destination in Morocco, despite the fact that neither the print magazine nor the brand Layalina had ever existed in Morocco.

World Cup: Limiting Assumptions vs. Site Search Reality

Having implemented the GA site search feature—indispensable, particularly for a content site—we were able to directly report on what our visitors were asking for explicitly. Since our target demographic was largely female, we were surprised to see a high volume of searches related to the World Cup in the weeks leading up to the event. The site search data had invalidated our assumptions, and the strong engagement with the World Cup content that we quickly produced further corroborated visitor interest in the subject. Sports-related content has since become a staple on layalina.com.

Year-Over-Year Growth

At 7awi, GA became the default screen on every monitor, with excitement for record-breaking days and a rush for on-the-spot meetings when traffic stalled or dipped. Over time, we were able to set targets based on year-over-year data to forecast growth and set revenue expectations. For New Year's Day, Valentine's Day, Ramadan, and other observances and events, our historical data helped us better focus on partnerships with rich advertisement solutions at the best times on the calendar. Building on traditions of spirituality, habits, and food—and our visitors' engagement with this content in previous years—our Ramadan package on layalina.com grew over 50% in new unique users in 2015 relative to the previous year and served as the destination for 25 consecutive campaigns that produced positive return on investment (ROI) in terms of advertising revenue.

Opportunities through Analysis

Two-and-a-half years later, 7awi's network has over 12 million unique users serving over 300 million pageviews every month. Expert data, proper analysis, and timely execution by a dedicated team are the key to 7awi's leadership among Arab online consumers, advertisers, agencies, and clients. Truly, without data and GA, we would have missed out on many opportunities.

DIMENSIONS AND METRICS

Now that we've reviewed several reports in GA, let's go back and consider the terms *dimensions* and *metrics*.

We can think of dimensions as descriptors about users and their actions that allow GA to classify our data.

How did visitors get to my website? *Source* and *Medium* are the dimensions that answer this question.

Which country is my website or app being accessed from? There's also a Country dimension.

Which pages were viewed? The URL of each page that is viewed is stored in two dimensions: *Hostname*, which corresponds to the full domain name, and *Page* (also referred to as *Request URI*, as we saw earlier), which corresponds to the portion of the URL after the domain (but without any GA campaign parameters).

Metrics are the numeric data reported against the dimension values.

How many times did visitors watch our video? If you've configured event tracking for video, as explained in Chapter 6, the Top Events report would normally display the name of the video as the *Event Label* dimension and the number of user interactions with the video as the *Total Events* metric.

Which mobile devices were used? In the Mobile Devices report, *Mobile Device Info* appears as the dimension, and the *Session* metric indicates how many times the device was used to access your digital property.

How many times was the Help screen viewed in our app? In GA app tracking, the Screens report lists *Screen Name* as the dimension values and Screen Views as a metric.

As you work with GA, it's helpful to approach your reports with the concept of dimensions and metrics in mind, especially as you begin to configure your own custom segments and reports.

GA includes more than 400 dimensions and metrics; you can see a complete list in the Dimensions & Metrics Explorer within the GA developer pages (`https://developers.google.com/analytics/devguides/reporting/core/dimsmets`). It's unlikely that you'll need to use every available dimension and metric, so this book will focus on those that are most critical and hardest to understand.

As a note, the top sections of the overview reports, such as the Audience Overview shown in Figure 2.2, display the metrics for all sessions rather than breaking down the metrics by dimension values in rows.

Primary Dimension

Continuing our discussion of dimensions, each report table in GA defaults to a *primary* dimension in the left column that organizes the table and breaks down the metrics into rows, as shown in Figure 2.10.

The Browser and OS report defaults to Browser as the primary dimension, but you can switch to several other dimensions, such as Operating System or Screen Resolution, as the primary dimension.

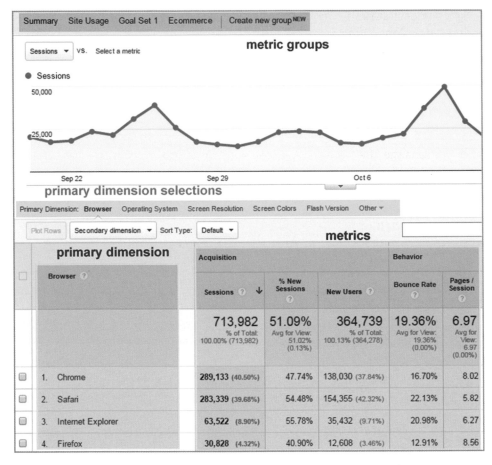

FIGURE 2.10 Within most table reports, you can display different primary dimensions and metric groups.

Metric Groups

In many of the Audience and Acquisition reports, *Summary* appears as the default metric group. Summary includes metrics from the other metric groups, such as Site Usage and Goal Set 1. You can click any of the metric groups to display them instead of Summary.

Secondary Dimensions

Most of the GA table reports allow us to use a secondary dimension. With this extremely useful feature applied, GA further breaks down the metrics based on all combinations or primary and secondary dimension values.

Let's demonstrate in the Landing Pages report, where we can add the following secondary dimensions, as just three examples:

- **Source/Medium.** Which traffic sources drove traffic to which landing pages?
- **Device category.** How many entrances occurred by landing page on desktop, tablet, and mobile?
- **Region.** How many entrances occurred by landing page by U.S. state (or Canadian province, etc.)?

As you analyze the GA table reports, you should take advantage of secondary dimensions regularly, as they provide opportunities for identifying the best- and worst-performing dimension combinations and can often provide greater insight than a primary dimension alone. In plain terms, Secondary Dimensions allow us to piece together more meaningful stories about what is and isn't working. In Figure 2.11, which combination of Landing Page and Source/Medium is achieving the lowest bounce rate?

	Landing Page		Source / Medium		Acquisition			Behavior
					Sessions ↓	% New Sessions	New Users	Bounce Rate
					279,664 % of Total 11.38% (2,457,847)	54.88% Avg for View: 49.88% (10.01%)	153,475 % of Total 12.52% (1,226,068)	25.06% Avg for View: 41.05% (-38.96%)
1.	/new-products		google / cpc		64,503 (23.06%)	77.72%	50,129 (32.66%)	16.83%
2.	/new-products		main-list / email		60,234 (21.54%)	37.88%	22,819 (14.87%)	42.59%
3.	/winter-sale		previous-purchaser-list / email		55,195 (19.74%)	48.48%	26,757 (17.43%)	12.95%
4.	/new-products		previous-purchaser-list / email		51,968 (18.58%)	57.33%	29,794 (19.41%)	11.04%
5.	/winter-sale		main-list / email		6,004 (2.15%)	39.92%	2,397 (1.56%)	48.15%

FIGURE 2.11 Landing Pages report, with Source/Medium set as secondary dimension.

Table Filters

The filter field appears directly above the metrics columns, as shown previously in Figure 2.11. We need to remember that this field directly relates to the primary dimension only: in this example, we could enter *winter* or *winter-sale* to filter the Landing Page dimension, but to filter by Source/Medium, or to filter by a metric threshold (for example, a bounce rate greater than 40%), we can instead click Advanced to access the advanced table filter panel as shown in Figure 2.12.

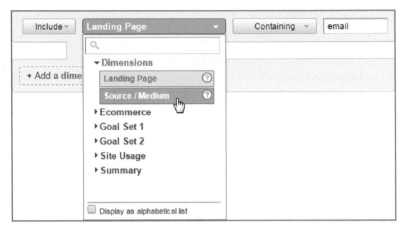

FIGURE 2.12 Since Source/Medium is applied to the Landing Pages report as a secondary dimension, we need to access the advanced table filter panel to filter the table by a complete or partial Source/Medium value, such as email. You can also use an advanced table filter to filter by a metric threshold (e.g., greater than 50% bounce rate).

Note

Filtering for Pages with a ? Character

If you have several pages listed as `/item.php?id=123`, `/item.php?id=456`, etc., and you filter the Pages report for all pages containing `item.php?id=`, the Pages report will display no data. In a view filter, characters such as `?` are interpreted by default as regular expression metacharacters and not as literal characters. In this regex notation, `?` means *zero or one occurrences of the previous character*.

To force GA to interpret the `?` as a literal character within the filter text, click Advanced, and change the Matching RegExp operator to any of the other operators, such as Containing, shown in Figure 2.12.

As another solution, you could add a backslash before the `?` (as in `item\.php\?id=`) to "escape" the `?` so it's interpreted as a literal character instead of a metacharacter. We review some additional regular expression basics in Chapter 9.

Terminology

Filter

Filter is used in GA to mean two quite different things. A *table filter* dynamically filters a table by primary dimension value or, in the case of an advanced table filter, by primary dimension, secondary dimension, or metric.

As discussed in Chapter 9, you can use *view filters* to hard-filter an entire GA view, including all reports within the view, to include or exclude a specific subset of data based on dimension values (device, geography, source, subdirectory, etc.) or to modify or completely rewrite certain dimension values (lowercase all campaign parameters, rewrite URLs to a human-readable format, etc.).

Though not referred to as filters in the user interface, segments provide a way of filtering that is in many ways comparable to view filters, but is dynamic and retroactive. We explore segments in Chapter 10.

Weighted Sort

By default, GA table reports are sorted in descending order according to the first column, but you can change the sort column by clicking the heading for any of the metric columns (and change from descending to ascending by clicking again).

Since we've been discussing landing pages and bounce rate in this chapter, we might want to click the Bounce Rate column heading in the Landing Pages report to easily identify the worst offenders. The problem, however, is that the default sort does not take sessions into account, so the sorting by bounce rate normally displays many one- or two-session landing pages with 100% bounce rate at the top of the report.

To make the sort more meaningful for percentage metrics such as bounce rate, % new visitors, and Ecommerce conversion rate, you can change the sort type from default to weighted, as in Figure 2.13. The weighted sort takes sessions into account and algorithmically displays the most critically high bounce rates relative to the number of sessions in which that page was accessed as the landing page.

	Landing Page	Sessions	Sessions	New Users	Bounce Rate
		2,481,729 % of Total: 100.00% (2,481,729)	49.74% Avg for View: 49.74% (0.00%)	1,234,396 % of Total: 100.00% (1,234,396)	41.71% Avg for View: 41.71% (0.00%)
1.	/lightweight-rubberized-canvas-messenger bag	192,131 (7.74%)	38.08%	73,160 (5.93%)	57.82%
2.	/premium-alloy-sport-performance-handlebars	42,231 (1.70%)	38.77%	16,373 (1.33%)	71.41%
3.	/clip-on-rear-bike-rack-and-fender-set	46,328 (1.87%)	42.30%	19,599 (1.59%)	60.40%
4.	/single-action-bike-pump-with-hose	128,937 (5.20%)	42.36%	54,616 (4.42%)	47.35%
5.	/micro-fiber-gel-adult-bicycle-suspension-seat	95,488 (3.85%)	40.03%	38,226 (3.10%)	48.23%

FIGURE 2.13 Weighted sort takes sessions into account to generate a more meaningful and actionable sort than straight ascending or descending order for metrics such as bounce rate.

Date Selection

The GA reports default to the 30 days preceding the current day. You can change the date selection to as short as a single day or as long as view inception to the current day. By default, the main over-time graph charts the selected metric by day, but you can change this interval to week or month (or hour in certain reports).

Most of the reports also allow you to compare two different time periods. For the most valid comparison, it is recommended to align the time periods to the same days of the week. If you select Previous Year from the Compare To time selection drop-down, the previous time period is selected by calendar date rather than day of the week, as illustrated in Figure 2.14. To align by day of the week, you can adjust the time selection by one day (or two days in the case of a leap year), so that you compare May 1–May 31, 2016, to May 3–June 2, 2015.

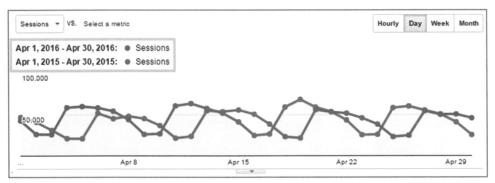

FIGURE 2.14 The Previous Year time comparison produces a one- or two-day offset by day of the week that you can adjust for better analysis.

Note

Seasonality and Yearly Comparison

When you reach the point of having captured more than one year of data from a clean and comprehensive GA implementation, you can begin comparing your performance to the same time period in the last year as a benchmark.

Let's say that on a website for accredited training programs in the medical field, you're tracking inquiries as leads, as shown in Table 2.1. GA indicates the following:

84 leads submitted June 1–30, 2016
64 leads submitted May 2–May 31, 2016

Was June 2016 a good month? Probably, but we still don't really know. If the interest in the training programs varies seasonally—as is the case for many businesses and organizations—the increase from May to June could have been due only to seasonality.

With this thought, you decide to compare this June to the period in the previous year corresponding by day of the week:

84 leads submitted June 1–30, 2016
57 leads submitted June 3–July 2, 2015

We can now say unequivocally that June 2016 was a great month, right? Well, very likely, but not conclusively. We still need to consider one more piece of data and confirm the *change in the change*:

55 leads submitted May 4–June 2, 2015

TABLE 2.1 Monthly Comparison Against Seasonality

	May Inquiries	June Inquiries	Change May–June
2015	55	57	2 (3.64%)
2016	64	84	20 (31.25%)

With data for these four months, we can say with reasonable certainty that June 2016 showed real improvement. The 84 inquiries not only indicated an improvement relative to the previous month and the same month in the previous year; it signaled an increase beyond the seasonal trend: 20 additional inquiries May-to-June 2016 versus two additional inquiries in the previous year.

Now is the time to celebrate and, more importantly, to further analyze traffic sources and landing pages (and to refer to your GA annotations, as discussed in Chapter 11, "Dashboards, Custom Reports, and Intelligence Alerts," to review any design changes, marketing campaigns, or influencer linking that could have contributed to the increase).

Note

How Long Will Google Analytics Keep My Data?

The GA terms of service oblige Google to maintain your GA data for at least 25 months. They have not been known to delete any data, even after many years of collection, but the agreement that you acknowledge when creating a GA account does allow Google to delete any of your GA data that is more than 25 months old. For GA 360, your data will be maintained for the duration of your contract. If you terminate your contract, you can extract your data, and then revert to the GA standard terms.

Table and Chart Display Options

Most GA reports default to a basic table format. If you hover over the small icons in the top right of the table, you'll see that this is called the Data display, as well as the names of the alternate formats in which you can present the same underlying report data. In total, most of the table reports in GA offer five display formats, as shown in Figure 2.15. A few other reports also offer a word cloud option.

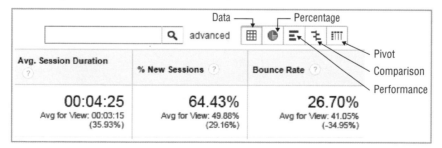

FIGURE 2.15 Most reports default to the Data display but allow you to present the same underlying data in four alternate formats.

Comparison Chart

The Comparison display charts the performance of each dimension row against the site average for a single metric. Figure 2.16 shows the Source/Medium report with the comparison display applied for bounce rate. In the case of bounce rate, lower is better and therefore indicated with green. In the case of a positive indicator such as Ecommerce conversion rate, green would appear on the right of the center line, red on the left.

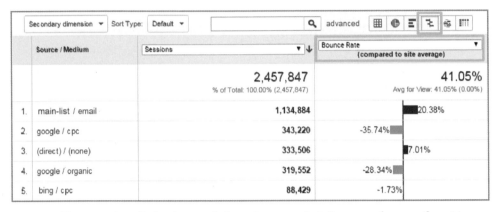

FIGURE 2.16 The comparison display charts each dimension row against site average for a specific metric, such as bounce rate in this case.

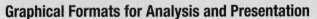

> ## Note
>
> ### Graphical Formats for Analysis and Presentation
>
> It's important to take advantage of the graphical formats not only for your own analysis, but also for communicating the GA data with colleagues and stakeholders. If, for instance, you're meeting with your designers to review landing page bounce rates and the potential improvements you could make (or initially test), or if you're advocating to your manager for design resources, the Comparison display will surely help to convey your message clearly and impactfully.

Percentage and Performance Charts

Similarly to the Comparison display, Percentage and Performance allow you to graph (as a pie chart or a horizontal bar chart, respectively) the performance of a single metric (sessions, in this case) against the dimension values in the report, such as the three dimension values (mobile, desktop, and tablet) in the Device Overview report in Figure 2.17.

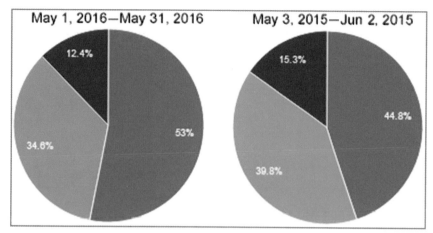

FIGURE 2.17 By switching the Mobile Overview report to Percentage display and comparing the corresponding period from the previous year, we can see the year-over-year metric percentages (sessions, in this case) for mobile (blue), desktop (green), and tablet (orange).

Pivot Table Display

The Pivot display allows you to focus on a single metric or pair of metrics for two dimension values. In Figure 2.18, we're inspecting sessions and bounce rate by OS and browser to isolate potential usability issues. You could actually apply a secondary dimension as well; in this way, Pivot is the only display in the built-in GA reports that allows you to display three dimensions simultaneously.

	Total		1. Chrome		2. Safari		3. Internet Explorer		4. Firefox		5. Safari (in-app)	
Operating System	Sessions	Bounce Rate	Sessions	Bounce Rate	Sessions	Bounce Rate	Sessions	Bounce Rate	Sessions	Bounce Rate	Sessions	Bounce Rate
1. Windows	181,427	47.31%	68,956	52.38%	57	35.09%	82,173	42.82%	26,452	48.46%	0	0.00%
2. iOS	109,123	68.72%	3,587	65.85%	93,978	66.79%	0	0.00%	0	0.00%	11,545	85.27%
3. Android	55,137	71.46%	46,506	71.09%	0	0.00%	0	0.00%	521	66.22%	0	0.00%
4. Macintosh	52,632	46.77%	16,466	48.12%	29,696	45.95%	3	0.00%	6,435	47.04%	0	0.00%
5. Linux	1,613	73.53%	759	70.36%	111	97.30%	0	0.00%	716	73.18%	0	0.00%
6. Chrome OS	1,549	56.17%	1,549	56.17%	0	0.00%	0	0.00%	0	0.00%	0	0.00%

FIGURE 2.18 Based on the session counts and the bounce rates in Pivot, it would be advisable to further investigate the high bounce rates for Chrome on Android and Safari on iOS.

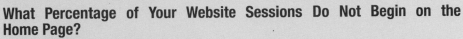

What Percentage of Your Website Sessions Do Not Begin on the Home Page?

In any of the report displays within the Landing Pages report, but particularly within the Percentage or Performance display, you can readily view the percentage of sessions that don't begin on the home page. A high percentage of sessions—even an overwhelming majority—that do not start on the home page is usually not a bad thing; in fact, it likely indicates a wealth of organic clickthroughs, deep-linked referrals from other websites, and paid campaigns driving traffic to designated landing pages.

If, in fact, the Landing Pages report does indicate that many or most of your sessions do not begin on the home page, you'll want to make sure not to confine your most critical functionality and messaging to the home page only. If you need to alert your website users of a planned outage or promote a new product or service, make sure that it is prominent on the top landing pages and/or the shared header or navigation.

Additional Reports

Now that we've reviewed the fundamental concepts and functionalities of GA reporting, let's examine some more specialized additional reports.

Search Terms Report

In GA, the Search Terms report is unique in that it displays actual proactive input from your website visitors. Within the report, you can also apply Start Page as a secondary dimension to view which terms your visitors are searching for on which pages.

The Search Terms and Start Pages data can provide many opportunities for website and marketing optimization:

- If your visitors are searching for a term that is not present on your website, you can develop content or even consider offering a corresponding product or service. (Earlier in this chapter, we learned about Anas Abbar's use of the Search Terms report for key insights into content development opportunities.)
- If visitors are searching for a term that is present on your website, you can optimize navigation from the start pages to the content that contains the corresponding search term, or incorporate the search term directly into the start pages.
- Based on the Search Terms report shown in Figure 2.19, you can also add keywords to your paid campaigns and even consider building out additional content for SEO.

Note that search results pages are sometimes indexed in the search engines, in which case the clickthroughs still do appear in the Site Search reports, with (entrance) as Start Page.

Also note that site search tracking is not enabled by default. Chapter 9 reviews site search configuration, which usually consists of one simple step.

Search Term ?	Total Unique Searches ↓ ?	Results Pageviews / Search ?	% Search Exits ?	% Search Refinements ?	Time after Search ?	Average Search Depth ?
	18,167 % of Total: 100.00% (18,167)	1.45 Avg for View: 1.45 (0.00%)	16.59% Avg for View: 16.59% (0.00%)	26.18% Avg for View: 26.18% (0.00%)	00:03:18 Avg for View: 00:03:18 (0.00%)	2.96 Avg for View: 2.96 (0.00%)
1. cavity	120 (0.66%)	1.57	8.33%	16.49%	00:02:42	2.16
2. crown	115 (0.63%)	1.26	4.35%	6.90%	00:03:04	2.15
3. insurance	98 (0.54%)	1.63	57.14%	7.50%	00:04:09	1.88
4. braces	95 (0.52%)	1.34	6.32%	11.81%	00:03:19	2.37
5. address	95 (0.52%)	1.26	15.79%	6.67%	00:02:03	1.74

FIGURE 2.19 The Search Terms report can provide input for website optimization, content development, and marketing.

Terminology

Keyword versus Search Term, Landing Page versus Start Page

In GA, *Keyword* refers to the phrase that a visitor entered into a search engine before an organic clickthrough (or potentially the matched bid term in the case of a paid clickthrough), while *Search Term* refers to a phrase that a visitor entered into your internal site search.

Landing Page refers to the first page that a visitor accessed in a session, while *Start Page* refers to the page on which a visitor entered a search term into internal site search.

Site Speed Reports

In usability studies, fast page load time has been shown to be a significant factor in user satisfaction and conversion rate, and it also serves, per the search engines themselves, as a strong signal for organic rankings. The Site Speed > Page Timings report (Figure 2.20) compares pages by average page load time. You can also view the Site Speed Suggestions report for specific recommendations on optimizing your page.

In additional to the Speed Suggestions report within the GA interface, you can analyze your website through the Google PageSpeed Insights (https://developers .google.com/speed/pagespeed/insights/), which provides specific recommendations for page load optimization on desktop and mobile.

Within Chrome, you can also refer to the Network tab in the developer console to view which specific page elements are loading the most slowly. Throughout the page speed analysis and optimization process, it is of course recommended that you work with your Web developers.

Secondary dimension ▾ Sort Type: Default ▾			🔍 advanced ⊞ 🕱 ⅲ
Page	Pageviews ▾ ↓	Avg. Page Load Time (sec) ▾ (compared to site average)	
	1,190,017 % of Total: 100.00% (1,190,017)	**4.16** Avg for View: 4.16 (0.00%)	
1. /home ⊕	66,119	-49.64%	
2. /services ⊕	50,610	100.13%	
3. /locations ⊕	32,478	17.29%	
4. /contact ⊕	10,968	-66.53%	
5. /apply ⊕	10,563	-28.22%	

FIGURE 2.20 Page Timings defaults to the Comparison display to illustrate page performance by load time.

Cohort Analysis Report

The relatively new Cohort Analytics report and Multi Session Analytics reports described later demonstrate the increasing orientation of GA toward user-based metrics as a complement to the session-based metrics that have dominated the reports until recently.

The Cohort Analysis report in Figure 2.21 displays the User Retention metric: the percentage of users in your cohort who returned during the given week since acquisition date. The cohort that first visited your website or opened your app May 11–May 17 is showing 5.89% User Retention in the second week since their acquisition date, higher than any of the other cohorts during week 2 since their own acquisition date.

	Week 0	Week 1	Week 2	Week 3	Week 4	Week 5	Week 6
All Sessions 815,830 users	**100.00%**	**6.97%**	**4.46%**	**3.81%**	**3.55%**	**3.45%**	**0.00%**
Apr 27, 2016 - May 3, 2016 140,987 users	100.00%	8.66%	4.44%	4.15%	3.26%	3.45%	0.00%
May 4, 2016 - May 10, 2016 131,927 users	100.00%	6.50%	4.73%	3.63%	3.82%	0.00%	
May 11, 2016 - May 17, 2016 139,499 users	100.00%	6.35%	5.89%	3.85%	0.00%		
May 18, 2016 - May 24, 2016 127,053 users	100.00%	6.60%	4.72%	0.00%			
May 25, 2016 - May 31, 2016 132,199 users	100.00%	6.69%	0.00%				
Jun 1, 2016 - Jun 7, 2016 144,165 users	100.00%	0.00%					

FIGURE 2.21 The May 11–May 17 cohort is showing the best user retention in week 2 since their acquisition date.

We could also display Goal Completions, Ecommerce Transactions, and Ecommerce Revenue as the metrics to confirm high performance of the May 11–May 17 during week 2 in terms of conversion. Going back to that week, you could evaluate any marketing campaigns or special offers that may have attracted or retained a greater proportion of qualified visitors and try to replicate that success: if something is working, do more of it. If we choose, we can also change the cohort interval—referred to as Cohort Size in the report—to day or month.

As highlighted in our discussion about Google Analytics Annotations in Chapter 11, it's critical to maintain a timeline of any factors that can influence usage and performance for your website or app—to help construct a story around your Cohort Analysis, and to interpret trends and anomalies in all of your GA reports.

For a discussion of long-term value by cohort, including offline revenue that your visitors generated after an initial online transaction, see Andrew Duffle's discussion in Chapter 15, "Integrating Google Analytics with CRM Data."

Multi Session Analytics Reports

The reports within the Multi Session Analytics section are also based on user rather than session. For instance, Multi Session Analytics > Engagement shows average cumulative pageviews and duration of sessions per user, and Multi Session Analytics > Ecommerce shows average Ecommerce revenue per user.

When you're viewing user-based reports, remain aware of the cookie dependency for all user-based metrics: if the user has deleted cookies or is using another browser or device, GA will attribute a returning visit to a new user. (For cross-device tracking, discussed in Chapter 12, GA can also recognize returning users across devices without the dependency on a single _ga cookie.)

REAL-TIME REPORTS

Within seconds of a receiving data for a tracked user action on a website or in an app, GA displays the data in the Real-Time reports. We won't rely on the Real-Time reports for close analysis, but, at a minimum, they can be interesting to view immediately after a feature update or a marketing campaign launch, and they're very useful for testing event, goal, and cross-domain tracking, as explained in Chapter 6 and Chapter 12.

Note that in the Real-Time Overview report shown in Figure 2.22, the active users count includes users who have generated a hit in the past five minutes. (This differs significantly from session timeout, which is set at 30 minutes by default, as previously discussed.)

FIGURE 2.22 The active user count in the Real-Time Overview is based on a five-minute window.

Krista's Top Tips and Resources for Google Analytics

Krista Seiden

Krista Seiden is an experienced leader in the digital analytics industry and a frequent speaker at industry events.

As an Analytics Advocate for Google, I'm regularly asked to teach, speak, and share what's new, interesting, and insightful in the analytics world. One question that I receive often is what are my top three tips for Google Analytics? I'd like to share those with you here:

Tip 1: Use Campaign Tracking (Well) to Understand User Acquisition

Campaign tracking is one of the easiest things to implement because it does not require any code on a page. It is simply made up of a string of parameters attached to the URL leading to your site. While it is easy to set up, I can't stress enough the importance of using a consistent naming convention and structure for your parameters. Done properly, it can help you understand not just where your users are coming from (email, social, search, etc.) but also what specific email/newsletter/keyword drove them there. This information is powerful for helping you allocate time, effort, and marketing budgets to the best-performing channels. Check out this template (`http://krsta.me/1NohsGw`) for setting up your own tags and my blog post (`http://krsta.me/1W6lZVu`) for campaign tagging best practices. (Campaign tracking is discussed in Chapter 7, "Acquisition Reports.")

Tip 2: Use Funnel Visualizations to Improve User Flow

Goal Funnels are an incredibly useful (and underused) feature that can help you identify where in your newsletter signup, Ecommerce shopping cart, information flow, etc. a user might be dropping off. You can then dig deeper on those steps to try to optimize the experience and increase user flow and retention. Check out my blog post for more on this: `http://krsta.me/1M73WDD`. (Goal funnels are discussed in Chapter 8, "Goal and Ecommerce Tracking.")

Tip 3: Use Site Search to Optimize Your Website

If you have a search box on your website, be sure to enable site search (two easy steps, outlined here: `http://krsta.me/1NUJ8G1`) in order to capture the keywords that users are searching on your site for. If you see a spike in a particular set of words, that could indicate that users are struggling to find certain content or that you should dedicate more prominent space on your site to such content. (Site search reports are also discussed in this chapter, and site search configuration is discussed in Chapter 9, "View Settings, View Filters, and Access Rights.")

Other Resources

On top of these tips, I'd like to share a few resources that may help you as you continue your Google Analytics education:

> The Google Analytics Academy (`www.analyticsacademy.withgoogle.com`) has five free courses to get you started with Digital Analytics:
> Digital Analytics Fundamentals
> Platform Principles
> Ecommerce Analytics
> Mobile App Analytics
> Google Tag Manager Fundamentals
> The GTM Solutions Guide details how to install GA via Google Tag Manager in a step-by-step, easy-to-digest way and is available in two places:
> Analytics help center, `www.support.google.com/analytics`
> GTM help center, `www.support.google.com/tagmanager`
> Follow our Google Analytics Advocate blogs for up-to-date content on everything analytics:
> Justin Cutroni: Analytics Talk, `cutroni.com`
> Avinash Kaushik: Occam's Razor, `www.kaushik.net/avinash`
> Daniel Waisberg: Online-Behavior, `online-behavior.com`
> Krista Seiden: Digital Debrief, `www.kristaseiden.com`

 **KEY TAKEAWAYS**

Session timeout is 30 minutes.   If more than 30 minutes elapse between two pageviews (or any GA hit type), GA considers the hits as part of two different sessions.

Session count is always higher than user count.   Since a single user can generate multiple sessions, session count is always higher than user count.

Time after final hit is not calculated.   GA cannot record the time of engagement with your website or app after the final pageview, screen view, or other hit type is sent. For this reason, and the many practical factors that can interrupt user engagement and inflate time between hits, you should interpret the GA time metrics comparatively rather than absolutely.

The final page/screen of a session is the exit page/screen.   A user does not have to actively navigate away from your website, close the browser, open another app, or quit the current app for GA to record an exit. The exit page or exit screen is, in all cases, the final page or screen in a session, even if the session just times out and the user then accesses another page or screen.

A bounce is a single-hit session.   While each session has an exit, a bounce occurs only in those sessions in which a user sends a single hit—normally a pageview or a screen view—to GA without any additional pageviews, screen views, events, or other hit types.

 ACTIONS AND EXERCISES

1. **Review the Locations reports.** Are the metrics in line with your expectations? Does the report indicate any marketing or sales opportunities?

2. **Review the Browser and OS and the Mobile Overview reports.** Which technology is underperforming in terms of bounce rate (goal conversion rate, Ecommerce revenue, etc.)? Review your website or app on these devices, etc., and identify the potential causes for the metrics as reported. (You can also use Chrome's device emulator to view your website on different types of devices.)

3. **Review the Landing Pages, Exit Pages, Navigation Summary, and Behavior Flow reports.** Which pages have the highest bounce and exit rates? Are the flows between the pages in line with your expectations, or do they indicate a problem with user experience and conversion?

4. **Apply secondary dimensions.** In several reports, apply secondary dimensions (such as Source/Medium as a secondary dimension in the Landing Pages report), and set advanced table filters that apply to the secondary dimensions. Which combinations show the best and worst performance? What opportunities do you see for optimizing marketing or design?

5. **Switch report display types.** In several reports, switch the report displays between Data, Percentage, Performance, and Comparison. In the Browser and OS report, apply the Pivot display with Browser as the primary dimension and OS as the pivot dimension, and with bounce rate and sessions as metrics, to identify performance issues.

Note

Implementation and Reporting Checklists

We've posted GA checklists at www.e-nor.com/gabook—one for implementation and several variations by industry for reporting—that you can refer to as you complete the chapters in the book and especially as you evaluate your current implementation for updates and you further develop your own reporting and analysis strategy.

3

Measurement Strategy

"The future belongs to those who can collect, aggregate, segment, integrate, visualize, and interpret data."

This core message was delivered by Web luminary Vint Cerf, VP and Chief Internet Evangelist at Google, during a Google Analytics (GA) partner summit at the Googleplex in Mountain View, California.

In the first two chapters of the book, we discussed some of the principles of analytics and optimization, and we reviewed the range of reporting that GA provides. In this chapter, we take a step back and consider the measurement strategy needed for a GA implementation and reporting practice that will help us secure our places in the future that Vint Cerf evoked in his keynote several years ago and that is rapidly emerging as today's data-driven reality.

OBJECTIVE: BUSINESS IMPACT

The overall objective of a measurement strategy is business impact. By defining a sound measurement strategy from the ground up, and by following through on your implementation, measurement, and optimization tasks, you can:

- Better understand your customers.
- Improve your website and mobile app performance.
- Maximize ROI from your marketing initiatives.
- Gain insight and generate recommendations for business improvement.
- Begin to move analytics from a one-off, afterthought project to an established measurement practice.
- Foster a mind-set of ongoing optimization.

The last two points are perhaps the most critical and elusive. While the analytics and optimization concepts are quite straightforward to grasp, changing an organization's culture to be data driven is anything but easy. Using the following approach can help you accomplish these objectives.

Optimization Framework

The optimization pyramid shown in Figure 3.1 serves as an overall guide for progressing from the gaps of the status quo to ongoing optimization and business impact.

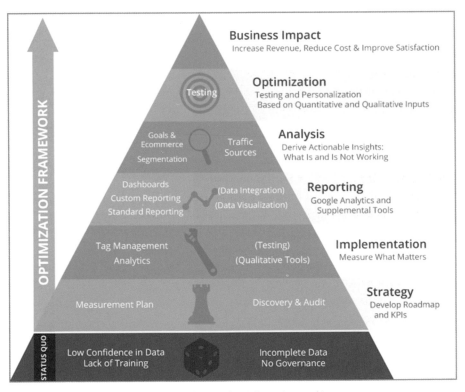

FIGURE 3.1 The optimization pyramid builds toward insight, action, and impact.

Assessing Your State of Analytics

Most organizations have already implemented some degree of Web or mobile analytics, so in most cases, rather that starting from scratch, the objective is to move your analytics program beyond the status quo.

In assessing the current state of your analytics, it's important to consider the following questions:

- **Current tracking code.** Are you using the most up-to-date version of the tracking code?
- **Desktop and mobile.** Are you currently tracking the desktop version of your website (and mobile versions)? Do you have separate mobile pages (on `m.yourdomain.com` or in a separate subdirectory) that need to be tracked?
- **Mobile apps.** Do you need to track any mobile apps?
- **Cross-device.** Do you need to track user journeys across different devices?
- **Cross-domain.** Do you need to track different domains, subdomains, or third-party processers?
- **Additional user interactions.** Does the current implementation capture all important user actions (such as video plays and file downloads)?
- **Taxonomy.** Does your data reflect your organization's classification for customers (such as subscription or membership level) and taxonomy for content (such as categories and authors)?
- **Individual tracking.** Do you need to track users individually but maintain anonymity and respect restrictions against capturing personally identifiable information (stipulated in the terms of service for tools such as GA)?
- **Validation against other systems.** Do you need to validate your data against back-end systems? (For Ecommerce, as an example, do transaction count and revenue in GA match your back-end system?)
- **CRM integration.** Do you need to integrate with CRM data (to measure customer long-term/lifetime value or marketing campaigns based on back-end data)?
- **Ad platforms and remarketing.** Do you have AdWords or DoubleClick campaigns running? Do you have remarketing/retargeting campaigns running through AdWords, DoubleClick, or another network?
- **Multi-channel attribution.** Do you examine the impact of multiple channels on your conversion instead of relying solely on last-touch attribution?
- **Account structure.** Does the current structure of your analytics account(s) effectively support your tracking and reporting needs?
- **Executive roll-up.** Would it be helpful to aggregate data from multiple websites or sources into a single report for managers and executives?

Process and Communication Challenges

As an outcome of the assessment, it typically becomes apparent that lack of data, tool inferiority, or vendor selection is not the issue. In most cases, the issues that most severely hinder a successful analytics program stem from insufficient measurement planning, confusion about roles and process ownership, communication gaps between marketers/analysts and IT, and/or inadequate management involvement.

The upcoming chapters will help you identify and fill gaps in your data collection, clarify responsibilities within your analytics practice, and strengthen confidence in your Web and mobile analytics throughout your organization.

For the remainder of the book, we focus primarily on GA, but we also discuss other tools and integrations with other data sets as part of an overall optimization framework.

> **Note**
>
> ## Who Owns Web Analytics?
>
> In the early days of analytics, when server log interpretation was all the rage, it perhaps made more sense for Information Technology (IT) to own analytics. Over the years, we've seen a shift of analytics ownership from IT to Marketing. Many marketing departments nowadays have IT resources reporting to the chief marketing officer. We believe this is a healthy shift.
>
> Unfortunately, some marketers still suffer from lack of IT support to get basic analytics and marketing tags implemented. Whether you have a dedicated IT staff in your marketing/analytics department or whether you rely on another department, it's key to get an executive champion to support your analytics effort and ensure IT resources and cycles are assigned not only during your analytics implementation project, but for ongoing enhancements and auditing.

Business and Marketing Discovery

As you're assessing the current state of analytics for your Web and mobile apps described earlier, you—as the analyst or marketer building your measurement strategy—should go back even a step further and reevaluate:

- what's important to your organization
- what's important to your customers
- the core, unique value proposition that your organization offers to the world
- what defines success for your organization
- how your organization is trying to achieve success

Your responses to these fundamental questions will inevitably help you clarify what you should be measuring and uncover gaps in your current analytics program.

Do not, however, undertake this foundational work on your own. Reach out and engage all stakeholders individually—this is the time to think both broadly and deeply. The basic question you want to ask is what matters most to them.

You may want to start by asking other analytics enthusiasts and early adopters of data technology, but be sure to consider the following stakeholders as well:

- business owners
- marketing teams (public relations, demand generation, content, social)
- product team
- design and user experience (UX) team
- Web/app developers

- customer support
- sales team

Each of these stakeholders can use data to make better decisions and help drive organizational excellence. Some might already know which metrics and key performance indicators (KPIs) are important to them. For a demand generation manager, KPIs around attribution of various campaigns to conversion is surely a critical focus, whereas performance metrics around browser and operating systems are probably more of interest to your designer.

Some stakeholders will need a little bit of guidance from you, so seek them out, ask questions, and help them to articulate their success metrics. Perspectives from all points within your organization are essential for establishing or reconstructing an effective measurement strategy, and in fact for driving ongoing optimization.

You can begin the discovery in person or you can initially engage stakeholders with a survey and then validate their responses during in-person meetings. In any case, proactively open the communication channels, speak with people face-to-face whenever it's feasible, and keep the dialogue flowing.

Direct input from your customer can also be extremely helpful during the discovery stage: what is most important to them?

> **Note**
>
> **Sample Discovery Survey**
> To download a sample survey that you can use during the discovery phase of your measurement planning, go to: http://www.e-nor.com/gabook.

MEASUREMENT PLAN

At this point, you should know your landscape very well. You've assessed the current state of your analytics, so you understand the breadth and quality of your data, and you've targeted the cultural and organizational hurdles that are impeding analytics progress. You've also engaged with stakeholders and identified their data collection priorities. You should be now ready to write your measurement plan.

We will use an example of a software company, and we will need to identify business objectives, KPIs, and performance targets. Let's define these three important components of the plan:

- **Business objectives.** This is what you want to achieve. For example, I want to sell more products; or capture more leads; or increase my in-app purchases by X%, increase my recurring revenue, and get more impressions/views of my ad-supported pages.

- **KPIs.** Once your objectives are defined, you want to measure progress; this is where KPIs come into play.
- **Performance targets.** The numbers that you need to accomplish to meet your business objectives. You may not yet know the current numbers if you have not yet measured, so you'd need to do an initial implementation to get a baseline. In any case, start with a baseline measurement, and then work to improve on an ongoing basis.

A few related notes:

- While we now more often hear about a mobile-only or mobile-first business (think HotelTonight, Uber, etc.), very few businesses are focused purely on Web play or mobile play, and thus when you're developing your measurement plan, include objectives, KPIs, and targets for both Web and mobile specifically.
  - Establish a process to integrate reporting so you see the full picture of online and offline.
  - To measure the full lead or customer journey, in most cases, you'll rely on GA and other systems, like your CRM system, marketing automation system, email marketing platform, etc.
- When it comes to digital, there is a ton of data available. Our colleague Tracy Rabold has an informative post, "KPIs vs. Metrics," that we encourage you to review: `https://www.e-nor.com/blog/digital-analytics/kpis-vs-metrics`.

We've included a sample measurement plan in Table 3.1.

TABLE 3.1 Measurement Plan with Defined Objectives, Key Performance Indicators, and Performance Targets

Objective	Action	KPI	Performance Target
1. Generate leads	Capture leads (get contact information)	"Request a consultation" form submissions	100 submissions per month
		Sign-ups for free site diagnostic tools	1,500 sign-ups per month
	Nurture leads (give potential leads useful information that makes them more likely to purchase in the future)	Whitepaper downloads	800 downloads per month
		Ebook downloads	150 downloads per month

TABLE 3.1 *continued*

Objective	Action	KPI	Performance Target
2. Build brand/ create awareness	Establish credibility as experts in online marketing	Traffic to blog	3% monthly increases in branded traffic
	Drive traffic to website through content generation	Visits to case studies and white papers section	2% monthly increases in pageviews
3. Sell books	Sell books in online store	Books sold in online store	100 monthly book purchases
	Give out samples of free content to move visitors toward a purchase	White paper downloads	800 downloads per month
		Ebook downloads	150 downloads per month

SIX STEPS FOR ANALYTICS EFFECTIVENESS

This book is designed to help you meet these six fundamental requirements for digital analytics effectiveness, quoted in the chapter introduction, as you implement Google Analytics.

Collect

In this chapter, we reviewed measurement planning—our journey to insight, optimization, and measurable impact has thus begun. In the next two chapters, we learn core GA implementation techniques and begin collecting data.

Beyond the most basic tracking, the book will detail the other types of data collection and customization—such as video plays and other non-pageload user interactions, Ecommerce, or cross-domain continuity—that you must consider as part of a complete implementation.

Aggregate

For our data to be most usable, we must eliminate unnecessary fragmentation (e.g., multiple URL entries in the GA Pages report for the same page content) and capture the data with classifications that reflect the way we view our organizations, our content, and our customers. Chapter 9, "View Settings, View Filters, and Access Rights," and Chapter 12, "Implementation Customizations," discuss data aggregation techniques that you can apply through view settings and filters, content grouping, and custom dimensions.

Segment

Data aggregation and segmentation may seem antithetical, but they are both essential for effective data analytics. During the data collection process, we consolidate and reclassify the data as needed. As part of analysis, we break our data into logical segments (such as buyer vs. seller visitor types) so we can view data in a tighter context that can generate better and faster insights. Chapter 9, "View Settings, View Filters, and Access Rights," and Chapter 10, "Segments," discuss hard-filtering data subsets and dynamically segmenting data through the built-in and custom segment functionality.

Integrate

Web and app analytics reside in the broader ecosystem of business and marketing analytics. Chapters 14 and 18 discuss integrations with Google AdWords, Google AdSense, and the DoubleClick platform to track search engine marketing and monetization ROI. In Chapter 15, "Integrating Google Analytics with CRM Data," we integrate your advertising and CRM data with your GA data so you can more accurately calculate marketing ROI and better correlate Web and app interactions with offline customer engagement and lifetime value.

Visualize

Communication of data and findings is essential to an effective analytics and optimization program, and, in many cases, visualization is essential to effective communication. As we explore the functionalities of the GA reporting interface in Chapter 6, we'll be able to quickly display our data in a graphical format that is in many cases more efficient and focused than the default table format—for your colleagues, managers, and clients, and for yourself. In Chapter 16, "Advanced Reporting and Visualization with Third-Party Tools," we pull data from the Google Analytics application programming interface (API) into third-party tools for rich, interactive visualizations.

Interpret

Interpret was the final imperative in Vint Cerf's statement. Understanding the causality behind the data—the why—is the most difficult and most important challenge we face as analysts. We'll interpret reports as we proceed through the book, and we'll also discuss qualitative inputs such as surveys and usability testing that can help us understand what is and is not working. We'll also consider the role of testing in validating the observations we have made from both the quantitative analytics data and qualitative inputs.

More than any other aspect of our role, interpretation will depend on your will to find meaning and opportunities within the data. Tools and books can help you, but the quest must be your own.

Push Off, Pedal, and Keep Going: Growing the Analytics Discipline in Our Company (and Your Company, Too)

Jon Burns

Jon Burns is Web Marketing Operations manager for a semiconductor company in San Jose, California.

Historically, our Web focus has been to support current customers with information and sometimes software for our products and also to provide presales information. We're just like many other organizations: we're trying to provide the right information to the right people at the right time through the buyer's journey.

Starved for Analysis and Insight

In 2012, I took over a Web team that was underinvested and starved for analysis and insight. In the area of analytics, there had been years of neglect—just monitoring pageviews and visitors, and making choices based on opinions and conjecture, not data.

Then one day it dawned on the folks at pay grades much higher than mine that they might like to know a little more about the hundreds of thousands of visitors coming to our sites each month. And so, to make a long story short, we chose to invest more in this whole Web analytics thing.

A Foundational Commitment to the Analytics Process

All too often, I've heard cases where companies have struggled to get their analytics off the ground for all kinds of reasons, even when funding wasn't the impediment. Investment in analytics is not just about licensing or salaries—it's also about investing time, investing attention, and investing in business processes.

And I believe that it was our commitment to the process that made the difference: not simply throwing money at a problem, hiring a consultant, and calling it solved, but taking the time to really learn the tools, analyze, gain insights, and drive real improvement.

Getting Started

At the beginning, it was not a smooth ride. As with a kid learning to ride a bike, there were bumps and bruises. When you're getting started, you might face data cleanup issues or deployment challenges with your developers. You might actually run into a manager who doesn't immediately see the value of the effort or of the desired end state. But we all need to start anyway. Push off. Pedal. And once you have started, keep going. Pedaling the bicycle should not be an afterthought to the process. Do the work to build a foundation of clean and accurate data.

Conversations at the Foundation of Data-Driven Culture

One of our early, critical moves in building a data-driven culture was simply to ask stakeholders what they hoped that the data would help them figure out. One day, we gathered the product marketers, corporate marketers, customer support teams, and investor relations into a room and simply asked them:

➤ What questions you are trying to answer?
➤ What do you want to find out about the site visitors?
➤ What validations do you need to help you make better choices in your area of the business?

continues

continued

To our surprise, they just wanted the basics. Confirm that the visitors are who we think they are. Tell us what they are doing. Which content is working, and which isn't. Where the trouble spots are. Are they getting what they need, and if they are not, tell us why, or help us figure out what really do need. The responses we heard that day became the foundation for our executive dashboards.

Quick Win for Data

My favorite metric in our executive dashboard is our "visits by customer" (i.e., client organization) metric, based on the domains that we see visiting the site. Because of our business model, the sales and marketing departments routinely voiced their belief that our customers never visited the site because they got all they needed from the sales and marketing folks that were managing the relationships with those customers. (See Figure 3.2.)

Service Provider	Acquisition
	Sessions
	16,981 % of Total: 100.00% (16,981)
1. (not set)	1,014 (5.97%)
2. time warner cable internet llc	508 (2.99%)
3. verizon online llc	445 (2.62%)
4. comcast cable communications holdings inc	264 (1.55%)
5. comcast cable communications inc.	227 (1.34%)
6. ip pool for iliad-entreprises business hosting customers	163 (0.96%)
7. internet service provider	153 (0.90%)
8. charter communications	143 (0.84%)
9. comcast ip services l.l.c.	131 (0.77%)
10. psinet inc.	130 (0.77%)

FIGURE 3.2 The Network report quickly dispelled the prevailing notion that existing customers didn't visit our website.

Well, how would you know that what you believed was not true? Turns out that it was indeed as absurd as it sounded. After just a few months, the GA Network report had put this silly notion to rest. The IP addresses that many larger companies use to access the Internet resolve back to the companies themselves, so the companies appear in the Network report, which in our case clearly indicated ongoing engagement with the website on the part of existing clients.

Unexpected Alignment

An interesting by-product of that first meeting: many parts of the organization realized that they wanted to understand the same things—that the investor relations folks were aligned with the customer service folks and the product marketers and so on. They went from a posture of "no one really gets what we do" to one of natural consensus. We almost high-fived!

Now you, as the analyst, have the whole organization on your side. You are no longer the problem; you are clearly making an effort to create a solution. And you can choose to see this as self-imposed pressure and expectation coming from those stakeholders. Or you can choose to see it as wind in your sails. Either way, it should work.

Make a Public Commitment, and Then Start Sharing

If you are having trouble getting started, do this:

1. Make a commitment.

   Set up that dynamic where now there is expectation and it's on you. There's nothing more motivating than that kind of social/professional pressure … something like an accountability partner. This dynamic can keep things moving, and create a snowball effect over time.

2. Share early, and share often.

   Next, don't lock the data away. Invite those stakeholders to get trained up on how to read those reports, dashboards, whatever it is. You'll build up other analysts in your organization, for those individuals who don't want to delve too far into the analysis themselves, you'll still build awareness of your analytics program, and they'll know whom to turn to for data to answer their questions.

3. Keep the data-driven decisions going.

   Finally, once you've got the tools and methods in place, use them. Every Web project has to have an analytics component. Whether it's a new landing page or an entire site redesign, analysts must be included, and the question must be asked: how will we use data to measure success? Analytics must have a seat at the table, every time. It's not an afterthought.

Now after two years, we've built the foundation, we've implemented enhancements, we're asking the questions we didn't know how to ask before, and we've got the dashboards and reports to answer them.

Recently, a request came in prefaced by "I don't know if it's possible to answer this but I was wondering … of the three embedded YouTube videos on this page, which one is the most popular to visitors of this page?" She had new content to add, needed to remove something to make it fit, and rather than just make a gut call, she asked for the data. And we had it for her. We could now clearly see which videos were being watched on this page, and for how long, so that choosing which one to remove became a no-brainer. If you see yourself in any part of this story, I hope I've provided some value or insight into what's possible. The first step might feel like a leap of faith, but then take another step, and keep going.

 **KEY TAKEAWAYS**

Measure what matters most.   Tie your measurement requirements and priorities to organizational objectives and initiatives.

A thorough assessment is key.   Audit and document what you have and don't leave any stone unturned: technology, implementation, customization, process, people, and skill-sets.

A measurement plan is as good as the time and effort you put into it.   Interview and listen to your stakeholders' needs, document the business and marketing questions data can help answer, and document all of that into your plan.

Go for business impact.   Don't settle for reporting on visits and pageviews. Track and report on data that your stakeholders obsess about.

Segment, segment, and segment some more.   You'll hear about it throughout this book, and we can't emphasize it enough. Aggregates will not take you far in your journey of optimization and insights.

 ACTIONS AND EXERCISES

1. **Engage your stakeholder.** Whether in your audit process or marketing discovery phases, ensure you reach out to get the buy-in from all stakeholders. Get an executive sponsor along the way—their support will be priceless.

2. **Complete the discovery survey.** Download and complete the discovery survey, available at www.e-nor.com/gabook.

Account Creation and Tracking Code Installation

I n the previous two chapters, we reviewed a range of Google Analytics (GA) reports and then took a step back to the measurement strategy phase of your GA program. This chapter walks through the creation of a GA account and a basic installation of the GA tracking code.

CREATING A GOOGLE ANALYTICS ACCOUNT

The only requirement for creating a GA account is an email address that's associated with a Google account. Any gmail address qualifies, as does any other email address with which you have created a Google account.

Creating a GA account is a quick and painless process, but it's important to understand the three levels of the hierarchy—account, property, and view—that are automatically generated with each new account.

Note

Create a Practice Account

Even if you're not directly responsible for implementation, the essential processes of creating an account and accessing the tracking code will help to anchor your reporting and analysis. If you're working within an existing implementation but have never or not recently created an account, we also recommend that you complete the steps in this chapter.

If you do not already have access to a Google Analytics account with the Google login that you are using, the steps for creating a GA account are as follows:

1. Go to: `http://www.google.com/analytics`.
2. Log in with your Google account as prompted.
3. Sign up for GA as shown in Figure 4.1.

If you have already created a GA account under the same login, you can select Create New Account from the account drop-down menu of the Admin screen, as shown in Figure 4.2. In either case, you can continue with step 4.

4. Specify your account and property settings as described below.
5. Click Get Tracking ID to complete the account creation.

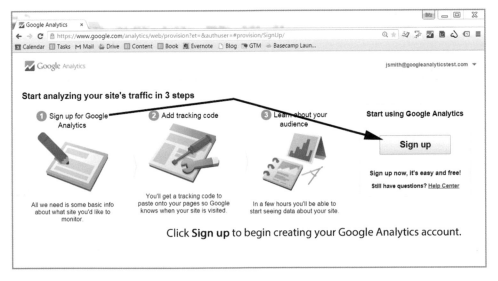

FIGURE 4.1 Google Analytics account sign-up screen.

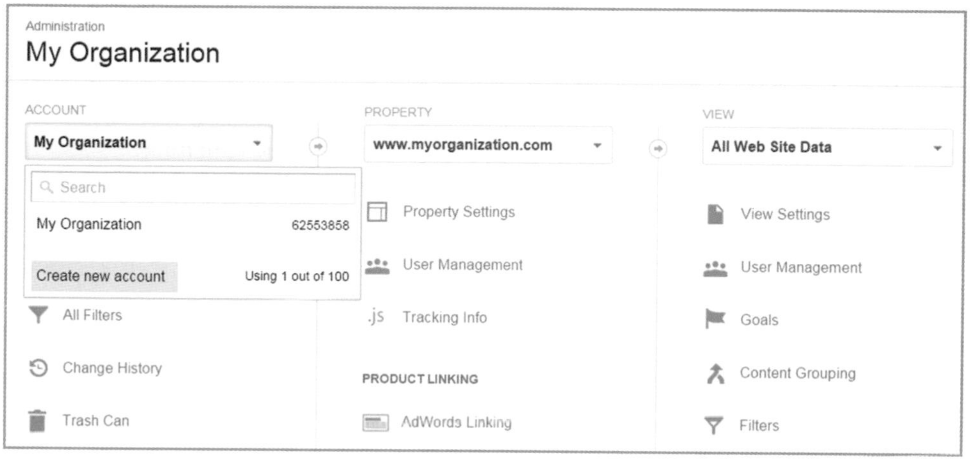

FIGURE 4.2 Creating a new account from the Admin screen.

Configuring Account and Property Settings

At the same time that you're creating a new account, GA automatically creates a new property within the account and a new view within the property. As shown in Figure 4.3, the majority of settings on the New Account screen relate to the property rather than the account.

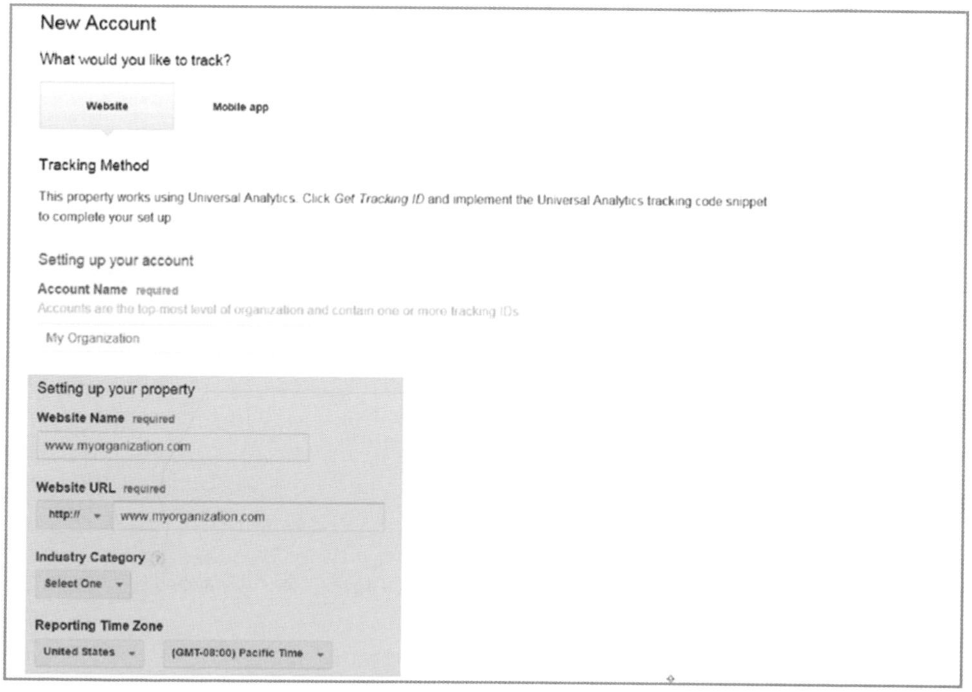

FIGURE 4.3 Account and property settings.

Account Settings

- **Website or Mobile App.** You can track websites and mobile apps as separate properties within the same account. For now, select Website to create a Web property as the first in the account.
- **Account Name.** Your account name can correspond to your organization, your department, or any logical grouping of websites and/or apps. If you have multiple accounts in your organization, the account name should clearly and logically differentiate this account from the others.

Property Settings

- **Website Name.** In most cases, it's recommended to use the website hostname (that is, the full version of the domain including the subdomain. such as www.mysite.com) in this field.
- **Website URL.** Repeat the website hostname in this field. If your pages are accessed through both `http://` and `https://`, you can keep the protocol drop-down set to `http://` and include the same tracking code on all pages.

    As an additional note, regardless of a property's Website URL setting, you'll be able to use this property's tracking code on different hostnames; specifying the one main hostname as Website Name and Website URL will not pose a problem. This may be counterintuitive, but it will be tremendously useful when we configure cross-domain and roll-up tracking in Chapter 12.
- **Industry Category.** This applies to the Benchmarking report discussed in Chapter 7.
- **Reporting Time Zone.** Match the time zone settings for any AdWords or DoubleClick accounts that you will link to this account.

After you have specified your new account and property settings, you can normally keep the four Data Sharing settings selected and then click Get Tracking ID (and agree to the terms of service). If, however, your organization might have strict policies on any type of data sharing, even in aggregated form, check with your legal/privacy specialists and disable any of the data sharing settings as needed.

The tracking code that appears next corresponds to the property, not to the account. In Figure 4.4, 62553858 represents the account, but UA-62553858-1 corresponds to a specific property within the account. If you set up another property for another website or mobile app within the same account, the ID for the new property will increment by one: UA-62553858-2.

Don't worry about copying the tracking code the first time you see it. You can always access it again under Tracking Info > Tracking Code within the property admin. Also, before you install the native tracking code shown in Figure 4.4, you should consider installing GA through Google Tag Manager as discussed in Chapter 5.

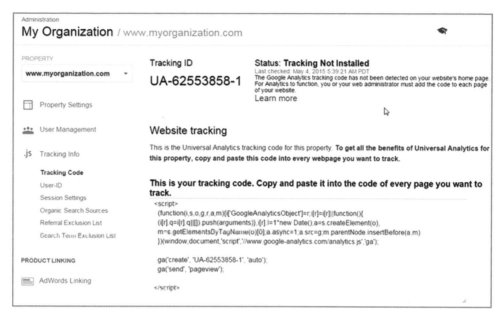

FIGURE 4.4 GA tracking code.

Account and Installation Terminology

Let's take a moment to review and compare some of the core terminology related to account, installation, and reporting options in GA.

Native versus Google Tag Manager

- **Native:** In a native deployment of GA, you include the tracking code shown in Figure 4.4 on all pages of your website. (For mobile apps, native deployment could be said to consist of tracking through the Android or iOS SDKs, as discussed in Chapter 13.)
- **Google Tag Manager (GTM):** When deploying through GTM, you include the GTM container on all pages of your website and add GA as a tag within the GTM container as discussed in Chapter 5. (You can deploy Google Analytics through other tag management systems as well.)

Classic versus Universal

- **Classic:** This term designates the previous version of the GA tracker in both native code and GTM. If your GA predates April 2014, it may be Classic. If you have a Classic installation and have not already migrated, see "Migrating from Classic to Universal" later in this chapter. The two Classic GA tracker variations are referred to as *asynchronous* and *traditional*.

- **Universal:** All new capabilities in GA are enabled through the Universal version of the tracker, whether the tracker is implemented through native code as described in this chapter, or through GTM as described in Chapter 5.

Google Analytics Standard (i.e., Nonpaid) versus Analytics 360

- **Google Analytics Standard:** This free version of GA offers a rich feature set and adequate storage for websites and apps that don't exceed 10 million sessions per month.
- **Analytics 360:** As discussed in Chapter 18, Analytics 360 (formerly called Google Analytics Premium) offers increased storage and custom dimension limits, faster processing, unsampled reporting for large data sets, retroactive custom funnels, data-driven attribution, a service-level agreement, and enhanced support. Analytics 360 is available as a paid option, and is the flagship service of the paid Google Analytics 360 Suite, which also includes Tag Manager (paid version), Optimize, Data Studio, Audience Center, and Attribution.

Standard (i.e., Built-In) versus Custom

- **Built-in:** The reports, dimensions, and metrics available to all GA users. You can access all built-in reports under Reporting in the top navigation. The regular, noncustom reports, dimensions, and metrics are often referred to as *standard;* in this book, we use the term *standard* primarily in reference to the nonpaid version of GA.
- **Custom:** Custom dimensions and metrics are those that you define and populate yourself. Custom reports are those that you define yourself (based on both regular and custom dimensions and metrics) and that you access under Customization in the top navigation.

Terminology

Standard

The out-of-the-box reports, dimensions, and metrics are often referred to as *standard* by GA practitioners. In this book, we use *standard* to refer primarily to the nonpaid version of GA and *built-in* to refer to the noncustom GA elements.

GOOGLE ANALYTICS ACCOUNT STRUCTURE

When you create an account, GA also creates a default property within the account and a default view within the property as described above and shown in Figure 4.5. Here are some key points about account structure:

- Under a single Google login, you can create as many as 100 GA accounts.
- A single GA account can contain as many as 50 properties.

- In most instances, a single GA property corresponds to a single website or mobile app. (For cross-domain and reporting, discussed in Chapter 12, you track more than one website or app in a single property.)
- Each GA property can contain as many as 25 views.
- The account creator (and any user with Manager Users rights) can provide access at the account, property, or view level to other Google logins.
- Any Google login can receive access to an unlimited number of accounts, properties, and views.

We discuss account access more thoroughly in Chapter 9.

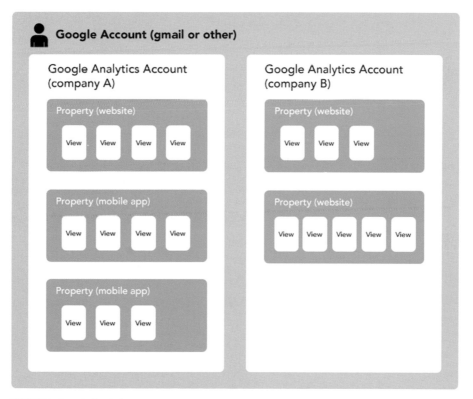

FIGURE 4.5 Google Analytics account structure.

New Property for Each Additional Website or App in an Organization

As discussed earlier, a property usually corresponds to a single website or mobile app. If you have to track a new website for your company or the same client organization, it's usually advisable to create a new property in an existing account rather than creating a new account and property. (You could also track multiple websites as a roll-up in a single property, as detailed in Chapter 12.)

Multiple Views per Property

If a single website or app normally corresponds with a GA property, why do we need multiple GA views?

Views provide outputs of the same raw feed of website or mobile app property data differentiated by data cleanup, data subsetting, and the addition of metrics such as goal conversion rate. As we will discuss in Chapter 9, "View Settings, View Filters, and Access Rights," our ability to create multiple reporting views for the data in each property is critical for a sound GA implementation.

INSTALLING THE TRACKING CODE

Once you have created a new account (or a new property in an existing account), there are two main approaches for populating data into GA:

- **Add the native tracking code.** Include the GA tracking code on every page of your site as outlined next.

- **Add a GA tag to Google Tag Manager.** Instead of installing the native GA tracking code, it may be better to add a GA tag through GTM, as outlined in Chapter 5.

Although you could use both approaches within a single website, you normally use just one or the other. You'll certainly want to avoid tracking the same hits to the same property through both the native code and GTM on the same page: this would count each hit twice and invalidate metrics such as bounce rate, goal conversion rate, and pages per session.

Note

We Strongly Recommend the Google Tag Manager Option

For the remainder of this chapter, we review the procedure for installing the native GA tracking code. For all but the most basic implementations, however, we recommend installation through Google Tag Manager, as detailed in Chapter 5.

The pageview data described below relates equally to native and GTM deployment of GA, and many of the verification tools and techniques apply to both approaches as well.

Placement of the Google Analytics Tracking Code

If you do opt for the native tracker, you should place the GA tracking code, seen in Code Listing 4.1, before the `</head>` tag on every page of your site. If, however, you need to place it at another point on the page (because of limitations in your content management system, for example), the tracking code will still execute, but you will run the slight risk of GA events not being tracked correctly if users initiate the corresponding actions before the page has parsed the main Google Analytics tracking code.

LISTING 4.1: Placement of the Google Analytics tracking code.

```
<html>
  <head>
    <title>Product Description</title>
    <script>
      (function(i,s,o,g,r,a,m){i['GoogleAnalyticsObject']=r;i[r]=
      i[r]||function(){(i[r].q=i[r].q||[]).push(arguments)},i[r].
      l=1*new Date();a=s.createElement(o),m=s.
      getElementsByTagName(o)[0];a.async=1;a.src=g;m.parentNode.
      insertBefore(a,m)})(window,document,'script','//www.google-
      analytics.com/analytics.js','ga');
      ga('create', 'UA-15155947-1', 'auto'); //replace with your
      property ID
      ga('send', 'pageview');
    </script>
  </head>
```

```
<body>
    <p>Here is bullet list about our product:</p>
    <ul>
        <li>relieves headaches</li>
        <li>fast-acting</li>
        <li>tastes great</li>
    </ul>
</body>
</html>
```

Advantage of Page Templates

If you have 2,000 pages on your website, it is unlikely that you'll have to add the tracking code manually to 2,000 pages. Most websites are constructed from templates (also referred to as master pages) that are shared among all pages of your website and that dynamically pull in page-specific data from a content management system or another back-end database (Figure 4.6).

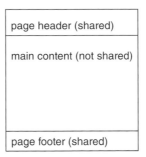

FIGURE 4.6 Most Web pages are constructed from shared templates.

Templates are a great help in implementing GA, because they allow you to propagate GA onto every page of your website by including the tracking code in perhaps as few as one single physical file on your Web server.

Note

Don't Forget to Tag Standalone Pages

Make sure you don't forget to add the tracking code to pages that don't use the same header and footer, such as no-header pages in a purchase path or simplified security, privacy, or terms of service pages.

Browser Requirements for Tracking

For GA to record data from a Web page, the following capabilities must be enabled in the browser:

- JavaScript
- cookies
- images

Fortunately, the percentage of visitors who do not support all of these browser functions is, by all accounts, very low: as high as 3% maximum, and perhaps even lower than 1%. Furthermore, even if you could track these visitors, it would probably not in most cases be advisable to focus a great deal of analytics or optimization effort on an audience segment that has deliberately opted out of a typical user experience.

JavaScript

JavaScript is a lightweight programming language that is used extensively to enhance Web page functionality. All components of GA tracking for a website are written in JavaScript, including:

- The GA tracking code snippet that you include on your page.
- The main analytics.js file that is referenced from the GA tracking code snippet.
- Any additional GA tracking that you perform on a page, such as Ecommerce transactions.

While JavaScript and Java are loosely related syntactically, they're different languages used for different purposes—don't use the terms interchangeably.

Cookies

When the GA tracking code executes, it first checks if the _ga cookie is present in the browser for the current website. If the cookie is not found, a new cookie is created. If the cookie is found, the session is recorded for a returning visitor in GA. The expiration date is set to two years from the current date in both cases.

If a visitor has disabled first-party cookies in the browser or has opted out of tracking as described below, the session is not recorded in GA.

If a visitor returns using the same browser and the same device within two years and has not deleted cookies, GA will recognize the visitor as returning.

It's worth noting that a single browser can store multiple _ga cookies: one for each GA-tracked website that a user has visited.

Images

Somewhat surprisingly, images must also be enabled for a browser to generate GA data. This is because analytics.js passes data back to the GA servers by requesting a single-pixel image file named `__utm.gif` and sometimes referred to as the *tracking pixel*. When analytics.js requests the tracking pixel, it appends GA data such as URL, timestamp, and browser version. You'll rarely, if ever, need to directly manipulate the tracking pixel, but it's useful to be aware of its behind-the-scenes data collection function.

Cookie Dependency

Many calculations in GA depend directly on detection of an existing _ga cookie in the browser for the given website. Any of the following conditions will cause a returning visitor to be recorded as a new visitor in GA:

- different device
- different browser on the same device
- user has deleted cookies since previous session
- previous session occurred in browser incognito/private mode

Any of the factors above would affect your GA reporting and functionality as follows:

- Returning Visitors skew lower.
- Count of Visits skews lower.
- Days Since Last Visit skews lower (more recent).
- Users skew higher.
- Cohorts appear more recent.
- Assisting channels in the Multi-Channel Funnel reports are lost.
- Members of Google Analytics Remarketing Audiences are lost.

Note

How Often Do Visitors Delete Cookies?

While it's hard to cite an exact figure, some research indicates that, on average, 30% of Web users delete their cookies at least once monthly.

Private Browsing

Let's review the impact of additional privacy settings on GA tracking.

Private/Incognito Mode

Google Analytics does track a visit from a browser that is set to private/incognito mode. (The name for this mode varies by browser.) The difference, however, is that the browser automatically deletes cookies following a private session, so any subsequent visits to a website would be tracked as new. (As an exception, private browsing in Firefox does block GA tracking.)

Do Not Track (Browser Setting)

If a user has enabled the Do Not Track browser option, Google Analytics still does track that user. You could choose to block tracking for do-not-track users, or you could use a custom dimension to record the percentage of do-not-track sessions. (For more on this discussion, see: `http://www.e-nor.com/gabook.`)

Google Analytics Browser Opt-Out

If, on the other hand, a user has added a specific GA opt-out browser extension/plug-in provided by Google or a third party, no data for that user will be recorded in Google Analytics.

As described in Holger Tempel's gaOptout discussion in Chapter 12, you can also build a selectable do-not-track option into your Web design If this is dictated by your industry or governing privacy laws.

> **Note**
>
> ## Privacy Policy
>
> The GA terms of service require that you advise your website visitors or app user that GA tracking is enabled and that you include an additional notice if Demographics and Interests or remarketing is enabled. See *Demographics and Interests* in Chapter 12 for boilerplate verbiage.

Intranet Tracking

Tracking intranet activity in GA—either natively or through GTM—is essentially identical to website tracking. The only specific requirement is that intranet users must also have outside Internet access so that the browser can reach analytics.js and the GTM container script on Google's servers.

> **Note**
>
> ## Can I Host *analytics.js* on My Own Web (or Intranet) Server?
>
> Downloading `analytics.js` and serving it from your own servers is not recommended. By instead allowing the native tracking snippet (or a GA tag in Google Tag Manager) to reference the current version of the file on Google's servers, you'll ensure immediate use of the up-to-date GA feature set.

Tracking from Mobile Devices

Since mobile and tablet browsers support JavaScript, cookies, and images, Web pages viewed on smartphones and tablets are tracked in GA the same way as on desktop. If you're using a responsive or adaptive website format, the same tracking code that records data in a desktop browser also records data in a smartphone or tablet browser.

If, however, you're redirecting your mobile visitors to standalone mobile pages, you must make sure to include the tracking code on those pages as well. No modifications to the tracking code itself are required for Web pages designed for mobile devices.

If you need to track websites from older WAP-based phones, sometimes referred to as "feature" phones, you can use the measurement protocol discussed in Chapter 17. The server-side code snippets that were formerly recommended for tracking feature phones have been deprecated.

Pageview Hits

If you parse out the readable English from the GA tracking code previously shown in Listing 4.1, you may notice the core ga('send', 'pageView') JavaScript function.

This function executes each time a page that has the tracking code loads and thereby sends data to GA, including:

- page URL and title
- visitor source
- visitor IP address, from which geo data is derived
- technology data, such as device type and browser version
- timestamp

No special configuration is required to capture this data: it is all recorded automatically when the tracking code executes. Illustrated in Figure 4.7, the data packet that encapsulates this information and sends it to Google Analytics is referred to as a *hit*. A hit is triggered by an interaction—in this case, a pageview. Different types of hits include events (for actions such as video plays or offsite links that don't cause a page load on your site), social interactions, and Ecommerce transactions, all of which will be discussed in upcoming chapters.

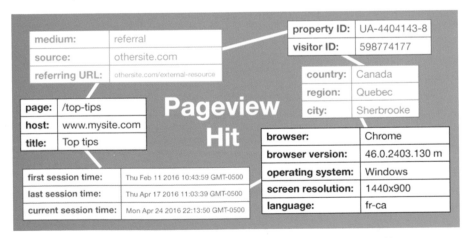

FIGURE 4.7 Pageview hit includes a great deal of data in addition to the page data itself.

Verifying Tracking Code Installation

To verify that the tracking code is installed on a page, and that GA is receiving data, you can:

■ Install and activate the Google Tag Assistant extension for Chrome, as shown in Figure 4.8, which will confirm the presence of the tracking code on the page.

FIGURE 4.8 Google Tag Assistant.

■ View the Real-Time reports, discussed in Chapter 2, "Google Analytics Reporting Overview."

■ Install and activate the GA Debug extension for Chrome, as discussed below.

Google Tag Assistant Record Feature

In addition to indicating the presence of GA and GTM on a Web page, Google Tag Assistant also allows you to record the tags that load as you navigate from page to page on a website. Furthermore, if you have access to a Google Analytics view that is populated with data from the website, you can display more detailed information about pageview and event hits that are generated.

In this way, Google Tag Assistant can be useful in verifying that a GA pageview is firing on the recorded pages, and even more useful in checking any event details that are generated while you are on the page.

You can take the following steps to create a recording in Google Tag Assistant:

1. Install the Google Tag Assistant extension for Chrome if you have not already done so.
2. In Chrome, click the Google Tag Assistant icon in the top right of your browser to display the Google Tag Assistant panel.
3. At the bottom of the panel, click **Record**.

4. Navigate through the website and (perform actions for which you have configured events).

5. At any time, click the icon to redisplay the panel and click **Stop Recording** and then Show Full Report. The Tag Assistant Report that appears by default displays information about each tag that was present when each page loaded.

6. Click into the section of the recording named **Google Analytics Report** to display details about the pageview and any events that were generated on each page that was recorded, as shown in Figure 4.9.

Note that the recording also displays custom dimensions included in the hit. (Custom dimensions are discussed in Chapter 12. To view the Google Analytics Report section, you must have access to a corresponding view in Google Analytics.)

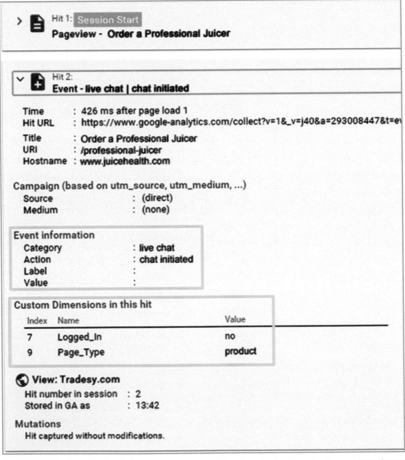

FIGURE 4.9 The Google Analytics Report section of the Google Tag Assistant recording shows the GA pageview and event hits that were generated on the page and displays additional details, such as event dimensions and custom dimensions.

Using Google Tag Assistant Recordings with GTM Debug

Google Tag Assistant recordings capture unpublished GTM tags that fire in Debug mode, including GA pageview and event tags. For instance, if you are debugging an event tag your live chat, you could:

- view the GTM debug panel to verify that the event tag is firing
- access the Google Analytics Report section of the Google Tag Assistant recording to verify that the event category and action (and label) dimensions are captured correctly

As mentioned previously, to verify the event tag that you're debugging, you could also check the Google Analytics Real-Time Events reports and also the output of the GA Debug extension in the Chrome console.

Saving and Sharing Google Tag Assistant Recordings

Google Tag Assistant allows you to save recordings. This feature might be especially useful for agencies (or even departments within one organization) that may need to verify tag execution on an authenticated or development website that they cannot access.

In this case, another user can save the Google Tag Assistant recording and forward you the recording file (named tag_recording.harz by default), which you can then load into Google Tag Assistant yourself by opening the Google Tag Assistant panel, clicking Record > View Recordings > Upload Report, and selecting the .harz file that was previously recorded. (To view the Google Analytics Report recording, whether the recoding was generated with live or GTM-debug GA tagging, you still do need access to a corresponding GA view.)

You can also use the Google Tag Assistant recording feature to verify fixes. Let's say, for example, you see that the thank-you page of your lead generation process is appearing prominently in your landing pages report. This page should not be serving frequently as a landing page; it should be preceded by several other pages in the session.

When you go through the lead generation process with Google Tag Assistant, you note, in fact, that the final page is included in a new session because a developer had inadvertently used campaign parameters in the internal redirect to the thank-you page. (In Chapter 7, we discuss campaign parameters—and why you should never use them for internal linking.)

Once you have removed the campaign parameters from the internal link, you can replay a .harz file saved out from the previous recording to verify that the clickthrough to the thank-you page is no longer starting a separate session.

Google Analytics Debugger (GA Debug) Extension for Chrome

The GA Debug extension for Chrome displays each dimension of the hits sent to GA. To activate GA Debug:

1. While in Chrome, perform an Extension search or a regular Google search for Google Analytics Debugger, install the extension as prompted, and click the icon to turn on the extension.
2. From the three-bar menu in Chrome, select More Tools > JavaScript Console.
3. Reload the Web page.

The Chrome JavaScript console should now display the pageview hit data, as shown in Figure 4.10.

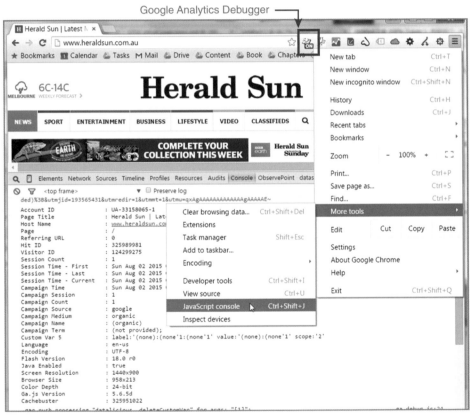

FIGURE 4.10 The GA Debug Extension displays GA hit data in Chrome's JavaScript console.

In Chapter 5, "Google Tag Manager," and Chapter 6, "Events, Virtual Pageviews, Social Actions, and Errors," we also use Preview and Debug mode in GTM to confirm pageview and event hits. Debugging options are also summarized at `http://www.e-nor.com/gabook`.

Removing Your Own Domain from Referral Exclusions to Identify Pages Missing Tracking Code

When you first create a property, GA automatically adds the website domain to the Referral Exclusion list, which you can access under Tracking Info in the Property panel of the Admin screen. It can be helpful to exclude your own domain, since your own site would otherwise appear as a referrer in the case of session timeout. That is, if a visitor views one page on your site and then accesses another page or generates an event after the session timeout (30 minutes by default), the new event or pageview will start a new session, and the source of that new session will be your own website rather than the traffic source that actually drove the visit. (Self-referrals would similarly occur at midnight, per the time zone indicated in your view settings, due to the midnight session reset discussed in Chapter 2, "Google Analytics Reporting Overview.") By excluding your own domain as a referrer, you maintain the session and the original, actual source of the visit.

The downside to excluding your own domain as a referrer is that GA won't indicate which pages on your site are missing the tracking code. If you remove your own domain from the exclusion as shown in Figure 4.11, every click back from a nontracked page to a tracked page will appear as a self-referral regardless of session timeout. You'd be able to spot these self-referrals quite easily in the Acquisition reports, click into your domain to display the Referrals Paths (i.e., the specific referring pages) from which the tracking code is missing, and fix the tracking gaps.

If, however, you're implementing cross-domain tracking as discussed in Chapter 12, "Implementation Customizations," you must exclude your own domain as a referral. In this case, you can instead use a tracking code verification resource listed at www.e-nor.com/gabook.

Referral Exclusion List ⓘ

Exclude these domains from your referral traffic. Users arriving at your site via any of these domains will not be counted as referral traffic in your reports.

+ ADD REFERRAL EXCLUSION	🔍 Search
Domain Name	
mysite.com	remove

FIGURE 4.11 It can be helpful to remove your own domain from the Referral Exclusion list to more easily identify pages that are missing GA tracking.

Migrating from Classic to Universal

If you're starting out with a new GA account or property, you won't need to migrate to GA Universal, since Universal is now the only version of the tracking code that is readily accessible. (GA Classic is still available through GTM but normally not used.) If, however, you installed GA native code before April 2014, you may still be using Classic and may therefore need to migrate to Universal.

> **Note**
>
> ## What makes Google Universal Analytics "universal"?
>
> While most GA functionality did not change from Classic to Universal, several features do put the "universal" into Google Universal Analytics, including the following:
>
> ➤ **Custom dimensions and metrics.** While GA Classic allowed only 5 custom variables per property, Universal allows 20 custom dimensions and 20 custom metrics. (Analytics 360 allows 200 of each per property.) By capturing dimension values and metrics that are specific to your users (no PII), your organization, and your websites/apps, you extend the GA data set to be even more meaningful for you. (Custom dimensions and metrics are reviewed in Chapter 12, "Implementation Customizations.")
>
> ➤ **Cross-device tracking.** Tracking logged-in users across different devices is also a "universal" aspect of GA Universal. (Cross-device tracking is also discussed in Chapter 12.)
>
> ➤ **Measurement Protocol.** Perhaps the most "universal" aspect of GA Universal is the Measurement Protocol, which allows you to send data to the Google Analytics servers through an HTTP request from any networked, programmed environment, without dependency on analytics.js or the Android or iOS SDK. (Measurement Protocol is discussed in Chapter 17. Though very powerful, it's also very specialized and not part of most GA implementations.)

How Can I Tell If I'm Still Using Classic?

The Google Tag Assistant extension for Chrome discussed earlier should indicate which version of GA is present on a page (Figure 4.12). If Code Version/Syntax appears as Asynchronous, Traditional, or anything other than Universal, the GA on the page is not yet

FIGURE 4.12 The Google Tag Assistant extension for Chrome indicates that the page still contains the GA Classic tracking code.

updated to Universal. Note that *Classic* will not appear as the code version; the term *Classic* is used to refer broadly to the asynchronous version of the tracking code that preceded Universal and to the "traditional" version of the tracking code that preceded asynchronous.

> ### Note
>
> ### Google Tag Manager versus Google Tag Assistant
>
> Be sure not to refer to *Google Tag Manager* and *Google Tag Assistant* interchangeably. Google Tag Manager is a Google's tag management system, which we use throughout the book. Google Tag Assistant is a Chrome extension that you can use to verify the presence of GA, Google Tag Manager, and other Google-related code snippets (such as DoubleClick advertising) on a Web page. You can use Google Tag Assistant on any Web page, whether or not you manage the page or the GA implementation for the website. For more on Google Tag Assistant, visit `www.e-nor.com/gabook`.

Also, the Classic and Universal versions of tracking use very different syntax. If the source HTML for one of your Web pages (or a standalone JavaScript file in which you have embedded the tracking code) contains the tracking code in the format shown in Listing 4.2, or in any format other than Listing 4.1, you are still using Classic and need to migrate to Universal.

LISTING 4.2: The Google Analytics Classic tracking code differs drastically in syntax from Universal.

```
<script type="text/javascript">
 var _gaq = _gaq || [];
 _gaq.push(['_setAccount', 'UA-43490834-2']);
 _gaq.push(['_trackPageview']);
 (function() {
  var ga = document.createElement('script'); ga.type = 'text/
javascript'; ga.async = true;
  ga.src = ('https:' == document.location.protocol ? 'https://ssl' :
'http://www') + '.google-analytics.com/ga.js';
  var s = document.getElementsByTagName('script')[0];
s.parentNode.insertBefore(ga, s);
 })();
</script>
```

If you have deployed Google Analytics through Google Tag Manager, and the GA tag type is not indicated as Universal Analytics, you're still using Classic, and you should migrate to Universal within GTM.

Migration Paths to Universal

Your migration to Universal depends on your current implementation and on whether you want also transition to GTM at the same time. The possible scenarios are:

- You're currently using Classic version of the native GA tracking code, and you're migrating to Universal native GA tracking code.
- You're currently using Classic GA tag in Google Tag Manager, and you're migrating to Universal GA tag in Google Tag Manager.
- You're currently using Classic version of the native GA tracking code, and you're migrating to Universal GA tag in Google Tag Manager.

As outlined in the third bullet, you can efficiently migrate from Classic to Universal and switch from native code to GTM as part of the same process (Figure 4.13).

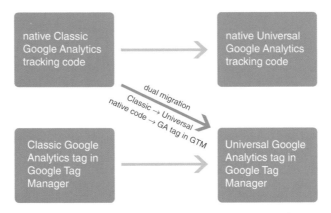

FIGURE 4.13   You can migrate to Universal and Google Tag Manager in the same process.

Warning	!
If you have scripted any events, social tracking, Ecommerce, or custom variables in GA Classic, you need to update them at the same time as you update the main tracking code to Universal syntax or switch to Google Tag Manager.	

By When Do I Need to Migrate?

If you determine that you are still using GA Classic, you should plan to migrate as soon as reasonably possible. The Classic tracking code will likely be supported through the first half of 2016 and beyond, but is now deprecated and could potentially be discontinued at any point. (The GA team will surely provide additional advance notice before discontinuing Classic completely.) Furthermore, new GA features are available through Universal only, not through the Classic version of the native tracking code, and not through the Google Analytics Classic tag in Google Tag Manager.

analytics.js Means Universal

The Universal and Classic tracking codes, respectively, call the analytics.js and ga.js JavaScript tracking file, which actually does all the work in sending the hit data to the GA servers. Particularly in the context of native tracking code (rather than Google Tag Manager), many of the GA help docs refer to *analytics.js* and *ga.js* to distinguish Universal from Classic, as shown in Figure 4.14.

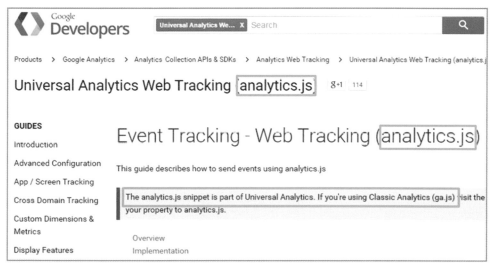

FIGURE 4.14 In documentation, analytics.js is often used to signify Google Universal analytics, while ga.js corresponds to Classic.

| GUEST SPOT | **Top 10 Google Analytics Gotchas** |

Brian Clifton

Brian Clifton is Director of Data Insights at Search Integration.

A paradox GA has suffered from since its launch in 2005 is that it is free. Being free is, of course, great for adoption—around 30 million websites now run GA (`http://trends.builtwith.com/analytics/ Google-Analytics`). To put this into context, prior to launch the total user base for all Web analytics tools was estimated to be between 30,000 and 50,000! However, the downside of this thousand-fold increase is the perception that *free* is synonymous with *cheap, superficial,* or even *easy.* As you already know, GA is not any of these.

In fact, GA is quite complicated—even hard, unless full-time analytics is your day job. By that, I mean hard to do it right so that your organization *trusts* the data, uses it to make *informed* decisions (not just prepare reports), and benefits from it by making *changes* to its digital strategy or approach.

continues

continued

In this section I discuss how to gain trust in the data by avoiding the common pitfalls and mistakes that can sabotage trust. As a practitioner, I come across all of the following on a regular basis. My reason for highlighting these is to help you jump-start your knowledge and gain a competitive advantage.

Here is my list of top 10 GA gotchas. Note that these are all important and, apart from item 1, are listed in no particular order:

1. Collecting personal information.
2. Assuming data quality takes care of itself.
3. Not separating customers from prospects (not segmenting).
4. Comparing your Ecommerce data with your back-end data.
5. Not cleaning your data (or creating a backup). (See Chapter 9, "View Settings, View Filters, and Access Rights.")
6. Not using the GTM to manage your setup. (See Chapter 5, "Google Tag Manager.")
7. Not defining goals (key visitor actions that have a real value to the business). (See Chapter 8, "Goal and Ecommerce Tracking.")
8. Not bothering with campaign tracking. (See Chapter 7, "Acquisition Reports.")
9. Using campaign tracking for internal campaigns. (See Chapter 7, "Acquisition Reports.")
10. Not keeping notes of change (not using chart annotations) (See Chapter 11, "Dashboards, Custom Reports, and Intelligence Alerts.")

Items 5 through 10 are discussed elsewhere in this book. Therefore, I focus on the first four items of my list.

1. Collecting Personal Information

Collecting personally identifiable information (PII) about your visitors in GA is strictly against Google's Terms of Service (`www.google.com/intl/en/analytics/tos.html`). This includes names, postal addresses, email addresses, Social Security/government ID numbers, telephone numbers, credit card information, social media names, and so forth. So you should never set out to deliberately track these in GA. For example, do not track the personal information of an Ecommerce transaction. However, the collection of PII often happens by mistake—because GA logs all URL parameters by default.

For example, a visitor has subscribed to your newsletter and you require them to confirm their email address by clicking a link you email them. That link can look like the following:

```
www.mysite.com/newsletter?subscriber=y&fname=brian&lname=clifton
```

When the visitor clicks this link, they are taken to your website where your back-end system confirms their address. However, the entire URL loaded in the visitor's browser is also captured by GA—including the parameters containing the name (`fname`, `lname`).

Another common way to capture PII unintentionally is from form submissions. If the form is processed by an HTML GET request, all of the information contained in the form fields is appended to the URL of the thank-you page—again all captured by GA.

Do You Collect PII?

Check your pageview reports (Behavior > Site Content > All Pages) for unintentional PII collected in URLs. As a tip, use the table filter of Figure 4.15 to quickly search all URLs for suspicious content.

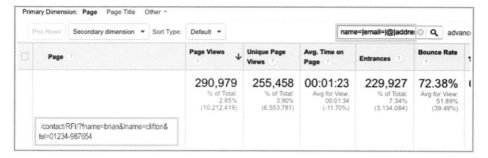

FIGURE 4.15 Using a table filter to check for PII within URLs.

An example search criteria could be:

```
name=|email=|@|address=|tel=|mobile=
```

Note that this is a regular expression (the default match type of table search) with the pipe character "|" meaning OR. If a captured URL contains any of these terms, it will show in the table. As you get to understand your URL structure, you can fine-tune the regular expression. See Chapter 9 for further details of regular expression usage.

To ensure that you haven't missed anything, choose a suitably long time period to check data (e.g., past six months).

If PII has been intentionally gathered, you will most likely find this in your Events reports (Behavior > Events > Top Events). Review the names captured in the Category, Action, and Label fields, shown in Figure 4.16.

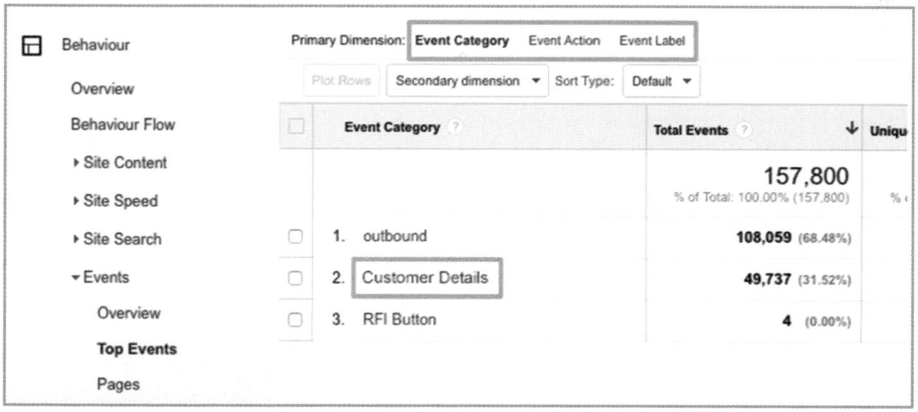

FIGURE 4.16 Checking event tracking parameters for PII.

If you run an Ecommerce site, check the Affiliation field, as shown in Figure 4.17.

continues

continued

FIGURE 4.17 Checking Ecommerce affiliation field for PII.

How to Remove PII

First, educate your Web development team in order to explain the consequence of PII being passed around in URLs (bad in general). It is better to avoid this altogether than have it happen and then try to remove it from GA, which is never a bulletproof solution.

Even then, add view filters to block any potential PII being collected. You will require Edit access to the view to do this. Chapter 9, "View Settings, View Filters, and Access Rights," discusses how to add filters to clean your data.

What If I Have Already Collected Personal Information?

It is, of course, always better to set up your GA account in a best-practice way to avoid this scenario. Therefore, ensure that you apply the filters described in this section as soon as possible. However, filters are not retroactive—they only work on data moving forward.

If the problem has already happened, add the filters described in this section and contact Google to explain the situation. In most cases, they will delete the range of data polluted by PII—that means all data from all sessions for the date range (not just the PII). Then educate your Web development team in order to avoid this happening in the future.

If you knowingly take no action or deliberately collect PII, Google reserves the right to close your account—meaning you lose all your data and setup information.

2. Assuming Data Quality Takes Care of Itself

My first gotcha is all about cleaning your data—specifically about the collection of personal information. However, the approach to cleansing is a part of an overall approach of good data governance and is applicable to *all* your data.

Why Data Governance Is Important

As mentioned in my introduction to this section, the issue everyone faces with digital measurement is trust. The most common question I hear form senior managers and data stakeholders is: "*How can we trust the data?*"

In the digital world, the vast majority of users remain anonymous—perhaps as many as 97% of them. According to the e-tailing group's 12th Annual Merchant Survey of 2013 (www.e-tailing.com/content/wp-content/uploads/2013/04/pressre-

`lease_merchantsurvey2013.pdf`), 46% of U.S. merchants report a purchase conversion rate between 1.0% and 2.9%.

Because anonymous traffic cannot be traced back to an identifiable person without breaking privacy laws, there is an inherent lack of trust in the data from people in the enterprise that do not work directly in digital analytics. Many such people consider 97% of the data as just noise—not worth the trouble to investigate it beyond the basic traffic volume numbers.

Such a lack of trust is valid unless you take control of your data—that is, perform a data quality health check audit. With a good solid platform of anonymous data, you can make huge improvements to the performance of your website. As the vast majority of anonymous website visitors are from prospects, often the improvement increase can be staggering—a 100% improvement to the bottom line is common, often significantly more. Therefore, data quality audits are well worth your investment.

Data Quality Health Check

The purpose of a data quality audit is to minimize the noise and inaccuracy of your GA data and maintain relevancy. The process is detailed but can be performed without the need to look at code. Figure 4.18 is a health check audit summary page taken from the book *Successful*

Data Quality Audit - Scorecard Summary

August: ~112k visitors, 157k visits
ToS = 3:08, p/v = 3.75, bounce rate = 45%, Adwords spend = not linked to GA
Reporting since March 2011

N/A = Not applicable

	Weight	Status	Weighted Score
1. Google Analytics Account Setup & Governance	1.0		5.0
2. GATC Deployment	1.0		10.0
3. AdWords & WMT Data	1.0		0.0
4. Site Search Tracking	1.0		0.0
5. File Download Tracking	1.0		0.0
6. Outbound Link Tracking	1.0		0.0
7. Form Completion Tracking	1.0		0.0
8. Video Tracking	N/A	-	-
9. Error Page Tracking	0.5		0.0
10. Transaction Tracking	2.0		0.0
11. Event Tracking (i.e. non-pageviews)	1.0		0.0
12. Goal Setup	1.0		0.0
13. Funnel Setup	1.0		0.0
14. Visitor Labelling	1.0		0.0
15. Campaign Tracking	1.0		5.0
Google Analytics Quality Score (out of 100)			**13.8**

Ideally, your normalized score would be 100. That is, a 100% complete best practice implementation of Google Analytics. Whilst that should be the long-term aim, a **score of 50** is required before you attempt any in-depth analysis of your data.

FIGURE 4.18 Sample health check audit summary.

continues

continued

Analytics. The summary is aimed at senior managers in order to get an at-a-glance understanding of the current data quality status.

The report summarizes all aspects of your setup, each row weighted according to their importance to your business. At the bottom of the table is a single numeric—your GA quality score (QS). This represents the overall quality of your data.

The health check audit report articulates what is working correctly, what is missing from your current data setup, and where the problem areas are, and it lets you focus on which areas to prioritize to meet the organization's data requirements.

In Figure 4.18, first look at the overall QS—the number in the last row (QS = 13.8). This ranges on a scale from 0 to 100, where 100 represents a best-practice setup for your organization. The data quality of this example is so low it is not credible for analysis. Further setup improvements are required first.

What Is a Minimum Value for the Quality Score?

Ideally, your quality score would be 100, a 100% complete best-practice implementation of GA. While that should be your long-term aim, I use the following general rule: until you achieve a QS of 50, don't attempt any analysis. A value below 50 leaves too many holes and caveats in the data.

When you can demonstrate a high score (QS > 80), you and your peers will have the confidence in the data that you need to base strategic decisions on it.

Once you understand your overall quality score, examine the rest of the scorecard table. It summarizes the 15 key items that make up a best-practice implementation by showing the weight (importance), its status (red, yellow, green), and the weighted score for each (weight × status). Clearly you want to have many greens in the Status column and be able to explain the yellow and red items in the report's supporting pages.

The weight of each of the 15 items in Figure 4.18 is determined by your business—it is the relative measure of the importance of tracking that particular item to you. A 0 represents no importance, and 1.0 represents the highest importance. A weight of 2.0 is reserved for transaction tracking, because of its special importance. For each non-green item in Figure 4.18, consider its weight. This is your priority list for work to be done to improve your QS.

Page 1 of the audit report (the scorecard summary) is the most important part of the report—as a manager, your focus is on this page. The remaining pages of the report explain why items receive a yellow or red status value.

More About the Quality Score Process

The methodology I developed for assessing and evaluating your GA quality score is detailed in the book *Successful Analytics: Gain Business Insights by Managing GA* (`BrianClifton.com/about-the-book`). You can download the complete example audit (summary and detail pages) report from `BrianClifton.com/audit-example`.

3. Not Separating Customers from Prospects (Not Segmenting)

Following a best-practice deployment of GA, your next step to gaining an understanding of your data is to segment your visitors. Segmentation is critical to success—without it, you are simply looking at an average of averages, effectively treating all your prospects and customers as the same.

Segmentation is a feature you use to group together visitors of similar behavior (segments). For example, a segment of visitors could be your *customers, high-value customers, subscribers, noncustomers,* or *engagers.* I use the term *engagers* to describe visitors who have done something on your site that indicates significant interest in you in terms of goals, Ecommerce, session duration, or page depth.

Downloading your brochure can signify engagement, as can filling in a contact request form, commenting on a blog article, or socially sharing your content. You can even combine these criteria into a sequence segment—visitors who match criterion X and immediately match criterion Y.

Segmentation is the technique employed to focus your analysis on groups of visitors who have similar characteristics—rather than on the whole data pot. The purpose is to improve the signal-to-noise ratio by bubbling up data points that otherwise lie below the surface (and potentially go unnoticed). Understanding how a handful of visitor segments behave is far more practical than trying to comprehend the thousands of individual visitor patterns that exist on your site.

An example Engagers segment is shown in Figure 10.10 within a broader discussion on segmentation.

4. Comparing Your Ecommerce Data with Your Back-End Data

If you have a transactional site, then, of course, you will want your transactional and product data as measured by GA to match the real numbers that your back-end system collects. However, in reality, due to any of the issues listed below, these never exactly match.

What Is an Acceptable Level of Difference?

Whether comparing GA Ecommerce data or other metrics against your back-end systems, I use a traffic light system to determine if a difference requires action:

- **GREEN:** Differences are within 5%. Acceptable; continue to monitor but a detailed investigation is not considered worthwhile.
- **YELLOW:** Differences between 5% and 10%. Warning: You may have a setup issue in GA. Replicate the issue using the transaction details from the back end that are not present (or correct) in GA. Review your transactional tracking code for correctness.
- **RED:** Differences greater than 10%. Urgent attention required. The performance metrics determining the success of your advertising campaigns may be completely wrong. Almost certainly an error with your GA setup.

These guidelines are on a *per metric* basis. That is, they are not a summation of the discrepancies found.

Causes of Ecommerce Discrepancies between Google Analytics and Back End

Any of the following factors can cause some degree of discrepancy between Ecommerce reporting in GA versus your back-end system:

- **Cross-domain tracking.** Transactions that are finalized on a payment gateway under a third-party domain (such as PayPal, Authorize.net, or WorldPay), requires you to configure cross-domain tracking. This involves adding your GA tracking code to your gateway template pages. If this is not permitted by your gateway provider, you must implement a workaround for Ecommerce tracking. Any problems with these configurations can prevent GA from correctly recording your transactions. (Vanessa Sabino examines GA tracking for checkouts and payment gateways in Chapter 8, "Goal and Ecommerce Tracking.")
- **Processing time.** Payment details may not be processed on the back end until next day (or next working day), or may be delayed due to batch processing.
- **Blocked tracking.** Although likely to affect only a small percentage of your audience, any visitor who blocks first-party cookies or has explicitly opted out of GA tracking will not appear in your GA reports, but will still generate transaction data with your back-end sales system.

continues

continued

➤ **Returns.** Product returns and order cancellations processed within your back-end sales system may not be accounted for in your GA reports.

Should You Process Ecommerce Returns in Google Analytics?

It is possible to account for returns within your GA reports by processing a *negative transaction*. However, I do not recommend this for two reasons:

➤ Aligning Web visitor data with internal systems is imperfect as a return usually takes place well after the original purchase—therefore, in a different reporting period. Viewing returns in your GA reports is generally more confusing than simply leaving the original transaction in place.

➤ Returns are not representative of your marketing or website effectiveness. For example, if I search online for "running shoes" and then make a purchase from your website, that is a perfectly good transaction—one that reflects a success for your website and its marketing. If subsequently I decide I don't like the shoes and return them, this would be because of the product (perhaps a quality issue). Just because I return my shoes does not mean the marketing investment for that product should change.

For a complete discussion on aligning GA and back-end Ecommerce data, see `Brian-Clifton.com/top-google-analytics-gotchas]`.

 **KEY TAKEAWAYS**

Only a Google login needed.   The only requirement for creating a GA account is a Google login. Any gmail login qualifies, but you can also use a non-gmail email address associated with a Google account.

100 GA accounts, 50 properties per account, 25 views per property.   For each GA login, you can create 100 GA accounts. Each GA account will contain one default property, and each new property will contain one default view. A single GA account can contain 50 properties, and a single property can contain 25 views.

Unlimited access to additional accounts.   Other GA users can give you access to an unlimited number of GA accounts, properties, and views.

Property: website or mobile app.   A website or mobile app corresponds to a GA property and not directly to a GA account.

Google Tag Manager deployment strongly advised.   You should consider deploying GA through Google Tag Manager instead of the native tracking code.

Universal migration.   If you're using tracking code that predates April 2014, you may still be running GA Classic and may therefore need to upgrade to Google Universal Analytics.

Dual Universal/GTM migration. You can perform a dual migration by updating to Universal and switching from native code to GTM as part of the same process.

Pageview hit. The core `ga('send ', 'pageView ')` function of the GA tracking code sends data not only about the page but also about the user's traffic source, device, and geographic location. In this way, each time a pageview action occurs on a tracked page, an entire pageview hit is sent to the GA servers.

 ACTIONS AND EXERCISES

1. **Create a new account as needed.** Review your measurement strategy as discussed in Chapter 3, "Measurement Strategy," and create a GA account and properties as needed. If you're just starting out with GA or making significant changes to the implementation, you should work first in a test environment before moving the changes to a production environment. (Environments are discussed in greater detail in Chapter 5.)

2. **Create a test account.** If your organization is already using GA, you probably will not need to create a new account or property, but you can still create a test GA account (with the organizational login or a separate login that you have associated with a Google account).

3. **Google Tag Assistant.** Add the Google Tag Assistant extension to Chrome. If you don't have Chrome, install it as a first step.

4. **Universal migration.** Determine if you're still running Google Analytics Classic (as native code or in Google Tag Manager) and, if so, plan your migration for as soon as reasonably possible.

5

Google Tag Manager Concepts

I n Chapter 4, "Account Creation and Tracking Code Installation," we created a new Google Analytics (GA) account and a new GA property within the account. We then copied the provided tracking code into our website template so each page would execute `ga('send', 'pageView')` on each page load and thereby populate our GA property.

We're now going to look at a different way to get data into GA: through a GA tag within Google Tag Manager (GTM). Note that Google Tag Manager does not replace Google Analytics: we're still going to need to create a GA account and property and still send a pageview hit to GA each time a page loads.

When we use GTM, however, we do not add the native code to our pages. Instead, we start with container code. It is through the container that we will add and modify GA. We'll also be able to use the container to add other types of marketing and analytics tags to our website.

Note

Examples in the Book Will Be Provided in Google Tag Manager

Because of the many advantages that GTM offers over native tracking, code implementation examples in the following chapters (e.g., for events, Ecommerce, or cross-domain tracking) will be provided in GTM format. Native tracking equivalents for all examples are available in the GA help docs, but they will not appear in the book.

GOOGLE TAG MANAGER CONCEPTS

Google Tag Manager is Google's free tag management solution. (GTM360, available as a paid option and included with GA360, includes support and may at some point offer additional features.) GTM makes it easier to add, delete, and update website tags without editing the website code directly and can thus empower more people in the organization—namely, marketers and analysts—to play a more direct role in the tagging process. There are a variety of other paid tag management solutions (such as Tealium and Ensighten) that offer the same core functionality as GTM, and you can certainly deploy GA through any of the other tag management systems.

In this chapter, we review some fundamental GTM vocabulary. If you are using another tag management system, the terminology may differ, but the concepts are the same regardless of the tool.

Account

The requirement for creating a GTM account is the same as for creating a GA account, as described in Chapter 4: you need only to have a Google account associated with either a gmail address or another email address.

Just as a GA property—rather than a GA account—corresponds to a website (or mobile app), a GTM container—rather than a GTM account—corresponds to a website (or mobile app). A GTM account relates more to the organization level: you may have a single GTM account that houses the five containers for three websites and two apps that your organization manages. In GA, we want to think more in terms of *properties* than accounts, and in GTM, we want to think more in terms of *containers* than accounts.

Note
Google Tag Manager for Mobile Apps
This chapter focuses primarily on GTM use within websites. In Chapter 13, "Mobile App Measurement," we discuss GTM as an option for tracking Android and iOS mobile apps in greater detail.

Container

It's helpful to consider a GTM container as just that: a container through which you add, remove, and modify marketing, analytics, and other types of tags on your website or in your app.

When you create a GTM account, a container is created automatically. Within the same account, you can create additional containers for other websites or apps.

For each Web container, GTM provides the container code for you to incorporate onto every page of your website. Once you have included the container code on your website, you can begin publishing tags to your site through the GTM.

In almost all cases, you add only one GTM container to a website or app. In some instances, however, it might be practical to include a single container in multiple websites or apps—for cross-domain or roll-up reporting, as examples discussed in Chapter 12.

The most essential concepts in GTM, as we continue to describe below, are:

- the container
- the tags that the container houses
- the triggers that fire the tags

Also covered below are variables and the data layer: somewhat more advanced as GTM functionality, but still essential.

Tag

In most cases, a tag within a Web container executes a JavaScript function related to analytics, website optimization, or advertising. More simply, we can basically think of tags as scripts.

The GA tag that we deploy through GTM serves as a replacement for the native GA tracking code. Note, however, that GTM does not replace GA; it just provides another way to record data into GA.

Terminology

Tag

In the course of this book, and throughout GA/GTM documentation, you'll notice *tag* used in three ways:

> **Google Tag Manager tag.** In most cases, a piece of JavaScript managed as a self-contained unit within GTM.
> **HTML tag.** Part of the HTML page markup, such as `<body>` (referred to as *open body tag*) or `</head>` referred to as *close head tag*).
> **Campaign tag.** You can add the campaign tags `utm_medium`, `utm_source`, and `utm_campaign` to inbound links so clickthroughs are tracked in the Campaigns report. Campaign tags are completely unrelated to the two preceding usages of *tag* and are often also referred to as *campaign parameters*. We discuss campaign tracking in Chapter 7.

Trigger

For a tag to fire, it must have an associated trigger. In the case of the main GA pageview tracker, you normally apply the built-in All Pages trigger. To fire a GA event tag to track an outbound link, you would normally define a trigger for a click to a URL that does not contain your own hostname and begins with `http` or `https`.

As an example trigger unrelated directly to GA, you could configure a visitor survey to pop up only when the page URL contains `/thank-you`.

Variable

Variables are temporarily stored values that you can use to both populate and trigger your tags. GTM provides a number of commonly used built-in variables, and you can also define your own. For example, you can trigger a GA event or virtual pageview when the built-in Click URL variable ends in `.pdf`, and you can also use the Click URL to directly populate the event or virtual pageview tag, as discussed in Chapter 6.

The model for defining your own variables is very flexible: as a few examples, you can read in a JavaScript variable or return the result of any JavaScript function (such as the current time), parse any value out of your page's markup or text (such as the heading or subject of a blog post), or output a value from a lookup table. In this and following chapters, we'll use several of the user-defined variable types shown in Figure 5.1.

FIGURE 5.1 While user-defined variables aren't needed in all cases, they provide much of GTMs flexibility for tags and triggers.

Data Layer

The data layer object stores information that you want to pass to GTM. The values that you store in the data layer often originate from your back-end data store but can also be derived from page elements and user interactions.

Variables and the data layer are more advanced as concepts in GTM than tags and triggers. For the most basic GA deployment through GTM, you don't need to define any of your own variables or work with the data layer, but we will see these topics in full action in Chapter 6, "Events, Virtual Pageviews, Social Actions, and Errors," Chapter 8, "Goal and Ecommerce Tracking," and Chapter 12, "Implementation Customizations."

BENEFITS OF GOOGLE TAG MANAGER

A tag management system such as GTM offers a range of important improvements over manual deployment of native JavaScript codes.

> **Note**
>
> ### Other Tag Management Systems
>
> If you're using a tag management system other than GTM, the tag management principles and most tag configurations reviewed in this chapter still apply, but the user interface will differ from GTM.

Management

As the name indicates at the most basic level, a tag management system helps you *manage* your tags. If you deploy all of your marketing and analytics codes through GTM, you can keep track of them at a glance. Though few developers, marketers, and analysts may admit it, many of us have included a variety of scripts on websites and have basically forgotten about them, at least for a period of time. With GTM, it's much easier to keep track of which scripts you have deployed and on which pages you have deployed them.

> **Note**
>
> ### Ghostery
>
> Want to quickly see how many tags are placed on a Web page? Install the Ghostery extension for Chrome and visit a few sites. The number of tags running on some pages may astound you and will surely demonstrate the utility of a tag management system.

Flexible Triggering

As discussed above, GTM offers a very flexible triggering model. This is a critical feature: you can keep all your tags organized within a single container, yet maintain complete control over the individual firing of each tag.

Because a tag requires a trigger to fire, you could temporarily disable a tag by removing all triggers (or applying a blocking trigger) but still maintain the tag in GTM for reference or future reactivation.

Templates and Open-Format Tags

GTM provides a variety of built-in templates, such as for GA, DoubleClick, or AdRoll retargeting, that you can configure and publish. As a note, many of the built-in GTM templates correspond to non-Google tools, and the list is growing gradually.

For tools that do not have a corresponding tag template (for example, a third-party heatmapping or survey tool), you can deploy code through the open-format Custom HTML Tag (which may have as easily been named Custom JavaScript Tag, since it houses JavaScript in almost all instances).

In fact, the Custom HTML Tag is not reserved for just third-party marketing and analytics codes: you could potentially use it to add any of your own JavaScript to any of your pages—for example, to update the text in a navigation menu when the change would otherwise be delayed until a code release.

Customizations and Updates

For template-based tags, updates become available directly in the tag interface. For example, if Google Analytics introduces any changes to the tracking code, those changes will update in the background through GTM. Similarly, any new tracking code configurations will be exposed in the GA tag within GTM: instead of manually updating your tracking code, you'll be able to change a configuration in the GA tag within GTM and republish.

Consistency with Structured Variability

Thanks to triggers, variables, and tag configurability, GTM offers a great degree of control and flexibility at the same time. If, for instance, you wanted to distinguish clicks on different signup buttons, you could consistently generate GA events with *signup* and *click* as the category and action but use a variable to dynamically populate the button size, color, or position. Since both data consistency and specificity are needed for good analytics, GTM's combination of control and flexibility is a great boon to GA implementation. (Chapter 6 explores GA event tracking in detail.)

Modularity and Reusability

The modular nature of GTM elements such as triggers and variables make them eminently reusable. Have you already defined a trigger for a survey tool to fire on your two purchase confirmation URLs? Use that same trigger to test a cross-sell popup for a new product. Want to populate the author for each of your blog posts as both a content group and a custom dimension in GA? Write one variable, and use it to populate both.

Greater Involvement of Marketing/Analytics Department

Another essential benefit of GTM: it can help to put more control of marketing and analytics code deployments into the hands of marketers and analysts and avoid the bottlenecks that hinder general website version releases. This is not to suggest that the marketing or business intelligence department should unilaterally or randomly add tags to the website. Regular communication with the developers and IT remains best practice—and in some cases, such as GA Ecommerce tracking through GTM, developer support is still required to populate the data layer—but with GTM, most marketing and advertising code updates do not have to fight for priority on the development list or get caught in a slow development cycle (Figure 5.2).

As two other potential workflows, marketers and analysts can add tags to GTM but leave the publishing to IT, or marketers and analysts can communicate tag requirements to IT, who can then add and publish the tags.

In any of the scenarios above, GTM offers a much more systematized process for including marketing and analytics scripts on your website, and, in many cases, it avoids the dependency on code pushes to make the changes live.

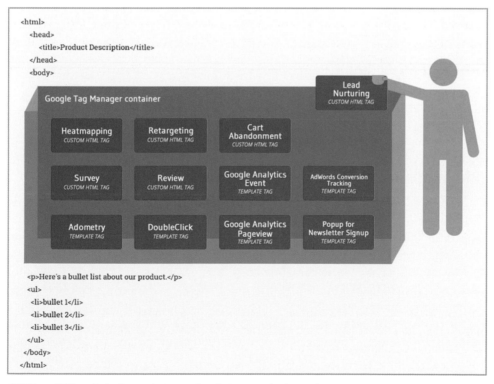

FIGURE 5.2 GTM can help the marketing and analytics team deploy analytics, optimization, and advertising scripts (even if IT retains control of publishing).

> **Note**
>
> ## Google Tag Manager and Governance of Data Collection
>
> As explained earlier, a tag management system such as GTM allows you to account for all, or at least most, tags that you have deployed to your website and to control access rights to tag modification and publishing. We can consider these practical, day-to-day benefits in the broader context of an enterprise data collection governance program: governance begins with knowing exactly what you're doing and where and how you're doing it. In the case of auditing or certification for security or quality management standards, the readily available tag and trigger inventory in GTM would greatly facilitate any required assessments.

CREATING A GOOGLE TAG MANAGER ACCOUNT AND CONTAINER

Before you can deploy GA or any other functionality through GTM, you must first create a GTM account. Your first container will be created automatically within the account—you'll then need to add the container code to every page of your website.

Creating an Account

To create a GTM account, go to `https://tagmanager.google.com`, and follow the prompts. In most cases, you can use your organization as the account name and your website as the container name (Figure 5.3).

Adding the Container Code to Your Website

Once you create your account and container, you'll be prompted to install the container code. You should ideally place the container code just after the `<body>` tag in your page template, as illustrated in Listing 5.1. This placement differs from the GA tracking code, which we're instructed to include before the `</head>`.

Why should we place the container code after <body>? This ensures that script dependencies are loaded in the <head></head> section of the page before the tags in the container begin executing. For instance, any jQuery code that you included in a GTM tag would need to use the main jQuery library, which you normally refer to from within <head></head>. Also note that you cannot place an <iframe>, such as the one referenced in the GTM container code, within the <head> section of an HTML page.

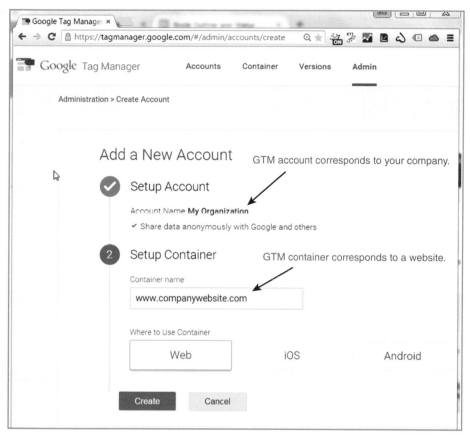

FIGURE 5.3 A GTM account normally corresponds to your organization, and a GTM container normally corresponds to a website or mobile app.

LISTING 5.1: Placement of the GTM container code in the HTML of your page template.

```
<html>
      <head>
              <title>Product Description</title>
      </head>
      <body>
<!- GTM ->
<noscript><iframe src="//www.googletagmanager.com/ns.html?id=GTM-
MZGZ83" height="0"
style="display:none;visibility:hidden"></iframe></noscript>
<script>(function(w,d,s,l,i){w[l]=w[l]||[];w[l].push({'gtm.start':
new Date().getTime(),event:'gtm.js'});var f=d.getElementsByTagName(s)[0],
j=d.createElement(s),dl=l!='dataLayer'?'&l='+l:'';j.async=true;j.src=
```

```
'//www.googletagmanager.com/gtm.js?id='+i+dl;f.parentNode.
insertBefore(j,f);
}) (window,document,'script','dataLayer','GTM-MMGZ83');</script>
<!- End GTM ->
                <p>Here's a bullet list about our product.</p>
                <ul>
                        <li>bullet 1</li>
                        <li>bullet 2</li>
                        <li>bullet 3</li>
        </body>
</html>
```

As discussed in Chapter 4, most Web pages are constructed from a single or small number of templates or master pages that are used throughout the site, so in most cases, adding the GTM container code is a quick process—just make sure to also add the container to any standalone pages that do not use your standard page template(s). (You can use Google Tag Assistant, first discussed in Chapter 4, to check for the GTM container code on any Web page. Additional tools for verifying the presence of the GTM tracking code on all pages are referenced at www.e-nor.com/gabook.)

The Web developers would still be responsible for the initial installation of the GTM container code. Once the container code is installed, direct reliance on developers may diminish for script additions, because the analysts and marketers will be able to add codes through GTM's Web interface as discussed above. We discuss GTM access rights and workflows later in the chapter.

Installing the GTM Container in WordPress

You can install the GTM container into WordPress in one of the two following ways:

- Open header.php and manually add the tracking code directly after the <body> tag, as shown in Listing 5.1.
- Install one of the several available GTM WordPress plugins.

If you use a GTM plugin, you'll need to configure the plugin with your GTM container ID. The plugin may offer some other options, such as automatic population of the data layer with variables for author, category, and login state, which you can use as custom dimension and content grouping values as discussed in Chapter 12, "Implementation Customizations."

A recommended, full-featured plug-in is Google Tag Manager for WordPress by Tamás Geiger.

DEPLOYING GOOGLE ANALYTICS THROUGH GOOGLE TAG MANAGER

As stated earlier, GA and GTM are separate systems. You don't need GTM to deploy GA— you could opt for native code tracking as described in Chapter 4—and you could use GTM to exclusively deploy tags other than GA. That said, GTM does provide a great deal of built-in GA tagging functionality, so, in addition to the GTM benefits enumerated earlier, we have another good reason to use GTM for our GA tracking needs.

It is important to remember that GTM does not replace GA; it just provides an alternate way to include the GA tracking on your Web pages. You will perform other aspects of your implementation—such as view filtering and goal configuration—as you would with a native deployment, and you will still use the GA reporting interface (or the GA API) in the same way once the data has been collected and processed.

Creating a Google Analytics Pageview Tracker

To create your GA pageview tag in GTM, take the following steps:

1. In Google Tag Manager, click into the container to which you want to add the Google Analytics tag.
2. In the left navigation panel, click Tags, and then click New.
3. Configure your tag as shown in Figure 5.4.
4. Save the tag.

Note that saving the tag does not make the tag active—you still need to publish the container as described below.

FIGURE 5.4 Configuration of a Google Analytics pageview tag in Google Tag Manager.

Note that we have not hard-coded the GA property ID into the tag but have instead created a very simple text-constant variable. We'll be able to use this same variable in our GA event, social, and Ecommerce tags. Also, if we want to initially capture GA data in a test property and then push to a production property, we'll be able to update the property ID variable without having to edit one or more GA tags.

Creating a variable for your GA property ID is a fast and straightforward way to begin taking advantage of the modularity and reusability that GTM offers, as shown in Figure 5.5. The variable is, however, wholly optional—you could certainly populate the Tracking ID field directly, though this is not quite considered best practice.

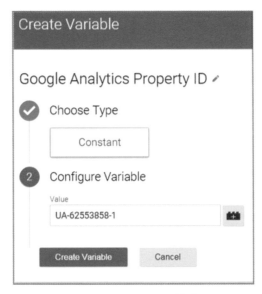

FIGURE 5.5 Simple text-constant variable for our GA property ID—not obligatory, but best practice.

Also note that we have selected Enable Display Advertising Features. This setting helps to ensure that the Demographics and Interests reports are populated, and it will also allow additional advertising functionality for AdWords and DoubleClick. Chapter 12 examines this and other tracking customizations in further detail.

Previewing/Debugging

If you have included the container code on your website as described earlier, you can view the tag in preview/debug mode, before you publish it, to make sure it's firing where you intended. If your tag is designed to make a visible change to the page, you can also see the change in preview mode. To view your tags in preview/debug mode as demonstrated in Figures 5.6 and 5.7:

1. Make sure you have included the GTM container code on the page you're debugging.
2. Click the down arrow on the right of the Publish button.
3. Click Preview.

FIGURE 5.6 Starting preview/debug mode.

FIGURE 5.7 The Google Analytics Pageviews tag is firing in preview/debug mode.

Publishing and Versioning

To make your GTM changes live, you must publish your container (after adding the container code to your Web pages).

When you publish your container, you'll automatically create a container version that will serve as a snapshot of the container's current state. GTM will keep track of each container version that you create, and you can revert to any container version if this ever becomes necessary (due to unintended side effects of a tag deployment, etc.).

Designating a Single Publisher

For many organizations, it is helpful to designate a single person or a very small team as responsible for publishing your GTM container. Because all tags within a container are published at the same time, the publisher should be aware of the status and function of each tag, trigger, and variable in the container at the time of publishing and remain in communication with IT and developers about the publishing (if the designated publisher is not part of the IT/development team directly).

If you do provide publish rights to an outside agency, they should understand the purpose and status of every element within your container. To avoid publishing tags that may not be ready for publishing, it's generally recommended that you restrict publish rights to a single outside agency at most.

All Tags Published Simultaneously

As previously mentioned, it's critical to remember that all tags within a container are published simultaneously. As a best practice, you can use a tag naming convention as in Figure 5.8 to readily assess publication readiness for each tag in a container. In the container shown, tags whose names do not begin with *ACTIVE* are not yet ready for publishing.

Another strategy might be to create a GTM folder named HOLDING and to move tags out of this folder only once they are ready to be published, such that the presence of any tags in HOLDING should indicate that the container should not yet be (re)published.

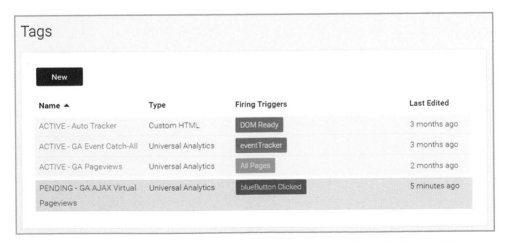

FIGURE 5.8 You can keep your tags prefixed with PENDING until they're ready for publishing, at which point you can prefix them with ACTIVE.

> ### Note
>
> ### Use GTM Folders to Organize Your Tags, Triggers, and Variables
>
> As mentioned above, you can create a folder called HOLDING in which you keep any tag, trigger, or variable that is not yet ready for your live environment. You could also use folders to organize your GTM assets by creator, department, or functionality (e.g., Google Analytics, Heatmapping and Surveys, etc.).
>
> The folders serve only to organize your GTM assets in whichever way makes the most sense for you; no functionality is changed by moving the assets between folders or changing a folder name, so feel free to organize and reorganize your tags, triggers, and variables as needed. Just remember, of course, to first confer with colleagues and clients who also have access to the container.

Google Analytics Tag as Equivalent to Native Google Analytics Tracking Code

So far, this chapter has covered all the basic steps for deploying GA through Google Tag Manager:

1. Create a GTM account and container.
2. Add the container code to all pages of your site.
3. Into the container, add a GA tag with the Track Type set to Page View.
4. Apply the All Pages trigger to the tag.
5. Save the tag, and publish the container.

So what have we accomplished? At this point, we're performing the same tracking as we did following the procedure for native code deployment detailed in "Installing the GA Tracking Code" in Chapter 4, and we are recording the same pageview hit data represented in Figure 4.7.

The GTM option may seem like more work than the native option, but the ease and flexibility that GTM provides will become clear when we discuss additional tracking requirements, such as event and cross-domain, in upcoming chapters.

Furthermore, now that we have a container in place, we can easily deploy and manage codes for many other purposes beyond GA.

ACCESS RIGHTS

User management in GTM is very straightforward, as described below.

Account Access

The user who has created the account can click User Management in the Account column of the Admin screen and provide other Google logins with the access levels shown in Figure 5.9.

FIGURE 5.9 Two options for account permissions (apart from no account permissions).

Account-level access does not automatically confer container-level access. Conversely, container-level access does not require any account-level access. In short, account access and container access are managed separately. (The GTM access model differs from the cascading access rights model for GA discussed in Chapter 9.)

Once you provide full account-level access to another login, that login has all the same admin privileges that you do—including account deletion and assignment of any account and container rights for any other login—so be judicious.

Container Access

For ongoing usage of GTM, container privileges, shown in Figure 5.10, are more relevant than account privileges.

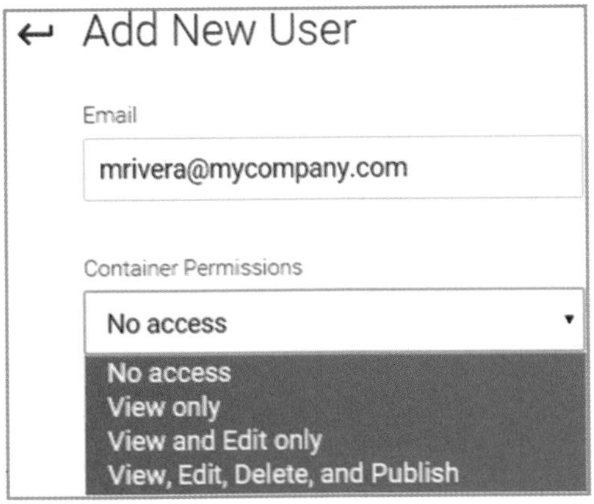

FIGURE 5.10 Container permissions.

Users with View and Edit Only access can create tags but not publish them. You should be extremely cautious with the View, Edit, Delete, and Publish role. Publishing tags is serious business, and the privilege should be extended only to the one person or few people who understand the technical function and the business requirement for each tag, trigger, and variable in the container at any point in time.

Warning   **!**

Exercise Extreme Caution for Container Publish Access

As an essential practice for GTM governance, only one person, or a very small number of people at most, should have publish rights to the container, and those individuals should understand the function and status of each and every element in the container. If your organization and one or more third-party agencies can add tags to the same container, you should maintain even more stringent control on publish access and processes.

Two-Step Verification

If you select two-step verification as an option in the account settings shown in Figure 5.11, additional authentication will be required for GTM users to:

- create or modify JavaScript variables or Custom HTML tags
- modify user settings

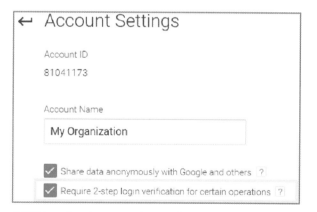

FIGURE 5.11 Google two-step login enforces additional security.

The two-step verification is used across multiple Google services; it is not specific to GTM. In addition to the password for login, the two-step verification requires entry of special security code sent via text, voice call, or the Google mobile app.

This additional security measure is a wise option. If unauthorized individuals gained access to your GTM, they could wreak havoc.

MIGRATING TO GOOGLE TAG MANAGER FROM NATIVE TRACKING

Once you decide to implement GTM, you should plan to migrate as much of your in-page tracking to GTM tags as possible. It goes against best practice to implement some of your analytics and advertising code additions in GTM while leaving others native.

For instance, it is not ideal to implement GA and retargeting through GTM while leaving your survey and shopping cart abandonment codes on your Web pages in native format.

While there are a few types of codes that you can't deploy through GTM (such as synchronously loading codes needed for split testing—see "Are There Tags That Google Tag Manager Does Not Support?" in the GTM online help docs), you should plan to deploy all your marketing and analytics codes, or at least as many as possible, through GTM and thereby take maximum advantage of the tool's fundamental *management* benefit.

Google Tag Manager and Universal Upgrade in One

As discussed in Chapter 4, if you're still using the Classic version of the GA native tracking, you can simultaneously migrate to Universal and switch to GTM by replacing your native GA code with the GTM container code and publishing a Google Universal Analytics tag to the container.

> **Warning**   **!**
>
> You must switch any GA events, social tracking, or Ecommerce tracking from native to GTM at the same time as you switch your main pageview tracking.
>
> If you have implemented custom variables for GA Classic (through GTM or native tracking), you must begin tracking the custom variables as custom dimensions in GA Universal.

Maintaining Native GA Code While Building Out GTM

If you are currently using the native GA tracking code, you can maintain it while you're building out the GA tracking through GTM:

1. Include the GTM container code in the page template for your test environment.
2. Keep the GA native tracking code in place in your test environment.
3. Configure GA pageview tracking within GTM. Where applicable, also configure GA event and Ecommerce tracking as described in Chapters 6 and 8.
   - As you configure the GA pageview, event, and Ecommerce tags in GTM, use a GA property ID separate from the property ID in the native GA tracking code.
   - To enable easy updating of your property ID in multiple GA tags, encapsulate the property ID in a text-constant variable as shown earlier in Figure 5.5.
4. Interact with your test environment to generate data in both GA properties simultaneously.
5. Create a custom segment based on hostname, e.g., *dev.mysite.com*, to view data for the test environment only. (Segments are discussed in Chapter 10.)

6. When the GA property tracked through GTM reaches data parity with the GA property tracked natively (i.e., the metrics in all reports look the same for a given time period):
    a. change the property ID of the GA tags in GTM to the property ID of the native tracker, and republish the container.
    b. simultaneously remove the native tracker
    c. replicate in your production environment

This process will verify that your GA tracking through GTM matches the native GA tracking that you're replacing and provide tracking continuity within your working property. In the upcoming section, we consider options for GTM containers and GA property IDs in your development and production environments on an ongoing basis, once you have migrated from native tracking to GTM.

GTM ENVIRONMENTS

The Environments feature in GTM allows you to publish your container to development and/or staging environments before publishing to your live environment. This feature eliminates the need to maintain separate containers for your development, staging, and live/production servers.

Creating a Custom GTM Environment

You can access the Environments panel from the Container column of the GTM Admin screen. Once there, you can click New to display the panel where you can create a new environment, as shown in Figure 5.12. As Destination URL, specify the hostname (or a subdirectory under

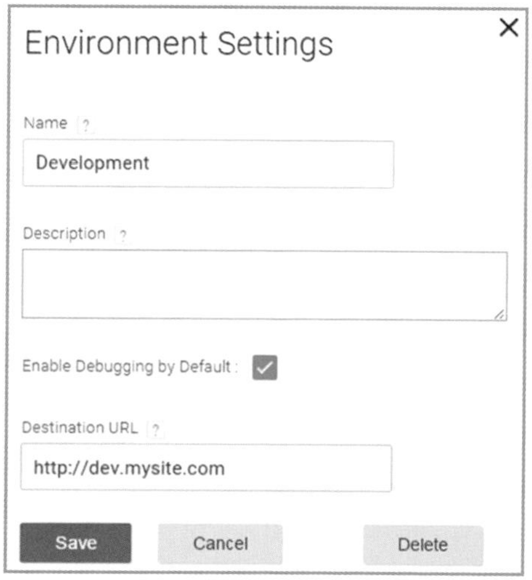

FIGURE 5.12 When you configure a new GTM environment, specify the hostname of your development or staging server (or a subdirectory under the hostname of your live environment) as the Destination URL.

the hostname of your live environment) on which the environment should activate. Select Enable Debugging by Default to display the Debug panel previously shown in Figure 5.7 when you access pages on the specified hostname; otherwise, only previewing (without debugging) will be enabled in the environment when you share it.

You can create a new GTM Environment for your development website, your staging website, and any other website instances that may be part of your development or QA process.

Once you create a new GTM environment, you're alerted to the two different ways in which you can preview and debug in that environment:

- **Snippet:** include an alternate version of the container code on the development/staging pages.
- **Preview link:** preview/debug the custom GTM environment by sharing a link instead of copying the alternate version of the container code onto your development/staging pages.

We discuss the environment sharing options in greater detail below.

FIGURE 5.13 The container's Environments panel lists the default environments as well as any custom environments that you have created.

Once you have created environments for Staging and Development and you have begun to publish to the environments as described below, the container's Environment panel will appear as in Figure 5.13.

In addition to any custom environments that you define, each container includes three default environments:

- **Live:** the version of the container published to your production environment.

- **Latest:** the last version of the draft container that you have saved, whether or not you have published it to the Live environment or any custom environment.
- **Now Editing:** the draft version of the container, which includes any changes since you saved the last version. When you publish the current draft of a container, a new version is created (if you have not already saved out the new version), and that version becomes the Latest environment, regardless of which environment (Live or a custom environment) you have published to.

Terminology

Container Versions and Container Environments

As we mentioned earlier in the chapter, a version is a snapshot of your container. If you are making a great deal of changes to your container, you can save multiple versions along the way, add notes, and republish any previously saved version if anything goes awry in a later version.

An environment corresponds to your live website and any other website contexts such as development or staging to which you need to publish your GTM changes separately. The latest published version and the in-edit version of the container are also listed as default environments.

A version resides within the context of an environment, and the same version can be published in multiple environments. In Figure 5.13, version 6 has been published to the Development Environment, but version 5 is the latest published to Staging and Live.

Sharing the Environment Through the Code Snippet

For this option, you select Get Snippet from the environment's Actions menu to copy a separate version of the container code, as shown in Figure 5.14, into your development or staging environment. Note that this snippet doesn't correspond to a separate container *per se*; rather, it's the Environment variation of the Live container. The container ID (*GTM-MHZM6G* in this case) itself does not vary.

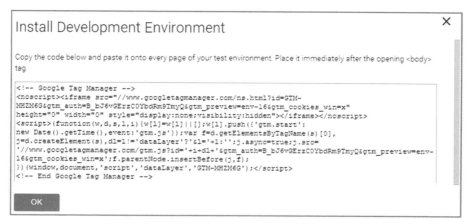

FIGURE 5.14 As one option for making the GTM changes in your Development environment visible to other users, you can ask your developers to copy the GTM environment snippet onto all development pages.

> ## Warning   !
>
> ### Don't Overwrite Your Live Container Snippet with a Development or Staging Environment Snippet
>
> If, as part of a website release, you overwrite the page template that contains the Live container snippet with a development or staging environment snippet, the latest version published to development/staging will be live in your production environment, ready or not. As a precaution, you can apply a blocking trigger for your live/production environment to any new tags, as described below. Once you have QAed the new tags, you can remove the blocking trigger and publish to the Live environment.

Sharing the Environment Through a Preview Link

If you did not use the version preview option previously available in GTM, it may be a bit surprising to learn that you can select Share Preview from an environment's Actions menu to share an environment preview with other users without actually making any update to the container code in the development environment. (The default snippet for the container, however, does need to be present on the page.) See Figure 5.15.

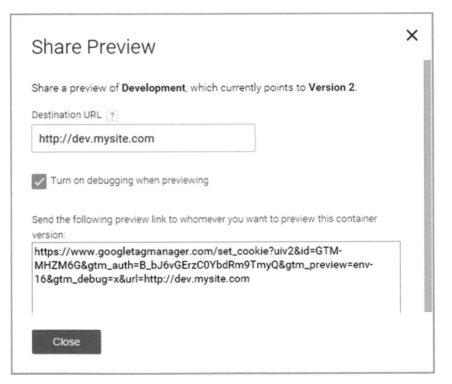

FIGURE 5.15 As long as the Live container code is present on the development page, you can share a link with other users that allows them to preview and debug changes in the GTM development environment that you have set up.

Because the preview link sets a cookie, you don't need to send out a new preview link each time that you publish to the container as described below. As long as the person with whom you shared the preview link is using the same browser and hasn't deleted cookies, the changes that you publish will be visible in the environment for that person.

Sharing preview links can present a bigger administrative burden than the snippet option if many people need to see GTM updates in your development and staging environments; in this case, the snippet might offer a better solution. An advantage of the preview links, however, is that you eliminate any risk of development or staging tags ending up in production before they're ready (because of the inadvertent snippet overwrite described in the previous section).

In addition to sharing a link for your custom environments, you can also share a link for the Latest and Now Editing default environments.

> **Warning** !
>
> ### Reset Link Also Invalidates the Container Snippet
> The innocuously named Reset Link item in the custom environment's Actions menu does more than invalidate any preview links that you have shared for the environment: it also invalidates the environment snippet. If you have added the environment snippet to your development or staging pages and select Reset Link, you—or your developers—will need to add the updated environment snippet if you still want changes to the development and staging environments to be visible.

Publishing to a GTM Environment

Whether you opt for the snippet or preview link approach, no changes will be visible on the development or staging pages until you publish a new version to one of the custom environments as shown in Figure 5.16.

If you're QAing the PDF event tracking that we set up in Chapter 6, a suggested workflow might proceed as follows:

1. Make the tag, trigger, and variable updates in GTM.
2. If there's any chance that you can overwrite the Live container snippet with a development or staging environment snippet, apply a blocking trigger for your live/production hostname to the new tag as described below.
3. Save the current container draft as a new version—let's say version 6, as shown in Figure 5.13.
4. Publish version 6 to the development environment as shown in Figure 5.16. (You can also select Publish To… in the Actions menu for the development environment in the Environments panel, or Publish To… in the Actions menu for a given version in the Versions panel and then select the development environment.)

FIGURE 5.16 You have the option to publish a container version to the Live environment or any custom environments that you have configured.

5. Verify that the event tracking is firing in the development environment. (See "Testing the PDF Event Tag" in the Chapter 6.)
6. Repeat steps 4 and 5 in the staging environment, along with any other QA processes that you normally perform before pushing changes to production.
7. If you have applied a blocking trigger for the live/production hostname to the tag, remove it now.
8. Save a new version of the container and publish it to the Live GTM environment.

The PDF tracking example cited above and outlined in Chapter 6 does not require developer involvement (for additional back-end data), so you would not necessarily need to coordinate the publishing to the different environments with any other code-level changes in those environments. If, on the other hand, the GTM changes that you make—let's say for a GA custom dimension that records a back-end customer status as described in Chapter 12—you'd need to work with your developers to coordinate your publishing to the GTM environments with their code-level updates in those environments.

Use Trigger Exceptions to Block Firing

Any trigger that you define in GTM can also serve as a trigger exception, that is, a trigger blocker that takes precedence over any other trigger applied to the tag.

If it's not feasible for you to maintain different container snippet variations in your live and development environments, you can prevent your tags from firing in your live environment by applying a blocking trigger based on the hostname of your live/production environment.

As emphasized earlier, if you are maintaining GTM development and staging environment snippets distinct from the Live GTM container snippet and there is any chance that the file in your development or staging environment that contains the snippet can be inadvertently pushed to production and thereby overwrite the Live container snippet, you can also keep a blocking trigger applied to all new tags until you have validated them in development and/or staging, at which point you can remove the blocking trigger and publish the container to the Live environment.

To create a live/production trigger and apply it to a tag as a blocking exception, take the following steps:

1. Within the GTM container interface, click Variables in the left navigation and enable the built-in Page Hostname variable as shown in Figure 5.17.
2. In the left navigation, click Triggers > New, and then configure the trigger for your live/production hostname as shown in Figure 5.18.
   a. Name the trigger Live Environment.
   b. In the Choose Event section, click Page View.
   c. In the Configure Trigger section, select Page View as the trigger type.
   d. In the Fire On section, click Some Pageviews.
   e. Configure the trigger as in Figure 5.18.

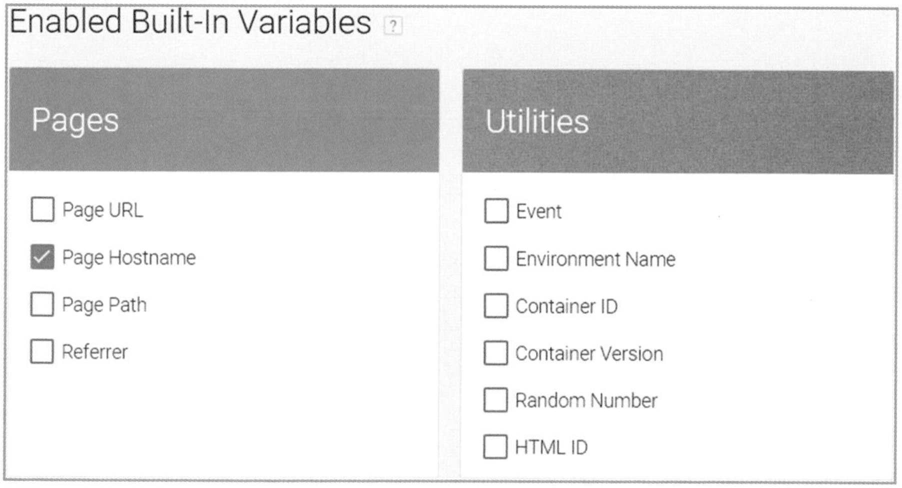

FIGURE 5.17 Page Hostname is a built-in variable that you must enable for use in triggers and tags.

3. Apply the trigger as a blocking exception:
    a. In the Fire On section of a GTM tag (a Google Analytics tag or any other), click Add Exceptions.
    b. Select the Live Environment trigger as an exception so it appears as in Figure 5.19.

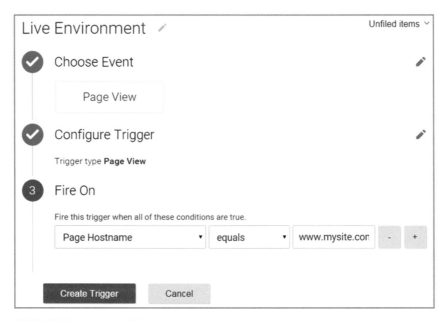

FIGURE 5.18 This trigger is defined to match the hostname in your live/production environment, but we use it as a trigger exception in Figure 5.19 to block tag firing.

Note

Block `mysite.com` and `www.mysite.com` with a Single Trigger

The trigger configured in Figure 5.18 would block a tag from firing on www.mysite.com but not mysite.com. If your live/production environment is accessible under both of these hostnames, you can define a single trigger using regular expressions:

```
Page Hostname - matches RegEx - ^(www\.)?mysite\.com$
```

This single regular expression will match only *www.mysite.com* or *mysite.com* as hostname. (For more about the useful text matching tricks that you can perform with regex, see "Regular Expressions in Google Analytics" in Chapter 9.)

Otherwise, you can define a separate trigger for each live hostname variation and apply both triggers as trigger exceptions.

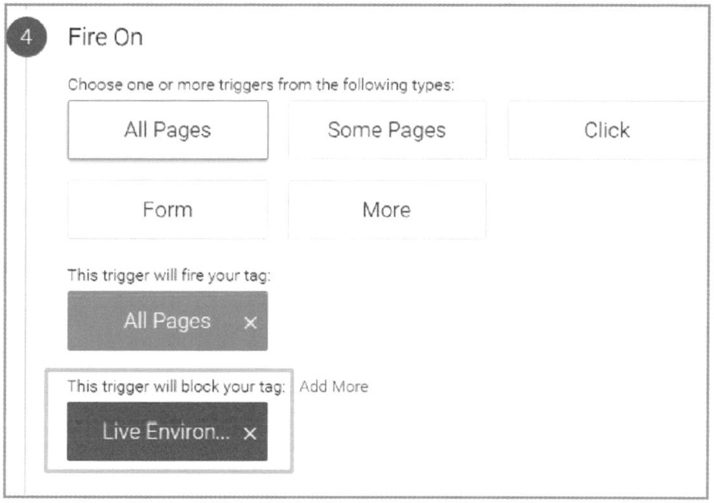

FIGURE 5.19 You can apply the Live Environment trigger as an exception until you're ready for the tag to begin firing in your production environment.

The trigger exception may be particularly helpful if you're managing many different triggers for your tags and/or your triggers already contain complex conditions and you prefer not to add and remove an additional condition to match hostname within the existing trigger. Also, you can easily scan the main Tags panel for any trigger exceptions that are applied without having to remember the any specific conditions within triggers, as illustrated in Figure 5.20.

FIGURE 5.20 Trigger exceptions, such as Live Environment in this example, appear prominently on the main Tags panel.

Once you're ready for the tag to fire in production, you can remove the trigger exception from the tag (and republish the container). If you want to block the tag in the development environment once you activate it in production, you can apply a blocking trigger based on the development hostname.

Separate GA Properties in Development and Production

Thus far, we have discussed distinct GTM container environments for development/staging and production, but we have not addressed another important option: tracking into the same or separate Google Analytics properties from the different environments. Either option is viable and requires specific implementation considerations, outlined in this section and the following.

To track your live and development/staging environments into separate GA properties, you can dynamically populate the Tracking ID field for a GA tag (shown first in Figure 5.4) with one of the variables shown in Figure 5.21 or 5.22. These variables accomplish the same objective: they return separate GA tracking IDs based on the hostname on which tag is firing.

FIGURE 5.21 Custom JavaScript variable for development or production Google Analytics property ID.

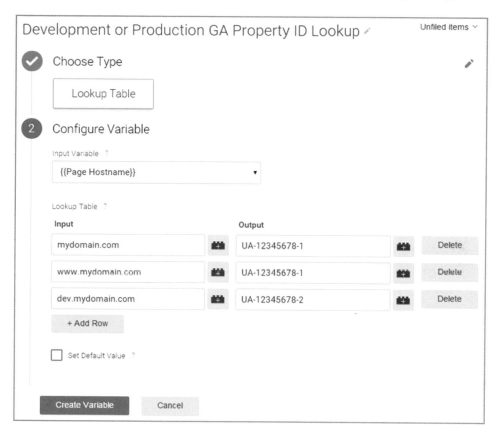

FIGURE 5.22 This lookup table returns the same outputs as the manual JavaScript variable shown in Figure 5.21.

As a prerequisite for this solution, you would of course have to create separate properties in GA and use their assigned property IDs in the variables.

Single GA Property in Development and Production

If you're using the same GA property for your production and development data, you can just configure your GA tag as outlined earlier in this chapter in "Creating a Google Analytics Pageview Tracker."

With the same GA property for development and production, it's best-practice to filter your development data out of your main GA views, either by excluding internal traffic or, even better, by explicitly excluding the hostname of your development and staging environments. You can also create a dedicated view that includes only traffic from your development and/or staging environments. Chapter 9 discusses views and view filters in detail.

Note

Which Workflow Options Should I Choose?

If you have already established an effective development-to-production workflow for GA and GTM, stick with it. There's no single correct solution.

If you're starting with a new implementation of GA and/or GTM, our recommended approach is outlined below.

➤ Use a single GTM container with separate environments created for development and/or staging.
➤ If it's feasible to update the container code in your development and/or staging environments, use the snippet option (rather than the preview link option) to share your development and/or staging changes for preview and debugging.
➤ If there's a possibility that a development/staging environment container will overwrite the Live container in a code push to production, apply trigger exceptions for your Live environment to all tags until they're ready to go to production.
➤ Maintain a dedicated GA property for your Live environment only.
➤ Maintain a dedicated GA property for your development and staging environments, or a separate property for each.

In any case, if you are building or changing your GA and GTM workflow, confer closely with developers, analysts, and marketers within your organization to determine which options make the most sense for you.

GUEST SPOT   **Working with Developers (When You're Not a Developer)**

Joel Michael

Joel Michael is Director of Consulting Services at E-Nor.

If you're a somewhat nontechnical person who wants more than a basic GA implementation, you're going to need to team up with your code-loving friends for at least some implementation tasks. The increased autonomy that GTM provides marketers and analysts doesn't mean you can do it all yourself. But with clear direction and the right attitude, you'll be able to guide your developers to track the elements on your site and/or in your mobile app and configure GA to get the business-changing knowledge you expect.

Developers Think Differently

You may feel that you don't speak their language. So you'll need to find some common ground. Consider using a specific GA report as an example to express the data you want your developer friend to send to GA. If you both work on the same apps and sites, you'll also have their features and functions in common. Again, be prepared for them to think about these differently from you, but take heart that you'll at least have some clue that you'll know what each other is talking about. By sharing a report (even if it is empty) and showing them that you want to see certain kinds of data from your site or app in this column or that column, you'll give them a point from which they can work backward to figure out how to give you what you want. Lather. Rinse. Repeat. Keep showing them examples—not only reports but GA documentation, blogs, and learning materials—until your requirements are understood.

Know the Terminology

It will also help both of you to use GA terminology. Get familiar with dimensions and metrics. Make sure you both use these terms. Further helping them to understand concepts like custom dimensions and events will also help them to know how to search for the appropriate development documentation.

When you provide instructions to your developer, be clear. Just because you found you have some things in common doesn't mean they can read your mind. Use the terminology you both understand to express their next steps. Don't make them have to think about what to do next. In other words, don't make the analysis problem you want to solve become their problem. Most likely, they'll be happy to help you implement an analytics solution as long as you own the problem and have made a good effort toward solving it.

Use Visuals and Provide Concrete Requirements

Demonstrate to your developer how you've helped them to help you. Provide the information that they will need to help you send to GA. Make it logical. Use spreadsheets to devise naming conventions of screen names, events, virtual pageviews, custom dimensions, and so on. In instances where this data is dynamic and needs to be pulled from back-end data sources or the Document Object Model (DOM), the documentation you provide will give them the context necessary to decipher their next steps.

Listen and Compromise, but Get What You Need

Sometimes the developers really do know better. When a developer questions your input, listen. If they aren't able to understand or meet your requirement, ask them for their recommendation on what to do. As the analyst, just make sure you don't compromise to the point that you lose the insight you want to gain. On the other hand, tracking something that no one cares about can cause confusion and simply wastes developers' and analysts' time.

Take on More Responsibility, but Keep Developers in the Loop

Sometimes you may be able to give your developers a break. Deploying GA through GTM is a great way to take on tracking responsibility. GA events, for example, discussed in the next chapter, can be conveniently taken off of your technical colleague's plate by even a novice GTM user.

Actually, deploying GA via GTM isn't a bad idea even when you are a master coder. With GTM, a tag containing GA tracking code can easily be dropped into the GTM container on the site/app by using the GTM interface, as we're beginning to see in this chapter.

The caveat for GTM is that for all of these tags to work, somebody has to place the GTM container code on the site/app in the first place, which will lead you right back to your developer friends. Once the GTM container code is installed, you'll have the flexibility to do more of the page tagging yourself, but be sure to stay in sync with your developers before publishing new tags through GTM. It's just good practice. Whether it's you or your developers doing the actual tagging and publishing, using GTM will be cleaner and easier than trying to manage multiple native codes randomly inserted into various pages and templates. Employing GTM and it's easy-to-use interface, developers, marketers, and analysts will all be able, at a glance, to know which tags are active on which pages at any time.

continues

continued

Get the Technical Implementation Done, and Start Providing Insights

As the analyst, your job is to share with your business colleagues the insight that drives business decisions. That's serious responsibility. Because it's so important, it's up to you to lead the team that will capture the data that delivers the insight. Don't expect that you can hand off the project to the developers for completion. Work with them to produce the implementation you need. They'll appreciate your guidance, and your colleagues on the business side will envy your ability to motivate.

So there you have it. It's not complicated. Be good to your developers and they will be good to you.

 # KEY TAKEAWAYS

More tagging control to marketers and analysts.   GTM can allow greater control of code additions on the part of marketers and analysts and speeds deployment outside of the development cycle, even if developers are adding and publishing tags.

Other tags—not just Google Analytics.   You can use GA to deploy not only GA but almost all type of analytics and marketing codes, as well as snippets of your own internal scripting.

Templated tags and Custom HTML tags.   With the exception of code that must execute synchronously, such as for split testing, you can add most types of scripts to your website through GTM. If a template is not available for the type of tag that you want to deploy, you can use the open-format Custom HTML tag.

Trigger flexibility.   A tag that is present in a container does not have to fire on every page that contains the container code. GTM triggers provide a flexible and straightforward mechanism for dictating tag firing and dormancy.

Control the publishing process.   By best practice, it's acceptable for multiple people to create tags within a container, but only a single individual, or a very small team, should have publishing rights.

 # ACTIONS AND EXERCISES

1. **Create a test GTM account and container.** You can create a test account and container to practice the procedures outlined in this chapter and in upcoming chapters. While you're experimenting, you don't have to worry about any unintended consequences: the container will remain completely inactive until you add the container code to Web pages and publish the container.

2. **Plan your switch to GTM.** If you have an existing native GA implementation, it is recommended that you switch, at some point, to a GTM implementation.

   A. **Take inventory of all other GA coding.** At the same time that you transfer your GA pageview tracking from native code to GTM as described above, you'll need to switch existing event, social, and Ecommerce tracking to GTM, as discussed in upcoming chapters. Review the corresponding reports to assess the current tracking. (The auditing tools listed at `www.e-nor.com/book` can assist in this process.)

   B. **Take inventory of all other marketing and analytics codes.** As a best practice, and with few exceptions, you should transfer native codes for other utilities (such as surveys or heatmapping) to GTM tags.

3. **Plan your development-to-production process.** Review the options for development and staging above for GTM and GA to begin planning the best process for your development workflow (once you have migrated from native tracking to GTM, as needed).

6

Events, Virtual Pageviews, Social Actions, and Errors

I n the previous chapters, we learned how to record pageviews in Google Analytics (GA)—by including the default GA tracking code on all pages of our website, or by including the Google Tag Manager (GTM) container code on each page of our website and then publishing a GA pageview tracker tag to the container. Either of these straightforward approaches will immediately begin populating your GA property with pageview data but will invariably leave big gaps in understanding the full range of your visitors' interaction with your Web pages.

To fill these gaps, you can configure events and also virtual pageviews and social tracking, all of which are covered quite thoroughly in this chapter, along with error tracking. Along the way, we'll get a great deal of practice with GTM skills beyond basic GA tracking.

Please note that this is a lengthy chapter that delves into fairly deep technical detail and introduces some more advanced GTM functionality, so if you are a marketer or analyst, you can read through the chapter to learn the fundamentals of tracking events, virtual pageviews, social actions, and errors and then work with your developers on the implementation procedures.

THE NEED FOR EVENT TRACKING

As illustrated in Figure 4.7, pageview tracking is quite comprehensive in the sense that each default pageview hit includes a wide range of dimension values that describe the page, the visitor's traffic source and geographic location, the technology that the visitor used to access the page, and the visitor's status as a new or returning visitor.

As comprehensive as a pageview hit is, it's important to recognize that a pageview hit is generated only when a page loads and that your GA property does not by default record any user interaction that does not cause one of your own GA-tracked pages to load. Event tracking also tends to play an important role in mobile app tracking, where there may be typically a great deal of interaction without a new screen load.

The Click Does Nothing

To elaborate on the preceding discussion, it's critical for anyone who works with GA, particularly on implementation, to understand this fundamental tracking concept: by default, no click action is tracked in GA. If a click accesses a page on your website and that page contains the GA tracking code or a GA pageview tag in GTM, GA records a pageview. The click is not directly recorded in GA: it's the pageview that results from the click that's recorded. By the same token, browser actions such as scrolling and hovering also go unrecorded in GA by default.

By reviewing Figure 6.1, we can begin to enumerate the many types of user interactions that are not recorded through the default pageview-based tracking code:

- non-pageview links:
  - offsite
  - `mailto:` (opens email client)
  - PDF, spreadsheet, PowerPoint/presentation
  - anchor within the same page
- social connect links
- social content links
- video
- hovering to display help or product variations
- live chat, map, or any other modal or nonmodal popup that doesn't appear as a separate document
- tabs
- list filters
- scrolling

FIGURE 6.1 This mockup represents a wide range of user interactions that are not tracked in GA by default.

Not pictured in Figure 6.1 are several other types of events that you may need to track:

- navigating to an image within a carousel
- comment submissions

- review/rating submissions
- completion of individual form fields or drop-down menu selections
- distinguishing between multiple links on one page that point to the same other page
- multistep/multiscreen process that does not involve a URL refresh, as discussed in *Virtual Pageviews for Multiple AJAX Screens* later in the chapter
- single-page Web applications
- any other interactions designed to use AJAX, jQuery (and other JavaScript libraries), or the HTML5 canvas element to update the page without a pageload

Figure 6.2 illustrates mobile (particularly smartphone) interactions that are not tracked by default, including:

- `tel:` links (prompts autodial)
- accordion menu
- portrait/landscape rotation
- pinching in and out

FIGURE 6.2 Several types of mobile interactions are not tracked in Google Analytics by default.

Note

tel: links

The most recent mobile browsers do not require you, as a Web page developer, to wrap a phone number side with a `tel:` link for the phone number to activate autodialing when clicked. If you do use `tel:` links for your phone numbers, however, you'll be able to easily configure event tracking for `tel:` clicks and then also configure goals based on the event data. From a functional standpoint, a `tel:` wrapper also allows to you to make any text click-to-call, even if all or some of the text is not a telephone number as in Figure 6.2.

DOM Listeners

We've identified a problem: many user interactions on desktop and mobile are not tracked by default. What's the solution?

The solution begins with another critical concept that underlies GA event tracking: you can code a response to any user interaction in the browser, whether the interaction generates a page load or not. As part of its broader role as a notation format for referencing and manipulating browser and page elements through JavaScript, the Document Object Model (DOM) provides a way for us to "listen" for user actions and code specific responses.

Following are some of the DOM listeners that we can implement:

- `onclick`
- `onmouseover` (hover over an element)
- `onmouseout` (hover away from an element)
- `onkeydown` (can check for a specific key)
- `onkeyup` (can check for a specific key)
- `onchange` (drop-down menu selection)
- `onfocus` (user clicks into a form field)
- `onblur` (user clicks away from a form field)
- `onscroll`

Unless you're a front-end Web developer, it's not necessary to memorize this list, but, as a GA practitioner, you should understand that you can use these listeners to execute additional scripting in the page. In GTM, clicks (and form submissions) will generally be the easiest type of action to listen for, but we'll still be able to configure extra scripting in response to other types of user actions.

In our case, this extra scripting will take the form of GA events and virtual pageviews, as the examples in this chapter will demonstrate.

Populating the Events Reports

Before continuing the discussion on event implementation, let's take a look at the Top Events report in Figure 6.3. The report displays Event Category as the default primary dimension, and we've added Event Action as the secondary dimension.

	Event Category	Event Action	Total Events ↓	Unique Events
			2,767,294 % of Total: 100.00% (2,767,294)	**1,102,907** % of Total: 52.52% (2,100,051)
1.	video	play	**412,821** (14.92%)	231,523 (11.99%)
2.	outbound-link	http://www.othersite.com	**263,861** (9.53%)	154,136 (7.98%)
3.	scroll	25%	**188,560** (6.81%)	127,067 (6.58%)
4.	pdf	annual-report.pdf	**159,129** (5.75%)	116,327 (6.03%)
5.	carousel	image-3	**124,284** (4.49%)	86,891 (4.50%)
6.	tab	product-specs	**113,280** (4.09%)	83,136 (4.31%)
7.	internal-banner	7-day-promo	**107,305** (3.88%)	62,599 (3.24%)
8.	scroll	50%	**104,812** (3.79%)	73,398 (3.80%)
9.	video	complete	**69,702** (2.52%)	51,199 (2.65%)
10.	accordion	open	**63,021** (2.28%)	36,033 (1.87%)

FIGURE 6.3 Top Events report, with Event Category displayed as primary dimension and Event Action displayed as secondary dimension.

> **Note**
>
> ### Unique Events
> The Unique Events metric represents the number of sessions in which the given event occurred at least one time. For instance, if a visitor generated a completion event for your video demo twice in one session, Total Events would increase by two, but Unique Events would increase only by one. (This is similar to the Unique Pageviews metric, which represents the number of sessions during which a specific page was viewed at least one time.)

To view the pages on which events have occurred, you can apply Pages as a secondary dimension (and filter on a primary dimension value as needed), as shown in Figure 6.4.

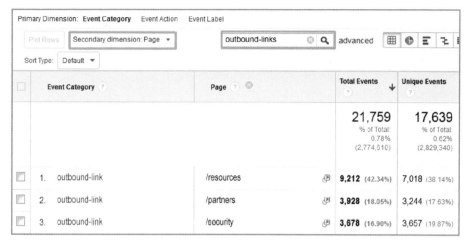

FIGURE 6.4 Pages applied as secondary dimension to the Top Events report.

GA provides multiple dimensions that we can populate to describe events:

- Event Category (mandatory)
- Event Action (mandatory)
- Event Label (optional but often used)

How do we record event data in GA? Let's start with a PDF link as an example. On your website, you have included a link to your catalog:

```
<a href="/catalog.pdf">Download our catalog</a>
```

Taking advantage of the `onclick` DOM listener listed above, we can execute additional code when a Web visitor clicks the link:

```
<a onclick="ga('send','event','pdf','click','/catalog.pdf');"
href="/catalog.pdf">Download our catalog</a>
```

The diagram in Figure 6.5 demonstrates potential event parameters for a video interaction.

FIGURE 6.5 An event call with Event Category, Event Action, and Event Label.

Note that we have a great deal of flexibility when populating events. In fact, we do not in all instances have to treat event *category, action,* and *label* literally. It can be perfectly valid to instead consider these three event parameters (or event *arguments*) as follows:

- Event Category: A general descriptor for the event.
- Event Action: A more specific descriptor for the event.
- Event Label: The most specific descriptor for the event.

To return to our PDF example, we could capture the catalog download as shown in Figure 6.6.

FIGURE 6.6 We could opt to record this event with Event Category, Event Action, and Event Label.

Since event label is optional, we could opt to record the PDF name as the event action and omit the label argument, as shown in Figure 6.7.

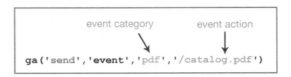

FIGURE 6.7 If Event Category and Event Action adequately describe the action, it's valid to omit Event Label, which is optional.

As two more examples of generating events with DOM listeners, you can use `onmouseover` as below to record a hover over a graphic (or any other visible HTML-element):

```
<img src="/group-photo.jpg"
onmouseover="ga('send','event','photo','hover',this.src);" />
```

And let's say that you've just added a suggestion field to a contact form on your website, and that you want GA to record completions of that field. Let's break down the following code block to understand how we can accomplish this event tracking:

- `textarea` is the HTML element that can render a wide, multirow field in a form.
- `onblur` is the DOM listener that fires when a page element loses the cursor (i.e., the user clicks somewhere else on the page or tabs to another field).
- `if(this.value.length > 0)` is a bit of extra JavaScript logic that tests if the length of the text in the field is greater than zero (that is, if it's not empty). We don't want to send an event for every `onblur` in the `textarea`—only when the visitor has entered a suggestion.

```
<textarea name="suggestion" cols="60" rows="10"
onblur="if(this.value.length > 0)
{ga('send','event','form','completed','suggestion');}" />
```

Will you need to set up this type of very specific event tracking on a regular basis? Perhaps not, but the previous example illustrates an important point: you can generate GA events for any user interaction on a Web page, and you can build in any front-end logic to determine if the event is recorded.

Later in the chapter, we'll learn how to use GTM to generate events for many types of user interactions without actually editing the page's HTML directly.

Don't Track Every User Interaction

None of the previous discussions are intended to imply that you should track every conceivable interaction between a user and your Web page. If data on image hovers would be useful for design, development, or content decisions (e.g., many users are hovering over the question mark help icon next to the product delivery options in the checkout form, so maybe you need to make that section clearer), it makes sense to track events for that user interaction. It is not, however, recommended to track every cursor movement on every page: you could deplete the GA hit limit for your property and create clutter that obscures the important data. Measure what matters.

To visually overlay user interaction trends on a page, you can possibly refer to the In-Page Analytics report within GA, but this report sometimes does not load correctly. As another option for displaying on-page interactions, you can use a third-party heat-mapping tool such as CrazyEgg or HotJar, discussed in Appendix A.

Consistency Is Critical

You may have already noted two fundamental differences between, on the one hand, event tracking and, on the other hand, pageview tracking as implemented through the native tracking snippet or GTM:

- You have to be more specific in dictating the conditions for event firing.
- For events, you're populating two or more dimensions with your own values; GA does not automatically pull them from the environment.

So you have full power to populate the event values in any way you choose, but with great power comes great responsibility. For your event reporting to be meaningful and usable it's critical that you adopt a consistent convention for your event category, action, and label values. More specifically, you must take care to avoid the metrics fragmentation as represented in Figure 6.8:

- Don't use two different values to refer to the same thing, as in play and played in rows 1 and 3.

- Don't vary case, as in rows 1 and 5.
- Don't swap the same values between different dimension slots, as in rows 2 and 4.

		Event Category ?	Event Action ? ⊗	Total Events ? ↓	Unique Events ?
☐				2,781,593	1,112,334
				% of Total: 100.00% (2,781,593)	% of Total: 39.21% (2,837,172)
☐	1.	video	play	2,042,979 (73.05%)	664,739 (59.43%)
☐	2.	link	pdf	263,667 (9.43%)	125,629 (11.23%)
☐	3.	video	played	187,326 (6.70%)	127,168 (11.37%)
☐	4.	pdf	link	81,339 (2.91%)	55,266 (4.94%)
☐	5.	video	Play	72,181 (2.58%)	34,520 (3.09%)

FIGURE 6.8 Metrics fragmentation due to inconsistent event naming.

The five rows in the report should have appeared as just two, but there's no way that we can consolidate retroactively. Right from the start, you must make sure to avoid unnecessary fragmentation when generating event data in GA. There isn't one right way to name your events; you can adopt whatever convention makes the most sense for you and your organization, but it's vitally important to adhere to that convention.

Fortunately, as we'll see a bit further on in the chapter, we can use GTM to enforce consistency in much of our event tracking.

EVENT TRACKING IN GTM

To continue our discussion on event consistency, let's consider a few specific points about the manual event tracking that we demonstrated previously in this chapter.

- You'd need to avoid errors in the code.
- You'd need to maintain consistency in the event category, action, and label parameters.
- It does not take advantage of any extensibility. For instance, you'd need to set up event tracking for each new PDF or outbound link.

So if you were thinking that the previous examples would be cumbersome and hard to manage on anything but a very limited scale, you were right.

Understand Manual Event Tracking, but Avoid It When You Can

It is important to understand the underlying mechanisms behind event tracking as demonstrated in the previous discussions, especially since manual event tracking may be the only option for certain user interactions that we need to record. What we want to do now, however, is take this nuts-and-bolts knowledge of manual event tracking and actually implement most of our events through GTM (and third-party scripts as needed) so the entire process is less invasive, more consistent, better managed, and faster.

Tracking PDF Downloads through GTM

In this example, we're going to perform the following actions to configure consistent and extensible event tracking for any PDF link on your website:

1. Enable the built-in Click URL variable.
2. Create a GA tag to generate PDF events.
3. Create a trigger that fires the tag on PDF link clicks.

These steps are explained below—they're all quite straightforward. It's recommended that you first implement these steps in a test environment as detailed in Chapter 5.

Enable the Click URL Variable

GTM variables, both built-in and custom, offer the ideal combination of flexibility and control. In the case of PDF tracking, the Click URL variable will offer the flexibility of dynamically populating the event label with the filename of the PDF, and the control of consistently retrieving this filename from the `href` value of the HTML link to the PDF.

GTM offers many built-in variables, but only a few are actually enabled by default. You can enable the Click URL variable by clicking Variables in the left navigation of your container and checking Click URL, as shown in Figure 6.9.

FIGURE 6.9 The *Click URL* variable is built into GTM but not enabled by default.

Create a Google Analytics Event Tag

Next step is to set up the actual GA event tag for PDF tracking. The Event tag will be somewhat similar to the GA pageview tag outlined in Chapter 5, "Google Tag Manager," with some additional considerations:

- **Tracking ID.** We can reuse the *Google Analytics Property ID* variable as shown in Figure 6.10, which we first used for basic pageview tracking. (If you're using a separate GA property for testing, you can specify the corresponding property ID for the event tag, either as a hard value or through a separate variable.)
- **Track Type.** Select Event.
- **Event Category.** In most cases, you'll "hard-code" a static event category—`link`, in this case.
- **Event Action.** In many cases, you'll also hard-code the event action, as we did with `pdf` in this example.
- **Event Label.** Because the event label should dynamically pull in the `href` value of the link to any PDF file, it would make little sense to hard-code the event label. Instead, we just use the *Click URL* variable enabled in the previous step.

Note that different configurations of this event tag could be equally valid. For instance, we could have used Courier as the Event Category and Click URL as the Event Action and left the Event Label blank, since it's not obligatory. In either case, we enjoy the consistency of static values and the flexibility of variables wherever either is needed.

As a note, if you need more than three dimensions to adequately describe your event, you can record the event with additional custom dimensions as described in Chapter 12, "Implementation Customizations."

We selected Enable Display Advertising Features to populate the Demographics and Interests reports, also discussed in Chapter 12. You can leave Event Value blank; it is usually left unpopulated.

Create a Trigger for PDF Clicks: Think in Patterns

As we have learned previously, a tag can be active only if you have applied at least one trigger to it. In plain terms, we want a click on any PDF link to trigger this tag. What is the common pattern that we can identify for these links? The filename always ends in `.pdf`.

If you are already thinking about using the *Click URL* variable for the trigger, your instincts are serving you well once again. To create the trigger:

1. In the Fire On section of the tag configuration, select Click.
2. Create the trigger as shown in Figure 6.11.
   a. In the Configure Trigger section, select Just Links from the Targets drop-down. (All Elements would also work in this case, but would not allow the checks described in the following step.)

FIGURE 6.10 Our PDF event tag uses two static values and one variable.

b. The Enable When setting is required when Wait for Tags or Check Validation is selected in section 2. Wait for Tags pauses the execution of the click action until any other GTM tag completes firing, and Check Validation suppresses the click event in case you have scripted the click action to return false under certain conditions. (You can similarly use Check Validation to block a Form Submission trigger if the form fails validation and you have coded the submit action to return false under this condition.)

In most cases, you can use the .* regular expression (that is, a dot followed directly by an asterisk) to match all pages for Enable When. If you have any trouble getting your Event tag to fire when following the debugging procedures outlined below, you can disable Wait for Tags and Check Validation, at least temporarily.

c. In Fire On, you specify the exact conditions that will cause the trigger to fire any associated tags.

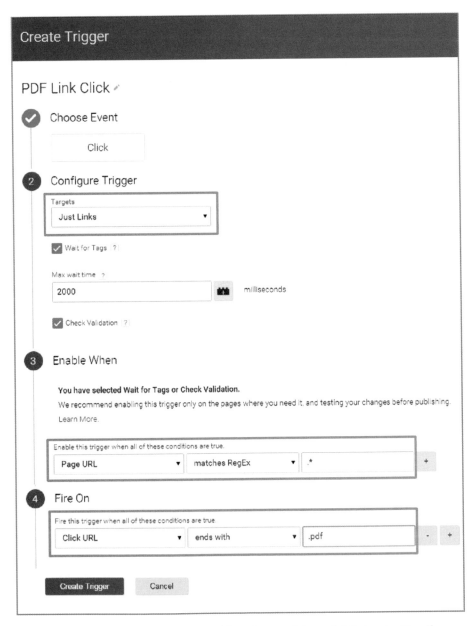

FIGURE 6.11 This trigger uses the *Click URL* variable to detect a click on a link that ends with *.pdf*.

If the links to your PDFs include a URL fragment following .pdf, you could instead configure the trigger in Figure 6.11 as *Click URL – matches RegEx (ignore case) – ^(.*)\.pdf* instead of using the *ends with* match. For more on regex, see *Regular Expressions in Google Analytics* in Chapter 9.

Tracking Other File Types and Offsite Links

Note that you could easily adapt our PDF tracking for clicks to other file types. For instance, to track downloads of Microsoft Excel spreadsheets, you could change the Event Action field in Figure 6.10 to **excel-spreadsheet** and the trigger in Figure 6.11 to **Click URL - ends with - .xlsx**.

To track offsite links, you could change the Event Action to offsite-link and configure the two condition trigger as in Figure 6.12.

Enable When		
Page URL matches RegEx .*		

4 Fire On

Fire this trigger when all of these conditions are true.

Click URL	does not contain	mysite.com	-
Click URL	starts with	http	- +

Create Trigger   Cancel

FIGURE 6.12 Two-condition trigger for clicks on offsite links.

GUEST SPOT   **GTM Triggers Under the Hood**

Simo Ahava

Simo Ahava is Senior Data Advocate at Reaktor.

Every single GTM *tag* requires a *trigger* to fire. Every single trigger requires a special Data Layer interaction, specifically an *event* (not the same as a GA event), to activate. This flow is central to how the rule-based logic of GTM works, and we'll explore this more below.

GTM wouldn't be a very special tool unless it automated a number of things. Most of the triggers you'll end up using are, in fact, automatic processes, where you only have to indicate the type of event you want to listen to, and GTM does the rest.

continues

continued

You can, and you most often will, also use custom code to fire your tags, and we'll take a look at how this works as well.

Google Tag Manager's Automatic Events

As previously mentioned, GTM automates a number of events, so that you can start tracking without adding any extra code to the site. When you create a new Trigger, you'll see a selection like the one shown in Figure 6.13.

FIGURE 6.13 The GTM events from which you can define a trigger.

Each one of these, except for the Custom Event, represents automated events that you can tap into and use to make your tags fire. In Table 6.1, I've listed the most common event types you'll use, what they'll look like in the Data Layer (I'll get back to this soon, I promise!), and what the triggers that listen for these events could be used for.

TABLE 6.1 Each Built-in GTM Trigger Type Listens for a GTM Event in the Data Layer (The GTM events do not correspond directly to any GA event tracking.)

GTM Event	Trigger Type	Appears in the Data Layer As	Triggered When	Useful For
Page View	Page View	`gtm.js`	The GTM library first loads	Firing your Page View tag, as this is the earliest moment in the page load when you can do so
	DOM Ready	`gtm.dom`	The page source has been read	Firing any tags which rely on something in the HTML source (e.g., the number of images, or the length of your header)
	Window Loaded	`gtm.load`	The page and all linked resources (images, files) have loaded	Firing tags that require all linked resources (e.g., the `jQuery` library) to be loaded first

TABLE 6.1 *continued*

GTM Event	Trigger Type	Appears in the Data Layer As	Triggered When	Useful For
Click	All Elements	`gtm.click`	A mouse click is registered on any element	Firing a tag when a specific tab or button, or any visible HTML element, is clicked on the page
	Just Links	`gtm.linkClick`	A mouse click is registered on a link element	Firing a tag when a link is clicked
Form	N/A	`gtm.formSubmit`	A form submission is registered	Firing a tag on a form submission, when you don't have a "thank you" page to use as a conversion goal

As I wrote earlier, GTM automatically listens for these events on the page. Thus, when you create a trigger, all you need to do is indicate which event you want to make your tags fire.

Remember that triggers let you delimit how tags are fired beyond just the Event selection. For example, if you want to fire a tag only when a link is clicked that does *not* point to `mydomain.com` (i.e., your website's domain), you'd use a Just Links trigger as shown in Figure 6.14.

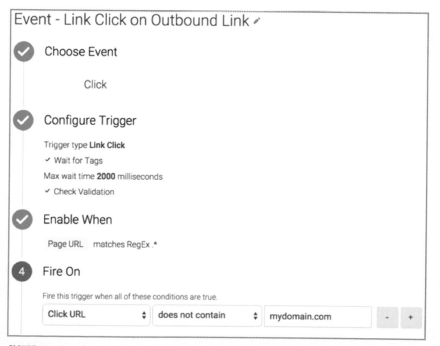

FIGURE 6.14 Based on a GTM click event, this trigger is configured to fire when a website user clicks on an outbound link.

continues

continued

Or if you want to fire a tag after someone has spent 30 seconds on the page, you could use a Timer trigger as shown in Figure 6.15.

Use the Fire On setting of the trigger to specify the conditions under which any tags that use this trigger should fire (in addition to the event type, of course).

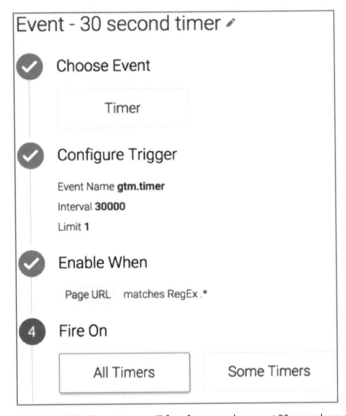

FIGURE 6.15 This Timer trigger will fire after a user has spent 30 seconds on a page.

As a special note, click propagation in the page's HTML differs for the All Elements and Just Links trigger types. All Elements would serve to fire a tag when any HTML element in the page is clicked, but it's very rigid in the sense that nesting is not recognized. The element that is the target is the element that was actually clicked, so if there is, for example, a nest like: `<div class="classname"><span>Hi</span></div>`, and you try to use `{{Click Classes}} contains classname` in your trigger, your trigger won't fire, as the actual clicked element will be the `<span>`, which does not have the `classname` class applied.

Just Links, in turn, looks up the DOM tree until it finds an `<a>` element, so it's much less rigid than All Elements. You can click on a nested element, and it will still return the link that's further out in the nesting hierarchy.

Custom Events in the Data Layer

When GTM records one of the automatic events, it actually pushes a message to the Data Layer, which then activates the triggers. For the events listed in Table 6.1, it's completely automated, so you don't have to worry about the Data Layer at all.

But every now and then you need to make a tag fire with some custom code, especially if you can't find an automatic event type that you could use.

Let's open with an example. Say you have a user login on your site. Once the user successfully logs in, you want to send their User ID to GA, so that you can benefit from the awesome user-centric reports, metrics, and dimensions. To accomplish this, you need to ask your Web developer to add the following custom code after a successful login:

```
dataLayer.push({
  'userId' : 'a143-bce4-fffd-a223',
  'event' : 'loggedIn'
});
```

This is a *Data Layer message*, where you pass both a `'userId'` key as well as an `'event'` key. The latter is, as you might have guessed, what you'll need to configure when you select the Custom Event trigger type, as shown in Figure 6.16.

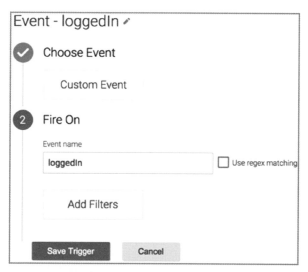

FIGURE 6.16 A Custom Event trigger listens for a variable named *event* to be pushed to the data layer with a specific value—*loggedIn*, in this case.

This trigger would fire a tag when a Data Layer message with `loggedIn` as the `'event'` key value is pushed. This is how the Custom Event Trigger works.

In fact, this is how *all* triggers in GTM work. It's just that with the automatic triggers, the Data Layer interaction happens without you needing to add any custom code on the site.

And to read the `'userId'` value in from the Data Layer and use in a GA tag, you could create a simple `DataLayer` variable in GTM.

continues

continued

Summary

It seems to me that the *Data Layer*, and how GTM both utilizes and depends on it, is one of the more difficult things to understand for GTM users. This difficulty stems from the fact that the Data Layer serves a dual purpose in GTM:

First, it's a *repository* of generic, semantic information. The data within is structured according to a specific syntax. This means that any application, platform, and library to which the website or mobile app is connected to can make use of this data. An example of this type of semantic information was introduced in the example above, where the User ID is one such piece of data we'd want to store in the Data Layer.

Second, the data layer is a *message bus*, which feeds commands to GTM so that GTM can, in turn, fire the tags within the container. Only messages where the `'event'` key is included have the power to fire your tags.

GTM gives you the powerful Custom Event trigger type, which you can use to fire tags on any `'event'` pushes you manually add to the code, and it also gives you a handful of useful automatic events, which you can utilize without any coding at all. The concept of the *event* is central to *everything* you want to do with GTM.

Testing the PDF Event Tag

To verify that our event is firing, we'll use three of the techniques first reviewed in Chapters 4 and 5 and shown again in Figures 6.17, 6.18, and 6.19.

Note

How Can I See the Event in the GTM Debug Panel If the Link Accesses Another Page or Resource?

If you're testing an event for a PDF or offsite link, you can command-click, control-click, or right-click the link to open the resource in a different browser window or tab and preserve the debug panel on the page that you're testing.

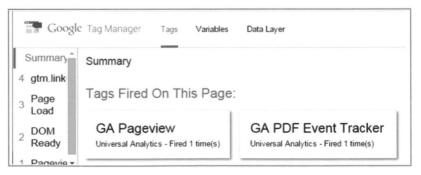

FIGURE 6.17 GTM Preview and Debug mode displays the initial pageview hit and then the event hit when you click the PDF link.

FIGURE 6.18 The GA Debug extension for Chrome that we first activated to verify pageviews in Chapter 4 can also display the event dimensions.

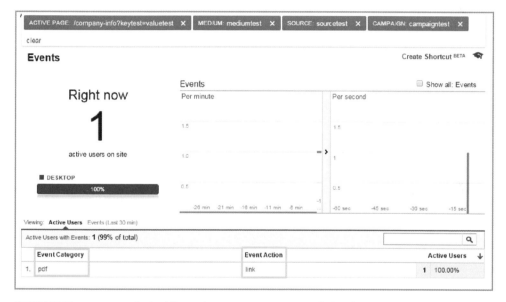

FIGURE 6.19 You can access the Real-Time > Events report in GA to verify that the event is firing.

Note

How Can I Isolate My Own Session within the Real-Time Reports?

If you're testing your event in a GA property that is receiving data from other visitors, your own activity may be difficult to spot in the Real-Time reports. You can, however, take either of the following approaches to identify your own activity within GA.

As a note, if your own sessions are filtered out of your working view through internal IP address exclusion as described in Chapter 9, "View Settings, View Filters, and Access Rights," make sure to look at an unfiltered view for the property.

Add a Dummy Name=Value Pair to the URL

For most URLs, you can add a dummy name=value pair to the URL when you access a page on your site, as follows:

```
http://www.mysite.com/company-info/?keytest=keyvalue
```

You can then access the Real-Time > Content report and click /company-info/?keytest=keyvalue to apply this Request URI as a dynamic filter for all the other Real-Time reports, including Real-Time > Events.

Add Dummy Campaign Parameters to the URL

As another option for isolating your own session, you can add dummy campaign parameters to the URL as follows:

```
http://www.mysite.com/company-info/
?utm_medium=mediumtest&utm_source=sourcetest&utm_campaign=
campaigntest
```

You can then access the Real-Time > Traffic Sources report and click the medium, source, and campaign values to apply them as filters.

Campaign tracking is detailed in Chapter 7, "Acquisition Reports."

The Request URI, medium, source, and campaign Real-Time filters all appear at the top of Figure 6.19.

Non-Interaction Events and Bounce

If a visitor lands on your home page and watches a video, does GA consider that session to be a bounce?

As we learned in Chapter 4, a bounce is defined as a *single-hit session*, so there's our answer. If a visitor lands on your home page and watches a video, GA does not consider that session to be a bounce, provided that you generate GA events for the video interactions. In this case, the page would generate a pageview hit, and the video would generate an event hit, and so the second hit would classify this session as non-bounce.

But what if the video played automatically 15 seconds after page load? In this case, the video play does not represent an additional user engagement, so the session should still count as a bounce until the visitor deliberately initiates another tracked interaction. You could still track this autoplay video as an event, without inadvertently lowering bounce rate, by selecting True as the Non-Interaction Hit value within the event tag configuration as shown in Figure 6.20.

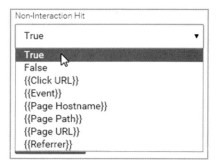

FIGURE 6.20 Set Non-Interaction Hit to True only for events that the visitor does not initiate.

Note that it is an exception to set Non-Interaction Hit to true: the overwhelming majority of events do signify user engagement. For these events, leave Non-Interaction Hit set to False so they will rightfully influence bounce rate (and session duration).

VIRTUAL PAGEVIEWS

Referring to non-pageview actions that appear in Figures 6.1 and 6.2 and other points earlier in the chapter, it's important to note that we don't need to track all of these actions as events. In some cases, we can—or should—opt instead for virtual pageview tracking.

Unlike events, which appear in dedicated Events reports, virtual pageviews are integrated into the Pages report that displays all our physical pageviews. In fact, once we record virtual pageviews, GA considers and represents them the same as physical pageviews.

Notice in Figure 6.21 that we've recorded a PDF download as a virtual pageview instead of an event as shown previously in Figure 6.10. Both approaches are equally valid. If you consider a clickthrough to a PDF to be an interaction that is unlike the regular pageviews that occur on your site, especially if you have configured your website to download the PDF instead of opening it directly in the browser, you may decide to track the PDF clicks as events. If, however, you consider the PDF view to be closely akin to a view of a Web page, you may opt instead to track it as a virtual pageview.

So how would we track the PDF click as a virtual pageview instead of an event? Let's start again with our basic HTML link to the PDF:

```
<a href="/catalog.pdf">Download our catalog</a>
```

	Page ?		Pageviews ? ↓
☐			**827,771** % of Total: 100.00% (827,771)
☐	1. /home	⊡	**143,713** (17.36%)
☐	2. /about-us	⊡	**90,772** (10.97%)
☐	3. /services	⊡	**83,044** (10.03%)
☐	4. /support	⊡	**64,642** (7.81%)
☐	5. /virtual/step-2	⊡	**27,013** (3.26%)
☐	6. /virtual/catalog.pdf	⊡	**15,950** (1.93%)
☐	7. /5-resources-for-pretecting-your-investment	⊡	**15,015** (1.81%)
☐	8. /virtual/step-3	⊡	**11,046** (1.33%)
☐	9. /privacy	⊡	**10,874** (1.31%)
☐	10. /virtual/step-4	⊡	**8,252** (1.00%)

FIGURE 6.21 Virtual pageviews appear integrated with physical pageviews in the Pages report.

And let's also look back to the main GA pageview tracking function first presented in Chapter 4:

```
ga('send','pageview');
```

When `ga('send', 'pageview')` or a GA tag in GTM executes, the Page dimension value (i.e., the Request URI) sent to GA defaults to the page that visitor is loading in the browser. When we generate a virtual pageview, we'll use the same function as with the physical pageviews, but we'll overwrite the default Page/Request URI with whichever value we choose, as in the following code:

```
<a onclick="ga('send','pageview','/virtual/catalog.pdf');"
href="/catalog.pdf">Download our catalog</a>
```

As we discussed for event category, action, and label, you should take care to name your virtual pageviews in a way that will facilitate your reporting. Although in no way obligatory, including `virtual` in the Page value of a virtual pageview will allow easy visibility and filtering of virtual pageviews within the Pages report. Furthermore, if we add `/virtual/` at the beginning of the Page value for all virtual pageviews to mimic the top level of a directory structure, we'll be able to easily create a view filter based on subdirectory to include or exclude all virtual pageviews within `/virtual`.

What steps would we need to take in GTM to implement virtual pageview tracking for PDF downloads? We'd need to set up a GA Pageview tag, but with settings that differ from the main pageview tracker that we configured in Chapter 5. There a few steps required in the process, which seems a bit involved but is actually quite straightforward and provides some good practice with built-in and user-defined variables. (And if you can complete these steps, you can congratulate yourself for having graduated from elementary to intermediate GTM skills.)

Specifically, we'll need to record a pageview for a page other than the default. As an option, we can also set a page title. The first step in completing this process is enabling the built-in Click Text as shown in Figure 6.22.

FIGURE 6.22 Enabling the built-in Click Text variables.

As the next step, we'll need to create an Auto-Event variable as follows. We can use an Auto-Event variable to retrieve an attribute of a clicked element when a built-in variable won't do the trick. In this case, we're using an Auto-Event variable to read the href value only: /catalog.pdf. We could have used the built-in Click URL attribute, but this actually pulls in the entire click URL, with the domain: `http://www.mysite.com/catalog.pdf`.

1. From the User-Defined Variables section on the bottom of the Variables panel, click New.
2. In the Choose Type section, click Auto-Event Variable.
3. Configure the variable to return the href attribute of the clicked link, as shown in Figure 6.23, and click Create Variable.

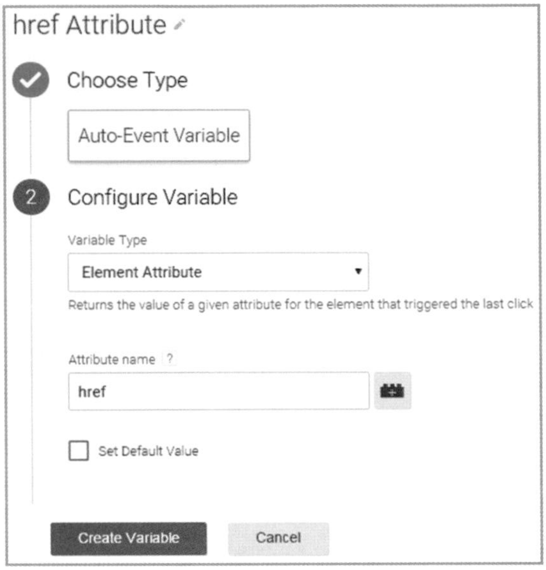

FIGURE 6.23 This variable returns the href value of the clicked link.

With our href Attribute variable ready to go, we can configure the virtual pageview tag itself as in Figure 6.24. The More Settings > Fields To Set section of the tag is configured to overwrite two dimensions that a GA tag would otherwise pull directly from the page: *page* (i.e., request URI) and *title*.

FIGURE 6.24 The *page* setting that overrides the default page URL is what distinguishes a virtual pageview from a regular physical pageview. Here we're also setting the page *title* to populate with the text of the clicked link.

Of these two, page is required for a virtual pageview; otherwise, the tag would populate the GA *page* dimension with that page that you're linking from instead of the page or resource that you're linking to. In a previous step, we configured the href Auto-Event variable to return the asset that we're linking to, and we've prepended */virtual* as a static string so the virtual pageview will be easier to identify in the Pages report as previously demonstrated in Figure 6.21.

We're also overriding the default page title with the Click Text variable that we enabled, prepended with *Virtual:* as a static string.

To fire this virtual pageview, we can save the tag with the same trigger that we used for PDF event tracking as shown previously in Figure 6.11. (We could have also defined our trigger as *{{href Attribute}} - ends with - .pdf*.) There is no need to maintain a one-to-one relationship between tags and triggers: to a single tag, you can apply multiple triggers, any of which would cause the tag to fire, and you can certainly apply a single trigger to multiple tags.

Once we save our tag, we can validate it the same ways that we tested our event tag earlier in the chapter: Preview and Debug mode in GTM, GA Debug extension for Chrome, and the GA Real-Time reports. Checking the Real-Time > Content report in Figure 6.25, we can see that the page and title dimensions have populated with the variables that we configured in GTM, and that static-text prepends will make it easy to identify the virtual pageviews among the physical pageviews. Both Page and Page Title will be available as primary dimensions in the GA Pages report.

Viewing: **Active Users** Pageviews (Last 30 min)	
Metric Total: **1**	
Active Page	**Page Title**
1. /virtual/catalog.pdf	Virtual: Download our catalog

FIGURE 6.25 The Real-Time > Content report shows that our virtual pageview tag configuration has successfully overwritten the default *Page* and *Title* dimensions.

Also note that this virtual pageview tag will work not only for this one link but for all links to .pdf files. As with our event tag, the variables that we use in the virtual pageview tag and associated trigger provide a winning combination of flexibility, extensibility, and consistency.

Virtual Pageviews for Multiple AJAX Screens

As mentioned earlier, virtual pageviews may be more suitable than events for tracking actions that are more akin to physical pageviews. In addition to the previous example of a virtual pageview for PDF clicks, we could also potentially configure tab navigation—especially if each tab displays a lot of its own content—and page scrolls as virtual pageviews. (Scrolling is discussed later in the chapter.)

The preeminent candidate for virtual pageviews, however, is a multiscreen process in which the URL does not change. In the early days of the Web, each new screen that the browser displayed usually required a full round trip to the server and new load of a different page for the screen to refresh.

For some time, however, we have seen the emergence of front-end Web technologies that allow page *updates* without page *loads*. This provides a more continuous and fluid end-user experience by avoiding the visible flicker that usually occasions complete page loads.

The HTML5 canvas element (which you can hand-code or now output from development environments such as Flash) and JavaScript libraries such jQuery all allow rich user interactions without page reloads. AJAX (which stands for Asynchronous JavaScript and XML) goes a step further by enabling actual round trips to the Web server (for processing and data transfer) without a page load. Multiscreen, single-URL end-user processes as demonstrated in Figure 6.26 and single-page Web applications are usually implemented in AJAX or a comparable technology.

FIGURE 6.26 In this multiscreen process, the screens update, but the URL does not change, and the page does not reload.

Apart from the fact that the screen refreshes serve as separate pageviews from a user experience standpoint, there is sometimes another compelling reason to opt for virtual pageviews instead of events: you can use both events and virtual pageviews as the basis for a goal, but you cannot use an event anywhere in a goal *funnel*. (Chapter 8 provides a detailed discussion of goal and funnel configuration. The Custom Funnel feature for Analytics 360 described in Chapter 18 does allow events as funnel steps.)

Referring again to Figure 6.26, you should ideally track the four-step process as a goal with three funnel steps so you can measure drop-off from screen to screen and begin to optimize for improved conversion rate. If you generate a virtual pageview for each of the steps (after the first step, which GA would record as a physical pageview when the URL first loaded), you'll be able to configure the screens as funnel steps leading to the thank-you page and view a Funnel Visualization report as in Figure 8.9.

Generating virtual pageviews will be somewhat more challenging for this multistep process than for PDFs, but with the help of some logic and another GTM variable, we'll devise a good solution.

Create the Lookup Table

As outlined below, we're going to use the text of each button as the key in a lookup table, from which we'll pull the page dimension to record for each virtual pageview.

1. Create an Auto-Event Variable as in Figure 6.27 to read the value attribute of the button, which appears as the button text. (We can't use the built-in Click Text variable in this case, since the text is not surrounded by an open and close HTML element.)

FIGURE 6.27 This custom GTM variable reads the *value* attribute of the button, which appears as the button text.

2. As shown in Figure 6.28, configure a lookup table variable that outputs different text values based on the Button Value variable created in the previous step. We can now use the Lookup for Checkout Virtual Pageviews variable as the page field in a virtual pageview tag similar to Figure 6.24.

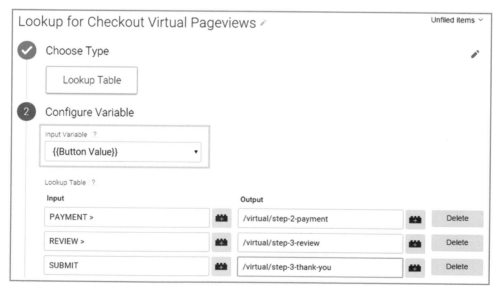

FIGURE 6.28 Instead of using the button text directly as the page dimension for the virtual pageview, we'll use the Button Text variable defined in Figure 6.27 as the input variable in a lookup table and retrieve better page dimension values to populate into our virtual pageviews.

3. Create a similar lookup table that also uses Button Text as the input but outputs the page title that we'll use in our virtual pageview tag.
4. Create a GA pageview tag similar to Figure 6.24, but use the two new lookup variables for as the page and title values in the Fields to Set section.

Create the Trigger

Before we configure the trigger, let's take a look at the HTML for the blue button on the checkout screens.

```
<input type="button" value="PAYMENT >" id="btn1001"
class="blueButton" />
```

In most cases, your HTML button will contain an ID and/or class attribute, both of which are used primarily for CSS styling but can also identify an HTML element for other purposes. You can use either of the attributes for GTM triggers. (Even without class or ID, you could base your GTM trigger on an Auto-Event variable for the style attribute of the clicked element. In the example below, we'll use the class attribute.

1. Enable the Page Path and Click Classes built-in variables.
2. Configure the trigger as in Figure 6.29.

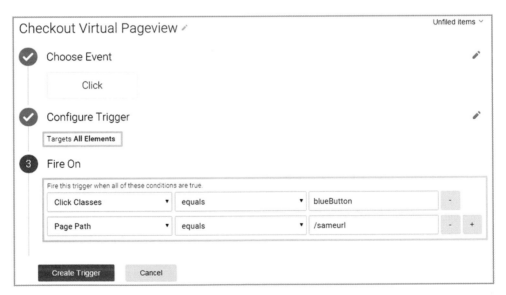

FIGURE 6.29 The trigger for the multiscreen virtual pageviews specifies conditions for the page path and the class name of the button on the form.

Once you have applied the trigger to your virtual pageview tag, you can test the tag using GTM Preview and Debug mode, GA Debug Chrome extension, and the GA Real-Time reports as described above.

Should You Use Events or Virtual Pageviews?

Referring again to the list of non-pageview interactions at the beginning of this chapter, it's generally considered standard practice to opt for events in most instances.

A compelling reason to opt for virtual pageviews is if you need to include the interaction anywhere in a goal funnel, as described earlier.

A compelling reason *not* to opt for virtual pageviews: if your pageview counts are closely monitored or audited and the virtual pageviews could be construed as willful pageview "inflation," or if for any reason you wish to keep any hits other than physical pageviews out of the Pages report, you should opt for events, which appear in their own reports and do not affect pageview metrics. (As mentioned earlier, if you prefix the page field of your virtual pageviews with /virtual, you'll be able to easily filter virtual pageviews out of any view by applying a subdirectory filter, while also maintaining an unfiltered view that displays your virtual pageviews. View filters are discussed in Chapter 10.)

Several aspects of events and virtual pageviews are compared in Table 6.2.

TABLE 6.2 Comparison of Events and Virtual Pageviews

	Events	**Virtual Pageviews**
Reporting	Appear in dedicated Events reports.	Integrated with physical pageviews in the Pages report; "inflates" pageviews.
Parameters passed	Usually described with three parameters: category and action are obligatory, and label is usually used; value is normally omitted, and non-interaction hit is normally left to the *false* default value.	Page parameter only.
Non-interaction	You can configure an event as a non-interaction hit that does not influence bounce rate or session duration.	Always counts as a pageview hit and lowers bounce rate, session duration, and time on page as calculated.
Goals and funnels	You can use events as goals, but you can't build a funnel that leads to an event-based goal, and you can't use events as funnel steps. (You can use events as part of the Custom Funnels feature in Analytics 360 described in Chapter 18.)	You can use virtual pageviews as goals and funnel steps, and you can build a funnel that leads to a virtual-pageview-based goal.

TRACKING GOOGLE ANALYTICS EVENTS THROUGH THE GOOGLE TAG MANAGER DATA LAYER AND CUSTOM EVENT TRIGGER

The event tag that we configured previously in Figure 6.10 and its associated trigger demonstrated two of the basic benefits the GTM provides: rule-based tracking, and variables. Once this tag and trigger are deployed, clicks on any PDF we add to any page will be recorded as events.

A slight disadvantage of this approach, however, is that we need to create a separate tag and trigger for each link type (such as offsite, mailto: or tel:). This is not a big drawback, and it would certainly be manageable to create a dedicated tag and trigger to track each link type as an event. You may have suspected, however, that there is an even more automated approach that will cover multiple file types, as described below.

In the following discussion, we're going to continue building out our GTM skills by considering three more important GTM concepts:

- **Data layer.** You can use the data layer page object to store variables (in the form of name: value pairs, such as `'eventCat':'Outbound links'`) that you can then read into your tags.
- **DOM Ready trigger.** We first learned about this trigger in Chapter 5, and we'll see it in action in the following example.
- **Custom Event trigger.** This special trigger is activated when the data layer is populated with an *event* variable—the actual name of the data layer variable is *event*.

Note

The *event* Variable in the Data Layer Does Not Necessarily Relate to a Google Analytics Event

As confusing as this may sound, it's critical to understand that the *event* variable in the data layer and the Custom Event trigger in GTM do relate directly to each other, but neither necessarily relates to a GA event. In our autotracker example below, we'll use the *event* variable to activate the Custom Event trigger applied to our GA event tag, but we could just as easily use this same *event* variable in the data layer and same GTM trigger to fire a GA virtual pageview, or even a non-GA tag.

We're also going to be configuring a GA event tag that reads the event category, action, and label from the data layer and is triggered by the special *event* variable in the data layer.

GUEST SPOT　**GA Event Autotracker: Use Only Two Tags to Track Multiple Types of Link Clicks as Events**

Ahmed Awwad

Ahmed Awwad is Analytics Team Lead at E-Nor.

To automate the process of tracking multiple link types as events, we have written a special script that we'll call the GA event autotracker. To implement the event autotracker, you can download the script at www.e-nor.com/gabook and follow the procedure below, in which we'll configure two tags, two triggers, and four similar data layer variables, as shown in Figure 6.30. (In the figure, we omitted one data layer variable, so three appear only.)

In setting up our event autotracker, we'll also be building some elements that we'll be able to reuse later in the book, such as the "catch-all" event tag, the custom event trigger, and the data layer variables. (These are the elements highlighted in yellow within the diagram, as well as the DOM Ready trigger.)

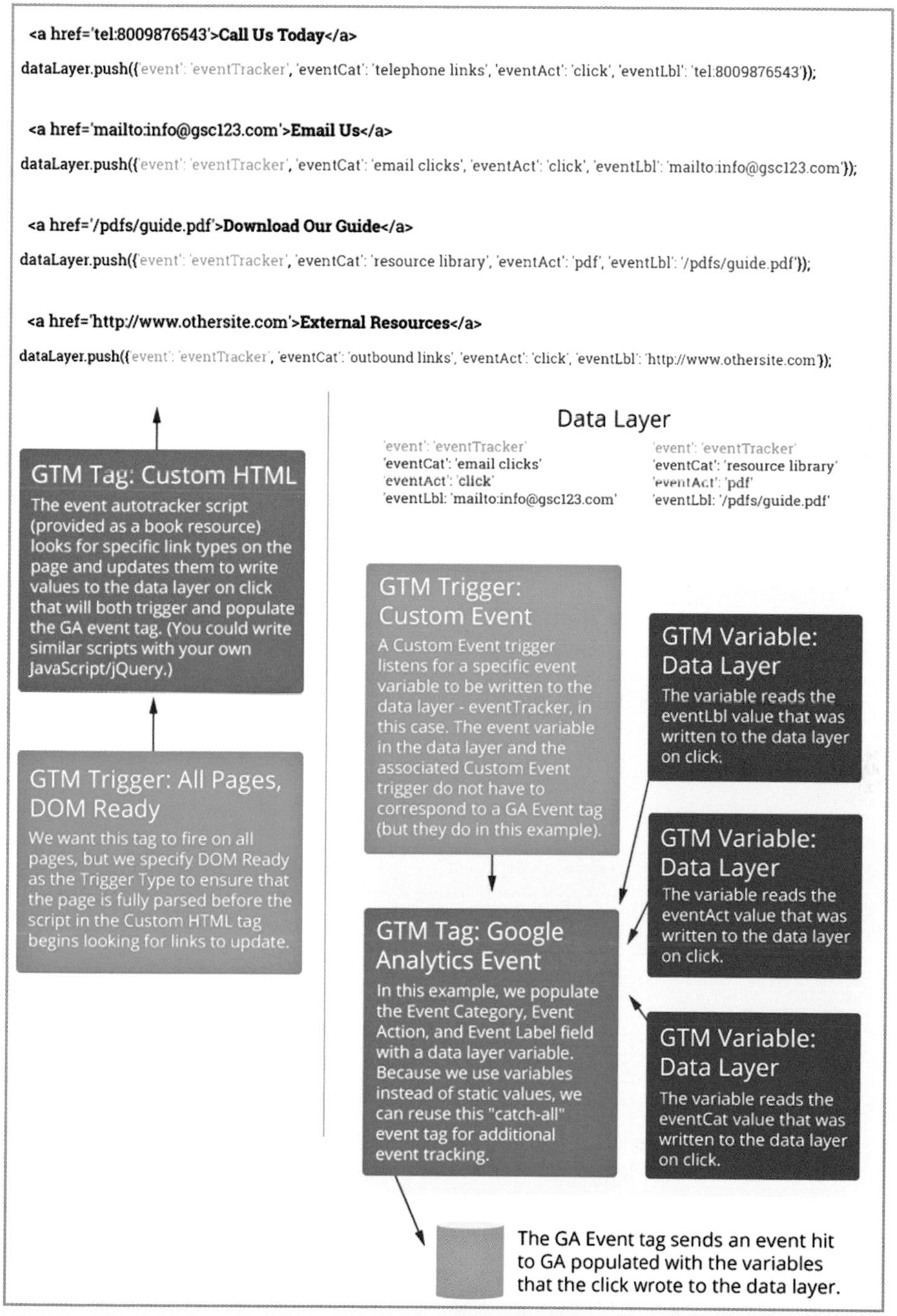

```
<a href='tel:8009876543'>Call Us Today</a>

dataLayer.push({'event': 'eventTracker', 'eventCat': 'telephone links', 'eventAct': 'click', 'eventLbl': 'tel:8009876543'});


<a href='mailto:info@gsc123.com'>Email Us</a>

dataLayer.push({'event': 'eventTracker', 'eventCat': 'email clicks', 'eventAct': 'click', 'eventLbl': 'mailto:info@gsc123.com'});


<a href='/pdfs/guide.pdf'>Download Our Guide</a>

dataLayer.push({'event': 'eventTracker', 'eventCat': 'resource library', 'eventAct': 'pdf', 'eventLbl': '/pdfs/guide.pdf'});


<a href='http://www.othersite.com'>External Resources</a>

dataLayer.push({'event': 'eventTracker', 'eventCat': 'outbound links', 'eventAct': 'click', 'eventLbl': 'http://www.othersite.com'});
```

Data Layer

```
'event': 'eventTracker'              'event': 'eventTracker'
'eventCat': 'email clicks'           'eventCat': 'resource library'
'eventAct': 'click'                  'eventAct': 'pdf'
'eventLbl': 'mailto:info@gsc123.com' 'eventLbl': '/pdfs/guide.pdf'
```

GTM Tag: Custom HTML

The event autotracker script (provided as a book resource) looks for specific link types on the page and updates them to write values to the data layer on click that will both trigger and populate the GA event tag. (You could write similar scripts with your own JavaScript/jQuery.)

GTM Trigger: All Pages, DOM Ready

We want this tag to fire on all pages, but we specify DOM Ready as the Trigger Type to ensure that the page is fully parsed before the script in the Custom HTML tag begins looking for links to update.

GTM Trigger: Custom Event

A Custom Event trigger listens for a specific event variable to be written to the data layer - eventTracker, in this case. The event variable in the data layer and the associated Custom Event trigger do not have to correspond to a GA Event tag (but they do in this example).

GTM Variable: Data Layer

The variable reads the eventLbl value that was written to the data layer on click.

GTM Variable: Data Layer

The variable reads the eventAct value that was written to the data layer on click.

GTM Tag: Google Analytics Event

In this example, we populate the Event Category, Event Action, and Event Label field with a data layer variable. Because we use variables instead of static values, we can reuse this "catch-all" event tag for additional event tracking.

GTM Variable: Data Layer

The variable reads the eventCat value that was written to the data layer on click.

The GA Event tag sends an event hit to GA populated with the variables that the click wrote to the data layer.

FIGURE 6.30 By configuring a few tags, triggers, and variables, we'll be able to track many types of clickthroughs as events.

continues

continued

Step1: Custom HTML Tag for Our Own GA Event Autotracker Script

While it's not necessary to understand every line of code in the autotracker script, it's helpful to note that it's designed to generate an event when you click any of the following types of link. (The | is regular expression pipe symbol, which means *or*.)

```
doc|docx|xls|xlsx|xlsm|ppt|pptx|exe|zip|pdf|js|txt|csv
```

If you parse the script a bit more, you'll see more specifically that `dataLayer.push` statements are preconfiguring each of these link types to populate the following variables into the data layer when clicked. (The variable values are shown for an outbound link in the example below.)

- ➤ `'event': 'eventTracker'`: This is the specially designated data layer variable for which we'll set up a Custom Event trigger that will fire our GA event tag; this variable name and value is the same for all link types in the autotracker script.
- ➤ `'eventCat': 'Outbound Links'`
- ➤ `'eventAct': 'Click'`
- ➤ `'eventLbl'`: Dynamically pulls in the link URL.

Step 2: DOM Ready Trigger for the Autotracker Tag Created in Step 1

As Simo Ahava outlined earlier in this chapter, you should use the DOM Ready trigger type for any tags that reference any element of the page's HTML. Our autotracker script searches all the HTML markup of the page for any instances of the link types shown above; if we mistakenly applied the default Page View trigger to this tag, we would risk missing links in portions of the page that the browser had not yet parsed. For this reason, our autotracker tag needs the DOM Ready trigger shown in Figure 6.31.

FIGURE 6.31 This DOM Ready trigger will ensure that the browser has parsed all HTML in the page before the script in the autotracker tag begins searching for links to configure to write to the data layer.

As a note, the autotracker script generates GA events for clicks to your social profile pages; you'll just need to add the URLs for your own social profiles to the top section of the script. (In the *Tracking Social Interactions* section later in this chapter, we'll also learn about tracking social clicks specifically as social hits instead of events, as another viable option.)

You can also change the variable for event category, event action, and event label values in the script as you prefer.

Step 3: "Catch-All" Google Analytics Event Tag

We could call this our "catch-all" event tag, or perhaps our event tag template, because it has no hard-coded values. As shown in Figure 6.32, it pulls all values from the data layer through data layer variables as described in the next step. To the tag, we'll apply a Custom Event trigger that activates each time the data layer is populated with the special *event* variable equal to *eventTracker*.

Note that the tag reads in a fourth variable—*event value*—which the autotracker configures as 0. You can change the script to populate a different number, but it's common in most event tracking to leave event value at 0 (or to not specify event value at all when you're recording the event).

FIGURE 6.32 This event tag will pull in values that the link clicks, as configured with the autotracker tag above, have populated into the data layer.

Step 4: Data Layer Variables

We'll need to create a data layer variable for each of the values that we have written to the data layer; these variables will read the specified data layer values into the catch-all event tag as shown in Figure 6.33.

FIGURE 6.33 Four simple data layer variables will read in the GA event values from the data layer, as shown here for event category.

continues

continued

Step 5: Custom Event Trigger for the Catch-All Event Tag

Finally, we'll create a Custom Event trigger to fire the catch-all tag. Again, a Custom Event trigger listens for a specific *event* variable to be written to the data layer—as `eventTracker` specifically for this trigger as shown in Figure 6.34.

Apart from achieving automated event tracking for many link types, this example covered several important GTM functionalities that you can reuse as needed for your own tracking requirements.

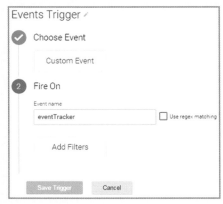

FIGURE 6.34 This trigger fires when the *event* data layer variable is populated as *eventTracker*.

Tracking Blog Comments as Events

Using the same principles that we discussed in the event autotracker setup above, you could generate an event each time a visitor submits a comment on your blog.

Let's say that the HTML for your comment box and submit button is written basically as follows:

```
<textarea id="comment" />
<input type="submit" id="submitButton" value="Post Comment" />
```

You could place the code in Listing 6.1 in a GTM Custom HTML tag and apply the DOM Ready trigger to the tab. This tag will then wait until the page is fully parsed before adding an onclick handler to the comment submit button that will populate the data layer with the event category, action, and label values. Our GTM event tag shown previously in Figure 6.31 will be triggered when the `eventTracker` event value is written to the data layer, and the tag will read in event category, action, and label values using data layer variables. Note that we'll populate the data layer only if the `textarea` is not empty, and that we'll write the first 200 characters of the comment as the event label. (Length of the event label dimension in GA is limited to 500 bytes, which should equate to nearly 500 characters, unless the event label includes many non-ASCII characters.)

LISTING 6.1: By placing this code into a Custom HTML tag and applying a DOM Ready trigger, you'll configure the blog-comment submit button to populate the data layer, using values that the event tag we configured in Figure 6.32 will read in.

```
<script>
$('input#submitButton').click(function() {
        var txtArea = $('textarea#comment').val();
        if (txtArea.length > 0) {
            dataLayer.push({'event': 'eventTracker',
'eventCat': 'blog', 'eventAct': 'comment', 'eventLbl': txtArea.
substring(0,200)});
            }
});
</script>
```

> **Note**
>
> ### jQuery + Data Layer + "Catch-All" Event Tag
>
> This blog comments example further illustrates some of the replicable GTM and event tracking principles we've discussed in the past two chapters. By using a bit of jQuery to insert listeners for any type of user action—such as clicking a button, hovering over a tool tip icon, or changing the selection in a drop-down menu—we can populate the data layer and use the same event tag, data layer variables, and custom event trigger as shown in Figure 6.30. For additional examples of jQuery that can take advantage of the catch-all event tag by writing to the data layer for user interactions, see www.e-nor.com/gabook.

Tracking Page Scroll and Video Embeds

Scrolling and video plays are among the important user actions that are not tracked by default. Scroll tracking is especially useful for blogs and content-focused websites, on which it's more critical to understand user engagement with the page itself rather than specific conversion steps. Below we look at two script resources that can respectively help you track scrolling and interactions with embedded YouTube videos.

GUEST SPOT   **Event Tracking for Scrolling and YouTube Embeds**

Mohamed Adel

Mohamed Adel is Analytics Implementation Engineer at E-Nor.

Outlined below are two additional script resources that we put together to automate event tracking for page scroll and interactions with embedded YouTube videos. Note that both solutions use jQuery, so be sure to load the jQuery library in the <head> section of your pages (before the GTM container in <body>).

continues

continued

Tracking Page Scroll

1. Download this script at `www.e-nor.com/gabook`.
2. Copy the script into a Custom HTML tag.
3. To the Custom HTML tag, apply a DOM Ready trigger. (You can also restrict the trigger to certain pages on your site, such as those that contain */blog/* in the URL.)

The script records the event category as *page interaction*, event action as *scroll down*, and event label as a scroll percentage, as shown in Figure 6.35.

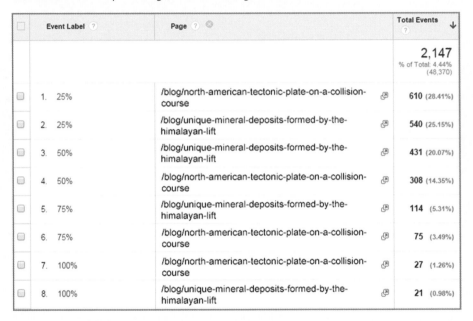

	Event Label ?	Page ? ⊗		Total Events ↓ ?
				2,147 % of Total: 4.44% (48,370)
☐ 1.	25%	/blog/north-american-tectonic-plate-on-a-collision-course	⊡	610 (28.41%)
☐ 2.	25%	/blog/unique-mineral-deposits-formed-by-the-himalayan-lift	⊡	540 (25.15%)
☐ 3.	50%	/blog/unique-mineral-deposits-formed-by-the-himalayan-lift	⊡	431 (20.07%)
☐ 4.	50%	/blog/north-american-tectonic-plate-on-a-collision-course	⊡	308 (14.35%)
☐ 5.	75%	/blog/unique-mineral-deposits-formed-by-the-himalayan-lift	⊡	114 (5.31%)
☐ 6.	75%	/blog/north-american-tectonic-plate-on-a-collision-course	⊡	75 (3.49%)
☐ 7.	100%	/blog/north-american-tectonic-plate-on-a-collision-course	⊡	27 (1.26%)
☐ 8.	100%	/blog/unique-mineral-deposits-formed-by-the-himalayan-lift	⊡	21 (0.98%)

FIGURE 6.35 By drilling down into the scroll event within the Top Events report and applying Page as a secondary dimension, we can gauge scroll depth on our blog pages.

Tracking Embedded YouTube

1. Download this script at `www.e-nor.com/gabook`.
2. Copy the script into a Custom HTML tag.
3. To the Custom HTML tag, apply a DOM Ready trigger.

This script records *play, pause, watch to end,* and several percentages completed as the event action and the name of the video as event label.

For YouTube embeds, you could also opt to code your own solution using the YouTube Player API. Other video hosting providers, such as Vimeo and Wistia, offer direct integrations into your GA property or similar APIs that you can use to listen on the back end for video interactions and generate corresponding GA events. If you're in the process of choosing a video host, be sure to verify the provision for GA tracking before you make the decision and enter into an agreement.

Using Events to Track Navigation

As a specialized and potentially very useful application of event tracking, you can populate an event category, action, and label to track each navigation click hierarchically and individually.

For instance, to track a click on the *Office Renovation* link under the *Services* menu in the top navigation of your remodeling company's website, you could populate the event into the data layer as shown in Listing 6.2.

LISTING 6.2: A click on this menu item populates the data layer with navigation details that GTM can read into a Google Analytics event tag.

```
<a href="/office-renovation" onclick="dataLayer.push({'event':
'eventTracker', 'eventCat': 'top navigation menu', 'eventAct':
'services', 'eventLbl': 'office renovation'});">Office Renovation</a>
```

Note that we're basically generating the event the same way as in the previous event autotracker and blog comment examples: in the data layer, we write event category, action, and label values that GA will read into the event tag using the data layer variables that we have also configured, and we also write the specialized *event* value, which does not relate directly to GA events but that we can use in a GTM Custom Event trigger (for any type of tag). A difference in this navigation example is that we're setting the `onclick` handler directly in the HTML, but we could have instead used jQuery within GTM Custom HTML tags as in the previous examples; the jQuery approach, however, might be less practical due to the large number of navigation links.

You would need to work with your developers to add the data layer code to each link in your navigation. The initial code changes would likely require a good bit of time and manual effort, but you would then be able to view your navigation data more easily in the Events and Pages reports (with secondary dimensions applied as needed, as illustrated in Figure 6.36) and in custom reports as described in Chapter 11, "Dashboards, Custom Reports, and Intelligence Alerts."

	Event Category ?	Page ?	Total Events ↓ ?
			12,809 % of Total: 1.35% (949,730)
☐ 1.	top navigation menu	/home	**12,053** (94.10%)
☐ 2.	left navigation menu	/home	**541** (4.22%)
☐ 3.	footer navigation menu	/home	**133** (1.04%)

FIGURE 6.36 Top Events report, with Page applied as secondary dimension, displaying the navigation data that we're populating into the data layer. You could drill down to Event Action and Event Label to show more granular navigation details.

> **Note**
>
> ### Do You Need to Know HTML and JavaScript to Use Google Tag Manager?
>
> To use GTM for some basic tasks, such as deploying a general GA pageview tracker as outlined in Chapter 5, you don't need to know much about the structure of Web pages (provided that a Web developer has already included the GTM container code in your page templates).
>
> As the GTM examples in the book become somewhat more involved, it's clear that some knowledge of HTML is very beneficial for many types of GTM tasks. HTML is very, very straightforward to learn, and it can make a useful and relevant addition to your professional toolkit, even if your focus is on analytics or marketing and not on implementation. Just a little bit of HTML will greatly enhance your GTM capabilities.
>
> A basic understanding of CSS selectors and the DOM (Document Object Model) is also very helpful for targeting specific page elements from GTM. These are also very straightforward topics that you can master with just a bit of time and focus.
>
> JavaScript proficiency is very helpful for configuring more complex GTM variables, but GTM does provide a great deal of built-in functionality that allows us to avoid hand-scripting in many cases. While JavaScript is indispensable for some GTM tasks, those tasks are not as common as those for which you need to know HTML, and JavaScript presents somewhat more of a learning curve than HTML.
>
> If you're going to be working with GTM regularly, learn some HTML and CSS selectors as a priority, and then undertake JavaScript (and the jQuery JavaScript library, which has achieved nearly universal adoption). You can find several good, free learning resources for all these skills, such as `codeacademy.com`.

TRACKING SOCIAL INTERACTIONS

Figure 6.1 includes two types of social actions that we may need to track in GA:

- **Social connect/follow actions.** Likes or follows of your organization's social profiles.
- **Social content actions.** Likes, shares, or tweets of your content.

We can track either of these types of social actions as either events or the more specialized social hit. Either approach is valid. Let's first consider social connects/follows.

Social Connects

The simplest way to record social connect actions (or, more precisely, clickthroughs to your social profiles after which the visitor, ideally, completes the connect action) would be to track them as offsite link events as discussed earlier in the chapter. You might, however, choose to track social profile clickthroughs separately from other, more general offsite links.

To track social connects within a separate event category, let's look at a simple example for tracking likes of your company's Facebook page.

Let's say that you have a link in your Web page footer to `https://www.facebook`
`.com/mycompany`.

You could set up a dedicated event tag as follows:

- Category: **social-profile.**
- Action: **like** (or **like-facebook-page**, to distinguish from content likes).
- Label: **facebook-page.**
- Trigger: **Click - Just Links - Enable When url matches Regex .* - Click URL equals https://www.facebook.com/mycompany**.

As another option, however, you could choose to track a social follow (or a social content action) with Track Type set to Social as in Figure 6.37. Setting the Track Type to Social populates the data into the Social > Plugins report rather than the Event reports.

FIGURE 6.37 A Google Analytics tag in Google Tag Manager with Track Type set to *Social* populates the Social > Plugins report.

Note that the Action Target parameter is optional. If not specified, it defaults to the URL of your current Web page. The purpose of Action Target is to indicate the asset that received the social attention, so in many cases, it's fine to leave the default. In this case, we have specified *facebook-page* to indicate that the target of the social action was your Facebook page itself rather than the Web page from which the Facebook click originated. (And we could always apply Page as a secondary dimension in the Social Plugins report to view the originating page.)

We'll set the trigger for this tag to Click URL equals `https://www.facebook`
`.com/mycompany`.

You may have observed that neither of these two preceding approaches is particularly efficient, since both would require you to set up a separate tag and trigger for each of your social profile links. That said, four or five additional GTM tags and triggers to track your social profile clickthroughs would not be unreasonable to configure and manage. (As a note, you could house all your social tags within a single GTM folder for better organization.)

The event autotracker example discussed earlier in the chapter provides a more streamlined solution to tracking your social profile clickthroughs as events. If you wanted to generate social hits instead of event hits for the social profile clickthroughs, you or your developer could adapt the script to populate the data layer with the following values:

- `event: socialTrigger`
- `socialNetwork: facebook`
- `socialAction: like` (or `like-facebook-page`)

You would populate the data layer in the same way for your other social profile links, and you would then need to set up corresponding data layer variables to populate the Network and Action fields in the GTM tag.

We'll use the data layer *event* value for our trigger. As mentioned previously in the chapter, *event* serves as a specially designated data layer variable that activates a Custom Event trigger once the variable is populated into the data layer. Again, the *event* variable in the data layer does not correspond directly to a GA event; in the current example, we're using the data layer *event* value as the trigger for a GA social hit.

To summarize, there are three basic options for tracking social connect/follow links:

- Track the same way as other offsite links events.
- Track as events, but within a separate category.
- Track as social hits.

The latter two options offer the slight advantage for separating social connects/follows from other outbound link events.

Social Content Actions

We also have the option of tracking content shares and content likes as events or social hits. In the example below, we'll track Facebook likes of a page on our website as social hits by populating event, social network, and social action variables into the data layer. Unlike the preceding social follow examples, we'll take advantage of a callback option to send our social hit only after confirming that the visitor has logged into the social network and completed the social content action: we won't have to just assume that the social action was completed.

Listeners and Callback Functions

Let's say that on your blog pages, you have the social content action buttons for Google Plus, Facebook, Twitter, LinkedIn, and Pinterest. To record the social hit only when the user has completed Facebook content like or a tweet, we'll bind a callback function to

the listeners that Facebook and Twitter provide. The listener executes the callback function once the user has actually signed into the social network and completed the like
or the tweet.

The callback is not related directly to GTM or GA; you could execute any JavaScript
code as your callback function. In our case, we'll write variable values to the GTM data
layer that we can read into a GA social hit tag.

Since callback is not available for LinkedIn and Pinterest, we'll set up tags with triggers based directly on the click action.

For Google Plus, you don't need to add any code to generate a social hit. For any site
that is tracked with GA, +1 actions will be recorded automatically (on callback) in the
Social Plugins report. (+1 actions for your organization's Google Plus page would not
be recorded automatically; you'd still need to track this action using one of the options
outlined above for tracking social follows.)

The fact that Google Plus content actions are tracked automatically in the Social
Plugins report provides an incentive for us to track our other social content actions as
social hits and not as events; in this way, all of our social content actions would be consolidated in the Social Plugins report.

Let's begin by setting up the callback for Facebook likes:

1. Create a Custom HTML tag for each listener/callback, as shown for Facebook in
   Figure 6.38. To each of these tags, we can apply the same DOM Ready trigger as in
   the event autotracker example earlier in the chapter to make sure the page is fully
   parsed before the listeners attempt to bind.
2. Create a Data Layer variable for each of the values (except *event*) that we populate
   into the data layer.
3. Create a single GA tag with Track Type *Social* that reads in the Data Layer variables
   as shown in Figure 6.39.
4. For the GA social tag created in step 3, apply a Custom Event trigger with Event
   Name set to *socialTrigger* (or whichever event value you populate to the data
   layer).

Note the Facebook callback does not respond to share actions. You may be able to
work with the Facebook SDK to create a share callback, or you can directly track clicks
on the Facebook share button by applying a trigger based the Click Classes or Click ID
variables, similarly to the approach described below for LinkedIn and Pinterest content
action tracking.

Using the snippets in Listing 6.3, you can create a similar Custom HTML tag for tweet
callbacks. Please note that the social networks may update these snippets periodically,
so it's advisable to refer to their developer resources for the most current version of each
script.

FIGURE 6.38 You can create this Custom HTML tag to set up the listener and callback for Facebook content likes.

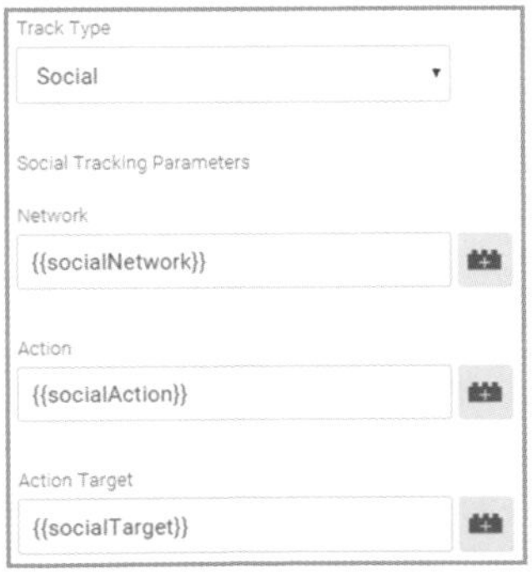

FIGURE 6.39 This Google Analytics social tag reads the values that we wrote to the GTM data layer from Facebook and Twitter callback functions as well as LinkedIn and Pinterest click actions.

LISTING 6.3: Similarly to the Facebook callback in Figure 6.38, this Twitter callback function is coded to write data layer values that GA social tag in GTM will read in through Data Layer variables.

```
<script>
//assumes you have initialized window.twttr as part of the standard
code for displaying the tweet button
if (typeof twttr !== 'undefined') {
  twttr.ready(function (twttr) {
    twttr.events.bind('click', trackTwitter);
  });
}
function trackTwitter() {
  dataLayer.push({
        'event': 'socialTrigger',
        'socialNetwork': 'Twitter',
        'socialAction': 'tweet',
        'socialTarget': window.location.href
      });
}
</script>
```

The LinkedIn `data-onsuccess` callback attribute no longer seems to be operational, and Pinterest does not offer a listener for callback. For LinkedIn shares and Pinterest pins, Listing 6.4 demonstrates scripts that will write GA data to the data layer as soon as the user clicks on the respective social button (with the assumption that most users actually complete the social action).

LISTING 6.4: Since callback is not available for LinkedIn, we can include this script in a Custom HTML tag and configure the trigger as in Figure 6.40 to write the values to the data layer as soon as the LinkedIn share button is clicked.

```
<script>
dataLayer.push({
    'event': 'socialTrigger',
    'socialNetwork': 'linkedin.com',
    'socialAction': 'share',
    'socialTarget': window.location.href
});
</script>
```

FIGURE 6.40 We can configure a trigger to isolate the LinkedIn share
button based on the *id* attribute of the corresponding <a> tag.

We can begin to configure the GTM trigger by choosing Inspect Element (not View
Source) from the right-click/context menu for the LinkedIn share button to display the
source HTML, and then following the procedure below:

```
<a id="li_ui_li_gen_1439046400859_0-link" href="javascript:void(0);">
```

1. Enable the built-in Click ID variable.
2. Create a new trigger.
3. Under Choose Event on the trigger setup screen, click Click.
4. Select Just Links from the Targets drop-down.
5. Configure the remaining settings as shown previously in Figure 6.39.

For Pinterest pins, we can basically follow the same procedure demonstrated in Listing 6.4 and Figure 6.39. Apart from the Pinterest-related values that we write to the data
layer, the main difference will be in the trigger, which we'll configure based on class value
instead of ID value. The tag below seems hard to parse, but we can easily enable the
built-in Click Classes variable and specify Fire On as *Click Classes contains pin_it_button*.

```
<a data-pin-href="http://www.pinterest.com/pin/create/button/"
data-pin-log="button_pinit_bookmarklet" class="PIN_1439052112077_
pin_it_button_28 PIN_1439052112077_pin_it_button_en_28_red
PIN_1439052112077_pin_it_button_inline_28 PIN_1439052112077_pin_
it_none_28" data-pin-config="none"><span class="PIN_1439052112077_
hidden" id="PIN_1439052112077_pin_count_0"></span></a>
```

As mentioned above, the Facebook Share button does not invoke the callback function. Facebook Share is identical for Facebook Like in terms of HTML and class name:

```
<span class="pluginButtonLabel">Like</span>
<span class="pluginButtonLabel">Share</span>
```

So how could we isolate the Share button as a trigger? We could not use the Click
Classes built-in variable: this could only match both Like and Share. Instead, we'll make
sure that the built-in Click Text variable is enabled as in Figure 6.22. We'll then configure a click trigger as in Figure 6.41 to fire the script in Listing 6.5 included in a Custom
HTML tag.

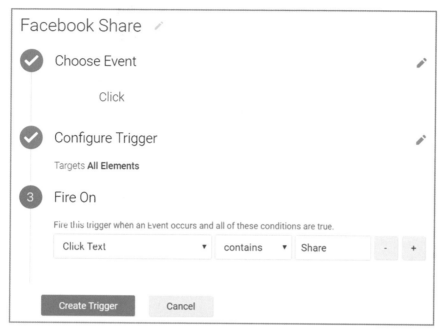

FIGURE 6.41 This trigger is using the built-in Click Text variable to isolate the Facebook Share button.

> **LISTING 6.5:** We can include this script in a Custom HTML tag and configure the trigger as in Figure 6.41 to write variables to the data layer that will generate a social hit for Facebook Share through our GA social tag configured in Figure 6.39.

```
<script>
dataLayer.push({
    'event': 'socialTrigger',
    'socialNetwork': 'facebook.com',
    'socialAction': 'share',
    'socialTarget': window.location.href
});
</script>
```

Distinguishing between Social Connects and Content Actions

In instances where a social action (such as *like* for Facebook or *+1* for Google Plus) could equally represent a social connect or a social content action, you can instead populate more specific values as shown in Table 6.3. The separate values would be even more useful if you're recording both types of actions as social hits (i.e., neither type as event) so you could readily distinguish social connects from social content actions in the Social Plugins report.

TABLE 6.3 Recommendations for Social Action Values to Distinguish between Connects and Shares

Social Network	Connect Action	Content Action
Facebook	like-facebook-page	like-content
Twitter	follow	tweet
Google Plus	plus-one-or-circle	+1 (automatic)
LinkedIn	connect	share
Pinterest	follow	pin

Social Plugins Report

GA populates the Social > Plugins report with any GA hits generated from GTM with Track Type set to Social. [The native equivalent `ga('send','social',network,action,target)` also populates the Plugins report.]

As the Plugins report in Figure 6.42 demonstrates, the Social Source dimension corresponds to the social network value that you provide in the social hit, and Social Entity corresponds to the social target value. By using specific action values as listed in Table 6.3, we can easily distinguish between follow and share actions, even without Social Entity selected as the secondary dimension.

FIGURE 6.42 The Plugins report is populated with social hits.

Google Analytics Tracking for Social Widgets

Some widgets such as ShareThis or WordPress plugins such as Sharrre that allow you to add social sharing buttons to your Web pages offer built-in or easily configurable GA integration. (ShareThis populates social sharing data into the Events reports; Sharrre populates Social Plugins.) You can review documentation or check with support for additional details. If you do opt for a social widget instead of adding social buttons manually, it's advisable to choose a widget that integrates easily with GA.

> **Note**
>
> ## Can You Create Goals from Social Actions?
>
> If you have tracked social actions as events, you can create goals for them just as you can for any other event, as described in Chapter 8, "Goal and Ecommerce Tracking." If you have tracked social actions as social hits, you won't be able to create corresponding goals, since there is no goal setup available for social dimensions or metrics. If it's critical that you track your social actions as goals, you can opt to track them as events.
>
> Clicks on the Google +1 button for your content are automatically tracked as social hits. If you wanted to create a goal for these clicks, you could use the same approach as for LinkedIn and Facebook Share clicks above to also generate events for the Google +1 clicks, and you could create a goal based on these events.

ERROR TRACKING

GA and GTM can track several different types of errors on your Web pages:

- 404 errors (page not found)
- 500 errors (server errors, such as uncaught exceptions in a database operation)
- JavaScript errors (script errors that occur in the browser environment)

Tracking 404 and 500 Errors

Our error tracking strategy for 404 and 500 errors will depend on the URLs and titles of the error pages. In all cases, however, we'll aim to record the error state as a pageview, either physical or virtual, so we can more easily isolate the referring pages that contain the bad links.

As a prerequisite, make sure that your error pages include the GTM container code so GA pageview tracking is occurring as on all other pages.

Error Indicated in URL

If the URLs of your error pages directly indicate the error as follows, you don't have to take any additional steps for basic error tracking:

```
http://www.mysite.com/404/y2k-update.aspx

http://www.mysite.com/505-error/quote-results
```

With URLs such as these, you'll be able to readily spot the errors as regular physical pageviews within the Pages report and perform the additional analytics and alert steps below.

Error Indicated in Title but Not URL

Many websites indicate 404 or 500 errors through text in the page title such as Page Not Found or 404, as in Figure 6.43.

FIGURE 6.43 Similarly to many websites, the page title indicates a request for a nonexisting page on the *London Times.*

To view the URLs corresponding to the error page titles, we could apply Page Title as a secondary dimension in the Pages report and filter for the error text as in Figure 6.44.

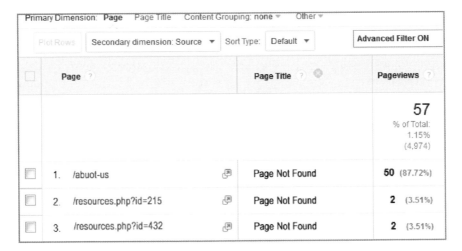

FIGURE 6.44 With Page Title selected as the secondary dimension and filtered, we can list the invalid page requests.

Error Not Indicated in URL or Title

Some Web servers are designed or configured to display a 404 or 500 error page as warranted but do not include an error indicator in either the URL or the page title. In this case, you or your Web developer will need to edit the 404 and 500 pages to provide GTM with some type of error indicator. You can do a great deal with GTM variables, but you do need the right inputs to start with.

A simple approach would be to add an event value to the data layer as shown in Listing 6.6.

LISTING 6.6: When added respectively to 404 and 500 error pages that do not already indicate the error in the URL or the page title, these snippets will provide the necessary inputs for tracking the errors through Google Tag Manager.

```
<script>
dataLayer.push({'event': '404-error'});
</script>

<script>
dataLayer.push({'event': '500-error'});
</script>

<!-these scripts should precede the GTM container->
```

Note that you are not placing this code into a GTM tag; you'll instead need to include this code directly in the source of the page, before the GTM container code (so when GTM is processing all tags and triggers for the page, the data layer is already populated with the *event* value).

To add an error indicator to the URL that you'll be able to view and filter in the GA Pages report, you'll create alternate pageview tags that will fire only when the `404-error` or `500-error` value is present in the data layer.

To summarize the procedure:

1. Write a *404-error* and *500-error* event value (or whichever values you choose—any text string will work) to the data layer higher in the 404 and 500 error pages than the GTM container code, as shown in Listing 6.6.
2. Create two Custom JavaScript variables in GTM that respectively prepend `/404-page-not-found` or `/500-server-error` (or whichever text you prefer as an error indicator) to the URL path, as shown in Figure 6.45. Note that you should not use the built-in Page Path variable in this case, since it would exclude the ? symbol and any characters following in the URL.
3. Create Custom JavaScript variables that also prepend error indicators to the page titles. (The DOM notation for the page title is `document.title`.)
4. Create two GA pageview tags that use the path and title variables created in the previous steps as shown in Figure 6.46.
5. To the two tags created in step 4, apply Custom Event triggers based on the `404-error` and `500-error` event values in the data layer similarly to Figure 6.47.
6. Block your main GA pageview tracker when either of the error triggers is activated (to avoid double pageview tracking), as in Figure 6.47.

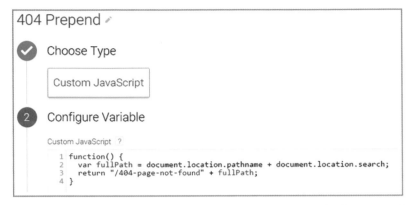

FIGURE 6.45 This Custom JavaScript variable prepends an error indicator to the document path.

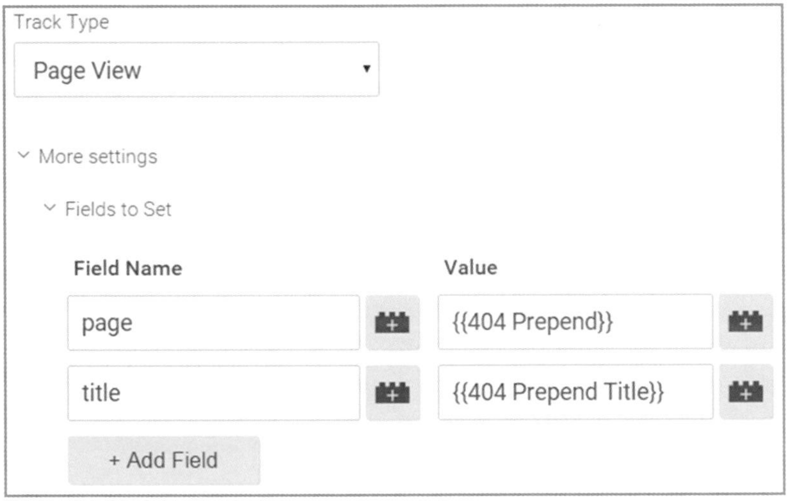

FIGURE 6.46 Instead of generating a regular GA pageview on our error pages, we'll trigger a pageview tag that overwrites that default page and title values with the error prepends.

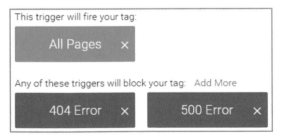

FIGURE 6.47 Add the 404 and 500 triggers as exceptions to the main GA pageview tracker to avoid double pageview counting.

View Referring Pages in the Navigation Summary

In all of the cases above, the error indicator will appear in the Pages report directly as the Page dimension and/or as the Page Title dimension. Once you've filtered for your bad page requests, you can then use the Navigation Summary shown in Figure 2.9 to determine which internal pages are calling the bad URLs.

To identify external referrals to bad URLs, you could apply Source/Medium, Campaign, or Full Referral as a secondary dimension in the Landing Pages report, as shown in Figure 6.48.

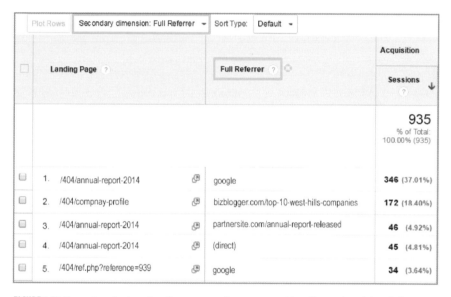

FIGURE 6.48 By sorting the Landing Pages report for your error identifier and applying Full Referral as a secondary dimension, you can see the external origins of bad requests.

Tracking Errors as Events

As an alternative or an addition to the error tracking options outlined above, you could track your errors as GA events, populating the event dimensions as follows:

- Event Category: **error**
- Event Action: **404** or **500**
- Event Label: **{{Page URL}}**

Your trigger would depend on which of three URL/title scenarios above apply:

- **Error indicated in URL.** Configure trigger as `{{Page Path}} contains 404 or 505` (or whichever text you have used).

- **Error indicated in title.** Set up a Custom JavaScript variable that returns `document` `.title`, and configure trigger as `{{Document Title}} contains Page Not Found` or `Server Error` (or whichever text appears in the `title` HTML tag of the error pages).
- **Error not indicated in URL or title.** Apply a Custom Event trigger based on an *event* variable that you have written to the data layer as shown in Listing 6.6.

Intelligence Alerts for Errors

Errors are logical candidates for custom intelligence alerts. In Chapter 11, we configure GA to send us a proactive email or text notification when our website or app reaches a specific error threshold.

Crawl Errors in Google Search Console

In addition to setting up error tracking in GA, it's recommended that you gain access (through validation or user addition) to Google Search Console, where you can view the Crawl Errors report. This report displays errors that Googlebot has experienced in crawling your Web pages, from either internal or external referring pages.

The Crawl Errors report, however, does not indicate how frequently actual users tried to access the problematic URLs, and it does not include errors for pages that reside behind a login and are therefore blocked from search engine spidering. GA can fulfill these two aspects of error reporting.

Chapter 7 reviews Google Search Console in greater detail.

Tracking JavaScript Errors

Google Tag Manager provides a built-in JavaScript error trigger and built-in JavaScript error variables that you can use to record JavaScript errors in GA, as outlined in the following procedure:

1. Enable the built-in JavaScript error trigger as shown in Figure 6.49.

FIGURE 6.49 Enabling the built-in JavaScript error trigger.

2. Enable the built-in Error Message, Error URL, and Error Line variables as shown in Figure 6.50.

FIGURE 6.50 Enabling the built-in JavaScript error variables.

3. Configure a GA event tag similarly to Figure 6.51. Be sure to set Non-Interaction Events to False so error tracking does not artificially lower bounce rate.

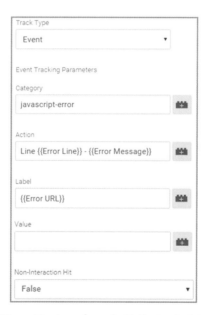

FIGURE 6.51 The GA event tag is configured with the JavaScript error variables enabled in Figure 6.50. Apply the trigger configured in Figure 6.49 to this tag.

4. Apply the JavaScript error trigger to the event tag.

   Confer with your developers as you configure JavaScript error tracking in GTM.

Viewing JavaScript Errors in the Events Reports

Let's say that you have added a mouseover script (natively or through GTM) to an image that is supposed to display a popup, but you have misspelled the JavaScript function that you're trying to call:

```
<img src="/images/starburst.png" onmouseover="specailOffer()" />
```

If you have configured JavaScript error tracking as shown above, the error would appear in the Top Events report as shown in Figure 6.52.

Event Action ?	Total Events ? ↓
	2,600,439 % of Total: 100.00% (2,600,439)
1. Line 25 - Uncaught ReferenceError: specailOffer is not defined	**456** (0.02%)

FIGURE 6.52 JavaScript error listed in the Top Events report.

Note that the JavaScript Error trigger can fire for a user interaction or a script that appears after the GTM container in the page, but it cannot fire for any JavaScript errors that occur before the GTM container, namely, JavaScript errors within the `<head>` and `</head>` tags.

The error trigger can activate for errors within JavaScript that you have deployed in a Custom HTML tag through GTM. The only small caveat is that the line number for the JavaScript error in your Custom HTML tag is reported relative to the tag and not to the entire page, such that the error line number would appear as 3 if the error occurs on the third line of your Custom HTML tag.

 **KEY TAKEAWAYS**

A click does nothing.   By default, GA does not record a click action *per se*; it records a pageview hit only if the click loads another page on your site that contains GA pageview tracking.

Opt for events or virtual pageviews.   For the many important user actions that are not tracked by default, you can opt for event or virtual pageview tracking.

Virtual pageviews for multiscreen processes.   The most suitable option for most untracked user actions is event tracking, but you might want to opt for virtual pageview tracking when the action is more akin to a physical pageview, as is the case in a multi-screen AJAX process in which the URL does not change.

Events as goals but not funnels.   You can use events as goals but not as a part of a funnel process. To include an untracked user action in any step of a funnel, track the action as a virtual pageview rather than an event.

Events appear in dedicated reports.   Events appear in their own reports, while virtual pageviews are integrated in the Pages report and serve otherwise as physical pageviews in GA. If there is any concern about pageview "inflation" due to virtual pageviews, opt for event tracking rather than virtual pageview tracking, or be sure to begin the Page dimension for your virtual pageviews with /virtual so you can easily apply a view filter to exclude your virtual pageviews as a subdirectory.

Be consistent in event naming.   Events require the event category and event action arguments, and usually include an event label argument as well. To avoid fragmentation of your event data, choose a consistent naming convention. GTM can greatly help you maintain consistency in your event naming.

Auto-Event variable for clicked element.   You can configure a GTM Auto-Event variable to read an attribute of a clicked element when the built-in GTM Click variables are not suitable.

Distinguish between social connect and social content actions.   When recording social actions, it's advisable to use different action arguments so your reports can readily distinguish between connect and content actions.

Record social actions as either event hits or social hits.   It's valid to record social actions as either GA event hits or GA social hits. If you record social hits, the data appears in the Social > Plugins report. Because Google +1 actions are automatically recorded as social hits, you may also decide to record your other social content actions as social hits so all social tracking is consolidated in the Social Plugins report.

Twitter and Facebook provide callbacks.   You can track tweets and Facebook content likes through callback functions that execute only when the user has logged into the social network and completed the action.

Check 404 and 500 errors in URL or title.   Many Web servers indicate 404 and 500 errors directly in the page URL or title. If your 404 or 500 error pages do not contain an error indicator in the URL or title, you can manually add a data layer event variable to the pages that you can then use to prepend an error indicator to the page and title dimensions in a virtual pageview, or to trigger an event.

Track JavaScript errors.   You can use built-in variables and the built-in trigger to track JavaScript errors through GTM, but this approach will not record errors in JavaScript that is embedded natively into your page and that executes immediately on page load.

ACTIONS AND EXERCISES

1. **Take inventory of all untracked user interactions.** Assess all important user interactions that are not currently tracked. Decide if you will track each action as an event or a virtual pageview.

2. **Establish a naming convention.** Provide consistent, hierarchical naming for your event categories, actions, and labels.

3. **Set up event tracking for a single link type.** As a proof of concept, set up event tracking for .pdf links, external links, and so on. When creating new tags, follow one of the testing scenarios outlined in *GTM Environments* in Chapter 5.

4. **Set up virtual pageview tracking for a single link type.** As a proof of concept, set up virtual pageview tracking for links to PDFs or another file type.

5. **Configure the event autotracker.** Create the tags, variables, and triggers required for the event autotracker, as outlined in this chapter. This will provide event tracking for outbound links, links to PDFs and other file types, mailto: links, tel: links, and—as a separate category—social follow links. Once you install the event autotracker, you can remove the tags for individual link tracking that you set up in steps 3 and 4.

6. **Configure social tracking.** If you're using the event autotracker, the social follow actions will already be tracked. If you're not using the event autotracker, create a plan for tracking your social follow actions. In either case, create a plan for tracking your social content actions.

7. **Assess 404 and 500 error tracking.** If there is an error indicator in the URL and or page title of your 404 and 500 error pages, you can track these errors in GA without further setup (as long as the pages execute basic GA pageview tracking). If neither the URL nor the title indicates an error, write an *event* variable to the data layer that you can use as a trigger to fire an alternate pageview tag; you can configure this tag to add an error indicator to the page and title dimensions. You can additionally opt to track 404 and 500 errors as GA events.

8. **Set up JavaScript error tracking.** Using the built-in trigger and built-in variables, set up JavaScript error tracking in GTM.

9. **Download the container export and sample pages.** From `www.e-nor.com/gabook`, download the GTM container export and the sample pages. You can create a new GTM container and select Import Container under in the GTM Admin screen to import the tags, triggers, and variables. If you have a test Web server to which you can upload pages, you can update the pages to use your container code, upload the pages, and then test out the configuration of the imported GTM container.

7

Acquisition Reports

At a basic level, most of Google Analytics (GA) boils down to two types of data: how your visitors are getting to your website (or to your mobile app or mobile app download), and how they're interacting with your website (or mobile app). In Chapter 6, "Events, Virtual Pageviews, Social Actions, and Errors," we learned how to use events, virtual pageviews, and social tracking to provide a more complete picture of visitor behavior. This chapter focuses on better acquisition tracking: we break down GA acquisition terminology and concepts, learn how we can help GA clarify the ambiguities in default acquisition reporting, and customize the GA acquisition reports to align most closely with our traffic sources.

ACQUISITION TERMINOLOGY AND CONCEPTS

Let's begin by reviewing some of the core acquisition terms and concepts in GA.

Medium and Source

All GA sessions are recorded with at least two dimension values that describe acquisition: *medium* and *source*. As illustrated in Figure 7.1, Medium is the most general dimension value that GA uses to designate traffic acquisition, and Source is more specific. While *source* is sometimes used more generally in discussion to mean *where your traffic is coming from*, within the GA interface it refers specifically to the actual Source dimension.

By default—that is, without campaign tagging, which we discuss later in this chapter—GA records all traffic with one of three medium values:

- **Referral:** clickthroughs from any website that GA does not recognize as a search engine. The source dimension for referral traffic would be the website where the clickthrough originated, such as `abc123.com` or `partnersite.pk`.
- **Organic:** clickthroughs from one of the many websites that GA recognizes as a search engine and assigns *organic* as medium. The source dimension for organic traffic would be one of the many websites that GA recognizes as organic search engines, such as `google`, `bing`, or `baidu`.
- **(None):** direct entry of a URL into the browser (and, by default, many other types of traffic that you don't want to appear as direct, as we discuss with campaign tagging later). All traffic recorded with `(none)` as the medium value is also recorded with `(direct)` as the source.

	Source / Medium ?	Acquisition		
		Sessions ? ↓	% New Sessions ?	New Users ?
		301,960 % of Total: 100.00% (301,960)	55.43% Avg for View: 55.28% (0.29%)	167,386 % of Total: 100.29% (166,909)
☐	1. google / organic	**147,302** (48.78%)	56.11%	82,647 (49.38%)
☐	2. (direct) / (none)	**73,673** (24.40%)	60.32%	44,438 (26.55%)
☐	3. mytopreferrer.com / referral	**14,883** (4.93%)	40.30%	5,998 (3.58%)
☐	4. baidu / organic	**9,633** (3.19%)	55.01%	5,299 (3.17%)
☐	5. yahoo / organic	**6,597** (2.18%)	54.33%	3,584 (2.14%)

FIGURE 7.1 All sessions have a source and medium value, as indicated in the Source/Medium report. Source is more specific, Medium more general, and both dimensions can be populated with either the default values or the campaign tag values that override the defaults.

If you wanted to display the Source/Medium report aggregated by the more general medium values, you could change the primary dimension of the report to just Medium.

Referrals

As mentioned above, GA considers referrals to be clickthroughs from any website that it does not recognize as a search engine, and it assigns a medium value of `referral` to all such traffic (unless you have overwritten medium and source with campaign tags).

Because the Referral Traffic report (labeled as Referrals in the left navigation) displays only sessions for which the medium dimension has been populated as `referral`, the report only lists Source as the primary dimension, as shown in Figure 7.2.

	Source ?	Acquisition		
		Sessions ? ↓	% New Sessions ?	New Users ?
		49,218 % of Total: 16.30% (301,960)	**46.32%** Avg for View: 55.28% (-16.21%)	**22,796** % of Total: 13.66% (166,909)
☐	1. mytopreferrer.com	**14,883** (30.24%)	40.30%	5,998 (26.31%)
☐	2. linkjuice.com	**1,936** (3.93%)	49.48%	958 (4.20%)
☐	3. facebook.com	**1,291** (2.62%)	15.49%	200 (0.88%)
☐	4. partnersite.com	**1,062** (2.16%)	48.02%	510 (2.24%)
☐	5. anysite.com	**853** (1.73%)	60.96%	520 (2.28%)

FIGURE 7.2 The Referrals report displays sessions recorded with *referral* as the medium value.

Full Referral Path

If you click into any of the sources listed in the Referrals report, you can see the specific page on which the link to your website was clicked, as shown in Figure 7.3.

Plot Rows	Secondary dimension ▼	Sort Type:	Default ▼	

	Referral Path ?	Acquisition		
		Sessions ? ↓	% New Sessions ?	New Users ?
		853 % of Total: 0.28% (301,960)	**60.96%** Avg for View: 55.27% (10.30%)	**520** % of Total: 0.31% (166,892)
☐	1. /resources/top-links	**297** (34.82%)	49.83%	148 (28.46%)
☐	2. /news/business-briefs	**279** (32.71%)	69.18%	193 (37.12%)

FIGURE 7.3 By drilling down into a referring source in the Referrals report, you can see the specific originating page, or *Referral Path*.

> **Note**
>
> ### Why Do Social Clickthroughs Appear in the Referrals Report but Under Social (not Referral) in the Channels Report?
>
> The Referrals report and the Channels report use different criteria to determine how sessions are displayed. The Referrals report only considers the medium value of *referral*, regardless of source. Social clickthroughs, by default, are recorded as the *referral* medium value; there is actually no *social* medium value captured by default.
>
> The Audience Overview and Channels reports, on the other hand, display traffic by Default Channel Grouping, which buckets traffic according to medium, source, and potentially other dimension values if you have edited or added any channel definitions. Default Channel Groupings are discussed in greater detail in this chapter, and in Chapter 9, "View Settings, View Filters, and Access Rights," we configure a view filter for changing the medium value of social clickthroughs from referral to social (so they are recorded as a separate medium and do not appear in the Referrals report).

Channels

The Acquisition Overview and Channels reports are organized by Default Channel Grouping. Designed as a more aggregated and user-friendly labeling than source/medium, the Default Channel Grouping contains nine channels, each of which is defined by medium, and in some by source as well.

As outlined in the "Default Channel Definitions" help article at `https://support.google.com/analytics/answer/3297892?hl=en`, GA offers the definition for the default channels:

- Direct
- Organic Search
- Referral
- Email
- Paid Search
- Other Advertising
- Social
- Display

Affiliates, an additional default channel that does not appear on the definition page, includes traffic for which medium value is *affiliate*.

It's important to note that even though GA applies these default channel groupings to inbound traffic, in many cases it is up to you to provide the right medium and source campaign tags to inform GA how to group the traffic. To revisit a previous example, the Email channel is defined as *Medium exactly matches email*. This is quite straightforward, but if your inbound links from an email opened in Outlook aren't campaign-tagged, the medium value will be recorded as `(none)`, and the resulting sessions will be grouped as Direct.

Any sessions whose medium and source values don't match any of the channel definitions appear in the Channels report as (Other).

Since we know where to look for the default channel definitions, there's no guessing about which medium (and source) values to use as our campaign tags so traffic is grouped correctly in the Channels report.

As we discuss below, GA users with Edit access to a view also have complete flexibility to edit channel groupings as needed.

Treemaps Report

As a relatively new Acquisition report, the Treemaps report uses size and color to illustrate a simple yet ingenious comparison of two metrics. In Figure 7.4, the comparison of Sessions (size) to Ecommerce Conversion Rate (color) indicates underperformance of Display channel, which is especially problematic, since it's a paid traffic channel.

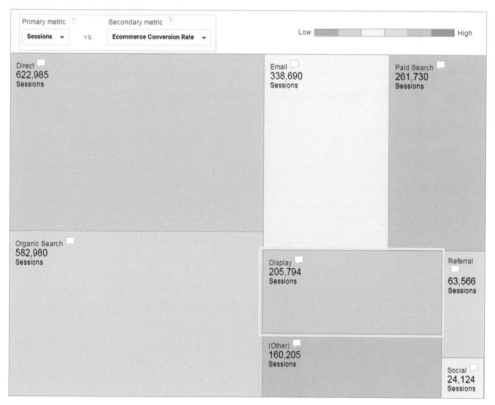

FIGURE 7.4 By comparing Sessions (size) to Ecommerce Conversion Rate (color) for each Channel, you can readily identify underperforming channels and the share of sessions that they account for.

Before you disable all your display campaigns, you can drill down to view a treemap that indicates Ecommerce Conversion Rate for specific display sources. You should also review the Multi-Channel Funnel reports as described in Chapter 9 to check if Display is providing Ecommerce conversion assists to other channels that are converting on last click.

In Acquisition > AdWords, there is also a dedicated Treemap report for AdWords search campaigns.

Campaigns

In GA, campaigns consist of clickthroughs on links that you have tagged with special parameters—`utm_medium`, `utm_source`, and `utm_campaign`—that overwrite the default medium and source attribution and also populate the resulting sessions into the All Campaigns report. As a crucial task for effective GA, campaign tagging is examined in detail below.

Note that the following discussion relates to campaign tracking for traffic to your website as reported in a GA website property. Chapter 13, "Mobile App Measurement," discusses campaign tracking for clickthroughs to Google Play or the iTunes Store for installation and also for clickthroughs directly to your app for reengagement.

CAMPAIGN TRACKING: GOOGLE ANALYTICS NEEDS YOUR HELP FOR ATTRIBUTION

By default, GA determines attribution based on the Referer [sic] header of each HTTP request. If there is no previous Web page—as is the case for a clickthrough from a link that appears in any application other than a Web browser—there are no referrer details in the request, so GA can only populate that session with (none) and (direct) as the medium and source values.

Any standalone email client application such as Outlook illustrates this problem. Let's say that you send out an email campaign to 10,000 email addresses on your list, which generates 600 clickthroughs from standalone clients and 400 clickthroughs from online clients such as gmail. GA will count the 600 clickthroughs from stand-alone email clients as direct, and the 400 clickthroughs from online email clients most likely as referral.

Let's also consider a banner campaign that drives traffic to your site from hundreds of different websites. Each of those clickthroughs is sending referrer information, but it would be pointless to try to identify each of the individual referring sites in the Referrals or Source/Medium report.

Note

Where Do You Set Up Campaigns?

There's no campaign setup *per se* in GA. A campaign consists only of clickthroughs on links to which you have added campaign tags as described below. Apart from the link tagging, no campaign configuration is required.

As a solution to the issues above, adding GA campaign parameters to appropriate inbound links provides three main benefits:

- It correctly groups your sessions within the Acquisition Overview and Channels report.
- It provides more specific listings in the Source/Medium report.
- It populates the All Campaigns report, so you can track specific traffic generation efforts separately from other types of traffic.

The tracking benefit extends to performance metrics in addition to sessions: with campaign tracking, you'll be able to much more cleanly track bounce, goal completions, and Ecommerce transactions by actual traffic source.

Terminology

Campaign *Parameters* = Campaign *Tags*

In reference to campaigns, *parameters* and *tags* are used interchangeably. As mentioned in Chapter 5, "Google Tag Manager," campaign tags have a very separate meaning from *tags* in the GTM context, which refer in most cases to a code snippet injected into the page, and from tags in the broader sense of HTML elements, as in *h1 tag*.

Whether we call them *campaign parameters* or *campaign tags*, their importance cannot be overstated.

Adding Campaign Parameters to Inbound Links

The process of campaign-tagging an inbound link is straightforward; you only need to add the following query parameters to the URL:

- **utm_medium:** the most general descriptor for the attribution; overwrites the default Medium dimension value
- **utm_source:** a more specific descriptor for the attribution; overwrites the default Source dimension value
- **utm_campaign:** the most specific descriptor for the attribution; this identifies the specific campaign and populates resulting clickthroughs into the All Campaigns

report. As a convention, you can include the date at the beginning of the campaign name, especially for frequent, short-duration campaigns. (Technically, utm_campaign is not required, but you can consider it obligatory in practice.)

You can manually add these campaign parameters to your URL, but you're instead advised to use a tool such as Google's or E-Nor's URL Builder (`https://www.e-nor.com/tools/url-builder`) to minimize errors.

Let's use an email newsletter as an example for campaign tagging. The email that you send to your customer list each month contains news summaries and a link back to your main news page. Instead of linking with a nontagged URL, you'll use the URL Builder for formatting a tagged link as shown in Figure 7.5.

Website URL *

http://www.mysite.com/news

(e.g. http://www.urchin.com/download.html)

Campaign Source *

main-list

(referrer: google, citysearch, newsletter4)

Campaign Medium *

email

(marketing medium: cpc, banner, email)

Campaign Name *

201605-newsletter

(product, promo code, or slogan)

GENERATE URL

http://www.mysite.com/news?utm_source=main-list&utm_medium=email&utm_campaign=201605-newsletter

FIGURE 7.5 A URL builder tool such as Google's helps you format campaign parameters in an inbound link.

By including the campaign parameters in the email link, we ensure that all resulting clickthroughs appear in Email as the Default Channel grouping, in the Source/Medium report as *main-list/email*, and in the campaigns report as 201605-newsletter.

Note also that you can use any of your pages—assuming that they all contain the GA tracking code—as your campaign URL. It is also routine to use the same landing page for multiple campaigns; the relationship over time is usually one-to-many.

> **Note**
>
> ## Parameter Order Doesn't Matter; Question Mark Does
>
> No specific order is required for the `utm_medium`, `utm_source`, `utm_campaign`, and other *name=value* query parameters. You will need to be sure, however, to use a question mark before the first *name=value* URL query parameter only and to then separate all query parameters with ampersands.
>
> For a URL such as `http://www.bicycleparts.au/product.aspx?partno=3498`, a campaign URL would be formatted with a single question mark as:
>
> ```
> http://www.bicycleparts.au/product.aspx?partno=3498&utm_source=-xyz-
> affilitate-network&utm_medium=affiliate&utm_campaign=comfort-seat
> ```
>
> In some cases, question marks won't work. This usually is when the website CMS uses question marks to show specific content, for example, webstore.com?product=womens &category=shoes. You can't add &utm_… to the URL because it would prevent the CMS from finding the page. In that case, you use the anchor character (#). In Google Analytics Classic, you had to implement the setAllowAnchor method in your tracking code in order to use the anchor. In Universal Analytics, you can use the anchor by default. (There is still a setAllowAnchor method, but it is now set to true by default.)
>
> In the webstore example, you could add campaign parameters as follows:
>
> ```
> http://www.webstore.com?product=womens&category=shoes#utm_medium=
> banner&utm_source=bestbannernetworks&utm_campaign=2016-summer-shoes
> ```

As another example, let's say that you're tweeting about a product release. You could specify the following parameters:

- utm_medium: **social**
- utm_source: **twitter.com** (You could also use **t.co**, which is, strangely, the default source value for untagged clickthroughs from twitter.com.)
- utm_campaign: **20160601-product-release**

Your formatted campaign URL would appear as:

```
http://www.mysite.com/product-release?utm_source=twitter
.com&utm_medium=social&utm_campaign=20160601-product-
release
```

Note

Can You Use Campaign Parameters in Short Links?

Yes. Add your campaign parameters to the original URL, and then paste the entire URL, with campaign parameters, into whichever link shortener utility you're using. The resulting short URL will expand to include the campaign parameters.

Table 7.1 lists many other types of traffic that require campaign parameters for accurate and specific attribution.

TABLE 7.1 Traffic Types That Need GA Campaign Parameters for Attribution Accuracy and Specificity

Traffic Type	Default Channel Grouping (without campaign tags)	Suggested utm_medium	Suggested utm_source	Notes
Email	Direct or Email	*email*	[email list]	If the clickthrough occurs from a standalone email client such as Outlook, GA counts the session as direct by default. If the clickthrough occurs from an online email client such as gmail or hotmail, GA will record the session as referral or direct by default.
Social	Direct or Social	*social, social-paid*	[social site]	If the clickthrough occurs from a social app and not a social website, GA counts the session as direct. Note that you can opt to track your paid social clickthroughs with social-paid as medium value, if you wanted to track these clickthroughs separately from nonpaid social and pay-per-click. Since *social-paid* as medium does not, however, match any of the default channel definitions, it would be recommended to define a new channel as described later in the chapter.

Table 7.1 *continued*

Traffic Type	Default Channel Grouping (without campaign tags)	Suggested utm_medium	Suggested utm_source	Notes
Pay-per-click/ SEM	Organic Search	*cpc* or *ppc*	[search engine]	If PPC traffic is not tagged, GA receives only the search engine as the referrer and therefore assigns *organic* as the medium. If you're running an AdWords campaign, you should use the Autotagging feature instead of any manual campaign tagging. If you're running a Bing Ads campaign, you can also enable Bing's version of Auto-tagging, described below.
Banner/Text Display Ad	Referral	*banner*	[ad network]	For non-AdWords display campaigns, *medium = display* will match the definition for the Display channel. The problem for AdWords display campaigns, however, is that the Display channel appears below the Paid Search channel in the Default Channel Grouping. Since all autotagged AdWords campaigns are recorded with *cpc* as medium, this will match the Paid Search channel, thereby short-circuiting the match for Display. To ensure that your AdWords display campaigns match the Display channel first, move it higher in your Default Channel Grouping, as shown in Figure 7.12.

continues

Table 7.1 *continued*

Traffic Type	Default Channel Grouping (without campaign tags)	Suggested utm_medium	Suggested utm_source	Notes
Retargeting ad	Referral	*retargeting*	[retargeting network]	Since *Medium = retargeting* does not match any of the default channel definitions, it would be helpful to also define a custom channel based on *Medium = retargeting*, as described below. Note, however, that Google AdWords remarketing campaigns are also recorded with *cpc* as medium, so your custom Retargeting channel should also include a rule to match the campaign name of your retargeting campaign as illustrated in Figure 7.12.
Press release	Referral	*press-release*	[press release platform]	Define a custom channel based on *Medium = press-release*.
Clickthrough from PDF	Direct	*pdf*	[type of document] such as *catalog*	Define a custom channel based on *Medium = pdf*. To track clickthroughs *from* your website to a PDF, you can use an event or virtual pageview as discussed in Chapter 6.
Clickthrough from mobile app	Direct	*app*	[name of app]	Define a custom channel based on *Medium = app*. You certainly can add campaign tags to links from your own apps to your website. If, on the other hand, third-party apps link to your website, you probably will not be able to have them use campaign tags, so that traffic will be recorded as direct.

Table 7.1 *continued*

Traffic Type	Default Channel Grouping (without campaign tags)	Suggested utm_medium	Suggested utm_source	Notes
Affiliate	Referral	*affiliate*	[affiliate network]	Clickthroughs with `utm_medium=affiliate` will match the default Affiliates channel.
Promo/vanity URL redirects	Direct	*vanity-url*	[context of redirect] such as *billboard* or *print* URL	Define a custom channel based on *Medium* = *vanity-url*.
QR codes	Direct	*qr-code*	[context of QR code] such as *mailing* or *print ad*	Define a custom channel based on *Medium* = *qr-code*.
SMS	Direct	*sms*	[SMS list]	Define a custom channel based on *Medium* = *sms*.

For the complete version of the campaign and channel matrix, visit `www.e-nor.com/gabook`.

Two Additional Campaign Parameters: *utm_content* and *utm_term*

When using the URL builder tool, you'll notice two additional, nonobligatory campaign parameters: `utm_content` and `utm_term`.

The `utm_content` parameter is not used in most campaign tagging situations, but it can be helpful to distinguish two inbound links in the same email (`utm_content=top` or `utm_content=bottom`), or as another example, to distinguish multiple creatives in the same banner campaign (`utm_content=leaderboard`, `utm_content=rectangle`, or `utm_content=skyscraper`). The value of `utm_content` is populated into GA as the Ad Content dimension, which you can access as a secondary dimension or configure as a primary dimension in a custom report.

The `utm_term` parameter is used for the bid term in pay-per-click campaigns. You do not normally have to configure `utm_term` manually; it is instead populated by AdWords Auto-tagging or automated campaign tagging from the Bing Ads platform, as described below.

As another, more specialized campaign tag, you can add `utm_nooverride=1` to prevent a clickthrough on the URL from overriding another traffic source. For more on `utm_nooverride=1`, see `www.e-nor.com/gabook`.

> **Warning**   !
>
> Don't use campaign parameters for any internal linking. Since GA recognizes only one medium and source value per session, an internal campaign-tagged link will automatically create a new session in which you won't be able to attribute any user actions, including goal completions and Ecommerce transactions, to the real medium and source of the visit.

To safely track clicks on specific page elements, you can use events, which do not affect attribution and do not break the session. Optionally, you can track performance of internal promotions as part of Enhanced Ecommerce implementation as discussed in Chapter 8, "Goal and Ecommerce Tracking."

Don't Campaign-Tag All Inbound Links

As important as it is to campaign-tag all traffic types listed in Table 7.1, it's not necessary to campaign-tag every inbound link. If, for instance, your website is listed in an industry directory, the Source/Medium and Referrals report will clearly indicate all sessions that this inbound link generates. It would not be harmful to add campaign parameters to the link, but you will not be gaining any benefit in accuracy or specificity, apart from listing this traffic source in the All Campaigns report.

Automated Campaign Tagging for Email

Most email platforms provide an option for automated GA campaign tagging: you can select GA campaign tagging as a configuration option, which prompts the email platform to automatically add `utm_medium`, `utm_source`, and `utm_campaign` to inbound links. (On some platforms, you can specify another utm_campaign value to overwrite the name of the email campaign.)

To distinguish between two links in the same email, as previously described, you'll probably need to disable the automated campaign parameters and manually configure each link instead so you can include `utm_content` in your inbound links.

On a related note, you'll want to remember to campaign-tag inbound links in emails that partners are sending out to their lists on your behalf. In most cases, they'll be able to enable tagging automation through their email platform as described above, but if automated tagging is not an option, do your best to make sure that the links to your site in their outgoing emails are manually campaign-tagged.

Automated Pay-Per-Click Campaign Tracking

For your AdWords campaigns there is a much better option than manual campaign tracking. You should instead, in most instances, opt for AdWords Autotagging, which is easily configurable from GA as explained in Chapter 14, "Google Analytics Integrations — The Power of Together," and reviewed below. Autotagging populates all five campaign parameters and a range of other useful dimensions listed in the "Benefits of Auto-Tagging" GA help page. Note that the 25-character AdWords ad title is passed as `utm_content`. (To distinguish between two AdWords ads with the same title within GA, you'd need to apply AdWords Creative ID as a secondary dimension, or as a primary dimension in a custom report.)

Linking Google Analytics to AdWords to Import Cost Data and Enable Autotagging   In the Property Admin, click Product Linking > AdWords Linking to link GA to an AdWords account. This link will automatically import AdWords cost data into the GA views you select as part of the linking process, and will also, by default, enable Autotagging. Once you enable Autotagging, you should not add the manual GA parameters to the destination URLs of your AdWords ads. As a note, you can also import GA metrics into the AdWords interface, as discussed in Chapter 14.

Clicks Tab: AdWords Cost Data in Google Analytics   If you have linked GA to AdWords as described above, the Clicks tab of the AdWords > Accounts and AdWords > Campaigns reports will display a range of cost-related metrics, including Cost, Cost per Click (CPC), Revenue per Click (RPC), and Return on Ad Spend (ROAS). RPC and ROAS are based on goal value and/or Ecommerce revenue. Keep in mind that ROAS does not take margin into account: if your CPC is 5USD and your margin per click is 4USD, you're losing money, even though ROAS based on total revenue or goal value may appear wildly successful.

Linking Google Analytics to Multiple AdWords Accounts   Note that if you link multiple AdWords accounts to the same GA views, each will be listed separately in the AdWords > Accounts report. This may be useful if, for example, your organization is directly managing an AdWords account and you're also working with an agency that's driving traffic from a separate AdWords account.

Also, if you use an AdWords manager account (MCC), you can easily link all the accounts under MCC to Google Analytics to keep the AdWords accounts in sync in both systems. The MCC-level tracking is beneficial if you want to do cross-account conversion tracking and remarketing. For more details, see "Linking Multiple AdWords accounts to Google Analytics" in the Google AdWords help pages.

Auto-Tagging Bing Ads   Bing Ads does not offer the same level of automated GA integration as AdWords in terms of additional dimensions and cost data, but you can enable Auto-tagging in the Bing Ads account settings to add `utm_medium`, `utm_source`, `utm_campaign`, and `utm_term` to campaign links (Figure 7.6).

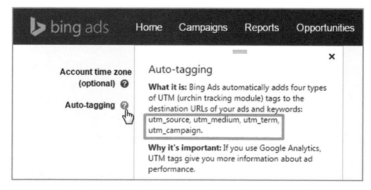

FIGURE 7.6 The tooltip for Bing Ads Auto-tagging indicates the four GA campaign parameters that will be added to inbound links.

> **Note**
>
> ## Campaign Tagging for Google Analytics and Adobe Analytics
>
> If you need to pass campaign parameters to GA and Adobe Analytics installations on the same website, you can keep Auto-tagging enabled for GA and manually add the Adobe Analytics campaign parameter (specified as CMPID in the example below), which incorporates source, medium, and campaign separated by underscores as shown below:
>
> ```
> http://www.mysite.com/promo-page?CMPID=google_cpc_20160524-buy-
> one-get-one
> ```

Consistency Is Critical

Whether manual or automated, the mechanics of campaign tracking are quite straight-forward. There is no technical difficulty in campaign tracking; the challenge lies rather in maintaining a consistent process and naming convention.

Beyond the Implementation Phase

It's important to recognize that campaign tracking is not part of the once-only implementation phase or periodic implementation updates in the same way as event tracking or goal configuration. Campaign tagging requires an ongoing effort on the part of everyone in your organization who drives traffic (with the exception of the SEO team), and the responsibility for upholding the campaign tagging process lies squarely within the marketing and analytics team, not with IT.

Naming Convention

There is no single campaign naming convention that we can point to as correct. What is most important is that you adopt a single naming convention and that you—and anyone else who is driving traffic and campaign-tagging inbound links—stick to it. Even if you remember to campaign tag for all scenarios outlined in Table 7.1, your analysis will be more difficult if you don't maintain your naming convention, particularly for `utm_medium` and `utm_source`.

Figure 7.7 demonstrates unwanted fragmentation with Source selected as the primary dimension in the All Campaigns report. Rows 1, 2, and 5 indicate the same traffic source and should have appeared aggregated for more efficient reporting, as is also the case for rows 2 and 3. Inconsistent campaign tagging has made two traffic sources appear as five.

In the case of the Facebook campaigns, you may want to standardize on *facebook.com* as `utm_source`, since it is also the source value captured for nontagged traffic from Facebook. You can also control the case consistency by maintaining your naming convention, or you can apply a lowercase filter for each campaign dimension as described in Chapter 9.

	Source ?	Acquisition		
		Sessions ↓ ?	% New Sessions ?	New Users ?
		1,252 % of Total: 0.43% (294,286)	**57.35%** Avg for View: 55.34% (3.63%)	**718** % of Total: 0.44% (162,855)
☐	1. facebook	**701** (55.99%)	58.20%	408 (56.82%)
☐	2. Facebook	**192** (15.34%)	66.67%	128 (17.83%)
☐	3. main-email-list	**98** (7.83%)	48.98%	48 (6.69%)
☐	4. main-list	**88** (7.03%)	45.45%	40 (5.57%)
☐	5. facebook.com	**40** (3.19%)	42.50%	17 (2.37%)

FIGURE 7.7 Source reporting fragmented due to inconsistent utm_source values.

> ## Note
>
> ### Campaign Consistency in the Enterprise
>
> To help maintain consistency in campaign naming, you can download a campaign spreadsheet at `www.e-nor.com/gabook`. This spreadsheet will allow you to keep track of the campaign parameters that you and your team have used, and it will also format your inbound links with the parameter values in the same way as the URL Builder tools. You could also use a Web-based spreadsheet to serve the same purpose.
>
> For medium and large companies, a centralized mechanism for keeping track of campaign naming is recommended, as is some form of training to increase adoption. You could work with your development team to develop this kind of tool, or you could use CampaignAlyzer[1] as a licensed platform that also offers link shortening and social sharing. A free trial is available at `campaignalyzer.com/gabook`.
>
> [1] Book authors are affiliated with E-Nor Inc., owner of CampaignAlyzer.

Using the Same Campaign Name for Different Sources and Mediums

If you're launching a campaign across different channels and websites, you have the option of using the same campaign name with different source and medium values, or you could choose to customize the campaign name per channel.

For example, if you're announcing the appointment of your new COO on Twitter, on Facebook, and by email, you could opt to use `20160610-coo-tw`, `20160610-coo-fb`, and `20160610-coo-main-list` respectively as the `utm_campaign` parameter, or you could just use `20160610-coo` in all three instances.

In the first scenario, as shown in Figure 7.8, the All Campaigns report, with Campaign selected as the default primary dimension, would immediately distinguish between the different sources for that same campaign, but you'd lose the campaign-level aggregation benefit.

	Campaign ?	Acquisition
		Sessions ? ↓
		135,081 % of Total: 5.77% (2,340,877)
☐ 1.	20160610-coo-tw	52,327 (38.74%)
☐ 2.	20160610-coo-fb	41,777 (30.93%)
☐ 3.	20160610-coo-main-list	40,977 (30.34%)

FIGURE 7.8 With separate campaign names for each traffic source participating in the same campaign, you can immediately identify the source, even with Campaign as the default primary dimension in the All Campaigns report.

In the second scenario, as shown in Figure 7.9, the campaign value would be aggregated by default for all three sources, which means that you—and all others viewing the report—would need to add Source as a secondary dimension to view metrics for the campaign traffic from the different sources.

	Campaign ?	Source ?	Acquisition
			Sessions ? ↓
			135,081 % of Total: 5.77% (2,340,877)
☐ 1.	20160610-coo	t.co	52,327 (38.74%)
☐ 2.	20160610-coo	facebook.com	41,777 (30.93%)
☐ 3.	20160610-coo	main-list	40,977 (30.34%)

FIGURE 7.9 The same campaign name offers the benefit of aggregated metrics for that campaign across different channels, but you'd need to add Source as a secondary dimension to identify the exact origin of the campaign traffic.

Either option has advantages and disadvantages, and both are perfectly valid. As stated earlier, there is not a single correct campaign-tag naming convention, but you should adopt your own convention and strive to maintain it with consistency.

Combining the Actual Referring Source with Campaign Parameters

As critical as campaign parameters are, their use does, in some instances, force a sacrifice: the loss of any actual referrer details, which are overwritten by the utm_source parameter. This issue might be especially troublesome in the case of press releases. If your press release is picked up by 50 online newspapers, you need to be able to aggregate all resulting traffic in GA, but you might also want to identify the publications individually.

With the help of a Custom JavaScript variable in Google Tag Manager, we can rewrite the page value passed to GA so that it combines the actual referring website with the campaign parameters when utm_medium=press-release (and otherwise leaves the URL unaltered in all other cases), so you achieve both the campaign aggregation and the referrer specificity that you need. You can then update your main GA pageview tracker as demonstrated in Figure 7.10 to set the campaignSource field to the value returned by the variable instead of the actual URL that appears in the browser.

FIGURE 7.10 You can use a Custom JavaScript variable in GTM to combine referrer into utm_source.

You can download the JavaScript that you'll need for the variable, and review the required tag and trigger modifications in detail at www.e-nor.com/gabook. An example resulting URL passed to GA appears below:

```
http://www.mysite.com/updates.php?utm_source=pr-
network-www.torontosun.com&utm_medium=press-
release&utm_campaign=20160718-product-release.
```

Importing Campaign Parameters

As an alternative to appending three campaign parameters to your inbound links, you can append a single utm_id parameter against which you can then import utm_medium, utm_source, and utm_campaign, as discussed in Chapter 17, "Data Import and Measurement Protocol." This approach provides greater discretion—the campaign is not revealed to the website visitor in the URL—and offers a viable solution for advertising platforms that allow a single campaign parameter only. (Keep in mind, however, that data import in GA standard is now-forward only, so if you're not using Analytics 360, you'd need to make sure to have the import already configured at the time that you launch your campaign.)

CHANNEL CUSTOMIZATIONS

As discussed previously in the chapter, channels in GA are buckets for your traffic based by default on medium and source primarily. The objective of channels is to provide higher-level, human-readable labeling as an alternative to the actual medium and source dimension values. By default, the same channel grouping is available to all users in the Acquisition and Multi-Channel Funnel reports, but there are several ways that we can customize the channels, as described below.

In a few instances throughout the book, we emphasize that you should make Google Analytics "speak your language." Channel customizations provide a way to label your traffic sources that resonates most naturally for your organization or your clients. How do you, your executives, your management, and especially your marketing team think about your visitor sources? Let your answer guide your channel customizations.

The channel groupings have been simplified in GA, but they're still a little tricky to understand. The key points are below.

Terminology

Channel versus Channel Grouping

A channel itself is a rule-based grouping or "bucketing" of traffic based on medium, source, and a few other dimensions values. A channel grouping is itself a set of channels. We can perform channel customization at two levels: we can customize, create, or reorder individual channels as in Figure 7.12, and we can also create a new channel *grouping* consisting of both custom channels and those that appear by default in the Channels report.

Note

Why Does (Other) Appear as a Channel?

If a session does not match the rules for any default or customized channel, it appears in the (Other) channel.

As a first step to minimizing the sessions that get classified as (Other), apply Source/Medium as a secondary dimension in the Channels report, as shown in Figure 7.11.

Now that we understand why this traffic—clickthroughs from an RSS feed—are not matching any of the channel definitions, we have two options for keeping these clickthroughs out of (Other):

➤ **Customize a default channel**: in this case we could add a rule to the default Social channel as in Figure 7.12 to pull in sessions in which medium exactly matches *feed*.
➤ **Create a new channel**: if we wanted to keep our RSS clickthroughs in a separate channel, we could define a new RSS channel as medium exactly matches *feed*.

Both of these options are described below.

	Default Channel Grouping	Source / Medium ⑦ ⊗	Sessions ⑦
☐	1. (Other)	feedburner / feed	**531** (37.35%)

FIGURE 7.11 Applying Source/Medium as a secondary dimension in the Channels report reveals Source/Medium values that did not match any of the default or customized channel definitions and therefore forced GA to bucket the traffic as (Other).

Customize a Default Channel

In Figure 7.11, we saw that Feedburner clickthroughs were bucketed into the (Other) channel because they didn't match any of the default channel definitions. If we want to include this traffic in Social, we can add an alternate match condition to the Social channel definition, as shown in Figure 7.12.

If you have Edit access to the view, you can modify the Default Channel Grouping by clicking Channel Grouping > Channel Settings in the view admin. As with all changes that will affect the reporting for everyone accessing the view, try all modifications of the Default Channel Grouping in a test view before your working view(s).

Reorder a Channel

As discussed in Table 7.1, AdWords Autotagging adds *cpc* as the medium for Google Display Network (GDN) and remarketing traffic. Since Display appears lower than Paid Search in the Default Channel Grouping, GDN traffic from AdWords, by default, matches Paid Search first and the match with Display is short-circuited.

If instead you want your GDN traffic to count toward the Display channel, you need to drag Display ahead of Paid Search, as in Figure 7.12.

> ## Note
>
> ### For Channel Matching, Order and Case Matter
>
> As demonstrated in Figure 7.12, we need to order our channel definitions such that a session matches a more specific condition before a more general condition. If we did not move Display ahead of Paid Search, our clickthroughs from the Google Display Network would match Paid Search first, and no further channel matching would take place. There is no overlap or subsetting among channels: each session can match one channel only. As soon as the session finds a channel top-to-bottom that it matches, a match is declared, and the session is bucketed within that channel, and not in any other.
>
> On a related note, if you used *Retargeting* instead of *retargeting* as `utm_medium` for your non-AdWords retargeting, the case variation would prevent the resulting clickthroughs from matching the new channel definition. Applying a lowercase filter to the Campaign Medium dimension as described in Chapter 9 would not help in this case: when your raw data is processed on the GA servers, channel matching occurs before view filters are applied. Be very aware of case as you're setting up actual campaign names in AdWords, applying campaign parameters (such as *utm_medium=retargeting*) to inbound links, and customizing channels in GA. To accommodate potential case inconsistency in past (and future) campaign parameters, you can add case variations and/or use regex in your channel match conditions.

> ## Note
>
> ### Annotate Changes to the Default Channel Grouping
>
> Since they do not apply retroactively, it's important to annotate changes to the Default Channel Grouping. If you're comparing the Display channel in June 2016 to the same time period in the previous year, it would be important to note that you added a new rule to the Display definition on May 15, 2016, and that you're therefore not quite comparing apples to apples. Annotations are demonstrated in Chapter 11.

Define a New Channel

In addition to customizing an existing channel as outlined in the previous procedure, you can add a new channel to the Default Channel Grouping. At the top of Figure 7.12, we're creating a channel to capture two different types of remarketing/retargeting traffic:

- **Remarketing traffic from AdWords:** Autotagging adds cpc as the medium to AdWords remarketing links, so resulting clickthroughs would, by default, match the Paid Search channel. We can instead define a new channel that would match all campaign names that contained *remarketing*. For this equation to work, we would certainly also need to include *remarketing* in the actual names of all remarketing campaigns administered through AdWords. (AdWords remarketing is discussed in Chapter 14.)

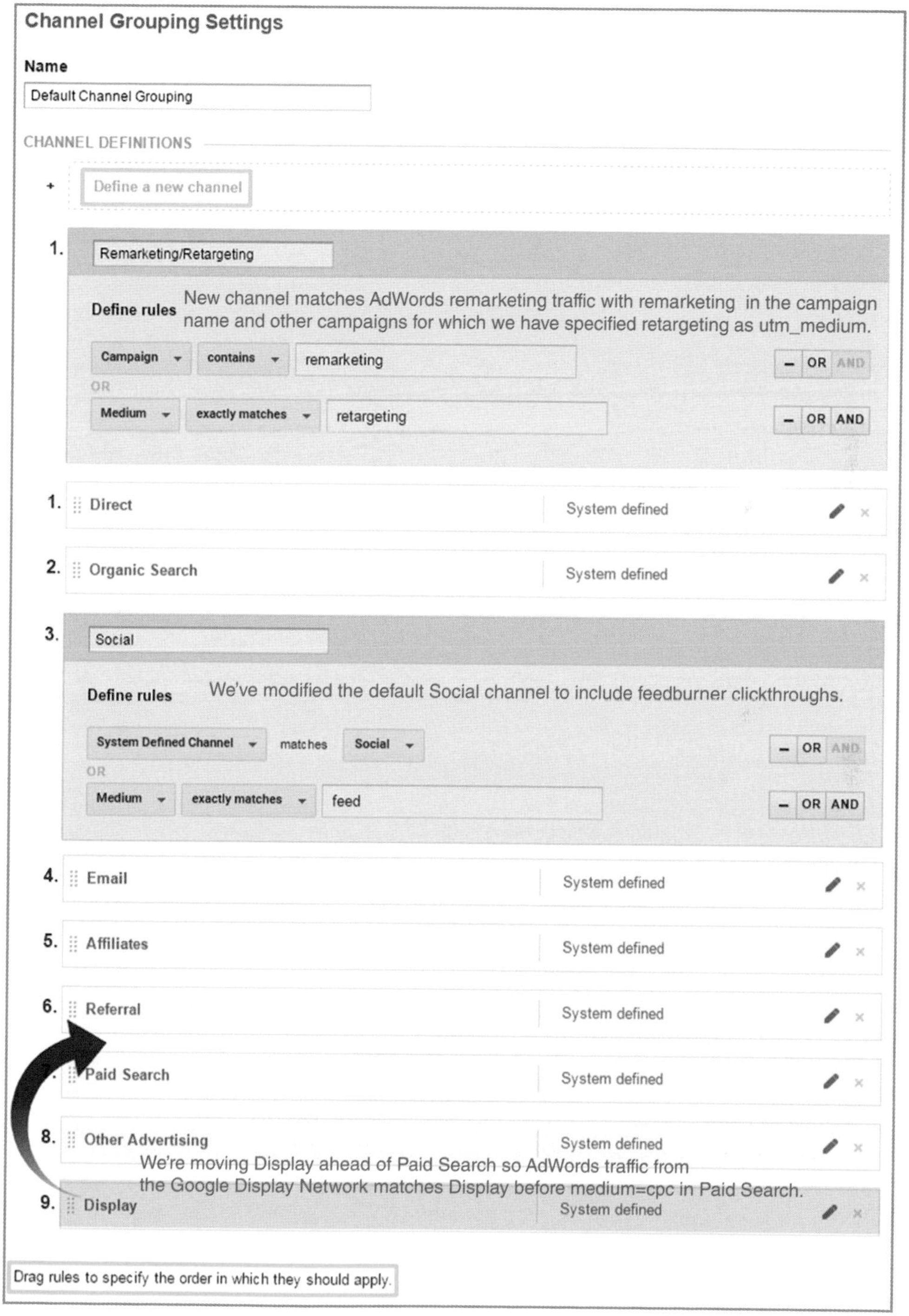

Channel Grouping Settings

Name

Default Channel Grouping

CHANNEL DEFINITIONS

+   Define a new channel

1.   Remarketing/Retargeting

Define rules   New channel matches AdWords remarketing traffic with remarketing in the campaign name and other campaigns for which we have specified retargeting as utm_medium.

| Campaign ▼ | contains ▼ | remarketing | − | OR | AND |

OR

| Medium ▼ | exactly matches ▼ | retargeting | − | OR | AND |

1.   ⠿ Direct   System defined   ✎ ×

2.   ⠿ Organic Search   System defined   ✎ ×

3.   Social

Define rules   We've modified the default Social channel to include feedburner clickthroughs.

| System Defined Channel ▼ | matches | Social ▼ | − | OR | AND |

OR

| Medium ▼ | exactly matches ▼ | feed | − | OR | AND |

4.   ⠿ Email   System defined   ✎ ×

5.   ⠿ Affiliates   System defined   ✎ ×

6.   ⠿ Referral   System defined   ✎ ×

.   ⠿ Paid Search   System defined   ✎ ×

8.   ⠿ Other Advertising   System defined   ✎ ×

We're moving Display ahead of Paid Search so AdWords traffic from the Google Display Network matches Display before medium=cpc in Paid Search.

9.   ⠿ Display   System defined   ✎ ×

Drag rules to specify the order in which they should apply.

FIGURE 7.12 On the Channel Grouping Settings screen, you can customize a default channel definition, create a new channel definition, and reorder the channel matching.

■ **Retargeting traffic from other networks:** For other retargeting networks, such as AdRoll, we can manually add *retargeting* as `utm_medium` to the inbound links and include another match condition in our new channel definition.

Retargeting and *remarketing* mean the same thing; the latter is Google's terminology. Match conditions for both appear in Figure 7.12.

> Note

Paid Branded, Paid Nonbranded, and Additional Custom Channels

GA provides a specialized but straightforward setup for breaking out paid branded and paid nonbranded ("generic") search engine clickthroughs. For more details, see "Brand and Generic Channels" in the GA help docs:

```
https://support.google.com/analytics/answer/6050679?hl=en&utm_id=ad
```

(Later in the chapter, we'll discuss the critical distinction between branded and nonbranded organic traffic.)

You could also define channels for the following types of traffic, again based on campaign parameters:

➤ specific email campaign types (e.g., newsletter) or email lists (e.g., main list)
➤ QR code redirects
➤ redirects of vanity/promo URLs used for print, radio, or television campaigns

> Note

Campaign Parameters and Channel Customizations Work Together

As demonstrated above, you can take advantage of campaign tagging and channel customizations to bucket your traffic in the Channels reports however you choose. Campaign parameters allow you to control the Medium, Source, and Campaign dimensions for much of your traffic, and you have full control over channel definitions and groupings. With these two capabilities, you can customize your channels in a way that is most useful and meaningful for yourself and all stakeholders.

Define a Custom Channel Grouping

In addition to creating or customizing individual channels, you can also create a custom Channel Grouping, that is, a customized set of channels. Custom Channel Groupings are probably not used as much as just custom channels within the Default Channel Grouping. Don't feel compelled to create any New Channel Groupings, but be aware of the functionality if you need to take advantage.

Also, while changes to the Default Channel Grouping apply now-forward only, a new Channel Grouping applies retroactively. (The downside of the dynamic retroactivity is that new Channel Groupings are also subject to sampling, which we discuss in Chapter 10.) The new Channel Grouping does not replace the Default Channel Grouping; it serves as an alternative to the default, and you can readily switch between the two (or however many you create; the limit is 50).

As examples, you could define a new Channel Grouping with just two channels: Paid Traffic and Unpaid Traffic. Or you could define a Channel Grouping that breaks out specific referrers or social sources—again, configure the Channel Grouping however makes the most sense for a top-level traffic labeling scheme.

To define a custom Channel Grouping:

1. In the View Admin, click Channel Grouping and then + New Channel Grouping.
2. Name your channel grouping, for example, *Paid and Unpaid Traffic*.
3. Define your channels.

Note that you don't need to redefine any of the predefined channels from scratch. To add Organic Search as a channel in your new Channel Grouping, set the rule to *System Defined Channel – matches – Organic Search*, for one example.

View-Level and Single-User Channel Groupings

In the procedure above, we began the process of creating a new Channel Grouping by clicking Channel Settings, shown in Figure 7.13, in the top section of the View Admin. To perform this action, you need to have Edit rights to the view, and, accordingly, this Channel Grouping will be accessible to everyone who accesses the view. The customizations to the Default Channel Grouping in Figure 7.12 also require Edit access, since they affect Channel reporting for everyone accessing the view. (We discuss access rights in Chapter 9.)

FIGURE 7.13 If you have Edit rights to the view, you can click Channel Settings in the top section of the View Admin to customize the Default Channel Grouping or create a new view-level Channel Grouping.

Each GA user with Read & Analyze access to the view also has the option of creating a new Custom Channel Grouping, as shown in Figure 7.14, that is accessible only to that user; it's a private, user-level Channel Grouping, as indicated in Table 7.2. The GA user who created the Channel Grouping can share it with other GA users through Share Assets in the View Admin. Even more significantly, if the user who created the Channel Grouping has Edit rights, that user can "promote" the Channel Grouping to view level after first using it privately, thereby making it visible to all GA users who access the view.

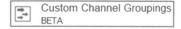

FIGURE 7.14 All users who have Read & Analyze rights to the view can click Custom Channel Groupings in the bottom section of the View Admin to create a private, user-level channel grouping.

TABLE 7.2 Channel and Channel Grouping Customizations

	Default Channel Grouping	New Channel Grouping (View-Level)	New Channel Grouping (GA-User-Level)
Where do you configure?	Admin > Channel Settings > Channel Groupings	Admin > Channel Settings > Channel Groupings > New Channel Grouping	Admin > Custom Channel Groupings
Access rights required to configure	Edit	Edit	Read & Analyze
Who can see it?	All GA users who can access the view	All GA users who can access the view	Only the GA user who created the grouping
Does it apply retroactively?	No	Yes	Yes
Available in custom reports, in segments, as a secondary dimension, through the API, and in Analytics 360 custom tables (to avoid sampling)?	Yes	No	No

Channel Customizations in the Multi-Channel Funnel and Attribution Reports

The Channel Customizations described above apply not only to the Acquisition > Overview and Acquisition > All Traffic > Channels report, but also to the Multi-Channel Funnel reports and the Attribution > Model Comparison Tool, which we discuss in Chapter 9. For Analytics 360, customizations to the Default Channel Grouping apply to the Data-Driven Attribution modeling discussed in Chapter 18.

TRACKING ORGANIC TRAFFIC

Organic traffic reporting in GA is problematic for the following two reasons:

- The keywords for most nonpaid clickthroughs from Google, Bing, and Yahoo are blocked from analytics tools and appear instead as *(not provided)*.
- "Organic" traffic encompasses two utterly different types of clickthroughs: branded/navigational searches for company name, product name, or domain name entered into a search engine, and nonbranded searches for an actual search term. Only nonbranded clickthroughs can be considered organic in the true sense. With most of our organic keywords reported as *(not provided)*, we can't distinguish branded from nonbranded organic traffic in GA.

In the sections below, we discuss these two issues in greater detail and also consider Google Search Console as a partial solution.

(not provided)

If you access the Campaigns > Organic Keywords report, it's highly likely that you'll see *(not provided)* recorded as the keyword for the greatest number of organic sessions, as shown in Figure 7.15.

Keyword ?	Source ? ⊙	Sessions ? ↓
		359,544 % of Total: 27.04% (1,329,613)
1. (not provided)	google	**276,090** (76.79%)
2. (not provided)	yahoo	**26,625** (7.41%)
3. (not provided)	bing	**23,613** (6.57%)

FIGURE 7.15 With Source selected as the secondary dimension, the Organic Keywords report shows *(not provided)* as the top keyword recorded for Google, Yahoo, and Bing.

Branded versus Nonbranded Organic Traffic

The distinction between branded and nonbranded organic traffic is fundamental. Let's say that your company is called Fallbreaker and that you manufacture and sell parachutes. If a searcher enters *fallbreaker* or *fallbreaker.com* into the search engine and then clicks through, you can consider the visit to be *branded organic*, also referred to as *navigational organic*. The searcher was already aware of your company, so you can celebrate your brand awareness, but you don't want to congratulate your SEO team just yet.

If a searcher enters *parachute* into the search engine and fallbreaker.com ranks high enough to earn a clickthrough, you can consider this a true, nonbranded organic session and an SEO success.

Before October 2011, when the Google search engine began blocking keyword data from Web analytics, it was very easy to distinguish branded from nonbranded organic clickthrough performance in GA: each keyword appeared with performance metrics such as bounce and goal conversion rate, and you could quickly define a branded organic segment (including medium = *organic*, keyword containing *F|fallbreaker*) and a nonbranded organic segment (including medium = *organic*, excluding keyword containing *F|fallbreaker*) that you could then apply to any of the GA reports. (Segmentation is discussed in Chapter 10.)

These segments were particularly useful when applied to Goal and Ecommerce reports and typically revealed much higher conversion rates for branded versus non-branded organic traffic. With nonbranded sessions isolated, you could measure and optimize true organic performance.

Note

Multi-Channel Funnel Reports Reveal Conversion Attribution before Final Branded Organic Clickthrough

In Chapter 8, we learn how the Multi-Channel Funnel reports avoid all-or-nothing last-click attribution and instead display the assisting channels that helped to generate conversions on returning visits from other channels. This would be especially relevant for conversions on returning organic sessions, most of which are likely to represent *branded* organic click-throughs after a previous visit from another channel, such as pay-per-click, which undoubtedly assisted with the conversion that occurred in the later organic branded session.

Google Image and Country-Specific Clickthroughs

By default, clickthroughs from Google image search results appear in GA with *google.com/imgres* as the source and *referral* as the medium. In Chapter 12, "Implementation Customizations," we configure a view filter that rewrites these values as *images.google.com* and *organic*.

On a similar note, clickthroughs from country-specific versions of the Google search engine, such as *google.co.jp* or *google.ng*, appear in GA with *google* as the source. In Chapter 12, we configure our GA property to record specific source values for search engines with country-specific top-level domains.

Google Search Console

Google Search Console (formerly known as Google Webmaster Tools) can help us to address the previously discussed (not provided) issue, at least partially. As a tool separate from GA, Google Search Console provides reporting on visitor interactions with the Google search engine leading up to the clickthrough to your pages, and it also reports on Google search crawler (dubbed *Googlebot*) activity on your website.

Specifically, the Search Analytics report in Google Search Console will help you with (not provided) by displaying impressions, clickthroughs, clickthrough rate, and average positions for nonbranded and branded keywords searches in Google that resulted in organic clickthroughs to your website. (See Figure 7.16.)

	Queries	Clicks ▼	Impressions	CTR	Position	
1	fallbreaker parachute ⬀	281	458	61.35%	1.9	»
2	fallbreaker ⬀	204	290	70.34%	1.0	»
3	parachute ⬀	145	25,637	0.57%	5.6	»

FIGURE 7.16 The Search Analytics report in Google Search Console displays impression and clickthrough data for branded and nonbranded keywords.

Linking Google Search Console to Google Analytics

You can choose Google Analytics Property from the gear menu in Google Search Console to connect to a GA property to which you have Edit access under the same login and thereby begin populating the Search Engine Optimization reports in GA.

This may at first seem like the perfect solution to the (not provided) issue, since it allows you to view complete Google organic clickthrough data within GA, but the solution is only partial: we still don't know post-clickthrough performance by keyword, since bounce rate and other performance metrics are not displayed.

As a fairly recent update, the Search Engine Optimization > Landing Pages and Geographical Summary reports show both Search Console and GA performance metrics such as bounce rate, goal conversion rate, and Ecommerce revenue. The Search Engine Optimization > Queries report, for its part, still only shows Search Console data for individual queries, so GA performance data by keyword has not been restored. For more details, see "Deeper Integration of Search Console in Google Analytics" on the Google Webmaster Central blog.

Google Search Console Verification and User Management

Before anyone can access Google Search Console data for your website, at least one person in your organization must add that property on the Google Search Console home page and then complete the verification process.

There are five different options for verification:

- HTML file upload
- addition of meta tag to home page
- shared Edit-level login for GA
- shared Publish-level login for GTM
- domain name registrar login

It's recommended that you first try the GA or GTM options if you have adequate access rights. If these verification options fail, as they tend to, ask other people in your organization (or client organization) who may already have access to Google Search Console—your SEO team is a good place to start.

The file upload verification option works consistently, but it requires direct access to the root directory of your website. Once one login is verified for your website, that person can provide access to others directly through User Management in the Google Search Console interface (but there's no harm if multiple people complete the verification process separately).

Note

Get Access to Google Search Console—It's Worth It

You may be able to easily gain access to Google Search Console, but do what's necessary in any case. Although the Search Analytics report does not completely fill the (not provided) gap, it provides hard data on Google search engine impressions and clickthroughs, which are important and relevant for many stakeholders in any organization.

Additionally, Google Search Console provides a range of other useful reporting, including URL Parameters (which we refer to in Chapter 9 for page consolidation in GA), broken links, and mobile usability (and ranking) recommendations.

Bing Webmaster Tools

Bing Webmaster Tools also offers a suite of reports about search engine activity that can complement Web analytics, and its inbound link reports are more comprehensive than their counterparts in Google Search Console.

Note

Clickthroughs from Search Engine Apps

Clickthroughs from the Google and Yahoo apps are tracked with Source/Medium values of *google/organic* and *yahoo/organic* respectively, with keyword as *(not provided)*. Clickthroughs from the Bing app are tracked with Source/Medium values of *(direct)/(none)*, with keyword *(not set)*, as it would be for any direct visit.

GUEST SPOT   Google Analytics Benchmarking Reports

Tracy Rabold
Tracy Rabold is a Digital Analytics Consultant at E-Nor.

The S&P 500 Index

Why the return on the S&P 500 Index works so well as a benchmark is that we know exactly what it is and we know exactly what is in our own portfolio, so we have a clean comparison.

Benchmarking Digital Performance

This is also why benchmarking digital performance—using data from others to ascertain your own performance—is fraught. Differences in site design or digital analytics tool implementation make comparisons shaky.

Google Analytics Benchmarking Reports

With some very simple manipulation of data from a Benchmarking report, I would conclude that it seems we are underserving our mobile device–using audience or, put another way, missing out on opportunities in mobile (Figure 7.17).

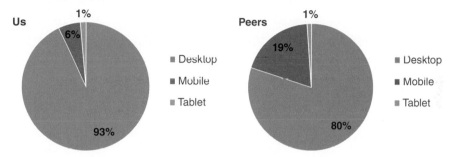

FIGURE 7.17 Based on data downloaded from Google Analytics Benchmarking reports. The data was downloaded to Excel from GA, where these two pie charts were created.

In this example, the dimension—device type—is basic GA that is not going to be affected by individual implementation or design issues.

What does give me pause here is "Peers." Who are our "peers"?

The peer group comprises organizations that have GA on their sites and have opted into benchmarking. There are two steps to opting into benchmarking for your site:

1. Toggle data sharing for Benchmarking to the on position in Account Settings.
2. Choose your organization's Industry Category from the drop-down in Property Settings.

GA will use the Industry Category you chose as the default in the Benchmarking report. However, it is possible to change the industry category (or vertical) to any industry and to drill down to a more specific industry subcategory (e.g., Baked Goods in Food) from within the Benchmarking report. In addition to customizing the peer group (Industry Vertical) from within a Benchmarking report, we can also customize by Country/Region and Daily Sessions (Size), as shown in Figure 7.18.

Channels		Aug
Email Export ▾ Shortcut	This report is based on 299,449 sessions (100% of sessions). Learn more	
Industry Vertical ⑦ **Baked Goods** ▾ Food	Country / Region ⑦ **California** ▾ United States	Size by daily sessions ⑦ **500-999** ▾

FIGURE 7.18 Drilldown options are at the top of each of the three benchmarking reports.

continues

continued

When I drill down to an Industry Vertical that better resembles my own, I come to a different conclusion: while we may be missing opportunities, we are not doing so bad, and tablet seems to be a bit more important than it did in the prior comparison, as you can see in Figure 7.19.

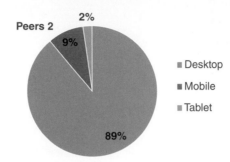

FIGURE 7.19 Based on data downloaded from GA Benchmarking reports after choosing a more granular Industry Vertical (i.e., a subset of the original). Data downloaded to Excel, where pie charts were created.

A Good Digital Performance Benchmark

Good digital performance benchmarking can be found using GA—or third-party data sources such as Comscore—for dimensions or metrics that are not, or at least less, subject to design or implementation differences—like Organic Search.

Similar to the device category example above, we could use Benchmarking reports to download and then calculate year-over-year or month-over-month percent change in Organic Search sessions. For more than two time periods, it would be necessary to download multiple reports (Figure 7.20 and Figure 7.21).

Organic Search	
Jul 1, 2015 - Jul 31, 2015	**39.20%** ⬆ 154,407 vs 110,923
Jun 1, 2015 - Jun 30, 2015	**25.61%** ⬆ 135,658 vs 108,002
% Change	53.09%

FIGURE 7.20 Sessions using time period comparisons with us on the left (July 2015 is 154,407) and peers on the right (July 2015 is 110,923).

We seem to have really outperformed our peer group as well as the overall U.S. search market in terms of June-to-July Comscore growth. Wow!

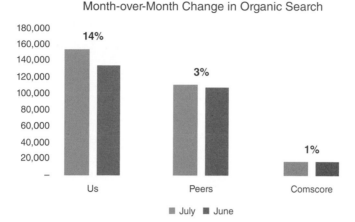

FIGURE 7.21 By using the GA benchmarking data and also benchmarking against a third-party data source, we can see that our own organic search growth exceeds that of our industry peers and of the Internet overall.

Direct Traffic and Attribution Precedence

Let's say that your company sells herbal supplements. On Tuesday, a Google search engine user searches for *echinacea* and clicks your AdWords ad (costing you 4USD, incidentally). The Source/Medium for the first sessions is *google/cpc*.

On Wednesday, remembering the 400mg echinacea supplements on your website, the same visitor enters your Web address directly into the browser (and purchases the echinacea this time). So the second-session Source/Medium would be *(direct)/(none)*—correct?

Actually, in most GA reports, the second session will also be attributed to AdWords and will appear with same Source/Medium values and channel grouping as the first session.

This makes sense. The second visit, though technically direct, is clearly attributable to the first visit, which was driven by AdWords. As long as the second session takes place on the same device and in the same browser, the user has not deleted cookies, and the browser in the first session was not set to private/incognito mode—private/incognito browsing automatically deletes cookies after a session—the second session will still count as *google/cpc*.

Other Source/Medium values have equal precedence and therefore overwrite each other, as demonstrated in Figure 7.22. For instance, if the second session above had been organic, a referral, or a campaign clickthrough, any of these sources would have appeared in GA for the second session and not *google/cpc*, the idea being that the nondirect returning source deserves credit—at least to some degree—for the returning session.

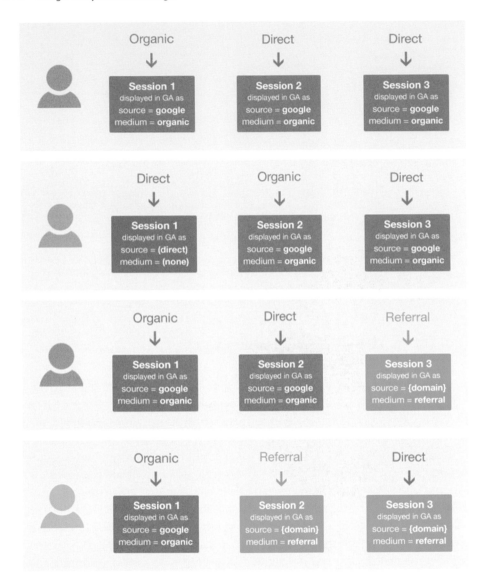

FIGURE 7.22 Direct sessions appear with the more specific medium and source values of a previous session.

In Traffic Info > Session Settings within the Property admin, you can see that Campaign Timeout defaults to six months. This determines how far back the GA reports will look back for a direct visit to pull in a more specific Source/Medium from a previous visit. You can easily change the Campaign Timeout if you choose, but it's generally recommended to keep the setting at the six-month default. (See Figure 7.23.)

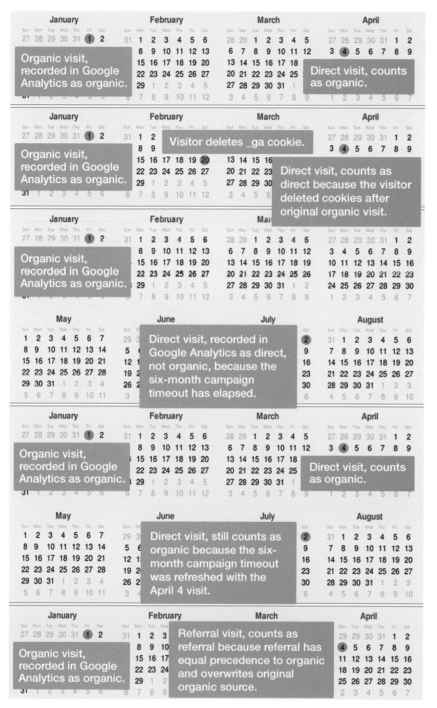

FIGURE 7.23 The Campaign Timeout—six months by default—determines the lookback for direct sessions to appear as a more specific previous traffic source. The six-month period is refreshed with each returning session.

Direct Sessions in the Multi-Channel Funnel Reports

As mentioned earlier in the chapter, the Multi-Channel Funnel reports display Source/ Medium details for all sessions during which a conversion occurred or that were followed by a returning session in which a conversion occurred. Unlike the Acquisition reports, the Multi-Channel Funnel reports assign equal precedence to direct traffic relative to other sources and do not therefore repeat Source/Medium from previous sessions for returning direct sessions. The Multi-Channel Funnel reports are discussed in greater detail in Chapter 8.

GUEST SPOT	https-to-http Referrer Loss

Hazem Mahsoub

Hazem Mahsoub is an Analytics Solutions Engineer at E-Nor.

It may be surprising to see in Table 7.3 that many clickthroughs from secure pages (i.e., pages accessed through the https protocol) to nonsecure pages (i.e., pages accessed through the http protocol) appear in GA as direct traffic. If all your pages are secure, this issue will not impact you, but if some or all of your pages are non-secure, you may be missing some referral data in GA.

TABLE 7.3 Referrer Information Passed or Blocked Based on Page Protocols

Protocols	Referrer Passed?
http to http	Referrer Passed
http to https	Referrer Passed
https to http	Referrer Blocked
https to https	Referrer Passed

   With the referrer information blocked, GA records https-to-http traffic with *(direct) / (none)* as Source/Medium dimensions in most instances.

   Links from some websites (google.com and facebook.com, most notably) are configured with the `content="origin"` attribute, which does preserve the referrer in https-to-http clickthroughs.

   For a complete discussion on this issue, see "https to http: Secure-to-Nonsecure Referrer Loss" on the E-Nor blog.

Note	

l.facebook.com and lm.facebook.com: Link Shim Referrals

In addition to *facebook.com* and *m.facebook.com*, it is likely that *l.facebook.com* and *lm. facebook.com* appear as sources in your GA reports. The second two sources indicate that Facebook has activated its Link Shim process during the clickthrough to protect the user from malicious links. The *l.facebook.com* and *lm.facebook.com* sources should not raise any concern; in fact, their presence in GA indicates that your website was evaluated favorably by Link Shim.

For analytics purposes, you can consider *l.facebook.com* as the equivalent of *facebook.com* and *lm.facebook.com* as the equivalent of *m.facebook.com*. You have the option to apply view filters to rewrite each of the two variations to a single source value. View filters are discussed in Chapter 9.

 **KEY TAKEAWAYS**

All sessions have medium and source dimension values.   All sessions are recorded in GA with a medium dimension and a source dimension, medium being a more general descriptor and source being more specific.

By default, GA recognizes three mediums.   Without the aid of campaign tagging, GA assigns all traffic one of three medium values: `(none)` for direct traffic, `organic` for traffic from known search engines, and `referral` for traffic from non-search-engine websites.

GA needs attribution help in the form of campaign parameters.   Campaign parameters, also called campaign *tags*, are critical for helping GA record attribution more accurately (in the case of clickthroughs from applications other than browsers) and more meaningfully (in the case of banner clickthroughs that are recorded by default as unrelated referrals, as one example).

Use an automated option for pay-per-click tracking.   For AdWords, it's strongly recommended in most cases to enable Autotagging instead of manually campaign-tagging the inbound links. Bing Ads offers an Auto-tagging feature that is similar (but that does not bring in the great deal of additional data that AdWords Autotagging does).

Channels are based on medium and/or source values.   The eight default channels that GA recognizes are based on medium or source values. (For instance, the Social channel is defined to include referring sources recognized as social websites and campaigns tagged with *social* as utm_medium.)

You can customize your channels.   You can customize the definition of an existing channel in the default channel grouping, you can create a new channel within the default channel grouping, or you can create a new channel grouping (i.e., as a set of channels) as an alternative to the default channel grouping. You can also reorder channels within the grouping to change matching precedence.

Most organic clickthroughs are recorded with *(not provided)* as keyword.   The vast majority of keywords from Google, Bing, and Yahoo organic clickthroughs appear in GA as *(not provided)*.

Direct traffic repeats a more specific medium and source values from a previous visit. For a default Campaign Timeout period of six months, GA repeats any other Source/Medium values (such as *google/organic* or *referral/abc123.com*). As an exception, the Multi-Channel Funnel reports treat direct traffic with equal precedence and do not pull in previous Source/Medium values as an overwrite for direct.

 **ACTIONS AND EXERCISES**

1. **Assess your campaign gaps.** Review your current traffic sources against Table 7.1 and the online resource to determine where you need to start using campaign parameters.

2. **Develop a consistent process and naming convention for your campaign tags.** Use the spreadsheet resource referenced in the chapter to maintain consistency in your campaign naming hierarchy. For an enterprise-wide campaign tagging strategy, consider CampaignAlyzer or an in-house solution.

3. **Enable automatic campaign tagging in your email system.** If your email system offers automatic campaign tagging for inbound links, take advantage.

4. **Customize your channels and channel groupings as needed.** Review the nine GA channel definitions, and revise default channel definitions, reorder channels to change matching precedence, and create new channels (for traffic from QR codes and URL redirects, as two examples) as needed.

5. **Get access to Google Search Console for your website.** If a colleague or client already has access to Google Search Console, ask that they grant you access through the User and Property Owners settings. If none of your associates already have access, complete one of the verification options yourself.

8

Goal and Ecommerce Tracking

A s first discussed in Chapter 2, "Google Analytics Reporting Overview," Google Analytics (GA) does not populate the Conversions reports at all until you take either or both of the following steps:

- tell GA which existing pageview or event actions constitute a goal conversion
- provide additional Ecommerce data beyond pageview and event tracking

In either case, you're enabling GA to measure success according to the specific key performance indicators (KPIs) that you identified for your website or mobile app as discussed in Chapter 3, "Measurement Strategy."

It's critical to configure goals and/or Ecommerce so your analytics can clearly tell you if your users are achieving these objectives.

GOAL TRACKING

In the following example, we set up a goal for a health tips email newsletter signup on a health insurance provider website—this is a primary action that the company executives and website designers want visitors to take, so we're going to track it as a goal.

As we configure our goals, we need to consider four options:

- goal type
- match type (for Destination goals only)
- funnel or no funnel (for Destination goals only)
- goal value

We discuss each of these considerations in the next sections.

Warning   **!**

Goals are not retroactive. All of the other warnings in this book are about the potential harm of doing something. This warning is about the potential harm of *not* doing something: setting up goals as soon as possible. Goal (and Ecommerce) setup does not apply retroactively, so make sure to configure goals (and/or Ecommerce) as an urgent implementation priority.

Configuring a Goal

Since goal configuration changes the underlying report data (by calculating conversion rate and related metrics) for everyone who accesses the corresponding GA view, you need Edit access to the view to set up a goal. We'll discuss access rights in Chapter 9, "View Settings, View Filters, and Access Rights."

Note

Create Your Goals in a Test View First

In Chapter 9, we discuss the best practice of maintaining at least three views for each GA property: a raw backup view, a test view, and one or more working views for your reporting. You should create goals in a test view first, let them run for a few days or a week to verify that your goal setup is working, and then recreate the goal in a working view, either manually or, preferably, by sharing the goal with yourself from the Share Assets panel as discussed in Chapter 11, "Dashboards, Custom Reports, and Intelligence Alerts," which you can also access from the View Admin screen.

On a related note, you cannot actually delete a goal once it's created; you can only edit it or turn off recording. We thus have another incentive for verifying goal configuration in a test view before creating the goal in a working view.

Twenty Goals per View

GA allows us to create 20 goals per view. This limit should suffice for most websites or mobile apps, since we don't want to track every user action as a goal, only those that indicate a central or supporting success relative to our KPIs.

If, however, you do need additional goal slots, you can always create a new view, apply the same view filters and settings, and set up more goals.

Goal Sets

As you create goals, GA by default populates the five goal slots in four goal sets in sequence. It's perfectly acceptable to stick with the default sequencing, but you could opt to group related goals within a goal set, which would allow you, for example, to choose Goal Set 2 as the metric group in the Source/Medium report and display the conversion rate per Source/Medium for each goal within the goal set.

As just stated, however, it's fine to stick with default goal sequencing. In most cases, you should analyze goals individually, so the initial grouping is not critical in most implementations.

Goal Type

Let's start by clicking Goals in the view column on the admin screen, and then clicking New Goal. An initial screen displaying goal template options such as Place an Order or Media Play can be helpful to provide additional ideas for goal tracking, but select Custom and click Continue to access the goal setup screen shown in Figure 8.1.

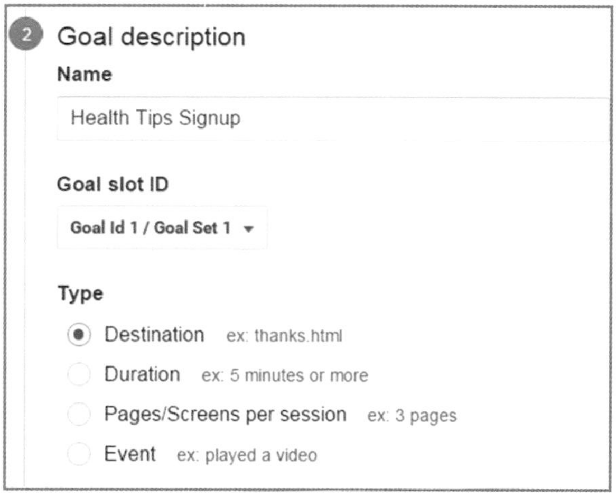

2 Goal description

Name

Health Tips Signup

Goal slot ID

Goal Id 1 / Goal Set 1 ▾

Type

◉ Destination   ex: thanks.html

◯ Duration   ex: 5 minutes or more

◯ Pages/Screens per session   ex: 3 pages

◯ Event   ex: played a video

FIGURE 8.1 As the first step of goal setup, specify the goal name and type. If you choose, you can also specify a goal slot other than the default.

Note that we have chosen Destination as the goal type. Destination is the most common goal type, since, in many cases, it's a specific pageview or screen view that signifies the goal completion.

You can also create a goal based on any action that you have tracked as an event, such as a video play or a click on a specific offsite link. As another goal option that we will not be discussing, Smart Goals are designed to be used for AdWords when you don't have actual GA goals or Ecommerce in place.

GUEST SPOT   **Seven Tips for an Effective Call to Action**

Tim Ash

Tim Ash is the CEO of the strategic conversion rate optimization agency SiteTuners, author of the bestselling books on Landing Page Optimization, and the founder and chair of the international Conversion Conference.

If you work in marketing or digital operations, the call to action (CTA) is something of a rock star. We test it. We revere it. We understand that a small lift it generates in clickthroughs can mean significant gains for the business.

However, despite the increased attention towards CTAs, compared to, say, 10 years ago, we could still be thinking about them and improving them quite a bit more.

The tips below for optimizing and testing your CTAs apply to lead-generation landing pages and more broadly to any Web page that has a call to action (as pretty much all Web pages should).

1. **Increase contrast:** as a general principle, it's important to have a mostly color-neutral presentation. Benign and boring works quite well for most sites, and you'll have more leeway to make the CTA more distinctive when using a "bland" page.

2. **Limit choices:** for your CTAs to be found and acted upon, you need to limit choices. Limit the potential actions of your visitors. One is ideal, and two potential actions can be forgiven if you absolutely need the second choice. Any more than that and you're just confusing your visitor. Remember: *if you prioritize everything, you prioritize nothing.*

3. **Use affordances:** visual affordances provide clues about what your visitors can do with screen elements.
   - ➤ *Shape:* rounded objects call a little more attention and convey a little more interactivity.
   - ➤ *Size:* greater sizes typically help give buttons more attention and hierarchical "weight."
   - ➤ *Position:* negative space around buttons help visitors understand that the area can be interacted with.

4. **Match intent:** Don't underestimate the importance of matching intent. You might be surprised to find a difference in clickthrough rates between the passive "Free Trial" and action-oriented, "Try it Free," or the generic "Submit" and more emotional "Help Tornado Survivors."

5. **Use graphics to make CTA explicit:** make sure the *picture in the background does not dominate the scene*, and that the *form is not so bland against the color graphic*. The CTA should naturally arise from the Zen-stillness of your page.

6. **Direct towards CTA with faces:** Visitors will always look at faces because they're a rich source of information about the environment. We have a general object recognition system, and near our emotional midbrain, we have a separate part for recognizing faces and people. That allows us to judge someone's attitude or aggression towards us, and this is all critical for social and survival reasons. On your page, the *direction of the gaze of the face matters*. Generally, rather than looking past your form or off the page, you want the face to signal something interesting on the page: your CTA.

7. **Keep it boring and short:** In the real world, you wouldn't want to be rude or too forward, so *don't ask for too much information too early in the process* when there's no obvious benefit for the customer to give up that information. To echo the tips above, it's critical that other graphic elements of your page don't compete with your CTA for attention, so visitors know right off the bat what they're supposed to do. (See Figure 8.2.)

FIGURE 8.2 MR Insurance Consultants' photo of a woman gazing towards the form directs the visitor's attention to the CTA area.

Engagement Goals

Because they're based on a threshold rather than a specific action, Duration and Pages/Screens per Session goals are referred to as *engagement goals*. Keep in mind that your Duration goals depend directly on hit timestamps. For example, if a visitor lands on a long blog page and spends 10 minutes scrolling and reading the blog post, but you haven't set up any event or virtual pageview tracking for scrolling (as described in Chapter 6, "Events, Virtual Pageviews, Social Actions, and Errors"), that session will not count toward a 5-minute Duration goal.

The Pages/Screens per Session goal type, for its part, depends only on pageviews (physical or virtual) or screen views and does not consider time on page/screen or session duration.

Match Type

Because we chose Destination as the goal type in the previous step, we must now specify the text string for the matching page(s) or screen(s) as well as the match type. The page or screen text string that you specify is compared to the Page or Screen dimension values as listed in the Pages or Screens report. The match type defaults to Equals To, but you can change this to Begins With or Regular Expression, as shown in Figure 8.3, so more than one Page or Screen value would count as a conversion.

FIGURE 8.3 For a Destination goal, you can choose one of three match types.

Match Type *Begins With*

Let's say that you manage a consumer credit website. The primary KPI for the website is the number of sessions in which a credit report is purchased. The user's selection of delivery method for the credit report—by mail, or as PDF attachment in an email—determines the confirmation URL that the user is directed to `/confirmation-mail` or `/confirmation-email`. In this case, we could easily configure a Destination Goal with Begins With as the match type and `/confirmation` as the Page field, since these two confirmation pages should satisfy the same goal.

Match Type *Regular Expression*

Begins With would not be suitable, however, if there were other pages that began with `/confirmation`, such as `/confirmation-contact-us` but that should not count as a goal match, or if the two URLs for the credit report confirmation appeared as `/mail-confirmation` and `/email-confirmation`. In these cases, we'd need the specificity that only a regular expression could provide.

In the second case, we could select Regular Expression as the Match Type and specify the Page field as follows:

```
\/(mail|email)-confirmation
```

The regular expression above uses the pipe metacharacter to signify `or`. At the beginning of the regular expression, we "escaped" the forward slash with a backslash to ensure that the forward slash is interpreted as a literal character.

Too much duplication between *mail* and *email* in the regular expression? We could rewrite the regular expression more efficiently using the ? quantifier metacharacter to signify *zero or one occurrences of the preceding character*:

```
\/e?mail-confirmation
```

Chapter 9 includes an overview of regular expressions.

Goal Value

Though not obligatory, Goal Value is very useful—especially if you do not have Ecommerce tracking enabled—since it allows GA to calculate metrics such as Page Value, which we discuss later in the chapter, and Per-Session Goal Value.

Goal values are not dynamic; the static value that you configure is used in each goal completion. (Goals based on events can pull in varying event values as the goal value, but event value is not normally specified as part of event tracking.) For purchases of products and services at varying price points, Ecommerce tracking, discussed later in this chapter, offers greater flexibility than goal tracking.

There is not necessarily a single correct approach, but some recommendations follow.

- **Single goal, actual value.** If you're configuring a goal to track the sale of only one product or service, populate the purchase price as the goal value.
- **Single goal, estimated value.** If you're configuring a goal to track a lead submission for £1,000 financial consulting engagement, and you close 10% of leads, populate £100 as the goal value.
- **Single goal, nonmonetized.** If you're tracking a goal that's not in any way monetized, populate an arbitrary value: €1 or €100 or €1,000 (as in Figure 8.4). The relative Page Value and Per Session Goal Value metrics will still be fully valid for comparison purposes.

FIGURE 8.4 Goal value is optional but usually recommended. Even in the case of nonmonetized goals, populating an arbitrary goal value such as US$1 or €100 will allow GA to calculate Page Value and Per Session Goal Value.

- **Multiple goals, actual or estimated values.** Set up the goals and populate individually with the actual or estimated values. You can also opt to duplicate any goal in a separate view to report on Page Value and Per-Session Goal Value based on Goal Value only for a single goal only.
- **Multiple goals, nonmonetized.** Set proportional goal values for each goal. If, for instance, you consider your Contact Us goal to be twice as important as your Mailing List Signup goal, you can assign respective Goal Values of $2 and $1. You can also duplicate the goals in separate views, again, for separate Page Value or Per-Session Goal Value metrics by goal.
- **Ecommerce and goals.** This is probably the trickiest scenario. If you're tracking Ecommerce and goals in the same main view, you may want to consider duplicating your goal in a separate view and specifying Goal Value for that goal in that separate view. This will allow GA to calculate Page Value separately for Ecommerce transactions (in the main view) and for goal completions (in the separate view). There's no need to refer to the separate view, however, for Ecommerce- and goal-specific metrics, such as Revenue and Per-Session Value for Ecommerce and Per-Session Goal Value for goal completions; GA will calculate these separately in the main view.

Note

Get Your Goals as Close to Brick and Mortar as Possible

One of the most elusive quests in analytics is correlating online website visits or mobile app usage with offline purchases. Although you cannot in most instances map a direct cause and effect, you can configure a goal for any user action that indicates a disposition towards a trip to the store. You must first make sure to set up event or virtual pageview tracking for actions such as click-to-call, getting directions, or *make this my store* that may not be tracked as physical pageviews, and you can then create corresponding Destination or Event goals as a very relevant performance indicator for online or in-app support of offline conversions.

Goal Funnel

Going back to the health tips newsletter signup, our Web designers envisioned the conversion process to consist of three pages:

- health tips page, with a link to the newsletter signup form
- newsletter signup form page, with delivery and subject selections
- signup confirmation page

We have already set the final step in the funnel as the Destination field in the previous example: the bottom of the funnel appears at the top of the goal configuration. We now need to just specify the first two funnel steps as in Figure 8.5.

FIGURE 8.5 Funnel configuration is possible for Destination goals only. Though a funnel is not required, it is recommended wherever designated steps precede the goal completion.

Note that, by default, the Funnel Visualization Report will display entries at any funnel step, not just the first. If you want to restrict the funnel to top-step entries only, you can set the Required? toggle for the first step to Yes. You could also create two goals with identical funnel steps but different first-step Required settings. (Instead of manually re-creating the goal, you can use the Share Asset feature to share the goal with yourself as previously mentioned and then just change the first-step Required setting in the new copy.) This would provide two different ways to view entries and completions in the same funnel for the same goal.

Funnel Is Recommended but Not Required

A funnel is not required to calculate Goal Conversion Rate. It is, however, required for the following reporting elements, so it is therefore recommended:

- Funnel Visualization report.

- Funnel Conversion Rate (appears at the bottom of the Funnel Visualization report).
- Goal Abandonment Rate (appears in the Goal Overview report).

While a funnel is recommended, and is required to populate the Funnel Visualization report and also to calculate the Goal Abandonment Rate and the Funnel Conversion Rate (which will be shown in Figure 8.9), it's not required to calculate the Goal Conversion Rate.

A goal funnel is not required to populate the Goal Flow report (Figure 8.10) for a given goal, but it makes the report more useful.

If you're unsure of your funnel steps, omit them at first, and proceed with your goal setup. Once the goal has been running for a period of time, you can view the Reverse Goal Path report (which will be shown in Figure 8.11) to understand the actual paths that visitors are taking to your goal completion pages or screens, and you can then map the most common path(s) as funnel steps in the original goal or in a new goal and thereby measure drop-off between the steps leading to conversion.

Note

You Can Use Virtual Pageviews in a Funnel, but You Can't Use Events

In Chapter 6, we reviewed many types of user actions that are not tracked by default but that you can track as events or virtual pageviews. While either option is valid, it's important to remember that you cannot use an event at any point in a goal funnel. If you were tracking a PDF download as an event, you could define a goal based on the event, but you could not build a funnel on top of the goal, and you could not use the PDF download as a funnel step leading to another destination page.

Since virtual pageviews are treated identically to physical pageviews once recorded in GA, you can specify a virtual pageview as a funnel step or as the page field in Destination goal on which you configure other pages as the funnel steps.

If you tracked each step (after the first physical pageview) in the multistep AJAX process shown in Figure 6.26 as a virtual pageview, you'd be able to define a corresponding goal and funnel.

Similarly, if the health tips signup form submission did not redirect to another page and therefore generate a physical pageview by default, you could generate a virtual pageview with the help of a GTM Form Submission trigger as listed in Table 6.1.

Goal and Funnel Reports

Once you have configured a goal, GA will start calculating goal-related metrics and populating the Goal Reports. We will discuss the goal reports as well as goal metrics that appear within other reports.

Goal Overview

It's usually advisable to analyze goals individually, so if you have multiple goals configured in the view, select a single goal for display as in Figure 8.6.

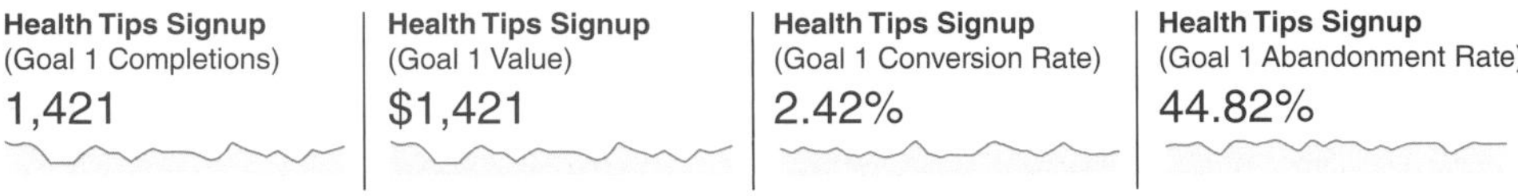

Health Tips Signup
(Goal 1 Completions)
1,421
Health Tips Signup
(Goal 1 Value)
$1,421
Health Tips Signup
(Goal 1 Conversion Rate)
2.42%
Health Tips Signup
(Goal 1 Abandonment Rate)
44.82%

FIGURE 8.6 Metrics in the Goal Overview report.

Conversion Rate: Perhaps Not What You Think

In the context of goals, a *conversion* is a *completion*. Although the two terms are used in different metrics, they represent the same concept. Let's continue by clarifying two potentially confusing points about goal conversions and conversion rate:

- **For a given goal, a single user cannot convert more than once during a session.** If you have two newsletter signups that lead to the same thank-you page, GA will record only one conversion for a session in which a user signs up for both newsletters. Conversely, one user can convert multiple times on the same goal, but only in separate sessions.
- **Goals metrics are based on sessions, not users.** Because conversion rates are based on sessions and not users, they can sometimes appear bleaker than they are in reality. If you see a 1% conversion rate for application submission on a mortgage website that you're analyzing, it does not mean that 1% of *people* are converting; it means that 1% of *sessions* included a conversion.

Especially for costly or complex propositions, it may take several return sessions for a user to convert, as we'll be able to see in the Multi-Channel Funnel reports discussed later. If you're presenting your conversion data at a company meeting and someone asks why only 1% of people are converting, that's your cue to briefly explain the concept of a session and clarify the definition of conversion rate, as shown in Figure 8.7.

50 goal completions
1,000 users
= 5% conversion rate
50 goal completions
5,000 sessions
= 1% conversion rate

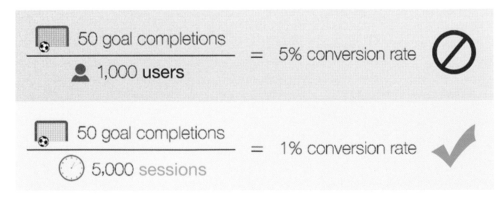

FIGURE 8.7 Since conversion rate is defined as conversions per session, it appears lower in all instances than if defined as conversions per user.

Why doesn't GA base conversion rate on users rather than sessions? While this would be useful, unique users as a metric is much more difficult to determine than sessions (because of multiple-device usage, cookie deletion, etc.), so conversion rate based on users would suffer a much greater margin of error. That said, we can, if we choose, create our own calculated metric for user-based conversion rate, as described in Chapter 12.

GUEST SPOT   **The Buyer Legend Precedes the Funnel**

Bryan and Jeffrey Eisenberg

Bryan and Jeffrey Eisenberg are the cofounders of training company BuyerLegends.com.

You can make money being average. We hope you aspire to be more than average.

In 2015, the average conversion rate of the nation's top online retailers was 3.32%. In 2001, we wrote:

Conversion rates are a measure of your ability to persuade visitors to take the action you want them to take. They're also a reflection of your effectiveness at satisfying customers, because for you to achieve your goals, visitors must first achieve theirs.

The top 25% of online retailers convert at 5.31% and the top 10% of online retailers convert at 11.45%. Amazon Prime members convert 74% of the time on Amazon.com, according to a 2015 study from Millward Brown Digital, compared to 13% for non-Prime members.

Companies that plan and optimize persuasive momentum usually convert 2 to 4 times better than their industry average.

The Difference between Average and Excellent

The companies that truly excel at conversion rate optimization have evolved a culture of customer-centricity; not at the manager or director level, but in the C suite. The best companies absorb CRO learnings and incorporate them into strategy and operational changes. That makes them superior, not just at fixing, but at creating relevant customer experiences that delight their customers.

They think about the sales funnel differently.

Conversion Funnels: Fixing a Flawed Metaphor

You've planned the campaign or the test.

You've designed the checkout or registration.

Now your customers come along and enter your funnel.

Let's get real: Your customer isn't truly in a funnel. There's no gravity compelling them through your experience like there is in a real funnel. There is only the customer's motivation and your understanding of that motivation to create persuasive momentum.

Your customers' journeys are their stories, *not* funnels. They could tell you the stories, just try asking them. And those stories don't always have happy endings.

Your customers' stories end happily when they are delighted. And for them that may mean buying from you or from a competitor. It's simply a matter of perspective.

Now you come along and interrogate your analytics to find out what your customers did.

Is this process so very different from what you do?

continues

continued

The most successful companies start with the story from the customer's perspective. They anticipate what needs to be measured in order for the analysts to understand the customer's experience.

Analysts must tell stories and businesspeople must measure accountability. If not their strategy isn't truly aligned with customers' needs.

It's time to perfect your concept of a funnel.

Start with a Story

Buyer Legends are measurable and accountable by design. A Buyer Legend is not a feel-good story; it's about your business. A Buyer Legend should describe in significant detail what actions you expect your customer to take, many of which are measurable.

Measure and Optimize Your Persuasive System

Whether or not you are aware, *your business has created a de facto persuasive system*. Buyer Legends is a process for creating a persuasive system that is intentional, measurable, and optimizable. That is why it is important for you to track both the micro and macro actions so that you are not just optimizing the final conversion but all the steps in between, where you can spot breakdowns in the system and fix them.

What Is Persuasive Momentum?

In our book *Waiting for Your Cat to Bark?*, we defined persuasive momentum as "the progressive decision-making process that aligns the customers' goals with our own business goals." Whether intentional or not, your business is operating a persuasive system.

Funnel visualizations are certainly a useful tool for analysis and optimization, but marketers who are stuck on the sales/conversion funnel metaphor, without considering user stories or persuasive momentum, work too hard for too little return. They pour more customers into the top of the funnel hoping more come out at the end.

Micro Actions vs. Macro Actions

Typically your conversion goals are the macro actions. It is dangerous to ignore micro actions; all the required smaller actions customers need to take to before they can take a macro action. Without persuasive momentum customers stop moving forward in their buying journey.

The Three Elements of Persuasive Momentum

No matter if the action is micro or macro, there is a simple formula that will help you identify persuasive momentum or the lack thereof.

- **Relevance.** Are you relevant to my wants/needs/desires (search query)?
- **Value.** Do I know why you are the right solution for me? Have you explained your value proposition/offer well?
- **Call to action.** Is it obvious what I need to do next? Have you given me the confidence to take that action?

Ask these questions of every touchpoint, and you will quickly find if your touch points are missing one, two, or all three of these components. We also call this "The Conversion Trinity," shown in Figure 8.8.

Relevance   Value   CTA

FIGURE 8.8 The Conversion Trinity: Relevance, Value, Call to Action.

A Legend for Your Customer's Buying Journey

Your Buyer Legend is a map of your customer's journey, and to read the map properly you need to have a legend.

Your hero is on a journey. You tell his or her story. Every successful customer journey needs a map and every map needs a legend. The journey's legend is the key to navigating the map. The components of a journey legend are described below.

Hero   This is the protagonist of your legend. All legends are told from the point of view of the hero.

Catalyst   This is the point at which the customer first identifies your company, product, and/ or service as a potential solution.

First Measurable Step   Here is where your customer enters the measurable portion of the journey.

Road Signs   These are points in the customer's path that are critical to their completion of the journey. These include information that, if not available, will most likely prevent the customer from completing the journey.

Detours   These are pathways that marketers must construct as solutions to forks in the road. They often go off the path in search of answers to concerns, alternative solutions, or just plain curiosity. So meet the customer along those wrong turns and guide them back onto the proper path.

Measurable Step   This is any step along the way that can be measured.

Fork in the Road   These are decision points in the person's path where a specific need or curiosity can take them off the ideal path in search of answers to a specific need, curiosity, question, or concern.

Destination   This is the final measurable step where the customer converts into a lead or sale.

Understanding the Value of Quantitative vs. Qualitative

As humans, and certainly as website visitors, our actions can be measured. This creates quantitative data that tells you *what* your customers are doing, and qualitative data can provide insight into *why* your customers are doing what they do. Quantitative data needs to make sense in the context of qualitative data: business needs both types of research to see the whole picture. So do not discount the value of focus groups, surveys, customer interviews, and even customer comments and reviews as you begin to craft your Buyer Legend.

continues

continued

With a combination of qualitative inputs and quantitative validation, you can start to build meaningful, user-focused Persuasive Momentum that delivers better experiences to your website visitors, generates greater success for your organization, and drives towards real, measurable excellence.

Note

Conversion Rate Optimization: When 1% Can Be 50%

Even with the understanding that conversion rates appear lower because they're based on sessions and not users, our job as analysts and optimizers is to never be satisfied with current goal and Ecommerce conversion rates. There is always lots of room for improvement, particularly if your organization has not yet made a focused effort in this regard.

In this book, we learn from Brian Clifton that U.S. merchants report a purchase conversion rate between 1.0% and 2.9% and from Bryan and Jeffrey Eisenberg that the top 10% of U.S. online retailers convert at 11.45%.

If you're already converting at 5% for a goal or Ecommerce, and, through a concerted effort on analytics and optimization, you increase your conversion rate to 6%, how much of an improvement does this represent? It's not 1%; it's *20%*. If instead you started at a 2% conversion rate, that 1% increase would represent a 50% improvement.

Also keep in mind that the margin in that additional 1% is likely greater than in the first 2% or 5%: you've invested more person-hours in analytics and optimization, but you haven't increased your marketing spend, your website hosting fees are the same, and it's not costing any more to keep the lights, heat, and water cooler going at your office. The 1% conversion rate gain represents a profound performance improvement and potentially a critical competitive advantage for your business.

Abandonment Rate

In Figure 8.6 (previously shown), why isn't abandonment rate the inverse of conversion rate? While goal conversion rate is based on all sessions and is not influenced by a funnel, goal abandonment rate is based only on the number of sessions in which the funnel was entered (but the goal was not completed). If you do not configure a funnel for a goal, GA will not calculate an abandonment rate for that goal.

Note

Abandonment Does Not Respect "First Step Required" in Funnel Setup

If you have selected First Step Required in your funnel setup, the Abandonment Rate in the Goal Overview report will not correspond accurately with the Funnel Visualization report shown in Figure 8.9. The Funnel Visualization report, including the Funnel Conversion Rate that appears at the bottom, does respect First Step Required, while Abandonment Rate does not, such that two funnel definitions that are identical except for First Step Required would display identical Abandonment Rates.

If you have selected First Step Required in your funnel setup, you can calculate Abandonment Rate as the inverse of the Funnel Conversion Rate (e.g., 100% – 67.97% Funnel Conversion Rate = 32.03% Abandonment Rate).

Funnel Visualization

GA offers two reports for goal funnels: Funnel Visualization and Goal Flow. These reports are very useful, but, as described below, some aspects of these reports are not readily apparent, particularly for Funnel Visualization.

Note that the Custom Funnel feature available in Analytics 360 and discussed in Chapter 18, "Analytics 360," is somewhat similar to goal funnels but is not necessarily related to goal completions and also, importantly, applies retroactively. Furthermore, the backfilling issue described in the sections below does not affect Custom Funnels, and you can also configure a Custom Funnel to include funnel completions during a single session or over multiple sessions.

Funnel Conversion Rate Is Based on Funnel Completions—Goal Conversion Rate Is Not

It may be surprising that GA calculates goal conversion rate without considering any funnel that you may have configured. If you have created two goals with the same

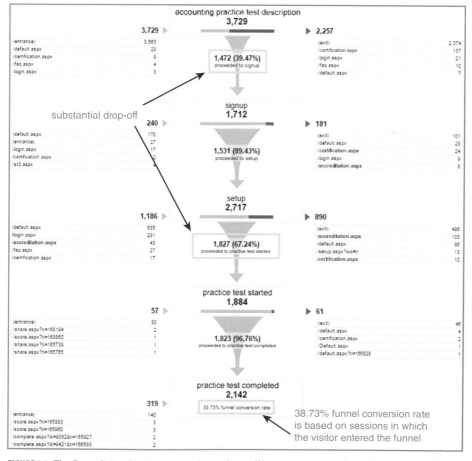

FIGURE 8.9 The Funnel Visualization report shows drop-off between steps and provides the overall funnel conversion rate.

destination page but funnels containing different steps, the abandonment rates for the two goals will certainly differ, but the conversion rates would be identical.

Funnel Step Completions Correspond to Unique Pageviews

As we discussed in Chapter 2, the Unique Pageviews metric represents the number of sessions in which a page was viewed at least one time. Funnel step counts are based on Unique Pageviews: if a user views a funnel page 1 time or 10 times before conversion during a session, the count for the funnel step will increase by one only.

Funnel Steps Don't Need to Be Completed Sequentially

Funnel steps don't need to be completed sequentially to count. If a user views other pages in between funnel steps, the step counts in the Funnel Visualization are still incremented normally. In fact, the funnel steps don't even need to be completed in the order you specified: if a user happens to view your third funnel step before your first funnel step, both steps are still incremented normally.

This might lead you to ask: what if step 3 actually does experience more pageviews than step 2? In this case, something strange and somewhat inexplicable called *backfilling* occurs in the Funnel Visualization report: step 2 will appear with a marginally *higher* unique pageview count than step 3 (minus the entries directly at step 3 if you have not made the first step required).

The good news is that backfilling does not occur in most funnels. The two following scenarios are the most susceptible to backfilling:

- an optional step that many users skip in a process
- a more specific page (such as an article category page) that leads to a more general page (such as newsletter signup page for all article categories)

How can you tell if your funnel is a victim of backfilling? You can check your funnel step counts against the Unique Pageview counts in the All Pages report: if a funnel step count is greatly inflated relative to Unique Pageviews in the All Pages report, backfilling is occurring in the Funnel Visualization report. Even quicker: check the Goal Flow report, described later, which is not subject to backfilling.

You Can't Apply Segments to Funnel Visualizations

Unlike most other GA reports, Funnel Visualization does not allow you to apply the segments discussed in Chapter 10, so you cannot therefore dynamically segment your funnel for visits from Chile and Argentina or organic clickthroughs from Bing, just as two examples.

Since you can apply segments to Goal Flow shown in Figure 8.10, you can refer to this report instead of the Funnel Visualization if you do need to segment. If, however, it is important for you to display the drop-off percentages of the Funnel Visualization report itself for a specific traffic segment such as those mentioned above, you can create a dedicated, hard-filtered view as described in Chapter 9, thereby ensuring that every report in the view, including Funnel Visualization, reflects only the subset of sessions after filtering.

FIGURE 8.10 Goal Flow report offers some advantages over Funnel Visualization but may require more interpretation.

Goal Flow

While the Goal Flow report populates for goals that don't have funnels configured, it's more useful for goals that do have funnels and serves as a good complement to the Funnel Visualization report in the following ways:

- **Segments**: unlike the Funnel Visualization report, you can apply segments to Goal Flow.
- **No backfill**: the backfill issue does not affect Goal Flow. (The First Step Required setting in the funnel setup also does not apply to Goal Flow.)
- **Level of detail**: you can apply a more aggregated or more granular level of detail to Goal Flow, which can help to illustrate skipping of funnel steps and even looping back to previous funnel steps.

With these advantages of Goal Flow over Funnel Visualization, what's the downside? The Goal Flow overall requires more interaction and interpretation, as shown in Figure 8.10. It's worthwhile for your own analysis but may be somewhat less suitable than the Funnel Visualization for a general audience.

> **Note**
>
> ### Funnel Visualization and Abandonment: Simple, Visual, and Emotional
>
> Though the Funnel Visualization has some drawbacks, it possesses a special power of demonstrating visitor progress and drop-off toward your goals—for yourself, for clients, and for any stakeholder in your organization. If you need support (in terms of development resources or usability testing to help determine the reasons for drop-off at specific steps) for your conversion optimization efforts, the Funnel Visualization report can help you communicate your message and get others on board.

Similarly, Abandonment Rate is a metric that we can all connect with viscerally and that every-one within a business can recognize as a negative indicator that you should work to minimize. You, as an analyst, can drill down to finer and more actionable detail, but make sure to first present analytics data (and conversion problems) to other stakeholders in clear and impactful terms.

Reverse Goal Path

The Reverse Goal Path report (Figure 8.11) shows the most frequent series of three pageviews or screen views that lead to a goal. You might wonder: if I have this report, why do I need the Funnel Visualization (or Goal Flow)? Notice that the Reverse Goal Path indicates only the most popular paths but does not show page-to-page drop-off (and also that it goes back three pages only). The Reverse Goal Path provides the best ideas for funnels if you have previously defined goals without them: set up a funnel for the most popular paths as reported view drop-off in the Funnel Visualization and Goal Flow reports, and begin to optimize for goal completions.

Goal Completion Location ⑦	Goal Previous Step - 1 ⑦	Goal Previous Step - 2 ⑦	Goal Previous Step - 3 ⑦	Practice Test Completed (Goal 1 Completions) ↓
1. /completed.aspx	/started.aspx	/setup.aspx	/description.aspx	214 (9.98%)
2. /completed.aspx	/started.aspx	/setup.aspx	/signup.aspx	142 (6.61%)
3. /completed.aspx	/started.aspx	/setup.aspx	/accreditation.aspx	95 (4.42%)

FIGURE 8.11 Reverse Goal Path report shows how visitors are actually getting to your goal pages.

Note

I See Where the Drop-off Is Happening—Now What?

Once you have identified the drop-off points in your funnel, you can review the page yourself and also conduct in-person and online usability testing as qualitative analysis to determine the potential cause of the drop-off at that funnel step. If there's a clear problem, such as a drop-down menu that's cut off on certain displays, go ahead and make the change. If the reason for the drop-off is less clear, create a hypothesis for improvement based on your observations, and, ideally, test one or more variations of the funnel step against the goal conversion. Tools and strategies for qualitative analysis and testing are presented in Appendix A.

GUEST SPOT   **Fixing the Biggest Blind Spot in Web Analytics: Phone Calls**

Irv Shapiro
Irv Shapiro is the CEO of DialogTech.

Let's talk about phone calls. In today's digital world, the roles that phone calls play in marketing and sales success have never been bigger. Inbound calls have reemerged as the most effective channel for generating high-quality leads and closing business.

Over 76 billion calls were made to businesses in the United States from search, social, and display advertising alone in 2014, and that number is expected to reach 162 billion by 2016, according to BIA/Kelsey. The surge in smartphone adoption and the continued growth in mobile advertising are partly responsible, driving a huge influx of sales calls into businesses. A 2013 study by Google found that 70% of mobile searchers call a business directly from search results. It makes sense: tapping a click-to-call link on your smartphone is much easier and more natural than trying to fill out a Web form on your device's tiny screen.

That same Google study also found that 61% say it's important that businesses give them a phone number to call, and 33% would be less likely to use and refer brands that don't. Consumers see phone numbers as a sign that a business is trustworthy.

The data on calls continues to mount. According to BIA/Kelsey, 66% of businesses consider inbound phone calls to be excellent leads, more than any other type. It makes sense, since inbound calls convert to revenue on average 10 to 15 times more frequently than Web leads. It's why marketers are spending $68 billion annually on ads to generate those sought-after inbound sales calls: Phone calls mean revenue.

The resurgence of the phone call is great news for marketers trying to drive quality leads to their sales teams, but it's also a problem if you are using GA to track engagement from your marketing. Let me explain.

"Help! I Don't See Phone Call Data in Google Analytics!"

For years marketers have been using GA to better understand activity on their website. In 2013, Google took their analytics platform to the next level with the release of Universal Analytics, which gives businesses the ability to view not just Web activity, but also data on offline interactions, mobile app traffic, and a wide range of custom dimensions and metrics—all in the same interface.

Being able to view online and offline data together can lead to truly amazing insights into how your online, mobile, and offline marketing channels generate leads and the path customers take in the buyer journey. But it only works if you are able to able to collect and pass that offline data to GA, and that's where the problems begin. GA can't collect data on phone calls by default, and if you aren't including call data in your marketing analytics, you could be missing one of the biggest drivers of quality leads, new business and revenue.

So how can you solve this problem? There is a technology called call tracking that can help. It eliminates the blind spot in Web analytics and conversion optimization by collecting detailed data on phone calls from your website and marketing campaigns and passing that data to GA. Taking advantage the GA Measurement Protocol discussed in Chapter 17, "Data Import and Measurement Protocol," call tracking technology can record data into GA for calls that occur on your website and even for marketing campaigns in which the target audience does not necessarily visit your website.

What Is Call Tracking?

Call tracking is a form of lead attribution and marketing analytics technology. Marketers use it to track inbound phone calls back to the specific marketing source that originated them and then follow those leads through the sales cycle to revenue.

Call tracking enables marketers to understand what marketing sources—including offline, online, and mobile ads, campaigns, keyword searches, Web pages, pieces of content, direct mail or email blasts, and social media sites—generate phone leads and revenue, and which don't. They can then use this data to make more intelligent decisions on everything from where and how to advertise, what content to create, what messaging resonates, and what search engine optimization (SEO) terms to target. Plus, the data enables marketers to more accurately prove to their executives (or to their clients, for agency marketers) how their work is driving leads and revenue.

continues

continued

How Does Call Tracking Work?

Call tracking technology works by giving you clean, trackable phone numbers (local, toll-free, or vanity) that you insert into your marketing material. When someone calls one of those numbers, call tracking knows exactly what source they're calling from and pins that source data with the lead information. If that lead goes on to become an opportunity or a customer, you can tie those events and revenue back to the original source, so you can understand and prove how your marketing is impacting lead generation and sales.

For offline advertising (sources like print ads, direct mail campaigns, TV or radio spots, billboards, or trade show materials), content marketing (eBooks, webinars, brochures, and videos) or email blasts, call tracking is a fairly basic concept. You simply:

1. Insert a trackable phone number obtained from the call tracking software into your marketing materials.
2. Attribute those numbers in the software to their respective source.
3. Tell the software where to route the call (more on those options later), and you're off. All calls will still come to you, and the callers won't know the difference, but you will be able to tie each call back to the specific source that originated it.
4. Use call tracking software to generate reports on the calls each source generates.

If you are using Google call extensions (the "Click" buttons that appear in your mobile paid search ads), you can also insert call tracking numbers in your ads to attribute calls from your call extensions back to the keyword search that generated them. Setting it up is either a manual, one-to-one process, or you can also use a call tracking provider (like DialogTech) to automate the entire process and save yourself a lot of time and effort.

DNI: Dynamic Number Insertion

For online and mobile sources such as search, social, or display ads where people visit your Web page first before calling, call tracking works a bit differently by using a technique called dynamic number insertion (DNI). DNI automatically displays a unique call tracking phone number (taken from a pool of numbers exclusive to your business) on your Web pages based on the visitor's specific referral source (site, keyword search, etc.). The visitor sees this special phone number the entire time they're on your site, and when they call you, the call tracking software will populate an event or custom metric into GA and thus tie that call to the proper referring source, including the specific keyword search they used to find you (if the visitor came from any paid search campaign or from an organic result on a search engine that shares that data).

Here's a summary of how DNI works:

1. First, you should include a phone number prominently on your Web pages for people to call.
2. You then add a small snippet of JavaScript code, provided by the call tracking software, to the page to enable the dynamic insertion over the phone number in HTML. JavaScript code can sometimes be inserted via a tag manager such Google Tag Manager, Ensighten, or Tealium with some call tracking providers (like DialogTech).
3. The code then automatically displays a unique phone number from a pool of numbers on your web pages for each visitor based on how they got there (i.e., Google or Bing keyword search, pay-per-click [PPC] ad, banner ad, referring website, social media post, etc.).
4. When the visitor calls the number, the phone lead is attributed in call tracking reports to the right referral source, including the exact keyword search.
5. After a certain period of time, the call tracking software returns that number to your pool so it can be assigned to another visitor. This way, you don't need (or have to pay for) thousands of unique numbers, making keyword-level call tracking both effective and affordable, even for big businesses and larger marketing agencies with hundreds of clients.

Integrating Call Tracking with Google Analytics

While not every call tracking technology integrates with GA, a few (like DialogTech) do, enabling you to add the critical phone data piece to Google's marketing analytics puzzle. By integrating your call tracking data with GA, you can view and analyze call data alongside Web traffic data to better understand how Web visitors and callers find your business and better measure campaign ROI.

GA users can view rich, context-specific call tracking data alongside your other online and offline marketing analytics, so you can get insight into things like:

➤ Which channels, ads, search keywords and marketing programs are driving Web visits and phone calls to your business.
➤ Which of your Web pages or videos visitors viewed before and after calling you.
➤ Which of your content they downloaded or items they purchased before and after calling you.
➤ Where people are calling from.

Figure 8.12 shows an example of a GA report. This is for a Pricing page. It shows all the traffic to that page for a given time frame, and what the users did next.

FIGURE 8.12 With the calls recorded in GA as events, the Behavior Flow report can indicate pages that were viewed (and other events that were generated) before and after the call.

continues

continued

Google Analytics Custom Reports with Call Tracking Data

As mentioned above, DNI normally integrates into GA by generating event hits or, in the case of DialogTech, a custom metric. Figures 8.13 and 8.14 are two custom reports that display our call metric by traffic source and by U.S. state.

This first report includes calls as a metric alongside website visits based on the channel that drove the website visit and call. It gives you a high-level understanding of which ones are driving the most overall engagement.

Default Channel Grouping	Sessions	DialogTech Calls	% New Sessions	New Users
	92,169 % of Total: 100.00% (92,169)	**5,711** % of Total: 100.00% (5,711)	**60.26%** Avg for View: 60.26% (0.00%)	**55,538** % of Total: 100.00% (55,538)
1. Direct	**32,975** (35.78%)	3,570 (62.51%)	51.65%	17,033 (30.67%)
2. Display	**27,971** (30.35%)	105 (1.84%)	66.64%	18,639 (33.56%)
3. Organic Search	**23,582** (25.59%)	443 (7.76%)	58.10%	13,702 (24.67%)
4. Referral	**3,885** (4.22%)	95 (1.66%)	72.28%	2,808 (5.06%)
5. Paid Search	**2,640** (2.86%)	722 (12.64%)	71.82%	1,896 (3.41%)
6. Social	**995** (1.08%)	14 (0.25%)	69.15%	688 (1.24%)
7. (Other)	**108** (0.12%)	724 (12.68%)	670.37%	724 (1.30%)
8. Email	**13** (0.01%)	38 (0.67%)	369.23%	48 (0.09%)

FIGURE 8.13 This custom report displays calls by Default Channel Grouping. You could create similar reports for calls by search engine or by new versus returning visitor.

Region	Campaign	Sessions	DialogTech Calls	% New Sessions	New Users
		3,255 % of Total: 3.53% (92,169)	**774** % of Total: 13.55% (5,711)	**59.82%** Avg for View: 60.26% (-0.73%)	**1,947** % of Total: 3.51% (55,538)
1. California	brand	**280** (8.60%)	4 (0.52%)	37.50%	105 (5.39%)
2. Texas	brand	**257** (7.90%)	2 (0.26%)	28.02%	72 (3.70%)
3. Illinois	brand	**240** (7.37%)	42 (5.43%)	51.67%	124 (6.37%)
4. Florida	brand	**182** (5.59%)	3 (0.39%)	37.36%	68 (3.49%)
5. North Carolina	brand	**167** (5.13%)	1 (0.13%)	19.76%	33 (1.69%)
6. New York	brand	**152** (4.67%)	2 (0.26%)	32.89%	50 (2.57%)

FIGURE 8.14 This custom Map Overlay report shows where website visitors and callers are located. This report is invaluable in helping you measure the success of your marketing at the local level. Understanding which geographies are driving the most calls can help you allocate budget to the right programs in the right areas.

What to Consider When Evaluating Call Tracking Technologies

Not all call tracking technologies are created equal. In order to select the right call tracking vendor, here are some questions to consider asking:

1. How Clean Are Your Call Tracking Numbers, Really?   Many call tracking vendors sell phone numbers that are "dirty," meaning they receive calls from past advertising campaigns with other businesses. If you use one of these dirty numbers to track marketing, it can ruin the validity of the data you pass to GA. Ask the call tracking vendor how they clean their numbers. Do they put their phone numbers through rigorous call cleansing processes before they give them to you, ensuring the accuracy of your data? If so, how?

2. Can Your Call Tracking Software Automatically Route Calls to the Right Call Center, Store, Dealer, or Agent?   Generating a higher volume of inbound calls is fantastic, but as a marketer, what you really want to do is drive opportunities and revenue. That means you need to be sure inbound calls are getting sent to the best call center, store, dealer or agent to convert them. Few call tracking vendors offer intelligent call routing options, so be sure to ask what they provide.

3. Will You Have the Proper Support to Help You Along the Way?   It's important to ask potential vendors what kind of support they offer, how much it costs, and if you are able to get them on the phone and get help when you need it. When working with a call tracking solution, proper implementation is key to getting the most value. This is true especially when you are tracking digital campaign sources like AdWords ads, as they can be complex and require specific expertise to configure. A vendor who has Google-certified call tracking specialists on staff and available to take your call will be a big benefit to you and to the overall value you receive from implementing call tracking.

4. Some Other Questions to Consider Asking Vendors
   - Can you track calls from Google call extensions at the keyword level?
   - Can I list more than one call tracking number on a single Web page for pages that list multiple business locations?
   - Do you offer "whisper" messages to announce how each caller found you to your agents before they accept the call?

Call Tracking and Google Analytics: A Match Made in Return on Investment (ROI) Heaven

GA is an amazing asset to marketers. Being able to view online and offline data together can lead to truly amazing insights into how your marketing is driving engagement, but only if you are able to able to collect and pass that offline call data to GA. By picking the right call tracking solution, you can reap the benefits of having complete, accurate call data in your GA reports. It really is a match made in ROI analytics heaven.

ECOMMERCE TRACKING

Goal tracking, while extremely useful, is not ideally suited for Ecommerce transactions that entail different products, quantities, and price points. To record the detail for these more varied types of transactions, Ecommerce tracking offers the needed flexibility.

We'll consider two types of Ecommerce tracking: basic Ecommerce, and Enhanced Ecommerce. As you might expect, Enhanced Ecommerce requires more setup than basic Ecommerce, but they both differ from goal tracking in this fundamental way:

you configure goals within the view admin screen and based on hits that are already captured as pageviews or events, while both types of Ecommerce tracking normally require you to work with your developers to push additional data into GA specifically about the Ecommerce transaction.

As a note, while Google Tag Manager (GTM) facilitates event tracking that might otherwise require code-level changes, GTM normally cannot help to automate Ecommerce tracking or avoid all code-level changes, since, in most implementations, you still need to populate Ecommerce-specific variables from the back end into the data layer as discussed below.

Configuring Basic Ecommerce Tracking

Setup for basic Ecommerce requires three steps:

1. Work with your developers to populate the data layer with Ecommerce transaction and product variables, normally on the purchase confirmation page.
2. In GTM, create a GA transaction tag and a corresponding trigger.
3. Enable Ecommerce Tracking in one or more views.

Each of these steps is detailed below.

Populate the Data Layer with Ecommerce Variables

This step represents most of the work in Ecommerce configuration. You'll need to work with your developers to populate your transaction confirmation page with specific back-end data for the transaction and one or more specific products.

You can use five variables for the transaction data:

- `transactionId` (required)
- `transactionTotal` (required)
- `transactionProducts` (optional, but used routinely)
- `transactionShipping` (optional)
- `transactionTax` (optional)

As noted above, `transactionProducts` is optional but is usually populated. Unlike the other transaction variables, which require a single value, `transactionProducts` requires one or more product objects that can take the following variables:

- `name` (required)
- `sku` (required)
- `price` (required)
- `quantity` (required)
- `category` (optional)

You could populate the data layer as in Listing 8.1. Note that the listing displays the output of server-side coding; you can work with your developers to actually pull the Ecommerce values from the back end and format as demonstrated.

LISTING 8.1: Populating the data layer with Ecommerce variables.

```
dataLayer = window.dataLayer
|| []; //this is the data layer initializer
dataLayer.push({
    'transactionId': '12345678',
    'transactionAffiliation': 'Natural Hair Care',
    'transactionTotal': 43.24,
    'transactionTax': 3.29,
    'transactionShipping': 7.98,
    'transactionProducts': [{
        'sku': '486GOU',
        'name': 'Aloe Wash',
        'category': 'Soap',
        'price': 11.99,
        'quantity': 1
    },{
        'sku': '574PRV',
        'name': 'Coconut Shell Scalp Scrub',
        'category': 'Shampoo',
        'price': 9.99,
        'quantity': 2
    }]
});
```

Note

Using Ecommerce Tracking for Detailed, Nonmonetized Conversions

Despite its name, you can use the GA Ecommerce (and even Enhanced Ecommerce) features to track nonmonetized conversions that are too detailed for goal tracking. A U.S. government agency has implemented GA Ecommerce to track orders of print publications, taking advantage of product variables such as name, quantity, and category, while providing stand-in values for the required price variable.

Create a Transaction Tag in GTM

In Chapter 4, "Account Creation and Tracking Code Installation," we discussed the concept of a hit as basically a packet of dimension values sent to GA. The primary hit types that we have examined thus far are pageviews and events, and we also discussed social hits in Chapter 6. We now get to work with another kind of GA hit: Ecommerce transaction.

To generate a transaction hit through GTM:

1. Create a GA tag.
2. Set the Tracking ID to the same value that we're using for pageviews and events (ideally by using the GA Tracking ID variable that we first created in Figure 5.5).
3. Set the Track Type to Transaction as shown in Figure 8.15.

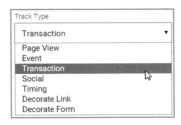

FIGURE 8.15 A GA tag with Track Type set to Transaction automatically reads Ecommerce variables that you have populated into the data layer.

You do not need to create GTM Data Layer variables: a GA tag with Track Type set to Transaction will automatically read in the Ecommerce variables named in the data layer as indicated above.

Populate the Data Layer Before the Transaction Tag Fires

To make sure that the Ecommerce variables are populated into the data layer as shown in Listing 8.1 when the GA Transaction tag fires, we can take either of the two following options:

- Populate the data layer with Ecommerce variables before the GTM container code occurs in the page; in this case, you could apply a basic Page View trigger to the Transaction tag, for example, {{*Page Path*}} *equals /receipt*
- Apply a DOM Ready trigger (first discussed in Chapter 5) to the GA Transaction tag so the page has been fully parsed when the tag looks for the Ecommerce variables in the data layer; an example trigger would be *Page View – DOM Ready – {{Page Path}} equals /receipt*

Reusing Existing Ecommerce Variables

If the variables that you need for GA Ecommerce tracking are already present on the page as different variable names, or if your environment blocks the dataLayer object, you can instead use an Enhanced Ecommerce purchase action with a Custom JavaScript variable (instead of using a GA Transaction tag). See *Reading Enhanced Ecommerce Data from Your Own Object Variable* below.

Enable Ecommerce Setting

As the final (and certainly the easiest) step for Ecommerce configuration, turn on the Enable Ecommerce toggle in the Ecommerce Settings for one or more views within the property for which you have performed the two previous steps.

Ecommerce Reporting

The variables listed above that you populate in Ecommerce tracking become available as dimensions and metrics within the several built-in Ecommerce reports that GA provides. Some of the metrics in the Ecommerce Overview report shown in Figure 8.16 require explanation.

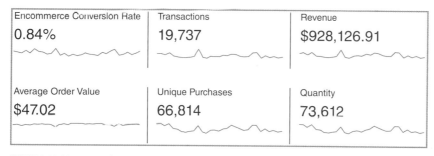

FIGURE 8.16   Metrics in the Ecommerce Overview report.

If you went to a hiking website that had GA Ecommerce enabled and you purchased one pair of hiking boots and two pairs of the same hiking socks, Transactions would increment by one, Unique Purchases would increment by two (two products included at least one time in the transaction), and Quantity would increment by three (three product units total in the transaction).

Similarly to goal conversions, a visitor can *convert* for Ecommerce one time only in a given session, meaning that Ecommerce Conversion Rate only considers if there is at least one Ecommerce transaction in the session. Additional transactions in the same session would not increase Ecommerce Conversion Rate but would increase other Ecommerce metrics (such as Revenue). In this way, GA recognizes a *conversion* for a given goal or for Ecommerce once per session only, but it will record multiple Ecommerce *transactions*.

Transactions with the same Transaction ID within the same session, however, are not double counted; to record additional transactions within a session, you must make sure to use different Transaction IDs.

In the Product Performance report, you can switch the primary dimension to view metrics by Product, Product SKU, or (if populated) Product Category. The Sales Performance and Transactions reports break down the metrics by date and transaction ID, respectively.

The Ecommerce Time to Purchase report shows the time lapse between the last non-direct session and the purchase. For further lookback, see the Time Lag report shown later in Figure 8.41.

Terminology

Value and Revenue Terminology

GA displays several metrics related to goal value and Ecommerce revenue:

Goal Value. The static monetary value per goal that we optionally specify in the goal configuration. The corresponding Goal Value metric in the reports corresponds to all goals in a view, whereas Goal 1 Value corresponds only to that goal.

Revenue. The monetary value of Ecommerce transactions.

Product Revenue. The Revenue metric minus tax and shipping.

Per Session Value. Average Revenue per session; this does not appear as Per-Session *Revenue*.

Average Order Value. Revenue per Ecommerce transaction.

Per Session Goal Value. Average Goal Value (for all goals in the view) per session.

Page Value. As discussed below, the total Revenue and Goal Value accrued after a given page was viewed at least once, divided by the number of unique pageviews for the page.

There are also several value-related terms in the AdWords reports, as discussed in Chapter 7, "Acquisition Reports."

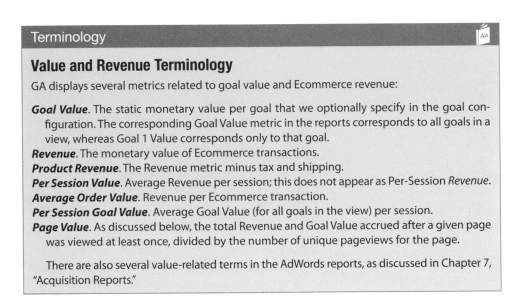

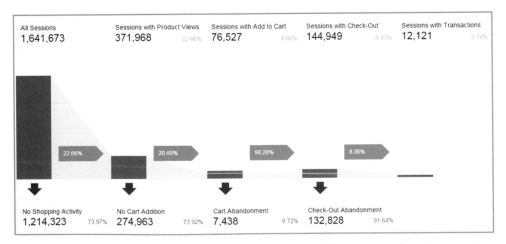

FIGURE 8.17 The Shopping Behavior report shows progress and drop-off from site entry through transaction.

Enhanced Ecommerce

While basic Ecommerce tracking provides much greater detail than goal tracking, it only measures the transaction itself. It still doesn't track the several steps that usually must precede an Ecommerce transaction: essentially, the Ecommerce funnel.

You can implement GA Enhanced Ecommerce tracking to populate a range of additional Ecommerce reports and metrics in GA; let's review the reports and metrics before examining the corresponding code requirements.

- **Shopping Behavior**: displays a five-stage funnel from session start to purchase (Figure 8.17).
- **Checkout Behavior**: displays up to eight funnel steps corresponding to the checkout process (Figure 8.18).
- **Product Performance**: to this report, Enhanced Ecommerce adds the Cart-to-Detail Rate and the Buy-to-Detail Rate as performance metrics after visitors have viewed a product details page (Figure 8.19).
- **Product List Performance**: shows performance from Impression through revenue by product, product list, and product list position (Figure 8.20).
- **Internal Promotion**: shows clicks and views for internal promotions (such as a banner) and performance metrics following the click (Figure 8.21).
- **Order Coupon, Product Coupon**: transactions by order-based coupons (e.g., 20% off your order) and product-based coupons (e.g., 20% off a specific item) submitted during checkout.
- **Affiliate Code**: revenue, transactions, and average order value for clickthroughs from affiliate programs.

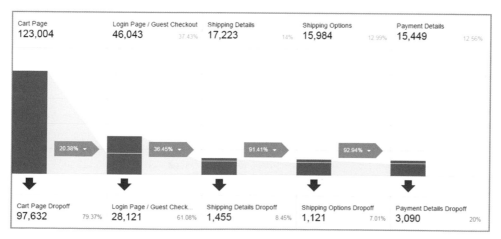

FIGURE 8.18 You can configure the Checkout Behavior report to display the specific steps within checkout.

Product ?	Shopping Behavior	
	Cart-to-Detail Rate ?	Buy-to-Detail Rate ?
	2.22% Avg for View: 2.22% (0.00%)	**0.91%** Avg for View: <0.91% (0.00%)
1. Sony Xperia Z3+ (Dual), 4G LTE, 32 GB, Black	6.87%	1.46%
2. Samsung Galaxy S6 Edge, 4G LTE, 64 GB, White	2.00%	0.36%
3. Apple iPhone 6 Plus, 4G LTE, 64 GB, Gold	0.01%	0.04%

FIGURE 8.19 With Enhanced Ecommerce implemented, the Product Performance report lists the Cart-to-Detail and Buy-to-Detail.

Product List Name ?	Product List Views ? ↓	Product List Clicks ?	Product List CTR ?	Product Adds To Cart ?	Product Checkouts ?	Unique Purchases ?	Product Revenue
	31,870,969 % of Total: 100.00% (31,870,969)	**677,173** % of Total: 100.00% (677,173)	**2.12%** Avg for View: 2.12% (0.00%)	**931** % of Total: 100.00% (931)	**1,068** % of Total: 100.00% (1,068)	**226** % of Total: 100.00% (226)	**$310.897** % of Total ($310.897)
1. Phones	**12,696,372** (39.84%)	180,636 (26.68%)	1.42%	764 (82.06%)	799 (74.81%)	119 (52.65%)	$109,373
2. Cases	**4,850,497** (15.22%)	98,874 (14.60%)	2.04%	102 (13.35%)	110 (10.30%)	41 (18.14%)	$10,390
3. Headsets	**2,348,651** (7.37%)	44,409 (6.56%)	1.89%	51 (5.48%)	60 (5.61%)	29 (12.83%)	$9,443

FIGURE 8.20 Product List report displays performance in terms of views, clicks, purchases and other metrics, broken down by the list parameters that you provide in the Enhanced Ecommerce code.

Internal Promotion Name ?	Shopping Behavior			Conversions eCommerce ▾		Transactions Per Internal Promotion Click ?
	Internal Promotion Views ↓ ?	Internal Promotion Clicks ?	Internal Promotion CTR ?	Transactions ?	Revenue ?	
	1,593,590 % of Total: 100.00% (1,593,590)	**47,953** % of Total: 100.00% (47,953)	**3.01%** Avg for View: 3.01% (0.00%)	**519** % of Total: 100.00% (519)	**$13,557.46** % of Total: 100.00% ($13,557.46)	**1.08%** % of Total: 100.00% (1.08%)
1. 10% off	**369,895** (23.21%)	7.639 (15.93%)	2.07%	55 (10.60%)	$1,630.64 (12.03%)	0.72% (66.52%)
2. free upgrade	**239,355** (15.02%)	9,467 (19.74%)	3.96%	138 (26.59%)	$3,250.85 (23.98%)	1.46%(134.68%)
3. one-day-only sale	**219,885** (13.80%)	6,103 (12.73%)	2.78%	89 (17.15%)	$2,477.83 (18.28%)	1.46%(134.74%)

FIGURE 8.21 Internal Promotion Report shows click and purchase metrics for internal promotional banners and text links.

Implementing Enhanced Ecommerce Tracking

Enhanced Ecommerce implementation is similar to basic Ecommerce in that you typically populate the data layer with back-end data that a GA tag in GTM will read in and record. If you currently track basic Ecommerce, you'll be able to migrate to Enhanced Ecommerce without losing the Ecommerce data that you've already captured.

As we'll soon see, somewhat surprisingly, you don't implement Enhanced Ecommerce using a GA tag with Track Type set to Transaction. Instead, the Enhanced Ecommerce variables are read from the data layer by a Page View or Event tag that you have enabled for Enhanced Ecommerce.

As we saw in the preceding section, basic Ecommerce implementation is more difficult than goal configuration since it normally requires your developers to populate the GTM data layer with additional data from the back end. Enhanced Ecommerce, for its part, is significantly more complex than basic Ecommerce and is undoubtedly the most challenging code-level aspect of GA implementation.

To make this topic more approachable, we review a high-level outline as well as specific code examples. For reference, we'll be using the very helpful and interactive Google Analytics "Enhanced Ecommerce" demo at `https://ga-dev-tools.appspot.com/enhanced-ecommerce/`. Please be sure to access this demo directly as we proceed through the examples.

Also refer to the Google Tag Manager "Enhanced Ecommerce (UA) Developer Guide " at `https://developers.google.com/tag-manager/enhanced-ecommerce` for additional detail on the Enhanced Ecommerce data objects.

What Data Do You Track for Enhanced Ecommerce?

From an implementation standpoint, we can consider Enhanced Ecommerce as tracking four types of occurrences:

- **Product Impressions:** the user was exposed to a product listing without accessing information about that product specifically. (If the user does click through to a product page, you'd capture product click and product detail actions separately from the impression, as discussed below.) You often record several product impressions (for all products on a page or screen) as an array at one time.
- **Product Actions:** for the many types of actions that the user can perform on a product or an array of products, you specify the following elements:
  Action—specific action that the user takes or experiences. Actions include:
  - Click
  - Detail
  - Add (to cart)
  - Remove (from cart)
  - Checkout
  - Checkout_option (discussed below)
  - Purchase
  - Refund

  ActionField—additional data that you can embed in some types of actions, such as checkout step for a checkout action or tax and shipping for a purchase action.

Products—the one or more products that the action applies to. For instance, you'd normally apply an add (to cart) action to a single product only but a checkout action to an array of all products in the shopping cart.

CurrencyCode—optional field to designate a currency from which the Ecommerce needs to be converted to match the currency setting in your GA view; especially useful if you process transactions in multiple currencies.

- **Promotion Impressions:** you can capture promotion impressions to which the user was exposed.
- **Promotion Clicks:** you can also capture clickthroughs on a promotion impression.

The sections below detail the tracking for these occurrences. Keep in mind that you are not required to implement all aspects of Enhanced Ecommerce at one time. You could start, for example, by tracking only product detail pageviews, adds to cart, and purchases, and later add impressions, promotions, and checkout steps. That said, it's advisable right from the start, while you're making the effort, to + implement tracking that will provide an actionable level of data for your Ecommerce analysis.

Note

Currency Conversion

As mentioned above, if you specify a currency code in your Enhanced Ecommerce data, GA will convert—based on active exchange rates—to the currency specified in your GA view.

It is helpful that we can avoid performing our own conversion, but, as Brian Clifton argues in "*A* Flawed Feature—The New Multi-Currency Support in Google Analytics," you may instead want to consider applying a static conversion rate on your own so your Ecommerce performance indicators are not subject to the vagaries of currency exchange rates. Please see the blog post at `https://brianclifton.com/blog/2013/02/15/multi-currency-support-in-google-analytics-a-flawed-feature/` for the full discussion.

Pageview or Event Tag for Enhanced Ecommerce

As demonstrated in Figure 8.15, we set the Track Type in the GA tag for basic Ecommerce tracking to Transaction; for basic Ecommerce, it's the Transaction tag that reads the Ecommerce data from the data layer and sends it to GA. As mentioned previously, however, you use a GA tag with Track Type set to either Page View (or App View in mobile app tracking) or Event to pass Enhanced Ecommerce data.

So which do you choose, pageview or event? In most cases, that depends on whether the user executed a specific step or if the user was just exposed to the product or promotion as part of the page (or screen) load.

You'd normally track product impressions and promotion impressions in a pageview tag. You'd also normally track a product *detail* action in a pageview tag. You can also use a pageview tag for product *add* to cart, *remove* from cart, *checkout*, and *purchase* if these occur on separate pages.

Figure 8.22 shows a Page View tag enabled to read Enhanced Ecommerce variables from the data layer.

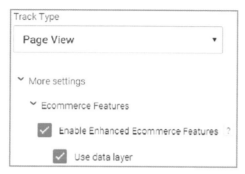

FIGURE 8.22 You can enable a Page View tag, as shown in this figure, or an Event tag to read Enhanced Ecommerce variables from the data layer.

Occurrences to Track with an Event Tag

If any of the actions mentioned previously occur on the original page without a new page load—common in AJAX-based checkout scenarios as demonstrated in Figure 6.26—you can track them instead with events.

You can also use an event tag instead of a pageview tag for product or promotion impressions that are not initially rendered on the page but are instead generated through additional user interaction—typically scrolling.

You'd normally track product actions that don't coincide with a pageview, and also promotion clicks, in an event tag.

Product and Promotion Impressions

As you use the Google Analytics Ecommerce demo, you can click the icons to view the code that executes on pageview or click and populates the data layer with Enhanced Ecommerce variables, as illustrated in Figure 8.23.

In Listing 8.2, we see that multiple product impressions (just two shown in the listing for brevity) and also the Back to School promo impression are pushed to the data layer. Since these impressions occur as soon as the page loads, and without further interaction on the part of the user, you can enable the GA pageview tag in GTM to read in this Enhanced Ecommerce data from the data layer. You should place the code in Listing 8.2 before the GTM container code (or set the pageview tag to fire on DOM ready instead of the default page load).

FIGURE 8.23 You can enable a Page View tag, as shown in this figure, or an Event tag to read Enhanced Ecommerce variables from the data layer.

LISTING 8.2: Populating the data layer with product and promotion impressions.

```
dataLayer = window.dataLayer
|| []; //initializer not shown in online example
dataLayer.push({
  "ecommerce": {
    "currencyCode": "USD",
    "impressions": [{
      "id": "9bdd2",
      "name": "Compton T-Shirt",
      "price": "44.00",
      "brand": "Compton",
      "category": "T-Shirts",
```

```
        "position": 0,
        "list": "homepage"
      },
      {
        "id": "6d9b0",
        "name": "Poyo T-Shirt",
        "price": "62.00",
        "brand": "Poyo",
        "category": "T-Shirts",
        "position": 3,
        "list": "shirts you may like"
    }], //see full product array in online demo
    "promoView": {
      "promotions": [{
        "id": "bts",
        "name": "Back To School",
        "creative": "HOME banner",
        "position": "right sidebar"
      }]
    }
  }
});
```

Note

Flushing the Data Layer

To prevent resending any Enhanced Ecommerce data that remains in the data layer from a previous interaction (e.g., product impression data populated on page load when you're now sending promo click data), you must flush the data layer after sending each Enhanced Ecommerce payload. For options on data layer flushing, see: www.e-nor.com/gabook.

Product Click

Listing 8.3 shows the code that is executed when a shirt is clicked. Note that it populates an optional *list* field.

Also note that the *event* field in the second line of the listing corresponds to a Custom Event trigger that you can apply to any tag, as first demonstrated in Figure 6.16. In this example, there would be a Custom Event trigger listening for "event": "productClick" in the data layer, at which point it would fire a GA event tag to which that trigger was applied that was enabled to read Enhanced Ecommerce data from the data layer.

Instead of setting up a new tag and trigger in GTM for each type of click action as in the online demo, we could reuse the "catch-all" event tag, data layer variables, and trigger that we implemented as demonstrated in Figures 6.32, 6.33, and 6.34. To take advantage of this existing infrastructure, replace "event": "productClick", with:

```
"event": "eventTracker", "eventCat": "ecommerce", "eventAct": "click",
"eventLbl": "product",
```

Note that the specific event category, action, and label values aren't that critical in themselves; we're just using the event tag to convey the Enhanced Ecommerce data, which will be the focus of our analysis rather than the event data.

LISTING 8.3: Populating the data layer with Ecommerce product click data, as well as the designated *event* variable that can fire a Custom Event trigger.

```
dataLayer.push({
  "event": "productClick",
  "ecommerce": {
    "click": {
      "actionField": {
        "list": "homepage"
      },
      "products": [{
        "id": "f6be8",
        "name": "Comverges T-Shirt",
        "price": "33.00",
        "brand": "Comverges",
        "category": "T-Shirts",
        "position": "2"
      }]
    }
  }
});
```

Promotion Click

If we click the small icon for the Back to School banner, we see the code in Listing 8.4. As in Listing 8.3, we can replace `"event": "promotionClick"` with four data layer variables that our existing catch-all event tag will use.

LISTING 8.4: Populating the data layer with Ecommerce promotion click data.

```
dataLayer.push({
  "event": "promotionClick",
  "ecommerce": {
    "promoClick": {
      "promotions": [{
        "id": "bts",
        "name": "Back To School",
        "creative": "HOME banner",
        "position": "right sidebar"
      }]
    }
  }
});
```

Note that the Enhanced Ecommerce promotion impressions and promotion clicks provide a safe way to track internal campaigns. In Chapter 7, we warned against campaign parameters for internal campaigns because they spawn a new session and break the attribution of subsequent actions to the rightful traffic source, so make sure to squelch any temptation to use campaign parameters in parallel with Enhanced Ecommerce promotions.

Product Detail

When the product detail page pictured in Figure 8.24 loads, the GA pageview tag will read the product detail, product impression (for the shirts listed on the bottom), and promotion impression data that we wrote to the data layer.

Product click and product detail may seem redundant, since one should lead to the other, but product click actions are used specifically to calculate the Product List Clicks metric that appears in the Product List report.

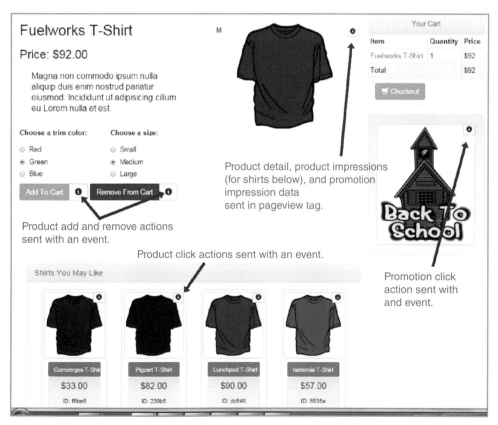

FIGURE 8.24 Product detail, product impression, and promotion impression data is recorded when this product description page loads.

Add and Remove (To and From Cart)

The code that is populating the add-to-cart action for the main shirt on the page appears in Listing 8.5. Note that the code for the remove action is identical, except *add* is replaced with *remove*. There is no reference maintained for the product that was previously added to the cart, so we must again specify all the product fields.

Also note that `"event": "addToCart"` and `"event": "removeFromCart"` differ in the online demo, but, again, the *event* variable in the data layer is just used to trigger a GTM tag, and we could instead push the four values used in our event catch-all tag, as in previous examples.

LISTING 8.5: Populating the data layer with add (to cart) action.

```
dataLayer.push({
  "event": "addToCart",
  "ecommerce": {
    "currencyCode": "USD",
    "add": {
      "products": [{
        "id": "bc823",
        "name": "Fuelworks T-Shirt",
        "price": "92.00",
        "brand": "Fuelworks",
        "category": "T-Shirts",
        "variant": "green",
        "dimension1": "M",
        "position": 0,
        "quantity": 1
      }]
    }
  }
});
```

Note

Custom Dimensions and Custom Metrics for Ecommerce Products

In Chapter 12, we'll learn how to record our own dimensions and metrics to capture data that GA would not record as a built-in dimension or metric. In Enhanced Ecommerce, we can create custom dimensions and metrics at product scope, for example, the *M* custom dimension value for men's clothing in Listing 8.4. We could also create a custom metric to capture a discount, surcharge, or extra tax for a product. Custom dimensions and metrics do not appear in any of the built-in reports, but you can use them in custom reports, which we discuss in Chapter 11.

You only have to record custom dimensions or metrics once per product within an Enhanced Ecommerce transaction, but it's not harmful to record them with multiple actions as is done in the Enhanced Ecommerce demo that we're exploring online.

Checkout Steps

We need to discuss checkout action somewhat separately from the other Enhanced Ecommerce actions because we're going to configure and populate multiple checkout steps that will appear in the Checkout Behavior funnel.

Let's first complete the required admin configuration. (As a note, even if we are not populating the Checkout Behavior funnel, we need to enable the Enhanced Ecommerce toggle as shown in Figure 8.25.)

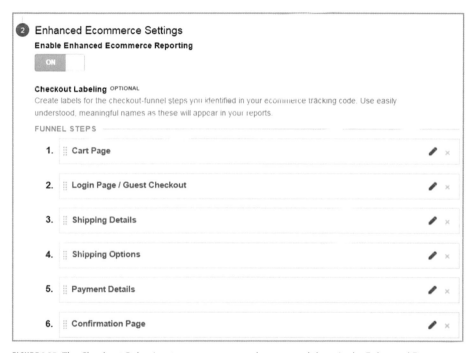

FIGURE 8.25 The Checkout Behavior steps appear as you have named them in the Enhanced Ecommerce Settings.

If we do want to populate the Checkout Behavior funnel, we must begin by adding the steps: note the correspondence with the names of the checkout steps in Figure 8.18. For the Ecommerce Demo, we would instead name steps that correspond to each of the tabs that represent different checkout steps. In this way, we can configure Checkout Behavior report to match our checkout steps as they occur in our own checkout process.

With our checkout steps set up, we can begin receiving checkout data, as shown in Listing 8.6 for the Shipping tab of the online demo. Note that for each of our checkout steps and our purchase action, we'd include all products in the cart. (We have only one product in the cart for our example.)

LISTING 8.6: Populating the data layer with the checkout action and checkout step 2 specified in the actionField.

```
dataLayer.push({
   "event": "checkout",
   "ecommerce": {
     "checkout": {
       "actionField": {
         "step": 2
       },
       "products": [{
         "id": "bc823",
         "name": "Fuelworks T-Shirt",
         "price": "92.00",
         "brand": "Fuelworks",
         "category": "T-Shirts",
         "variant": "red",
         "dimension1": "M",
         "position": 0,
         "quantity": 1
       }]
     }
   }
});
```

Checkout Options

You can record additional user input in the checkout process, such as the credit card selection that appears in Figure 8.26. As indicated in Listing 8.7, we don't need to include product information with a checkout_option action; we just need to associate it with a checkout action for which you have specified the same step number: step 3, in the example.

Because the checkout_option check step corresponds to a checkout step that you've already recorded, you typically record a check_option in a separate GA event or potentially at the time that the following checkout step is recorded. (In this way, you'd record checkout_option for step 2 at the same time as checkout step 3.)

FIGURE 8.26 You can capture selections in the checkout process such as credit card as Enhanced Ecommerce checkout options.

LISTING 8.7: Populating a checkout option.

```
dataLayer.push({
  "event": "checkoutOption",
  "ecommerce": {
    "checkout_option": {
      "actionField": {
        "step": 3,
        "option": "Mastercard"
      }
    }
  }
});
```

Purchase

The purchase action is similar to the checkout action in that you apply it to all products that are in the cart. You use the actionField to specify additional detail about the purchase.

Coupon

When recording a purchase, you have the option of applying a coupon value at the transaction or product level, both shown in Listing 8.8.

LISTING 8.8: Purchase data, with optional coupon details, populated into the data layer.

```
dataLayer.push({
  "event": "transaction",
  "ecommerce": {
    "purchase": {
      "actionField": {
        "id": "6172c619-a62f-40c0-bba8-aeff7f7a6c54",
        "affiliation": "Online Store",
        "revenue": 102,
        "tax": 5,
        "shipping": 5,
        "coupon": "SummerSale"
      },
      "products": [{
        "id": "bc823",
        "name": "Fuelworks T-Shirt",
        "price": "92.00",
        "brand": "Fuelworks",
        "category": "T-Shirts",
```

```
            "variant": "red",
            "dimension1": "M",
            "position": 0,
            "quantity": 1
            "coupon": "RedShirtPromo"
        }]
    }
  }
});
```

Record Confirmation Step with Purchase

Don't forget to record a confirmation step as the last step of your checkout process (so it appears in the Checkout Analysis report). You can send a confirmation checkout step along with your purchase when your thank-you page loads.

The online demo takes a different approach: it records the purchase when the user clicks the Purchase button on the Review Cart tab and then records the confirmation checkout step by itself when the Confirmation tab loads. Either approach is good, but there's a slight risk with the latter of recording a few Purchase clicks as purchases even when the purchase does not complete because of a credit card decline, etc. (To mitigate this risk, you can select the Check Validation option in a Form or Click - Just Links trigger in GTM—this will block the trigger from firing if the form submit or link click returns false.)

Reading Enhanced Ecommerce Data from Your Own Object Variable

If your Ecommerce data is already present on the page, or if for any reason you cannot use the data layer object, Figure 8.27 demonstrates a Custom JavaScript variable that you can set up to populate a JavaScript object with the same name/value pairs that you would otherwise populate into the data layer. Figure 8.28 illustrates a Page View or Event tag that uses the Custom JavaScript variable instead of the data layer to read Enhanced Ecommerce data.

As a related note mentioned in Chapter 6, you can rename the two instances of `dataLayer` in the GTM container code if this variable name is already in use for another purpose. If, for example, you changed the name in the container snippet to `gtmDataLayer`, you'd use that variable name to populate the GTM data layer for Enhanced Ecommerce and so forth.

```
ecommerceData ✎

✓  Choose Type

   ┌─────────────────────────┐
   │  Custom JavaScript      │
   └─────────────────────────┘

2  Configure Variable

   Custom JavaScript  ?

    1  function() {
    2    var ecommerceData = {
    3      "ecommerce": {
    4        "currencyCode": existingCurrencyCode,
    5        "add": {
    6          "products": [{
    7            "id": existingId,
    8            "name": existingName,
    9            "price": existingPrice,
   10            "brand": existingBrand,
   11            "category": existingCategory,
   12            "variant": existingVariant,
   13            "dimension1": existingCustomDimension,
   14            "position": existingPosition,
   15            "quantity": existingQuantity
   16          }]
   17        }
   18      }
   19
   20    };
   21    return ecommerceData;
   22  }
```

FIGURE 8.27 This custom JavaScript variable rewrites existing Ecommerce data from the page into the format that GTM can consume.

```
˅ Ecommerce Features

    ✓  Enable Enhanced Ecommerce Features  ?

    ☐  Use data layer


    Read data from variable
    ┌──────────────────────────────────────┐
    │  {{ecommerceData}}                  ▾ │
    └──────────────────────────────────────┘
```

FIGURE 8.28 We can configure a Page View or Event tag to read Enhanced Ecommerce data from a Custom JavaScript variable instead of from the data layer.

Enhanced Ecommerce in Testing and Live Environments

In Chapter 5, we learned about the Environments feature in GTM that allows you to publish a single container into development, staging, and live environments.

Because Enhanced Ecommerce (as well as basic Ecommerce) relies both on code-level changes within the page and on tag changes within the container, you'll need to coordinate your development-to-testing and especially your testing-to-live updates so you're pushing code at the same time as you're publishing to the Live environment in GTM.

As detailed in the Chapter 5 discussion, you can use a GTM Custom JavaScript or Lookup Table variable to dynamically track your Enhanced Ecommerce transactions to a dedicated development and/or test GA property from a development/test hostname (e.g., test.mysite.com) and to your main/live GA property from your live hostname.

Ecommerce and Enhanced Ecommerce Tracking in Mobile Apps

As, we'll learn in Chapter 13, the two basic GA tracking options for mobile apps are the GA SDK or the GTM SDK (either for iOS or Android in both cases). If you're using a GTM SDK, the process is similar to Ecommerce or Enhanced Ecommerce tracking for a website as detailed above.

For basic Ecommerce tracking through GTM:

1. Use a GA tag with Track Type set to Transaction.
2. Populate the data layer with the designated Ecommerce variables.

For Enhanced Ecommerce tracking through GTM:

1. Use one or more tags with Track Type set to App View (meaning screen view) or Event.
2. Select the Enable Enhanced Ecommerce Features setting and Use Data Layer settings, as shown previously in Figure 8.22.
3. Populate the data layer with the designated Ecommerce variables.

For code examples, see:

- Google Tag Manager for Android—Enhanced Ecommerce (`https://developers.google.com/tag-manager/android/v4/enhanced-ecommerce`)
- Google Tag Manager for iOS—Enhanced Ecommerce (`https://developers.google.com/tag-manager/ios/v3/enhanced-ecommerce`)

For Ecommerce and Enhanced Ecommerce tracking through the GA SDKs, see:

- Enhanced Ecommerce Tracking—Android SDKv4 (`https://developers.google.com/analytics/devguides/collection/android/v4/enhanced-ecommerce`)
- Enhanced Ecommerce Tracking—iOS SDK (`https://developers.google.com/analytics/devguides/collection/ios/v3/enhanced-ecommerce`)

This documentation is current at the time of writing; you can check for any updates. You can use the demonstrated syntax to write to the data layer for basic or Enhanced Ecommerce tracking.

If you're using the third-party cart for in-app purchases, ask your provider the questions listed in Integrating with "Third-Party Shopping Carts" below.

GUEST SPOT **The Last Concession: Advanced Technique for Tracking Build & Price Leads with Google Analytics Enhanced Ecommerce**

Stéphane Hamel

Stéphane Hamel is a distinguished thought leader in the field of digital analytics.

Some time ago, after implementing analytics on a complex build-and-price workflow for an automotive website (navigation shown in Figure 8.29), I was tasked with analysis. The workflow involved typical model selection/transmission/colors/accessories/extended warranty, and ultimately enticed the visitor to stay in touch by getting some financing, finding a dealer, printing a nice personalized brochure, or saving their dream car configuration for later.

FIGURE 8.29 Which are the last accessories that car purchasers sacrifice?

While digging into the data, I had one of those "aha!" moments.

Think of the above scenario—what is your behavior? If you are like me and most people I have watched using this type of tool over the years, you start with your dream car and quickly realize you will have to make some concessions.

Analyzing what gets added and removed from a build and price tool can be very time consuming and complex, and can lead to analysis paralysis. However, the last item, option, or feature the user conceded is worth a lot of money! If you can uncover a pattern based on this information, you'll know exactly how to subtly tap into a new segment of previously hidden opportunities—and ultimately grow revenue.

At the aggregate level, this gained knowledge can inform new marketing campaigns and promotions. At the individual level, this invaluable piece of information can be leveraged to know exactly what to upsell to the client! Note that this technique isn't against GA's Personally Identifiable Information restriction. The only thing we're adding is a fake product to the enhanced Ecommerce purchase. The one-to-one tie-in with a specific prospect/client happens in whichever sales or CRM system the organization is using on the back end.

Build and price tools aren't limited to automotive websites. Think of vacation packages, computers, phone and cable services, and more.

continues

continued

Solution

The concept builds upon the Enhanced Ecommerce tracking presented in this chapter, except that instead of actual orders, we track "leads." The main differences are:

➤ Track add/remove from cart for each option, feature, or item.

➤ Persist the information about the last item removed from the cart—you can use a cookie or HTML5 localStorage to do that. You might also want to keep this item in a custom dimension, and its value in a custom metric, both with a session scope—see the Conceded Accessory dimension and the Conceded Value metric in Figure 8.32.

➤ When the user converts (the Enhanced Ecommerce *purchase* action), you will also include a very special product to your purchase: the last concession item you kept in your back pocket! You will change two things: the price will be 0, and the Enhanced Ecommerce variant will be *concession*.

Caveat

Lead tracking: anytime you look at Ecommerce reports, you will have to remember those are not actual sales! You have a couple of options here:

➤ **Configuration value.** If you are OK seeing the extra Ecommerce revenue reported (which, for a car manufacturer website, would tally several millions of dollars!), leave it as is.

➤ **Lead value.** If you consider a lead is worth $100, use this as the purchase value of the main item, and set all other items to be free. Also set a custom metric for each item with their actual value.

➤ **Fractional value.** If you consider a configuration is worth something but the exact value depends on the selected options, use 1/10 or even 1/100 of each cart item value.

Analysis

You now have detailed data about the build-and-price flow and selected configurations in your Ecommerce reports. Following are some examples of the analysis you can perform.

Most Conceded Items

Under the Product Performance report, you will be able to view which configuration items are most popular (regardless of package). By adding a secondary dimension for Product Variant, as in Figure 8.30, you will see how many times a specific item was conceded. The next step is to understand *why*: Why is this popular item not making the cut? Is it too expensive? Not compatible with another item? Replaced with a lower-cost item?

Lost Opportunity/Share of Wallet

What's the value of items being abandoned? How much more money could you make if those items were included? If you had to discount those items, what would be the tipping point where the customer would keep it in the build?

Product	Product Variant	Sales Performance			
		Product Revenue ↓	Unique Purchases	Quantity	Average Price
		$751,546.08 % of Total: 100.00% ($751,546.08)	26,551 % of Total: 100.00% (26,551)	26,551 % of Total: 100.00% (26,551)	$28.31 Avg for View: $28.31 (0.00%)
1. Door Edge Guards	concession	$43,428.60 (5.78%)	220 (0.83%)	220 (0.83%)	$197.40
2. Body Side Moulding	concession	$33,278.69 (4.43%)	261 (0.98%)	261 (0.98%)	$127.50
3. Moonroof Visor	concession	$23,775.35 (3.16%)	115 (0.43%)	115 (0.43%)	$206.74
4. Rear Underbody Spoiler	concession	$13,681.35 (1.82%)	184 (0.69%)	184 (0.69%)	$74.36
5. Engine Block Heater	concession	$12,716.96 (1.69%)	61 (0.23%)	61 (0.23%)	$208.47

Secondary dimension: Product Variant ▼

FIGURE 8.30 Product Performance report, filtered for *concession* as the Product Variant secondary dimension value.

Custom Funnel

You could use the Custom Funnels feature (included in Analytics 360 and outlined in Chapter 18) to mimic an Enhanced Ecommerce shopping or checkout funnel, but for the build-and-price process.

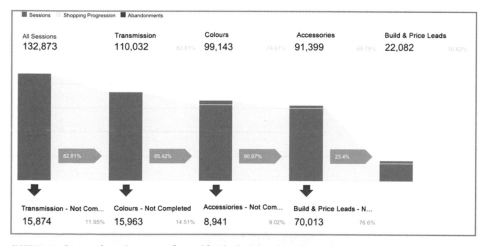

FIGURE 8.31 Custom funnel steps configured for the build-and-price process.

continues

continued

Lead Generation

Last but not least, pass the "last concession item" down to your CRM or lead management platform and use it to upsell or simply better serve your customers! (To enable the data integration, you could store the back-end lead number in GA as a custom dimension, as shown in Figure 8.32. Integrating GA and CRM data is discussed in Chapters 15 and 17.)

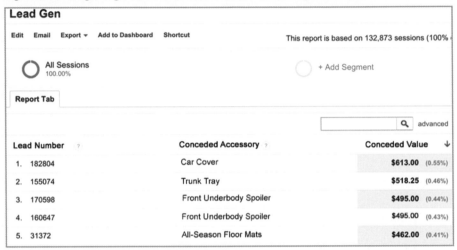

FIGURE 8.32 Custom report containing lead number imported from CRM, Conceded Accessory custom dimension, and Conceded Value custom metric.

Related Items

You can activate the Related Products feature under Ecommerce Settings in the View Admin. Related Product data then becomes accessible only through the reporting API after 30 days, and provided there are enough products and transactions recorded. (See `https://support.google.com/analytics/answer/6223409?hl=en`.)

Once enabled, you will gain a unique view of the most popular configuration packages, as demonstrated through the GA Query Explorer in Figures 8.33 and 8.34. You will find out which model/color/accessories work well together. You will also have the ability to see which accessories were considered as part of those popular packages, but later conceded (by looking into the Product Variant dimension).

FIGURE 8.33 This query configuration in the Google Analytics Query Explorer includes the *relatedProductName* dimension as well as the *relatedProductQuantity* and *correlationScore* metrics.

Queried Product Name	Related Product Name	Correlation Score	Queried Product Quantity	Related Product Quantity
Hybrid Sedan	Car Cover	0.025491	1,075	1,005
Sport Coupe	Car Cover	0.024756	688	1,005
Front Underbody Spoiler	Rear Underbody Spoiler	0.024756	5,178	715
Sport Coupe	Moonroof Visor	0.024172	688	758
Door Edge Guards	Body Side Moulding	0.024256	1,967	1,188

FIGURE 8.34 The Query Explorer results list both car models and accessories as the primary dimension and the most often coinciding accessory as secondary dimension, with the Correlation Score indicating the frequency of the car/accessory or accessory/accessory combination. The correlation score ranges between 0 and 1, the higher value meaning that the correlation is stronger.

Segmenting and Remarketing Based on Shopping and Checkout Behavior Funnels

In Chapter 10, "Segments," we'll see how segments can narrow the audience we're analyzing to highlight significant points in the data. As a preview, let's consider segmentation scenarios for the Shopping Behavior and Checkout Behavior funnels:

- **Create a segment based on abandonment (or continuation) at a funnel step.** We can create a segment from any point in either of the funnel and then apply it to other reports. In Figure 8.35, we're creating a segment for all shopping cart abandoners. We could also create a counterpart segment: visitors who continued to checkout. If we applied both of these segments to the Mobile Devices report, for example, we could see which devices experience the most abandonments.
- **Create a segment based on other report data and apply to the Enhanced Ecommerce reports.** As a complementary approach, we would create a segment based on a mobile device (Android tablets, for example) and apply this segment to the Shopping or Checkout Behavior funnels, or any of the other Enhanced Ecommerce reports.

As we learn in Chapter 14, GA remarketing audiences for AdWords are defined essentially the same way as segments, and dynamic remarketing will allow us to display specific product details in our remarketing ads.

FIGURE 8.35 You can easily create custom segments or remarketing audiences from any continuation or abandonment point in the Shopping Analysis or Checkout Analysis funnels.

MULTI-CHANNEL FUNNEL REPORTS

Goal and Ecommerce metrics also appear outside of the conversion reports, as in the Source/Medium report shown in Figure 8.36. The conversion data in this report seems quite straightforward, and we might be tempted to say that Google organic traffic drove 4,766 lead submissions.

FIGURE 8.36 Based only on last-click attribution, goal and Ecommerce data in the Source/Medium report does not apportion credit among multiple channels for the conversions.

Before feeling confident in this observation, however, we need to recognize that some or many of these 4,766 conversions should be attributed, at least in part, to other traffic sources.

Last-Click Attribution

Most of the GA reports display conversion data according to last-click attribution: the source that drove the converting visit receives credit—all credit—for the conversion, even if one or more previous sessions were driven by a different channel. (The exception is a returning direct visit, which pulls in the more specific previous source and medium values, as demonstrated in Figures 7.22 and 7.23.)

As an example, for the 4,766 lead submissions attributed to Google/organic, many of the converting sessions could have been preceded by a clickthrough from a paid campaign or an email. When we remember from Chapter 7 that much of the traffic reported as organic in GA is *branded* organic, and therefore not truly organic but navigational and very similar in essence to direct traffic, it's even more of an inaccuracy to give Google/organic full credit for the 4,766 lead submissions.

Multi-Channel Funnel Reports

As discussed below, the Multi-Channel Funnel (MCF) reports provide a more complete picture of your visitors' journeys to conversion. In fact, you should devote a large part of your conversion analysis to the MCF reports, especially if you are responsible for driving traffic to a website.

> ### Note
>
> ### Credit Where Credit Is Due
>
> Outside of the MCF reports in GA, last-click channels obscure the first-click and assisting channels that generated the sessions prior to conversion on a returning session. If you're running pay-per-click, retargeting, email, or any other campaign that consumes time and money, make sure to inspect the MCF reports to understand which channels are assisting conversions. Even if you cannot attribute a specific percentage of credit for the conversion to the assisting channels, you'll at least know how often these channels are generating sessions that precede the converting return sessions.

Assisted Conversions

The Assisted Conversions report shown in Figure 8.37 is indispensable for demonstrating the traffic sources that drove initial and assisting sessions for visitors who ultimately converted in a returning session, in many cases from another traffic source.

As shown in Figure 8.38, the top portion of the MCF reports provide many configurable options:

- **Conversion:** MCF reports default to all goals and Ecommerce transactions, but you can narrow focus to a smaller conversion selection.
- **All/AdWords:** You can display the MCF reports for AdWords (so that the Assisted Conversion report, for example, defaults to AdWords campaign as the primary dimension).

MCF Channel Grouping ?	Assisted Conversions ↓	Assisted Conversion Value	Last Click or Direct Conversions	Last Click or Direct Conversion Value	Assisted / Last Click or Direct Conversions
☐ 1. Direct	47,078 (27.55%)	$344,616.55 (27.87%)	56,901 (29.36%)	$298,974.31 (31.97%)	0.83
☐ 2. Email	41,408 (24.23%)	$269,376.90 (21.79%)	51,888 (26.77%)	$217,737.80 (23.28%)	0.80
☐ 3. Paid Search	31,396 (18.37%)	$221,026.72 (17.88%)	39,682 (20.47%)	$191,229.22 (20.45%)	0.79
☐ 4. Organic Search	24,092 (14.10%)	$159,175.90 (12.87%)	31,054 (16.02%)	$114,963.68 (12.29%)	0.78
☐ 5. Referral	12,369 (7.24%)	$125,048.96 (10.11%)	3,336 (1.72%)	$23,712.61 (2.54%)	3.71
☐ 6. Other Advertising	10,398 (6.08%)	$96,266.48 (7.79%)	8,757 (4.52%)	$80,353.14 (8.59%)	1.19
☐ 7. Display	2,453 (1.44%)	$10,525.76 (0.85%)	1,108 (0.57%)	$2,967.39 (0.32%)	2.21
☐ 8. (Other)	1,128 (0.66%)	$6,971.59 (0.56%)	683 (0.35%)	$3,195.59 (0.34%)	1.65
☐ 9. Social Network	590 (0.35%)	$3,441.97 (0.28%)	425 (0.22%)	$2,151.51 (0.23%)	1.39

FIGURE 8.37 The Assisted Conversions report indicates how often a channel provided a conversion assist prior to a converting return session. A value greater than 1 for Assisted/Last Click or Direct Conversions indicates that the channel is stronger for assists than for the converting sessions.

- **Lookback Window:** the default is a 30-day lookback, but it can be useful to extend the lookback to the maximum 90 days for a more complete attribution story. (If one of your visitors converts on an organic clickthrough today, wouldn't you want to know if that visitor clicked through from your email campaign 89 days ago but did not convert at that time?)
- **First Interaction Analysis:** the MCF reports default to Assisting Conversion Analysis, but you can change the display to First Interaction Analysis. (First Click Conversions are a subset of Assisted Conversions, not separate from Assisted Conversions.)
- **Conversion Segments:** you cannot apply the same segments to the MCF reports that you can to other GA reports. You can, however, apply built-in and custom Conversion segments, such as *Last Interaction Is Organic Search*. (As stated earlier for Funnel Visualization, if you need to view the MCF reports for a specific portion of your traffic, such as a country or a source, you can set up a dedicated filtered view, as described in Chapter 9.)

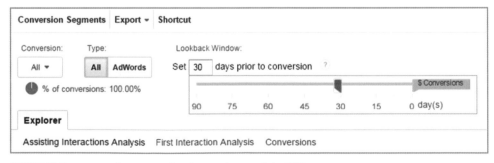

FIGURE 8.38 You can configure several options at the top of the MCF reports.

Top Conversion Paths

The Top Conversion Paths report does not relate to the pages viewed before a conversion; *path* in this context refers to the channels that drove the sessions leading to and including conversion as shown in Figure 8.39. Note that in the Top Conversion Paths report as well as the other MCF reports, Direct has the same precedence as the other channels; it is not overwritten by a more specific channel from a previous session as in the Acquisition reports.

Paid Search
Organic Search
569 (0.58%)
Email × 2
Direct
565 (0.57%)

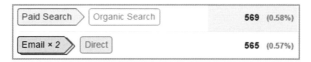

FIGURE 8.39 These two rows from the Top Conversion Path report show, respectively, that 569 conversions occurred on an organic search clickthrough preceded by a paid search clickthrough and that 565 conversions occurred during a direct session preceded by two email clickthroughs.

You can display the Top Conversion Paths report with other primary dimensions selected, such as Source/Medium, as illustrated in Figure 8.40, or Campaign.

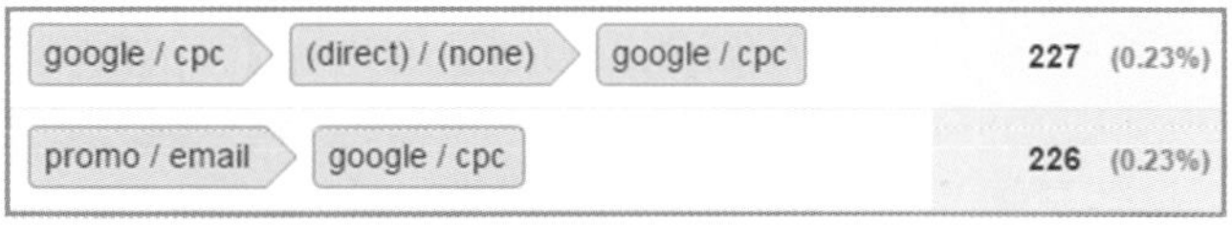

google / cpc
(direct) / (none)
google / cpc
227 (0.23%)
promo / email
google / cpc
226 (0.23%)

FIGURE 8.40 You can set the primary dimension in the MCF reports to Source/Medium, as above, or to Campaign.

Time Lag

The Time Lag report, shown in Figure 8.41, indicates how long it takes for the conversions to occur relative to the first session.

Note that the Multi-Channel Funnel reports don't exist in GA mobile app views, but if you have Ecommerce or Enhanced Ecommerce tracking configured for a mobile app, the Ecommerce > Time to Purchase report can provide similar data to Time Lag (but for Ecommerce transactions only, not for goal completions).

Time Lag in Days	Conversions	Conversion Value	Percentage of total (Conversions / Conversion Value)
0	650,351	$238,217.50	64.36% / 64.64%
1	31,951	$13,252.50	3.16% / 3.60%
2	22,014	$9,495.00	2.18% / 2.58%

FIGURE 8.41 This portion of the Time Lag report indicates that 35.64% (the inverse of 64.36%) of conversions occurred more than one day after the initial session.

Path Length

As in Top Conversion Paths shown above, the *path* in the Path Length report, shown in Figure 8.42, refers to the channels that drove one or more sessions that (eventually) led to a conversion.

Path Length in Interactions	Conversions	Conversion Value	Percentage of Total ■ Conversions ▢ Conversion Value	
1	505,850	$183,082.00	50.06% 49.68%	
2	186,540	$67,365.50	18.46% 18.28%	
3	90,799	$34,453.25	8.99% 9.35%	

FIGURE 8.42 This portion of the Path Length report indicates a nearly even split between conversions that occur on the first visit and conversions that required two or more sessions.

Attribution Model Comparison Tool

Attribution modeling is the art/science/practice of experimenting with different ways to assign conversion credit to marketing channels based on factors including position in the conversion path, attributes of user interactions, and engagement metrics to better show the value of marketing investments across the conversion funnel.

You can use the model comparison tool to compare channel performance according to different built-in (or custom) models. In Figure 8.43, we're comparing the number of conversions that would be attributed to each channel according to different attribution models:

- **Last Interaction:** all conversion credit to the last interaction that drove the converting session.
- **First Interaction:** all conversion credit to the first interaction that drove an immediate conversion or preceded a conversion on a return session.
- **Linear:** conversion credit divided equally by each session that led to a conversion.

	MCF Channel Grouping	Spend (for selected time range)	Last Interaction		First Interaction		Linear	
			Conversions	CPA	Conversions	CPA	Conversions	CPA
1.	Direct	—	524,164.00 (46.64%)	—	373,096.00 (33.20%)	—	385,618.13 (34.31%)	—
2.	Organic Search	—	224,684.00 (19.99%)	—	286,134.00 (25.46%)	—	206,132.68 (18.34%)	—
3.	Display	$2,987.59	126,529.00 (11.26%)	$0.02	212,403.00 (18.90%)	$0.01	340,062.05 (30.26%)	<$0.01
4.	Email	—	117,448.00 (10.45%)	—	115,344.00 (10.26%)	—	91,353.88 (8.13%)	—
5.	Paid Search	$69,031.72	72,915.00 (6.49%)	$0.95	93,924.00 (8.36%)	$0.73	60,016.05 (5.34%)	$1.15

FIGURE 8.43 In this example we're using the Model Comparison Tool to compare channel performance using First Interaction, Last Interaction, and Linear models.

Figure 8.44 shows all available built-in models. Note that you can create your own models or customize any of the built-in models based on session recency before conversion, level of user engagement during the session, and many other factors.

Note also that the Data-Driven Attribution model, discussed in Chapter 18, is available in Analytics 360 only.

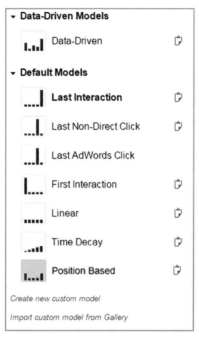

FIGURE 8.44 Built-in attribution models.

Note

Attribution Modeling and Assumptions

The built-in and custom attribution models basically represent assumptions (e.g., if I gave all conversion credit to the first interaction, how many conversions could I attribute to email?). There are some assumptions, however, that are better than others. If you run multi-channel, integrated marketing programs then you have at least two (and likely many more) channels driving ad impressions and site interactions leading to conversion activity. If that's the case, we can definitely say that the assumptions built into single touchpoint conversion models are not as good as models that potentially give credit to all touchpoints that contributed to a conversion.

As an exception, the Data-Driven Attribution model (available only in Analytics 360 and discussed further in Chapter 18) bases conversion credit on algorithms rather than assumption.

The Assisted Conversion report discussed earlier does not assume that one model is more valid than the other—instead, it just displays all channels that it can objectively demonstrate, through GA data collection, to have driven a session that led to an eventual conversion. For more on attribution modeling, see www.e-nor.com/gabook.

Custom Channel Groupings

Note

Cookie Dependency

Keep in mind that the MCF reports depend on cookies If a user deletes the _ga cookie between sessions or returns with a different device or browser, GA will not be able to make a connection with a previous session. Therefore, in reality, path lengths and time lags are longer, and there are more conversion assists than GA is able to report.

In addition to conversion assists traceable through the _ga cookie, a user-id-enabled view for cross-device tracking can also show conversion assists based on login in the converting session and previous sessions. Cross-device tracking is discussed in Chapter 12.

Page Value

The Page Value metric that appears as the last column in the All Pages report is perhaps the most misunderstood (and underappreciated) metric in GA. In general, we can say that Page Value indicates how much support a page is providing to goal (Destination and Event type, primarily) and Ecommerce conversions.

For each page, Page Value is calculated as:

$$\frac{Goal\ Value + Ecommerce\ Revenue\ Accrued\ After\ (or\ on)\ the\ Pageview}{Unique\ Pageviews}$$

As we remember from Chapter 4, the Unique Pageviews metric represents the number of sessions in which the page was viewed at least one time. When calculating Page Value, a page counts in the denominator of our equation only once, even if it was viewed multiple times in a session. Similarly, Goal Value and Ecommerce Revenue is added to the numerator only once, even if the page was viewed multiple times before the conversion took place, and the full Goal Value or Ecommerce Revenue is credited regardless of how many pageviews interceded between the given page and the conversion—as long as the conversion was completed after at least one of the pageviews occurred.

Figures 8.45 and 8.46 illustrate Page Value respectively for Ecommerce and for a non-monetized lead generation goal to which we have assigned a goal value of $1. Note that even based on an arbitrary goal value in the second example, Page Value helps to identify pages that are—and are not—supporting the conversion process.

Ecommerce - Camping Equipment			
Session 1	/about-us	/product-announcements	/money-back-guarantee	$40
Session 2	/free-shipping	/product-announcements		
Session 3	/about-us	/free-shipping	/privacy-policy	$20
Session 4	/free-shipping	$40	/product-announcements	
Session 5	/privacy-policy	/about-us	/money-back-guarantee	
Session 6	/product-announcements	/privacy-policy	$10	
Session 7	/about-us	/privacy-policy	/money-back-guarantee	
Session 8	/product-announcements	/free-shipping	$50	/privacy-policy
Session 9	/product-announcements	/money-back-guarantee		
Session10	/product-announcements	/free-shipping	/product-announcements	$30

Page	Ecommerce Revenue Contributed	Total Sessions	Page Value
/about-us	$60	3	$20.00
/free-shipping	$120	3	$40.00
/money-back-guarantee	$40	4	$10.00
/privacy-policy	$30	4	$7.50
/product-announcements	$130	7	$18.57

FIGURE 8.45 With Page Value based on actual Ecommerce revenue, we see that the Free Shipping page seems to be helping Conversions more than Privacy Policy.

Does Page Value provide an absolutely objective comparison of your pages' conversion impact? Not completely, of course. Visitors who viewed the Privacy Policy page in Figure 8.43 may have already been experiencing some anxiety and have therefore been less likely to convert, while those viewing the Free Shipping page may have been seeking affirmation on a purchase that they had already nearly decided on.

Nonetheless, Page Value can provide an important aid to conversion analysis and optimization. If your Advisory Panel page has the highest Page Value as in Figure 8.44, you can revise your home page variation to more prominently display or link to Advisory Panel information, or—even better—you can set up an A/B test variation with these changes and measure the difference in conversion rate.

Lead Generation - Financial Planners				
Session 1	/adivsory-panel	/charitable-giving	/money-back-guarantee	$1
Session 2	/office-locations	/charitable-giving	/code-of-ethics	
Session 3	/yearly-performance	/office-locations	/yearly-performance	$1
Session 4	/office-locations	$1	/charitable-giving	
Session 5	/yearly-performance	/advisory-panel	/code-of-ethics	$1
Session 6	/charitable-giving	/yearly-performance	/office-locations	
Session 7	/advisory-panel	/yearly-performance	/money-back-guarantee	
Session 8	/charitable-giving	/office-locations	$1	/yearly-performance
Session 9	/charitable-giving	/advisory-panel		
Session 10	/advisory-panel	$1	/office-locations	/yearly-performance

Page	Goal Value Contributed	Total Sessions	Page Value
/advisory-panel	$3	4	$0.75
/charitable-giving	$2	6	$0.33
/code-of-ethics	$1	2	$0.50
/office-locations	$2	5	$0.40
/yearly-performance	$2	6	$0.33

FIGURE 8.46 Even with Page Value based on an arbitrary goal value of $1, we can see which pages are likely helping lead submissions.

Conversely, if a page that you expected to help conversions is displaying a low Page Value, review the page for potential improvements or consider directing traffic away from that page and towards a page that is achieving higher Page Value.

Distinguishing between Goal Value and Ecommerce Revenue within Page Value

As shown above, Page Value calculation is based on all Goal Value and Ecommerce Revenue accrued in the given sessions, so how can you display Page Value based on one goal or Ecommerce revenue?

There are two approaches: segments or separate views. Let's say specifically that within the same view, we have:

- Ecommerce tracking
- one goal configured with a £10 Goal Value

If you wanted to display Page Value based on either Ecommerce transactions or Goal completions alone, you could apply custom segments as shown in Figures 8.47 and 8.48 to remove sessions in which the goal conversion or the Ecommerce transaction occurred. (We discuss segments in Chapter 10.)

FIGURE 8.47 To display Page Value based only on Ecommerce Revenue, we can apply a filter to exclude sessions in which the goal conversion occurred.

FIGURE 8.48 To display Page Value based only on the Goal Value that we configured, we can apply a filter to exclude sessions in which Revenue (i.e., Ecommerce revenue) is greater than 0.

You may have noticed in the segments above that we would be inadvertently excluding, in both cases, those sessions in which both the goal and an Ecommerce transaction took place. Though this would probably not significantly skew our analysis, we always have the option (with Edit rights to the property) to create two additional views: one to track the goal only, and one to track the Ecommerce transactions only. In this way, Page Value as reported in these dedicated views would be based on all Ecommerce transactions or all completions of the £10 goal.

INTEGRATING WITH THIRD-PARTY SHOPPING CARTS

If you're working with a third-party Ecommerce platform (or planning to), you'll want to make sure to verify the level of GA support that the platform offers, for tracking in general and Ecommerce specifically. For hosted platforms such as Shopify, BigCommerce, and Volusion, cross-domain support is also a consideration, since you'll want to make sure to maintain the session between your own domain and the hosted cart domain. (Cross-domain tracking is discussed in Chapter 12.) For self-hosted platforms such as Magento, cross-domain tracking does not pertain, since users won't traverse domains for the Ecommerce functionality.

GUEST SPOT **GA Tracking Questions to Ask Your Ecommerce Provider**

Vanessa Sabino
Vanessa Sabino is Data Analysis Lead for Shopify.

Using a hosted checkout/shopping platform to power your Ecommerce is a great way to build a site to promote your offerings and generate sales online without having to worry about infrastructure. In some cases, this also means a big part of the GA implementation will be done for you.

continues

continued

Here are a few items that you should verify to ensure your online store is collecting high-quality data that will help you understand your customers.

Does Your Platform Offer Any Kind of GA Integration?

If there is a place to enter your GA Property ID, the platform will probably track at least the pageviews for your site. But check which version of the tracking code is being used: if they don't support Universal Analytics (analytics.js), there are many new features that will be unavailable to you.

Is There Ecommerce Tracking?

If you want to see your sales in GA, you'll need to enable Ecommerce tracking, which can be done from the Admin in your GA account. You also need to ensure that data is being sent from the order confirmation page, which includes the transaction ID, products that were sold, quantity, price, and so on.

Ideally, your checkout platform provider should automate the Ecommerce coding and data population. If, however, the platform provider does not automatically configure GA Ecommerce for you, do they provide a way for you to add this code manually? In this case, you'll need to edit the HTML of the page to insert JavaScript code. You'll also need to have variables (such as product ID and tax) available that contain all the required information to create a transaction in GA.

Is There Support for Enhanced Ecommerce?

Even better than the standard Ecommerce tracking is the new Enhanced Ecommerce option for Universal Analytics. This collects Ecommerce-related data for the entire session, not just the final purchase. This data includes product views, items added to cart, and different check-out steps.

Does the Checkout Happen in a Different Domain from Your Storefront?

In order to transmit information securely during checkout, the URL needs to have a valid secure sockets layer (SSL) certificate. Depending on the platform or subscription plan that you select, this may be achieved by having the checkout flow in a shared domain that belongs to the platform (such as `tshirtstore.platform.com`) instead of your own store domain (such as `www.tshirtstore.com`) (Figure 8.49). In this case, make sure the cross-domain tracking is working properly. When you first go from your own domain to the checkout domain, you should see a `_ga` parameter in the end of the URL containing a set of numbers. This will enable GA to recreate the cookie in the new domain in a way that you are still identified as the same user. Otherwise, your GA reports will show one user ending their visit in the previous page and a new user starting a new visit on the checkout page, which would make you completely miss the original traffic source of a sale. (For further details on cross-domain tracking, see Chapter 12, "Implementation Customizations.")

FIGURE 8.49 In some checkout configurations, your shopping cart resides on your main storefront domain while checkout (including payment) and confirmation reside on a separate checkout domain.

Is Your Payment Gateway Under a Domain Separate from Your Checkout Platform?

If the customer is taken to a completely different site to enter their payment information, such as PayPal, there isn't a lot you can do to track what is happening there. But make sure everything is set up to take the customer back to your thank-you page on the hosted platform after the payment is completed, as this is the ideal place to trigger the Ecommerce tracking (Figure 8.50). In some cases, you have to set an Auto Return URL on the configuration page of the payment gateway as in Figure 8.51, but depending on the integration between your platform and payment gateway, this may not be necessary, as the return URL could be generated automatically for you.

Also make sure you add your payment gateway domain to the Referral Exclusion List under Tracking Info in your GA property settings.

FIGURE 8.50 Another possible configuration is the payment gateway that resides on a third domain, separate from the checkout domain.

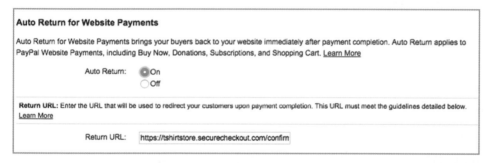

FIGURE 8.51 For some payment gateways, you need to configure the URL that the user will be redirected to on the secure checkout site after payment on the payment domain.

Ask the Right Questions

Whichever checkout and payment configuration you're considering, make sure to ask about GA Ecommerce and cross-domain tracking. With the right configurations, you'll be able to fully understand the performance of your online store and drive ongoing improvement.

 KEY TAKEAWAYS

Goals and Ecommerce tracking are not retroactive.   Don't delay in setting up a goal for any action or engagement level that represents a success in terms of your KPIs, and Ecommerce (or Enhanced Ecommerce) for transactions that include a variety of products, price points, and so on.

Four goal types.   You can create goals based on a pageview or screen view (physical or virtual), an event, or threshold of engagement (that is, pages/screens per session, or session duration).

Three match types for Destination goals.   You can use the *Equals To* match type to match a single Page or Screen dimension value only, or you can use *Begins With* or *Regular Expression* for multiple pages or screens to count as a completion of the same goal.

Goal funnels are recommended but not required.   If your conversion process is designed to include a series of pages or screens, create a Destination goal with a funnel.

Conversion rate is based on sessions.   Conversion rate is calculated as conversions per session and therefore appears lower than if it were calculated as conversions per user.

Funnels do not affect conversion rate.   Funnels populate the Funnel Visualization report and determine Abandonment Rate and Funnel Conversion Rate, but they do not affect Goal Conversion Rate. The only factor for calculating conversion rate for a Destination goal is the number of sessions in which the Destination page or screen was viewed.

Unlike goal tracking, Ecommerce tracking requires additional code.   While goal tracking depends only on an Admin configuration and the page or event data that is already being recorded, the greater detail in Ecommerce tracking usually depends on additional back-end transaction data written to the data layer. For this reason, you normally need to work your developers to implement Ecommerce tracking.

Enhanced Ecommerce provides reporting on actions leading to the transaction.   While Ecommerce reporting is much more detailed than goal reporting in terms of transaction data, it does not provide direct insight into the steps leading to the transaction. The additional coding steps required for Enhanced Ecommerce provide richer reports, including product impressions and adds-to-cart, promotion clicks, and checkout abandonment.

Use a test view first.   Configure goals, Ecommerce, and Enhanced Ecommerce in a test view before your working view(s).

Multi-Channel Funnel reports show channels that assist conversions, not just Last-Click Attribution.   The MCF reports provide critical reporting on the channels responsible for non-converting sessions that preceded converting return sessions from other channels.

Attribution models represent assumptions.   With the exception of the algorithmic Data-Driven attribution model available in Analytics 360, each attribution model represents shows how conversion credit would be allocated to channels if a certain assumption (e.g., each session deserving equal credit) were true. Data-Driven attribution, available in Analytics 360, algorithmically assigns different percentages of credit to assisting channels.

Page Value indicates goal and Ecommerce support.   You can interpret Page Value as an indicator of the support that a page—especially if it's not designed as part of the conversion process—is providing to goal completions and Ecommerce transactions.

 ## ACTIONS AND EXERCISES

1. **Articulate the KPIs for your website or mobile app.** Revisiting our discussion in Chapter 3, "Measurement Strategy," make sure you have a very clear idea of a successful session.

2. **Set up goals, Ecommerce, or Enhanced Ecommerce.** For your KPIs and any user action that indicates an increased level of interest (such as a contact-us submission), set up a goal or Ecommerce to correspond. If you can't currently set up Enhanced Ecommerce tracking where it would be ideal, set up Ecommerce tracking; if you can't set up Ecommerce tracking, set up a goal.

3. **Create goal funnels.** Create funnels for your destination goals. You can review the Reverse Goal Path report for existing goals and map the most common paths to conversion as actual funnel steps and thereby measure step-to-step drop-off.

4. **Determine goal values.** Using the guidance offered in the chapter, set suitable goal values for your goals. This is particularly important if you do not have Ecommerce tracking in place.

5. **Confer with your third-party shopping provider.** If you're choosing or currently using a third-party provider for Ecommerce processing, determine their support for GA pageview, Ecommerce/Enhanced Ecommerce, and cross-domain tracking as applicable.

6. **Review the Multi-Channel Funnel Reports and the Attribution Model Comparison Tool.** Once goals and/or Ecommerce tracking are in place, review the MCF reports and the Model Comparison Tool. Which channels are performing best for the converting visit? Which channels are assisting conversions?

View Settings, View Filters, and Access Rights

n this chapter, we're going to learn about the settings and view filters that you can apply to the raw, unfiltered property to modify, consolidate, or completely rewrite the incoming data and to create focused subsets of the data.

Since you may want to provide certain individuals with access only to the subsets of your data rather than to all data that you collect in the property, we're also going to discuss Google Analytics (GA) access rights at the account, property, and view level.

WHY DO WE NEED MULTIPLE VIEWS?

In Chapter 4, "Account Creation and Tracking Code Installation," we learned that:

- A GA property normally corresponds to a single website or mobile app.
- Data collection is associated with a specific property ID (also called a *tracking ID* or *UA number*), and website and mobile app data therefore flows into GA at the property level (rather than at the account level).

Since data collection occurs at the property level, we might at first wonder why we need multiple views at all, but, as we learn some of the basic concepts behind views, we soon realize the critical role played by the view level of the account hierarchy.

As demonstrated in Figure 9.1, views allow us to alter the raw, underlying property data in the following ways:

- **Data cleanup and consolidation.** Exclude your own internal website traffic from tracking, consolidate URLs and case variations, and rewrite any dimension value.
- **Configuration for additional metrics.** Configure goals and site search.
- **Data subsets.** Create subsets of the raw data by including or excluding a subdirectory, a geographical area, or another type of dimension value. As discussed later in the chapter, you can take advantage of dedicated views and restricted privileges to selectively control access to specific portions of your GA data.

The same principles apply for views within a mobile app property, but some of the potential view settings and filters, such as URL consolidation and site search configuration, would not pertain.

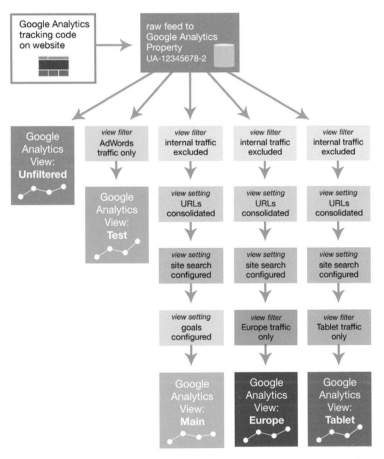

FIGURE 9.1 In Google Analytics, a view is a representation of property data that has been processed with different settings and filters.

BEST PRACTICE: WORKING, TEST, AND UNFILTERED VIEWS

When you create a new account, or just a new property within an existing account, GA automatically creates a single view called All Web Site Data or All App Data within the property. It's considered best practice to perform at least some data cleanup on your raw property in your working views, and it's also considered best practice—or rather a critical precaution—to try view settings and filters in a test view before applying to a main working view. If you're applying view settings and filters to any view, it's also imperative to maintain a raw view to which you apply no view settings or filters.

To create a new view, you only need to select Create New View from the view drop-down on the Admin screen as shown in Figure 9.2. You can rename All Web Site Data or All App Data to *01 Working*, *01 Main*, or **Main,* as a few examples, to keep that view at the top of the list. There's not a single correct convention for view naming, so name them as makes senses for you and your organization.

Note that you need Edit access at the view level to change any view settings and Edit access at the property level to create a new view.

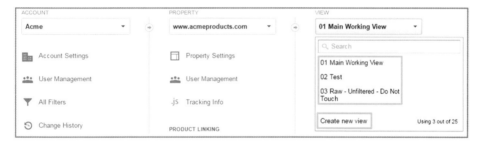

FIGURE 9.2 As an essential practice for Google Analytics, you should maintain a test view, an unfiltered view, and one or more working views for each property.

> **Warning** !
>
> **Don't change view settings or add filters before creating test and unfiltered views.** In the next sections of this chapter, we'll change view settings and add view filters. It's important to take advantage of these capabilities, but don't make any changes until you create, in addition to your main view, a test view for validating settings, filters, and goals, as well as a backup view that you maintain as a raw property feed without any view settings, view filters, or goals. As an extra precaution, you can even create two raw views to maintain a backup of your backup.

VIEW SETTINGS

Several of the view settings rewrite or exclude data that's delivered in the raw property feed. In this way, they are very similar to the actual rewrite and exclude filters that we'll examine later in the chapter. As a specialized setting, site search tracking is also configured at the view level.

Before we explore the view settings highlighted in Figure 9.3, here are a few quick notes on some of the more administrative view settings:

- **Name.** For your first three views (main, test, and backup), the names shown above are suitable; you can name additional views to describe the filtering or configuration that you have applied (e.g., North America Only).
- **Website's URL.** Inherited from the property; you can leave this as is.
- **Time Zone Country or Territory.** As best practice, match the time zone in any AdWords accounts that you have linked to the property so reporting by hour of day is aligned as much as possible.
- **Currency Displayed As.** Determines only the currency symbol displayed for Ecommerce revenue, goal value, and so on.

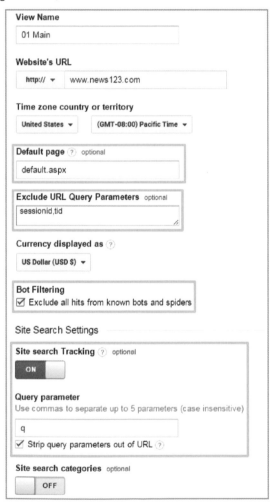

FIGURE 9.3 Example view settings.

Default Page

Does the top page in your Pages report appear as a single forward slash? We may recognize / as the home page, but you can rewrite / into a more meaningful Page dimension value.

Before you specify the default page in the view settings, you need to check your reports to determine which one of two scenarios pertains to your Pages report:

- **Rewriting and consolidation.** If your home page is accessible to visitors as both / and `/default.aspx`, and therefore appears in the Pages report as either of these two dimension values as in Figure 9.4, specify *default.aspx* (without the forward slash) as the default page in the view settings. This will rewrite all instances of / to / `default.aspx` and thereby consolidate the reporting with all other instances of `/default.aspx` that were recorded with the pageview. (We'll address the case variations in our upcoming discussion on view filters.)

	Page ?		Pageviews ? ↓	Unique Pageviews ?	Avg. Time on Page ?	Entrances ?	Bounce Rate ?
			34,345 % of Total: 100.00% (34,345)	**25,840** % of Total: 100.00% (25,840)	**00:01:39** Avg for View: 00:01:39 (0.00%)	**12,861** % of Total: 100.00% (12,861)	**45.73%** Avg for View: 45.73% (0.00%)
☐	1. /	⊡	**4,357** (12.69%)	2,455 (9.50%)	00:01:07	3,350 (26.05%)	43.78%
☐	2. /default.aspx	⊡	**4,306** (12.54%)	3,510 (13.58%)	00:01:21	2,319 (18.03%)	48.46%
☐	3. /Default.aspx	⊡	**3,227** (9.40%)	2,604 (10.08%)	00:02:09	425 (3.30%)	52.37%

FIGURE 9.4 Because these three Page dimension values represent the same actual page, they fragment the metrics in the Pages report.

- **Rewriting only.** Many websites are configured to redirect the default home page (such as `index.html`, `index.php`, `default.aspx`, etc.) to just the domain, such that users who may attempt to access `http://www.`*`yoursite`*`.com/`*`index.php`* are redirected to `http://www.`*`yoursite`*`.com`, which would generate a pageview for /. If this is the case—that is, you have no instances of `index.html`, `index.php`, or `default.aspx` already recorded as the Page in GA—you can rewrite / to any value you choose. You could, for example, specify *home* as the default page, which would rewrite all instances of / to /home.

A bit surprisingly, the Default Page setting applies not just to / but to all pages that end with /. If you specify *home* as the Default Page, all URLs that end in / will also be rewritten, such that `/topics/` would be rewritten as `/topics/home`.

If you don't see / in your Pages report, and if none of your Page dimension values end in /, you can disregard the Default Page setting.

> **Note**
>
> ## Fight URL Fragmentation: Consolidate Multiple Pages that Represent the Same User Experience
>
> If users are accessing your home page as both `www.yoursite.com` as `www.yoursite.com/index.php`, do we want to see both `/` and `/index.php` as page values in GA?
>
> In a word, no. You'll always be able to see the actual user-facing Page (aka *Request URI*) in your raw view, but in your working views, it's much more useful to consolidate these Page dimensions, since they both represent the same end-user experience. *If multiple Request URIs represent the same end-user experience, you should consolidate them into a single Page in GA.*
>
> As another means of Request URI consolidation, we'll also discuss the Exclude URL Query Parameters setting. The lowercase filter, also coming up in this chapter, can help to consolidate not only the Request URI but other dimensions such as campaign name.
>
> Overall, however, fragmentation plagues Request URI more than any other dimension. It's not always a problem, but where it is a problem, it tends to be a big one. In many GA implementations where everything else is correct, URL fragmentation produces tens of thousands or sometimes hundreds of thousands of separate Request URIs. Make it a priority to consolidate your home page and any other pages as needed.

Exclude URL Query Parameters

It's easy to misconstrue the name of this setting. It does not serve to exclude URL query parameters in the sense of blocking data from the view (as an actual exclude view filter would); instead, it removes URL query parameters from multiple URL variations and consolidates them into a single Request URI. We can thus think of *Exclude URL Query Parameters* as *Strip URL Query Parameters*.

This setting does not apply to all websites. If you do not use any query parameters in your URLs, this setting does not pertain to you. (You still may have fragmented request URIs, but if the fragmentation is not caused by *name=value* query parameters as shown below, you'll instead need to apply a rewrite filter as described later in the chapter.)

Also, if your URL parameters do determine significantly different page content and therefore a different end-user experience, you certainly do not want to remove and consolidate. Let's say, for example, that you have the following two URLs on your learn-how-to-paint website:

- `/article.jsp?id=123` (about brushstrokes)
- `/article.jsp?id=456` (about oil paint)

Since, in this case, the `id` query parameter dictates different page content, we definitely would not want to strip it out of the URL. If we chose, we could rewrite each URL to a more human-readable format using a view rewrite filter, or we could rewrite the URLs in Google Tag Manager (GTM) before even sending the hit to GA, but we'd certainly want to maintain two separate URLs in GA for these two different page experiences.

Here's where the URL Query parameters become a problem: when they don't change any of page content, or do not change the page content significantly enough for the URLs to be analyzed separately. Let's say that after a user logs into your website, a `sessionid` parameter is added to the URL as follows:

- `/account-settings/?sessionid=123` ("Hello, Nigel")
- `/account-settings/?sessionid=456` ("Hello, Sandra")

The `sessionid` parameter is not in any way a bad thing from a Web coding standpoint; it allows each page to display a personalized welcome message in the top navigation. The problem from a GA standpoint is that we don't need to know if the account settings page showed a greeting for Nigel or Sandra; we only need to know that the account setting page was accessed in these two sessions. Therefore, it's not useful—in fact, it's a serious hindrance for analysis—to have multiple URLs for the same content and user experience. (However, as we discuss in Chapter 12, we do want to use custom dimensions to distinguish between authenticated and unauthenticated sessions and to record additional, non-PII data from the back end about authenticated users, such as customer level.)

This is where the Exclude URL Query Parameters setting comes in. By listing `sessionid` and any other parameters that do not determine different page content and create Page fragmentation as illustrated in Figure 9.5, GA strips the query parameter— actually, the entire *name=value* pair—from the URL, thus consolidating pageviews and all other page-related metrics, as you can see in Figure 9.6.

FIGURE 9.5 Without consolidation of Pages through Exclude URL Query Parameters, the unfiltered view for this website shows 21,679 Page (aka Request URI) variations.

FIGURE 9.6 By specifying Exclude URL Query Parameters, we have consolidated the 21,679 Request URI variations in Figure 9.5 down to just 51, with the same number of total pageviews in both cases.

Note

Refer to the URL Parameters Report in Google Search Console

In Chapter 7, "Acquisition Reports," we reviewed the Search Analytics report within Google Search Console and emphasized the importance of gaining access to Google Search Console for the same websites for which you have GA access. Another benefit of Google Search Console is the URL Parameters report, shown in Figure 9.7, which serves as a great starting point for identifying query parameters that you should exclude in GA.

continues

continued

Parameter	URLs monitored ▲	Configured	Effect	Crawl	
sessionid	69	Jan 19, 2016	None	Representative URL	Edit / Reset
di	26	Apr 11, 2016	None	Let Googlebot decide	Edit / Reset
cnt	10	Apr 14, 2016	None	Every URL	Edit / Reset

FIGURE 9.7 The URL Parameters report in Google Search Console can help you identify the query parameters that you need to list in Exclude URL Query Parameters.

The Crawl column displays one of three statuses:

➤ **Representative URL.** Googlebot thinks that the URL parameter does not determine different page content, so you should probably consolidate in GA.
➤ **Every URL.** Googlebot thinks that the URL parameter does determine different page content, so you should probably not consolidate in GA.
➤ **Let Googlebot decide.** Googlebot isn't sure, so you'll need to investigate.

Regardless of the three statuses in the URL Parameters report, you should confer with your Web content and development teams before listing a parameter in Exclude URL Query Parameters, and definitely do not update this setting in your main working view(s) before validating in your test view.

As another note, any settings in the URL Parameters report in Google Search Console affect only the Google search engine, and the Exclude URL Query Parameters setting affect only GA. The consolidation concepts are the same for SEO and analytics, but there is no cross-functionality between the two environments.

Exclude URL Query Parameters for PII Blocking

In Chapter 4, "Account Creation and Tracking Code Installation," Brian Clifton's top 10 gotchas included a strategy for detecting and preventing personally identifiable information (PII) in GA. If PII is sent to GA following a query parameter such as `name`, `lname`, `fname`, `email`, `address`, `tel`, or `mobile`, you can list these parameters in Exclude URL Query Parameters. You'll not only be removing PII; you'll also be consolidating your Request URIs.

Site Search Tracking

We first saw the Search Terms report in Figure 2.19. This report provides explicit data and unique insights on what your visitors are searching for. None of the Site Search reports are populated by default. In the Site Search Tracking view settings, you can tell GA which URL query parameter signifies a search results page.

If, for instance, we were configuring site search in a GA implementation for amazon.com, our first step would be to perform a search and inspect the URL of the search results page, as in the following example of a search for *big query*:

```
http://www.amazon.com/s/ref=nb_sb_noss_1?url=search-
alias%3Dstripbooks&field-keywords=big+query
```

We can start by identifying the ? and & symbols—the ? demarcates the query string from the domain and path portions of the URL, and the & symbols demarcate the query parameter *name=value* pairs from each other. Here we can see that `field-keywords` is the query parameter we'd need to specify in the Site Search view setting.

The URL of the search results page for *economy* on the Chicago Tribune website readily indicates that we'd need to specify `Query` as the Site Search Query parameter.

```
http://www.chicagotribune.com/search/dispatcher.front?Query=economy&
target=all&spell=on
```

If your site search includes a category option that is displayed in the URL as a separate *name=value* pair, you can configure the Site Search Category parameter in addition to the Site Search Query parameter. (Site Search Category is available as a primary dimension in the Search Terms reports and as a secondary dimension throughout GA.)

Note that we can use the Site Search Query parameter setting only if the search page URL includes the search parameter as the name and the search term as the value in a *name=value* pair. If the search term appears in the URL in another format, we'll instead need to use a view filter as shown in Figure 9.12.

Bot Filtering

You can select the checkbox under Bot Filtering, shown previously in Figure 9.3, to remove all GA data generated by bots and spiders that have been compiled into the frequently updated IAB/ABC International Spiders & Bots List.

While many bots and filters cannot execute JavaScript, others can, and can therefore execute the GA tracking code and send hits to GA. Bot Filtering removes this data from the view.

Some bots and spiders are perfectly legitimate, and some not. While search engines and site monitoring bots serve aboveboard purposes, other bots operate illicitly. The most grievous bot and spider transgressions occur on publishing sites that run CPM (i.e., cost per thousand impressions) advertising: in some cases, bots are thought to represent one-third of the activity on a website, thus inflating pageview counts, benefitting the ad networks and the publishers, and costing the advertiser money for ad "impressions" that were never seen by human eyes.

In this way, bot and spider activity may account for a significant portion of your Web analytics data. On other websites, they have minimal impact on analytics. In either case, you can follow the steps below to determine if bots and spiders are inflating your GA data to any extent:

1. In the view settings of your unfiltered view, click Copy View.
2. Name the view Bot Filtered.

3. Check the Bot Filtered checkbox in the view settings of the new view.
4. After one or two weeks, note the difference in pageviews and sessions between your unfiltered view and the Bot Filtered view.
5. Check the Bot Filtered checkbox in the view settings of your main view.
6. Create an annotation, as described in Chapter 11, "Dashboards, Custom Reports, and Intelligence Alerts," to record the date of the change to your main view.

If you noted a significant difference in the bot-filtered view, you may want to alert your Web developers and anyone who is responsible for any CPM campaigns you may be running on your own site as a publisher. (If you're an advertiser, you may want to verify that your network has implemented controls to prevent you from paying for bot and spider impressions.)

VIEW FILTERS

As mentioned previously, many of the view settings that we reviewed in the preceding sections serve as filters in that they exclude sessions or rewrite a dimension value. Beyond the view settings, GA provides rich functionality for view filtering. Table 9.1 summarizes the types of filtering that you can perform on a view.

TABLE 9.1 Summary of View Filter Functionality

Filter Functionality	Example
Include sessions that match a rule.	Include Device Category = tablet only.
Exclude sessions that match a rule.	Exclude internal IP addresses.
Modify a dimension value.	Lowercase Campaign Name.
Rewrite a dimension value.	Add Hostname to the Page dimension.

Excluding internal IP addresses, lowercasing dimension values, and even prepending the hostname name to the Page (used often in cross-domain or roll-up reporting, as discussed in Chapter 12) can all be considered forms of cleanup or enhancement: they're not creating a view that is fundamentally different from the raw property feed.

The first filter in Table 9.1, on the other hand, alters the raw property feed more drastically by allowing only a subset of data into the view.

Despite their dynamic-sounding name, view filters permanently alter the view data for the duration that they're applied. Let's say, for example, you're tracking the Android and iOS versions of your mobile app into the same property. You create a view on July 1 and apply a filter to a mobile app view to include traffic only from Android OS, and you then remove that filter on July 31. Data collected in the view from August 1 forward will include Android and iOS, but iOS is gone forever within the view for July.

By the same token, filters are not retroactive. If the Android/iOS property mentioned in the example above has been collecting data for one year and you then apply an Android filter, the iOS data will remain in the view for the time that the filter was not applied.

Since view filters do permanently alter the underlying property data that the view receives, you need Edit rights to create and apply them, as discussed later in the chapter.

The "Segments vs. Filtered Views" section in Chapter 10 compares view filters with custom segments, which serve as a retroactive and dynamic equivalent of the permanent, now-forward data subsetting that view filters perform.

Next, we demonstrate setup for several different types of filters. As we've highlighted before, do not apply any of these filters to any working view, especially not your main view, before trying them in a test view.

Exclude Internal Traffic by IP Address

Because IP address is available for filtering (even though it's not available in the reporting interface or through the API), you can identify sessions that originate from within your own organization's IP address range(s) and exclude those sessions from your working views.

Your network admin should be able to inform you of the IP address range that your organization uses to access the Internet from your own office; an example would be 32.161.79.1 to 32.161.79.18. Knowing the IP address range, you have two options for excluding your internal traffic:

- a predefined filter: Exclude—Traffic from the IP Addresses—That Begin with—32.161.79
- a custom filter

The predefined filter would work well overall, but it would be a little broader than necessary since it would exclude all 255 IP addresses that matched the first three octets instead of excluding the 18 IP addresses in your range only.

We can still avoid creating 18 separate filters for each of the IP addresses we need to exclude. Fortunately, a single regular expression will allow us to create a single filter that matches all 18 IP addresses but no more. You can use RegexIP (`http://www.regexip.com`) to generate a regular expression that you can then use in an exclude view filter as shown in Figure 9.8.

If your IP address range is expressed in CIDR format (e.g., 25.32.210.1/28), you can use a tool such as `http://www.ipaddressguide.com/cidr` to display the beginning and end IP addresses of the range that you can then enter into the RegexIP tool.

Once you have the regex for your IP address range:

1. In the view column of the Admin screen, click Filters.
2. Click + Add Filter.
3. Configure the filter as in Figure 9.8.

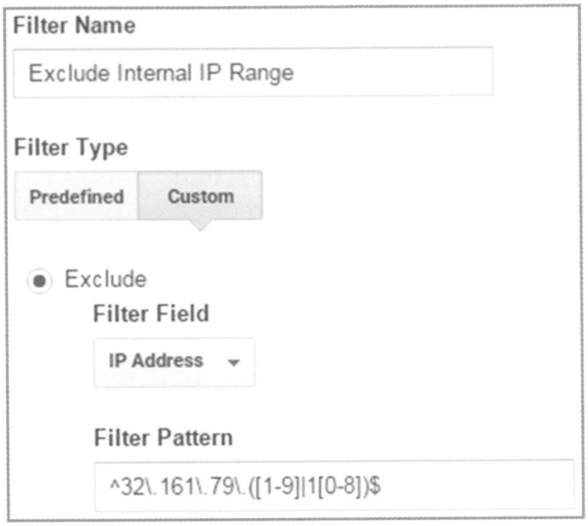

Filter Name

Exclude Internal IP Range

Filter Type

Predefined   Custom

⦿ Exclude

   Filter Field

   IP Address ▾

   Filter Pattern

   ^32\.161\.79\.([1-9]|1[0-8])$

FIGURE 9.8 Single filter to exclude sessions originating from any IP address within a range.

If your organization uses noncontiguous IP addresses for Internet access, you can potentially configure an exclude filter for internal traffic based ISP Organization or ISP Domain instead of IP Address. Your network admin can advise.

If you're accessing the Internet from outside your own organization's networks, it's difficult to exclude your traffic by IP. Since individual, home-based IP addresses tend to be assigned dynamically, a single filter to exclude your sessions is not feasible in most cases.

As another potential option for excluding your own traffic from a GA website property, post a dedicated page for which you configure Google Tag Manager to record a user-scope custom dimension and then exclude that custom dimension from your working views. This would be a somewhat special case, however, and would probably be worth the extra overhead only if you and colleagues also working from home offices were significantly inflating sessions, pageviews, and especially any conversions.

To filter out traffic from IPv6 addresses, see "Exclude IPv6 Addresses" in the GA help pages.

> **Note**
>
> ## Regular Expressions in Google Analytics
>
> Regular expressions, or *regex*, are text-matching notations that you can use for several purposes in GA—such as view filters, table filters, goals, and custom segments—as well as many other environments independent of GA.
>
> You will probably not need to use regex in GA every day, but when you need regex, it's quite indispensable, and although it can get quite complex, most of its uses in GA require only the basics. In fact, the regular expression that we populated into the Filter Pattern field in Figure 9.8 encapsulates much of what we need to know about regular expressions in GA and provides a good opportunity to review in Table 9.2 what we learned about regular expressions in Chapter 2, "Google Analytics Reporting Overview," and Chapter 8, "Goal and Ecommerce Tracking."

TABLE 9.2 Overview of Regular Expressions in Google Analytics

Regex Metacharacter or Sequence	Interpretation
^	The beginning-of-string anchor excludes any matches with strings that have text preceding the ^ character. For this reason, 132.161.79.8 or 232.161.79.11 would not match: `^32\.161\.79\.([1-9]|1[0-8])$` The regex tries to "find itself" within the match string and will generate a positive match if it locates its text pattern at any position within the match string unless you specify a beginning-of-string and/or end-string anchor as part of the regex.
$	The end-of-string anchor excludes any matches with strings that have text following the $ character. For this reason, 32.161.79.80 or 32.161.79.117 would not match: `^32\.161\.79\.([1-9]|1[0-8])$`
|	Probably the most frequently used regex metacharacter in GA, the pipe symbol means *or*. The parentheses in a regular expression such as (*bing|yahoo*) serve to group the *or* options and are not interpreted literally.
[–]	Brackets serve to group single-character options. For instance, `[b6x]` would match a single instance of *b* or 6 or *x*. Brackets with a hyphen allow a match for a character within the range represented. `[a-e]` matches a single lowercase character within the range, `[B-G]` matches a single uppercase character within the range, and `[3-9]` matches a single digit within the range. Note that regex treats all characters as text, so `[15-20]` would not be a valid regex notation to match any numeral between 15 and 20. With our understanding of the pipe symbol, the brackets, and the hyphen, we can read the `([1-9]|1[0-8])` portion of our IP exclude filter to represent a match for the a single character in the range 1 through 9, or 1 followed by a single character in the range 1 through 8. In this way, we're specifying a match for 1 to 18 as the value for the final octet of the IP address.
.	The dot metacharacter matches any single character.

continues

TABLE 9.2 *continued*

Regex Metacharacter or Sequence	Interpretation
\	The back slash, called the *escape* character, allows the following character in the regex to be interpreted literally instead of as a metacharacter. Thus, when we escape the dot characters in the IP address, we're performing a bit of extra regex hygiene to prevent a match for any other character (besides a literal dot) in the position of the dot.
?	The ? quantifier allows a match of zero or one of the preceding character (or zero or one of multiple characters in parentheses). If you wanted to filter a table for *car* or *cars* but not *card* or *cart*, you could specify cars?$ as the regular expression. The ? would mean a match for zero or one preceding *s* characters, and the $ end-of-string anchor would cause the *d* or *t* to invalidate the match.
*	The * quantifier allows a match of zero occurrences, one occurrence or multiple occurrences of the preceding character, such that .* means zero or more occurrences of any characters: in other words, a wildcard for matching any text string, even an empty one. You can use parentheses with .* as in (.*) to form a capturing group that extracts the wildcard string for reuse, as demonstrated in Figure 9.12 and Figure 12.26.

Regular expressions take some practice before they become intuitive. While it's not necessary to remember all the notations, it is important to know that you can always rely on regex for more specialized text matching needs in GA. The Regex101 website serves as an outstanding resource for testing your regular expressions and learning more about the subject.

Rewrite Medium to *social* for Social Sources

As discussed in Chapter 7, "Acquisition Reports," traffic from websites that GA recognizes as social networks are still recorded with referral as the medium in most instances. (This differs from traffic from websites that GA recognizes as search engines, for which the medium is recorded as organic.) If we wish to record social traffic with social as the medium instead of referral (or feed or twitterfeed, as may also be the case), we can configure a rewrite filter as in Figure 9.9.

Note that we use an advanced filter to match two dimensions (and output to one). In this example, we can disregard Extract A and Extract B—we're using the two fields only for matching, and not for copying to the output field (as we do in Figure 12.26).

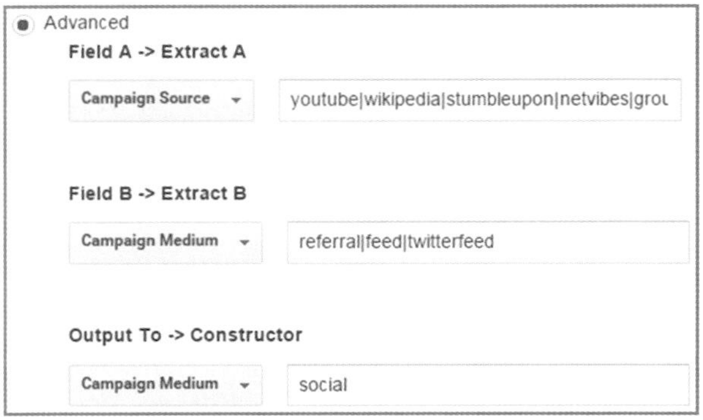

Advanced

Field A -> Extract A

Campaign Source ▾   youtube|wikipedia|stumbleupon|netvibes|grou

Field B -> Extract B

Campaign Medium ▾   referral|feed|twitterfeed

Output To -> Constructor

Campaign Medium ▾   social

FIGURE 9.9 This filter rewrites the medium of social clickthroughs to social.

The full string used for Campaign Source as follows is also available at www.e-nor .com/gabook:

```
youtube|wikipedia|stumbleupon|netvibes|groups\.google|bloglines|
groups\.yahoo|linkedin|facebook|webmasterworld|del\.icio\.us|digg|fe
edburner|twitter|technorati|blog|faves\.com|wordpress|newsgator|prwe
b|econsultancy|toprankblog|forums\.searchenginewatch|t\.co|plus
.(url\.)?google|feedly
```

Several regex metacharacters discussed previously are used in this filter: pipe (|), escape (\), and zero-or-one quantifier (?). Notice also that you don't need to specify the full domain names: any text string between two pipes can "find itself" anywhere within the source dimension text string, such that the technorati portion of the regular expression would match *www.technorati.com* as the Source dimension.

There's no need to rewrite the medium to social for the traffic to be correctly classified as Social in the Default Channel Grouping, but this filter will allow us to immediately identify social traffic wherever Medium is displayed. Note also that you can omit *feed* from Field B if you intend to break out your RSS traffic as separate channel as described in Chapter 7, or you could define your channel based on Source rather than Medium.

This filter will not in any way replace the need for campaign parameters in social clickthroughs from a Twitter app, a Facebook app, or any other social app: without URL parameters to specify medium, source, and campaign, GA will classify these click-throughs as direct, also as discussed in Chapter 7.

Note

Filters in the Real-Time Reports

While include and exclude filters apply to the Real-Time reports, filters that rewrite a dimension value are not yet applied when a session appears in the Real-Time reports. With the social rewrite filter in Figure 9.9 applied to a view, a clickthrough from the LinkedIn website would still appear in the Real-Time > Traffic Sources report as Referral, but, after the filters come into play during the GA data processing phase, the medium value for the same session would appear as social in the Acquisition reports.

Lowercase Filters

As we saw in Figure 9.4, GA treats case variations as separate dimension values. To reconcile these variations, we could apply a lowercase filter to Request URI as shown in Figure 9.10.

FIGURE 9.10 This filter consolidates case variations in the Pages report and anywhere else that Request URI appears.

It's quite common practice to lowercase the following dimensions (or *Filter Fields*, as dimensions appear in the custom filter setup) so they're consolidated in all reporting:

- Request URI
- Search Term
- Campaign Medium
- Campaign Source
- Campaign Name

> ### Note
>
> #### SEO Consideration: Lowercase Request URI or Not?
>
> While consolidation of Request URI variations for the same physical page is certainly beneficial within GA, there's a special reason to consider omitting a lowercase filter for Request URI: case variations can be indexed separately by the search engines. If the *Wall Street Journal* links to www.yoursite.com/Top-story, the *Washington Post* tweets www.yoursite.com/top-story, and the search engines are interpreting these pages differently, you're dissipating precious link equity and competing against yourself for ranking.
>
> A GA view filter will certainly not reconcile the case variations for the search engines: as discussed earlier in the chapter, the same URL consolidation principles apply to search engine indexing and to analytics, but the tools for these environments function independently. If you lowercase Request URIs in GA, you may therefore hide an SEO issue that you'd otherwise be able to alert your SEO team to.
>
> If you worked with your developers to instead control the actual URL case variations such as with 301 redirects, URLs would be consolidated for the search engines and GA alike.

Include Traffic to a Specific Subdirectory

Let's say that you run a website about video production. The two primary experiences that your website offers to visitors are tutorials, all housed in the /tutorials directory, and sales of video equipment, all housed in the /products directory. If your tutorial and product sales teams want to see activity only in their own subdirectories, or if, for any reason, one team should not have access to the other team's Web analytics, you can easily create two new views and apply a predefined subdirectory filter to each, as shown in Figure 9.11.

FIGURE 9.11 This filter will allow only traffic within the */tutorials/* subdirectory to appear in the view.

Note that specifying a subdirectory in a view filter produces a very different result from specifying a subdirectory as the Page field of a custom segment. If we defined a custom segment as *Page— contains— /tutorials/*, your reporting would show all activity for all sessions that included at least one pageview within the `/tutorials/` subdirectory, as discussed in Chapter 10, "Segments," while a view filter for the `/tutorials/` subdirectory would not allow any activity outside of that subdirectory into the view.

Hostname Filters

Figures 12.26 and 12.28 demonstrate the use of the Hostname dimension in a rewrite filter (to prepend the hostname to the request URI, as in *www.mysite.com/page*) and in an include filter (to include only one subdomain, such as news.mysite.com, in the view).

As stated about Google Tag Manager and GA implementations in Chapter 5, "Google Tag Manager," we generally recommend a single GTM container but separate GA properties in your production and development environments, but if you are using a single GA property across environments, you can also create separate views and apply an include hostname filter for *www*.mysite.*com* and *dev*.mysite.*com* as respective examples.

Configure Site Search for Nonstandard Search Results URLs

When we reviewed the Site Search view settings earlier in the chapter, we saw that this configuration works only if the search parameter appears within the URL of the search results page as the name in a *name=value* querystring pair. For a search results URL such as below, we need to follow a different procedure for GA Site Search configuration.

If, for example, a search for *wireless router* on your website leads to the following search results URL, we would configure site search with the advanced filter shown in Figure 9.12.

```
http://www.mundonetworking.com/search/results/wireless+router
```

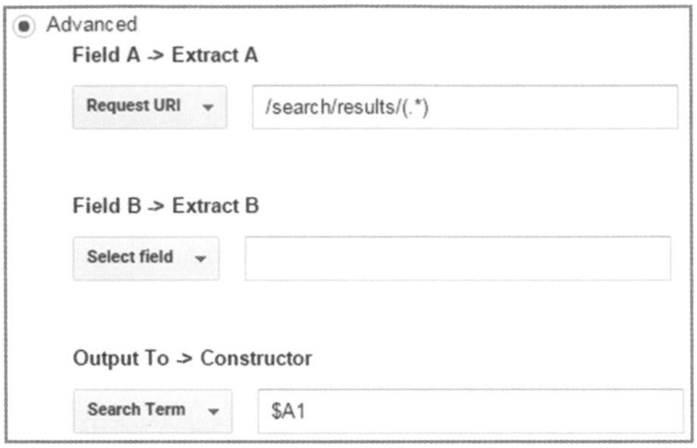

FIGURE 9.12 The (.*) regex capturing group serves to extract the search term from the Request URI, so we can then output it into the Search Term dimension.

As we'll discuss below in "Filter Execution Order," if you have this Search Term extract filter and a Search Term lowercase filter applied to the same view, make sure to position the lowercase filter after the extract filter so it can lowercase, as needed, all search terms received as output from the extract filter.

Exclude Referral Spam

Referral spam is generated in GA by spam bots designed to populate your Source/ Medium and Referral reports with spam domains (such as *semalt.com*) in the hopes that you, while reviewing your reports in GA, will click through. Apart from inflating your session and user count, these fake sessions increase your bounce rate and lower your conversion rates as reported.

At this time of writing the book, a referral spam solution is expected to become available directly within Google Analytics. In the meantime, see "How to Remove Referral Spam from Google Analytics" on Brian Clifton's blog. (Brian's blog post also steps through custom segment setup for excluding referral spam from GA data that has already been recorded. We discuss custom segments in the next chapter.)

Filter Execution Order

When you apply multiple filters to one view, each succeeding filter receives as input the output of the previous filter. You can click Assign Filter Order as shown at the top of Figure 9.13 to change the order of filter execution.

Rank ↓	Filter Name	Filter Type	
1	Include New Zealand	Include	remove
2	Include Australia	Include	remove

+ ADD FILTER | Assign Filter Order | Q Search

FIGURE 9.13 Because include filters are not cumulative, users from Australia will never make it into this view.

Filter order is normally not a primary consideration for filters that relate to different dimensions, but for filters that apply to the same dimension, we need to fully understand how include filters work.

Include filters do not work cumulatively: *include* means *exclude everything else*. Once you apply an include filter for one dimension value—such as *New Zealand* as Country in Figure 9.13—you lose the sessions that match all other dimension values. In this case, once the New Zealand filter executes, sessions from Australia are irrevocably excluded.

A regular expression will save the day in this case as well. By including both New Zealand and Australia separated by the regex pipe symbol, we'll be able to apply a single filter as shown in Figure 9.14 to include website visitors or mobile app users from both countries.

FIGURE 9.14 The regex pipe symbol allows us to include two or more dimension values within the same include filter.

If you wanted instead to exclude New Zealand and Australia from your view, either approach would work. Since exclude filters can function in series, you could apply separate exclude filters for the two countries, or you could apply a single filter that uses the pipe symbol.

> **Note**
>
> ## You Can Create 25 Views per GA Property—Take Advantage
>
> In most GA implementations, there are not as many views as there should be. As mentioned, your baseline should be three: working, test, and unfiltered. Beyond these three, you should

continues

continued

> not hesitate to create additional views as needed based on a specific subdirectory, device, source/medium, or, geographic location.
>
> In reports where the segments (discussed in Chapter 10) are not available, view filtering can also fulfill the same role as built-in or custom segments. For instance, you could apply the built-in Tablet Traffic segment to the Referral Traffic or Content Drilldown reports, but what if you wanted to view only tablet sessions in the Funnel Visualization or Multi-Channel Funnel reports, to which you cannot apply the usual GA segmentation? If you create a new view and apply an include filter for tablet, every report that anyone accessed in the view will display data only for tablets.
>
> Unlike segments, which are retroactive, view filters apply now-forward, so it's recommended to assess your need for additional views early in your implementation and create any that might be useful. If you create a view that you and your team end up not using, delete the view—no harm done.
>
> The capability to create additional views exists in GA for a reason; don't be afraid to use it.

Applying the Same Filter to a Different View

We've stressed the importance of trying your filters in a test view before applying to a working view. To facilitate this best practice, GA allows you to copy filters between views: no need to re-create a view that you've already applied to another view within the property.

If you have validated lowercase filters for campaign medium, source, and name in your test view, you can perform the following steps to replicate them in your main working view (or any other view):

1. In the view column of the Admin panel, select your working view and click Filters.
2. Click + Add Filter and select Apply Existing Filter as in Figure 9.15.
3. Select one or more filters that exist in the property but are not yet applied to your working view.

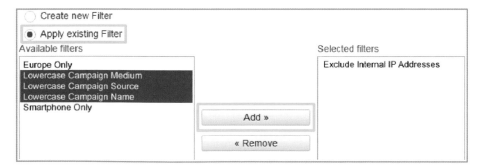

FIGURE 9.15 Once you have created a filter view, the Add Filter to View panel allows you to apply it to any other view in the property.

While it would certainly be considered best practice to apply cleanup filters (such as lowercase) to all views except your unfiltered view, you'd apply the specialized filters (such as Europe only) more selectively. As stated previously, different combinations of filters and settings applied to the same raw property feed illustrate the fundamental purpose of GA's multiple-view functionality.

ACCESS RIGHTS

Access rights management in GA is both flexible and quite straightforward. When you (as an individual) create a GA account, you can manage GA user access by clicking User Management in the Admin panel at all three levels of the account hierarchy:

- Account
- Property
- View

Access rights work top-down: rights that you grant to a user at the account or property levels flow down to the lower levels. Furthermore, you can't apply more restrictions for a user at a lower level than the level of access that you have provided at a higher level.

At each level of the account hierarchy, you can assign as many as four permissions, as shown in Figure 9.16 and detailed below. Of these permissions, you should consider Manage Users and Edit to be administrative and grant them very judiciously.

Add permissions for:

cthompson@company.com

User e-mail that is registered in Google accounts

Read & Analyze ▼

☐ Manage Users
☐ Edit
☐ Collaborate
☑ Read & Analyze

☑ Notify this user by email

Add   Cancel

FIGURE 9.16 At each level of the account hierarchy, you can assign four levels of privileges.

The requirement for a user to be given any level of access to GA is the same as for creating a GA account to begin with: a gmail address, or any email address that the user has associated with a Google account.

The permissions also work somewhat top-down: if you provide Edit or Collaborate access to a user, the lower permissions are selected automatically. Manage Users does not select any of the lower permissions, but it's routine to grant the other three levels of access to accompany Manage Users.

Manage Users

This permission allows other GA users to manage permissions in turn. Assign this permission only to fully trusted parties.

Edit

The Edit permission allows a GA user to dictate how data is captured and processed. Edit has different meanings at different levels of the account hierarchy; Table 9.3 lists several privileges that Edit access includes at each level.

TABLE 9.3 Edit Permissions at Account, Property, and View Levels

Account Level	Allowed through Edit Permission
Account	■ Manage account settings ■ View Change History ■ Manage Trash Can ■ Create new property
Property	■ Manage property settings ■ Customize tracking ■ Configure custom dimension and metrics ■ Import data ■ Create remarketing lists ■ Create new views
View	■ Manage view settings ■ Create and apply view filters ■ Create goals ■ Customize default channel groupings ■ Configure content groupings ■ Configure calculated metrics

Collaborate

The Collaborate permission can be a bit confusing, mainly because it means two things depending on whether or not the user created the asset at hand:

- If you have Collaborate permissions, you can share a Dashboard, Custom Segment, or Annotation with other GA users who have Collaborate or only Read & Analyze access.
- If the GA user with whom you have shared a Dashboard, Custom Segment, or Annotation also has Collaborate access, that user can edit or delete the asset.

The sharing option for dashboards and annotations is illustrated in Figure 11.2 and 11.12 respectively. You can share a segment from the Segment Availability popup as shown in Figure 9.17.

FIGURE 9.17 If you share a custom segment, other GA users with Read & Analyze rights to the view will be able to apply the segment to reports, and GA users who also have Collaborate rights will be able to edit or delete the segment.

Read & Analyze

This level of access formerly appeared in GA as *View Reports Only*. While still designating the most basic rights, the current name—Read & Analyze—hints at the many capabilities that this permission enables.

Read & Analyze users can create:

- Custom segments
- Custom reports
- Personal channel groupings
- Dashboards
- Intelligence alerts
- Private annotations
- Shortcuts

We discussed personal channel groupings in Chapter 7. We'll explore custom segments in Chapter 10 and the other capabilities listed above in Chapter 11.

Data Subset Access Control through View Filters and User Permissions

Earlier in this chapter, we learned how to apply an include filter to create a subset of the raw property. If we had to report on activity from a specific referring website, and we wanted to share with the website owners the GA data only for the sessions resulting from clickthroughs from their website, we could take the following steps:

1. Create a new view and name it Partnersite Clickthroughs.
2. Apply an include filter to the view as shown in Figure 9.18.

FIGURE 9.18 You could create a view containing data only for sessions that originated as clickthroughs from another website and then assign rights to that view only.

3. Click Manage Users in the View Admin, and assign Read & Analyze permission, possibly with Collaborate, to individuals at the partner organization.

> **Warning**   **!**
>
> **Deletion happens: be smart with access rights.**
>
> ➤ Be very careful when granting Edit and Manage Users Rights, particularly at the account level. If you provide Edit rights and Manager Users rights to another GA User at the account level, that user could edit or delete any element within the account and could also remove or revise your own access and thereby prevent you from accessing Change History or the Trash Can in the Admin screen.
> ➤ Be proactive and preemptive with GA access rights when individuals leave your organization, especially if not by choice.
> ➤ As relationships evolve or potentially terminate with providers and partners to whom you may have allowed any level of GA access, update permissions accordingly.
> ➤ The Manage Users screen does not allow you add a name as a label for an email address of a user that you add. If you feel that you will not be able to recognize an individual by email address at any point in the future, you can maintain a separate record that matches email addresses to names and organizations.

No Direct Access

No Direct Access is clearly not an actual access level that you can assign in GA, but it should be a consideration in some cases. Since you, as the reader, have taken the initiative to acquire this book and read it to this point, you understand that it takes some time, effort, and specialized skills to navigate and interpret GA reports effectively.

If an executive, a manager, a colleague (especially outside of marketing/analytics), or anyone within a client organization might be overwhelmed with the GA interface—or, more seriously, make ill-advised business decisions based on faulty report interpretation—it might be more appropriate, efficient, and safe to configure one or two dashboards or custom reports to be emailed to that individual on a weekly or monthly basis as described in Chapter 11.

User Management for Agencies

When managing analytics for websites and apps belonging to many organizations, consider these factors:

- You can create only 100 GA accounts under a single Google login, but other GA users can provide that single login with access to a large number of GA accounts, properties, and views. (For Analytics 360 clients, make sure to check with Google directly or your GAP reseller on settings and thresholds for the number of accounts, properties and views that you can create under a single login. Your total hit volume plays a factor here.)
- Once a Google login is granted all four permissions at the account, property, or view level, that login has the same rights within that account, property, or view as the GA user who created it.

With these two points in mind, it may make more sense for clients to create a GA account or property under a client login and to then provide full access to your agency, as we first discussed in Chapter 4. As one benefit, you won't need to be concerned about reaching the limit for GA account creation under a single login; as another, you'll eliminate the chance of inadvertently providing one client with access to another client's data. By the same token, if you're working with an analytics or digital marketing agency to assist you with GA, it's recommended that you create new accounts and properties as needed and then grant access to individuals at the agency (instead of the other way around).

CHANGE HISTORY

The Change History panel (Figure 9.19) shows detailed a record of all account, property, and view changes that GA users with Edit and Manage User rights have performed.

Date ↑	Changed By	Change
Jun 22, 2016, 6:34:33 PM	jkhan@ctrnews.com	Ecommerce reporting enabled for view "01 Main" on Property "ctrnews.com".
Jun 22, 2016, 6:32:47 PM	bhill@ctrnews.com	Read & Analyze permission granted for cdinardo@ctrnews.com on Account "CTR News".
Jun 19, 2016, 1:22:43 AM	ncruz@ctrnews.com	View "International News Subdirectory" created.

FIGURE 9.19 The Change History documents configuration and permissions changes at the account, property, and view levels.

TRASH CAN

GA users can no longer immediately delete an account, property, or view. A user must instead move an account, property, or view to the Trash Can as shown in Figure 9.20, from which it can be restored within 35 days by a GA user with Edit access to the account, after which the trashed item is deleted permanently.

FIGURE 9.20   GA users with Edit access to the account have 35 days to restore a trashed item.

When an account, property, or view is moved to the Trash Can, GA users with Edit access to the account receive a notification, as shown in Figure 9.21.

FIGURE 9.21   View deletion notification.

🔑 KEY TAKEAWAYS

View settings and filters transform the raw property feed.   View filters and many view settings serve to clean the property data, add metrics such as goal completions, or create subsets of the data. The reason for multiple views is primarily to represent differ-ent filtered output of the same raw property data.

Consolidate Request URIs as warranted.   If you have tens or hundreds of thousands of rows in the Pages report, your data likely suffers from fragmentation of the Page (aka Request URI) dimension: multiple Request URIs representing the same content and user experience. Start with the URL Parameters report in Google Search Console, and populate Exclude URL Query Parameters accordingly.

Filters and view permissions for controlled access to data subsets.   If it's not appropriate for all GA users to access all data recorded in the property, you can use a view filter to create a subset of your property data and then provide access only to that view.

Don't be afraid to create new views, but be sure to validate with view filters and settings.   Take advantage of the 25 views that you can create in each property. Create a test view and a backup view within each property, and carefully validate view settings and filters in the test view before copying to a working view.

Unlimited account access.   You can be given access to an unlimited number of accounts, properties, and views.

Be very cautious with Edit and Manage Users access.   Provide Edit and Manage Users rights, especially at the Account level, to trusted parties only.

Deletions restorable from the Trash Can for 35 days.   If you have Edit access at the account level, you can restore a trashed account, property, or view within 35 days.

 ## ACTIONS AND EXERCISES

1. **Create test and backup views.** Create a test view and a raw, unfiltered backup view for each GA property that you manage. You can also provide view names that keep your views in order, with your main view on top.

2. **Exclude internal traffic.** Consult with your network admins on your company IP address ranges, and create an exclude filter for your internal IP addresses accordingly. As another potential option, you may be able to filter internal traffic by Internet service provider (ISP) Domain or ISP Organization.

3. **Configure site search tracking.** If you provide a site search function on your website, use one of the two methods outlined in the chapter to configure site search tracking.

4. **Consolidate URLs.** Use the Default Page and Exclude URL Query Parameters to consolidate URL variations as needed.

5. **Apply lowercase filters**. Lowercase Campaign Medium, Campaign Source, and Campaign Name, and also Search Term if site search tracking is enabled.

6. **Test bot filtering.** Create a copy of your unfiltered view, check the Bot Filtering checkbox, and note the difference in sessions and pageviews after a week or two before enabling bot filtering your one or more working views.

Segments

At an eMetrics conference back in 2008, the early days of Web analytics, conference chair Jim Sterne asked a panel of industry thought leaders about the number-one thing that analytics platforms are missing.

"Segmentation," they answered, almost in unison. Some also added that aggregation "stinks" (but used a more colorful term).

Fast forward to today: Web analytics platforms—and Google Analytics (GA) specifically—have done a great job at allowing marketers to slice and dice the data in almost every way possible and to get to insights much more quickly than with the default reporting aggregates.

In this chapter, we cover the power and the ease of segmentation in Google Analytics.

SEGMENT TO FOCUS AND AMPLIFY

In analytics, aggregation can hinder insights. When you apply a segment to your GA reports, you're viewing a cohesive subset of data, based on visitor characteristics or behavior, that will allow you to detect trends that would otherwise remain hidden and to measure and optimize for performance in a more focused and meaningful way (Figure 10.1).

FIGURE 10.1 Segments focus your analysis on visitor subsets.

If, for example, your boss is still not convinced of the need to invest in a mobile marketing and analytics strategy, you can apply the built-in Mobile Traffic segment to easily isolate mobile visits in Audience Overview, Landing Pages, Source/Medium: the segment stays applied in almost any report you access, so you can readily see if mobile traffic is trending up (while mobile bounce and conversion rates may not be improving). By applying a segment, you've gained an insight that you can act upon concretely for business improvement. Your argument is settled, and you can get your mobile budget allocation approved.

Applying a Built-In ("System") Segment

You can apply two different types of segments to your reports: built-in segments, and custom segments that you or another GA user has defined.

To apply a built-in segment:

1. At the top of a GA report, click Add Segment.
2. In the left section of the segments panel, click System to display only the system (i.e., built-in) segments as in Figure 10.2.
3. Select a segment, such as Mobile Traffic.

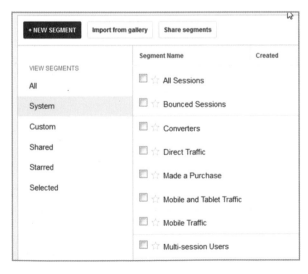

FIGURE 10.2 System (or "built-in") segments listed in the segment panel.

Once we apply a segment to one report, it stays applied even as we navigate among different reports across properties and accounts. You can apply as many as four segments to a report at one time.

Below we discuss several additional built-in segments.

Non-Bounce Sessions

Why might you want to exclude bounced sessions from your reports? The answer is straightforward: to focus your analysis on visitors who demonstrated an initial level of engagement and therefore better represented your true target audience.

We're not by any means recommending complacency about your bounce rate. Bounce rate is normally a negative indicator, especially for a transactional website, and you would not want to see your Bounce Rate metric increasing year over year. That said, a certain amount of bounce is always to be expected: such as from errant organic searches, outdated referrals, and so forth. By excluding these sessions from your analysis, you're tightening the focus to visitors who were, so to speak, really supposed to be on your website to begin with.

With the Non-Bounce Sessions segment applied in Figure 10.3, we amplify the representation of the conversion rate metric and thereby highlight trends more saliently than with only the default All Sessions segment applied. This metric amplification, a key benefit of segments, is explored in greater detail later in the chapter.

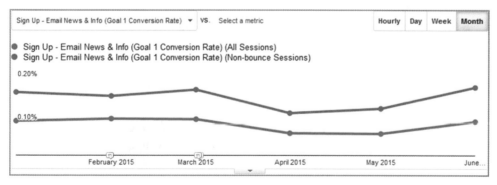

FIGURE 10.3 The conversion rate trend is more pronounced within the Non-Bounce Sessions segment than within All Sessions.

Conversion-Related System Segments

Which pageviews and events occurred most frequently in sessions that included goal completions? Where were the greatest number of exits in non-converting sessions?

Five of the built-in segments relate to goal conversions and Ecommerce transactions:

- **Sessions with Conversion**
- **Sessions with Transaction**

- **Converters:** Similar to Sessions with Conversion, but with the scope set to User instead of Session. (Segment scope is discussed later in the chapter.)
- **Made a Purchase:** Similar to Sessions with Transaction, but with scope set to User instead of Session.
- **Non-Converters:** Users who did not complete a goal or an Ecommerce transaction in any session, as defined in Figure 10.4.

FIGURE 10.4 By making a copy of the built-in Non-Converters segment, we can see that it encompasses users who completed neither a goal nor an Ecommerce transaction.

When you apply the Sessions with Conversion segment to the Pages report, you can see which pages were the most viewed during converting sessions. Similarly, Sessions with Transaction segments for sessions that included an Ecommerce transaction. You can apply the Non-Converters segment at the same time as any of the converter segments to compare pageviews against any of the converter segments. If the top pages in the converter segments are helping, or at least coinciding, with conversions and transactions, you can make these pages even more accessible in your website navigation.

Conversely, the Non-Converters segment mentioned above isolates users who have not converted or transacted in any session, as shown in Figure 10.5. After you apply this segment to the Exit report, how can you improve the top exit pages for non-converters? Better value proposition or call to action?

Page		Exits		Pageviews	% Exit
Non-Converters		631,782 % of Total: 31.48% (2,007,207)		1,529,232 % of Total: 12.34% (12,395,141)	41.31% Avg for View: 16.19% (155.13%)
1. /home		269,813 (42.71%)		421,558 (27.57%)	64.00%
2. /payment		60,688 (9.61%)		78,566 (5.14%)	77.24%
3. /search-results		15,326 (2.43%)		51,122 (3.34%)	29.98%
4. /news-summary		13,914 (2.20%)		40,730 (2.66%)	34.16%
5. /bios		13,859 (2.19%)		47,374 (3.10%)	29.25%

FIGURE 10.5 Applying the Non-Converters segment to the Exit Pages report highlights opportunities to optimize the payment and search results pages.

Creating a Custom Segment

As we saw earlier, many of the built-in segments are very useful, but the real power of segments comes with the custom segments that you define yourself. Let's broadly consider two kinds of segments: we'll call them *characteristic segments* and *behavior segments*.

Characteristic Segments

For characteristic segments, you can very easily define a segment based on a value that you see in the Audience or Acquisition reports, for instance:

- **Ontario (province of Canada).** Define a segment based on the Region dimension.
- **Old versions of Internet Explorer.** Define a segment based on Browser and Browser Version dimension.
- **Referrals from a partner website.** Define a segment based on Source dimension.

All of these examples are based on a dimension value: geography, technology, and traffic source characterize the entire session.

To define a segment for visitors from `partnersite.com`:

1. Access the segment panel shown previously in Figure 10.2.
2. Click New Segment.
3. At this point, there are two places you can find the dimension to define your segment: in the top five sections of "starter" sections (Demographics through Traffic Sources or Ecommerce), or under Advanced > Conditions. These options are basically equivalent, but we usually recommend to go straight to Advanced > Conditions. There you'll find all the same dimensions as in the starter sections, and you'll also be able to select Users or Sessions scope and create a segment based on a custom dimension value, all of which we will discuss below.
4. For our example shown in Figure 10.6, we'll select *Source* as the dimension, we'll keep the match drop-down set to *contains*, and we'll enter *partnersite.com* into the value field. Notice that we could also create an inverse segment by selecting *Exclude* instead of *Include* from the available drop-down.

FIGURE 10.6 You can start your segment definition in one of the top sections, such as Traffic Sources, or in Advanced > Conditions, where additional options are available.

Behavioral Segments

Behavioral segments may be a harder to understand at first than characteristic segments, but they can be even more critical for determining your success factors and identifying your different audience constituencies. As a note, the behavioral segments we're discussing here do not correspond directly with the Behavior section of the new segment panel shown in Figure 10.6.

In a behavioral segment, we're using a single hit-level action—in most cases, a pageview or an event—to identify entire sessions or even multi-session users.

Let's say that you run a website that promotes tourism to Denmark. Three months ago, you posted a new page with a prominent link from the home page: "Top 10 Reasons to Visit Denmark This Year." Your design and content team put considerable effort into this page, and everyone wants to know if it's helping to increase information requests and mailing list signups.

You create two segments: one that includes sessions in which a Top 10 Reasons pageview occurred as in Figure 10.7, and an inverse session that excludes sessions in which the pageview occurred (in other words, all sessions in which the pageview did not occur).

FIGURE 10.7 A segment based on the Page dimension includes all data from the sessions in which the page was viewed at least once.

It's critical to reiterate that a segment defined as *Page – exactly matches – /top-10-reasons* does not just include that page. If it did, it would serve little purpose, since the Pages report already displays metrics for that page. Instead, this segment identifies all *sessions* in which this page was viewed at least one time. If you defined a segment as *Page – contains – /product*, you would not just match pages with */product* in request URI;

instead, you'd match all *sessions* that included at least one view of a page with */product* in the request URI.

When applied to the Goals reports, our two segments demonstrate a possible correlation between the Top 10 Reasons page and the goal completion: the email signup conversion rate for the Top 10 Viewed segment is 1.45% while only 0.73% for the Top 10 Not Viewed segment, as shown in Figure 10.8.

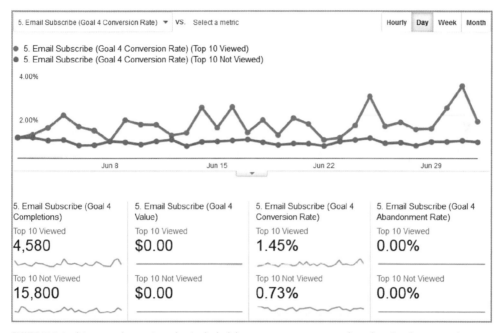

FIGURE 10.8 In this example, sessions that included the promo page generated nearly twice the conversion rate of sessions that did not include the promo page.

Is it invalid from a statistical or psychographic standpoint to attribute the increase in conversions to the Top 10 Reasons pageviews? Perhaps: in logical terms, the visitors who were most likely to convert could have also been the most likely to access the Top 10 Reasons page. However, the correlation is very compelling, and we might plausibly attribute the conversion increase, at least in part, to the Top 10 Reasons page, and make an effort to drive more traffic there. At a minimum, we have identified an excellent hypothesis for testing: the Top 10 Reasons to Visit Denmark Page increases our email signups. (We'll discuss testing techniques in Appendix A.)

To validate that the Top 10 Reasons pageview occurred before the conversion, we can create a segment with a specific step order. Note that you can specify whether or not the steps could have been separated by other interactions; for many types of analysis, direct succession is not as relevant as the completion of the steps in an overall order, so we can keep the default *is followed by* setting rather than change to *is followed immediately by* (Figure 10.9).

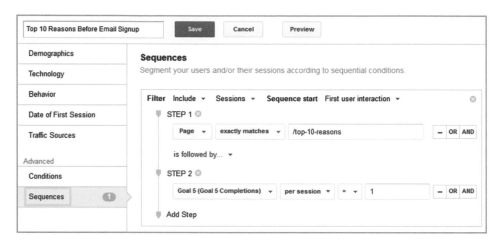

FIGURE 10.9 This sequence segment will tell us the number of sessions in which the Top 10 Reasons pageview preceded the email signup.

Based on the success of the Top 10 Reasons page, you decide to invest €10,000 of your marketing budget in a Top 10 Reasons video. How will you measure the video's effectiveness? Assuming that you have tracked video interactions as GA events, you could again create two segments—sessions with the video play and sessions without the video play—similar to Figure 10.14, and you could again validate the sequence with a Sequence segment similar to Figure 10.9.

Additional Custom Segments

In addition to the segments discussed above, you can define the following segments to focus your analysis.

Sessions with/without Login   If your logged-in users are redirected to a page such as `/logged-in` or `/welcome`, you can create login and no-login segments based on that page. If your logged-in visitors are not redirected to a special page, you can record a custom dimension (or an event) as part of the login process as described in Chapter 12, "Implementation Customizations," and then create a segment based on that custom dimension (or event).

High-Value Ecommerce   Sessions (or users) with Revenue greater than a specified amount.

Non-Bounce Non-Converting Sessions   Copying the built-in Non-Bounce Sessions segment as a basis, we can define a segment that helps us identify pageviews and exit pages for sessions in which the visitor was motivated enough not to bounce but not motivated enough to convert.

Home Page Not Viewed   The Landing Pages report immediately indicates the percentage of sessions that did not begin on the home page, but you can also create a segment to display the number of sessions that did not include the home page at all. If a significant portion of your sessions do not pass through the home page at all, you need to make sure that critical messaging and navigation options are not restricted to the home page, since many of your visitors will never see the home page.

Note

"Engagers" Segment

Figure 10.10 shows an example *Engagers* segment from Brian Clifton, which you can apply to your reports to help identify interested visitors and begin to "improve the signal-to-noise ratio."

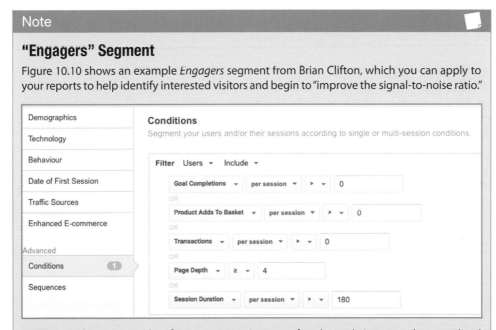

FIGURE 10.10 This segment identifies engagement in terms of goal completion, started or completed Ecommerce transactions, page depth (unique pageviews of different pages), or session duration. Note that the *Product Adds to Basket* metric may appear as *Product Adds to Cart* depending on localization.

You can apply this segment to the Location, Mobile Devices, or Source/Medium report (as shown in Figure 10.11) for a better understanding of your engaged visitors: the country they're located in, the technology they're using, and the traffic sources that are generating their visits.

By applying the Engagers segment to the Source/Medium report, we see that our AdWords (i.e., google/cpc) traffic accounted for only 15.65% of overall sessions but 21.95% of engaged sessions for the time period. To drill down for further insight, we could view our reports with any number of more specific segments applied, such as the Goal Overview report with an AdWords

continues

continued

(source = `google`, medium = `cpc`) segment applied, or we could analyze goal and Ecommerce metrics in the AdWords Campaigns report even without applying additional segments. In either case, the Engagers segment can provide the first indication of the factors behind successful visits.

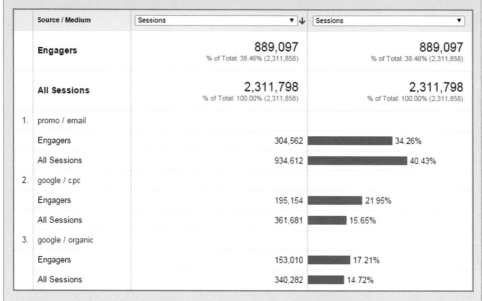

FIGURE 10.11 Engagers and All Sessions segments applied to the Source/Medium report, with the report display set to Performance.

Tie Sessions Together with User Scope

When you're defining a custom segment, the Advanced > Conditions or Sequences options shown in many of the preceding screen shots provide the choice between two scopes: Sessions (the default) and Users. (Note that *Scopes* does not appear as a label within the user interface.) This distinction may seem trivial, but it's quite profound, as it allows us to connect actions in one session with outcomes in a later session.

As an example, let's say that your content team is putting a great deal of time and effort into your blog, and the */blog* section of your website is beginning to get organic rankings and trackbacks/pingbacks, but you also want to gauge how much of your blog traffic also reaches the main part of your website.

You decide to create a sequence segment: *Landing Page – contains blog*, followed by *Page – does not contain – blog*. If, however, you don't change the scope from the default of Sessions to Users, you may be missing important insights. With the scope set to User (and Sequence Start set to "First user interaction") as in Figure 10.12, you can see users who first landed on a blog page but then accessed pages on the main part of your website, even during subsequent sessions.

Sequences

Segment your users and/or their sessions according to sequential conditions.

Filter	Include ▾	Users ▾	**Sequence start** First user interaction ▾		⊙

STEP 1 ⊙

Landing Page ▾	contains ▾	blog	—	OR	AND

is followed by... ▾

STEP 2 ⊙

Page ▾	does not contain ▾	blog	—	OR	AND

Add Step

FIGURE 10.12 By changing the segment scope from Session to User, we can trace activity on the main part of our website back to landing pages on the blog, even from a previous session.

As another scope example, let's say that you run a mortgage website. Your primary conversion occurs when your visitor completes an online mortgage application. When you check the Multi-Channel Funnel > Time Lag and Path Length reports, you observe that many conversions are occurring after the first session, as shown in Figure 10.13.

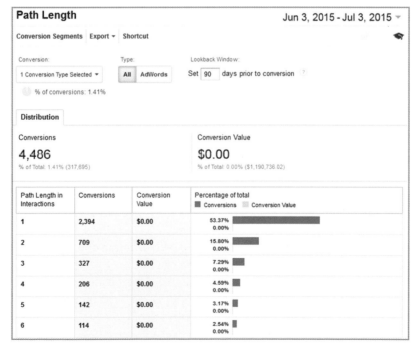

FIGURE 10.13 This Path Length report demonstrates that many mortgage seekers are converting after the first session.

Your next investigation: which interactions may be helping conversions in later sessions? Is the mortgage calculator on the home page engaging visitors to return and apply for a mortgage? Similarly to the segments we defined earlier in this chapter for individual sessions in which the "Top 10 Reasons to Visit Denmark" promo page was or was not viewed, we can define segments based on mortgage calculator submissions during any of multiple sessions from the same user (assuming that you're capturing the calculator interactions as GA events or virtual pageviews). See Figures 10.14 and 10.15.

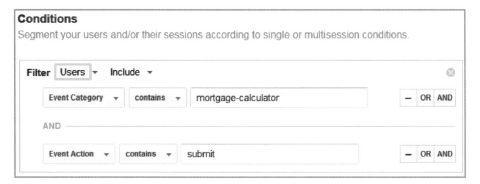

FIGURE 10.14 This behavioral segment matches any user who submitted a mortgage calculation in any session.

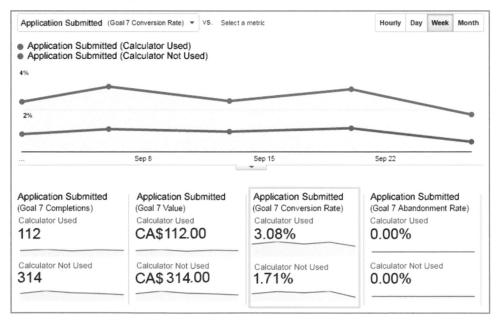

FIGURE 10.15 Users who submitted a mortgage calculation generated a considerably higher conversion rate.

We could further validate the order of these interactions—that is, that the calculator interactions preceded the goal completions—by creating two sequences at Users scope: one in which the mortgage calculator event did precede the goal completion, and one in which no mortgage calculator event followed the goal completion. When applied to the Audience Overview report, these segments would clearly indicate which came first for most users.

As a note, if the mortgage calculator interaction occurred primarily in the same session as the mortgage application conversion, conversion rate might display lower with a user-scope segment than a session-scope segment. This is due to the fundamental conversion math demonstrated in Figure 8.7: since the denominator in conversion rate is sessions and not users, a user scope segment pulls in more sessions, thereby potentially lowering the conversion rates that the goal or Ecommerce reports display.

User Scope and Cookie Deletion

Keep in mind that the multisession connection of Users scope depends on the _ga cookie. If a visitor to the mortgage site uses the calculator and then returns to the site on a different device or browser or after having deleted cookies, the Mortgage Calculator segment defined above would not be able to recognize any calculator events from previous sessions. (Cross-device tracking, discussed in Chapter 12, can also associate multiple sessions with the same logged-in user.)

MAPPING CUSTOMER CONSTITUENCIES AS CUSTOM SEGMENTS

Two of your top priorities as an analyst and optimizer are to:

1. Create GA segments for your different visitor constituencies.
2. Perform most of your ongoing analysis within the segments and not within the aggregate data.

What are your customer or visitor constituencies? They're the designations you already use for your customers or visitors. As a basic example, let's consider the two basic constituencies on `airbnb.com`:

- **(Potential) hosts:** website visitors who want to list a residence as a rental.
- **(Potential) renters:** website visitors who want to rent out someone else's residence.

These two different visitor blocs have completely different objectives, so it would make little sense to analyze their behaviors and conversions as one aggregate. But how can you separate these two visitor groups?

FIGURE 10.16 You can identify the constituency of potential hosts on airbnb.com by a clickthrough on Become a Host, which accesses the */rooms/new* page.

In many cases, visitors' own actions signal the constituencies to which they belong. On `airbnb.com`, we can define a reasonably accurate potential-host segment based on visitors who click the Become a Host button shown in Figure 10.16 and thereby access the `/rooms/new` page, as shown in Figure 10.17. To define a segment for your potential renters, change the segment definition in Figure 10.17 from *Include* to *Exclude*. In both cases, we can set the scope to Users, also as shown in Figure 10.17.

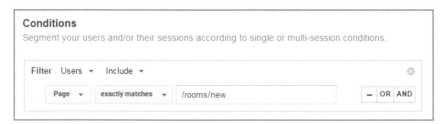

FIGURE 10.17 Potential Host segment based on a */rooms/new* pageview.

If you're the person at Airbnb responsible for room listing conversions, the Potential Host segment provides the context that you need. Why should you measure conversion rate against a general audience, most of whom were never potential converters for that goal? With other visitor types excluded from your segment, you'll get a much clearer indication of your conversion rate in this logical context, and you'll much more easily be able to detect fluctuations of the amplified conversion rate within a segment than of the nonsegmented conversion rate diluted by traffic that is not relevant for the goal, as you can see in Figure 10.18.

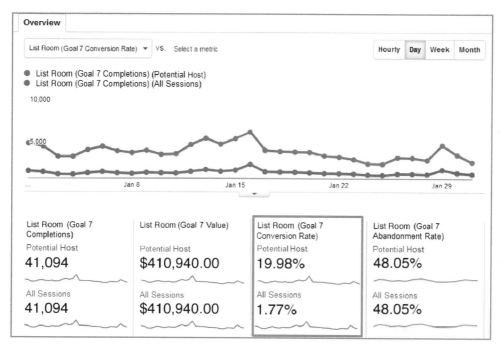

FIGURE 10.18 Though the number of goal conversions for the List Room goal is the same for all sessions and for potential hosts, the conversion rate for the List Room goal has a much more focused context within the Potential Host segment.*

The Potential Host segment would benefit our analysis within other reports as well. With the Potential Host segment applied, we could access the Channels report to see which traffic channels are sending the most visitors who click Become a Host, or we could view the Goals > Overview report to see if visitors who clicked Become a Host completed other goals besides List Room.

You could also define a Potential Renter segment as the inverse of the Potential Host segment in Figure 10.17: just *exclude* users who have accessed the */rooms/new* page. You could then more meaningfully evaluate your Rent Room goal within the Potential Renter segment, the same way that we evaluated the List Room goal within the Potential Host segment.

As another example, a health insurance website may have five very different types of users, as indicated in Table 10.1.

---

* As a disclaimer, Figure 10.18 and the associated discussion do not represent actual GA data for Airbnb.

TABLE 10.1 Customer Constituencies for a Health Insurer Mapped to Google Analytics Segments

Constituency	Conversion	Segment Description	Segment Definition
Human resource managers or representatives at a client company	**Enroll employees:** It's three times as expensive for your insurance company when your client companies enroll a new employee by phone or mail, so your main conversion for HR managers or representatives is to enroll new employees online.	Anyone who enters a human resource login is redirected to the /group-management page on your website, which no other type of user sees.	Page – exactly matches – /group-management
Medical provider (doctor, hospital, therapist)	**File a claim:** Online claims filing is also much more cost-effective than paper or phone claims, so your main conversion for health care providers is to complete a claim filing online.	Anyone who enters a medical provider login is redirected to one of the pages on your website that begin with /provider, which no other type of user sees.	Page – starts with – /provider
Existing health insurance policyholders	**Watch a video:** To encourage policyholders to eat right, exercise, and stay healthy, your main conversion for policyholders is to watch at least 75% of your Fitness Facts video.	In the same scripting that displays a Welcome message when a policyholder logs in, you and your developers can populate a custom dimension named Login Type as policyholder. Since regular policyholders (i.e., not human resource or medical provider) are not redirected to another page, we cannot define this segment based on Page as in the previous two segments.	Custom Dimension Login Type – exactly matches – policyholder (We discuss Custom Dimensions in Chapter 12.)
Existing health insurance policyholders—cobranded referrals	Same as above	The insurance company has an agreement with a health care provider for single sign-on (SSO) and cobranding the header (with logos and messaging) when visitors click through from that medical care provider's website.	Source – contains – medicalprovider.com

TABLE 10.1 *continued*

Constituency	Conversion	Segment Description	Segment Definition
Individual potential customers	**Purchase a policy:** Your primary goal for direct consumers is to purchase a health policy.	You can define your potential direct customers as any visitor who does not login and therefore doesn't match any of the four segments above.	Inverse of the four segments above

For two of the segments above (human resource and health care provider) all we needed for our segment definition was a page that only that type of visitor can ever access. During the course of a session, all logged-in providers—and only logged-in providers—view at least one page that contains */provider* at the beginning of the Request URI. The segment is there waiting to be defined, based on the data that we're already capturing in GA.

Since existing policyholders are not redirected to a specific page on login, it will take a little more implementation work before we can define our segment. The steps, however, are straightforward: once you have worked with your developers to push a variable named *policytype* with the value *policyholder* (just as examples) into the data layer when the policyholder logs in, we'll be able to populate the custom dimension in GA and define our segment based on the custom dimension as described in Chapter 12.

It's not always necessary to identify our constituencies based on behavior or a custom dimensions in the examples above: in the case of the referrals from the medical provider website, `medicalprovider.com` as a source defines our segment very neatly.

Individual potential customers match none of the criteria of the other four visitor groups, and that's just how we can define that segment: as the inverse of the other four.

> Note
>
> ## Segment or Else!
> Are all these custom segments worth the hassle?
>
> If this point is not yet abundantly clear: yes, segments—particularly segments mapped to your user constituencies—are absolutely, positively worth the time you invest to set them up. In many cases, you can easily define segments based on the page, source, technology, and geo data that you're already capturing. Even for segments such as the existing health insurance policyholders in Table 10.1 that require a bit of coding effort for a custom dimension, the analytics payback will exponentially compensate the initial setup effort.
>
> If you deal with only one basic user type, custom segments may be less of a priority. If, on the other hand, you and your organization have designed different pages, experiences, or conversions for different audience types, it is imperative that you perform much of your analysis with your own custom segments applied.
>
> Your million-dollar (-pound, -euro, etc.) insight is not likely to happen while you're swimming in aggregated data; it will come from focused segmentation.

Segment Availability for Other Views and Users

By default, a custom segment that you create in one view is also available to you in any other view. You can opt to restrict the segment to a single view, or to make it visible to other GA users and editable for users with Collaborate rights to the view, as shown in Figure 10.19.

FIGURE 10.19 Custom segment options.

You can also share segment configurations with other GA users either from the Share Assets screen that you access from the View admin or directly from the segments panel that you access from a report. The procedure for sharing assets is detailed in Chapter 11, "Dashboards, Custom Reports, and Intelligence Alerts."

By clicking Import from Gallery at the top of the segments panel, you can also import and apply segments that other GA users have contributed to the Solutions Gallery.

> **Note**
>
> ## Don't Be Afraid to Use Segments
>
> After our previous exhortations, we offer this assurance: don't be afraid to apply built-in segments, to import segments from the gallery, or especially to define your own custom segments. The segments will not permanently alter any of the underlying report data, and they will be visible only to you by default.
>
> As long as you understand how the segmentation works, don't hesitate to create new segments as the analysis warrants, even several dozen segments in the course of a year even for a single GA property or view. Any segment that you define remains available in your custom segment pool, and if you never need to use a certain segment again, just delete it—no harm done.

Remarketing with Google Analytics Segments

Custom segments can be an extremely useful tool not only for analysis but also for marketing. If, for instance, you create a segment for visitors who view three pages or more but do not convert, you can then use that segment—or *audience*, as a segment is called for remarketing—to trigger banner displays through the Google AdWords Display

Network or the DoubleClick banner platform. You can also take advantage of Remarketing Lists for Search Advertising (RLSA) by using your GA remarketing lists to influence bids, text, and keyword matching through AdWords for searches on Google. We discuss remarketing and RLSA in Chapter 14, "Google Analytics Integrations."

Multi-Channel Funnel Conversion Segments

The system and custom segments that we've examined thus far do not apply to the Multi-Channel Funnel reports discussed in Chapter 8. In these reports, such as Top Conversion Paths below, you can apply built-in or custom segments based on the traffic sources that drove goal or Ecommerce conversions. With the First Interaction Is Paid Advertising conversion segment applied (and the lookback window set to 90 days) in Figure 10.20, we can see that paid advertising served as the first touchpoint for 9.72% of eventual conversions.

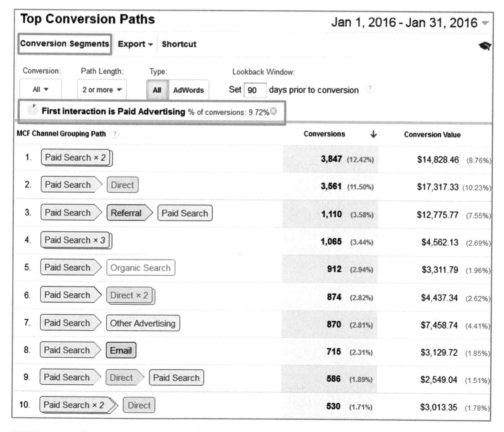

FIGURE 10.20 In the Multi-Channel Funnel reports, you can apply specialized segments based on the traffic sources that generated conversions.

The segment availability settings shown previously in Figure 10.19 do not apply to the Conversion Segments in the Multi-Channel Funnel reports. Any custom Conversion Segment that you define will be accessible to you in other views, properties, and accounts, but not to any other GA user.

SAMPLING

As useful as segments are, we must remember an important caveat: segmenting your reports can cause sampling. Sampling is triggered when both of the following conditions are in play:

- You are using GA standard, and you're reporting on a time period that contains more than 500,000 sessions in the view. (At the time of writing, the thresholds in Analytics 360 are 200 million, 50 million if the date selection includes the current day, and 1 million if only the current day is selected. These thresholds are likely to keep increasing or possibly even be removed. For data that is more than 6 months old, the Analytics 360 sampling threshold is reduced to 1 million sessions, but longer lookbacks with the higher thresholds may also roll out in the future.)
- You apply a segment or a secondary dimension to a built-in report, or you access a custom report. (We discuss secondary dimensions in Chapter 2 and custom reports in Chapter 11.)

Segments, secondary dimensions, and custom reports force GA to make on-the-fly calculations. If the sessions in the selected time period surpass the thresholds stated above, these calculations are made only on a subset of the data and then multiplied back out to equal the original number of sessions.

As a simplified example in Figure 10.21, AdWords campaign 2 generated the greatest number of clickthroughs from Malaysia in actuality. When, however, you define a segment for visitors from Malaysia and apply it to your custom report, campaign 1 shows twice as many clickthroughs as campaign 2, because the final data that you see in the reporting interface is based on a disproportionate sample—25% in this case—that was multiplied by four to equal the original number of sessions in the unsampled data.

How do we know when sampling is in effect? Let's say that we wanted to display a list of our best-selling products on tablet devices. Figure 10.22 shows that when we applied the built-in Tablet Traffic segment to the Product Performance report, the sample size has dropped from the unsampled default of 100% to only 5.05% of sessions.

Sample Size and Cardinality

Notice that 5.05% indicates the *sample* size, not the *segment* size. The 8.01% segment size in Figure 10.22 is calculated from the 5.05% sample size. Since there are only three device categories—desktop, mobile, and tablet—the Tablet Traffic segment size

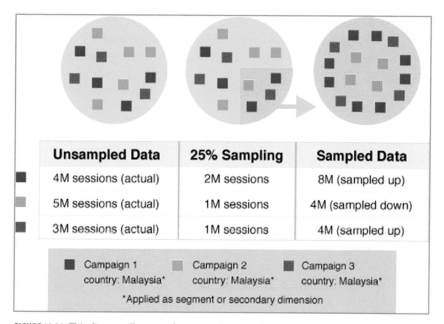

FIGURE 10.21 This diagram illustrates how sampling can skew your reporting.

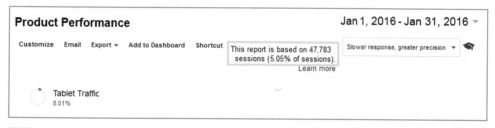

FIGURE 10.22 When we apply the built-in Tablet Traffic segment, the sample size drops from 100% to 5.05%.

itself is probably quite accurate based on only 5.05% of data. Where sampling really becomes an issue is when the sampled report involves a data dimension with many possible values—that is, a *high-cardinality* dimension—or a metric for an infrequent occurrence.

For example, even though the overall 8.01% segment size is reasonably accurate, reporting for hundreds of different products by tablet may be very skewed when based on just 5.05% of actual data. Sampling is especially likely to skew reporting for a high-ticket product that sells infrequently, or for a special goal such as a partnership or sponsorship inquiry that visitors submit only occasionally.

Basically, the smaller the sample size and the more granular or sporadic the data, the more of a problem sampling is going to pose. New versus returning session breakdown based on 60% of your data will be quite accurate, but a 2% sample size can seriously distort the calculation for entrances on 100 different landing pages.

Happily, the GA engineers are making significant improvements in this regard, so sampling is progressively occurring less in GA user interface overall.

If there's a segment that you use repeatedly, such as all visitors from South America, you can avoid sampling by creating an equivalent filtered view, as discussed in Chapter 9.

Accessing Unsampled Data

If you're using Analytics 360, you have the option to export an unsampled version of any sampled report as comma- or tab-separated values as shown in Figure 10.23. In approximately one hour, the exported file appears in your Google drive (`https://drive.google.com`) under the same login that you use for GA.

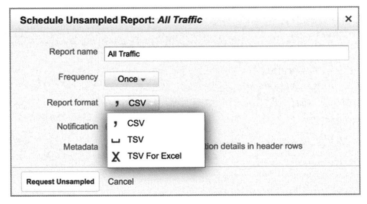

FIGURE 10.23 With Analytics 360 you can export unsampled data as comma- or tab-separated values.

For immediate access to unsampled data (when sampling would otherwise occur), you can also preconfigure Custom Tables to avoid sampling for any combination of dimensions, metrics, and segments that falls within the Custom Table definition. Chapter 18 reviews unsampled export and Custom Tables in greater detail. Also refer to the discussions on the Unsampled Request API in Chapter 16.

SEGMENTS VERSUS FILTERED VIEWS

We previously noted a parallel between segments and the view filters discussed in Chapter 9: both can serve to focus your reporting on a narrower subset of the full data capture. Table 10.2, however, outlines several critical differences.

TABLE 10.2 Comparison of View Filters and Segments

	View Filters	**Segments**
Access rights	Edit access required at the view level to create or apply a view filter.	Only Read & Analyze access required to create or apply a segment.
Availability/ Visibility	View filters affect reporting for anyone who accesses the view.	Default visibility for segments is set to an individual GA user across views.
Reports covered	Apply to all data and all reports that you access in the view.	You can apply segments to most reports in the view, but they are not available in the Funnel Visualization or the Multi-Channel Funnel reports.
Retroactivity	Apply to your data now forward.	Retroactive.
Permanence	Permanently alter underlying report data for the time that they are applied.	Do not alter underlying view data. You can apply and remove them dynamically.
Behavior	You can define a filter for all activity within a subdirectory but not for other specific behaviors.	You can define a "behavioral" segment that includes all other hits occurring in the same session that your specified pageview or event occurred in. You can also extend the scope from Sessions to Users.
Sampling	Do not cause sampling.	May cause sampling if the sampling conditions described above are met.

To elaborate on consideration listed in the table, segments provide somewhat more behavioral flexibility than view filters. While view filters allow you to include pageview hits that occur only within a certain subdirectory, segments allow you to include or exclude all hits in a session based on a single specific pageview or event. In cases where your audience constituencies identify themselves by accessing a specific page or generating a specific event, it will be feasible to create a corresponding segment but not a corresponding view filter.

 KEY TAKEAWAYS

System versus Custom Segments.   GA provides a range of built-in ("system") segments. You can create your own custom segments by copying and modifying a system segment, or you can start from scratch.

Characteristic and Behavioral Segments.   You can base your custom segments either directly on a session-level characteristic such as source, technology, or geographic location, or a hit-level behavior such as a pageview or an event that serves to identify the entire session. By applying behavioral segments, you can draw plausible correlations between actions (such as watching a video) and outcomes (such as submitting a lead form) and support them with Sequence segments.

Skip the "starter" conditions.   In the New Segment panel, the Conditions selection will provide all of the options available in the "starter" sections, plus some additional options, such as custom dimensions and user scope.

Sequences.   As another option for custom segments, you can identify visitors who completed a series of actions within a single session or across multiple sessions.

Retroactive, personal, nonpermanent.   Custom segments are analogous to view filters, but custom filters apply retroactively and are available only to you by default, and you can dynamically add and remove segments in your reports without affecting underlying view data.

Focus and amplify.   Apply segments to focus your analysis and amplify data points and trends that may otherwise remain undetected in aggregated data.

Map visitor constituencies.   If you offer distinct experiences to different types of customers and website visitors, determine the criteria (such as source, pageview, event, or custom dimension) that you can use to map these constituencies as GA segments, and perform much or most of your analysis within these segments.

Aggregates stink.   To reiterate and summarize, actionable insights are much more likely to arise from segmentation than from default data aggregation.

 ## ACTIONS AND EXERCISES

1. **Review all system segments.** Before you define your custom segments, review the built-in system segments. For each of the system segments, analyze at least one report after applying the segment.

2. **Review the conditions available for a new segment.** From the segment panel, click New Segment, review the "starter" conditions (Demographics through Traffic Sources or Ecommerce), and all options available under Conditions.

3. **Create three custom segments based on session characteristics.** Create segments based on source, technology, or geographic data, and apply them to your reports.

4. **Create two segments based on behavior.** Create two segments based on a pageview or an event, and create the inverse of those two segments as well. (For example, sessions in which the visitor viewed the promo page versus session

in which the visitor did not view the promo page.) Apply the segments to your reports, especially your goal or Ecommerce reports if either is configured. If you see a possible correlation between the behavior and a goal or Ecommerce conversion, create a corresponding Sequence segment to validate that the pageview preceded the goal completion or Ecommerce transaction.

5. **Change the scope of your behavioral segments to Users.** How does user scope affect the metrics displayed in your goal and Ecommerce reports? Keep in mind, as discussed in the chapter, that conversion rate can actually appear lower if most conversions occurred in the same sessions as the behavior (such as a video play or a pageview of a specific page), but the conversion rate will appear higher if most conversions for the users occurred in different sessions from the behavior in the segment definition.

6. **Create segments for each of your visitor or customer constituencies.** Determine the criteria that you can use to create segments for each of your customer or visitor groups. If you're unsure of which groups you need to account for, speak with your colleagues, managers, and executives.

7. **Begin generating any custom dimension (or event) data needed for your segments.** If you need custom dimension data to base a segment on—for example, logged-in users who aren't redirected to a designated page and cannot therefore be segmented by a Page dimension value—work with your development team to code the custom dimension, and then define the segment. If you need event or virtual pageview data for a behavioral segment—for example, a session in which a video was completed or a PDF was downloaded—configure the event or virtual pageview as a priority, and then define the segment.

Dashboards, Custom Reports, and Intelligence Alerts

n this chapter, we review dashboards and custom reports that you can configure to your own specifications, and we also discuss the automated emailing option that you can apply to dashboards, custom reports, and also the wide range of standard (i.e., built-in) Google Analytics (GA) reports that we've seen in previous chapters.

We also review the important custom Intelligence Alerts feature that allows to you receive notifications for specific changes in your GA metrics, and we'll learn how to create simple yet extremely helpful annotations to maintain a timeline of factors that could affect your GA data.

DASHBOARDS

Dashboards are a very important GA feature to which we could devote a lengthy discussion, but, because the dashboard functionality is very flexible and largely very straightforward, we'll just call out the trickier points, keep it fairly brief, and leave you to explore this feature directly.

Creating a Dashboard

Once you click Dashboards > Private > + New Dashboard in the left navigation, you're presented with three options, as shown in Figure 11.1:

- Blank Canvas
- Starter Dashboard
- Import from Gallery (the shared GA Solutions Gallery)

FIGURE 11.1 Options for creating a dashboard: Blank Canvas, Starter Dashboard, and Import from Gallery.

The first two options are self-explanatory. The Import from Gallery option allows you import dashboard configurations that other GA users have shared in the GA Solutions Gallery. Once you import a dashboard from the gallery—on its own or in a group of assets—the dashboard configuration populates with data from the view into which you have imported it.

In a new or existing dashboard, you can add widgets by clicking + Add Widget in the dashboard itself or by clicking Add to Dashboard in any report. To each dashboard, you can add up to 12 widgets, which you can rearrange by dragging and dropping and also by clicking Customize Dashboard and selecting a different layout. Each widget is very configurable in terms of metrics, report linking, format, and filtering. As mentioned above, the GA dashboard functionality is very flexible. (For nearly limitless formatting options and much greater dashboard interactivity, see the Tableau discussion in Chapter 16, "Advanced Reporting and Visualization with Third-Party Tools.")

You do not need Edit rights to the view to create a dashboard; you only need basic Read & Analyze access. If you decide that you don't want a dashboard that you've created, you can click Delete Dashboard. Under your GA login, you can create as many as 20 dashboards.

Sharing

By default, dashboards are private. For other GA users to see the dashboard listed in the left navigation, you can click Share Object in the Share menu, shown in Figure 11.2 (provided that you have Collaborate access rights in the view). At that point, the dashboard moves from Private to Shared in the left navigation and becomes visible to any GA user who accesses the view. Other GA users who have Collaborate rights can edit or delete the shared dashboard, while users who have only Read & Analyze access can only view the dashboard.

FIGURE 11.2 If you have Collaborate permission in the view, you can Share Object to move the dashboard from private to shared.

In the event that you want to share the dashboard configuration with another GA user so that they can import it into another view (or into the same view if your dashboard is still private), you can click Share Template Link in the Share menu and forward the template link in a regular email.

Export and Email

Although we're examining the export and email functionalities in the context of dashboards, they apply to almost all of the built-in reports reviewed in this chapter and throughout the book, and also to the custom reports discussed later.

You can export a dashboard as a PDF and most of the other GA reports as a PDF or in one of several data formats, such as CSV. (In Chapter 10, we also discuss the Unsampled Data export available to Analytics 360 users.)

These same formats are also available for emailing the dashboard or report as an attachment. You can email one time only, daily, weekly, monthly, or quarterly. (Note that the time interval defaults to Weekly, so if you intend to send the email out at the current moment, be sure to set Frequency to Once.) Any segments that you apply to a dashboard stay applied for export and email, but time comparisons can shift.

To remove or edit email scheduling, access Scheduled Emails from the View Admin column.

> **Note**
>
> ### Use the Email Feature in Your Role as Communicator and Agent of Change
> Take advantage of the email feature to send the most relevant dashboards, custom reports, and or built-in/standard reports to different stakeholders in your organization (or to clients).

continues

continued

> You should make sure that the metrics are relevant for the recipient, but also remember that, apart from the specific data points, the regularity of the emailed dashboard or report will keep others engaged in the analytics process, and they'll immediately know whom to seek out with questions about website or mobile app activity.
>
> In some instances, you'll be able to answer their questions readily. In other instances, you'll need to dig deeper and explore aspects of the data and use cases that you haven't considered on your own. The result? You've met a challenge and enhanced your analytics know-how, you've empowered your colleague, manager, or client with a data-driven insight, and you've probably created some value for your organization or your client's: win-win-win.
>
> To follow general etiquette for automated emailing, just remember to ask for permission first, but *keep other people engaged in your analytics work*.

CUSTOM REPORTS

Similarly to dashboards, we could devote many pages to the very important custom reporting feature in GA, but custom dashboards are also quite straightforward to configure, so we'll just review some basics, and you can then try them out directly and take advantage of them frequently.

You create custom reports for different combinations of the dimensions and metrics that we've seen in the built-in reports, and we can hard-filter by any dimension value (e.g., traffic from a specific source or device).

Custom reports are sometimes most useful for the data that they *do not* contain. Since a basic custom report definition requires only a single dimension and a single metric, you can create custom reports as streamlined versions of the built-in reports. This tight focus can be especially beneficial for presenting GA data to others in your organization and to clients. As we strive to communicate as effectively as possible, and custom reports allow us to remove distractions and highlight what's relevant.

Let's say, for example, that your sales manager has asked for a breakdown of Ecommerce performance by U.S. metro area (corresponding directly to DMA, or Designated Marketing Area for radio and television broadcasting). To create a focused custom report to meet this requirement, you could take the following steps:

1. Click Customization in the top navigation.
2. Click New Custom Report.
3. Configure the custom report as in Figure 11.3.

As with dashboards, you do not need Edit access in the view to create a custom report—only basic Read & Analyze access. Custom reports are visible only to you, but you can share the configuration with other GA users.

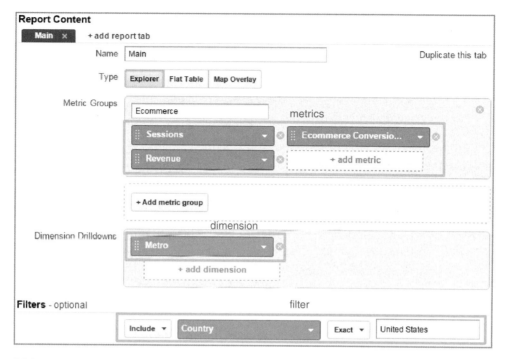

FIGURE 11.3 Custom report configured with three metrics, a single dimension, and a filter.

As we see in Figure 11.4, the resulting report communicates the data that your sales manager needs, without any clutter. As a note, we could have added another filter to exclude (not set) as Metro, but it may also be useful for your sales manager to see how many visits originated outside of any defined metro area. With a custom report, we'd have the flexibility to deliver the report either way.

	Metro	Sessions ⬇	Ecommerce Conversion Rate	Revenue
		2,349,527 % of Total: 97.11% (2,419,490)	0.85% Avg for View: 0.83% (2.22%)	$928,917.22 % of Total: 98.52% ($942,846.03)
☐ 1.	(not set)	236,863 (10.08%)	0.87%	$99,516.53 (10.71%)
☐ 2.	New York NY	139,775 (5.95%)	0.97%	$68,077.85 (7.33%)
☐ 3.	Chicago IL	128,259 (5.46%)	0.65%	$38,228.38 (4.12%)
☐ 4.	Dallas-Ft. Worth TX	110,665 (4.71%)	0.61%	$32,114.23 (3.46%)
☐ 5.	Los Angeles CA	100,384 (4.27%)	0.75%	$36,793.90 (3.96%)

FIGURE 11.4 Streamlined report, customized for the recipient.

Note that there are three formats available for custom reports:

- **Explorer:** similar to the built-in reports, with a main over-time graph and drill-down for multiple dimensions.
- **Flat Table:** simplified format, without a main over-time graph, and with side-by-side display for up to five dimensions.
- **Map Overlay:** geo and table format.

Custom Funnel, an additional custom report format available in Analytics 360 properties, is discussed in Chapter 18.

Note that custom dimensions, custom metrics, and calculated metrics, discussed in Chapter 12, "Implementation Customizations," do not appear in the built-in reports but are available for your custom report configuration. Furthermore, built-in dimensions such as Day of Week Name that do not appear as a primary dimension in any of the built-in reports are available for you to configure as a primary dimension in a custom report as illustrated in Figure 11.5.

	Day of Week Name ?	Sessions ? ↓	Lead Submitted (Goal 10 Completions) ?	Lead Submitted (Goal 10 Conversion Rate) ?
		1,092,265 % of Total: 100.00% (1,092,265)	47,571 % of Total: 100.00% (47,571)	4.36% Avg for View: 4.36% (0.00%)
☐	1. Tuesday	202,166 (18.51%)	9,056 (19.04%)	4.48%
☐	2. Monday	183,309 (16.78%)	8,167 (17.17%)	4.46%
☐	3. Wednesday	181,261 (16.59%)	8,416 (17.69%)	4.64%
☐	4. Friday	174,793 (16.00%)	7,538 (15.85%)	4.31%
☐	5. Thursday	162,575 (14.88%)	7,538 (15.85%)	4.64%
☐	6. Saturday	96,399 (8.83%)	3,407 (7.16%)	3.53%
☐	7. Sunday	91,762 (8.40%)	3,449 (7.25%)	3.76%

FIGURE 11.5 In custom reports, you can use built-in dimensions such as Day of Week Name that do not appear as primary dimensions in the built-in reports.

As a caveat, if the time period selected for a custom report includes more than 500,000 sessions (or 200 million sessions in Analytics 360), the custom report is subject to sampling. (Sampling is discussed in Chapter 10.)

Note

Custom Funnels: Easy, Useful, Underutilized

Given the ease of custom report configuration, there's no excuse to use a built-in report—for your own analysis, and especially for reporting to other stakeholders—when a custom report would be more suitable.

Avinash Kaushik has stated something along these lines: *If you tell me that you're a Google Analytics user but that you never use custom reports, I'll think less of you.* Listen to Avinash, and use custom reports.

GUEST SPOT   **Finding the Story in Your Data**

Meta S. Brown

Meta S. Brown is a consultant, speaker, and writer who promotes the use of business analytics.

While we are learning to analyze data using methodical, orderly processes, it's common to get in the habit of communicating in the same style. We say what we've done, in the order we did it, showing all of our work as we build to a conclusion. This style of communication isn't effective in a business environment.

The audience for our presentations consists of executives, coworkers, clients, and perhaps even members of the general public. These audiences don't like presentations that sound like homework.

Here's how many people explain a common data analysis result:

I looked at our latest numbers in Google Analytics and saw that the bounce rate for our site is XX%. (The analyst shows a slide featuring the entire GA page in question. The bounce rate is there, but it's just a tiny part of the image.)

So I drilled into the data. First I created a segment for desktop browsers and applied it to the Landing Pages report. (Analyst posts another slide, with another page from GA. This one has bounce rates for lots of segments, many of them on one page, in type that's small and hard to read at a distance.) *Bounce rate for IE was YY%, bounce rate for Chrome was ZZ%, bounce rate for Firefox was AA%,*

Blah, blah, blah …

… so then I applied the built-in Mobile traffic segment and created two new segments, one for iPhone and one for Android smartphones, and just look at this! (Analyst posts yet another slide of GA. This one has bounce rates for mobile on various platforms. Nothing on the slide is highlighted.)

Blah, blah, blah …

… and so I've shown that it is critical that the developers make these changes to the Android mobile platform.

Wait, what was that? We need changes? On what platforms? But the decision maker left for another meeting five minutes ago, the development group is very busy, and pretty much

continues

continued

nobody in the room really followed the whole presentation. So nobody is going to be making those changes.

This story, if you call it that, is about the person who did the analysis. "I did this" and "I did that" are not phrases a decision maker wants to hear. Slides of Web analytics reports such as Figure 11.6 are not things decision makers want to see. And executives are not known for patience; they want you to get to the point very quickly. So what's the right way to get the point across, grab the decision maker's attention, and hold interest? Tell a real story. A story about someone important to the executive (hint: a story that's not about you).

	Sessions ↓	% New Sessions	New Users	Bounce Rate
Desktop	1,123,874 % of Total: 60.23% (1,866,058)	26.19% Avg for View: 26.44% (-0.97%)	294,290 % of Total: 59.64% (493,411)	47.00% Avg for View: 45.94% (2.30%)
Mobile Traffic	543,615 % of Total: 29.13% (1,866,058)	26.37% Avg for View: 26.44% (-0.26%)	143,364 % of Total: 29.06% (493,411)	44.17% Avg for View: 45.94% (-3.86%)
iPhone	276,389 % of Total: 14.81% (1,866,058)	29.16% Avg for View: 26.44% (10.30%)	80,608 % of Total: 16.34% (493,411)	47.35% Avg for View: 45.94% (3.05%)
Android Smartphone	226,245 % of Total: 12.12% (1,866,058)	23.41% Avg for View: 26.44% (-11.45%)	52,974 % of Total: 10.74% (493,411)	49.90% Avg for View: 45.94% (-13.15%)
1. /signup-form				
Desktop	632,253 (56.26%)	20.98%	132,671 (45.08%)	49.52%
Mobile Traffic	76,195 (14.02%)	48.59%	37,026 (11.88%)	70.42%
iPhone	28,561 (10.33%)	29.48%	8,419 (10.44%)	52.02%
Android Smartphone	29,436 (13.01%)	60.80%	17,896 (9.24%)	96.10%

FIGURE 11.6 A data point in a report, such as the 96.10% bounce rate for Android phones on the signup page, may not be clear or impactful for executives, coworkers, or clients.

Look at your data and ask yourself, "What human experience is reflected in this data?" Say what happened, from the point of view of the person who experienced it. Perhaps you'd say it like this:

Sunil saw our ad on his Android phone and clicked through to one of our mobile landing pages. It got his attention right away, and he liked what he saw. He was ready to buy, but when he tried to fill out the form, he could not enter his information in the fields.

He really wanted to buy, so he reloaded the page. He tried again, but the form still didn't work. He reloaded again and again, but the form still didn't work properly and he could not buy the product.

Nobody leaves the room while you tell a brief and compelling story like that.

This little tale has all the parts required of any story. It has a hero, Sunil. The hero has a goal, to buy the product in the ad. The story has a beginning (he sees the ad), a middle (he clicks the Buy button and tries to buy), and an end (he doesn't buy).

The ending isn't happy. Your audience may not like that. That's OK. Your audience may argue and force you to prove that this story really happened. That's OK, too. In fact, that's terrific, because now they may actually pay attention when you present some numbers. Not all the numbers, but a few, selected, relevant numbers.

Data storytelling is compelling for the same reasons that any kind of story is compelling. It's about someone who interests us. It's believable (your stories must be true, and you must have the data to prove it). And it's in story form, the form our brains are designed to understand and recall.

How the Hero Gets a Name

The data doesn't usually reveal much about a visitor who didn't buy. In the example, the only information that the data reveals is the visitor's behavior, and that's a pretty common situation. Yet a compelling story must have a hero, not a generic "user," but a specific person.

How can you put a name to your hero, while keeping your story a true story?

> ➤ **Real examples.** We're not allowed to store personally identifiable information (PII) within GA, but you may be able to identify a real person who has had the experience you're describing. How? Through back-end registration data, customer service records, or anecdotal evidence.
> ➤ **Personas.** Marketers and developers often use "personas," imaginary customers or users who represent a typical or targeted segment. Personas usually have their own names, and some even come with detailed behavioral and demographic descriptions.
> ➤ **Other information sources.** Use sources other than your reports to get information about visitors. These could be formal qualitative inputs such as surveys or usability tests, or as informal as asking coworkers what they know about your customers.

In the example, the hero is named "Sunil." Why? Because the product is one with special appeal to young men, and is known to attract buyers from diverse ethnic backgrounds.

Remember, data stories must be true stories. Use the best evidence that you have to select a name that's right for your own data story hero.

SHORTCUTS

As we've seen in previous chapters, there is a great deal of custom configuration that you can apply even to the built-in reports: filtering, sorting, different display types (such as Comparison or Pivot), and segmentation. To save a report configuration, click Shortcut at the top of a built-in or custom report, and provide a name for the shortcut.

The shortcut will appear in the left navigation panel. Note that this shortcut is yours only. In fact, due to the potential dependency of the shortcut on custom reports and segments that other users may not have access to, you cannot share shortcuts as a GA asset.

INTELLIGENCE ALERTS

Clicking Intelligence Events in the left navigation accesses the Intelligence Events Overview Report. (*Intelligence Events* and *Intelligence Alerts* are used interchangeably as terms.) This report defaults to the Automatic Alerts: changes in your data that GA has detected as out of the norm. It's a good idea to take a quick look once a month and see if there is a spike or a drop that might require additional investigation, or maybe a referral from an influencer that you didn't catch on your own.

As perhaps the most important aspect of Intelligence Alerts, it is strongly advised that you set up Custom Alerts to actively monitor specific metrics changes. As a recommendation for a basic monitoring to start off with, you can create the following set of alerts:

- 10% weekly increase and decrease in sessions.
- 10% weekly increase and decrease in conversion rate for Ecommerce and each goal.
- 10% weekly increase and decrease in Ecommerce revenue.
- 10% weekly increase and decrease in goal completions.

To create an Intelligence Alert for a 10% weekly increase in sessions, we can take the following steps:

1. Click Intelligence Events > Overview > Custom Alerts > Manage Custom Alerts.
2. Configure the Intelligence Alert as shown in Figure 11.7. Note the following options:
   - **Period:**
     - Day (compared to previous day, same day in the previous week, or same day in the previous year)
     - Week (compared to previous week)
     - Month (compared to previous month, or same month in the previous year)
   - **Email:** Your login email address, and any other emails that you specify. When the Intelligence Alert is triggered, an email such as in Figure 11.8 will be forwarded to you and any other email addresses that you have specified
   - **Filtering:**
     - All Traffic
     - Custom segment that you've already defined
     - Filter that you apply just for the alert
   - **Metrics:** Site usage, goals, Ecommerce, etc.
   - **Condition:** Absolute threshold, absolute change, or percent change

As a note, daily alerts set for small variability could potentially trigger too frequently and without great importance, which could reduce your attention to the alerts and cause you to miss those alerts that are significant. Monthly alerts, on the other hand, may be too infrequent. If a form submission that you're tracking as a goal stops working—we've seen this happen—on the first day of the month, it would be unwise to wait till the end of the month before receiving an alert.

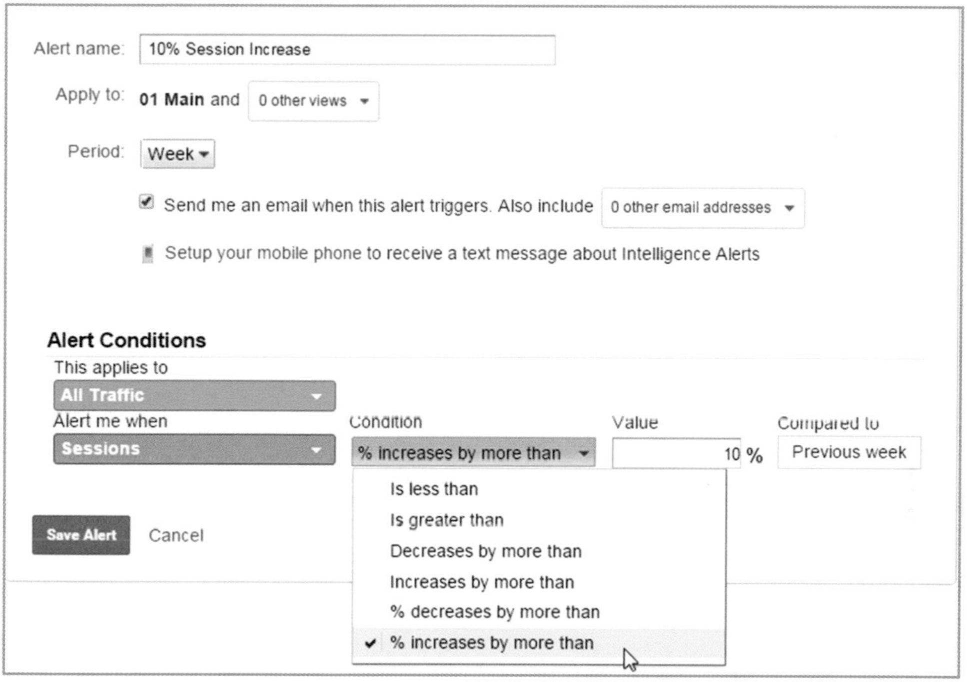

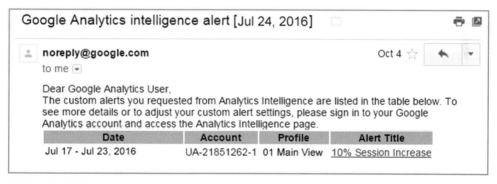

FIGURE 11.7 Configuring an Intelligence Alert to monitor a 10% weekly increase in sessions.

FIGURE 11.8 10% Session Increase Alert received by email.

In this case, a daily alert might in fact be appropriate: check if goal conversion rate or goal value = 1 on any day for that goal. As a note, you'll notice that the goal completion metric is not available in the Intelligence Alert configuration, but you can use goal value as a proxy for goal completions (if you have specified a goal value in your goal setup), or you can use goal conversion rate. (Goal value is discussed in Chapter 8, "Goal and Ecommerce Tracking.")

For most Intelligence Alerts, it's probably best to use percentages rather than absolute values so that the monitoring is always based on a relative and dynamic comparison.

For example, if we set an alert for Ecommerce revenue < $10,000 for a given week when your average weekly revenue is $12,000, but one year later your average weekly revenue is $25,000, you could drop by over half of your normal weekly revenue without receiving an alert. On the other hand, setting an alert for weekly revenue decreased by 2,000 relative to the previous week could become too narrow and sensitive a margin if your average weekly Ecommerce revenue multiplies over time.

An absolute value could be appropriate, however, in an alert such as in Figure 11.9, which will notify us when the number of pageviews with "Page Not Found" in the Page Title exceeds a specific threshold for the time interval—daily could be suitable in this case. If there were a 404 indicator directly in the URL, you could have created the alert based on the Page dimension rather than Page Title. (Error tracking in GA is discussed in Chapter 6, "Events, Virtual Pageviews, Social Actions, and Errors.")

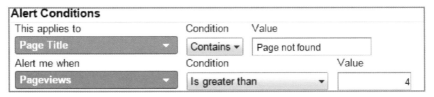

FIGURE 11.9   10% Intelligence Alert configuration for Page Not Found.

> ## Warning   !
>
> ### Don't Rely Only on Intelligence Alerts for Mission-Critical Notifications
>
> It's important to recognize that daily alerts may not be triggered before an entire day of data processing has occurred. If you configure a daily Intelligence Alert for pageviews = 0 to monitor if your website is accessible, downtime could go undetected for more than 24 hours, or at least for the several hours it may take GA to process your data. It's not a bad idea to configure such an alert as a supplemental notification, but the responsibility for minute-to-minute monitoring remains with IT.

Intelligence Alert Follow-Up

If we think back to our discussion about seasonality in Chapter 2, "Google Analytics Reporting Overview," it may not be very surprising to learn than many or most of the alerts that we receive are indicative only of normal traffic and usage variations, but how can we distinguish between regular trends and actual anomalies—good or bad—that warrant further analysis?

We can start with some of the techniques that also appeared in the seasonality discussion. If you have more than a year of GA data collected with a relatively unchanged implementation, you can compare to the same time period in the previous year. If you note the same trends in the previous year as in the second-to-last week shown in Figure 11.10, a weekly alert about a 10% lead submissions increase was probably due to seasonality. As you continue to drill down into your reports (to check the sources of the conversions), you'll likely confirm that the increase for that week was due to regular yearly trends.

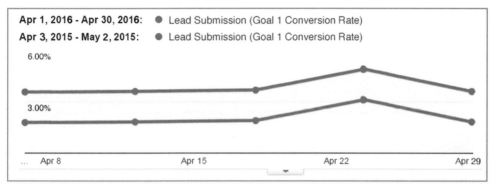

FIGURE 11.10 This time comparison on the Goal > Overview report likely indicates that the weekly alert we received this year was due to a seasonal trend.

If, however, we see in the Goal > Overview report that the alert did not signal the same yearly trend, we certainly need to dig deeper, starting with the following procedure:

1. Access the Source/Medium report.
2. Set the time comparison.
3. In the main over-time graph, set the metric to Goal 1.
4. Use the Plot Rows feature to chart the metric for specific Source/Medium rows.

You may find that the increase was due to a single Source/Medium. Figure 11.11 shows that the spike in lead submissions was attributable to your weekly newsletter for your real estate company, as an example. The newsletter is sent primarily to website visitors who have provided their email addresses but have not actually become leads; as analyst and optimizer, you can now review the newsletter for the messaging that may have produced the jump in conversions, and your marketing teams can aim to replicate that messaging and measure the impact in other marketing channels. Was the newsletter that generated the increase in leads about financing for rehabilitating older residential properties? You can try similar messaging in your PPC and social campaigns, and monitor the response in terms of clickthroughs and completed lead submission goals.

We can perform this type of analysis in GA even if we don't have solid data for the same month last year, but it often becomes somewhat easier and more effective if we can begin with a year-over-year comparison.

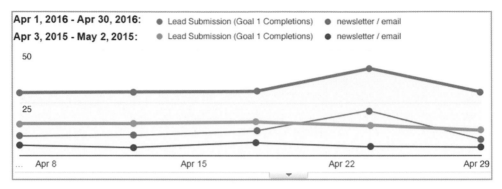

FIGURE 11.11 This time comparison on the Goal > Overview report, with Plot Rows applied, shows that the one-week spike in goal completions was due to increased performance from a specific traffic source rather than a seasonal trend.

ANNOTATIONS

Simple yet critical, Google Analytics annotations allow to you integrate a timeline of the many factors that could affect usage and reporting, such as:

- Website and app design updates
- New content or functionality
- Marketing campaigns
- News mentions and other relevant news events
- Weather
- Planned maintenance windows
- Cyberattacks and unplanned outages
- Changes to your GA configuration itself, such a new filter to exclude internal traffic or a new custom dimension

You can create an annotation as illustrated in Figure 11.12.

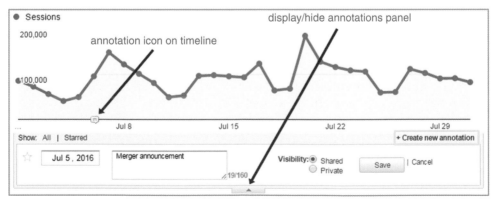

FIGURE 11.12 From the main over-time graph in any Google Analytics report, you can display the annotations panel to create a new annotation.

As a few additional notes:

- **Visible across reports but not views.** An annotation that you create in one report will be visible in other reports within the same view but not in other views within the same property. If you and your team routinely work with multiple GA views, it's recommended to designate a single main view in which everyone on the team creates annotations. (As noted below, however, they'll need Collaborate rights to create a shared annotation.)
- **For private annotations, Read & Analyze rights needed only.** You need only Read & Analyze rights to create a private annotation; Edit rights are not required. If you have Collaborate rights to the view, your annotations default to Shared visibility, as shown in Figure 11.12. All other GA users with access to the view will see your shared annotations, and those GA users who have Collaborate access to the view will be able to edit or delete any annotation that you have shared.
- **Complete list available from the Admin screen.** In the view column of the Admin screen, you can click Annotations to display a complete list of shared annotations and your private annotations created within the view.

Note

Maintain a Chronology

The GA annotations feature is particularly useful because individual annotations are displayed in line with the main report graph, but even if you don't use the annotations feature, make sure that you and your team maintain a fairly comprehensive timeline, even if it's in a separate spreadsheet.

How can you measure the impact of a design change or a marketing campaign if you don't remember when it happened? Don't rely on memory or retroactive scrambling: maintain a timeline. In many instances, a simple date can make the difference between confusion and insight.

KEY TAKEAWAYS

You can set automated emails for dashboards, custom reports, and built-in reports to colleagues, clients, and other stakeholders.   In addition to the once-only option, you can set the emails to go out on a daily, weekly, monthly, or quarterly basis.

Custom reports provide flexibility and streamlining.   Custom reports allow you to combine built-in dimensions and metrics and custom dimensions and metrics in a streamlined format that eliminates any data that is not relevant to the recipient.

Annotations provide an important timeline.   The annotation feature allows you to record any of a variety of factors that could affect your GA data.

 **ACTIONS AND EXERCISES**

1. **Create dashboards.** Create a dashboard from the starter dashboard and at least one by importing from the GA Solutions Gallery. Create a dashboard from scratch that includes up to 12 widgets that are relevant for your KPIs and analysis.

2. **Create three custom reports.** Create at least three custom reports.

3. **Configure automated report emails.** Request permission from three colleagues or clients for you to send them a dashboard or report through monthly email automation. Make sure that the built-in report, custom report, or dashboard that you email contains only data that is relevant to the recipient. Each month, or at least periodically, schedule a few minutes to review the report with the recipients to identify opportunities for further analysis and for optimization actions.

4. **Create Intelligence Alerts.** Create a basic set of Intelligence Alerts as outlined above, as well as any more specialized Intelligence Alerts, such as for Page Not Found.

12

Implementation Customizations

I t's a recurring theme: customizations in Google Analytics (GA) beyond the default implementation facilitate better analysis and greater insights. We've already examined several key steps in surpassing default data collection and reporting: event and virtual pageviews to track non-pageview interactions, goal and Ecommerce configuration to track successes, campaign parameters to clarify acquisition, and view filters or segmentation to amplify trends within a data subset.

In this chapter, we consider some important additional customizations that will allow GA to more closely reflect our organizations and our customer experiences and thereby make the reporting even more comprehensive, meaningful, and actionable.

CUSTOM DIMENSIONS

As we first saw in Figure 4.7, GA records many dimensions with each hit, so we do not, for example, need to explicitly tell GA the visitor's operating system or the title of the page viewed. This is certainly a benefit, but let's consider a broader issue: by default, GA captures a certain number of predefined dimensions only. This default data set does not always provide the information that you need about your visitors, your organization, or your content.

By taking advantage of custom dimensions, you can extend the default GA data set to encompass dimensions that are specifically about your organization, your content, your products, or your customers.

The limit per property for custom dimensions—that is, the number of different custom dimension slots you define, not the different values that you can populate for each custom dimension—is 20 for GA standard and 200 for Analytics 360. (The same limits apply to custom metrics, which we discuss below.)

> **Warning**   !
>
> ## Don't Store Personally Identifiable Information as a Custom Dimension
>
> It is a direct violation of the GA terms of service to store personally identifiable information such as name, email, street address, or social security/government ID number anywhere in GA. It is not recommended to store date of birth, which is not personally identifiable information (PII) unto itself but can approach PII when combined with other data that you can store as a custom dimension.
>
> In Chapter 15, "Integrating Google Analytics with CRM Data," we learn acceptable practices for storing unique but anonymous identifiers in GA that we can use to merge GA data with personally identifiable information (outside of GA only).

Custom Dimensions: Article Author and Category

As a classic example of custom dimension usage, let's consider a blog or a website that publishes articles. When we're analyzing such a site, it would be useful to report metrics such as pageviews by category and author. Although we might somehow assume that GA captures the article category and author, this is not the case. These data points may appear in the Request URI that's captured by default, but, otherwise, GA has no reliable way of recording this data on its own. It's up to you to explicitly instruct GA to capture this data as custom dimensions that you can then use in your analysis (Figure 12.1).

Built-In Dimensions			Custom Dimensions	
Page	**Source**	**Screen Resolution**	**Author**	**Category**
/plant-your-eggplant	google	1280x800	Carl	vegetables
/the-dirt-on-topsoil	google	1920x1080	Dean	supplies
/hoe-hoe-hoe	(direct)	1366x768	Sheryl	supplies
/peppers-mild-to-wild	gardenglobe.com	360x640	Carl	vegetables
/knot-not-hoses	yahoo	1366x768	Sheryl	supplies
/autumn-bulb-planting	t.co	2560x1440	Dean	flowers
/four-leaf-clover	main-email-list	1920x1080	Carl	flowers
/heirloom-rutabagas	turniptribune.com	1366x768	Dean	vegetables
/guard-your-gardenias	facebook.com	1440x900	Carl	flowers
/let-us-eat-lettuce	(direct)	1366x768	Sheryl	vegatables

FIGURE 12.1 Custom dimensions allow you to record elements such as article author and category, which GA would not specifically capture by default.

Implementation for custom dimensions involves two basic steps:

1. Configure the custom dimension in the property admin.
2. Record the custom dimension value with a hit.

As we'll see below, the first step is quite straightforward, while the second step may require a little bit of consideration and development work.

Setting Up the Custom Dimension in the Property Admin

Because custom dimensions affect the data that all GA users see in any view within the property, you must have Edit access at the property level to complete the procedure below.

1. In the Property column on the Admin screen, click Custom Definitions > Custom Dimensions > + New Custom Dimension.
2. For Name, enter **Author**.
3. For Scope, select Hit.
4. Repeat the process, but with **Category** as the Name in step 2.

Custom Dimension Scope

That's all there is to the admin setup for custom dimensions. Before we move on to the harder part—populating the custom dimensions—let's discuss each of the four options that you can select for custom dimension scope. (For additional illustration of custom dimension scope, see "Custom Dimensions & Metrics" in the Google Analytics help pages: `https://support.google.com/analytics/answer/2709828?hl=en`.)

Hit   As we saw in Figure 4.7, a hit describes each packet of data, such as a pageview or an event, that we send to GA. In our first example, our custom dimensions relate to specific article pages of blog posts, so they correspond to the pageview hit, and we'd therefore need to set the Scope to Hit. If you were specifying a custom dimension associated with an event, such as the author of a PDF download that you're tracking as an event, you'd also use Hit as the Scope.

Session   Session scope is suitable for an extra descriptor that you want to set about the session. If, for example, your mobile app users can display your screens in French, German, or English, you could set a Language Selected custom dimension at session scope (in addition to the built-in Language dimension that GA populates by default based on the user's browser setting). You need to set a session-scope custom dimension only once per session. If you set a session-scope custom dimension with a different value during a single session, the previous value from that session is overwritten.

User   Conceptually, session and user scope are closer to each other than either is to hit scope. A user-scope custom dimension is useful for designating a status that spans multiple sessions. For instance, you could set a user-scope custom dimension for *purchaser* custom status at the time of purchase; this would allow you to track purchaser activity even on return non-purchase visits—provided (for a Web property) that the visitor was using the same browser and the same device and did not delete cookies between sessions.

As another use case for user-scope custom dimension, let's say that you store four customer status values on your back-end system based on your customers' first purchase date: *less-than-1-month, 1–6-month, 6–12-month, 1-year-plus*. You can work with your developers to read the customer status from the back end (or to generate it dynamically from the back end based on date of first purchase) each time that a user logs in. The developers could write customer status to the data layer (or even to a simple JavaScript variable) on the page so you can read it into a custom dimension slot within your GA pageview tag in Google Tag Manager (GTM), as discussed later in this chapter. The advantage of user scope over session scope in this case: even if a visitor does not log in during a given session, the custom dimension will carry over from a previous session (again, in the case of a Web property, provided that the `_ga` cookie is present in the browser).

Product   Product scope relates directly to a product in a basic or Enhanced Ecommerce transaction. While Enhanced Ecommerce already provides `product variant` as a "wildcard" variable that you can populate with any product data, you may have a need for additional slots. If, for instance, your online store sold vehicle accessories, you might want to use variant to store the make of the vehicle (Citroën, Hyundai, or Chevrolet), so you could use a custom dimension to store the type of vehicle (sedan or coupe).

Populating the Custom Dimension

Let's return to our author and category examples. We've already set the custom dimensions up in the admin—that was the easier part. Now we have to populate the custom dimensions.

The most essential point about custom dimension implementation is that custom dimensions are not sent to GA on their own, but rather as part of a hit (even for custom dimensions set to a scope other than hit). The custom dimensions are recorded the same way that the page, traffic source, and screen resolution values are recorded: as part of a hit encapsulating many dimensions. A custom dimension extends the data set recorded in a hit, but it does not constitute a hit unto itself.

All that said, how do we add the custom dimension to the hit? Here's the first question you'll want to ask in the case of our previous example: Do the author and category already appear somewhere in the text or markup of the page or in the URL? If yes, you can use a GTM variable to read the value.

If author and category text doesn't appear anywhere on the page, in the page source, or in the URL, you will need to ask your developers to bring them from the back end into the page as data layer variables (as shown in Listing 12.1) (or regular JavaScript variables).

LISTING 12.1: Populating the data layer with variables that we'll use as custom dimensions.

```
<script>
          dataLayer.push({'author': 'Sheryl', 'category': 'supplies'});
</script>
```

We can use the author and category variables configured either as in Figure 12.2 or as in Figure 12.3 to populate the custom dimensions within a GA tag in GTM.

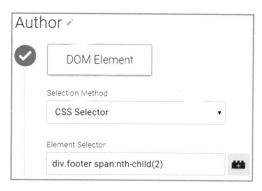

FIGURE 12.2 We're reading the author value from the page text—specifically, the second span tag within the div tag that has *footer* as class.

FIGURE 12.3 If author and category don't appear in the page, and you instead work with your developers to populate them into the data layer, you can read them in with simple GTM data layer variables.

> **Note**
>
> ## Retrieving Author and Category in WordPress
>
> The Google Tag Manager plug-in for WordPress by Tamás Geiger, which we first mentioned in Chapter 5, populates `pagePostAuthor` and `PageCategory` values into the data layer (along with many other values, such as `pagePostDate`), which you can read in with a Data Layer variable similar to Figure 12.3.

Ensure that the Custom Dimension Values Are Available When the Tag Fires

If we're sending the custom dimensions as part of a pageview hit, we'll need to make sure that the data layer reference in Listing 12.1 appears above the GTM container code in the page so the data layer is already populated when the GA tag fires.

As another option, we can apply a DOM Ready trigger to the tag, as we saw in Chapter 5, "Google Tag Manager," and Chapter 6, "Events, Virtual Pageviews, Social Actions, and Errors." By using the DOM Ready trigger type, we'll make sure that the data layer has been populated with the author and category values before the GA pageview tag tries to read them in as data layer variables (Figure 12.4). And if we're reading author and category from anywhere within the page text or markup, we'll certainly want to make sure to use the DOM Ready trigger type; otherwise, the GA pageview tag could fire and try to pull in author and category text as custom dimensions before the page text has even been parsed in the browser.

FIGURE 12.4 You populate custom dimensions within a GA tag (usually pageview or event) in GTM. The index corresponds to the order in which you created the custom dimensions in the property admin. The dimension values are normally set to GTM variables that read from the data layer or the page text/markup.

Custom Dimension in Apps

The way you have implemented overall GA tracking for your mobile app will dictate how you will populate any custom dimensions from your app. If you are tracking your app through GTM, you can use GTM variables to read in custom dimensions that you have populated into the data layer or that serve as the return value of a function call. If, instead, you're tracking your app through the iOS or Android SDKs, you can include the custom dimensions within the hits you record programmatically. (We discuss mobile app tracking in Chapter 13.)

> **Note**
>
> **Taking Advantage of Existing Taxonomies and Classifications, aka *Making Google Analytics Speak Your Language***
>
> While custom dimensions may at first seem somewhat complex, they're actually quite straightforward to implement in most cases. Creating the actual taxonomy for all of the articles on an information-based website, as an example, would normally take much more thought and effort than getting that taxonomy into GA. If you have already completed a taxonomy for all the pages on your website, or if you've already coded the back-end logic to store customer status, you've already done the heavy lifting.

Populating this data into GA should then be a relatively easy task in terms of both back-end coding and GTM setup, but the benefits are great, because you'll be enabling GA to more clearly reflect your world. If colleagues and managers are asking how Carl's blog posts are performing or if the one-year-plus customers are making additional purchases in your app, you can answer those questions if you have communicated your own organizational classifications into GA as hit-level, session-level, and user-level custom dimensions. In this way, custom dimensions represent a very meaningful and valuable step beyond a basic GA implementation.

Using the Custom Dimensions within the GA Reports

You won't directly find Custom Dimensions within the left navigation of the GA reporting interface; instead, you can use Custom Dimensions primarily in the three following ways:

- as a dimension in a custom report, as shown in Figure 12.5
- as a secondary dimension within built-in (and custom) reports
- in a segment definition

Author	Pageviews ↓	Bounce Rate
1. Carl	117,511 (49.55%)	41.59%
2. Sheryl	94,239 (39.74%)	55.30%
3. Dean	25,410 (10.71%)	48.39%

FIGURE 12.5 In this custom report, we've defined Author as the primary dimension.

Custom Dimensions are also available for export through the GA APIs, as demonstrated in Chapter 15, "Integrating Google Analytics with CRM Data."

Custom Dimension: Login Status

Another piece of data that GA cannot determine on its own—even though it somehow seems that it would—is login status. By setting *logged-in* as a session-scope custom dimension, we can see differences in behavior between visitors who are and are not logged in.

Since a user generally logs in once only during a session, and since a session-scope custom dimension does not need to be sent with every pageview hit, we can consider using a one-time event to record the custom dimension at the time of login. You can work with your developer to execute the code in Listing 12.2 when the user logs in: the code will populate the `eventTracker` value for the `event` variable into the data layer, which will fire the Custom Event trigger applied to the "catch-all" event tag that we first discussed in Chapter 6. The other values that we're populating into the data layer include the event category, event action, and `loginStatus`, which we can read into the event tag with GTM Data Layer variables. (Keep in mind that event label is optional, so we don't need to populate it in this example.)

LISTING 12.2: Instead of using a pageview to record the custom loginStatus custom dimension, we're opting for an event.

```
<script>
dataLayer.push({'event': 'eventTracker', 'eventCat': 'login',
'eventAct': 'log-in', 'loginStatus': 'loggedIn')});
</script>
```

We can now perform three additional steps to populate the custom dimension value into GA:

1. Configure the custom dimension in the Property admin, setting the scope to Session.
2. Set up a GTM Data Layer variable to read in `loginStatus`.
3. Modify the catch-all event tag in Figure 6.31 to read in the loginStatus Data Layer variable as a custom dimension, as we did for author and category in Figure 12.4.

If we're populating the custom dimension only when a login occurs, the value would be `(not set)` for all non-login sessions. If you so chose, you could use a view filter as described in Chapter 9, "View Settings, View Filters, and Access Rights," to rewrite `(not set)` to `notLoggedIn` for the loginStatus custom dimension.

You could use an approach similar to Listing 12.2 to read in customer status/designation from your back end system on login and record as a custom dimension, as the example custom report in Figure 12.6 demonstrates. As mentioned earlier, however, a user-scope custom dimension would be more suitable for customer status, and this scope would allow GA to record this custom dimension even for interim sessions in which a login did not occur.

Customer Level (Back-End)	Sessions ↓	Ecommerce Conversion Rate	Transactions	Revenue
1. silver	1,147,205 (46.72%)	0.45%	5,206 (24.42%)	$249,507.65 (25.05%)
2. gold	342,799 (13.96%)	1.33%	4,561 (21.40%)	$201,512.94 (20.23%)
3. platinum	331,551 (13.50%)	0.65%	2,143 (10.05%)	$96,261.86 (9.67%)
4. bronze	322,260 (13.12%)	0.91%	2,946 (13.82%)	$131,001.52 (13.15%)

FIGURE 12.6 In this custom report, we're reporting Ecommerce metrics by Customer Status, which we read in from the back end and stored in GA as a user-scope custom dimension.

> **Note**
>
> ### Firmographics Data as Custom Dimensions
>
> The Marketo marketing automation platform can inject firmographics data (such as specific organization or job role) into GA as custom dimension values. For more on firmographics integration, see *Marketing Automation and Personalization* in Appendix A.

Custom Dimension: Form Selection

Another handy use case for custom dimensions is the storage of form selections. A lead generation form on your website, for example, could contain a variety of drop-downs, radio button selections, or text fields such as:

- Age group
- Gender
- Occupation
- Industry
- Product or service interest
- Postal code

To generate a custom dimension that records industry selection, we can add the script in Listing 12.3 into a GTM Custom HTML tag. Since this script uses jQuery to find and configure the Industry drop-down to write to the data layer when the selected value changes, we'll certain want to apply a DOM Ready trigger to the Custom HTML tag so the drop-down element has been parsed before the Custom HTML tag fires. Since we're writing *eventTracker* as the *event* variable, our "catch-all" event infrastructure will again be activated.

LISTING 12.3: You can add this script in a Custom HTML tag to record selection from an Industry drop-down as a custom dimension in GA.

```
<script>
$("#ddIndustry").change(function () {
        var industry = $(this).find('option:selected').text();
        dataLayer.push({'event':'eventTracker','eventCat':'industry',
        'eventAct':'select','eventLbl':industry});
});
</script>
```

GUEST SPOT   Calculated Metric and Custom Dimensions for Hotel Bookings

Matt Stannard

Matt Stannard is CTO of 4Ps Marketing

Calculated Metric for Effective Booking Conversion Rate

If the only visitors who can book a room are those who have already conducted a room search during the session, it can be more helpful to report an effective booking conversion rate based on room search completions than the conversion rate default, which GA always bases on overall sessions. (This is a preview of calculated metrics, which we'll configure later in the chapter.)

By reporting bookings based on search sessions rather than all sessions, we're achieving the same benefit discussed in the Chapter 10, "Segmentation": we're amplifying data points and trends. For instance, with higher percentages for Effective Booking conversion rate (rather than overall Booking conversion rate), we can more easily spot the dip in booking conversion rate that appears on May 29, row 5 in the custom report shown in Figure 12.7, and we might correlate this dip to the price increases that the booking engine dynamically generated on that day.

Calculated metrics are discussed later in this chapter.

	Date	Sessions	Room Search (Goal 1 Completions)	Booking Completed (Goal 2 Completions)	Effective Booking Conversion Rate
		1,866,123 % of Total: 100.00% (1,866,123)	12,519 % of Total: 100.00% (12,519)	2,516 % of Total: 100.00% (2,516)	20.10% Avg for View: 20.10% (0.00%)
☐	1. 20160602	66,546 (3.57%)	449 (3.59%)	99 (3.93%)	22.05%
☐	2. 20160601	83,179 (4.46%)	560 (4.47%)	110 (4.37%)	19.64%
☐	3. 20160531	49,217 (2.64%)	463 (3.70%)	91 (3.61%)	19.65%
☐	4. 20160530	91,243 (4.89%)	749 (5.98%)	179 (7.11%)	23.90%
☐	5. 20160529	34,568 (1.85%)	278 (2.22%)	24 (0.95%)	8.63%

FIGURE 12.7 This custom report displays Effective Conversion based on Room Search completions rather than all sessions, thereby amplifying the conversion rate and highlighting the May 29 dip.

Custom Dimensions to Track the Differential between Search Date and Check-In Date

A custom dimension for Check-In Date can provide an excellent way to produce a Quote-to-Check-in-Date Differential report that demonstrates how long before a potential hotel stay are users performing their room searches. The concept is to chart a 365-day check-in projection to help inform room pricing and booking promotions.

You need to export the default date dimension that is captured with each event (or goal completion) that you are recording for searches as well as the Check-In date, which you can capture as a custom dimension. Within a spreadsheet program such as Google Sheets or MS Excel, you can subtract event or goal date for room search from provided check-in date to calculate the lead-up times.

As the actual hotel in our current discussion was an international hotel, we were able to compare search patterns of the U.S. and European users, for example, as shown in Figures 12.8

and 12.9. Noting the pronounced difference in search-to-check-in times for the United States and Europe, we were able to advise management and the marketing team at the hotel (our client) to adjust pricing and the time frames for their campaigns accordingly.

As a note on the export, if you are using Excel, SEO Tools for Excel (`http://tiny.cc/ga-seotools`) allows you to automate importing data through the GA API, and for Google Docs, there is an automated script available in the Google Developer help article entitled "Automated Access to Google Analytics Data in Google Sheets" (`http://tiny.cc/ga-googledoc`).

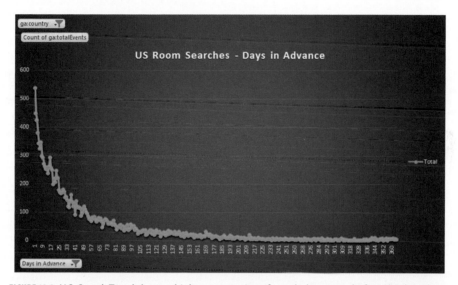

FIGURE 12.8 U.S. Search Trend shows a high concentration of search dates soon before check-in dates.

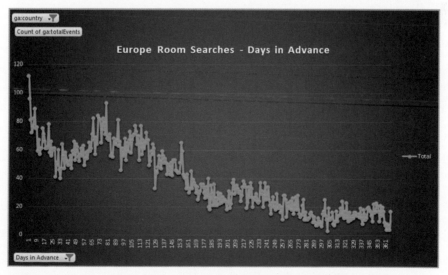

FIGURE 12.9 Europe Search Trend shows searches occurring longer before check-in dates.

CONTENT GROUPING

Content grouping is similar conceptually to hit-level custom dimensions for pages. A significant difference is that content groupings are available within two of the built-in reports: Pages and Landing Pages.

Let's consider the same use case for content groups as we did for custom dimensions in Figure 12.1. Instead of—or in addition to—using hit-level custom dimensions to capture article author and category, we can use a similar process to populate content groups, as described below.

Primary Dimension: Page Page Title **Content Grouping: Sport** (Content Group) ▾ Other ▾		

Plot Rows   Secondary dimension ▾   Sort Type: Default ▾

	Consumer (Content Group) ?	Pageviews ? ↓	Unique Views 1 (Consumer) ?	Avg. Time on Page ?
		5,548,775 % of Total: 100.00% (5,548,773)	930,317 % of Total: 100.00% (930,317)	00:01:19 Avg for View: 00:01:19 (0.00%)
☐ 1.	Football	3,788,681 (68.28%)	0 (0.00%)	00:01:09
☐ 2.	Basketball	611,962 (11.03%)	339,636 (36.51%)	00:01:46
☐ 3.	Baseball	310,840 (5.60%)	136,859 (14.71%)	00:01:45
☐ 4.	Hockey	275,006 (4.96%)	140,662 (15.12%)	00:01:42
☐ 5.	(not set)	176,826 (3.19%)	77,667 (8.35%)	00:01:42

FIGURE 12.10 In the Pages report, we have selected Sport as the content grouping to display metrics for four content groups that we have populated.

Configuring the Content Grouping

Somewhat surprisingly, you configure a content grouping in the View Admin and not the Property Admin. To create the content grouping, click Content Grouping > + New Content Grouping, supply a Name such as *Sport,* and click Save.

Populating the Content Groups

In most cases, you'll populate the content groups similarly to custom dimension population in Figure 12.4; that is, we add the content group to the pageview hit.

As explained above for the category or author custom dimension, we can configure a GTM variable to read in the sport from anywhere in the page text or markup. If the sport doesn't already appear anywhere in the page, your developers can write the sport to the data layer, from which you can read it with a data layer variable similar to Figure 12.3. The same considerations outlined above regarding the DOM Ready trigger would apply for content group population.

FIGURE 12.11 With Sport set up as the first-slot content grouping in the View Admin, we can read the sport value into the Pageview tag as a DOM Element or data layer variable as shown in Figures 12.2 and 12.3.

Populating the Content Group Based on Rules or Extraction

When you're creating a content grouping in the View Admin, you see that direct population of the content group name as shown in Figure 12.11 is not the only option—you can also populate the content groups based on matching or extraction from page URL, page title, or screen name.

While this is useful, you may want to consider that content grouping may be slightly less of a priority if, for example, you can also view all pages related to basketball just by filtering the default Pages report. Also, if your URL structure is already very hierarchical, content grouping may be somewhat redundant. If all of the pages on your website that deal with basketball were already located in the `/basketball` directory, the Content Drilldown report would essentially provide metrics by content group.

For more information on the extraction method, see "Capture Groups and Content Grouping" in the GA help pages (`https://support.google.com/analytics/answer/3333221?hl=en`).

Note

Should You Opt for Custom Dimensions or Content Groups?

In the page classification examples that we have been considering, it's quite comparable—in terms of reporting benefit—to use either hit-level custom dimensions or content groupings. One advantage of content groups, however, is their availability within the built-in Pages, Landing Pages, and Behavior Flow reports. You'd still be able to configure a comparable custom report that use custom dimensions, but the content groups may be more visible than the custom reports for less experienced GA users in your (or a client's) organization.

The limit of five for content groupings within a view—not five content groups, but five content groupings—is usually sufficient. But if you happen to need more than five different ways to classify your page, you should opt for hit-level custom dimensions, since you can configure as many as 20 custom dimensions per property in GA Standard and 200 in Analytics 360.

Sampling and Use Outside of GA

Content groups are subject to sampling within the GA reporting interface. Also, while content groups are now available through the Core Reporting API, they aren't exposed to BigQuery. Thus, if you've licensed Analytics 360 and plan to export unsampled data to BigQuery (or another environment), custom dimensions will provide a better solution.

Use Both?

Since the processes of populating a custom dimension and a content group are similar, and since they both offer some advantages and disadvantages, there's no harm in populating both at the same time so you can then use either as suitable.

CUSTOM METRICS

It can be argued that your GA implementation is not complete without at least a few custom dimensions (or content groups) to reflect your own organization. Custom metrics, conversely, are more specialized, and their use cases more limited.

That said, they can serve a unique and critical purpose in certain tracking scenarios. Let's say that Health Canada, the public-facing digital service of the Health Ministry, has just created an initiative called *Canada Walks/Canada Se Promène* for Canadians to commit to walking a certain number of kilometers per week for exercise. Citizens can visit the Health Canada website and sign up to receive weekly email reminders for their walks.

On the signup form, would-be walkers can enter the number of kilometers they pledge to walk each week. This detail will be included in the reminder emails.

If you were responsible for analytics on the Health Canada website, you could take advantage of a custom metric as follows to track the number of weekly walking kilometers pledged and then configure a custom report as in Figure 12.12.

	Region ?	Sessions ? ↓	Kilometers Pledged
		50,028 % of Total: 1.43% (3,506,570)	**2,090,778** % of Total: 100% (2,090,778)
☐	1. Ontario	**25,735** (51.44%)	**996,081** (47.64%)
☐	2. British Columbia	**5,868** (11.73%)	**203,921** (9.75%)
☐	3. Quebec	**5,231** (10.46%)	**289,497** (13.87%)
☐	4. Alberta	**4,460** (8.92%)	**194,455** (9.30%)

FIGURE 12.12 Kilometers Pledged appearing as a custom metric in a custom report.

Configuring the Custom Metric

To configure the custom metric to record the kilometers pledged:

1. In the property admin, click Custom Definitions, Custom Metrics, + New Custom Metric.
2. For Name, enter **Kilometers Pledged.**
3. For Scope, select Hit.
4. For Formatting Type, select Integer.

Populating the Custom Metric

Populating a custom metric is similar to populating a custom dimension: we'll need to include it in a GA tag—usually a pageview, event, or Ecommerce transaction—as a custom metric value.

In this example, we do read the custom metric directly from a page element through a Custom JavaScript variable, but if the kilometers pledged had not been available in the DOM, we would have had to work with our developers to first write to the data layer so we could read it with a Data Layer variable.

1. **Variable.** Create the variable shown in Figure 12.13 to read the value from the Kilometers Pledged form field.
2. **Tag.** Create a GA event tag as in Figure 12.14 that reads the variable in as a custom metric and populates it into the first custom metric index in the property, which we configured above. (You can specify any suitable values for Event Category, Event Action, and Event Label.)

FIGURE 12.13 This Custom JavaScript variable reads the value of the kilometers field of the walk pledge signup form.

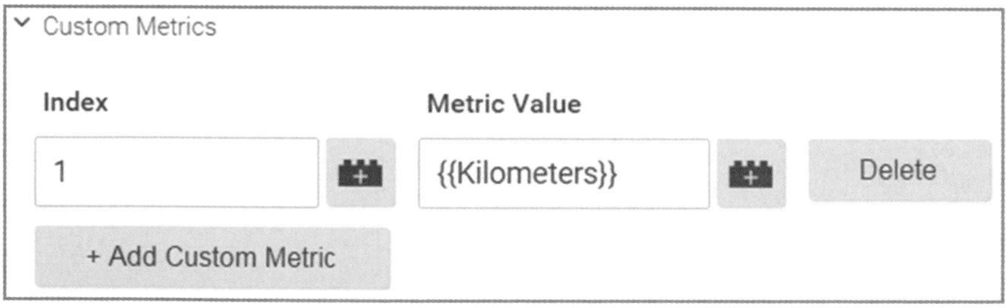

FIGURE 12.14 In the GA Event tag, we're populating the Kilometers variable as a custom metric.

3. **Trigger:** Enable the built-in Form ID variable, and apply the form trigger shown in Figure 12.15 to the event tag.

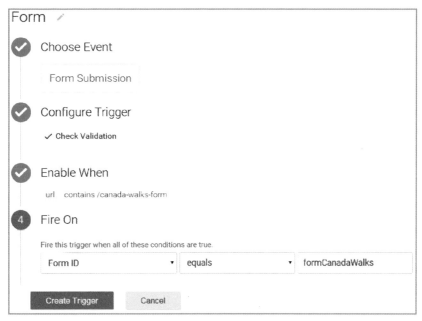

FIGURE 12.15   This trigger will fire the Walk Signup event when the signup form is submitted.

As a different approach, we could have opted for a bit of jQuery in a Custom HTML tag to write the kilometers pledged to the data layer on form submit, along with the other data layer variables needed to active and populate the catch-all event.

Formatting Type and Scope

In addition to *Integer*, the other custom metric Formatting Types available for custom metric setup are *Currency* and *Time*, and the other Scope besides *Hit* is *Product*. As two additional examples of custom metric, you could configure a Time custom metric with Hit scope to record total hours of video watched or a Currency custom metric with Product scope to record discount amounts in Ecommerce transactions.

Also note that all custom metric Formatting Types represent totals, not percentages or ratios. If we wanted to instead calculate the number of kilometers pledged per user or form submission, we would need to use our custom metric within a calculated metric formula. Calculated metrics are discussed below.

CALCULATED METRICS

In additional to custom metrics, which you configure and populate directly as discussed in the previous section, you can now also calculate new metrics based on existing metrics (both built-in and custom) and numeric constants. Many of the examples of custom metrics, such as those below, involve conversions (goal and Ecommerce) and/ or users (instead of sessions).

Conversion Rate Based on Users

Although we may be inclined to think casually of conversion rate as the number of *people* who complete a goal, it's critical to remember that conversion rate in the built-in GA reports is based on *sessions* rather than users. As Figure 9.6 demonstrates, this definition can make conversion rate seem surprisingly low to managers, clients, and so on, especially for a more ponderous or complex conversion.

The Multi-Channel Funnel > Path Length report indicates the number of times that visitors return before completing a goal, but we can also create a calculated metric that is based on users as detailed below. In our example, we'll calculate user-based conversion rate for submission of an application for a training program enrollment application.

1. In the View column of the Admin screen, click Calculated Metrics.
2. Configure the calculated metric as shown in Figure 12.16.

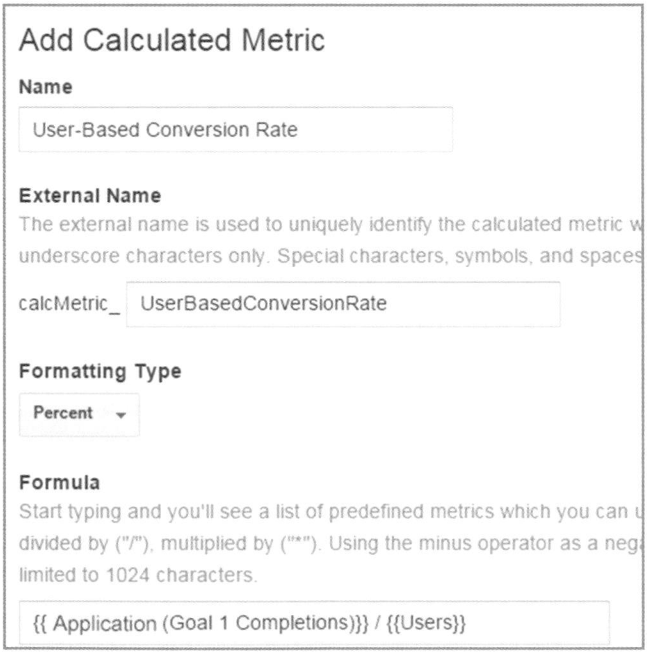

Add Calculated Metric

Name

> User-Based Conversion Rate

External Name
The external name is used to uniquely identify the calculated metric w
underscore characters only. Special characters, symbols, and spaces

calcMetric_ | UserBasedConversionRate

Formatting Type

> Percent   ▾

Formula
Start typing and you'll see a list of predefined metrics which you can u
divided by ("/"), multiplied by ("*"). Using the minus operator as a neg
limited to 1024 characters.

> {{ Application (Goal 1 Completions)}} / {{Users}}

FIGURE 12.16 Calculated metric for Goal 1 Conversion Rate based on users rather than sessions.

We'd need to keep in mind that the number of users reported in GA is still higher than the number of individuals who are visiting your website (due to cookie deletion, etc.), but conversion rate based on users rather than sessions may be significantly higher than the built-in session-based conversion rate and would provide a closer approximation of the percentage of individuals who are converting. In a GA mobile app property, the Users metric is likely a fairly accurate indication of the number of people who are actually using your app, so built-in metrics based on Users in mobile app properties should reflect per-person metrics fairly accurately.

For more on user-based conversion rate, see `www.e-nor.com/gabook`.

Non-Bounce Conversion Rate

As we saw in the Non-Bounce Sessions discussion in Chapter 10, "Segments," it can be useful to evaluate performance based on non-bounce sessions, particularly for websites: since our website will always experience some degree of bounce, why not instead track metrics for those users who were engaged enough to view another page or complete an action that you have tracked as an event?

We could certainly apply the built-in Non-Bounce Sessions segment to any of the goal reports, but we could also create a calculated metric specifically for non-bounce conversion rate as shown here.

```
{{Lead Submitted (Goal 1 Completions)}} / ({{Sessions}} - {{Bounces}})
```

Several additional considerations about calculated metrics should be noted:

- To configure a calculated metric, you must have Edit access at the view level.
- In a calculated metric definition, you can include built-in metrics, your own custom metrics, and numeric constants.
- Formatting types include integer, percent, float, currency, and time.
- Once you create a calculated metric, you can't rename it, but you can delete it.
- Calculated metrics are retroactive.
- Calculated metrics don't appear in built-in reports, but you can use them in custom reports (and query them through the GA Core Reporting API).

DEMOGRAPHICS AND INTERESTS

As discussed in Chapter 2: "Google Analytics Reporting Overview," the Demographics and Interests reports are not enabled by default. To enable the Demographics and Interests reports, you should only have to toggle the Enable Demographics and Interest Reports to the ON position in the Property Settings. Within each view, you'll also need to enable the Demographics and Interests reports as prompted the first time that they are accessed.

If for any reason, the Demographics and Interests reports to not begin populating, you can select the Enable Display Advertising Features checkbox in the GA tags in

Google Tag Manager, as shown in Figure 5.4 and in many of the other GA tags throughout the book (and then republish your container, of course). (This setting appears as Enable Advertising ID Features for GA tags in a mobile app container.)

Privacy Policy

To remain in compliance with the GA terms of service when enabling the Demographics and Interests reports, you should update your privacy policy similarly to the following to reference the DoubleClick cookie and demographics and interests information.

This website uses the first-party Google Analytics cookie only to track your return visits but not to identify you personally by name, email, or any other data. This site also uses the third-party DoubleClick cookie to enable reporting on demographics and interests information (such as age, gender, and favored product categories), but, again, not in any way that is associated with personally identifiable information.

If you enable remarketing as discussed in Chapter 14, see "Policy Requirements for Google Analytics Advertising Features" in the Google Analytics help docs for privacy policy requirements.

Along these same lines, it's advisable to check with your legal or compliance advisors before enabling Demographics and Interests or remarketing in GA.

If you do not enable Demographics and Interests or remarketing, the terms of service still require you to include basic verbiage about the first-party Google Analytics cookie, as shown in the example above, for overall tracking.

For mobile app tracking, change the *cookie* references in the privacy policy to *anonymous identifiers*.

ENHANCED LINK ATTRIBUTION

Thus far in the book, we have not discussed the Behavior > In-Page Analytics report. The report can be problematic (especially across domains and http/https pages), and, overall, GA is not a full-featured overlay reporting tool such as CrazyEgg, Hot-Jar, or SessionCam. That said, In-Page Analytics can be useful so it makes sense to enable Enhanced Link Attribution in the GA Pageview tag in Google Tag Manager as shown in Figure 12.17.

Enhanced Link Attribution offers two main benefits to the In-Page Analytics reports and to the Page Analytics plug-in for Chrome, which generates overlay reporting very similar to In-Page Analytics (and which tends to work more reliably):

- **Show different percentages for two or more links that direct to the same other page.** If, for instance, you have an About Us link in both your header and footer, Enhanced Link Attribution allows GA to display different click percentages (3.0% and 0.5%, for example) instead of 3.5% for both links.

- **Show click percentages on JavaScript-driven page elements.** Enhanced Link Attribution also allows GA to display separate click percentages for elements in a JavaScript drop-down menu and other JavaScript-driven page elements.

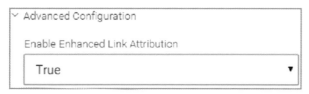

FIGURE 12.17 You can easily enable Enhanced Link Attribution in the GA pageview tag in GTM.

As a related discussion, see Appendix A for Alex Harris's guest spot on using both quantitative GA data and third-party overlay reporting for quick wins in landing page optimization.

TRACKING INFO CUSTOMIZATIONS

You can configure the following customizations under Tracking Info in the Property Admin.

Session Timeout

In Session Settings, you can change the session timeout from the default of 30 minutes to a minimum of 1 minute through a maximum of 4 hours. If your website or app is designed for steady user interaction—for active stock quoting, as an example—and a break in activity of even less than 30 minutes might logically signal the end of a session, you could consider decreasing the session timeout. If, however, your user experience is designed for long durations on a single page or screen, you could increase the session timeout to align with practical usage.

In the latter case, however, you would probably want to send additional hits to GA, even while the user is on the same page, by configuring event tracking for page scroll or for video view percentages (as discussed in Chapter 6). With additional hits being sent to GA even while the user remains engaged on a single page or screen, it would be unnecessary to increase the session timeout, since the default 30-minute timeout would refresh with each hit.

It is normal practice overall to leave session timeout to the 30-minute default. If you change this setting in an existing implementation, make sure to create an annotation as described in Chapter 11 to refer to when you're analyzing session counts over a period that straddles the change.

Campaign Timeout

Campaign timeout is illustrated in Figure 7.23. The Campaign Timeout, which appears in Session Settings, determines the duration for which a direct session will appear in the GA reports as a more specific traffic source from a previous session. While you can change the Campaign Timeout to a longer or shorter window for the direct override, it is considered normal practice, as with session timeout, to maintain the default.

As a note, the Campaign Timeout does not affect the Multi-Channel Funnel or Attribution reports, since these reports do not apply the direct override.

Organic Search Sources

GA maintains a list of search engines against which it compares incoming traffic. If it finds that the clickthrough originated from one of the websites on the search engine list, that session is assigned the `organic` medium rather than `referral`. This list is comprehensive, but if you do happen to see websites in your Referrals report that you instead want GA to consider as search engines, you can add that domain (`newsearchengine.com`, for example) as an organic search source.

Recording Country-Specific Search Engines

It may be a bit surprising that, by default, clickthroughs from google.in or google.it appear in GA with a source value of just `google`, and that fr.yahoo.com appears as `yahoo`.

To break out country-specific search engines as their own sources, you can list them as separate Organic Search Sources, as shown in Figure 12.18.

Search Engine Name	Domain Name	Query Parameter	Path		
⠿ Google UK	google.co.uk	q		edit	delete
⠿ Yahoo UK	uk.yahoo.com	p		edit	delete
⠿ Google India	www.google.in	q		edit	delete
⠿ Google Canada	google.ca	q		edit	delete

FIGURE 12.18 For country-specific search engines to appear as sources in GA, you need to add them as organic search sources.

Recording Google Image Search as a Source

The procedure for recording clickthroughs from Google images is not as straightforward as for country-specific search engines: adding images.google.com as an Organic Search Source does not work.

By default, Google image clickthroughs are recorded with `referral` as the medium and `google.com/imgres` or `google.co.uk/imgres` as the source. To rewrite the medium to `organic` and the source to `images.google.com`, `images.google.co.uk`. or any other country-specific Google image search results page, we can apply the filters shown in Figure 12.19 and Figure 12.20 to our view. (As emphasized in Chapter 9, you should always validate view filters in a test view before applying them to any working view.)

FIGURE 12.19 This first filter matches the original source and medium values for Google image clickthroughs and rewrites the medium as *organic*.

FIGURE 12.20 With medium rewritten to organic, this second filter still matches the original source, and the output constructor adds *com* or *co.uk* extracted as the wildcard in Field A.

Referral Exclusion List

When a clickthrough occurs from a domain included in the Referral Exclusion List, GA does not begin a new session, and the medium and source values of the current session are maintained. Referral exclusions have two general use cases:

- **Detour to another domain.** If, for instance, your checkout path diverts users to a third-party service on another domain (such as PayPal) before they return to your own site (for confirmation, etc.), you'll need to make sure to list that other domain as an exclusion—otherwise, when the user returns to the confirmation page on your site, a new session will start, with medium as `referral` and source as the domain of the other website.

- **Cross-domain tracking.** As discussed later in this chapter, we'll also use referral exclusions to maintain session, medium, and source (and campaign as applicable) across domains as part of cross-domain tracking.

Search Term Exclusion List

The Search Term Exclusion List allows you to specify organic keywords—normally, the branded/navigational keywords that we discussed in Chapter 7, "Acquisition Reports"—that will prompt GA to count the organic clickthrough as direct. With most organic clickthroughs, even most organic branded clickthroughs, now recorded with *(not provided)* as the keyword, the utility of the Search Term Exclusion list has become very limited. (In other words, just keep it blank; it no longer has much of an effect.)

CROSS-DOMAIN AND ROLL-UP REPORTING

In most cases, a single GA property corresponds to a single website (or app), but this does not always need to be the case. There are two overall use cases for tracking more than one website within a single property:

- **Cross-domain.** Needed when there is a continuity of user experience across two domains that you manage, such as www.mysite.com and www.myblogsite.com or www.myproductsite.com.
- **Roll-up.** Suitable when there is an organizational need for integrated reporting on two or more domains that are unrelated from a user standpoint.

To assess your need for cross-domain or roll-up reporting, you can ask the following questions:

- **Do I need to track multiple domains?** If not, neither cross-domain nor rollup tracking pertains.
- **Do the two or more domains offer a continuous user experience (in terms of branding, process, navigation, etc.)?** If so, you should implement cross-domain tracking.
- **Are the two or more domains separate in terms of user experience?** If so, it's perfectly acceptable and routine to track each domain in a separate GA property. If, however, you must provide consolidated, multidomain reporting within the

organization (to upper management, for example), roll-up reporting offers the right solution.

Cross-Domain Tracking

There are a couple of fundamental yet surprising facts about GA tracking that we must consider to before configuring cross-domain tracking.

Surprising fact 1: The tracking ID for any property will track data from any domain.   Yes, that's correct. If I create a new property, and set the Website URL to `http://www.abc123.com`, and the Property ID for that property is UA-12345678-1, I can deploy a GA tag in GTM on `www.xyz456.com` with the property ID set to UA-12345678-1, and GA will still record data, even though the tracking is occurring on a completely different domain.

Surprising fact 2: Surprising fact 1 is not enough for cross-domain tracking.   Once recovered from the first surprise, we may want to believe—since any tracking code will record data on any domain—that all we need to do to implement cross-domain tracking is to track with the same property ID on multiple domains. This is largely true for roll-up reporting, as we discuss later, but for cross-domain tracking to work correctly, there are some straightforward but important additional configurations required, as outlined below.

Maintaining the Session

The key concept in cross-domain tracking—and the differentiator from roll-up— is session maintenance. Using the same default GA tracking on two or more related domains such as `site.com`, `blogsite.com`, and `productsite.com` would cause the following problems:

- **New session.** As soon as the user traversed domains, the first pageview on the second domain would be considered part of a new session by a new user (since GA will create a separate cookie for the second domain with a different client ID).
- **Original Source/Medium lost.** As arguably an even graver problem, the original Source/Medium is lost in the new session on the second domain, replaced with `site.com/referral`. If we have designed our user experience to flow from site.com to productsite.com as in Figure 12.21, it's basically useless to attribute user actions on myproductsite.com, including conversions, to mysite.com/referral. If a conversion takes place on myproductsite.com, we need to be able to attribute that conversion to AdWords or an email campaign or whichever source/medium origi- nally drove the visit to `mysite.com`.

Outlined next are two additional steps you'll need to take for cross-domain tracking (in addition to the recommended view filter shown in Figure 12.27, later in this chapter).

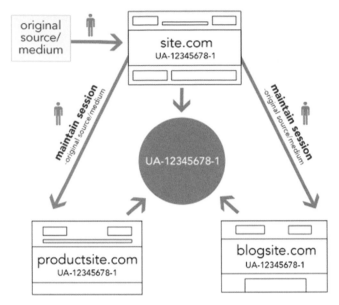

FIGURE 12.21 For cross-domain tracking, you must make configuration changes to maintain the session when the user crosses domains.

Cross-Domain Settings

To maintain the session in cross-domain tracking, you'll need to make changes to the GA pageview tag in GTM as indicated in Figures 12.22 and 12.23. By setting `allowLinker` to `true`, GA will actually add the client ID from the first domain to the URL when the user clicks a link between domains, and GA will then read the same client ID out of the URL and into the `_ga` cookie on the second domain, thus identifying a single user who has traversed domains.

FIGURE 12.22 For cross-domain tracking, specify a value of true for allowLinker in the GA tag.

FIGURE 12.23 In Auto Link Domains, list the domains that you need to track across.

In addition to these settings in the GA tag in GTM, you'll need to add the domains to the Referral Exclusion List in the Property Admin as discussed above.

Verifying Cross-Domain Tracking

You can take the following steps to verify that cross-domain tracking is working correctly.

1. **Check for the client ID in the URL.** When you click from site.com to productsite .com or blogsite.com, the URL should contain the client ID as well as a hashed time-stamp (which appears as `1362114490410` in the example URL below). As a note, GA expires the client ID portion of the URL after two minutes based on the time-stamp; this ensures that the same client ID won't be used repeatedly in case the user shares the URL.

   ```
   http://www.productsite.com/?_ga=1.182699591.1412315536.136
   2114490410
   ```

2. **Check the Real-Time reports.** Start by identifying your own session in the Real-Time reports as described in the "How Can I Isolate My Own Session within the Real-Time Reports?" sidebar in Chapter 6. When you click between domains, verify the following:

   - Active Users count does not increment.
   - Medium and source do not change—if you see `referral` as the medium and `site.com` as the source, cross-domain tracking is not working correctly.

Note

Cross-Domain Tracking and Hosted Ecommerce Providers

As discussed in Vanessa Sabino's "GA Tracking Questions to Ask Your Ecommerce Provider" sidebar in Chapter 8, cross-domain tracking is an important factor for tracking a hosted Ecommerce platform on a separate domain. Make sure to inquire with your current provider or with any you may be considering.

Roll-Up Reporting

As mentioned previously, the concept of roll-up applies when the reporting needs to be aggregated within a single property for domains that are completely separate in terms of branding, offerings, and user experience and that do not link to each other.

Let's say that the Amalgamated Turbines Corporation maintains three websites: windturbine.com, jetturbine.com, and industrialfan.com. Since these sites are designed for completely different audiences, there's no reason to link between them or to set up cross-domain tracking.

Managers and executives, however, may want to see consolidated reporting for all three sites: this is the purpose of roll-up reporting. You can implement roll-up reporting by including the identical GA tracking code on all three websites; none of the additional configurations mentioned above for cross-domain are necessary for roll-up. It is, however, still recommended to apply the hostname filter shown in Figure 12.24.

As another option for rollup, you could configure the GTM containers on each of the websites with two sets of GA tags: one that tracks to the rollup property, and one that tracks to a property for that website only, in which case we would not need to create separate views with filters as in Figure 12.29.

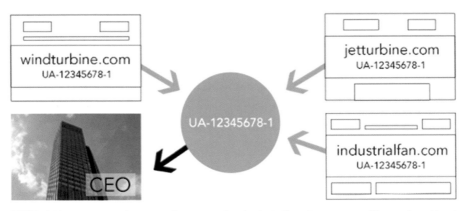

FIGURE 12.24 You can implement roll-up reporting by including the same tracking code, without modifications, in two or more websites.

Mobile App Roll-Up

You can create a roll-up of one or more apps in the same way as for websites: use the same property in multiple apps. Note, however, that for the recommended filters shown in Figure 12.27 and Figure 12.29 later in this chapter, you'd need to use Application Name in place of Hostname.

Theoretically, you could roll up a Web property with a mobile app property, but since the reports, metrics, and terminology reflect only one property type or the other, it's quite awkward to include Web and app data within a single property and generally not recommended.

As a separate discussion later in this chapter, we'll learn about cross-device tracking. For cross-device tracking as well, it's strongly recommended to maintain a Web property (accessed on desktop, tablet, or smartphone) separately from a mobile-app property (accessed on tablet or smartphone).

Subdomain Tracking

If you need to track multiple subdomains, such as www.mysite.com and news.mysite .com, you can begin by again asking some basic questions about user experience and reporting needs.

- **Do the two or more subdomains offer separate, unlinked user experiences?** If so, you can track the two subdomains as completely separate properties. As another option, you could essentially create a roll-up of the subdomains by including the same property ID in the GA tracking for the two subdomains, and you can ensure that separate cookies are written for each subdomain by specifying *www.mysite.com* and *news.mysite.com* for as the respective cookieDomain values in the Fields to Set section of the GA tags within GTM for the two websites. In this way, the subdomains would appear as referrers to each other when users crossed subdomains (that is, the session would not be maintained), but the roll-up property would still provide consolidated reporting across the subdomains.
- **Do the two or more domains offer a continuous user experience (in terms of branding, process, navigation, etc.)?** For subdomains, this will often be the case. You can use the same tracking code on the multiple subdomains, but you'll need to set the cookieDomain to *mysite.com* as shown in Figure 12.25 to prevent GA from writing separate cookies for each subdomain. As a note, *auto* as a cookieDomain value is also intended to set the cookie domain to the root domain, but since *auto* may function differently in certain cases—specifically for two-part top-level domains such as .co.uk—it's advisable to hard-code the cookie domain for tracking across subdomains.

FIGURE 12.25 To keep the same cookie across subdomains, set cookieDomain to your root domain.

Applying View Filters to Disambiguate Domains

A downside to including multiple domains or subdomains in a single property is that the pages are not distinguishable by domain or subdomain—within the Pages report, for example, as shown in Figure 12.26—unless you add Hostname as a secondary dimension or apply an individual Hostname as a custom segment.

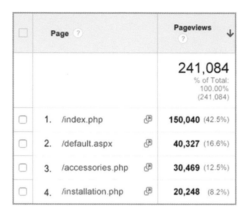

	Page ⑦		Pageviews ⑦ ↓
☐			241,084 % of Total: 100.00% (241,084)
☐	1. /index.php	🗗	150,040 (42.5%)
☐	2. /default.aspx	🗗	40,327 (16.6%)
☐	3. /accessories.php	🗗	30,469 (12.5%)
☐	4. /installation.php	🗗	20,248 (8.2%)

FIGURE 12.26 By default, you can't distinguish between different domains or subdomains unless you add Hostname as a secondary dimension or an individual hostname as a custom segment.

For the full domain name to appear as the Page (also called *Request URI*) value, we can apply a view filter as shown in Figure 12.27. Note that we're extracting the entire Hostname and original Request URI as (.*) regex capturing groups and outputting both into the final Request URI. With the filter applied, the Page dimension values are disambiguated as in Figure 12.28.

```
◉ Advanced
    Field A -> Extract A

    Hostname  ▾    (.*)

    Field B -> Extract B

    Request URI  ▾    (.*)

    Output To -> Constructor

    Request URI  ▾    $A1$B1
```

FIGURE 12.27 Custom view filter that prepends hostname to Request URI.

	Page ?		Pageviews ? ↓
☐			**241,084** % of Total: 100.00% (241,084)
☐	1. www.windturbine.com/index.php	⬚	**83,635** (34.7%)
☐	2. www.jetturbine.com/index.php	⬚	**66,405** (27.5%)
☐	3. www.industrialfan.com/default.aspx	⬚	**40,327** (16.6%)
☐	4. www.jetturbine.com/accessories.php	⬚	**30,469** (12.5%)
☐	5. www.windturbine.com/installation.php	⬚	**20,248** (8.2%)

FIGURE 12.28 With the view filter in Figure 12.25 applied, GA includes hostname in the Page dimension.

Dedicated View for Each Domain or Subdomain

As an additional best practice when you're tracking more than one domain or sub-domain in a single property, you can create dedicated views for each domain or sub-domain by applying a view filter that includes only a single hostname as shown in Figure 12.29. By applying the filter shown previously in Figure 12.27 to our main view and also creating dedicated views for each domain and subdomain, we have the best of both worlds: aggregated (but disambiguated) reporting across domains and sub-domains, and dedicated reporting for each domain or subdomain.

In the case of roll-up reporting for apps, you can use Application Name in place of Hostname for the filters shown in Figure 12.27 and Figure 12.29.

⦿ Include

Filter Field

Hostname ▾

Filter Pattern

(www\.)?windturbine\.com

FIGURE 12.29 With this view filter applied, we'll display data for *windturbine.com* only (with or without *www.*).

> **Note**
>
> **Should You Use the Same or Different GTM Containers in a Cross-Domain or Roll-Up Scenario?**
>
> In the case of cross-domain tracking (for websites that you manage directly), it's generally advisable to use the same GTM containers on the different domains, since they represent a unified user experience. In the case of roll-up reporting, separate GTM containers may be somewhat more suitable, especially if many of the other analytics and marketing codes deployed through GTM are intended only for a single domain.
>
> If you do you use a single GTM container for either cross-domain or roll-up, or across subdomains, you will be able to apply hostname-based GTM triggers to any of the other tags to control the websites they fire on. For mobile app tracking, you can use the built-in App Name variable in GTM triggers to fire tags in individual apps that share a GTM container with other apps.

CROSS-DEVICE TRACKING WITH USER ID

Life used to be simple (only a few years ago): people accessed your website from one device—namely, their desktop computers. You measured their actions, and that was the end of it.

Nowadays, visitors frequent your site from their laptops at work, then during lunch they'll check a promotion on their smartphones, and in the evening, on their tablet, they're convincing their significant others of the dire need that led them to buy your product.

It's great that these visitors had such an affinity with your brand and ended up making a purchase. By configuring cross-device tracking in GA, you can follow the journey throughout the Awareness-Consideration-Purchase cycle—as long as the user is authenticated, as we'll see below.

> **Terminology**
>
> **User ID and Cross-Device**
>
> Within Google Analytics, User ID and cross-device are always used in the same context. The Cross-Device reports appear only within a User-ID-enabled view, and it's the User ID that you pass to GA to populate the Cross-Device reports that we review below.

Authentication Required

Cross-device tracking is extremely useful and quite straightforward to configure, but it does not perform magic. As mentioned above, this feature works in an environment where you have an authenticated user experience (i.e., users are signing in). The authentication provides the common key that enables the cross-device tracking.

Admin Setup

Similarly to custom dimensions, custom metrics, and content groups, which you must first set up in the admin interface and then populate within hits that you send to GA, cross-device tracking also requires Admin setup followed by a User-ID value passed in the GA hits. In the case of cross-device reporting, we'll create one or more User-ID-enabled views for the property. When GA then receives hits that contain User ID, it will populate the Cross-Device reports within the User-ID-enabled views.

To set up a User-ID-enabled view that will display the Cross-Device reports:

1. In the Property Admin, click Tracking Info > User-ID.
2. Agree to the User-ID Policy, which prohibits you from passing PII to GA as the User-ID value.
3. Keep Session Unification set to ON. (This will allow GA to pull in hits from an authenticated session before the login occurred.)
4. Click Create to create the User-ID-enabled view.

Populating the User ID

For this step, you'll need to work with your developers to retrieve a unique but anonymous id for each logged-in user and typically write that ID to the data layer from the back end so we can pull it into GA through GTM. Note that you will need to include the User ID in every hit that you send to GA, so you should update all your GA tags—pageview, event, social, and Ecommerce—to read in the User ID as shown in Figure 12.30 so that these hits will be included in the User-ID-enabled view.

FIGURE 12.30   For a hit to be included in the User-ID-enabled view (and therefore the Cross-Device reports), you need to populate the userId field, with a unique User ID that your developers have normally pushed into the data layer from your authentication system.

Send User ID with Each Hit While the User Is Authenticated

Sending the User ID to GA with each hit requires two overall steps, described next.

Persist User ID

Since the User ID is required for each GA hit (to appear in the cross-device reports), the User ID must be accessible on each page while the user is authenticated. We can't just write the User ID to the data layer when the user logs in and then access the User ID in the data layer again on subsequent pages: the GTM data layer is flushed as soon as the user accesses another page. (The GTM data layer for mobile apps, conversely, does persist across screens. Cross-device tracking for mobile apps is discussed below.)

Depending on your authentication system, you might define the GTM {{User ID}} variable that appears in Figure 12.30 as follows:

- **Data layer:** you can work with your developers to push a User ID value to the data layer each time that a user accesses a page while authenticated. This is perhaps the most common solution and would offer the best option if your organization did not wish to expose a User ID value on the page, in the markup, in the URL, or in a cookie. From the data layer, you could read the User ID with a Data Layer variable.
- **DOM Element:** if the User ID is exposed on the page or in the markup, you can read it in through a DOM Element variable in GTM.
- **URL:** if the User ID appears as a query parameter (e.g., `http://www.mysite.com/?userid=123xyz`), you can parse it out through a URL variable in GTM with Component Type of the variable set to Query. If the User ID appears as a fragment (e.g., `http://www.mysite.com/#123xyz`), set Component Type to Fragment.
- **Cookie:** if for any reason it was not feasible to write the User ID to the data layer on each page load, you could store the User ID in a cookie when the user first authenticated and then read the cookie into your GA tags with a Cookie variable in GTM.

Unset the User ID on Logout

As soon as the user logs out, you are no longer permitted (by the GA terms of service) to send User ID with the hit, so you must make sure that you can no longer read it in through any of the variables listed above. If you have stored User ID in a cookie, you must delete the cookie on logout. If you have stored it in the GTM data layer for a mobile app, set the user ID variable in the data layer to *undefined* as soon as the user logs out.

Update All GA Tags to Send userId

As mentioned above, for each GA tag in GTM—including pageview, event, Ecommerce, and social—you should populate the userId field as shown in Figure 12.30. Again, this extra field will pertain only to User-ID-enabled views; in all other views, it will be ignored.

Note

Website and Apps in Cross-Device Tracking

While you could theoretically implement integrated cross-device tracking for authenticated website and app usage across different devices, the downside is that each User-ID-enabled view resides within a property that is designated for either Web or mobile app tracking, so pageviews would appear as screen views (or vice versa), and so forth.

You can, however, use basically the same steps to set up cross-device tracking for a mobile app that is accessed by an authenticated user on multiple mobile devices. In this way, you could configure separate Cross-Device reports for mobile app access and website access only.

As mentioned above, the data layer in GTM for mobile apps is persistent, so you could write the User ID to the data layer once only on login and then read it repeatedly into GA screen view tags, event tags, and so on.

Additional Considerations for Cross-Device Tracking

Keep the following in mind:

- Read and agree to the User ID policy. (You have to agree to it before you enable it, as detailed in the setup procedure above.) If your developers are on a time crunch, ensure you have signoff from your legal department ahead of getting the developers involved.
- Again, don't pass PII as a User ID.
- Use a clear and meaningful naming convention for the User-ID-enabled views, for example, *User ID Main*, or *User ID Europe Only*.
- You can configure goals, view filters, view settings, content groupings, AdWords linking, and Remarketing (discussed in Chapter 14) for a User-ID-enabled view just as you would for a non-User-ID-enabled view.
- The maximum lookback for the Cross-Device reports is 90 days.

Cross-Device Reports

Once the User-ID implementation and configuration are completed, you'll get to enjoy the three Audience > Cross-Device reports within the User-ID-enabled view.

Device Overlap

As shown in Figure 12.31, the Device Overlap report can display not only device overlap between sessions for authenticated users (who generated at least one session during the selected time period); it can also display which combination of devices across sessions drove revenue.

Device Paths

More granular than the Device Overlap report, the Device Paths report shows specific pass-offs from one device to another (before or during the selected time period). If we examine row 9 in Figure 12.32, for example, we see that 112 users generated (during the selected time period) one or more sessions on Desktop, then one or more sessions on Mobile, and then one or more sessions on Desktop, for a total of 1,641 sessions and $69,281.35 in revenue.

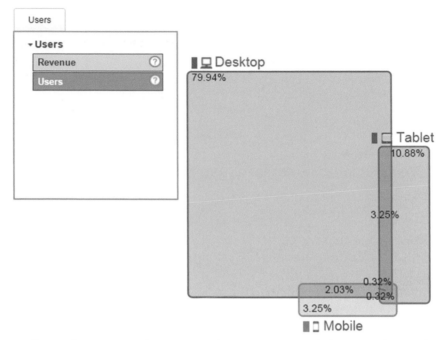

FIGURE 12.31 The Device Overlap report can display overlap not only for sessions but also for revenue that was accrued in different combinations of cross-device sessions.

Steps in path	Users ↓	Sessions	Average Duration of Sessions per User	Revenue
	36,133 % of Total: 100.00% (36,133)	171,766 % of Total: 100.00% (171,762)	00:07:30 Avg for View: 00:07:30 (0.00%)	$14,848,334.71 % of Total: 100.00% ($14,848,334.71)
1. Desktop	**29,503** (81.69%)	133,951 (77.98%)	00:07:19	$12,171,148.87 (81.97%)
2. Tablet	**4,009** (11.10%)	15,887 (9.25%)	00:07:11	$1,358,910.15 (9.15%)
3. Mobile	**1,203** (3.33%)	4,603 (2.68%)	00:08:03	$328,555.80 (2.21%)
4. Tablet Desktop	**178** (0.49%)	949 (0.55%)	00:07:43	$105,279.04 (0.71%)
5. Desktop Tablet	**139** (0.38%)	698 (0.41%)	00:07:36	$124,632.54 (0.84%)
6. Desktop Tablet Desktop	**128** (0.35%)	1,394 (0.81%)	00:10:12	$104,294.25 (0.70%)
7. Desktop Mobile	**119** (0.33%)	690 (0.40%)	00:07:43	$79,453.66 (0.54%)
8. Mobile Desktop	**113** (0.31%)	743 (0.43%)	00:07:38	$12,845.60 (0.09%)
9. Desktop Mobile Desktop	**112** (0.31%)	1,641 (0.96%)	00:10:54	$69,281.35 (0.47%)
10. Tablet Desktop Tablet	**77** (0.21%)	740 (0.43%)	00:08:19	$50,434.80 (0.34%)

FIGURE 12.32 The Device Paths report breaks down Users, Sessions, and Ecommerce metrics by pass-offs between device categories.

Acquisition Device

The Acquisition Device report in Figure 12.33 displays three rows only, corresponding to each of the three device categories. Row 2 indicates that 763 users who originated on Tablet (before or during the selected time period) generated $574,402.72 in revenue (during the selected time period) on Tablet and $158,868.20 on other devices.

Originating Device ?	New Users ? ↓	Sessions ?	Revenue From Originating Device ?	Revenue From Other Devices ?
	5,847 % of Total: 100.00% (5,847)	14,315 % of Total: 100.00% (14,315)	$4,322,366.49 % of Total: 100.00% ($4,322,366.49)	$1,299,246.19 % of Total: 100.00% ($1,299,246.19)
1. Desktop	4,827 (82.56%)	11,858 (82.84%)	$3,636,821.86 (84.14%)	$1,095,474.35 (84.32%)
2. Tablet	763 (13.05%)	1,910 (13.34%)	$574,402.72 (13.29%)	$158,868.20 (12.23%)
3. Mobile	257 (4.40%)	547 (3.82%)	$111,141.91 (2.57%)	$44,903.64 (3.46%)

FIGURE 12.33 The Acquisition Device report shows revenue generated on the originating device or other devices per device category.

Based on the Device Path and Acquisition Device report, you could potentially allocate additional PPC or other marketing budget to the device category that is performing best for acquisition leading to revenue (on the same device or other devices). If one device category is performing best in Revenue from Other Devices, you can target more of your remarketing to that device category.

Advanced Session Stitching

The session stitching that is enabled by default when we create a User-ID-enabled view ties in hits that were sent to GA before the login occurred in any unauthenticated session. For an advanced technique that allows you to associate entire unauthenticated sessions with authenticated sessions, see "Advanced Session Stitching and Cross Device Attribution using Custom Dimensions in Google Analytics" on the E-Nor blog.

User ID as a Custom Dimension

In addition to passing a user's unique, anonymous identifier to the GA's designated userId field for cross-device tracking, pass it also to a Custom Dimension to enable additional analysis. Once you have this identifier captured in a Custom Dimension, you can use it as a secondary dimension, in a custom segment definition, or in a custom report (whether or not you have enabled User ID for cross-device tracking in the view). You could, for instance, view traffic sources or device type for any user ID applied as a custom segment. (This type of analysis by individual ID is generally most useful in conjunction with back-end data also associated with that ID.)

Even more importantly, once populated as a Custom Dimension, the User ID would also be exposed through the API, which means that we could export from GA and integrate with CRM data for long-term lead qualification and customer value analysis as described in Chapter 15. (The designated userId field for cross-device tracking is, in fact, available for export to BigQuery for Analytics 360 users but is not accessible through the API. Even for Analytics 360, it's recommended to store the User ID variable in a separate Custom Dimension.)

In this way, we can have User ID perform double duty: populated into the designated userId field for cross-device tracking, and populated into a custom dimension (called *User ID*, *Visitor ID*, or any meaningful name) for use within the GA user interface and especially as a key for GA/CRM integration.

Even though you must populate User ID for cross-device tracking on a hit-by-hit basis, and only while the user is authenticated, you could opt to configure the User ID custom dimension at user scope for more complete GA data (including unauthenticated sessions following an authentication) for CRM integration.

GUEST SPOT   **Google Analytics and Data Privacy**

Holger Tempel

Holger Tempel is founder of the German company webalytics GmbH.

Google Analytics uses the device's Internet protocol (IP) addresses to geographically locate the user that accesses the Web server's pages. In countries of the European Economic Area many people are more and more concerned about data privacy, especially with regards to Internet usage and trackable behavior. This is because they think that an IP address itself is already PII. While IP address is not visible in the GA user interface or API, GA does, by default, store a visitor's complete IP address and uses it to determine the location information that is presented.

Whether or not IP address does actually constitute PII, privacy laws in Europe are very strict, and the governments of several European countries—Germany in particular—pressured Google to integrate a solution for this dilemma. In addition, they also demanded a solution for the users to be able to opt out of the tracking at all.

And back in 2010 Google integrated a function called `anonymizeIp`. In a nutshell: this function zeroes the last octet of an IP address and therefore makes sure that the IP address of any visitor will not be unique anymore.

In conjunction with `anonymizeIp()`, Google also released a browser add-on tool for the most common browsers, which, once installed, enabled the user to generally opt out of any tracking done with GA. But due to the increase of mobile devices usage and the variety of different browsers—which could not all be covered by that browser add-on tool—there was a need for change again. So Google integrated the possibility to opt out for each website individually.

Implementations of `anonymizeIp()` and tracking opt-in are outlined next.

Check the Need for Data Privacy Compliance

For country-specific guidance, you need to check with the commissioner of data protection if your website falls under the regulatory for data privacy compliance. As a rule of thumb, your website needs to fulfill the European data-privacy compliance if one of the following is true:

> Your website is run on servers in Europe.
> Your website offers content dedicated to European citizen (even if your website is run on servers outside Europe).
> Your company runs an office in Europe that is listed on your website.

If any of the conditions above applies to your website, you might need to complete the following steps:

1. Sign the Data Processing Amendment and send it off to Google.
2. Implement *anonymizeIp* to make sure that the IP addresses of your website's visitors will be anonymized.
3. Adjust your data privacy declaration.
4. Implement a possibility for each user to opt-out the tracking—on desktop PCs as well as on tablets, game consoles, and mobile devices.
5. Delete illegitimately collected data by deleting the corresponding property.

If you want to be sure to fulfill all requirements for being data privacy compliant in Europe, you should make sure to be compliant with the German laws and regulatory—it's the most restrictive in Europe and covers all aspects of data privacy.

Sign the Data Processing Amendment

The GA Data Processing Amendment is meant for businesses established in the territory of a member state of the European Economic Area or Switzerland, or that, for other reasons, are subject to the territorial scope of the national implementations of Directive 95/46/EC. It covers the GA account with all contained Properties and Views.

To accept the Data Processing Amendment is an optional procedure that does not affect the functionality of GA in any way. But because anonymizing the IP address of a user's device is accomplished after the IP address has been collected there's the need for an additional contract when using GA in Europe—the so-called data processing amendment. You can review and accept the data processing amendment from the bottom of the Account Settings.

In Germany, there's a need for signing an additional data processing contract. The link to the corresponding document is available when the terms of service are being displayed while setting up the account. If you website falls under the data privacy regulatory of Germany you need to download the document, fill in the form, print, sign, and send it off to Google.

Implement *anonymizeIp*

Each device has to have an IP address assigned to be able to communicate with each other. Therefore, each IP address on the Internet is unique and consists of four numbers—so-called *octets*. If you change the IP address, it doesn't represent the original device anymore. In the example below, you'll see how `anonymizeIp` works on an IPv4 address but it will also work with IPv6 addresses.

continues

continued

What Does anonymizeIp Do?

Now, how does `anonymizeIp` work? Below, you'll find the IP address for a device in Germany, Europe.

173.194.113.191

IP addresses are used to establish the communication between devices on the Internet. If you change the IP address of a device, it doesn't specifically represent this particular device anymore.

And this is exactly how `anonymizeIp` works: it changes the last octet of the IP address by replacing the original number with a zero (0).

This can also be done with many IP addresses no matter from which network they originate. Each and every IP address's last octet will be zeroed out by that function. After this anonymization, it seems that the first, second, and third group of IP addresses are all the same.

This approach obviously cuts both ways. On one hand, it's not possible to identify a particular device anymore, so you've satisfied this regulatory requirement. One the other hand, however, the data accuracy will blur with regard to geographic localization.

Why is that? Well, let's assume that the lower group of IP addresses in the example above could be geo-localized like this:

64.4.11.37 → Sunnyvale
64.4.11.38 → San Jose
64.4.11.39 → Santa Clara

And now let's further assume that 64.4.11.0 could be geo-localized to "Palo Alto." If you now use `anonymizeIp`, all hits originating from devices with IP addresses from this group would be anonymized to 64.4.11.0 and therefore geo-localized to "Palo Alto."

Let's have a closer look to what has to be done to make use of `anonymizeIp`.

What Kind of Modifications Have to Be Done to Use anonymizeIp?

While you can certainly add `anonymizeIp()` to native GA tracking code, the easiest way to implement `anonymizeIp` is to enable this option in your GA tags within GTM as shown in Figure 12.34.

Field Name		Value
anonymizeIp	🔳	true

FIGURE 12.34 To anonymize IP, you must set the *anonymizeIp* field to *true* in your GA tags within Google Tag Manager.

Adjust Data Privacy Declaration

In countries of the European Economic Area, there might be—and in Germany, there definitely is—also a need to adjust the website's data privacy declaration. This means that you have to inform the user that you are going to track the user's behavior when interacting with your website. Additionally, you have to point out the possibilities of opting out from being tracked with GA.

Implement *gaOptout*

In addition to the use of `anonymizeIp`, you'll have to offer a link to allow your visitors to opt out from GA tracking directly on your site. So it's necessary to also implement an option for that.

Even though Google already released a browser add-on for the most common browsers this would not help if the user visits a website with a nonsupported browser, a mobile device or a game console. This is why Google released an opt-out feature for digital property owners to implement.

What Does gaOptout Do?

`gaOptout` enables the user to opt out from GA on a specific site by simply clicking on a link on the site. In the case of a website, once the user clicks the `gaOptout` link, a cookie will be created telling the tracking snippet not to send data to GA anymore. The cookie expires in 2100, so it will work forever or until the user cleans the browser's cookies.

What Kind of Modifications Have to Be Done to Use gaOptout?

The implementation of `OPT-OUT` consists of two steps. First, you'll need to implement a link that enables the user to opt-out from GA tracing. Second, you'll have to implement some additional code in the source code of your website's pages.

Create an *opt-out* Link

You can use the script for the `opt-out` link directly from the example on the GA developer forum (`https://developers.google.com/analytics/devguides/collection/gajs/#disable`) and create a corresponding link in the footer of your website's pages.

This link's code should look like this:

continues

continued

```
<a href="javascript:gaOptout()">Click here to opt-out of GA</a>
```

Implement the *opt-out* Script

The function that is called with the opt-out link mentioned above is not yet implemented in the GA tracking snippet. So you need to insert it into your website's code before the GA tracking snippet.

The function's basic code to opt-out looks like this:

```
<script>
// Set to the same value as the web property used on the site
var gaProperty = 'UA-XXXXXX-YY';

// Disable tracking if the opt-out cookie exists.
var disableStr = 'ga-disable-' + gaProperty;
if (document.cookie.indexOf(disableStr + '=true') > -1) {
  window[disableStr] = true;
}

// Opt-out function
function gaOptout() {
  document.cookie = disableStr + '=true; expires=Thu, 31 Dec 2099
23:59:59 UTC; path=/';
  window[disableStr] = true;
}
</script>
```

To make this opt-out code work, you need to change the UA number in the third line to your own GA account. For details on offering opt-out for GA as implemented through GTM, see www.e-nor.com/gabook.

Delete Illegitimately Collected Data

Here's the last topic on how to be data privacy compliant in the European Economic Area—and probably the most painful for your company.

If you find out that you have to sign the data processing amendment for your GA account for the reasons mentioned above and you have already collected data for this particular account, you might already be in trouble.

Up to the point of signing the data processing amendment, all of the already collected data have been collected illegitimately and therefore need to be deleted. And to delete illegitimately collected data, you need to delete all GA Properties for the corresponding GA account. This is because the data processing amendment is signed for a GA account and not only for a single property.

Besides this big loss of valuable and actionable data, you also have to set up all of your filters, users, permissions, and so on again for new properties, which might be very costly and time consuming. Confer with your organization's attorneys before deleting any GA properties or accounts.

 **KEY TAKEAWAYS**

Custom dimensions help GA speak your language.   Custom dimensions allow you to extend the default GA data set and more closely align your reporting with your organization, your offerings, and your users. They're an important customization for a next-level GA practice.

Content groups are similar to hit-level custom dimensions.   Content groups play a similar role for page data as hit-level custom dimensions. The setup process is also very similar, and you can in fact populate a custom dimension and content group with the same data within the same GTM tags.

Take advantage of existing taxonomies.   If you have already classified your pages (by author, category, etc.), most of your work is already done. The steps for reading in an existing taxonomy as custom dimensions and/or content groups is quite straight-forward, especially if the text already appears in the page text or markup.

Cross-domain tracking is for unified user experiences; roll-up is for integrated reporting.   While cross-domain tracking and roll-up reporting both integrate data from multiple websites (or mobile apps in the case of roll-up) into a single property, cross-domain tracking is intended for multiple websites that constitute a unified user experience, while roll-up serves only to integrate reporting for multiple websites (or apps).

You can implement cross-device tracking for logged-in users.   By passing a User ID to GA on login, you can populate specialized cross-device reports within a User-ID-enabled view. You can use the same unique but anonymous back-end user identifier to populate the designated User-ID dimension for cross-device reporting and also a visitor ID custom dimension for integrating GA and CRM data, as described in Chapter 15.

 ACTIONS AND EXERCISES

1. **Assess the need for custom dimensions and/or content groups.** If you have an existing taxonomy, or if executives or managers are asking for metrics broken down by dimensions that don't exist in GA by default, you should probably make custom dimensions and/or content grouping a priority.

2. **Enable Demographics and Interests.** Enable Demographics and Interests, and update your privacy policy as indicated in the chapter (and check with your legal or compliance department beforehand).

3. **Enable Enhanced Link Attribution.** The In-Page Analytics report can be problematic, but it's still worthwhile to enable Enhanced Link Attribution in the GA pageview in GTM to benefit this report and the Page Analytics plug-in for Chrome.

4. **Assess the need for cross-domain or roll-up for separate domains.** If you need to track several domains, determine if you need to implement cross-domain or roll-up, or if tracking within separate properties is suitable.

5. **Assess the need for tracking multiple subdomains in a single or separate properties.** If you need to track several subdomains, determine if you should track within a single property (as a unified user experience) or if you should track in separate properties. You can also opt to track multiple subdomains into the same property but essentially create a subdomain "roll-up", similar to a roll-up of separate domains, by specifying a separate cookie domain in the GA tags for each domain.

6. **Implement cross-device tracking.** If your website offers a login, you can implement cross-device tracking as outlined in the chapter.

Mobile App Measurement

TRACKING MOBILE APPS

Mobile analytics while conceptually similar to Web tracking, is infinitely more complex. As the online world moves increasingly to mobile environments, it's crucial that businesses adapt not only their online presence to include mobile, but also their measurement strategy.

WHY IS MOBILE IMPORTANT

There are now more users on mobile than on desktop devices. A recent study, shown in Figure 13.1, by Marketing Land shows the rapid growth of mobile in the last few years. The trendline is startling and this will only grow, particularly with the astounding rate of mobile adoption in emerging markets.

Crucial to your overall marketing strategy, mobile analytics helps you understand:

- How often people interact with your app.
- What information in the app is important to them.
- Which devices are popular so you can optimize the app accordingly.
- How to best engage with consumers.

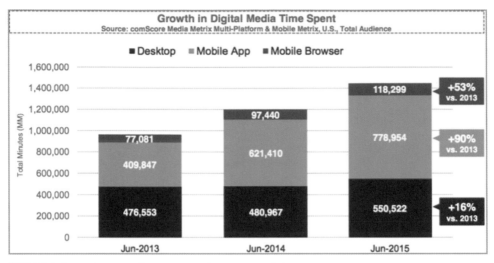

FIGURE 13.1 The striking growth in time spent by users in mobile apps.
Source: http://marketingland.com/apps-eat-digital-media-time-with-top-3-capturing-80-percent-143555

MOBILE STRATEGIES

The world of mobile is unique in that it encompasses two very different, equally impor-tant and complementary platforms. Users interact with organizations on their mobile devices using both browsers and apps. When we speak of mobile analytics, we are referring to both mobile apps and mobile Web. This may still be a point of confusion, so let's take a second to clarify. Mobile apps, of course, are standalone applications like Shazam and Maps that are downloaded and perform specific functions in a user inter-face very similar and consistent with the underlying operating system (iOS or Android). Mobile Web, on the other hand, refers to Web pages viewed in mobile browsers (as opposed to in an installed application). Most websites developed for desktop brows-ers are not very attractive or usable when accessed in a mobile browser. Organizations have typically addressed this issue in one of the two following ways, as first discussed in Chapter 4:

- redirect mobile users to a mobile-specific site (typically a different subdomain such as `m.example.com`)
- use responsive design to adapt content to the screen size of the user's device.

From a measurement perspective, it's important to note that instrumentation of analytics on mobile Web environments follows the same methods as for standard web-sites, as explored throughout this book. Mobile apps, however, require integration with Google Analytics mobile software development kits (SDKs), which we discuss as the primary focus of this chapter.

WHAT TO MEASURE

Before we delve into GA implementation for mobile apps, let's consider performance metrics from a mobile-app perspective. Often, organizations use the Number of Downloads as the be-all and end-all of mobile metrics. While knowing the number of downloads is interesting and a good reference point, you're doing yourself and your organization a major disservice if your measurement strategy is centered around number of downloads only. There are many more interesting bits of information that you should also be looking at which will significantly impact your business. For example, it's important to know how, when, where and by what audience your app is being used. Not only will this confirm whether your users are using the app as you think they are (or disprove your theories), but it's very empowering information as well, because it instantly will help point to insights and business actions you can take to improve performance.

There are many laundry lists of mobile metrics available online. Instead of recycling that information, we'll focus on a few really useful metrics that you should incorporate into your mobile measurement strategy.

In order to get a heartbeat of your app and a report on performance at both aggregate and granular levels there are some very fundamental metrics that require your attention. Table 13.1 breaks down the various reports/metrics available within Google Analytics (GA), specific to mobile apps, on which we can focus.

TABLE 13.1 Key Mobile Metrics to Focus On

Metric	Description
Active Users	The most fundamental metric in mobile analytics. Often dismissed, but serves as the foundation of all mobile segmentation, engagement and acquisition analysis.
Session Length	Measured as the period of time between app open and close. Indicates how much time users are spending in your app. Segmenting by your users, you can see which audiences are spending the most time in the app.
Session Interval	Session interval helps you understand user behavior and optimize your app accordingly. Defined as the time between the user's first session and their next one, this metric identifies the frequency with which your users use your app.
Acquisition	While this isn't really a metric, we're mentioning it here to emphasize its importance. Knowing where groups of users are originating from to download your app, and which campaigns are working well, is crucial to any successful mobile strategy.

continues

TABLE 13.1 *continued*

Metric	Description
Retention	In a sense, Retention measures how "sticky" your app is. Technically, Retention is the percentage of users who reopen your app within a certain time frame after initial open. Retention analysis is also referred to as cohort analysis, which is a useful method of analyzing not only the success of your app releases, but also your campaigns.
Lifetime Value (LTV)	LTV has historically been the big daddy of mobile metrics, measuring the actual monetary value of a user during the user's "lifetime" with your app. Looking at LTV by various user segments helps you identify which groups of users are most loyal, and thus most important to you, but also which ones are good candidates for upselling opportunities.
Average Revenue per User (ARPU)	As the name suggests, this metric indicates the amount of revenue generated by a user on average within a specific timeframe. It is calculated by dividing the total revenue generated within a specific timeframe by the total number of active users within that time frame.
	Used in conjunction with cost-based metrics, it can be used to measure success of campaigns. For example, if the average cost metrics are higher than the average revenue per user, you have work to do!
Cost per Install (CPI)	This metric is specific to marketing channels in which there is a cost for advertising as opposed to organic search, where this is no cost. It measures the cost for each installation resulting from your advertising campaigns.
Cost per Loyal User (CPLU)	Similar to CPI, this metric identifies the cost for each active user resulting from your advertising campaigns.
App Crashes	A metric essential to understanding the performance of your application. Looking at this metric alongside other low-performing metrics for specific user/device segments may reveal problem scenarios in your app that need to be resolved.
Devices and Operating Systems	Bundling these into one category but no less important than the others mentioned. While not a metric, these dimensions provide particularly revealing information about your users. For example, is your app most popular amongst iPhone users? Amongst users with the latest devices? Are there specific devices/OS versions where your app crashes more than others?
Geography	Geo data may provide you with insight into possible language options for your app. Alternatively, you might perhaps learn that the app tends to crash or function slowly in certain regions, resulting in diminished usage.

Segmentation

The reports and metrics identified above form just the foundation of your mobile analytics strategy. The real gems of information are revealed only when you combine the above data with more advanced analysis techniques.

As discussed in Chapter 10, segmentation is necessary for better analysis; this applies to mobile apps as fundamentally as to websites. Segmenting your user behavior allows you to see user activity within geographic, demographic, and technology (device type, app version, etc.) dimensions and draw distinctions between each of these groups of users. You can also segment on user actions (e.g., the concept of a nervous window shopper—someone who entered the in-app store many times but backed out of the purchase screen at least three times).

MOBILE CONFIGURATION IN GOOGLE ANALYTICS

Setting up GA to receive data from mobile devices is fairly straightforward. This setup will enable several mobile-specific reports, as well as a range of reports that we have already examined for website reporting.

As we saw in Chapter 9, the requirement for creating a mobile app property is the same as for creating Web property: edit access to the account.

The first step is thus to create a mobile app property, as shown in Figure 13.2.

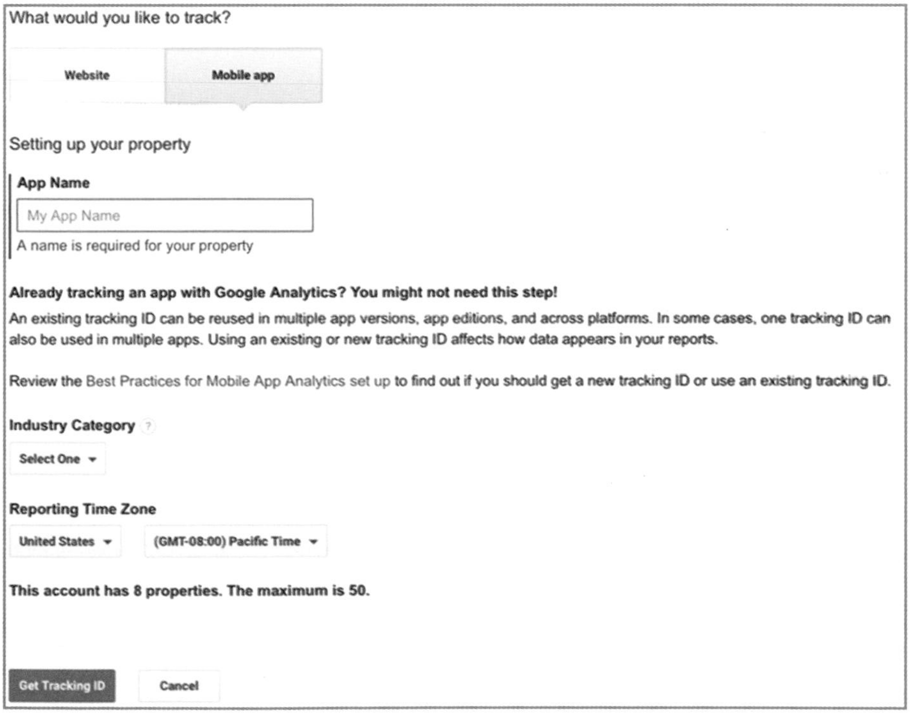

FIGURE 13.2 Adding a mobile property.

SETTING UP GOOGLE ANALYTICS IN YOUR APP

How do you actually go about setting up your app to report information to GA? The process is relatively straightforward but does require a development background.

Unlike analytics implementation for websites, Mobile Analytics requires more development knowledge and an understanding of how to integrate with an SDK provided by Google.

Deploying Google Analytics to Your App

We discuss two options for deploying GA to your mobile app:

- Via a mobile operating system SDK (Android or iOS).
- Via the Google Tag Manager (GTM) for Mobile SDK (Android or iOS).

Instead of detailing the specific integration steps, which you can find in Google's documentation, we'll focus on detailing why you would choose one option versus the other.

Should I Deploy via the Mobile SDK or GTM SDK?

Let's consider some of the potential advantages of GTM for mobile app tracking.

Easy Audit

As with the use of GTM on websites explored in Chapter 5 and through much of this book, GTM allows you to easily audit which tags are firing under which conditions for your mobile app. Since tracking with the GA SDK is implemented only at code level (at least for GA events and Ecommerce, even if you're using the autotracking option for screen views), auditing of your GA SDK tracking implementation might pose more of a challenge.

Tagging Flexibility

If you are writing from your mobile app to the data layer to trigger and populate a GA event tag in GTM, for example, you could decide to use those same data layer values to instead trigger and populate a GA screen view tag with a custom dimension in GTM, all without directly updating your app. We further discuss this advantage below.

Dynamic App Updates and Testing

As shown in Figure 13.3, you can use a GTM Value Collection variable to dynamically update your app without having to rebuild and resubmit application binaries to the app marketplaces, which can be an ordeal, particularly for Apple. (The app must, however, already be coded to read from the Value Collection. You could also activate different Value Collections based on a GTM Function Call variable that returns the value of a function coded within your app.)

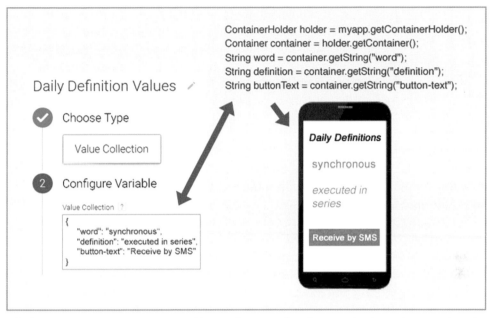

FIGURE 13.3 The GTM Value Collection variable provides a major benefit to app developers by giving them the ability to bypass the app marketplace review processes and update elements of their app easily.

You can similarly configure GA Content Experiments for your mobile app through GTM. For more on dynamic updates and testing for your app through GTM, see `www .e-nor.com/gabook`.

GA SDK Built Into GTM SDK

The GA SDK is actually built into the GTM SDK, so you can benefit from GTM but still take advantage of the GA SDK if this is ever necessary.

Mobile apps differ from websites in the sense that once you update your website, it's updated for all users who access your website. Releasing a new version of your app doesn't in any way guarantee that your user base will upgrade. Mobile apps are static in nature and require the user to accept the update. In other words, it's very likely and common for your user base to be running multiple versions of your app. GTM for Mobile helps mitigate this drawback by allowing developers to make app configuration and analytics updates by publishing new container versions through the Web-based GTM interface, as detailed above.

In addition, you can leverage the functionality of GTM to dynamically deploy other tracking tags and pixels within your apps, such as for DoubleClick remarketing or third-party conversion pixels. Developers can push important events into a data layer and then later decide which tracking tags or pixels should be fired—by a Custom Event trigger, as described in Chapter 6.

It should be noted that an implementation using the GTM SDK will without question take more time overall since you're essentially introducing a communication layer between the app and GA and therefore responsible for both the coding aspects and the tagging aspects.

The GTM implementation could also become more exhaustive than the mobile SDK option, since you could theoretically capture every finger tap, swipe, or other interaction as a data layer event and later decide how you'll consume these data layer events as Custom Event triggers to fire GA (or other) tags within GTM, but we recommend keeping it simple by focusing only on those user actions that are important to measure now or may be in the foreseeable future. In any case, GTM does provide the flexibility for you to decide how (and if) to consume the triggers and data that you write to the GTM data layer from your mobile app code.

For instance, let's say that you're populating the data layer with an *event* variable (for a Custom Event trigger), as well as eventCat, eventAct, and eventLbl variables that you originally intend to read into a GA event tag in GTM. After the app is live, however, you realize that you instead want to track the action as a screen view so that you can use the action as a step in a goal funnel, you'd be able to trigger a GA screen view tag instead of GA event tag in GTM without rewriting any of the original code that's populating the data layer.

One advantage that the GA SDK for Android offers is the ability to configure ga_autoActivityTracking in track_app.xml (for Android). This avoids the need to explicitly code screenview tracking, and by specifying screenName tags in track_app.xml, you can map your activity class names to more human readable screen names in your GA reporting. In GTM, this automated screen tracking isn't as easily available, but instead a GTM tag would need to configured to fire for each screen. Since there aren't that many screens in a typical app, individual screen tracking is not much of a burden, so the benefits of opting for the GTM SDK normally far outweigh the downsides, that is, an extra layer of implementation (and potentially debugging), and lack of auto screen tracking for Android.

For reference, links to the full set of instructions for each SDK are provided below for the releases current at the time of publication—please be sure to refer to documentation for updated releases as needed:

Deploying Google Analytics via the Mobile OS SDK
- Android: `https://developers.google.com/analytics/devguides/collection/android/v4/`
- iOS: `https://developers.google.com/analytics/devguides/collection/ios/v3/`

Deploying Google Analytics via the Google Tag Manager for Mobile SDK
- Android: `https://developers.google.com/tag-manager/android/v4/`
- iOS: `https://developers.google.com/tag-manager/ios/v3/`

For more on initializing the GTM container object in Android, see "Overview of Code to Load the Container" in the Google Analytics for Android course on Udacity.

Crashes and Exceptions

For more details specifically on tracking crashes and exceptions in mobile apps, see `www.e-nor.com/gabook`.

> **Note**
>
> **Tracking Non-Android and Non-iOS Mobile Apps**
>
> As mentioned in Chapter 17, since the GA and GTM SDKs are available only for Android and iOS, Measurement Protocol is our option for tracking mobile apps running on operating systems such as Windows and BlackBerry.

ACCOUNT STRUCTURE BEST PRACTICES IN MOBILE PROPERTIES

In April 2014, Google announced a new feature that allows you to track Web and app data in a single view. The premise behind this type of roll-up reporting is that, in theory, you can have a true count of logged-in users that is de-duplicated across your devices. Google can take data from two different properties and aggregate them into a single view. (We discuss roll-up reporting in Chapter 18.)

As with anything else, though, the ability to do something doesn't necessarily mean you should. To maintain a clean view of your data and enable easy scalability and reporting, use the following guidelines, based on "Best Practices for Mobile App Analytics" in the GA help docs (`https://support.google.com/analytics/answer/2587087`):

- **Track different apps in separate properties.** Each app should be tracked in its own unique property to avoid data being combined in unintentional ways. This will also help avoid sampling since the single-app views will contain less data than a roll-up. (Sampling is discussed in Chapter 10).
- **Track different platforms of an app in different properties.** Each app platform should be isolated to its own property as well. For example, an Android version of an app should be tracked in its own property, and iOS should likewise be in its own property. Combining these typically doesn't yield any tangible benefits other than the total users metric (which can easily be calculated outside of GA or in a roll-up like

the type discussed earlier). Combining app platforms within a single property would be particularly problematic if they're very different and would cause anomalies in reporting.

- **Track app editions based on feature similarities.** App editions can be tracked in either one or separate properties depending on the level of uniqueness. For example, if you have any app called "Crazy App" and then another called "Crazy App: Crazier Edition," and if the user experience of these apps is basically the same with some feature differences, then it's fine to report them to the same property. If there are significant differences, then it's best to keep them separate.
- **Track different app versions in the same property.** Version tracking is already a default attribute captured by GA, so it's not necessary to report different versions to separate properties. Combine them and let GA break this down for you as needed. Besides, seeing a version usage report of your app is extremely interesting!

REAL-TIME APP REPORTING

In GA for Web, Real-Time reports show you data about your users as they traverse the site (after a few seconds of delay). How do Real-Time reports work for apps? Slightly differently. We've isolated the data in the following examples to highlight the differences.

In the Real-Time Overview report, you see how many active users there are, how many screen views the app is getting "per minute" and "per second." The metrics work in the following ways:

Scenario 1:
- The app is launched and the user navigates through a typical variety of screens and icons, links. This navigation results in data being generated in GA.
- When you check the "Per Second" window of real-time reporting, nothing shows up. Something must be wrong—right?
- You escalate to your developers so they can correct the problem. They check the code and the GA View configuration and report back "no problem found."
- You run the test again and watch closely. After about two minutes, activities appear in the "Per Minute" window showing activities that happened two minutes earlier (see Figure 13.4). What happened?
- This is as real-time as you are going to get. Not good? Sorry—it's by design. Read on to find out why.

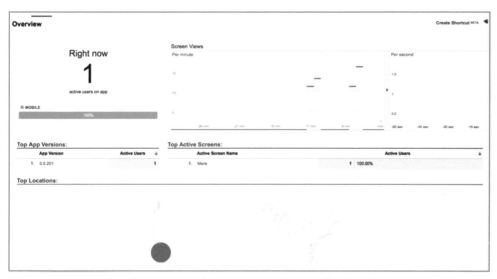

FIGURE 13.4 Real-Time data showing up roughly two minutes after actually taking place.

Data Dispatch

A process called *data dispatching*, often used in mobile analytics and in our specific GA example, is playing tricks on us. As defined by Google: "As your app collects GA data, that data is added to a queue and periodically dispatched to GA. Periodic dispatch can occur either when your app is running in the foreground or the background." Since mobile devices must manage the consumption of battery, CPU processing, and network bandwidth by mobile apps, dispatching is used to reduce overhead and strain on the device, resulting in a smoother end-user experience.

In iOS, the default dispatch is *2 minutes*—see "iOS Dispatching" in the GA help docs: `https://developers.google.com/analytics/devguides/collection/ios/v3/dispatch.`

For Android, the default dispatch is *30 minutes*—see "Android Dispatching" in the GA help docs: `https://developers.google.com/analytics/devguides/collection/android/v4/dispatch.`

While you can adjust the data dispatch delay and thereby refresh the Real-Time reports more frequently, as detailed in the help docs, it's not recommended to increase the data dispatch rate to the point where it may impact app performance: user experience should always trump measurement.

Scenario 2:

- The app was launched and a number of screens and elements were clicked.
- The app was killed—all within less than two minutes. Interestingly, the activities showed up right away in the Per Second window.

- After a minute or two, the activities showed up in the Per Minute window as shown in Figure 13.5.

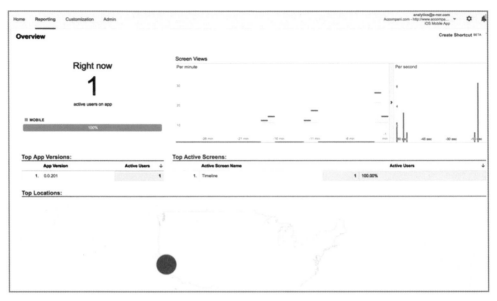

FIGURE 13.5 Data appearing in the Per Second window immediately, instead of after a dispatch-related delay.

Why did the activity show up within less than two minutes in the Per Second window and (pretty much less than two minutes) in the Per Minute window?

The batch is transmitted after a set delay. However, if the app is terminated before that time frame, data will be submitted right away. In this case, since the app was terminated prior to the two-minute mark, the batch was transmitted and (after some processing time) showed up in the Per Second window. In the minute window, after the processing time and minute intervals, the Real-Time activity will be visible.

INTEGRATIONS

There are several integrations available within Google Analytics for mobile apps. Let's discuss a few of these.

AdMob Integration to Google Play and iTunes

AdMob is Google's mobile advertising platform, designed to work with mobile apps.

While some mobile app users may find in-app ads intrusive, the revenue generated by AdMob (as shown in Figure 13.6) enables developers to offer their apps for free (or at a lower cost than they would otherwise need to charge).

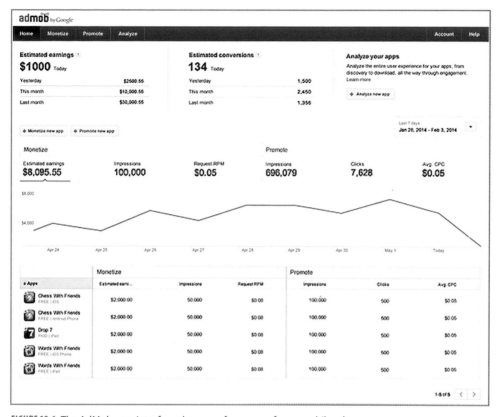

FIGURE 13.6 The AdMob user interface shows performance of your mobile ads.

Advertisers who have integrated AdMob and GA can see both AdMob data and GA data within the AdMob interface, and create or optimize AdMob campaigns accordingly. Now AdMob users can access.

Setting up the AdMob integration with GA is a fairly simple process:

1. Sign in to your AdMob account at `https://www.google.com/admob/`.
2. Select the Analyze tab.
3. Select appropriate account information:
   - Select "New" if you've never used GA before or if you prefer to create a new account. Be sure to review the data-sharing settings and Terms of Service, and then select the checkbox to agree.
   - Select "Existing" if you already have a GA account with which to analyze your app(s). Select the account from the drop-downs and enable Edit permission at the account level.
   - Upon selecting an existing GA account, you'll notice that a new roll-up property and view will be created. The new view (called All Apps) is the view that will

provide AdMob with aggregated data from all of your linked app properties. The data from this view will be visible in the "Analyze" tab.

4. Click Continue.
5. Under the "Start Analyzing your App" section, click Continue to proceed.
   - Select your app as shown in Figure 13.7.

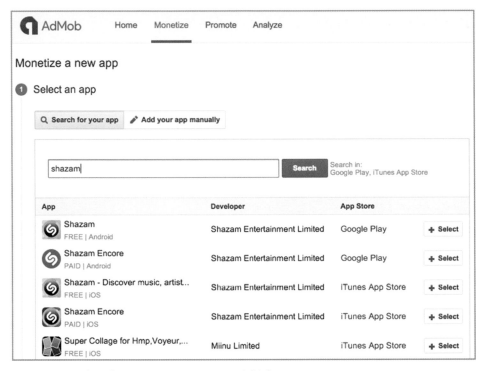

FIGURE 13.7 Searching for an app to connect to your AdMob account.

6. In the Apps Setup pop-up, you'll see a list of your apps. For any apps that don't have a GA tracking ID next to them, click "Set up Tracking ID."
7. From here, you can choose either to "Create a new tracking ID" if you prefer to use a new GA account, or you can "Use an Existing Tracking ID."
8. Click "Done" once you've completed associating a tracking ID with your app(s).

It typically takes up to 24 hours for GA data to start showing up in the Analyze tab within AdMob.

Google Play & Apple Store Integration

Integrating the major mobile app stores with your GA account can answer the following questions:

- How do users discover your apps?
- What devices do they use?
- How often do they return?
- How many times were your apps downloaded?

Google Play Integration

For instructions on mapping Google Play app activity to a GA property, follow these steps:

1. Sign in to your GA Account.
2. Click the Admin tab.
3. From the dropdown menus at the top of each column, select the appropriate Account and Property.
4. Select "All Products."
5. This page will show the products that your property is currently linked to. Scroll down to the Unlinked Products section, and find the Google Play entry as shown in Figure 13.8.
6. From here, click the Link Google Play button.
7. On the next screen (see Figure 13.9), select the apps to integrate with and click Continue.
8. Click Enable Link to complete the integration.

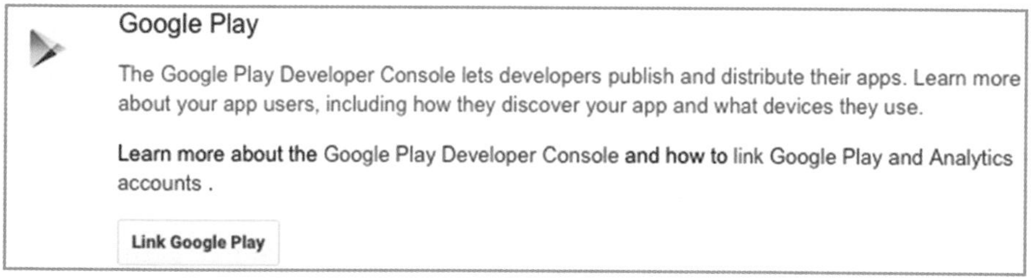

Google Play

The Google Play Developer Console lets developers publish and distribute their apps. Learn more about your app users, including how they discover your app and what devices they use.

Learn more about the Google Play Developer Console **and how to** link Google Play and Analytics accounts .

Link Google Play

FIGURE 13.8 The starting step for linking Google Play to Google Analytics.

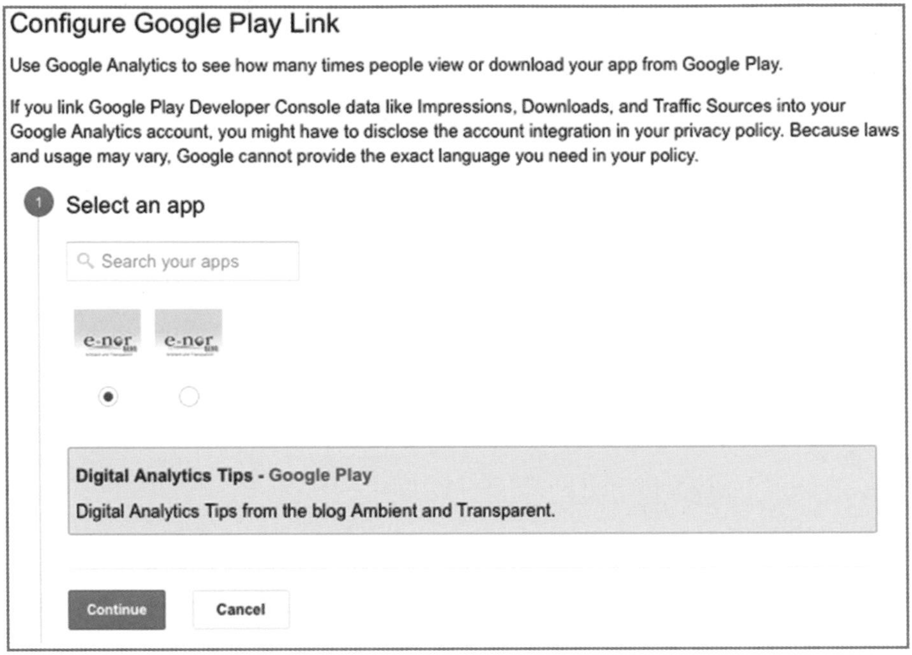

FIGURE 13.9 Configuring the Google Play/GA link.

Apple App Store Integration with Google Analytics

The iOS integration with GA is quite different from Google Play integration with GA.

To track installs, an app developer typically uses an Ad Network (or multiple Ad Networks) to set up an app download campaign. For install tracking on iOS, GA relies on Apple's resettable Identifier for Advertising (IDFA) to match app sessions to campaigns. To accomplish this, GA relies on Ad Networks to provide and send the IDFA and other campaign information to GA when an app user clicks on an ad.

Ad Networks can use the following methods to enable iOS install tracking in GA for their customers:

- Redirect
- Asynchronous ping

Both approaches yield the same iOS install data; your choice will depend largely on which of the two is supported by your ad network. Following we summarize Redirect and Asynchronous Ping as detailed in "iOS Install Tracking" in the GA help docs.

Redirect

The *redirect* method uses a campaign URL that points the user to the GA click server, which will then redirect the user to the app's iTunes page. The URL will look similar to the following: `click.google-analytics.com/redirect?param1=value1&` `param2=value2`.

The high-level steps for this method are:

1. The Ad Network forms the URL and sets the query string parameters to include campaign information and the IDFA.
2. When the user clicks the ad, the user is redirected to GA, which collects the IDFA and other parameter values.
3. The user is then redirected to the app's iTunes page.
4. If the user installs the app, it will be matched to the campaign from the ad clicked in step 2.

An example redirect URL:

```
http://click.google-analytics.com/redirect?
   tid=UA-1234-1                              // Google Analytics Tracking ID
   &idfa=BBA44F63-E469-42BA-833A-2AC550310CB3  // Identifier for Advertising (IDFA)
   &aid=com.bundle.myapp                       // App ID
   &cs=network                                 // Campaign source
   &cm=cpc                                     // Campaign medium
   &cn=campaign_name                           // Campaign name
   &url=https://itunes.apple.com/us/app/myApp/id123?mt=8
```

Asynchronous Ping

The ping method requires the Ad Network to make a direct request to the GA server when a user clicks an ad. The ping URL will look similar to the following:

```
click.google-analytics.com/ping?param1=value1&param2=value2
```

The high-level steps for this method are:

1. The user clicks the ad, which brings the user to the app's iTunes page.
2. The Ad Network pings the GA server with query string parameters that have been set with campaign information and the IDFA.
3. GA collects the IDFA and other parameter values from the ping request.
4. If the user installs the app, it will be matched to the campaign from the ad clicked in step 1.

MOBILE CAMPAIGN TRACKING

Campaign tracking is often one of the most overlooked areas of analytics, particularly for mobile apps, yet it's also one of the most beneficial. It certainly takes some work, and more importantly some thought and diligence to implement, but it provides the benefit of accurate attribution data, as shown in Figure 13.10. Following we outline Android and iOS campaign tracking procedures—for install and for reengagement—as specified in the GA help docs.

	Source / Medium ?	New Users ?	↓ Sessions ?	Avg. Session Duration ?
		292,067 % of Total: 92.75% (314,884)	**1,815,648** % of Total: 92.39% (1,965,139)	**00:06:32** Avg for View: 00:06:32 (-0.09%)
☐	1. (direct) / (none)	**280,408** (96.01%)	1,741,483 (95.92%)	00:06:33
☐	2. cnn.com / banner	**5,150** (1.76%)	28,205 (1.55%)	00:05:17
☐	3. facebook.com / social	**3,879** (1.33%)	27,353 (1.51%)	00:06:59
☐	4. google / organic	**2,428** (0.83%)	17,051 (0.94%)	00:06:05
☐	5. twitter.com / social	**77** (0.03%)	463 (0.03%)	00:05:22

FIGURE 13.10 The Google Play Sources report clearly shows which referral sources are driving traffic.

Mobile apps can receive incoming links from the same sources as Web (referral, direct, email, social), but also from another mysterious source—other apps! Without proper tracking of referring links, companies would have very little insight into where users are originating from, and ultimately wouldn't be able to effectively determine which marketing efforts are working well, and which aren't.

Android

The following options are available for attribution of campaigns and traffic sources to user activity within your Android mobile app.

Google Play Campaign Attribution for Download Tracking

This very useful feature enables you to see which campaigns and traffic sources are sending users to download your app from the Google Play store.

One of the additional data points that Google Play will allow you to view is the number of app downloads. By leveraging the campaign parameters, you not only see the aggregate number of downloads but also the distribution of those downloads by campaign. To measure app downloads by originating campaign we must add campaign parameters to the download URL provided by Google Play; the Google Analytics receiver will then parse this information and pass it along to GA when your app is downloaded.

GA campaign integration for Google Play downloads requires two overall steps:

1. Add the Google Analytics receiver to your AndroidManifest.xml file. The receiver allows the app to "receive" and parse the campaign parameters and relay them to Google Play.
2. As mentioned above, add GA campaign parameters to the Google Play download URLs you use in your campaigns.

For more details, see "Google Play Campaign Attribution" in the Google Analytics help docs for Android (`https://developers.google.com/analytics/devguides/collection/android/v4/campaigns`).

General Campaign and Traffic Source Attribution for Post-Install Tracking

The above method facilitates tracking of app downloads and install attribution. Figure 13.10 illustrates how users found your app and downloaded it.

What about tracking the effectiveness of the app post-install?

Once an app is installed, it can be launched by links from ad campaigns, websites or even other apps installed on your device. In order to properly attribute this type of post-install referral to the app, you must manually configure your app to process the campaign tracking parameters by using the `setCampaignParamsFromUrl` method, as shown in Listing 13.1.

LISTING 13.1: Using setCampaignParamsFromUrl to enable post-install campaign tracking for Android.

```
// Get tracker.
Tracker t = ((AnalyticsSampleApp) getActivity().getApplication()).
getTracker(
    TrackerName.APP_TRACKER);
// Set screen name.
t.setScreenName(screenName);

// In this example, campaign information is set using
// a url string with Google Analytics campaign parameters.
// Note: This is for illustrative purposes. In most cases campaign
//       information would come from an incoming Intent.
String campaignData = "http://examplepetstore.com/index.html?" +
    "utm_source=email&utm_medium=email_marketing&utm_campaign=summer" +
    "&utm_content=email_variation_1";

// Campaign data sent with this hit.
t.send(new HitBuilders.ScreenViewBuilder()
    .setCampaignParamsFromUrl(campaignData)
    .build()
);
```

For more details, see "General Source Campaign & Traffic Attribution" in the Google Analytics help docs for Android (`https://developers.google.com/analytics/devguides/collection/android/v4/campaigns`).

Google Play URL Builder

The Google Play URL builder (Figure 13.11) helps construct a URL that will ensure all required parameters are captured correctly.

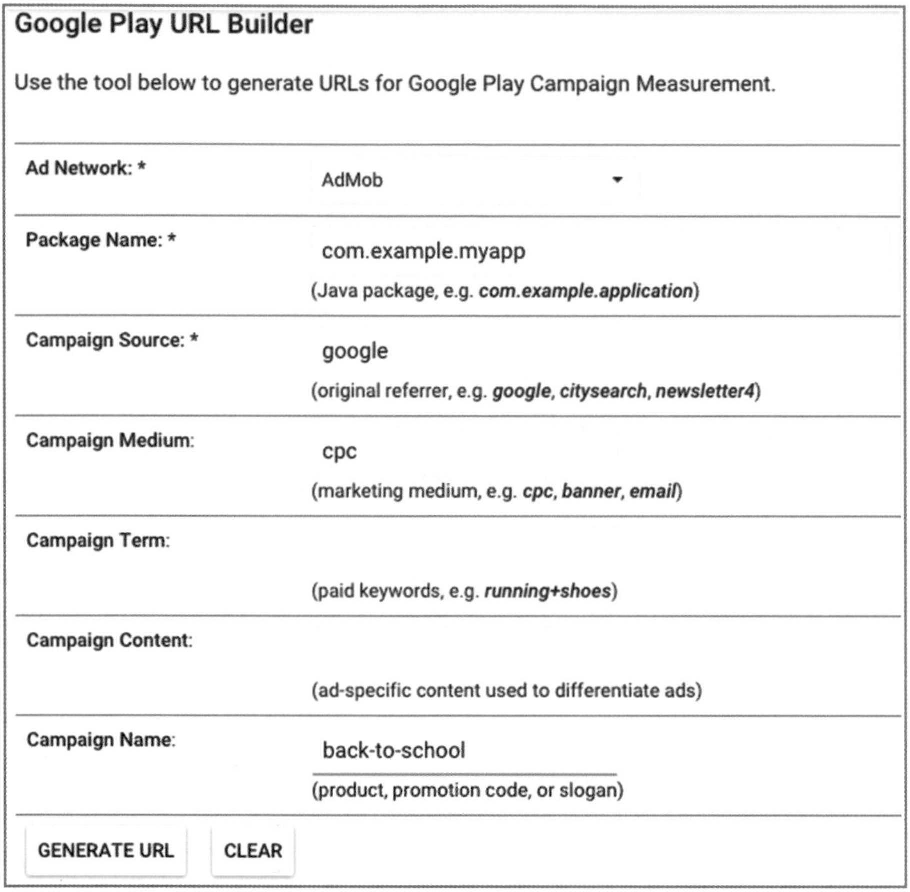

Google Play URL Builder

Use the tool below to generate URLs for Google Play Campaign Measurement.

Ad Network: *   AdMob   ▼

Package Name: *   com.example.myapp
                     (Java package, e.g. *com.example.application*)

Campaign Source: *   google
                     (original referrer, e.g. *google, citysearch, newsletter4*)

Campaign Medium: cpc
                     (marketing medium, e.g. *cpc, banner, email*)

Campaign Term:
                     (paid keywords, e.g. *running+shoes*)

Campaign Content:
                     (ad-specific content used to differentiate ads)

Campaign Name: back-to-school
                     (product, promotion code, or slogan)

GENERATE URL   CLEAR

FIGURE 13.11 The Google Play URL builder inputs the required campaign information and builds a URL that can then be used in marketing materials.

You can access the Google Play URL builder here: `https://developers .google.com/analytics/devguides/collection/android/v4/ campaigns#google-play-url-builder`.

The result of the above URL building process is: `https://play.google .com/store/apps/details?id=com.example.myapp&referrer=utm_ source%3Dgoogle%26utm_medium%3Dcpc%26utm_campaign%3Dback-to- school%26anid%3Dadmob`.

Notice how all the fields in the form above are automatically appended to the URL. Imagine doing this manually. Not fun.

As mentioned in Chapter 10, you can shorten your campaign-tagged URLs with a utility such as goo.gl or bit.ly. The clicked, expanded URL will contain the original campaign parameters and be processed by GA accordingly.

iOS

The following options are available for attribution of campaigns and traffic sources to user activity within your application.

iOS Install Campaign Measurement

Similar to the Google Play campaign attribution, iOS install campaigns allow you to view which campaigns, sites, and apps are sending traffic to iTunes to download your app.

Google Analytics provides the ability to capture downloads in iTunes for popular mobile ad networks and to generate custom URLs for any additional networks and referrals.

To configure iOS Install Campaign Measurement:

1. Ensure Google Analytics is implemented in your iOS app (with minimum one screen being tracked).
2. Confirm iOS Campaign tracking is enabled (under Property Settings in the GA admin).
3. Confirm that the application ID reported in GA matches your actual app ID. (You can view the application ID in GA by choosing custom report with App ID as dimension and Sessions as metric.)
4. Enable Identifier for Advertiser (IDFA) collection.
5. Check demographics report to confirm IDFA is being sent (if data is present, it's working).
6. Ensure iOS campaign tracking URLs are correct.

Full instructions for this process can be found here: `https://developers.google.com/analytics/devguides/collection/ios/v3/campaigns#ios-install`.

General Campaign and Traffic Source Attribution for Post-Install

iOS post install tracking is conceptually similar to what we discussed in the section of post-install tracking for Google Play. The purpose of this, of course, is to ensure post-install launches of your app are attributed correctly.

Once an app is installed, it can of course be launched by links from ad campaigns, websites or even other apps installed on your device. In order to properly attribute this type of post-install referral to the app, you must set campaign fields within the tracker directly.

The simplest approach for doing this is to use `[GAIDictionaryBuilder setCampaignParametersFromUrl:urlString]`, where `urlString` is a string representing a URL that may contain Google Analytics campaign parameters.

For more specifics and detailed instructions, please see: `https://developers.google.com/analytics/devguides/collection/ios/v3/campaigns#general-campaigns`.

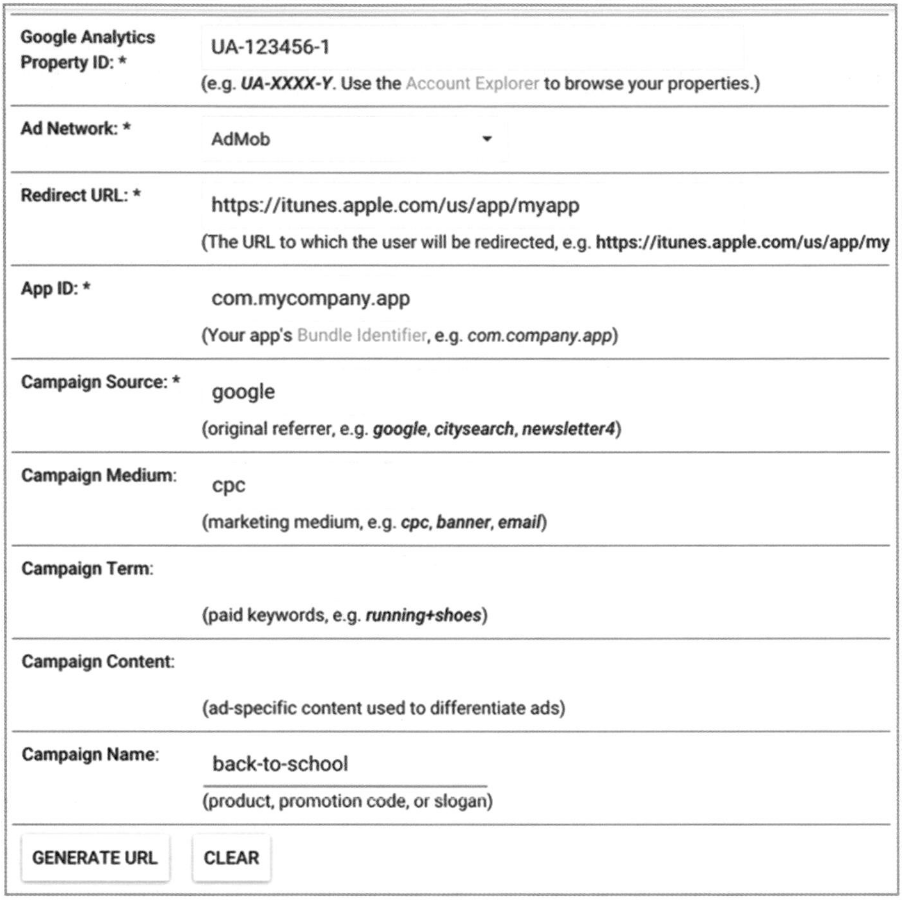

Google Analytics Property ID: *	UA-123456-1
	(e.g. *UA-XXXX-Y*. Use the Account Explorer to browse your properties.)
Ad Network: *	AdMob ▾
Redirect URL: *	https://itunes.apple.com/us/app/myapp
	(The URL to which the user will be redirected, e.g. **https://itunes.apple.com/us/app/my**
App ID: *	com.mycompany.app
	(Your app's Bundle Identifier, e.g. *com.company.app*)
Campaign Source: *	google
	(original referrer, e.g. *google, citysearch, newsletter4*)
Campaign Medium:	cpc
	(marketing medium, e.g. *cpc, banner, email*)
Campaign Term:	
	(paid keywords, e.g. *running+shoes*)
Campaign Content:	
	(ad-specific content used to differentiate ads)
Campaign Name:	back-to-school
	(product, promotion code, or slogan)
GENERATE URL CLEAR	

FIGURE 13.12 The iOS version of the URL builder requires a couple of more iOS specific fields to ensure data is mapped to GA correctly.

iOS Campaign Tracking URL Builder

Just like with Google Play apps, we strongly recommend using a tool to facilitate building of campaign tracking URLs.

The iOS Campaign Tracking URL Builder (see Figure 13.12) can be found here: `https://developers.google.com/analytics/devguides/collection/ios/v3/campaigns#url-builder`.

This results in the following URL: `https://click.google-analytics.com/redirect?tid=UA-123456-1&url=https%3A%2F%2Fitunes.apple`

```
.com%2Fus%2Fapp%2Fmyapp&aid=com.mycompany.app&idfa={idfa}&cs
=google&cm=cpc&cn=back-to-school&anid=admob&hash=md5 .
```

Similar to Google Play campaign tracking URLs, the campaign parameters are appended to the URL along with additional information needed specific for the Apple App Store.

While campaign parameters take an otherwise elegant URL and turn it into a monstrosity, the URLs can be minimized using popular URL shorteners to reduce their footprint and make them easier to read.

MOBILE PRIVACY

Whether it's reading books, playing games, listening to music, taking photos, getting directions, monitoring health/fitness activity, banking, or even remotely starting our vehicles, mobile devices are becoming the hub from which we control and perform many of these activities. As such, mobile devices contain very private information about their owners, the applications they use, the content they consume, and the places they visit.

With the increasing usage of mobile devices and the amount and type of data being stored on them, mobile devices are, of course, subject to the identical privacy risks of the Web, plus some additional vulnerabilities specific to the mobile sphere.

Google has several policies governing any application that leverages either of the mobile SDKs (or even Measurement Protocol, discussed in Chapter 17). These are listed below:

- You must make sure you have full rights to use this service, to upload data, and to use it with your Google Analytics account.
- You must clearly provide notice to your end users about the functions and features of Google Analytics being leveraged. This is for the purpose of obtaining consent from the users, or provide them with the opportunity to opt out from tracking.
- In scenarios where an SDK being used to implement audience reporting (i.e., demographics and interests data display in GA) or remarketing (or other Google Analytics Advertising Features), then the following policies must be respected:
  - Policy for Google Analytics Advertising Features: `https://support.google .com/analytics/answer/2700409`
  - Google Play Developer Program Policies: `https://play.google.com/ about/developer-content-policy.html`

As emphasized throughout the book, we are strictly forbidden from capturing personally identifiable information (PII) in GA. In the event that any PII is uploaded to Google Analytics (inadvertently or otherwise), your Google Analytics account can be shut down or all data erased from your property for the duration of the violation.

App Measurement for App Improvement

Smita Dugar

Smita Dugar is a consumer insights professional and leads digital and marketing analytics initiatives at TiVo.

Statista research is projecting more than 268 billion app downloads and more than 76 billion in revenue (from paid-for apps, in-app purchases, and advertising) worldwide in 2017.

As market researcher and digital analyst at TiVo, I'm responsible for analyzing and optimizing the adoption and performance of our TV experience mobile apps within this rapidly evolving and expanding—and extremely competitive—app universe. Below are some of the key optimization insights that I've gained using Google Analytics for mobile apps.

App Graveyard

The dramatic adoption and revenue statistics quoted above gives rise to an unavoidable corollary: punishing competition. Even by May 2015, some of the numbers were daunting:

➤ 1.5 million apps in Google Play
➤ 1.4 million apps in Apple App Store

I have lost count of the apps I have on my mobile devices, and yes, I installed yet another app to keep track of my usage! Android users have about 95 apps installed on their phones, but only about a third of them get used on a monthly basis. Consider these statistics:

➤ 27 apps used on average by each user monthly
➤ half of apps lose half of their peak users within three months
➤ 25% of installed apps used once only (!)

Metrics that Matter

The key app metrics at different stages of the user experience include those listed in Table 13.2.

TABLE 13.2 Key Metrics for App Tracking

Adoption	Engagement	Performance	Outcome
▪ Installs/ Uninstalls ▪ App visitors ▪ Growth rate ▪ Retention rate ▪ Acquisition channels	▪ App usage (MAU/DAU) ▪ Frequency ▪ Depth ▪ Time spent ▪ Behavioral screens, flows ▪ Geo/Demographics	▪ Error rates ▪ App load time ▪ Crashes	▪ Conversions ▪ Revenue/LTV ▪ Ad monetization ▪ In-app purchases ▪ Advocacy (Satisfaction/ Reviews)

Not every metric above would be relevant for all apps. The bottom-line requirement, of course, is to measure what matters most to your business objectives. Most of these metrics are available in GA, with the exception of some like:

➤ Advocacy: Reviews are available in the app stores, and satisfaction ratings can be collected through in-app intercept surveys. Tools like Apptentive, Surveymonkey, Polljoy, Helpshift, and a myriad of others support in-app feedback.

➤ Ad monetization: If you use ad networks like AdMob for in-app advertisements, you can get ad revenue data from their reports.

I will elaborate on a couple of these KPIs. **Retention rate** is the number of people using an app after downloading it within a specific period of time. Retention rate is a key metric of app success, because it costs far less to retain existing users than acquiring new ones.

Retention Rate = (Original Customers at the beginning of a period – Customers Lost during that period) / Original Customers

So if you had a total of 50,000 users at the beginning of the month, and 20,000 uninstalled, the retention rate would be (50K – 20K)/50K = 60% (which is pretty darn good).

There is a big variation in mobile app retention by type of app and industry, with the lowest rates hovering around 10% and the highest above 50% retention after one month. (Source: Mixpanel). Some general benchmarks for monthly retention rates are:

➤ News apps: 45%
➤ Music/entertainment apps: 30%
➤ Games: 15%

Engagement Rate (DAU/MAU): The Daily Average User to Monthly Average User Ratio is a great measure for stickiness. In other words, it tells you if your app is "top-of-mind" or not.

For games and most apps, DAU/MAU of 15% is considered to be pretty good (most apps struggle to get to that number!). For social apps, like a messenger app, a successful one would have a DAU/MAU closer to 50%. Facebook's overall ratio was 64% in early 2015.

Audience Overview Segmented by iOS Device

Users	Sessions	Screen Views	Screens / Session
iPad	iPad	iPad	iPad
92,016	645,302	1,366,587	2.12
iPhone	iPhone	iPhone	iPhone
138,803	720,317	1,930,926	2.68

FIGURE 13.13   The Audience Overview report indicates more sessions per user on iPad.

By defining two basic custom segments for iPad and iPhone, we can note some interesting differences in overall app usage patterns between the two devices. While iPad accounted for fewer unique users during the selected time period, the session per user are higher. What may seem surprising is that iPhone users generated significantly more screen views in approximately the same number of session, but because of the smaller form factor, some larger iPad screen elements had to be split into two screens, so more screen views are required on iPhone for the equivalent experience.

continues

continued

App Versions

Your designers and developers invest a great deal of time and effort in app version upgrades. How quickly are they being adopted? We have been very happy to see that the overwhelming majority of our app users are upgrading to the new app versions within one week of release.

Event Tracking

For a new implementation, you'll want to make sure to configure events for important

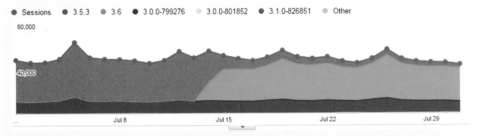

FIGURE 13.14 The app versions report shows fast adoption of the new version release.

interactions that won't be tracked as screen views, *important* being the operative word. If a user interaction will not influence your analysis or help to generate actionable insights, don't track it. As has been said before, measure what matters.

FIGURE 13.15 With event tracking implemented, we can see which screens are generating the most video plays.

Design Changes Based on Screen and Event Data

Our Google Analytics app tracking has prompted a range of design improvements, including revamping the app-based remote.

Button Repositioning and Scrapping the Gesture Remote

Speaking generally about Web, app, and software development, we sometimes develop features that we believe will be interesting, helpful, and widely used, but, of course, we must consult with our data to validate or invalidate our hopes and assumptions. Google Analytics demonstrated that there were several buttons and areas of the TiVo app remote that were being used sparsely, prompting us to redesign the remote experience in both Android and iOS implementations.

 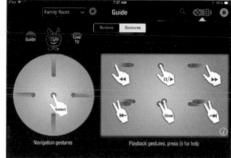

FIGURE 13.16 iPad remote screens, prior to redesign. Google Analytics showed very low usage of the Gesture Remote on the right relative to the Button Remote on the left.

FIGURE 13.17 Android redesign based on data from iOS.

continues

continued

Testing and Surveys

While analytics plays a central role in optimization, it's important to incorporate qualitative input into your process of ongoing improvement. At TiVo, we have gained important insights through synergy of analytics, usability testing, and surveys. This trifecta of behavioral, qualitative, and observational data is responsible for higher retention and engagement rates of the app.

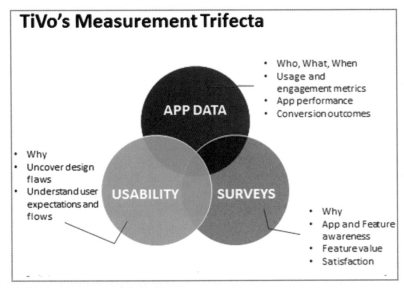

FIGURE 13.18 TiVo's Measurement Trifecta.

Since analytics has sometimes disproved our assumptions as demonstrated in the examples above, we routinely test important feature changes in the prototype stage before proceeding with development.

We make a lot of decisions based on usability from where to place buttons, what to call them, font sizes, navigational hierarchies, affordance, and so on. While testing an early version of our Android app we found that most people prefer to use the landscape version of the Guide, regardless of the size of the tablet (even on a 7" tablet). This insight is helping us make better decisions as we rework some of our app designs.

If you don't have usability researchers in-house, there are several firms that do usability testing on a modest budget (Usertesting, Userlytics, Applause, UserZoom, etc.).

Using Surveys for Feedback Gathering and Satisfaction Measurement

While reviews in the app store are informative, surveys allow us to get a granular measurement of whether users are aware of certain app features, and which features they find more important. We also use surveys to scope out feature concepts prior to development.

Our surveys are usually conducted with subscribers (app users as well as nonusers), and sometimes also prospective customers (sourced from a survey research panel).

"Learning Loop"

How do we avoid the app graveyard? In most part, by sticking to the basic imperatives of analytics and optimization:

- ➤ a comprehensive yet focused implementation
- ➤ emphasis on the metrics that matter
- ➤ qualitative inputs and additional tools to further understand user experience
- ➤ a constant striving for learning and insights
- ➤ updating the app to best serve our customers

In *Lean Startup*, Eric Ries depicted this virtuous circle (see Figure 13.19) in even more basic terms, as shown below.

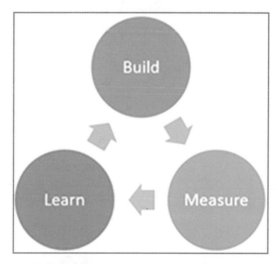

FIGURE 13.19 Eric Ries's Learning Loop can apply to analytics and optimization for your digital properties.

Through this steady, iterative process based on quantitative plus qualitative inputs, we can use better serve our users and help to build a competitive advantage.

 KEY TAKEAWAYS

There's more to Mobile App strategy than app downloads.   Look at your Active Users, Session Length, Session Interval, Lifetime Value, as well as other available metrics to gauge app and campaign performance.

Report on app crashes and exceptions.   Implement tracking of crashes and exceptions for immediate insight into problem areas.

Consider using GTM to deploy GA to your app.   The benefits far outweigh the additional time it will take to instrument your app.

Configure your GA account to view Mobile and Web properties separately.   Steer clear of combining these two data sets in the same property. While you could conceivably roll them up for aggregate reporting, it's best to isolate them.

Leverage integrations with AdMob, Google Play, iTunes.   Setting up these integrations can provide a significant amount of insight into where downloads are coming from, as well as which campaigns are working best.

Mobile campaign tracking.   Enable your app to relay the necessary campaign parameters to Google Play or iTunes to enable you to maintain accurate referral attribution, both for downloads and for clicks back to an app that the user has already installed.

 ## ACTIONS AND EXERCISES

1. **Take inventory.** If you don't have app tracking in place yet, take inventory of the screens and actions that you need to track, and decide on the GA or GTM SDK option. (As stated previously, the GTM SDK is recommended.)

2. **Set up campaign tracking.** Take the steps outlined in the chapter to enable campaign tracking both for initial downloads and for post-install clickbacks.

3. **Use the GA reports for optimization.** While this chapter has focused on implementation, the discussions in previous chapters—about custom reporting, segmentation, goal and funnel configuration and analysis, and other reporting functionalities—equally apply to GA mobile properties.

Google Analytics Integrations—The Power of Together

While Google Analytics (GA) is indispensable for gaining actionable insights on your website and mobile app activity, the truth is that we don't live in a silo. Marketers and analysts deal with many other systems, each with its own focus and data. In this chapter, we'll examine the integrations between GA and other Google services and several useful integrations outside the Google ecosystem.

Keep in mind that the primary goal of the integration is not to match or reconcile the data from two different sources, but rather to provide additional context, connect the elusive dots and derive more actionable insights. Let's walk through a simple and common example. Say you see a huge spike in traffic coming from Paid Search. Not only that but you're also seeing more conversions. A good thing, definitely. But what if the cost of this increased traffic was significantly higher than what you're willing to pay for? What if these additional conversions are cost prohibitive? Having the AdWords cost data readily available in the GA reports would enable faster decision making, and would save you the time to log into AdWords, search for the specific campaign of interest, and dig for the specific report just to find this one piece of information.

In this chapter, we cover three main integrations:

- Google AdWords (including remarketing)
- Google AdSense
- Third-party platforms and applications

With the complexity and power of the Google AdWords platform, we dedicate a good portion of this chapter to the AdWords integration, highlight key benefits of AdSense integrations for publishers and media sites, and then show examples of useful integrations with third-party platforms such as email, social, and data visualization.

> **Note**
>
> ## Integration Gotchas: Data Variance
>
> When working with GA and other platforms, it's sometimes hard to decide where to pull your reports from, especially for common metrics and dimensions. In general, and from a purely reporting and trending perspective, you'd want to have one system to report from, that is, one "source of truth," and use other systems to provide additional context, and in some cases data validation.
>
> When working with different data sources, reports won't align 100% due to a number of factors, including tool configuration (e.g., one system might be filtering a subset of the traffic), the method of data collection or errors in collection, terminology, and definitions, among other factors.
>
> Another general guideline when working with multiple data sources is to look for consistency within each data source. When data sources don't align, you can still rely on trends and comparisons within each for valid and actionable analysis instead of focusing your efforts on reconciling the offsets. If, however, one data source shows much greater fluctuation, it's recommended to place more confidence in the data source that is reporting with more constancy and less variability.

ADWORDS

According to Google, "over a million businesses rely on Google AdWords to connect with customers." Businesses small and large have embraced AdWords, as it brings more accountability to marketing and it allows marketers to target the right people at the right time on the right device.

The AdWords platform provides detailed reporting, including a plethora of reports to assist AdWords account owners in measuring and improving the performance of their paid search campaigns. The native AdWords metrics and dimensions provide thorough reporting primarily on the preclick aspects of your campaigns: Impressions (how many times your ad was shown), Clicks (how many times your ad was clicked on), Cost per Click, and so on. You can also report on "conversion" in AdWords (with some configuration), but rich user-behavior data, once a user clicks on your ad, is housed in GA. Linking your AdWords account with GA account will reveal the full picture of the user journey.

> **Note**
>
> ### Benefits of Linking AdWords and GA
>
> ➤ See your GA goals and Ecommerce transactions in AdWords as conversions.
> ➤ See GA user behavior/engagement next to AdWords metrics.
> ➤ Create remarketing lists in Analytics to use in AdWords audience targeting.
> ➤ View preclick data such as Impressions and Costs in GA.
> ➤ See AdWords campaign contribution to the conversion path in GA (in the Multi-Channel Funnel Reports discussed in Chapter 8).

AdWords Data in GA

Under the GA Acquisition > AdWords as shown in Figure 14.1, you'll see a list of important AdWords dimensions available for you to report and segment on.

FIGURE 14.1 AdWords reports available in GA under the Acquisition reports.

GA Data in AdWords

In addition, once the account linking is completed, you can see GA data in the AdWords interface. Your role and function will influence what system you use for reporting. If you are a media agency or the person in charge of managing AdWords campaigns, you probably spend most of your time in the AdWords interface and having GA data, such as bounce rate and session duration, available in AdWords enhances your analysis of AdWords campaign performance without requiring you to log into GA as frequently.

Namely, you can display the following GA metrics within your AdWords reports:

- Bounce Rate
- Average Session Duration
- Pages/Session
- % New Session
- Goal Completions and Conversion Rate
- Ecommerce Transactions and Conversion Rate

Linking AdWords and GA

"Link Google Analytics and AdWords" in the Google AdWords help docs provides step-by-step instructions: `https://support.google.com/adwords/answer/1704341?hl=en`.

The linking process is very straightforward. For large organizations, the most challenging part is typically finding who has Edit/Admin in both systems, as you need Administrative access to the Google AdWords account and Edit access to the GA property.

Auto-Tagging

In Chapter 7, "Acquisition Reports," we covered the importance and process of adding campaign parameters to inbound links (`utm_medium`, `utm_source`, and `utm_campaign`). AdWords campaigns need to be tagged as well, but the good news is that you have an option to allow Google to do all the heavy lifting for you, and that option is called *auto-tagging*. By keeping auto-tagging in your AdWords account settings, you'll ensure that your campaigns will show up properly in GA. (See Figure 14.2.)

While you are in the Preferences section of the AdWords configuration, make sure your time zone settings reflect your business needs and align to the time zone indicated in the View Settings of your corresponding GA property. The time zone preferences that you set in AdWords will override the settings you have in GA after the accounts are linked.

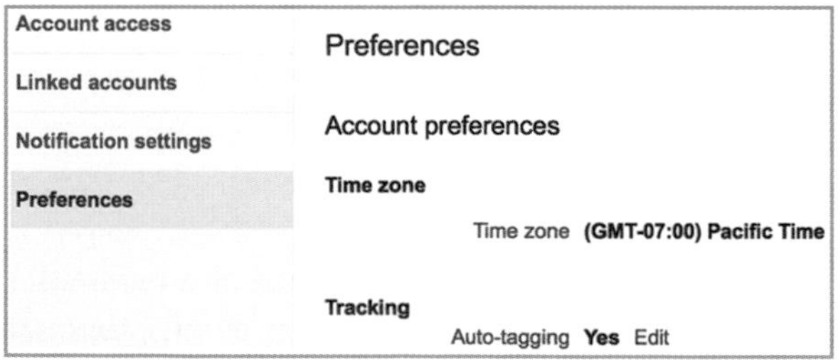

```
Account access              Preferences

Linked accounts

Notification settings       Account preferences

Preferences                 Time zone
                                   Time zone   (GMT-07:00) Pacific Time


                            Tracking
                                   Auto-tagging   Yes   Edit
```

FIGURE 14.2 In Google AdWords Settings > Preferences, ensure that auto-tagging is set to "Yes."

Manual Campaign Parameters

For specific scenarios, turning off auto-tagging might be preferred (e.g., your CMS is conflicting with the AdWords `gclid` parameter), and in this case you should follow the manual campaign tagging convention that was discussed in Chapter 7. If you launch a campaign called "back-to-school" in August 2017, you could configure your campaign parameters as follows:

- `utm_medium=cpc`
- `utm_source=google`
- `utm_campaign=20170801-back-to-school`

What Is "Not Set"?

What if you don't see your AdWords data in GA or you're seeing "not set" in the AdWords reports within GA? There is something probably wrong in either the auto-tagging or the account linking. Here is a guide for the four possible scenarios:

A. AdWords and GA accounts are *not* linked.
  1. *Auto-tagging is off:* You can't see cost data, and if you are manually tagging your campaign URLs, you'll see the data for the AdWords campaigns in GA.
  2. *Auto-tagging is on:* You can't see cost data.

B. AdWords account and GA accounts *are* linked.
  1. *Auto-tagging is off:* Cost data will appear in the "Clicks" reports in GA and if you're manually tagging, you'll see AdWords campaign data in the GA reports.
  2. *Auto-tagging is on:* Cost data will appear in the AdWords Campaigns reports in GA. (This is the optimal AdWords-to-GA integration.)

Large organizations might have one or more AdWords manager accounts (MCCs) or multiple AdWords accounts running various campaigns for different markets or products, or different campaigns are run by different agencies. GA integration with AdWords allows multiple AdWords accounts and MCCs to be integrated with a single GA property. The process to link additional AdWords accounts is the same as the process mentioned earlier to link one AdWords account.

Google Display Network Campaigns

Many advertisers leverage the Google Display Network (GDN) to expand their reach and show their messages to new potential customers. You can select from a set of topics, keywords, or specific pages and sites, and Google AdWords will serve your ads on these sites or apps. You can also use GA audiences to remarket on the GDN, as discussed below.

In GA and in the AdWords reports, you can see a set of very relevant GDN dimensions readily available, including the keywords, sites (placements), topics, interests, age, and gender. (See Figure 14.3.)

| Display Keywords | Placements | Topics | Interests and Remarketing | Age | Gender |

FIGURE 14.3 Display Targeting dimensions are available in the GA AdWords reports.

It's important to note that GA uses the same age, gender, and interests categories that you see in AdWords when you set up your targeting options in AdWords GDN to target ads on the Google Display Network. So your analysis and insights about a specific age group or gender, for example, can be applied with confidence to your AdWords Display campaigns. If, for example, your 55–64 age band or Travel Buffs Affinity Category is already generating the highest Ecommerce conversion rate, it would make sense to target on the GDN accordingly to attract more of the same types of users.

Attribution Beyond Last Touch

Another hidden gem in the AdWords and GA integration is the ability to see AdWords campaigns (search and GDN) in the Multi-Channel Funnel (MCF) reports. Not only will you see which channel or campaign directly drove a converting visit, but you'll see all the touch points leading to such conversion to assess and optimize how your channels are supporting your campaigns goals.

If your ad was presented to a user but wasn't clicked, the "Impressions" will show in the MCF reports. If someone saw your ad and later visited the site directly, their interaction is "Direct," and if you have rich media ads, you can include interaction with rich media (and YouTube videos) to the conversion paths. (See Figure 14.4.)

FIGURE 14.4 In the MCF reports, you can choose which interaction you want to include in your reports and analysis.

An example of MCF reports that show all the interactions is the Top Conversions Paths report. It includes all the interaction types mentioned, namely, "Display" when someone clicks on an ad, "Display" with an "eye" is when it's an impression-only contribution (the user didn't click on the ad), or "Display" with the "movie" symbol, meaning the user interacted with a rich media ad.

Of the 10 paths shown in Figure 14.5, 6 had Display in the mix and in total contributed to a significant number of conversions.

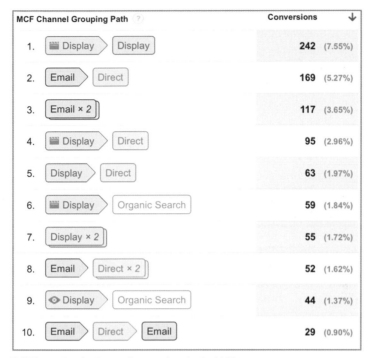

MCF Channel Grouping Path	Conversions	
1. Display > Display	**242**	(7.55%)
2. Email > Direct	**169**	(5.27%)
3. Email × 2	**117**	(3.65%)
4. Display > Direct	**95**	(2.96%)
5. Display > Direct	**63**	(1.97%)
6. Display > Organic Search	**59**	(1.84%)
7. Display × 2	**55**	(1.72%)
8. Email > Direct × 2	**52**	(1.62%)
9. Display > Organic Search	**44**	(1.37%)
10. Email > Direct > Email	**29**	(0.90%)

FIGURE 14.5 Display Network campaigns in the MCF reports.

GA Conversion versus AdWords Conversion

"Should I also include the AdWords tracking pixel?" This is a very common question that we hear from GA users and in training workshops. The short answer is: yes, do add the AdWords conversion tag to your site or mobile app (through GTM) or record conversions from your mobile app through the AdWords API or AdWords SDK for Android or iOS. It allows the person managing your AdWords campaigns to optimize the performance of their campaigns, especially if they are accustomed to reporting in AdWords without considering the GA metrics.

Expect to find differences between AdWords clicks and AdWords-pixel-based conversions (on the one hand) and Google Analytics sessions and conversions (on the other hand). For more on this topic, see "Data Discrepancies between AdWords and Analytics" at: `https://support.google.com/analytics/answer/1034383`.

AdWords Remarketing with Google Analytics Audiences

The principles of AdWords remarketing (normally called retargeting on equivalent non-Google platforms) are logical and straightforward:

1. A visitor comes to your site.
2. The visitor does not convert.
3. The visitor subsequently visits another website that participates as an advertiser in the vast Google Display Network.

4. At this point, that visitor may click on the ad and return to your website via the landing page in your remarketing campaign settings.

5. Ideally, the visitor now completes the conversion process that was previously undiscovered, ignored, or abandoned.

You can also remarket to visitors who *have* converted, but with offers for additional products or information resources instead of an encouragement to complete an abandoned conversion. You can similarly remarket to mobile app users who have not converted or who have not interacted with your app for a certain time period. If you've licensed Analytics 360, you can also use GA remarketing audiences in DoubleClick Bid Manager and DoubleClick Campaign Manager, discussed in Chapter 18.

AdWords versus GA for Remarketing Audiences

You don't actually have to create your remarketing audiences in GA; you also have the option to create them directly in AdWords. (In GTM, you can add a Google AdWords Remarketing tag, separate from the Google AdWords Conversion tag, to a website or a mobile app container.) Creating your remarketing audiences in GA, however, offers the following advantages:

- **Rich segmentation options.** Since you can create a remarketing audience in GA from any segment definition, you can take advantage of all GA segment options (reviewed in Chapter 10, "Segments") for GA-defined remarketing audiences.
- **Audience based on drop-off in Ecommerce or Custom Funnel.** As an extension of the previous point, if you have implemented Enhanced Ecommerce in GA, you can create remarketing audiences (or just segments) based on any drop-off (or continuation) point in the Shopping Behavior or Checkout Behavior funnels. If you have licensed Analytics 360, you can similarly create remarketing audiences (or just segments) based on any step in any custom funnel that you define, as discussed in Chapter 18.
- **Single tracking code.** To create remarketing audiences directly in AdWords, you must include the AdWords Remarketing tag on your website. If you create your remarketing audiences with GA, you don't need the AdWords pixel for remarketing—you need only to link GA to AdWords.

Terminology

Segment versus Remarketing Audience

You can think of *segments* and *remarketing audiences* as synonymous in different contexts. For instance, you could create an *Abandoner* segment for all sessions in which the user viewed the first page of your checkout process but not the second and apply that segment to your Acquisitions reports to see which traffic sources are sending the most abandoners.

You could define your remarketing audience the same way—the Audience Builder screen is largely identical to the new segment screen—or even create your remarketing audience directly from the segment that you have already defined; this remarketing audience would isolate the same users, but in real time on the Google Display Network rather than within your GA reporting.

Creating a Google Analytics Remarketing Audience for AdWords

When you're making a GA remarketing audience for AdWords (after you have linked GA to AdWords), you can use one of the built-in segment conditions such as Returning Users, but in many or most cases, the built-in segments are too broad, and you'll want instead to define more specific audiences based on characteristics (such as acquisition, device, or location) or by behavior (pageview, event, goal, or Ecommerce transaction) completed or not completed. As mentioned above, you can also base a remarketing audience on any existing segment, either built-in or custom.

Note that you must have Edit rights to the GA property to complete the following procedure for linking a GA audience to AdWords:

1. Link your GA property to Google AdWords as described previously in the chapter.
2. In the Property Admin column, click Remarketing > Audiences, and enable both the Remarketing and the Advertising Reporting Features settings.
3. In the Property Admin column, click Remarketing > Audiences.
4. Select the destination AdWords account.
5. At this point, you have three options for your remarketing audience:
   - choose a general built-in audience
   - import a segment (built-in or custom)
   - define a more specific audience from scratch, as shown in Figure 14.6

FIGURE 14.6 In the Audience Builder, we're targeting visitors who viewed a lead form but did not submit the lead in any session.

6. The membership duration defaults to 30 days. It might be useful to extend the duration to a longer time frame, particularly for more complex or costly conversions. (Maximum is 540 days, and truncated to maximum of 180 days for Remarketing Lists for Search Ads [RLSA], which we discuss later.)

7. You can also change the lookback window from a default of 7 days to 14 or 30 days. (The lookback window relates to multiple actions over several sessions at Users scope, such as *pageviews* > 10.)

8. Once you save your new remarketing audience, you'll be prompted to create an AdWords campaign that uses this audience. You can opt to create the campaign at this time, or you can choose to target that remarketing audience when you create remarketing lists at a later time, as shown in Figure 14.7.

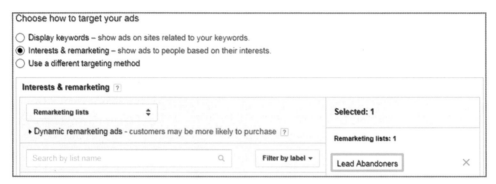

FIGURE 14.7 Once you've created a remarketing audience in GA, you're prompted to create an associated AdWords campaign. You can also choose the remarketing audience for an AdWords campaign that you configure at a later time.

Once your remarketing list includes 100 users (or, more accurately, 100 unique cookies), the Google Display Network will begin serving the corresponding AdWords campaign(s) to the remarketing audience.

> **Note**
>
> ## Session Scope versus User Scope
>
> As with segments, you have the option of changing the default scope from Sessions to Users when defining remarketing audiences. User scope is often the better choice, as exemplified in Figure 14.6. If we had left the scope at Sessions, we would have retargeted any users who viewed the lead form and did not convert during the same session, even if they did convert on a returning session.

Dynamic Remarketing

Dynamic remarketing allows you to display remarketing ads with specific details about the product or service that a visitor viewed on your website or in your app. As described below, the setup for dynamic remarketing is considerably more complex than for the basic "static" remarketing discussed thus far.

1. **Preliminary linking and feature enabling.** Link GA to Google AdWords, and enable Remarketing and Advertising Reporting Features as described above.

2. **Custom dimension(s) for dynamic remarketing.** To enable dynamic remarketing through GA, we'll need to add a minimum of one custom dimension (such as product ID), based on business type, to our basic pageview tracking. (Custom Dimensions are discussed in Chapter 12, "Implementation Customizations.")

3. **Dynamic Attributes.** For Google AdWords to map the custom dimension(s) described above to a record in the product or service feed described below, navigate to Remarketing > Dynamic Attributes in the GA Property Admin, and create a Dynamic Attribute Linking as shown in Figure 14.8 for the custom dimension(s) populated per the previous step.

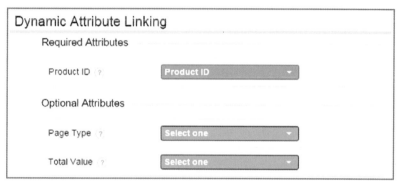

FIGURE 14.8 The Dynamic Attribute Linking that you configure in the property ties a custom dimension value to a record in your product or service feed; AdWords can then read that record to dynamically display specific content in the ad.

4. **Remarketing audience.** We can define our actual remarketing audience for dynamic remarketing the same way as for static remarketing; the dynamic key for the remarketing will be delivered to AdWords by the Dynamic Attribute described above.

5. **Product or service feed.** This feed contains complete product details, such as listing name, price, image URL, and clickthrough URL. The dynamic attribute(s) that you provided to AdWords in step 3 above will be used to match a listing in your feed and thus incorporate dynamic content into your AdWords remarketing ads. AdWords provides feed templates that you can populate for different business types (such as Real Estate, Flights, or Local Deals) and then upload to Business Data in your AdWords Shared Library. (Note that for Retail, you must instead upload your feed to the Merchant Center and link Merchant Center to AdWords.)

6. **Campaign and dynamic ads.** Create a Google AdWords campaign with the business type setting corresponding to the custom dimension(s) and Dynamic Attribute(s) specified in the previous steps. Target the campaign to the remarketing audience defined above, and create your dynamic ads.

Note

Google Merchant Center

As noted above for dynamic remarketing, you must create the product or service feed for Real Estate, Travel, and most business types directly in Business Data within the AdWords Shared Library, but for retail products, you create the feed in the Google Merchant Center and then link AdWords to the Merchant Center so AdWords can retrieve the dynamic ad content based on the product ID that you configure as a custom dimension and Dynamic Attribute in your GA Website or app property.

In addition to serving as the repository for retail dynamic remarketing ads, the merchant center also powers Google Shopping and AdWords Product Listing Ads (PLAs). For more information, see "About Merchant Center" in the AdWords help pages.

For more details on dynamic remarketing, see "Dynamic Remarketing, Step-by-Step" and "Dynamic Remarketing with GA" in AdWords help. Note that custom dimension and Dynamic Attribute configuration described above for dynamic remarketing with GA supersedes the Tag Your Website step (for dynamic remarketing with the AdWords pixel) in the first help article.

Smart Lists and Similar Audiences

When you're configuring your remarketing campaigns, you can take advantage of two particular kinds of algorithmic assistance.

Smart Lists

You can select Smart List as a built-in Recommended Audience in GA. In the case of smart lists, your remarketing will be targeted to Web users who—based on historical data from websites like yours—may be the most likely to convert on a return visit.

Similar Audiences

As another example of machine help, you can enable Similar Audiences in your AdWords campaigns to target Web users who visit the same types of websites as your visitors but who have not yet visited your site. Similar Audiences is enabled directly through Google AdWords, not GA.

Remarketing in Mobile Apps

You configure remarketing for apps following the same steps outlined above. You could, for example, remarketing to app users who viewed a certain screen, did or did not complete a goal, or even just opened your app (*Count of Sessions > 0*). The members of your remarketing audience would then see the ads from your AdWords mobile app campaign when viewing apps that participate in the Google Display Network.

Note that app remarketing is based on mobile advertising IDs (rather than cookies, which apply in the Web context only.)

AdWords has an "Estimated Conversion" metric that provides conversion data when Google believes that the conversion on one device (e.g., desktop) is associated with an ad clickthrough on another device (e.g., tablet); see "About 'All Conversions'" and the AdWords help pages (`https://support.google.com/adwords/answer/3419678?hl=en`).

Remarketing on YouTube

For YouTube, you have the option to remarket based on previous YouTube video views, and you can also remarket based on remarketing audiences defined in GA (or defined within AdWords using the AdWords tracking pixel).

Remarketing Lists for Search Ads (RLSA)

The remarketing campaigns discussed thus far run on the Google Display Network. As a somewhat newer remarketing option, you can now also use remarketing lists for search campaigns. RLSA works by combining the two following factors to help optimize your search campaigns:

- **Intent.** Search term entered into the Google Search engine.
- **Behavioral signal.** A previous activity on your website, as captured in a remarketing audience.

RLSA offers two basic options:

- **Target and Bid.** You define a campaign that displays only to keyword searchers who are part of your remarketing audience (i.e., they have already visited your website). As part of the campaign configuration, you can customize:
  - **Ad text.** *Come back and convert!*
  - **Keywords and keyword matching.** Since you'll be bidding only for searchers who have already visited your site, you may want to expand your keywords or broaden the match types.
  - **Bids.** For the same reason as above, you may want to bid higher on RLSA campaigns than on non-RLSA campaigns.
- **Bid Only.** The campaign can display to all searchers regardless of remarketing audience membership, but you increase the bid for higher visibility of your ads to your remarketing audience, as shown in Figure 14.9.

Set bid adjustment (1 audiences selected)

The bid adjustment below will replace current bid adjustments

Increase by ▾   50 %

Example: A $10.00 bid will become **$15.00**.

FIGURE 14.9 For Bid-Only RLSA, you only increase bidding for your remarketing audience.

Note that not all GA remarketing audiences are eligible for RLSA, and that RLSA does not activate until the corresponding remarketing audience comprises 1,000 cookies. For more information about RLSA, see *Improving Your Search Campaigns with Remarketing Lists for Search Ads* on YouTube.

| GUEST SPOT | **Best Practices and Expert Tips for Remarketing** |

Dan Stone

Dan Stone is the lead product manager for user-centric analysis and audience marketing at Google Analytics.

Remarketing with GA is an incredibly powerful way to re-engage with your users across Google display and search ads (using Remarketing Lists for Search Ads, or RLSA), and reach them with the perfect message at each micro-moment during their conversion journey.

But when first starting out, building your audience strategy from GA 250+ dimensions and metrics can be a little intimidating. Here are some best practices to help you hit the ground running, along with some expert tips once you're ready to up-level your remarketing game.

You can also read more about client successes with remarketing at www .thinkwithgoogle.com/products/remarketing-with-google-analytics.html.

Setting Up for Success

➤ Ensure your entire app, desktop site, and mobile site are tagged with GA, that you've enabled Remarketing in your GA Property's data collection settings, and that you're importing conversions from GA to AdWords in order to use Conversion Optimizer. Conversion Optimizer in AdWords enables you to focus on cost per acquisition (CPA) rather than clicks (CPC) or impressions (CPM). For more information on Conversion Optimizer, see "About Conversion Optimizer" in the AdWords help pages (https://goo.gl/kQt11c).

➤ Go broad before going narrow. Start out with an all-users audience, and an audience for each stage in your conversion funnel (e.g., category page viewers, product or offer page viewers, cart abandoners, and past converters) before segmenting further.

➤ Create a dedicated campaign for GDN Remarketing. For RLSA, you can use an existing search campaign.

➤ Pair remarketing with Conversion Optimizer and use target CPA (cost per acquisition) or ROAS (return on ad spend) bidding for best results.

➤ In Display, make sure to include all ad sizes and formats, including text, mobile, and HTML5. Also be mindful of any language, location, or placement exclusions you're using that may further reduce your coverage—remember that these are users who have already demonstrated an affinity for your brand.

➤ In Display, remember to match your audiences with great creative. If you have many different products or services, consider using dynamic remarketing on the Google Display Network to show the most personalized ad possible without having to create an audience for each individual product. You can map your existing GA data to be used for AdWords dynamic remarketing from the GA Admin interface.

➤ Use Similar Audiences and auto-targeting to expand your remarketing lists to reach new customers.

Expert Tips

➤ In general, any data in GA can be used in Remarketing. This includes native GA data like language, location, traffic source, campaign, purchases, as well as any data that you've imported into GA through custom variables, dimensions, metrics, whether set through the tracker, measurement protocol, or processing-time data import.

➤ Some of the most successful uses of remarketing involve combining your own customer data with your GA site data. For a guide on how to import data from your CRM system, check out `https://goo.gl/nVc4ew`.

➤ While most definitions work in Remarketing exactly as in Segmentation, definitions using an Exclude filter, like nonpurchasers or users not seen in 30 days, will not work as expected, since Remarketing is always evaluating in real time and does not go back and check later if a condition is no longer true. Instead, create a custom combination of lists in the AdWords interface. Nonpurchasers, for example, can be created by subtracting a "Purchased last 540 days" audience from an "All Users last 540 days" audience.

➤ There is a Remarketing section in the GA Solutions Gallery for crowd-sourced remarketing ideas (`https://goo.gl/blk2OQ`).

➤ When using user-scoped definitions, you might see a "Lookback days" box. This allows you to tell GA the time window over which to evaluate the audience definition. Using this drop-down, you could create an audience for users who purchased twice over the last 7 days, or over the last 30 days—it's up to you.

➤ Remember that each layer of segmentation adds complexity, so try to segment only when you want to interact with an audience differently (like using a stronger call-to-action on display for customers who are close to purchasing) or when you can profitably afford to bid a lot more on an audience (like bidding up in RLSA for customers whom you know are price insensitive). In general, we look at segmentation along two dimensions: behavioral signals (like funnel stage) and demographic signals (like customer segment). For example, you might have two customer segments (business travelers, leisure travelers) and five funnel stages (visitors, product viewers, cart abandoners, first-time purchasers, repeat purchasers), resulting in 10 audiences to represent each distinct customer segment (the *who*) at each purchase stage (the *when*). As you refine your strategy, keep in mind that each list needs to reach 100 users on display and 1,000 users on search before it will serve. If you're using conversion optimizer, each list must have 15 (ideally 50) conversions per 30 days before conversion optimizer can learn to use it.

➤ The best Similar Audiences often come from the most targeted lists. Remember to look for these in the AdWords shared library section, particularly for high-value lists like "business travelers" or "premium customers."

> **Terminology**
>
> ### Programmatic Advertising and User Centricity
>
> The term *programmatic advertising* refers broadly to rule-assisted and especially algorithm-assisted advertising. We can consider AdWords remarketing as the first stage to programmatic advertising to the extent that we're using previous visitor behavior to dynamically control ad display. With RLSA, we're going a step further by using visitor behavior to change bids, change ad creative or expand search term matching.
>
> If you have an Analytics 360 license, you can go a step further in programmatic advertising: use GA remarketing audiences through DoubleClick Bid Manager (DBM) to target and update bidding in real time through AdWords and the range of additional advertising networks that DBM reaches. DBM and DoubleClick integration with GA are discussed in Chapter 18, "Analytics 360."
>
> In any case, all of these types of programmatic advertising represent an evolution toward user-centricity: analytics and marketing no longer siloed but instead working in tandem to provide relevant messaging to end users and potential customers.

ADSENSE

In this chapter, we've covered Google AdWords with a lot of detail, but what if your business model is based on ad-supported content, as in the case of media and publishers sites?

If you're in the publishing business, your revenue may primarily come from displaying ads on your site or in your app. The more impressions you generate and the more clicks on those display ads, the more money you make: AdSense is Google's product that enables you to do just this.

To measure ad performance for your publisher website or mobile app, AdSense provides reports, accessible as shown in Figure 4.10, on a range of metrics including Impressions, Pageviews, and Clicks to Creative sizes (the sizes of ads served), to engagement and estimated revenue metrics. In addition, publishers have access to data on ad "Viewability" where, according to the Interactive Advertising Bureau (IAB), "50% of the ad's pixels are visible in the browser window for a continuous one second." Publishers can use this data to enhance the likelihood that ads will be viewed and clicked.

Benefits of GA Integration

Why integration? It's all about better monetization! Having the ability to look at site performance metrics next to the native AdSense metrics allows you to see what pages and content users engage with. Additionally, and as importantly, the sources of traffic that bring highly engaged users who consume your content and engage with your money-making ads.

The ability to analyze your AdSense performance metrics and earnings by location, traffic source, and other GA dimensions (as shown in Figure 4.11) is one of the key benefits of this integration.

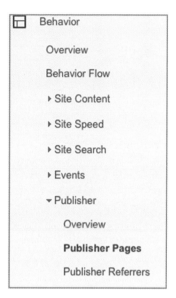

FIGURE 14.10 AdSense reports are available in GA under the Behavior > Publisher reports.

Linking Accounts

Since Google owns both AdSense and GA, the integration of the two platforms is very straightforward (as with AdWords/GA integration).

You just need to make sure that you're using a Google account that has Admin access in AdSense and Edit access in GA. On your GA Property Settings panel, you can then follow the few steps to enable this integration as described in "Link Analytics and AdSense" in the AdSense help docs:

```
https://support.google.com/adsense/answer/6084409
```

Sample Reports

Once the accounts are integrated, you'll see your AdSense metrics in the GA interface.

Another way to approach the data is to look at your revenue by page category. Say you're the monetization manager for the *New York Times* and you want to report on AdSense Revenue by Content Category (politics, business, science, sports, art, etc.); if you've set up a Custom Dimension to identify the type of each page, as described in Chapter 12, you'll be able to call the associated AdSense metrics by content category as shown in Figure 14.12.

You can easily create a custom report to include the GA dimension of interest to you and tie it to the AdSense revenue, including traffic sources, campaigns, and other initiatives you have to drive traffic to the site, and you want to measure its monetization effectiveness.

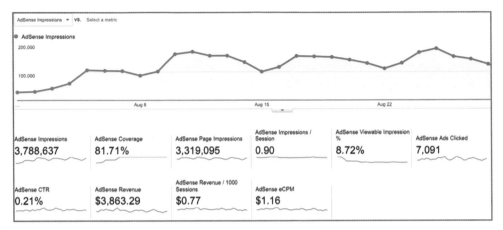

FIGURE 14.11 The AdSense Overview report shows key metrics such as Revenue and eCPM (revenue per 1,000 pageviews).

Category Type	Publisher Impressions ↓	Publisher Viewable Impressions %	Publisher Clicks	Publisher Revenue
	2,832,768 % of Total: 99.99% (2,833,047)	**48.68%** Avg for View: 48.68% (0.00%)	**10,852** % of Total: 100.00% (10,852)	**$19,812.77** % of Total: 99.99% ($19,815.11)
1. politics	**1,209,275** (42.69%)	56.03%	3,726 (34.33%)	$8,353.08 (42.16%)
2. business	**1,098,595** (38.78%)	42.53%	4,730 (43.59%)	$7,388.51 (37.29%)
3. science	**439,314** (15.51%)	45.92%	2,030 (18.71%)	$3,428.23 (17.30%)
4. sports	**62,165** (2.19%)	50.01%	104 (0.96%)	$462.25 (2.33%)
5. arts	**15,137** (0.53%)	24.20%	250 (2.30%)	$115.42 (0.58%)

FIGURE 14.12 AdSense metrics are segmented by Content Category. Politics and Business (first and second row) bring in over 77% of the revenue.

DoubleClick for Publishers and DoubleClick Ad Exchange

For publishers, GA offers two types of DoubleClick integrations:

- If you're a user of the DoubleClick Ad Exchange (which has all of Google AdSense inventory plus other ad networks and agencies), you can also integrate with GA (in the GA Admin > Ad Exchange Linking).
- If you're a DoubleClick for Publisher user and have Analytics 360, there is a native integration (as covered in Chapter 18).

YOUTUBE IN GA

No matter what business vertical you're in, video is (and should be, if not already) part of your marketing mix. Brands large and small have set up their own YouTube channels to produce engaging content about their brand, products, and services.

As with other digital marketing channels, video is very measureable and you'll be remiss not to measure how users interact with your video content.

In Chapter 6, "Events, Virtual Pageviews, Social Actions, and Errors," we covered the techniques and best practices to report on video consumption (track play, percent completion, etc.). Furthermore, by creating a behavioral segment as described in Chapter 10, you can go beyond just reporting on video plays and completions and instead begin to gain insight into the impact of video interactions on your conversions.

In this section, we cover a native integration between YouTube and GA.

YouTube Analytics

YouTube offers its own set of metrics, namely YouTube Analytics. You can easily report on video viewership, subscribers, and minutes watched, as well as engagement metrics such as likes, dislikes, and comments and some demographics information such as gender and geography. YouTube has been improving these reports and also allows channel owners to export the data into comma-separated values (CSVs) and to obtain the data through the YouTube application programming interface (API).

GA YouTube Channel Page

In addition to YouTube Analytics itself, one easy way to report on visits to your channel page is to integrate your channel with GA.

The setup is very straightforward:

1. Create a new property in GA. (You can use an existing property, but a separate, dedicated property for YouTube is recommended.)
2. In YouTube under Advanced Settings, paste the tracking ID into the GA Property Tracking ID field.
3. Click Save and you're done.

Note

What the YouTube GA Integration Is _Not_

When you add the GA ID to the YouTube channel, you're not tracking all your videos and the various integrations with the YouTube channel; the integration is merely a means to report on visits to your channel page. It would be beneficial if Google would enable full integration, but as of now, we can use the current, limited data that the integration provides.

It's best practice to create a separate GA property for the YouTube channel page tracking. Otherwise, if you use your main website or app property, you'd be mixing data from two different entities (your site and the YouTube channel page), which in most cases is not recommended.

ANALYTICS 360 INTEGRATIONS

Analytics 360 offers unique additional integrations with Google products, namely:

- DoubleClick Campaign Manager (DCM)
- DoubleClick Bid Manager (DBM)
- DoubleClick for Search (DS)
- DoubleClick for Publishers (DFP)

The details of these integrations are covered in Chapter 18.

ADDITIONAL INTEGRATIONS

So far, we've covered integrations with other Google products, namely AdWords, AdSense, and YouTube. But the digital marketing ecosystem expands well beyond Google.

Since GA is almost a default Web analytics platform, it makes sense for many marketing-related platforms and tools to integrate with GA. The level of integration varies from one platform to another, but, in general, third-party platforms are aiming to provide more context about the user journey (in the form of GA data) within the platform's own reports and user interface. The Google Analytics Partner Services and Technologies portal lists a wide range of platforms and tools that integrate with GA: `https://www.google.com/analytics/partners/search/apps`.

Most of these platforms provide detailed instructions on how to integrate with GA. Below we've outlined sample integrations with commonly used platforms.

> **Note**
>
> **In Platform Selection, Consider GA Integration**
> In your selection of third-party digital marketing platforms and tools, consider GA integration as one of the vendor selection criteria.

eMail Service Providers

eMail service providers such as ExactTarget, Responsys, MailChimp, and others provide their own analytics for metrics such as email opens, email clicks, number of subscribers, number of unsubscribes, and so on.

As it relates to GA, verify if the vendor provides a mechanism for easy campaign parameter setup (as discussed in "Automated Campaign Tagging for Email" in Chapter 7), and also if you can dynamically incorporate GA goal and Ecommerce data into the reporting on the email platform. In addition, some email providers allow you to pass in specific parameters such as a Subscriber ID in the email links. You can then capture Subscriber ID as a GA custom dimension and perform visitor-level analysis of content consumption and conversion, and also merge exported GA data with email data. (Chapter 15 discusses the integration of GA data with other data sources.)

You must, of course, ensure that a subscriber ID that you capture as a custom dimension does not contain any PII. Furthermore, if any of the clickthrough URLs from your email platform include PII such as an individual email address, you must strip the PII from the Page dimension in GA as described in "Exclude URL Query Parameters for PII Blocking" in Chapter 9.

Social Media Platforms

The broad range of available social media plug-ins, tools, and platforms offer different specializations. Some platforms focus on content publishing and workflow such as HootSuite, some specialize in social sharing such as ShareThis and AddThis; some focus on measurement and reporting such as SimplyMeasured; and others focus on qualitative reporting for sentiment and opinion mining such as CrimsonHexagon.

Many of the social platforms provide GA integration in the sense that you can see GA metrics within the user interface of the social media platform. The benefit is that you see your site engagement metrics (e.g., number of sessions, from GA) next to the number of retweets or new subscribers or shares (social analytics metrics), so you can better correlate your social activities and site activities.

Testing

As discussed in Appendix A, testing should be a key component of your digital optimization strategy. One powerful testing platform with a large market share is Optimizely. Complex statistical analytics supports the A/B testing reports that a platform like Optimizely offers, but the platform provides marketers with a streamlined user interface and easy-to-use reports on the experiments you're running.

When you integrate GA with Optimizely, you'll have the added benefit of segmenting your users based on the experiment they belong to. For example, if you're running an A/B test in which variation A has a "Buy Now" call to action and variation B has a "Save 20% Now" call to action with incentive, you can easily create a custom segment in GA for each variation based on the variation reference stored in GA as a custom dimension. You can then compare the performance of the two (or more) variations not only in terms of the experiment objective(s), but all other metrics in GA as well.

The new Optimize testing platform, offered as part of the Google Analytics 360 Suite, provides the additional benefit of tight integration with Google Analytics audiences, goals, and Ecommerce tracking and can also take advantage of the Google Tag Manager data layer for targeting.

Voice of Customer—Customer Feedback

In addition to quantitative data, marketers who want to get a better understanding of *why* users behave in a certain way can take advantage of qualitative analytics platforms that provide survey tools, aka Voice of Customer (VoC). Some of the leading systems in this space include ForeSee Results, OpinionLab, iPerceptions, Qualaroo, and others.

VoC platforms provide data such as survey response rates and survey completion rates, and they of course capture all the answers and long-form feedback that customers provide. Many of these platforms also integrate with GA. One powerful but perhaps underutilized integration is the ability to create GA events for the questions and the answers presented to the user when using your site or app. To learn more about using VoC in your optimization program and integrating VoC with GA, see "Enhancing Google with Customer Surveys" by Duff Anderson in Appendix A.

Marketing Automation

Platforms like Marketo, Eloqua, and Pardot and others also integrate with GA.

For example: Data from Marketo, including user profile information and "firmographics" (i.e., characteristics about target companies) can appear as GA custom dimensions. Examples of firmographics data include industry vertical, company name, or company size. Equipped with this new data in GA, marketers can now segment their traffic by industry vertical (e.g., software, retail) and also determine if they're driving traffic from their named accounts or target companies.

To read more about integrating firmographics information into GA, see "Marketing Automation and Google Analytics: Integration and Personalization" by Mike Telem in Appendix A.

Paid Search Management Platforms

Platforms such as Acquisio and Marin Software allow you to manage, report, and optimize the performance of your paid search campaign and paid social campaigns, all from a single interface in which you can also display GA performance data such as goal completions per campaign.

BI/Data Visualization

Most leading Data Visualization and Business Intelligence (BI) platforms—Tableau, QlickView, PowerBI, and others—have direct connectors to GA. More details on these tools are included in Chapter 16, "Advanced Reporting and Visualization with Third-Party Tools."

KEY TAKEAWAYS

We don't live in silos and data shouldn't either.   Connecting data from different sources adds more context to your reports and analysis and provides greater opportunity for broader insights.

You're missing out if you're not remarketing.   Done right, re-engaging your users through remarketing strategies has the potential to boost your campaign ROI since you can base the targeting on user characteristics and behavior and also dynamically display specific product or service details in your remarketing creatives.

Don't sweat small data discrepancies when comparing data from different systems.   If there are consistent offsets between multiple data sources, you can use all data sources directionally rather than interpreting any of them completely literally. If one data source shows much more variability than another, consider the more constant data source as your "source of truth."

ACTIONS AND EXERCISES

1. **Examine your GA reports and Admin section** and ensure all applicable Google integrations are enabled and data is appearing in the GA reports accordingly.

2. **When selecting a digital marketing platform** for email marketing, social media, marketing automation, and so on, get an understanding of available GA integrations and the level of effort required to ensure the integration is set up properly.

15

Integrating Google Analytics with CRM Data

A s critical as Web analytics data is, it can never provide a complete picture of customer analytics. Through cost-data import and Google AdWords auto-tagging, we can determine cost per lead conversion, but how do we know if those leads were qualified? Google Analytics (GA) Ecommerce tracking can readily reveal the revenue that our email and social campaigns have generated, but how can we assess the long-term value that each of these channels provides? How can we determine the content on our site that is driving our best customer engagements overall?

Integration between Web (or mobile app) analytics and data stored in your organization's customer relationship management (CRM) system is the key to understanding complete, long-term return on investment (ROI) of our digital properties and our marketing channels.

LONG-TERM PERSPECTIVE

As stated above, the main purpose of integrating GA and CRM data is to provide a more complete, long-term perspective on the marketing channels and content interactions that first engage your customers when they visit your website or download and use your mobile app. This integration can be particularly helpful in the following scenarios:

- **Business-to-business (B2B).** Long sales cycle in which the customer interaction moves from website or mobile app interactions to direct contact with the sales team.

- **Software-as-a-service (SaaS).** Subscription-based model in which customers either cancel or renew.
- **Ecommerce.** Customer may transact one time only or multiple additional times online or offline.

In this chapter, we'll measure cost per acquisition for qualified B2B leads and examine long-term or lifetime customer value.

CALCULATING COST PER QUALIFIED LEAD

As anyone who has ever worked with lead generation knows, all leads are not created equal. Many leads are submitted as just general inquiries and don't really indicate any serious level of engagement. In the use case below, we'll switch the focus from leads to *qualified* leads and obtain a much more realistic calculation of marketing ROI.

B2B Use Case: Qualifying Leads for Memory Chips

As a B2B use case, let's say that you're the Demand Generation manager for an enterprise product that your company, Pro Processors, sells: memory chips for servers. You don't sell to consumers but to companies like Google, Facebook, and Amazon. A lot is at stake, since a typical deal could bring in tens of millions of dollars and take your salespeople three to six months to close.

Keep the CPA under $500

In terms of demand gen, the marketing manager has tasked you with generating qualified leads and to keep the cost per acquisition (CPA) under US$500, and herein lies the problem. You interpret *cost per acquisition* to mean *cost per lead,* but it would be much more business-focused to think in terms of cost per *qualified* lead.

In any case, your memory chips have just been reviewed very favorably in an industry report, so you decide to leverage the report as a multi-channel marketing campaign. The research institute that produced the report does not offer the report directly on its own website, but you have secured the right to post it for download on proprocessors.com.

You work with your design team to create a dedicated landing page as shown in Figure 15.1 that features the report, and you set up the following campaigns to drive traffic:

- AdWords search ads
- LinkedIn sponsored ads
- Twitter promoted tweets
- Facebook paid ads

FIGURE 15.1 To download the report, visitors must submit a lead form.

CPA Based on Total Leads, Qualified and Unqualified

When you're setting up and initially evaluating your campaigns, you do everything you're supposed to. For starters, you make sure to add GA campaign parameters in Table 15.1 to the inbound campaign links (and, for AdWords, you've enabled auto-tagging). For example, the link from your LinkedIn campaign is formatted as:

```
http://www.proprocessors.com/chip-report?utm_source=linkedin&utm_
medium=social-paid&utm_campaign=2016q2-chip-li
```

TABLE 15.1 Campaign Parameters for the Lead Generation Channels

Campaign Channel	utm_medium	utm_source	utm_campaign
AdWords	cpc	google	Memory Chip Report
LinkedIn	social-paid	linkedin	2016q2-chip-li
Twitter	social-paid	twitter	2016q2-chip-tw
Facebook	social-paid	facebook	2016q2-chip-fb

You have also set up a goal for the lead submission. You specify */chip-report-thank-you* as the destination of your Chip Report goal and */chip-report* as the preceding funnel step.

You launch the campaigns. After they've been humming along for a month, you analyze the results first results. Because you have used campaign parameters, the GA Campaigns report shown in Figure 15.2 cleanly displays the lead generation goal completions for each of the campaign channels.

| Campaign ? | Conversions | Goal 2: Chip Report ▾ |
	Chip Report (Goal 2 Conversion Rate) ?	Chip Report (Goal 2 Completions) ?
1. 2016q2-chip-li	20.75%	11
2. Memory Chip Report	12.06%	7
3. 2016q2-chip-fb	8.57%	6
4. 2016q2-chip-tw	6.67%	6

FIGURE 15.2 The Campaigns report displaying goal completions for your four campaign channels.

Remembering that the Campaigns report is based only on last-click attribution, and noting two assists for the Chip Report goal in the Multi-Channel Funnel > Top Conversion Paths report shown in Figure 15.3, you split the credit for two of the last-click LinkedIn conversions with Facebook and Google AdWords.

You also notice that a Google AdWords campaign clickthrough later resulted in a conversion from a Google organic return visit. Since this return visit likely resulted from a branded, navigational search prompted by the initial paid visit, you give Google AdWords full credit for this lead as well.

Campaign (Or Source/Medium) Path ?		Conversions ↓
1. 2016q2-chip-fb › 2016q2-chip-li		1 (3.32%)
2. Memory Chip Report › 2016q2-chip-li		1 (3.32%)
3. Memory Chip Report › (google / organic)		1 (3.32%)

FIGURE 15.3 The Top Conversion Path report indicates which campaign channels might also deserve credit for conversion assists.

You open a spreadsheet and plug in the cost data and the lead conversions for each, as in Table 15.2. It seems like you've achieved your objective: the cost per lead is below $500 for each channel, but don't celebrate yet. (As a note, all data within this chapter is fictitious and does not reflect on the comparative performance of any marketing channel referenced as part of this use case.)

Cost per Qualified Lead

Before you share the CPA with the managers, you run a report in the CRM system. You're disappointed to see that the sales team has marked only very few of the leads as qualified. When you check the notes fields in the report represented in Table 15.3, you learn

TABLE 15.2 Cost per Lead (Qualified and Unqualified) by Campaign Channel

Campaign Channel	Cost (US$)	Leads	Cost (US$) per Lead
AdWords	$1,458	8.5	$172
LinkedIn	$1,678	10	$168
Twitter	$908	6	$151
Facebook	$1,193	6.5	$184
All	*$5,237*	*31*	*$169*

TABLE 15.3 Sample CRM Records Lacking Campaign Channel Data

Name	Qualification	Notes
Dolores Grant	Unqualified	Interested in consumer only
Heather Quinn	Qualified	2–4-month time frame
Ray Ramirez	Unqualified	Supply chain incompatibility
Keith Hansen	Unqualified	Spam
Sonny Carter	Unqualified	Wanted to sell us life insurance
Bruce Kozar	Qualified	Hot to trot
Ellen Tedesco	Unqualified	Dep't reorg., budget in question
Larry Cahill	Unqualified	Left company

that some of the leads were looking for consumer products, some didn't have the budget, some were vendors trying to pitch their own products, and some were just spam.

You realize that if you want to understand real ROI, you need to match the campaign channels with qualified leads, but there's a big issue: the campaign data resides in GA, while the lead qualification data resides in your CRM.

Note

CRM Integration and PII

You may already have spotted a potential problem: once you integrate GA and CRM, you can match any GA data—such as visitor source, device, and behavior—with personally identifiable information (PII) such as name and email address.

However, as long as the integration between GA data and PII does not occur directly within GA, you have not violated the GA terms of service. In the first integration example below, we're writing visitor source information directly into the CRM. In the other examples, we're writing a unique but anonymous identifier to both GA and CRM, and later joining the data sets outside of GA based on that identifier. In neither case is PII stored directly within GA.

Correlating Campaign Channels with Qualified Leads

To associate the campaign and lead qualification data, you can take one of two approaches:

- **Record the campaign data directly in the CRM.** When you submit a lead from your website to your CRM, you can pass your campaign information to be stored directly with each lead in the CRM.
- **Store a visitor ID in both GA and the CRM.** You can store a unique but non–personally identifiable ID in GA and your CRM. This ID can then serve as the key on which your exported GA and CRM data. This approach, discussed in more detail later in the chapter, allows you to integrate other types of GA data (in addition to acquisition) with your CRM data.

Note

Client ID, User ID, and Visitor ID

As described below, each of these terms has a specific meaning in GA.

Client ID

The client ID, often referred to as *cid*, represents a specific browser. When a visitor accesses a GA-tracked website, the GA tracking code writes the _ga cookie to the browser, which stores the cid in the format 1589402201.1369649169. The tracking code then reads the cid for each subsequent hit, thereby associating multiple hits to the same session, and multiple sessions to the same user. For mobile apps, client ID is based on the specific app running on an individual device.

User ID

GA designates the user ID dimension for you to populate with a lead or customer ID from your CRM and thereby identify the same logged-in user across multiple devices. User ID and cross-device tracking are discussed in Chapter 12, "Implementation Customizations."

Visitor ID (or another named Custom Dimension)

Because Client ID and User ID are not available in the API, we cannot rely on them for CRM integration. We must instead make sure to store a common key, once a user logs in or submits a form, so we can later associate sessions in GA with records in our CRM. We can store this key in a custom dimension named Visitor ID, or any name that you choose.

When you're populating the Visitor ID, there are three overall options:

- ➤ Read the lead or contact ID from your CRM when record is created after a lead submission or transaction, and record it in GA as a custom dimension. As discussed in Chapter 12, you can use the same back-end value to populate User ID and the Visitor ID custom dimension to enable both cross-device tracking and CRM integration.
- ➤ Read the client ID from the _ga cookie, and record it in GA as a custom dimension and in your CRM. If you begin storing the client ID even before authentication or form submission, you'll later be able to associate even previous unauthenticated sessions with your CRM data.
- ➤ Randomly generate a unique text string, and record it in GA as a custom dimension and in your CRM.

The implementation checklist available at www.e-nor.com/book reviews these options and best practices for integrating GA and CRM data.

The Salesforce example provided by Allaedin Ezzedin takes a hybrid approach: we pass campaign data into the CRM directly, and also pass the visitor ID to enable further integrated analysis of GA and Salesforce data. While the example focuses on leads, we could use the same procedure to record campaigns or other traffic sources for completed Ecommerce transactions.

GUEST SPOT   **Recording Google Analytics Campaign Data in Salesforce**

Allaedin Ezzedin

Allaedin Ezzedin is Digital Analytics Manager at E-Nor.

Before we review the process for recording GA campaign data in Salesforce, please note that most of the steps also apply if you're using a CRM system other than Salesforce. The procedures for reading the campaign data from cookies, generating and storing a visitor ID, and populating the hidden form fields should be fairly identical regardless of the CRM. The steps for creating and populating custom fields would vary by CRM.

1. Create Custom Salesforce Fields

As a first step, you need to create custom fields in Salesforce for campaign medium, campaign source, campaign name, and visitor ID, as shown in Figure 15.4.

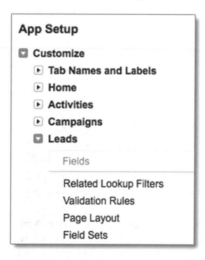

FIGURE 15.4 Creating fields in Salesforce to store campaign fields and visitor ID.

2. Create Hidden Fields in Your Lead Form

The hidden fields that you create in your lead form will convey the campaign and visitor ID values to Salesforce:

```
<form name="leadForm" action="/scripts/sfleadform.php"
method="POST">
```

continues

continued

```
        <input type="hidden" name="medium" id="medium">
    <input type="hidden" name="source" id="source">
    <input type="hidden" name="campaign" id="campaign">
    <input type="hidden" name="visitorID" id="visitorID">

        . . .
        </form>
```

You should also configure any necessary logic to pass the values of the hidden fields to their corresponding fields within SalesForce when the form is submitted.

3. Add the *salesforce.js* Code to Google Tag Manager

To read the GA campaign values that will go into Salesforce, download `gasalesforce.js` from `www.e-nor.com/gabook` and save it into Google Tag Manager as a Custom HTML Tag that is triggered on all pages. Alternatively, you could upload the file to your Web server and just reference it from a Custom HTML Tag.

If you inspect the code, you'll notice that it references ga.js, the tracker for GA classic. While `analytics.js`, the tracker for GA Universal, writes only the single `_ga` cookie, `ga.js` writes multiple cookies, including the `__utmz` cookie. It is from `__umtz` that our `gasalesforce.js` code will parse the campaign medium, campaign source, and campaign name.

Note that this code would also read medium and source values for direct, organic, and referral traffic; there would just be no campaign value if the traffic was not driven by inbound links containing campaign parameters. Note also that the code in gasalesforce.js can read additional cookie values such as session count and pageview count, which don't pertain directly to our use case on lead qualification for the memory chip manufacturer.

4. Populate the Campaign Values into the Hidden Form Fields

In the Custom HTML Tag into which you've copied the `salesforce.js` script, you need to add a bit of extra code to populate the campaign values into the hidden form fields with the medium, source, and campaign values that the script has read in from `__utmz` so these values will be passed into Salesforce on form submit as illustrated in Figure 15.5.

5. Generate a Visitor ID

The one value that we haven't yet determined is visitor ID. As mentioned previously, we don't need the visitor ID—either in Salesforce or GA—just for Salesforce to store our campaign values. However, by recording the visitor ID in both Salesforce and GA, we'll be able to perform additional integrations of the data sets at other times.

You can use any logic to generate a visitor ID, as long as it is unique and it is not personally identifiable. If your website is already coded to generate a unique ID for each visitor at the start of a session, it's best to use that existing unique ID as the visitor ID that you pass into Salesforce.

As another option, you can use the client ID value of the `_ga` cookie, such as `1355402211.1434649167`, that GA uses to recognize hits and sessions generated from the same browser client. This client ID is not stored in GA by default, but you can use it as the visitor ID value that will facilitate joins between GA and Salesforce data. You could also potentially generate a random, unique ID, but client ID can easily serve this purpose.

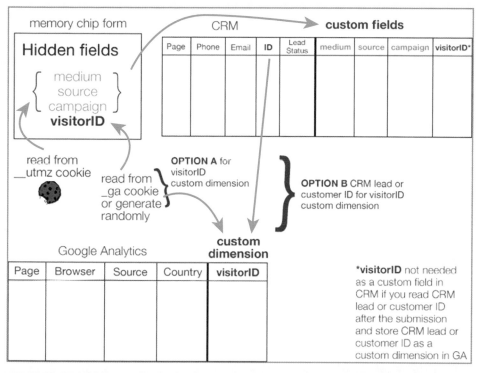

FIGURE 15.5 The lead form contains the hidden fields that we populate with campaign values to pass to Salesforce custom fields. For storing a common ID in the two data sets, there are two options: generate on the client side and pass into Salesforce, or read from Salesforce.

Once you have the visitor ID, you need to store it in its corresponding hidden form field along with the campaign values, and to store it in a GA custom dimension as described below.

6. Record the Visitor ID as a Google Analytics Custom Dimension

In our main GA pageview tracker within GTM, we can populate visitor ID as a custom dimension. It's best to set the scope of the custom dimension to User instead of Session so we'll be able to use this custom dimension as the key to identify all of a user's sessions in case we decide to merge CRM data into GA as described in Chapter 17, "Data Import and Measurement Protocol." Note that {{visitorID}} in Figure 15.6 is not available as a built-in GTM variable; you must define it yourself with the same logic that you used to generate the visitor ID for the hidden form field.

7. Make Sense of the Data!

Now that we have successfully collected campaign (and visitor ID) data in GA, we can use it for better intelligence. In the case of our memory chip lead, we'll be in a much better position to calculate the true ROI of our campaign channels, as shown in Figure 15.7.

continues

continued

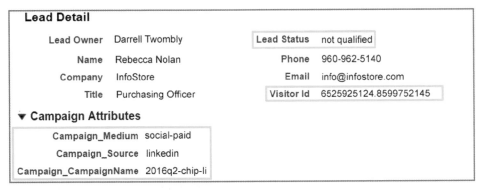

FIGURE 15.6 Recording visitor ID as a custom dimension in the main Google Analytics pageview tag.

Lead Detail

Lead Owner	Darrell Twombly	Lead Status	not qualified
Name	Rebecca Nolan	Phone	960-962-5140
Company	InfoStore	Email	info@infostore.com
Title	Purchasing Officer	Visitor Id	6525925124.8599752145

▼ **Campaign Attributes**

Campaign_Medium	social-paid
Campaign_Source	linkedin
Campaign_CampaignName	2016q2-chip-li

FIGURE 15.7 Campaign data and visitor ID stored in custom Salesforce fields. The Sales team can update the Lead Status field to *qualified* as warranted.

Let's say that in the case of the memory chip leads, you're now directly storing campaign data in your CRM—which is Salesforce in our example. Now that your CRM records contain both marketing and lead qualification fields, you can begin to calculate marketing ROI based on qualified leads instead of all leads.

You let the campaign run for another month, and then you pull a new report from your CRM, as represented in Table 15.4.

You now tabulate your qualified leads and calculate a much more meaningful cost per acquisition for each marketing channel, as shown in Table 15.5.

TABLE 15.4 Sample CRM Records Containing Campaign Channel Data

Name	Qualification	Notes	Campaign
Nicholas Prince	Unqualified	Wants too much customization	2016q2-chip-li
Laura Kwon	Unqualified	Assigned to another project	2016q2-chip-fa
Jason Peralta	Unqualified	Spam	2016q2-chip-tw
Amy Burnett	Qualified	Needs to be expedited	Memory Chip Report
Deepa Kumar	Unqualified	Unaffiliated industry	2016q2-chip-tw
Greg Hodges	Qualified	Multiple shipments	2016q2-chip-fa
Reid Porter	Unqualified	Just wanted to read the report	Memory Chip Report
Brian Apfel	Unqualified	Was looking for our competitor	2016q2-chip-li

TABLE 15.5 Cost per Qualified Lead by Campaign Channel

Campaign Channel	Cost (US$)	Qualified Leads	Cost (US$) per Qualified Lead
AdWords	$1,458	4	$364
LinkedIn	$1,678	3	$559
Twitter	$908	2	$454
Facebook	$1,193	2	$596
All	$5,237	11	$476

You can now report to the marketing manager that the overall CPA, based on qualified leads, is below $500, and you can consider steering more of your ongoing budget toward the campaigns that are showing better ROI.

One element, however, is missing from our previous analysis. Because the campaign values that we stored in Salesforce are based only on last-click attribution, no credit is given for earlier visits that eventually led to a lead submission on a return visit from a different campaign channel, but we'll address this gap below.

JOINING GOOGLE ANALYTICS AND CRM DATA WITH VISITOR ID

In the Salesforce example, we were able to match marketing channels to qualified leads by directly recording campaign data within Salesforce for each lead submission. As stated previously, however, there is another approach that you can use for integrating GA and CRM data:

1. Store the same anonymous but unique visitor ID in both GA (as a custom dimension) and your CRM (possibly as a custom field).
2. Using the visitor ID for the join, merge the GA and CRM data in one of the three following environments:
   - **CRM:** Import from GA into CRM.
   - **GA:** Import (anonymous data only) from CRM into GA.
   - **Separate environment:** Import from both GA and CRM into a third environment such as a spreadsheet, a relational database, or BigQuery.

Exporting Google Analytics Data

You can export as many as 5,000 rows (as comma-separated values [CSVs] and other data formats) directly from any GA table report. If you need to export more than 5,000 rows, you can export in batches, starting at row 1, and then row 5001, and then row 10001, and so on.

If you use the Google Analytics Spreadsheet Add-on, you can export up to 10,000 rows at one time into a Google sheet document, from which you can easily export as CSV. The add-on also allows scheduled automation.

As two additional options for more automated export from GA, you can use Shuffle-Point or Analytics Canvas, both discussed in Chapter 16, "Advanced Reporting and Visualization with Third-Party Tools."

Importing Google Analytics Data into CRM

Once you have imported GA data into your CRM, you can join any GA dimensions with any CRM columns. In the previous lead qualification example, instead of writing the Google campaign data directly to Salesforce with each lead submission, we could have instead just written the visitor ID to the CRM (and also stored it in GA as a custom dimension) and then joined the GA campaign data and the Salesforce lead qualification data, as shown in Table 15.6.

TABLE 15.6 Google Analytics Campaign Name Imported into CRM and Joined on Visitor ID

Name	Qualification	Visitor ID	Campaign
Nicholas Prince	Unqualified	1355402211.1434649167	2016q2-chip-li
Laura Kwon	Unqualified	1584125471.5412645325	2016q2-chip-fa
Jason Peralta	Unqualified	6521425124.8541252145	2016q2-chip-tw
Amy Burnett	Qualified	9852541414.5412548589	Memory Chip Report

If we have been storing client ID as the Visitor ID custom dimension even for unauthenticated sessions, as outlined later in the chapter and in the implementation checklist at `www.e-nor.com/book`, we could run a report to display previous sessions, from the same campaign or different campaigns, that preceded the returning sessions in which the lead submission occurred. Table 15.7 indicates that one of our qualified leads first clicked through on our LinkedIn campaign before returning the next day from the AdWords campaign and converting. We're thus getting a more nuanced understanding of our campaign performance, and we're in fact emulating the multisession scope that the GA Multi-Channel Funnel reports provide, but in this case we're also benefitting from the additional perspective that the CRM qualification field offers.

TABLE 15.7 Google Analytics Campaign Data for Converting Click and Previous Sessions, Joined to CRM Lead Qualification Data

Name	Qualification	Visitor ID	Campaign	Session Timestamp
Nicholas Prince	Unqualified	2514258565.2511425474	2016q2-chip-tw	2016-06-02
Nicholas Prince	Unqualified	2514258565.2511425474	2016q2-chip-li	2016-06-07
Laura Kwon	Unqualified	2548169369.2478968569	2016q2-chip-fa	2016-05-31
Laura Kwon	Unqualified	2548169369.2478968569	2016q2-chip-fa	2016-06-01
Jason Peralta	Unqualified	6521425124.8541252145	2016q2-chip-tw	2016-06-01
Nicholas Prince	Unqualified	2514258565.2511425474	2016q2-chip-li	2016-06-07
Amy Burnett	Qualified	9652312125.5747425369	2016q2-chip-li	2016-06-05
Amy Burnett	Qualified	9652312125.5747425369	Memory Chip Report	2016-06-06

Merging Google Analytics Behavior and Audience Data with CRM Data

Medium, source, and campaign are certainly not the only types of GA data that you can merge with CRM data. As other examples, you could merge pageview, event, or custom dimension data with CRM data to measure its impact on lead quality or order value. You could also merge GA audience characteristics such as device category.

What if we wanted to correlate CRM lead quality with video interactions on the memory chip landing page shown previously in Figure 15.1? As long as you have captured the video interactions as GA events, you could merge the event data with the lead qualification data as in Table 15.8 to measure potential impact.

TABLE 15.8 Event Data for Video Interactions Joined with CRM Lead Qualification Field

Name	Qualification	Visitor ID	Event Category	Event Action	Event Label
Glen Garcia	Qualified	3652154012.3256201845	video	25%	chip-choices-video
Glen Garcia	Qualified	3652154012.3256201845	video	50%	chip-choices-video
Glen Garcia	Qualified	3652154012.3256201845	video	completed	chip-choices-video
Dan Khan	Unqualified	3251012458.2215425489	(not set)	(not set)	(not set)
Teresa Baron	Unqualified	2545814247.3625212045	(not set)	(not set)	(not set)
Brett Jordan	Unqualified	2548756523.8563220212	video	25%	chip-choices-video
Kim Clarke	Unqualified	3621875456.8541024579	(not set)	(not set)	(not set)
Natalie Pham	Qualified	2145841233.8569874124	video	25%	chip-choices-video
Natalie Pham	Qualified	2145841233.8569874124	video	50%	chip-choices-video
Keith Halstrom	Qualified	9865851201.8412026958	video	25%	chip-choices-video
Keith Halstrom	Qualified	9865851201.8412026958	video	50%	chip-choices-video
Keith Halstrom	Qualified	9865851201.8412026958	video	completed	chip-choices-video

The video interaction seems to correlate strongly with lead qualification. Of course, the visitors who were most qualified may also have been the most likely to view at least 50% of the video, but it still seems that it would be logical for you, as an analyst and optimizer, to recommend that your designers make the video more prominent on the memory chip landing page pictured in Figure 15.1.

The example in Table 15.9 shows order value by device category—desktop, tablet, or mobile (smartphone)—for leads who later finalized a transaction through the sales team. Tablet is showing the highest average order value, so it would make sense to target more of your AdWords and Facebook ad budgets to tablet. (You could, of course, also add source, medium, and campaign columns for further analysis.)

TABLE 15.9 Order Value by Device Category

Name	Order Value (US$)	Visitor ID	Device Category
Todd Melchior	$390	5154945989.6545125541	Mobile
Pamela Fischer	$1,230	8575125426.7414512124	Tablet
Brenda DiMaio	$209	8636954159.2541259632	Desktop
Tom Krantz	$890	1478524569.5264585856	Tablet
Oliver Despres	$750	2356265365.5965636415	Desktop
Helen Matsui	$768	2548698585.5874514868	Tablet
Cedric Nejame	$439	2321245236.9856541472	Desktop
Alice Danielson	$387	2541256985.6985681245	Mobile

Using CRM ID as Visitor ID in Google Analytics

In the preceding examples, we generated the visitor ID on the client end and populated it into GA as a custom dimension and into the CRM as a custom field. For the visitor ID value, we actually didn't create anything new; we just read in the client ID that GA stores in the _ga cookie.

As another option, we could retrieve the lead or customer ID from the CRM an pass it back to the page—probably as a GTM data layer variable or a plain JavaScript variable—for you to record into as a GA custom dimension with the next pageview or event. This option is also illustrated in Figure 15.5.

For instance, in the memory chip example, instead of passing a client-generated visitor ID to the CRM as a hidden field in the lead form, you could have instead read the CRM lead ID as soon as the lead was created, saved it to the page as a variable, and populated this value into GA as the visitor ID custom dimension.

If the lead submission redirected to a separate thank-you page, you could populate the visitor ID as a custom dimension in the new pageview hit—just make sure to set the variable value higher up on the page than the GTM container.

If, however, the lead submission did not redirect to a new page but instead just displayed a confirmation message on the same page without a page reload, you could still pass the visitor ID as a custom dimension in a GA Event tag in Google Tag Manager (GTM) as follows:

1. When the lead is created in the CRM, retrieve the lead ID value from the new CRM record as outlined in Listing 15.1, and set that as a GTM data layer variable while also writing the other data layer variables that our catch-all event tag, first discussed in Chapter 6, depends on.

LISTING 15.1: Populating a GTM data layer variable with the CRM lead or customer ID.

```
function myLeadSubmssion() {
    //server-side logic for lead creation is completed
    var crmLeadID = getLeadID(); //implement this function with the
code requried to get lead ID from CRM
    dataLayer.push({'event':'eventTracker',
    'eventCat':'lead', 'eventAct':'submit',
    'eventLbl':'memory-chip','visitorID':crmLeadID});
}
```

2. Set up Visitor ID as a custom dimension, as described in Chapter 12.
3. Reconfigure the catch-all event tag to check for visitor ID as a data layer variable (Figure 15.9) to populate into the custom dimension (Figure 15.8). (If the visitor ID is not present in the data layer the other times we use the catch-all event tag, the custom dimension will just not be populated.)

FIGURE 15.8 This Google Analytics Event tag in GTM will set the visitor ID custom dimension.

With the CRM lead or customer ID now recorded in GA as a custom dimension, we'll be able to perform all of the same joins demonstrated earlier in the chapter when we instead generated the visitor ID generated from the client side and passed it into the

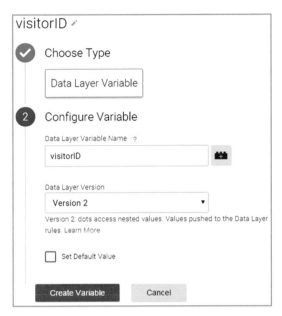

FIGURE 15.9 You can configure this GTM variable to read the *visitorID* value that we retrieved from the CRM so we can populate the visitor ID custom dimension into our catch-all event tag in Figure 15.8.

CRM. Starting from either the website or the CRM, the objective is to store a common visitor identifier in both data sets.

Note, however, that if we want to associate previous unauthenticated sessions with our CRM records, and we're using a back-end value for our Visitor ID custom dimension, we'll also need to store client ID as a separate custom dimension for authenticated and unauthenticated sessions, as outlined later in the chapter and in the implementation checklist at www.e-nor.com/gabook.

Associating Unauthenticated Sessions with CRM

As mentioned at several points in the chapter and illustrated in Figure 15.5, one of the options for associating GA with CRM is to read a CRM ID into GA as a custom dimension once a user has submitted a form or otherwise authenticated. While this approach is perfectly valid and frequently implemented, it does have one subtle but significant drawback.

GA uses the same Client ID to recognize a return user across multiple sessions, independent of whether or not the user authenticated during any of the sessions. Since Client ID is not, however, exposed as an exportable dimension through the API, we would not be able to associate a back-end Visitor ID custom dimension for authenticated sessions with any Client ID dimension for authenticated and unauthenticated sessions, and we would therefore not be able to associate original unauthenticated sessions (and the channels that generated these sessions) with CRM metrics such as long-term value. The back-end Visitor ID, stored in GA as a custom dimension, would allow us only to associate authenticated (or post-authentication) sessions with our CRM data.

To solve this issue, we can take two approaches:

- Begin storing Client ID as a custom dimension (named Client ID or Visitor ID) in GA even for unauthenticated sessions, and pass that same value into your CRM once form submission or authentication occurs.
- Begin storing Client ID as a custom dimension (named Client ID) in GA even for unauthenticated sessions, and store a back-end ID in GA as a separate custom dimension (named Visitor ID) once form submission or authentication occurs. Table 15.10 illustrates an analysis based on these two custom dimensions, which were both included in the join.

Either way, you'll be able to tie CRM long-term value or lead qualification all the way back to first click attribution, whether or not the user authenticated during that session.

TABLE 15.10 First-Click Campaign for an Authenticated or Unauthenticated Session Associated with 12-Month Custom Value

Name	12-Month Sales (US$)	Visitor ID (back-end)	Client ID	First-Click Campaign Channel
Glen Garcia	$430,000	gg094329843	3652154012.3256201845	2016q2-chip-fa
Natalie Pham	$445,000	pn432094328	2145841233.8569874124	2016q2-chip-tw
Keith Halstrom	$930,000	hk439029384	9865851201.8412026958	2016q2-chip-li
Amy Burnett	$200,000	ba394302489	9652312125.5747425369	Memory Chip Report
Greg Hodges	$390,000	hg832742938	2514585101.2584575632	2016q2-chip-fa

Note

Begin Storing Common Visitor ID in Google Analytics and CRM

Even though you may not see an immediate need to merge GA and CRM data, that need will arise as you delve into cost per acquisition per marketing channel, website content correlation with customer lifetime value, and any insight that requires the joined data sets. By storing the CRM's customer ID as a custom dimension in GA, you'll be well positioned to analyze the two joined data sets in the future.

To be able to associate both unauthenticated and authenticated sessions with CRM data after a submission or login does occur, and thereby report on all traffic sources leading to an eventual conversion, you can begin storing the unique ID from the _ga cookie as a custom dimension for unauthenticated sessions. For further discussion, see the "Google Analytics and Google Tag Manager Implementation Checklist" at www.e-nor.com/gabook.

Joining GA and CRM Data in Third-Party Tools and within GA

Earlier in this chapter, we noted that you can perform the GA/CRM data joins in the CRM, in a storage environment, or within GA. In Chapter 16, we merge GA and CRM data within BigQuery storage, and in Chapter 17, we merge some non–personally identifiable data from the CRM back into GA.

<table>
<tr><td>GUEST SPOT</td><td>The Case for Implementing Long-Term Value (LTV) Alongside Cost per Acquisition (CPA) to Gain Competitive Advantage</td></tr>
</table>

Andrew Duffle

Andrew Duffle is Director FP&A, Analytics & Optimization at APMEX.

Traditionally, marketing success has been based on a CPA model or an instant ROI proposition. Modern marketing has evolved to relationship building and creating experiences to generate long-term value in the customer base.

Queue the LTV model using GA merged with your CRM.

A Long-Term Value model should be applied under the assumption that the initial order generated from a customer is only a portion of the value that is attributable to a particular source. Traditionally, marketing departments only manage media spend through CPA, giving little to no benefit for the relationship created after acquisition. In a market that favors your particular business, the efficiency of your media spend can be astonishing in the short term, but over the past couple of years, it has become more difficult to maintain that efficiency of media spend for traditional Ecommerce companies in a highly competitive landscape.

As a marketer, you have always tried to know something your competition doesn't. Now you have the ability to quantify what an investment today could mean for you company tomorrow. Adopting an approach of managing CPA but focusing on LTV will lead to long-term stability and increased focus on media management.

Assumptions

Yes, assumptions.

- ➤ **Ecommerce transaction ID.** In GA, you have set up Ecommerce or Enhanced Ecommerce (as described in Chapter 8, "Goal and Ecommerce Tracking") and you are recording your CRM transaction ID as the Ecommerce transaction ID in GA. Since the Ecommerce transaction ID is stored in both data sets, we can use it as the join to compare original traffic sources (from GA) by long-term value (from CRM).
- ➤ **CRM can relate orders to customer.** You have a CRM system that will allow you to relate the first order and subsequent orders to the same customer and determine the acquisition date of a customer. My personal experience suggests using the month of a customer's first order as an acquisition date that will remain with the customer throughout the life of the model.
- ➤ **Margin calculation.** Within your CRM system you are able to get an accurate or at least fair estimate of the margin on a particular order.
- ➤ **Long-term period.** There needs to be an agreed-upon long-term period to focus on. Each company has to determine the period that is right for them: a lot of time this ends up being more a qualitative exercise. I have tended to always end up around 18 months. After 18

continues

continued

months, the trend, in my experience, is that the purchasing patterns have become less predictable and have a lower average order value.

Create a Custom Report

When you have determined that you have the ability to record and obtain the information above, create a custom report in GA, as shown in Figure 15.10. In this model, the Source/Medium associated with the initial acquisition will receive all credit for the LTV of a customer. We'll then be able to join this export with CRM margin data as shown in Figure 15.11.

Source	Transaction ID	Product Revenue
1. dfa / cpm	10216820	$4,116.00 (0.69%)
2. (direct) / (none)	10212194	$3,010.46 (0.58%)
3. google / organic	10249817	$2,978.00 (0.37%)
4. google / cpc	10212032	$2,558.00 (0.34%)
5. newsletter / email	10250414	$2,358.00 (0.33%)

FIGURE 15.10 We'll export this GA custom report and join with CRM data based on transaction ID. In this model, the customer long-term value will be associated with the Source/Medium of the customer's original online transaction.

	A	B	C	D	E
1	Source / Medium	Transaction ID	Product Revenue	Acquired Date	Margin Dollars
2	dfa / cpm	10216820	4116.00	3/31/2016	36.77
3	(direct) / (none)	10212194	3010.46	4/20/2016	26.32
4	google / organic	10249817	2798.00	8/12/2015	106.39
5	google / cpc	10212032	2558.00	12/23/2015	80.27
6	newsletter / email	10250414	2358.00	4/2/2016	30.14

FIGURE 15.11 Spreadsheet joining GA custom report export with CRM acquired date and margin dollars.

As a note, you can export a maximum of 5,000 rows of data from GA standard. If you're using GA at the Analytics 360 level, you can export up to 3 million rows through Unsampled Export.

Note that the acquired date field never changes for a customer and the margin dollars are relational to the order ID. Every time a customer makes a new order, the margin dollars will increase for the corresponding original visitor source.

Building the LTV Model

With this data, you can start to build out your LTV model. I encourage companies to maintain a model similar to the one presented below.

Below are some quick notes on building the model shown in Figure 15.12. You can download the corresponding template at www.e-nor.com/gabook.

➤ The column labeled Month is an indicator of the month a customer was acquired or the cohort period assigned to a group.

- Media/marketing cost in this example is the same as a traditional CPA model: what was the marketing expense associated with acquiring these customers in the month acquired?
- Month 0 profit per user is simply the profit made on customers during the acquisition month. It is very common for this to be the most profitable period for new customers.
- The CPA is a traditional marketing KPI that is taking the media cost per new customer into account. CPA and Month 0 profit per user are nice to have side by side. As marketers, the more investment we can recoup immediately for the business, the better, and it really illustrates the importance of a LTV model if the investment is not recouped fast enough to meet business requirements.
- New Customers is simply the number of newly acquired customers in a particular period. This number will never change for a cohort. It is literally a direct reference to the number of customers you are tracking together for a life cycle.
- The columns labeled 0–17 are the 18 months or periods that you will track customers through, where 0 is equal to the month acquired.
- At the bottom of the model, the row labeled LTV Profit per User is calculated by taking the vertical total of months 0–17 divided by the number users associated with the profit dollars. Example: Column 0 is the total of all the profit dollars in the column divided by the total of all the customers in the new customer column. However, in column 17 you will only take the total of $444 profit divided by the 550 customers that generated that profit.

Month	Media Cost	Month 0 Profit / User	CPA	New Customers	0	1	2	3	4	5	6
Dec-14	$38,897	$140	$52	744	$104,394	$16,303	$9,115	$8,002	$3,118	$7,158	$5,656
Jan-15	$47,010	$159	$66	717	$114,109	$25,361	$9,053	$8,249	$9,407	$2,822	$4,782
Feb-15	$47,029	$123	$42	1,127	$139,143	$21,841	$9,145	$8,449	$5,516	$3,996	$6,395
Mar-15	$43,679	$166	$51	856	$142,349	$26,451	$9,377	$7,275	$7,812	$4,033	$5,855
Apr-15	$36,896	$121	$52	710	$85,723	$25,568	$9,575	$7,950	$8,081	$6,555	$4,222
May-15	$44,000	$125	$60	729	$90,850	$16,540	$9,246	$5,328	$8,012	$5,305	$2,513
Jun-15	$37,017	$154	$57	650	$100,122	$21,208	$8,263	$8,826	$7,563	$3,001	$2,053
Jul-15	$12,007	$408	$34	350	$142,666	$10,271	$9,441	$5,555	$4,919	$7,116	$3,306
Aug-15	$44,087	$165	$66	667	$110,049	$15,590	$8,274	$9,207	$6,591	$4,537	$4,176
Sep-15	$34,785	$124	$59	591	$73,503	$15,552	$9,355	$6,114	$6,289	$6,619	$4,490
Oct-15	$31,538	$102	$35	910	$93,233	$34,812	$15,941	$11,724	$4,991	$2,443	$3,362
Nov-15	$13,459	$120	$28	483	$57,797	$19,860	$14,051	$6,107	$5,966	$6,288	$6,880
Dec-15	$14,227	$106	$26	537	$57,087	$18,681	$8,684	$4,759	$4,320	$6,681	
Jan-16	$27,460	$116	$37	744	$86,458	$17,358	$11,775	$10,804	$16,350		
Feb-16	$26,214	$112	$43	613	$68,921	$26,830	$20,823	$14,596			
Mar-16	$23,885	$128	$35	674	$86,044	$25,344	$25,133				
Apr-16	$23,368	$100	$35	660	$65,779	$28,414					
May-16	$38,226	$147	$35	1,086	$159,406						
				Profit per User	$138.36	$31.12	$16.87	$11.79	$10.08	$7.35	$6.39
				Adj. for Time Value	$138.36	$30.66	$16.37	$11.27	$9.50	$6.82	$5.84

FIGURE 15.12 Six-month close-up of 18-month value model. (Download the spreadsheet template at www.e-nor.com/gabook.)

From your data set, the acquired date becomes the group where you continuously add new data. Example: customers who completed their first order in April 2014 and ordered again during June14 will have the contributed margin dollars from the month of June added in the column labeled 2. In the model presented above, customers acquired in April 2014 have a full 18 months of data compared to customers acquired in September 2015 who only have one month's worth.

continues

continued

In most implementations of an LTV model like the one presented here, the model maintains the signature triangular shape. To maintain this effect in every period, you will have a cohort meeting the specified life cycle and a new cohort being acquired. After you have determined your data limitations and start to move into implementation, a best practice will be to build a LTV model for every acquisition channel. In most instances, models will be built for channels including Pay per Click (PPC), Display, and Organic. When acquisition channels are compared, you will quickly start identifying efficiency trends of different channels and different cohorts.

LTV by Channel

After multiple periods of tracking well defined cohorts, a natural and very insightful way to review your LTV data is a graph similar to Figure 15.13. (As a note, the marketing channels in this figure differ somewhat from the earlier examples.) You can see the Payback Period highlighted as the total amount we would be willing to invest to acquire a new customer. The Long-Term Value section is used as an additional justification of marketing spending today for future benefit.

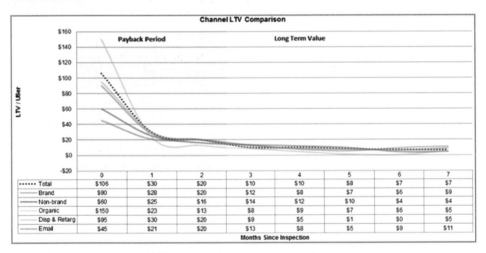

	0	1	2	3	4	5	6	7
Total	$106	$30	$20	$10	$10	$8	$7	$7
Brand	$90	$28	$20	$12	$8	$7	$6	$9
Non-brand	$60	$25	$16	$14	$12	$10	$4	$4
Organic	$150	$23	$13	$8	$9	$7	$6	$5
Disp & Retarg	$95	$30	$20	$9	$5	$1	$0	$5
Email	$45	$21	$20	$13	$8	$5	$9	$11

FIGURE 15.13 Payback period and lifetime value by marketing channel.

Continuous refinement and analysis of your LTV model will lead to additional discoveries about the quality of customers associated with a traffic source. While no company should ever base all marketing spend on one model, you can quickly see the value of investing in a more expensive acquisition program after considering a more modern LTV approach to media spend management and there determining which channels are ultimately performing the best.

 **KEY TAKEAWAYS**

Lead qualification.   When calculating ROI/CPA on your lead generation campaigns, consider lead qualification status that your sales team updates in your CRM. This may be especially applicable in for B2B and other typically long sales cycles.

Lifetime value.   By merging GA and CRM data, you can begin to calculate longer-term value for repeat Ecommerce transactions or for SaaS/subscription renewals.

Recording campaign information directly to CRM.   Using the process outlined in the Salesforce example, you can write GA acquisition data directly to your CRM with lead submissions or Ecommerce transactions. Although a common visitor ID by itself would allow you to merge any GA data with your CRM data, recording your GA acquisition data directly to your CRM would make this data immediately visible in your CRM lead or customer records. It's important to remember, however, that the acquisition data in this case would be based only on last-click attribution: the channels that drove a session prior to the converting return session would not receive any credit for the conversion.

Recording a visitor ID in GA and CRM.   You can record a common visitor ID in GA and your CRM that will allow you to join GA and CRM data in within the CRM, within GA, or in a separate environment. Even if you do not have immediate plans to merge your GA and CRM data, you can begin recording the same visitor ID in both environments so you can retroactively join the data at a later date.

Visitor ID not available in GA data by default.   There is no visitor/user ID stored by default in the GA data to which you have access. For this reason, you must store a visitor ID as a custom dimension in GA to enable merges with CRM data. You can populate the visitor ID custom dimension with the client ID that you read in from the _ga cookie, a random/unique value that you generate from your own algorithm, or the customer/lead ID from your CRM. The last case is the most common for logged-in users, and can be most efficient since it takes advantage unique customer key already resides in the CRM record, but it would require you to store a separate ID for unauthenticated sessions in a separate custom dimension if you also wanted to associate unauthenticated sessions with CRM data.

No PII data in GA.   The GA terms of service prevent us from storing personally identifiable data within GA, so we could not record PII such as name, email or government-issued ID number as any part of the visitor ID custom dimension.

Same user ID for cross-device tracking and GA/CRM merges.   In many cases, the logged-in user ID that you pass to GA for cross-device tracking can also serve as the common visitor ID that you store as a GA custom dimension for join with CRM data.

 ACTIONS AND EXERCISES

1. **Get access to your CRM.** If you don't already have access to your organization's CRM, obtain read/reporting access so you can view customer and lead records.

2. **Speak with your sales and customer relations team.** Speak to managers and other colleagues who are familiar with the sales cycle, repeat business, and so on.

3. **Store a common visitor ID in GA and your CRM.** Using the examples in this chapter, plan your steps for storing a common visitor key in GA and your CRM. In many cases, the visitor ID that you record to GA will be the customer or lead ID in your CRM.

4. **Decide how to associate unauthenticated sessions with CRM data.** To associate unauthenticated sessions (and thereby first-click traffic sources) with CRM data, decide which of the two approaches outlined previously is the most suitable for your organization: storing the GA client ID (or an ID that you generate) as a GA custom dimension and, when the user authenticates, as a field in your CRM, or maintaining two custom dimensions in GA—one for the client ID (populated in GA during all sessions) and the other for the CRM ID (populated in GA during and after authenticated sessions.)

5. **Write GA campaign data directly to your CRM.** Using the gasaleforce.js code reference in the Salesforce example, you can also make a plan to write GA campaign/acquisition data directly to your CRM so it's immediately accessible (without a merge based on visitor ID).

Advanced Reporting and Visualization with Third-Party Tools

n this chapter, we turn our focus to advanced reporting techniques, including data extraction and cleanup, as well as reporting automation. We'll also continue our discussion of data integration from Chapter 15.

To put it bluntly, advanced reporting—and report automation specifically —can be a bit of a bird's nest. Advanced reporting is a series of sometimes very manual steps that combine to form a report/chart/dashboard or enable deeper *ad hoc* analysis. The end product, which may look simple and elegant, is the outcome of a complex process.

With all the data being collected and all the different segmentation features available in GA, you would think that reporting and dashboarding data would be a problem solved long ago. Advanced reporting, however, remains one of the biggest challenges facing organizations today. Certainly, GA (among other tools) makes it easy to construct a basic report. Designing a reporting solution, however, that takes data sampling and automation into consideration is an entirely different matter. An effective report has the following characteristics:

- It takes data accuracy into consideration (no sampling).
- It has an elegant and simple presentation.
- It is automated so it doesn't require hours and hours of construction time.
- It delivers at strategic intervals in an easy-to consume format.
- Most importantly, it provides business insight.

Producing a report or dashboard that excels in all the above areas can be a daunting obstacle to overcome for many organizations. Analysts often spend countless hours manually copying data from various analytics tools, pasting it into Excel or Power-Point, cleaning it up, and then building an unusable and unattractive report, which is then emailed to stakeholders, usually without providing additional context about the data.

The reality is that it takes a significant amount of time and effort to work with the data contained in analytics tools, extract it into a format we can work with, make it report-friendly so that the report viewers will understand it, and then share it with our users through automation. Remember the time you put together a report of your Top 10 Landing Pages and the number 1 viewed page was "/"? The analysts, of course, know that "/" represents your home page, but this isn't something that most people, particularly executives, will know or even should be expected to know. If you have not already rewritten "/" in your GA view settings as described in Chapter 9, rewriting it now to a more report-friendly name that management will easily be able to interpret has a profound impact. It's our responsibility as architects of the reporting solution to construct the report in a way that is easy to consume for its intended audience. Sounds simple enough, right? Well, it kind of is, but combine this with the many other similar data inconsistencies that exist, and it's not so straightforward to do this in an automated way.

At a recent conference on sports analytics, one of the speakers was the Director of Analytics for an NBA (the U.S. National Basketball Association) team. In addition to offering many valuable analytics insights, he said, "What do you think I spend 90% of my time doing? I'm basically cleaning up data in spreadsheets." That really cemented for me just how important it is for us to leverage tools that can automate as much of the data extraction, cleanup, and visualization process as possible. Analysts shouldn't be spending their time copying and pasting data, renaming data, and building graphs and charts. Analysts should spend their time mining for insights and discovering trends and patterns that can impact the business.

In this chapter, we cover how to get data out of GA, the limitations of each method, and the factors to consider along the way to help guide us through the maze. At the end of the chapter we discuss three advanced use cases for extracting and visualizing GA data.

FRAMING THE ISSUE: HOW TO GET DATA OUT OF GA

There are several ways of getting data out of GA. We'll focus on the methods that are most effective in supporting our goal of automated reporting.

Core Reporting API

The GA Core Reporting API (`https://developers.google.com/analytics/devguides/reporting/core/v3/`) provides a basic querying system to request metrics and dimensions in the form of tabular data from GA. It can access the majority of report data contained within GA. The returned data will look and feel similar to what you would see within the interface, and enable you to build dashboards, and automate reporting tasks outside of the GA interface. For example, you can leverage the API to extract and integrate GA data into a Web page, or Excel, or any other application. Note that the Core Reporting API is the only automated extraction method available to GA Standard users.

Following is an example of a query to the Core Reporting API. In this example, we are querying for the top 10 Channels during the last 30 days.

```
https://www.googleapis.com/analytics/v3/data/
ga?ids=ga%3A73156703&start-date=30daysAgo&end-date=yesterday&metric
s-ga%3Asessions%2Cga%3AbounceRate&dimensions=ga%3AchannelGrouping&s
ort=-ga%3Asessions&max-results=10
```

The result of this query is shown in Figure 16.1.

Default Channel Grouping	Sessions	Bounce Rate
Organic Search	27637	41.003003220320586
Direct	10562	50.77636811209998
Social	9960	63.32329317269077
Referral	7534	23.719139899123974
Branded Paid Search	4145	34.571773220747886
Other Paid Search	2461	60.05688744412841
Display	1730	78.90173410404624
Generic Paid Search	1045	70.23923444976077
(Other)	20	65
Email	14	57.14285714285714

FIGURE 16.1 Output of a typical query to the Core Reporting API.

Unsampled Request API

The Unsampled Request API differs from the Core Reporting API in that it allows you to access unsampled data. While the Core Reporting API allows you to dynamically combine metrics and dimensions, the Unsampled Request API instead allows you to access predefined Unsampled reports in comma-separated values (CSV) format.

Third-Party Tools

Analytics Canvas

Analytics Canvas is a tool that can be used to automate the extract, transform, load (ETL) process. It can connect directly to GA via the Core Reporting API as well as the Unsampled Request API, and to GA data that has been stored in BigQuery. It can also connect to many types of databases and to Excel files. Data can then be modified as needed and automatically uploaded to a database of your choice.

The software requires a Windows-based computer that would need to have access to all data sources. You would need to set up Analytics Canvas to connect to, manipulate, and then automatically push data to the desired output location.

Other tools that offer more advanced but conceptually similar functionality within Analytics Canvas include Informatica, SQL Server Integration Services (SSIS), IBM Info-Sphere, SAP Data Services, and many others. Analytics Canvas is primarily designed to work with analytics and marketing data sources and is well suited for GA purposes.

Tools such as SSIS are good at extraction and transformation from internal databases, but either don't offer connections to GA/BigQuery or offer limited functionality (with respect to GA).

Analytics Canvas can connect to the GA data using three methods:

- Core reporting API
- Unsampled Request API
- BigQuery

Not only will Analytics Canvas offer direct connectivity to GA, but since it's designed primarily to be used for analytics data, it offers the ability to extract unsampled data, something that other ETL tools typically don't.

For GA Standard users who are restricted to using the Core Reporting API only, Analytics Canvas leverages a creative method of addressing data sampling called Query Partitioning. This effectively segments a query into smaller chunks to reduce the number of sessions within each chunk. For example, if your reporting period were one year, Query Partitioning would split up the query into 12 smaller queries. The process is transparent to the user other than that it takes longer to execute the query. It's a clever way of mitigating the effects of sampling, but as the word *mitigate* suggests, it only reduces the effects of sampling; it doesn't eliminate. Depending on the volume of data being reported on, Query Partitioning may have a major or perhaps a marginal effect on your data.

A sample of a "Canvas" is shown in Figure 16.2.

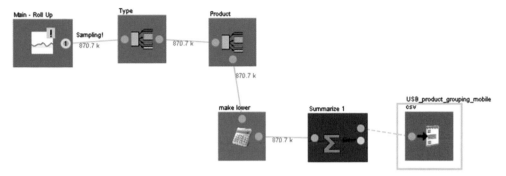

FIGURE 16.2 The visual blocks within the canvas make it extremely easy to follow the extraction and transformations occurring within your data set.

BigQuery

BigQuery is a querying tool that leverages the power and speed of Google's cloud infrastructure to store and query billions of rows of data in seconds. Initially developed as an internal tool to serve Google's internal technology stack, it works amazingly fast and enables complex data processing and segmentation.

BigQuery is a different product entirely from GA—the two aren't directly related. However, there is an integration available between Analytics 360 and BigQuery. As part of the integration, GAP exports data to BigQuery on a nightly basis. Not only is the majority of existing GA data available in BigQuery, but BigQuery's robust structure enables us to see deeper, more granular hit-level data. The additional layer of data enables us to understand and analyze user behavior with respect to sequence and the order in which activities were performed in a session.

BigQuery is one of several storage options within the Google Cloud Platform, as shown in Figure 16.3.

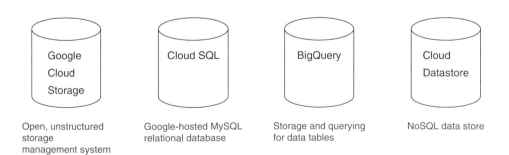

FIGURE 16.3 The Google Cloud Platform.

Is BigQuery a Relational Database?

Although BigQuery is designed to run SQL-like queries, it cannot be considered a relational database management system. Relational Database Management Systems (RDBMSs) such as Oracle, SQL Server, DB2, or MySQL are designed to efficiently perform all CRUD operations (create, read, update, delete), BigQuery is designed primarily for storage and the read operation—specifically, to run faster queries on extremely large data sets while avoiding the sampling that an RDMBS may apply.

We explore some advanced use cases for BigQuery later in this chapter.

For the datasets, tables, rows, and columns available for GA data exported to BigQuery, see "BigQuery Export Schema" in the GA help docs:

```
https://support.google.com/analytics/answer/3437719?hl=en
```

Tableau

Tableau is the recommended tool for visualizing the reports. Tableau is one of the leading data visualization tools on the market today and is extremely powerful at dashboard creation, ad hoc analysis, and the building of a self-service reporting solution.

GUEST SPOT   **Google Analytics Breakthrough: From Zero to Business Impact**

Jeff Feng

Jeff Feng is a Product Manager at Tableau Software.

Tableau is an interactive data visualization tool that helps people understand their data by providing an easy-to-use, drag-and-drop interface. We believe that data analysis should be about asking great questions, so we strive to enable the people who know the data best to quickly and easily answer their own questions of the data.

Tableau provides native connectivity to GA using their Core Reporting API, enabling users to create in-memory extracts of their data. As shown in Figure 16.4, Tableau provides many unique benefits for the analysis of GA data including the ability to:

➤ Mash up GA data with offline data, customer records, demographic data, and social media data without needing to move data from other data sources.
➤ Use drag-and-drop operations to build highly dynamic and interactive custom dashboards.
➤ Discover deeper insights about your data with point-and-click advanced analytics or new calculations.

In particular, the ability to blend GA data with other data sources is especially powerful.

GA is extremely powerful unto itself, and Tableau's objective is to provide even richer insights through integration with other enterprise data sources and to present the answers to the full spectrum of your data questions quickly and dynamically, with great visual appeal and the utmost clarity.

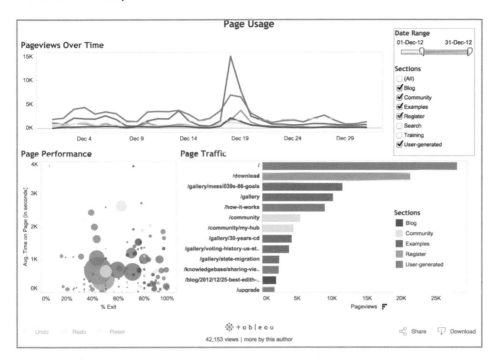

FIGURE 16.4 Tableau and integrate GA and other data sources with flexible, stylized, and interactive formatting options.

Tableau has three components:

- **Tableau Reader:** This is freely available for download and install. Its only function is to enable the user to view Tableau report files, similar to Adobe Reader for PDF files. If a file-sharing report distribution system is used, end users must install Tableau Reader to open the native-format Tableau files. Tableau Reader is available in both Windows and Mac versions.
- **Tableau Desktop:** This is the report-building environment of the Tableau suite. A select group of users who are well trained in Tableau will typically have access to this

software and will be able to view the raw data from each data source. Within this environment, report builders can either perform *ad hoc* analysis, or build reports/dashboards/visualizations to be shared as files (opened by Tableau Reader above) or published to the Web-based Tableau Server (mentioned below). Tableau Desktop is available in both Windows and Mac versions.

- **Tableau Server:** The Web-based Tableau Server acts as a publishing environment for Tableau reports. This software would be installed on a central Web-server within your network. Report builders would build reports and publish to this server, to be consumed by end users. End users would log in (in their browser since it is Web-based, eliminating the need for the Tableau Reader) and view reports/dashboards/visualizations as allowed by a role-based permissions model. (Tableau Server is currently available for Windows servers only.)

What Factors Dictate Which Tool to Use?

A considerable factor in devising a reporting solution is resolving the issue of the many disparate data sources that are not able to expose data in a way that allows the data to be pulled automatically. To facilitate an end-to-end automation process, we recommend the acquisition of a middle-layer tool called Analytics Canvas (aka Canvas), described earlier.

With all these tools available to use, it of course gets hard to determine which tool to use. There are several factors that impact the solution we should use, but one of the primary factors is sampling, discussed in Chapter 11. Since sampling in GA directly affects the quality and integrity of your data, Table 16.1 may help in determining which tools to use, or at least in eliminating options.

TABLE 16.1 A Summary of Available Data Extraction Methods/Tools, and Ideal Uses

Extraction Method	Sampling	Notes
Core Reporting API	Subject to same sampling thresholds as GA Standard interface (500,000 sessions within reporting period). 10,000 rows maximum returned per query.	Tools such as Canvas can help mitigate (not eliminate) effects of sampling by using the Query Partitioning Feature.
Unsampled Request API (Analytics 360 only)	Provides access to preconfigured unsampled reports.	Great way of exporting Unsampled data but limited access makes this a bit cumbersome. Unsampled reports must either be manually downloaded from within the tool (or emailed), or accessed via Google Drive account as CSV files.

TABLE 16.1 *continued*

Extraction Method	Sampling	Notes
BigQuery (Analytics 360 only)	Provides access to unsampled hit-level data.	Can be used in two models: 1) as a data hub where you can upload additional data sources and join with GA data; 2) as a vehicle for accessing unsampled hit-level GA data.
Analytics Canvas	Can connect to Core Reporting API, and Unsampled Request API for fully Unsampled data, as well as BigQuery.	Works in tandem with visualization tool. By itself, it only provides a facility to extract and transform data.
Tableau	Contains a connector to access GA data but prone to significant sampling issues.	Much better solution is to feed data to Tableau via integration with Analytics Canvas, or to use the automated export from Analytics 360 to BigQuery and connect to BigQuery from Tableau.

ETLV—THE FULL REPORTING AUTOMATION CYCLE

ETL stands for extract, transform, load. It is a BI-oriented process to load data from the source system to the target system to enable business reporting. We added a V at the end to make this process a little more current and complete. The V stands for visualize, of course!

The overall solution will function as follows:

1. Extract the data.
2. Transform the data.
3. Load the data into a reporting platform.
4. Visualize.

This process is illustrated broadly in Figure 16.5.

There are several factors that need to be considered in the ETLV process to extract/obtain data from heterogeneous data sources, modify (transform) it, and then load it into a data-reporting tool for visualization in an automated way. We've broken down some of the factors in Table 16.2.

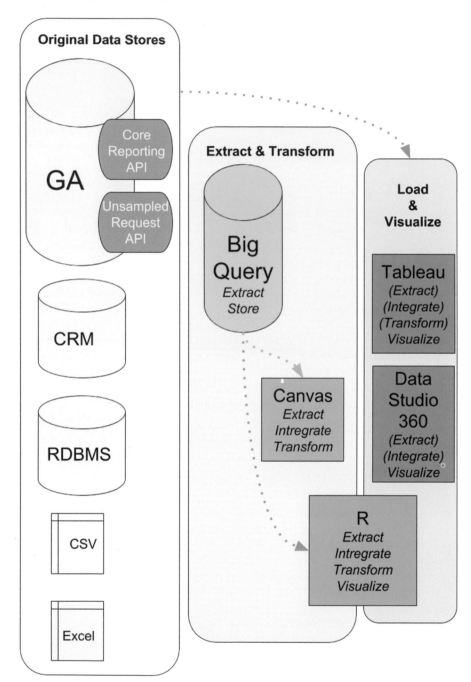

FIGURE 16.5 Data flow through ETLV.

TABLE 16.2 Factors at Each Stage of an Automated ETLV Reporting Solution

Factor	Considerations
Phase: Extract	
Data Sources	Typical business may need to pull data from platforms such as Google Analytics, WebTrends, Adobe Site Catalyst, Marketing Automation tools like Marketo or Eloqua, CRM tools like SalesForce, Display Advertising data such as AdWords, DoubleClick, AdMob, E-Commerce Data, App data (from Apple Store or Google Play), or any number of internal databases.
Format	What format is the data stored in, and how is it exposed will dictate the method we use to extract the data.
Frequency	How often is the data made available or refreshed?
Time Frame	Is the data made available in incremental chunks (daily, weekly, or monthly extracts) or as a full extract?
Phase: Transform	
Cleanup	How much sanitization, data filtration, and renaming (to make data understandable by its intended audience and report-friendly) is needed?
Structure	This step accounts for any calculation (e.g., calculating bounce rates, de-duplicating of data, summing/aggregation) or other calculations based on business logic.
Data Integration	Are there any common keys available to Join data sources together, or facilitate data widening via a lookup or mapping file?
Phase: Load	
Frequency	How "fresh" does the data need to be? For monthly reports, this typically isn't a concern, but for daily reports it can pose a big challenge.
Import Type	Will data be loaded incrementally? Or will the entire data set be overwritten with each cycle?
Format	What is the output of the load process? In other words, where is the data being sent for final reporting? Excel? Tableau? Data Studio 360? Some other reporting or visualization tool?
Phase: Visualization	
Governance	Who will be viewing the data, and which reports should they have access to?
Distribution	Will the reports be shared via email? On a network shared drive? Or will users login to a web-based system and view reports there?
Software	Which software have you already invested in to build reports with? Selection of software will depend highly on the reporting requirements but also on the willingness of end users to learn a new tool, and of reporting champions to enforce a particular tool/platform.

Before deciding on a solution or any one tool, it's recommended that you take a step back and evaluate your organization's reporting needs. By going through the above table and getting a better understanding of your data sources and how much data cleanup is needed, your organization will be far better equipped to make a solid business decision and build a reporting solution that will deliver insights with the speed, agility, and depth needed.

ADVANCED USE CASES FOR BIGQUERY/TABLEAU

Let's take a step away from the architecture of reporting and review some examples of reports that we can build using two tools available to us in the overall ETLV stack: BigQuery and Tableau.

Use Case 1: Path Analysis

As we mentioned earlier, the data available in GA is very aggregate in nature. You can see overall traffic by Campaign, Top Landing pages by Campaign, and so on. You can also drill into Users who performed certain actions on your site or mobile app. What you can't easily do within the GA interface is determine the order in which users, in aggregate, performed certain actions (even though we can refer to the User Explorer report for the series of actions completed by individual, anonymous users). For example, do the majority of users view a video first or download a PDF document prior to converting on your lead submission goal? The flow reports currently available in GA, while useful, don't always answer these types of questions about aggregate, hit-level flow through our websites and apps.

Enter BigQuery.

As part of the integration with Analytics 360, the data exposed to BigQuery includes a layer of data that isn't available within the GA interface. This hit-level data includes time/ sequence information so we can do exactly this type of flow analysis. Within BigQuery we can drill into this data for a specific user (based on user ID) or even a specific user session (similar to the User Explorer report in GA).

In order to do this, let's first find a user who was fairly active. To keep things simple, we'll just focus on one day of data.

Here is a simple query to find us just the right user session to dive deeper into:

```
SELECT CONCAT(fullVisitorId, STRING(visitId)) AS userSession,totals.
hits FROM [8839142.ga_sessions_20150920] order by totals.hits desc
LIMIT 100
```

The results are shown in Figure 16.6.

With 80 hits, the session in row 1 shows a high level of engagement. Let's go find out what pages this user looked at in this specific session. Actually, let's take it one step further and combine this with the order in which pages were viewed as well.

Row	userSession	totals_hits
1	8145577972766963426144274088I	80
2	58181865585942738431442755338	40
3	27328100088140737481442756504	17
4	56931057507440682961442768534	16
5	52465718007105126291442810155	13
6	75537273304561498571442815847	12
7	17268076316175367251442792084	12
8	81455779727669634261442737263	11
9	10756412833193996981442809110	10
10	72196124314062243551442808697	9

FIGURE 16.6 Results of a simple query to extract total hits by visit ID.

Here is the query:

```
SELECT hits.hitNumber,hits.page.pagePath FROM [8839142.ga_
sessions_20150920] where visitid=1442740881 and hits.type='PAGE'
LIMIT 100
```

The results of this query are shown in Figure 16.7.

Row	hits_hitNumber	hits_page_pagePath
1	1	/blog/social-analytics/3-steps-to-track-social-media-in-google-analytics
2	16	/index.jsp
3	17	/blog
4	20	/blog/google-analytics/google-analytics-account-configuration
5	25	/blog
6	27	/blog/google-analytics/benchmarking-reports
7	31	/blog
8	32	/blog/google-analytics/creating-remarketing-audiences-from-google-analytics
9	38	/blog

FIGURE 16.7 Looking at the hits generated during an individual user's session.

We can now see the sequence of pages this user looked in his or her session:

1. Viewed Social Analytics blog post.
2. Navigated back to the home page (probably to learn more about our company).

3. Went to the main blog page.
4. Read GA account configuration blog post.
5. Back to the main blog page.
6. Read Benchmarking reports blog post.
7. Back to the main blog page.
8. Read Creative Remarketing blog post.
9. Back to the main blog page.

You could also look at this data in aggregate path analysis to get a sense of what engaged users are looking at within your site or mobile app (since this methodology could be used on screens as well as pages). For examples of aggregated visualizations, see www.e-nor.com/gabook.

Use Case 2: Ecommerce

Let's say you run an E-commerce store and want some more information on how your users interact with your products. We'll start with a simple query: which products were purchased on a particular day? We'll use a fictitious sporting goods store in our example.

```
SELECT hits.item.ProductName as Product, hits.item.itemQuantity as
Quantity, hits.item.itemRevenue as Revenue
FROM [hockeystore:049725.ga_sessions_20150901] where hits.item
.ProductName!='null' and totals.transactions>0 order by hits.item
.itemRevenue DESC LIMIT 100
```

The results are shown in Figure 16.8.

The product called Skates earned a lot of units on this day. What if we were to answer the following business question: for users who purchased Skates, what other products did they purchase?

Here is the query to show this info:

```
SELECT
 hits.item.productName AS other_purchased_products,
 COUNT(hits.item.productName) AS quantity
FROM [hockeystore:049725.ga_sessions_20150901]
WHERE
 hits.item.productName IS NOT NULL
  AND hits.item.productName !='Skates'
  AND fullVisitorId IN (
 SELECT
  fullVisitorId
 FROM [hockeystore:049725.ga_sessions_20150901]
 WHERE
  hits.item.productName CONTAINS 'Skates'
  AND totals.transactions >= 1
```

```
GROUP BY
  fullVisitorId
  LIMIt 100)
GROUP BY
  other_purchased_products
ORDER BY
  quantity DESC;
```

Ignoring the complexity of the query itself, the point is that it shows us "people who bought a product called Skates also purchased the following products," as illustrated in Figure 16.9 and Figure 16.10. That is immensely useful data and can form the basis of a recommendation engine to cross-sell other products.

Row	Product	Quantity	Revenue
1	Helmets	5	58374.5
2	Skates	2500	40675
3	Sticks	4	37980
4	Gloves	25	29122.25
5	Pucks	1	23925.8
6	Jersey	20	23795.8
7	Shoulder Pads	20	23681.8
8	Knee Pads	20	23615.8
9	Elbow Pads	20	23589.8
10	Hockey Pants	20	23373.8
11	Socks	11	21690.79
12	Equipment Bags	15	20998.95
13	Hockey Tape	16	19116.64
14	Skate Laces	1000	18960
15	Mouthguards	1000	18310
16	Skate Tools	15	17542.35
17	Training DVDs	10	15780

FIGURE 16.8 Results from a query showing products purchased from a sporting goods store on a single day.

Row	other_purchased_products	quantity
1	Helmets	16
2	Shoulder Pads	13
3	Jersey	5
4	Hockey Tape	3
5	Skate Laces	2

FIGURE 16.9 Results of the query showing which other products were purchased by customers who purchased Skates.

FIGURE 16.10 Queries for also-purchased products could serve as the basis for a recommendation engine.

Use Case 3: Advanced Funnel Analysis

Funnels are an oft-asked-about feature of GA. The funnel features in GA are useful but lack some key features such as the ability to segment the funnel on the fly or to retro-actively apply the funnel to historical data. Typically this type of analysis can be done outside of Google Analytics.

The following is a contribution from James Standen, founder of Analytics Canvas discussing how to do such funnel analysis by leveraging Analytics Canvas.

GUEST SPOT   **Advanced Funnel Analysis—The Next Level**

James Standen

James Standen is founder and CEO of nModal Solutions Inc.

It is possible to move beyond Google Analytics' built-in funnel capabili-ties and have a much more sophisticated view of the funnel by using GA integration capabilities.

There are a number of major limitations for funnel reports in GA, some of which are:

➤ Difficult to use segments.
➤ Difficult to see evolution over time.
➤ (GA Standard)—No way to do funnel analysis on historical data.

It is possible, however, by using the powerful integration available in GA, to pull the data out of GA, and perform much more advanced funnel analysis. We will be able to create not just a single view of a funnel for an entire period, but see the exit rates by step over time as they evolve, and segment the funnel—so, for example, we can see how funnel performance changes by time of day, traffic source, and so on.

We will look at two advanced techniques:

➤ **Core Reporting API.** Available for both GA Standard and Analytics 360 accounts, by doing a number of queries and combining the results together, it is possible to build more advanced funnel analysis.
➤ **BigQuery.** Available for Analytics 360 only, with some fancy SQL footwork almost anything is possible with BigQuery—we'll look at some examples.

Both of these techniques are available in Analytics Canvas, a third-party tool created by Google partner nModal Solutions. Analytics Canvas provides a visual environment that lets users extract data from GA in sophisticated ways, and then clean, merge, and combine this data with other data sources and then deliver it to databases, to reports, or to visualization tools such as Tableau.

Using the Core Reporting API

By making a number of queries to the core reporting API, it is possible to get the advanced funnel information that is available within the GA interface, only from the Custom Funnel in Analytics 360, and in fact to get more detailed and segmented data of any given funnel.

continues

continued

Each query is created by using a segment that gets the number of sessions that have certain characteristics. When put together, a complete picture of the funnel activity is available.

First, a series of funnel steps must be defined. In Analytics Canvas this is done using the funnel query user interface (Figure 16.11). In this case we are only using `pagePath`, but a number of other options also exist. Notice also that there is a Segment tab. With this, we can overlay a segment onto the funnel—something not possible in GA Standard.

Funnel Definition	Time Period	Segment	Additional data	Detect Sampling

	Add new funnel step definition		Create a list of funnel steps, top to bottom.		
✗	pagePath ▼	Contains ▼	/checkout/customer-info/	Name:	Customer Information
✗	pagePath ▼	Contains ▼	/checkout/product-selection/	Name:	Product Selection
✗	pagePath ▼	Contains ▼	/checkout/payment-details/	Name:	Payment Details
✗	pagePath ▼	Contains ▼	/checkout/confirmation/	Name:	Confirmation

FIGURE 16.11 Funnel configuration in Analytics Canvas.

Once these steps are defined, then behind the scenes, for each step, three core reporting API queries are done. They are as follows:

➤ The number of sessions that went to the step and to no previous steps. This gives us the number of sessions that entered the funnel directly at this step.
➤ The number of sessions that went to the step and to a previous step. This gives us the number of sessions that made it to this step from some previous step.
➤ The number of sessions that went to the step but did not go to any later step. This is a very important one—this tells us how many sessions exited at this step.

The result of these three queries gives one row in the result data set—when we run them for each step in the funnel we get the following: A complete step by step funnel analysis (Figure 16.12). The example data set therefore would require $3 \times 4 = 12$ core reporting API calls.

FunnelName	FunnelStep	FunnelStepName	FunnelStepLabel	EnteredDirectly	FromPrevious	Total	WentToLaterStep	Exited	Conversion
Purchase Funnel	1	Customer Information	01 Customer Information	23	0	23	10	13	FALSE
Purchase Funnel	2	Product Selection	02 Product Selection	1	10	11	6	5	FALSE
Purchase Funnel	3	Payment Details	03 Payment Details	0	6	6	5	1	FALSE
Purchase Funnel	4	Confirmation	04 Confirmation	2	5	7	0	0	TRUE

FIGURE 16.12 Funnel analysis.

Where it becomes really powerful is if we add in the date—now, we can look at the change in the funnel over time. By adding segments, we can see how different segments interact with our funnel, and identify issues based on traffic source, or technical issues such as browser that might be increasing funnel exit rate at specific steps.

For example, we could even look at funnel performance by segment, by hour of the day across different days of the week—all these types of queries are supported by the Core Reporting API using this method.

Analytics 360—BigQuery, the Ultimate Funnel Analysis

As you would expect, the ultimate funnel analysis is only available with Analytics 360. This is made possible by the BigQuery integration with Analytics 360, discussed earlier in the chapter. When an Analytics 360 account has its BigQuery integration set up, all the detailed hit-level data is transferred every day into tables in BigQuery. As a result, there are no real limits to the potential analysis—the only thing standing between you and your data is writing the right BigQuery SQL query.

The types of queries might be to identify user trips through the funnel that involved backtracking—where users were confused or missed something, and by analyzing these interactions make the funnel clearer.

Analytics Canvas generates the BigQuery SQL required to implement an enhanced version of the funnel report we just looked at and returns the data directly into Canvas (Figure 16.13).

FIGURE 16.13 Analytics Canvas can generate BigQuery SQL.

Again, because we are using BigQuery, we can add as many columns as we like—no limits on dimensions or metrics, and within the SQL, the WHERE clause gives us lots of options for segmentation. The result is that it is possible to generate data sets that represent funnel performance, set up in a dimensional model that lets you slice and dice as needed. In fact, BigQuery can handle so much data that you can create segment tables (lists of millions of sessions or users that satisfy a given criteria), and then join this table to the funnel table to get a completely segmented set of funnels to analyze.

The key to the SQL structure is the use of FLATTEN to get a table of the hits involved, then do a series of tests, and sum up the total sessions for each test. In the above example, we are looking at the funnel by medium, and so have aggregated away the visitID, but if you had left that in and written the result to a BigQuery table you would have a generated a complete

continues

continued

funnel analysis at the individual session level. While a detailed analysis of the SQL involved is beyond the scope of this overview, the full SQL query that is generated by Analytics Canvas is available in the tool, so you can see the structure, and modify it as needed.

The final, ultimate goal is to create such a data set and visualize it in a tool such as Tableau—where it is possible to explore a multifaceted data set and its funnel performance at multiple levels, drilling down even to the individual session/user level.

Whether you are using GA Standard or Analytics 360, these techniques, and tools such as Analytics Canvas and Tableau, can provide significantly enhanced access to your funnel, and provide new opportunities for insight to let you optimize.

As a note, if you have licensed Analyics you can take advantage of the Custom Funnel feature discussed in Chapter 18.

GUEST SPOT | **Accessing GA Data with R**

Eric Goldsmith

Eric Goldsmith is the Data Scientist for TED Conferences.

The GA graphical user interface (GUI) works well for many use cases. But if you find yourself running up against functionality limits, such as the need to:

➤ Use more than two dimensions (Custom reports allow up to five and the API allows up to seven in a single query).
➤ Generate complex, calculated metrics (Simple calculated metric functionality in the GUI was being beta-tested when this was written).
➤ Combine GA data with external data sources.
➤ Report across multiple GA Properties.
➤ Create more sophisticated visualizations.
➤ Mitigate the impact of data sampling.

Then accessing GA data through a specialized tool or programmatically is the logical next step. Google provides two programmatic access methods:

➤ The Core Reporting API: `https://developers.google.com/analytics/devguides/reporting/core/v3/)`
➤ The BigQuery API: `https://cloud.google.com/bigquery/docs/reference/v2/`

Both are general purpose, and nearly any programming language can be used. But one language that is exceptionally capable at data manipulation is R (`https://www.r-project.org/about.html`).

The following sections will focus on the mechanics of using R for accessing and visualizing GA data. For information on learning to use R, there's plenty of help online:

```
http://tryr.codeschool.com/
https://www.datacamp.com/
http://dss.princeton.edu/training/RStudio101.pdf
https://support.rstudio.com/hc/en-us/sections/200107586-Using-
  RStudio
```

You can download the unabridged version of "Accessing GA Data with R," including the use of R with the GA Core Reporting API, at `www.e-nor.com/gabook`.

Using BigQuery

If you are a GAP customer, you can export your GA data to Google's BigQuery (`https://support.google.com/analytics/answer/3437618`) and gain access to the raw, unaggregated data that is not subject to sampling.

Using BigQuery is quite different from using the Core Reporting API: there are pros and cons to each, but that discussion is outside the scope of this introduction.

Installing Needed Packages

The `bigrquery` package (`https://cran.r-project.org/web/packages/bigrquery/index.html`) is available from CRAN.

```
install.packages("bigrquery")
```

Querying GA Data

BigQuery uses an SQL-like language (`https://cloud.google.com/bigquery/query-reference`), often referred to as BQL. To obtain the number of homepage pageviews from different device types in the United States, trended over the last 30 days, as shown in Figure 16.14, the code looks like this:

```
library(bigrquery)

project <- "xxxxxxxxx"
dataset <- yyyyy

query <-
 "SELECT DATE(date) AS date, device.deviceCategory AS
deviceCategory, COUNT(hits.type) AS pageviews
 FROM (TABLE_DATE_RANGE([%s.ga_sessions_], TIMESTAMP('%s'),
TIMESTAMP('%s')))
 WHERE hits.type = 'PAGE'
  AND hits.page.pagePath = '/'
  AND geoNetwork.country = 'United States'
 GROUP BY date, deviceCategory
 ORDER BY date, deviceCategory;"

bql <- sprintf(query, dataset, startDate, endDate)
data.bq <- query_exec(bql, project = project)
```

The project and data set values above are obtained during the BigQuery Export (`https://support.google.com/analytics/answer/3416092`) setup process.

Visualization

A box plot is helpful to visualize data distribution:

```
# Boxplot
ggplot(data.bq, aes(x = deviceCategory, y = pageviews, group =
deviceCategory, fill = deviceCategory)) +
 geom_boxplot() + guides(fill = FALSE)
```

continues

continued

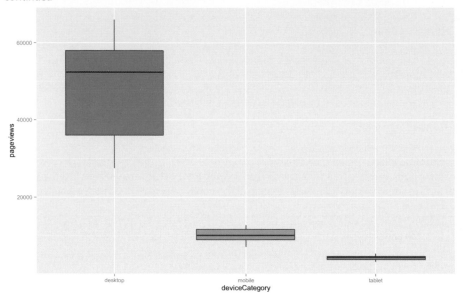

FIGURE 16.14 Pageviews by device type.

Next Steps

The material above barely scratches the surface of what's possible with GA data and R.

R can be used for interactive exploration of data, or scripted program execution. R scripts can be used for anything from data manipulation pipelines, to automated report generation via tools like knitr (*http://yihui.name/knitr/*), and even for building Web applications via tools like Shiny (*http://shiny.rstudio.com/*).

With these tools, connecting GA data with other data sets (e.g., content or customer data from external MySQL databases) becomes easy, allowing exploration, reporting, and visualization of bigger-picture relationships that might otherwise remain hidden.

GUEST SPOT   **ShufflePoint**

Mike Anderson

Mike Anderson is Data Integration and Visualization Specialist at E-Nor.

ShufflePoint has long been a great tool for accessing GA data. ShufflePoint uses a powerful Analytics Query Language (AQL) to access the GA Core Reporting API, allowing for data extraction without the need to use the GA interface. This provides numerous possibilities for automating your data extraction.

Why ShufflePoint?

For companies who are constructing Excel reports with their GA data, there may be no better tool than ShufflePoint. It's easy to use, easy to learn, and very powerful. Raw data can be easily extracted directly to Excel and then visualized for quick and cost-effective reporting automation for GA data.

It doesn't have the robustness and customization of Analytics Canvas and it certainly can't be used as a visualization tool like Tableau or Data Studio 360, but if Excel is your primary reporting platform, ShufflePoint is a solid choice for extraction from GA.

Using ShufflePoint

ShufflePoint offers two methods to access your GA data:

- a nice graphical, browser-based Web interface
- the ability to connect and run queries directly from Microsoft Excel

Web Interface

The primary method of using ShufflePoint is via their Web interface (see Figure 16.15), which provides an intuitive drag-and-drop method for creating queries. You can simply drag and drop your dimensions and metrics to the column and rows and the AQL query will be written for you. At the same time, it also provides direct editing of the query using their AQL for the savvier user.

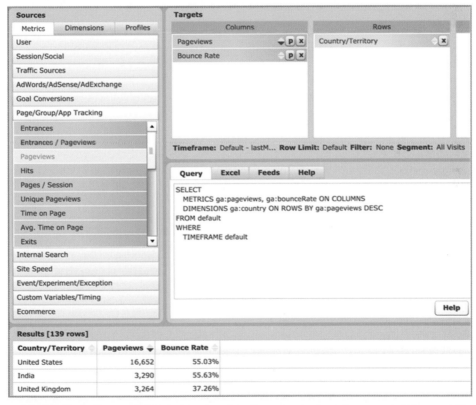

FIGURE 16.15 The Shufflepoint Web based user interface allows easy drag and drop query building capability.

Example AQL Query:

```
SELECT
  DIMENSIONS ga:Month ON COLUMNS
  METRICS ga:sessions, ga:pageviews, ga:bouncerate,
ga:pageviewsPerSession, ga:avgSessionDuration ON ROWS
```

continues

continued

```
FROM 45076979
WHERE
  TIMEFRAME lastMonth
```

Within the Web interface, you can run the query and return results in real time, which also allows for copying and pasting the extracted data from the Result window. This can be an efficient method for those who only need to run a few queries and then copy paste the data into a spreadsheet or an email.

Excel Data Connection

For larger, more complex reports that involve dozens of queries, ShufflePoint truly provides easy data extraction through a native data connection in Microsoft Excel®. This connection requires no additional software, and allows for executing and refreshing your queries directly within your spreadsheets.

This can be extremely time-saving for refreshing numerous queries and instantly formatting your data, once the queries have run. This also means that your charts and graphs will dynamically update when queries are refreshed. Entire reports can be refreshed and automatically formatted to suit your needs.

One of our favorite reasons for using this method of extraction is that Excel and PowerPoint already have object linking built in. A live object link from Excel can be embedded into your PowerPoint. This means that once you have finished running your ShufflePoint queries, the next time you open your PowerPoint deck, all of your GA data is instantly updated into your Power Point report. No more copy and paste.

Features of ShufflePoint

Reducing Sampling

One of the most important features of ShufflePoint is the ability to help reduce, or eliminate altogether the amount of sampling your queries may return from the GA Core Reporting API. ShufflePoint offers the ability to "partition" or loop through your query in smaller chunks by week, month, or year, resulting in the query returning the entire time frame's data set but broken down by the isolated date method chosen. This can be extremely helpful when querying large timeframes to help mitigate sampling.

Dynamic Filtering

Ever needed to create a filter on the fly? Directly within your ShufflePoint AQL query, you can define your own custom filter without needing to setup a Segment within the GA interface first. This also allows for easily editing the filter on a query-by-query basis, thus not affecting the filter of other queries, or requiring you to set up numerous segments.

Time Frame Comparisons

When building GA reports, time frame comparisons are extremely useful to help easily determine the percentage of change from one week to the next, one month to the next, etc. When defining the time frame of your query, ShufflePoint offers the ability to compare time frames and instantly return a percentage of change between the time frames. This can be very helpful when using the Excel integration because you can use conditional formatting on your time comparison column to easily change the percentage of change from red to green adding nice visual context to the time frame comparison without much work.

KEY TAKEAWAYS

Data visualization complements the reporting available in the Google Analytics user interface.   While Google Analytics has a robust interface, many advanced use cases require pulling data out of GA and into a data visualization tool, particularly when we need to integrate with other data sets.

Sampling can severely and negatively impact your data quality.   Sampling is something you should pay attention to since it impacts the quality of your data. Be aware of what causes sampling and which of your reports may be impacted by it.

Hit-level data in BigQuery opens up a new world of analysis.   BigQuery facilitates very granular level of data analysis not available natively in Google Analytics. Learn this product—it's the future.

Plan your report automation road map.   True report automation nirvana can only be achieved with careful thought and attention given to the variety of factors driving reporting within your environment.

ACTIONS AND EXERCISES

1. **Is your data sampled?** Check a few of your reports in GA to see which are sampled and which are not. You can check this by looking at the sampling indicator at the top of each report.

2. **Extract data outside GA.** Using the methods defined in this chapter, try to get data outside of GA using the available export or API functionality (or via a tool).

3. **Visualize.** Use this data to create a visual by building a chart in any visualization tool—Excel, Tableau, and so on.

Data Import and
Measurement Protocol

Thus far in the book, the discussions about Google Analytics (GA) data capture have centered around the GA JavaScript tracking code, analytics.js. Whether placed on the page directly or deployed through Google Tag Manager as we have demonstrated and recommended, tracking code execution tends to be our primary mental paradigm for GA data capture. In Chapter 13, we also worked with the Android and iOS SDKs to record mobile app data into GA.

In this chapter, we look at the two options beyond analytics.js and the SDKs for getting data into GA: data import (through the GA user interface or through the API), and the Measurement Protocol (MP), which allows any programmed, networked environment to push hits into GA in the form of basic HTTP requests.

We'll use data import in most cases to add dimensions to analytics.js and mobile SDK hits; using the Measurement Protocol, we'll record new hits.

DATA IMPORT

The data import feature in GA may seem somewhat complicated at first, but it's actually quite straightforward and very flexible. In each case, you're generating a .csv (comma-separated values) data file and importing built-in or custom dimensions against a common key in GA.

Several data import scenarios are outlined next.

> **Note**
>
> ### Processing-Time, Query-Time, and Retroactivity
>
> Perhaps unintuitively, data import in GA usually means adding data to hits as they're captured going forward only; this *processing-time* data import applies on a now-forward basis only (until you remove the import configuration from the data import setup). This means that some types of data import are more useful and practical than others, and that you should aim to set up your data import sooner rather than later and begin extending your hit data early on.
>
> Cost data import, discussed below, does apply retroactively. If you have Analytics 360 you can also take advantage of *query-time* data import to dynamically add data to existing hits.

Importing CRM Data into Google Analytics

In Chapter 15, "Integrating Google Analytics with CRM Data," we recorded GA campaign information directly in our CRM (Salesforce) so we could correlate our medium, source, and campaign values with the lead status that our sales team assigned in the CRM. We also recorded a common visitor ID in both GA and our CRM to enable additional joins between the two data sets within the CRM, within a separate environment, or within GA.

We can take advantage of the GA data import feature to accomplish the join within GA. (Since the imported data would need to apply retroactively, this scenario would require query-time import available in Analytics 360. The content, product, and geo imports that appear later in the chapter would be suitable as processing-time or query-time import and would therefore also be applicable to GA Standard.) In this example, we'll take the following steps to import lead status from the CRM for further correlation with GA data. Note that you need Edit access at the property level to perform the following procedure:

1. Create a *Lead Status* custom dimension in GA.

    The data that we're pulling in from Salesforce is the qualification status that our sales team assigned to each lead. Since there is not currently a slot for this data in GA, we'll need to create a custom dimension as in Figure 17.1 to populate as the objective of the data import.

    Let's say that we had previously created five other custom dimensions in the GA property and that this is the sixth. When we're importing the CRM data into GA, we'll add `ga:dimension6` as a heading to the lead status column to match it to the lead status custom dimension.

2. Create the data set schema in GA.

    Before we can import our CRM data into GA, we need to create a data set to receive the CRM data and define a schema to map the data import. In most cases, you'll designate a single key field that will serve as the join between the data sets and one or more target fields to populate in GA from the imported data.

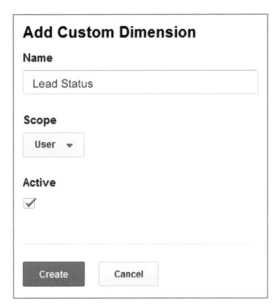

FIGURE 17.1 Creating a custom dimension to receive the lead status value during data import.

A. In the Property Admin, click Data Import.
B. For Import Behavior, select Query Time.
C. For Data Set Type, select User, and click Next Step.
D. On the following screen, name the data set Lead Status, and select one or more views to import the customer relationship management (CRM) data into. (You're advised to import first into a test view, verify import in the test view, and then import into one or more working views.)
E. In the next step, designate the common field/dimension to be used as the join in the import and, under Imported Data, one or more target dimensions to copy the new data into, as shown in Figures 17.2 and 17.3.
F. For Overwrite Hit Data, you can select No, since there will be no lead status associated with any of the visitor IDs at this point. For future imports in which Lead Status may have changed for some visitorIDs, you can select Yes for Overwrite Hit Data.
G. Click Get Schema to confirm the heading names that we'll need to add to our exported CRM data in step 3. In the lead status example, you'll configure the schema as either `ga:dimension4, ga:dimension6,` or `ga:userId, ga:dimension6,` depending on where you stored your visitor ID from the CRM (and assuming that you created the lead status custom field in the sixth custom dimension slot as in the example). If you previously stored the CRM visitor ID as both the User ID (for cross-device) and your Visitor ID custom dimension for CRM integration, you can use either as the key in your schema.

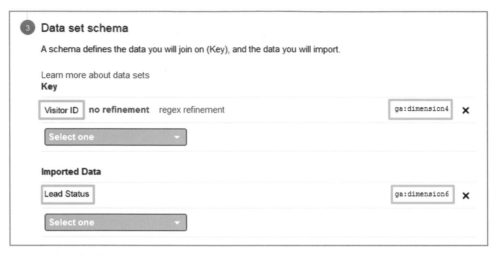

FIGURE 17.2 For the data set schema, you'll designate a key, which normally consists of a single dimension, such as the visitor ID that you created as a custom dimension, as well as one or more target fields to import against the key.

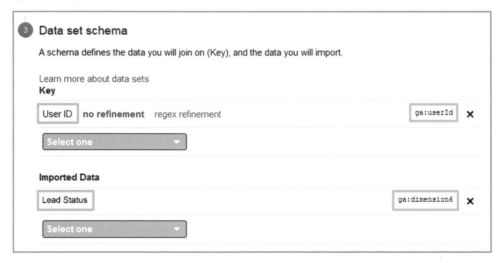

FIGURE 17.3 This schema is similar to Figure 17.2, but as the key, we're using the User ID dimension that you can populate for cross-device tracking but that can also serve to join your CRM and GA data.

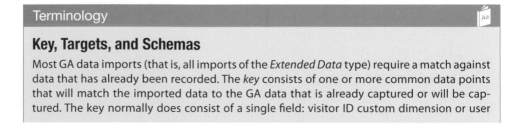

Terminology

Key, Targets, and Schemas

Most GA data imports (that is, all imports of the *Extended Data* type) require a match against data that has already been recorded. The *key* consists of one or more common data points that will match the imported data to the GA data that is already captured or will be captured. The key normally does consist of a single field: visitor ID custom dimension or user

ID for a User data import, as shown in Figure 17.2 and Figure 17.3, page/request URI for a Content data import, and campaign ID for a Campaign data import, as three examples.

The *targets* are the one or more GA dimensions that will receive the other data points in the imported data set, which are matched against the common key. As a target, you can designate a built-in dimension, such as Campaign Medium, Source, and Name in the case of a Campaign data import, or a custom dimension such as lead status in Figures 17.2 and 17.3.

Together, the key and one or more targets constitute the *schema*, or the expected structure of the imported data that we're mapping into GA.

3. Export CRM data.

In Salesforce, as an example, we can create a report that contains one of two field sets, following the schema in either Figure 17.2 or 17.3.

- **Visitor ID and lead status.** Again, if the common key that we stored in both GA and Salesforce was a client-generated ID (such as the client ID value of the GA _ga cookie), you need to export the visitor ID custom field that you populated into the Salesforce lead through a hidden field on the memory chip lead form.

- **Lead ID/Customer ID and lead status.** If, instead of passing a client-generated visitor ID to your CRM when a lead or purchase form was initially submitted, you retrieved the lead or customer ID from your new CRM record and recorded it in GA as the visitor ID custom dimension or the cross-device user ID, export this lead/customer ID and lead status.

When you export your CRM report as comma-separated values (CSV), you'll generate a file similar to Listing 17.1. For our example, we'll call this file `sf-export-lead-status.csv`.

Note that you must add the heading row yourself. This schema example corresponds to Figure 17.2.

LISTING 17.1: Visitor ID and lead status exported from the CRM as comma-separated values.

```
ga:dimension4,ga:dimension6
8575125426.7414512124,qualified
2351526532.8748574856,unqualified
3625325410.3621014101,qualified
8547512450.6958215485,unqualified
5693210174.6958745615,unqualified
5235651548.2514548845,qualified
5645461021.8645456120,unqualified
4561230223.7845613123,unqualified
8564612310.8964564103,qualified
4564613123.7841312301,unqualified
```

4. Upload the `.csv` file.
    A. In the property admin column, click Data Import.
    B. For the Lead Status data set listed in Figure 17.4 that we defined previously, click Manage uploads.
    C. Click Upload file, select sf-export-lead-status.csv, and click Upload.

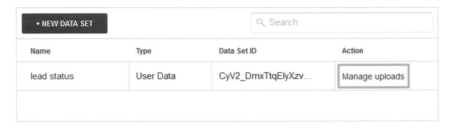

FIGURE 17.4   You import the CRM data into the data set defined in step 2.

Once the import is completed, you'll see a confirmation, as in Figure 17.5.

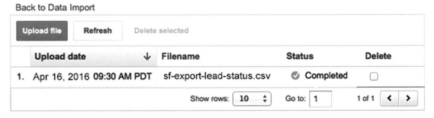

FIGURE 17.5   Data import confirmation for the lead status data set.

Uploading through the Management API

Note that you can also import data through the GA Management API instead of through the GA user interface. The management API would be a better option in scenarios where automation is desired. If data is being uploaded to GA on an *ad hoc* or infrequent basis, then the interface method works perfectly. If the upload is frequent or if a hands-off approach is desired, then the capabilities facilitated by the management API become much more attractive.

Using Imported Data in Google Analytics Reports

In many cases, such as the lead status example outlined in the previous section, the new data is imported into one or more custom dimensions. While custom dimensions do not appear by default in any of the built-in GA reports, you can apply custom dimensions as secondary dimensions in the built-in reports and use custom dimension to define a custom segment or custom report as discussed in Chapter 10, "Segments," and Chapter 11, "Dashboards, Custom Reports, and Intelligence Alerts."

We could apply our imported Lead Status data as a custom dimension in the Campaigns report as displayed in Figure 17.6. This report displays some of the same data as Table 15.4, but here the merge between CRM and GA data has occurred within GA and not the CRM or a separate environment.

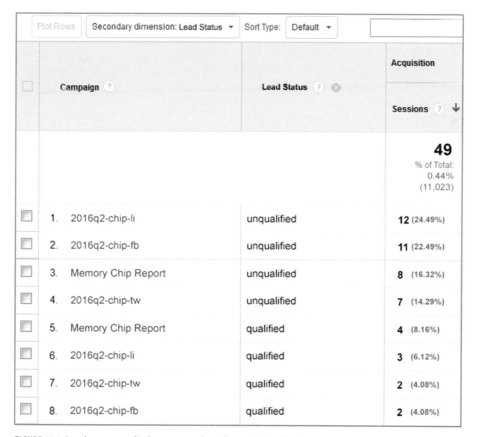

FIGURE 17.6 Lead status applied as a secondary dimension in the Campaigns report.

Importing Content Data into Google Analytics

It was in Chapter 12, "Implementation Customizations," that we first discussed the classic examples of content dimensions that GA can't record without help from you: author and category on blog or article pages. GA has no way to capture this data by default, so we populated the data layer with author and category variables from your content management system (CMS) since they did not already appear on the page, and we recorded author and category as custom dimensions with the pageview hit.

If, for any reason, your developers were not in a position to write that back-end data to the data layer so you could record it as a custom dimension with each hit, you could, instead, perform a data import for author and category against the page.

As mentioned above, GA Standard supports only processing-time imports other than Ecommerce refunds and cost data, so it would be beneficial to import this data as early as possible if you're using GA Standard. (With Analytics 360, you can take advantage of query-time import to add data to hits that have already been processed.)

> ## Note
>
> ### Extended Data Import versus Hit Data Import
>
> Almost all types of GA data import serve to add new dimension values to hits that are being processed. For this reason, the feature was previously called *dimension widening*: you're not creating a new hit but adding dimensions to an existing hit.
>
> The exception is Ecommerce refund data, for which you can perform actual hit data import. Both types of data import are outlined in "About Import Data" within the Google help docs.
>
> As mentioned previously, Extended Data import applies on a go-forward basis only (unless you have Analytics 360, in which case you can take advantage of query-time import to apply to data that has already been captured). Cost data import does apply retroactively in GA Standard or Analytics 360.

The procedure for importing content data is similar to importing user data as seen in the previous CRM example, but instead of matching on a visitor ID custom dimension or user ID, we'll match our content on the Page dimension, or a portion of it.

To perform the author and category import, take the following steps:

1. Create two new custom dimensions, one for author and one for category, with the scope set to Hit as shown in Figure 17.7.

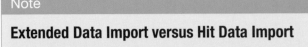

FIGURE 17.7 When you create the Author and Category custom dimensions, specify the scope as Hit.

2. Analyze the CMS key value relative to the GA Page dimension.

Before we create a data set and associated schema in GA, let's consider the CMS export, especially the key, and how the key is represented in the page URL.

Your CMS is essentially a database that injects content into the page. Each page on your website exists as a record in your CMS. When a Web visitor requests a page on your website, the CMS (1) reads the page key from the URL, (2) pulls the corresponding fields from the CMS into a page template, and (3) sends the resulting HTML for the page to the requesting browser.

As a simple example, let's say that three URLs in the news section of your meteorology website appear in the following format:

```
/news/article.php?articleId=3293
/news/article.php?articleId-4588
/news/article.php?articleId=5214
```

The corresponding row in your CMS might be structured as in Table 17.1, with the `articleId` parameter in the URL serving as the unique key in the CMS.

TABLE 17.1 Sample Content Management System (CMS) Records

Article ID	Title	Meta Description	Main Content	Author	Category
3293	Winter Outlook 2017	Long-range forecast for winter 2017	It appears that winter in the northern hemisphere …	Andrew Cullen	Forecasts
4588	Worldwide Water Update	Comprehensive water study	As we analyze hydrological data from around the world …	Stacy Hamida	Hydrology
5214	Typhoon Watch	Latest tracking for Pacific cyclones	This typhoon season in the Pacific is proving to be very active …	Andrew Cullen	Cyclones

3. Define the data set and associated schema in GA.
   A. In the Property column of the Admin screen, click Data Import.
   B. For Data set type, select Content Data.
   C. Select one or more views to import the data into.
   D. For Key, select Page. In many cases, the key in the imported data set will correspond only to a portion of the Page value rather the full Page value as detailed in Table 17.2.

E. Under Imported Data, set the newly defined Author and Category custom dimensions as the import targets. In this case, *Author* and *Category* were the fourth and fifth custom dimensions that you defined in the property, so you'll specify `ga:dimension4` and `ga:dimension5` in the header row of the `.csv` import file.

F. Keep the overwrite option set to No unless you're performing an additional import and any previous author or category values that may have changed in the interim.

TABLE 17.2 Key Refinements for Page Dimension

Page dimension in GA	`/news/article.php?articleId=5214`
Key in CMS	`5214`
Refinement	`query refinement: articleId`
Page dimension in GA	`/news/typhoon`
Key in CMS	`typhoon`
Refinement	`regex refinement: \/news\/([^\/]+)`

Since the key values previously listed in Table 17.1 correspond only with the value of the `articleId` query parameter in the Page dimension, we can specify `articleId` as the query refinement. This refinement applies only when your CMS key appears as the value in a *name=value* pair. The key in the data set configured in Figure 17.8 uses a query refinement on `articleId`.

If, instead, your CMS records were identified with a text key such as `typhoon`, and that text was incorporated into the Page value but not with the *name=value* format, you could instead use regex refinement to isolate the key within the URL pattern. In the regex refinement example in Table 17.2, `\/news\/` identifies the static pattern of Page value, and `([^\/]+)` represents the dynamic portion of the Page value that corresponds to the CMS key.

You could also use a regex refinement to match a single CMS key to multiple page variations, such as `/news/article.php?articleId=5214` and `/news/article.php?articleId=5214&sessionId=12374`, but, ideally, you should instead make every effort to consolidate your Page values by using the Exclude URL Query Parameters view setting as discussed in Chapter 9, "View Settings, View Filters, and Access Rights."

4. Export the article ID, author, and category columns from your CMS, and add a header row to match the schema.

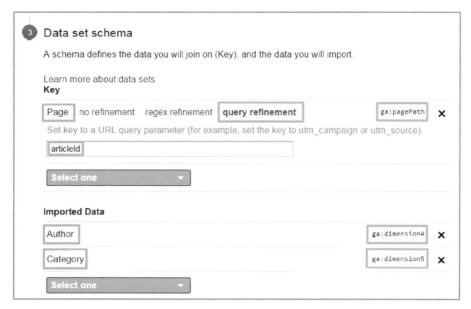

FIGURE 17.8 In the schema for the CMS data import, a query refinement is applied to match only the *articleId* value in the Page dimension.

> **LISTING 17.2:** Sample rows for the three columns that you've exported from your CMS and to which you've added a header row to match the data set schema that you've defined in GA.

```
ga:pagePath,ga:dimension4,ga:dimension5
3293,Andrew Cullen,forecasts
4588,Stacy Hamida,hydrology
5214,Andrew Cullen,cyclones
```

5. Upload the `.csv` file shown in Listing 17.2 as in the lead status example above.

This data import populates author and category just as if we were recording custom dimensions with each pageview on the meteorology website, and we can now create a custom report to display performance by author and category.

Importing Campaign Data into Google Analytics

In Chapter 7, "Acquisition Reports," we discussed the extreme importance of using the `utm_medium`, `utm_source`, and `utm_campaign` URL parameters to more accurately record our traffic sources and to populate the campaigns report with accurate, structured campaign data as in Listing 17.3.

LISTING 17.3: URL containing campaign parameters.

```
http://www.mysite.com/?utm_source=main-list&utm_medium
    =email&utm_campaign=20150501-newsletter
```

There is, however, another option for populating campaign parameters into GA: you can pass a single `utm_id` parameter in the URL, as shown in Listing 17.4, and then import the campaign parameters—and custom dimensions as an option—against this ID as the key, as shown in Listing 17.4.

LISTING 17.4: URL containing a single utm_id parameter.

```
http://www.mysite.com/?utm_id=198
```

Why might you use the simplified campaign parameter format in Listing 17.4? For one thing, it can be a bit compromising to explicitly display campaign parameters for your website visitors to plainly see. In most instances, direct indications of marketing descriptions can only be a distraction from the user and brand experience that you aim to provide. In other cases, you might be dealing with advertising platforms that allow a single campaign ID only.

To import campaign data:

1. Create a new data set and select Campaign Data as the Data set type.
2. Define the schema as in Figure 17.9. Note that we have created a Campaign Group custom dimension, which you can use (in a custom report or segment, or as a secondary dimension) to distinguish between product campaigns and informational resource campaigns. Also, as mentioned in Chapter 7, campaign name is not actually mandatory for campaign tracking, but it's always recommended as best practice.
3. Populate a `.csv` file as in Table 17.3.
4. Import the `.csv` file as in the lead status and author/category examples earlier in the chapter.

Importing Cost Data into Google Analytics

By linking your Google AdWords and GA and enabling AdWords auto-tagging as described in Chapter 14, "Google Analytics Integrations—The Power of Together," you can view AdWords cost data within GA. While GA does not offer direct integrations with other paid advertising, you can manually import cost data from other platforms such as Bing or Facebook.

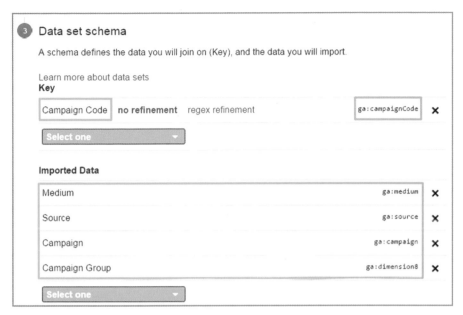

FIGURE 17.9 With utm_id populated as the ga:campaignCode key dimension, you can import campaign medium, source, and name, and also custom dimensions such as campaign group.

TABLE 17.3 Representation of the Key, Campaign Parameters, and a Custom Dimension to Match the Schema in Figure 17.9

ga:campaignCode	ga:medium	ga:source	ga:campaign	ga:dimension8
198	email	asia-list	20160701-newsletter	info-resource
199	qa-code	catalog	20160705-spring-discount-code-qa	product
200	email	europe-list	20160708-newsletter	info-resource
201	social	facebook	20160709-spring-discount-code-fb	product
202	social	linkedin	20160710-spring-discount-code-li	product

Importing cost data is fairly similar to the data imports we reviewed previously in this chapter, but a few special considerations are detailed in the following procedure.

1. Create a new data set and select Cost Data as the Data set type.
2. Define the schema as in Figure 17.10.

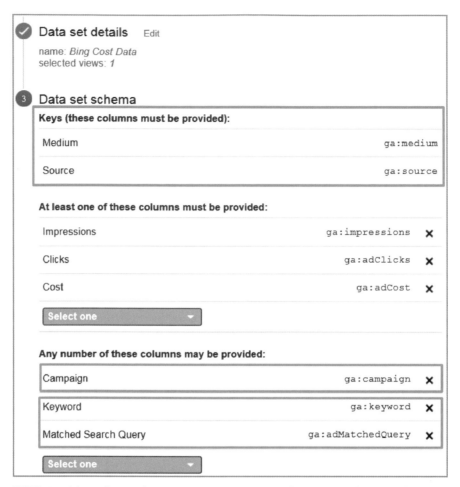

FIGURE 17.10 Schema for cost data import. Campaign is among the nonrequired import values, but for many cost data imports, it will serve as the *de facto* key.

- Note the key is automatically defined as the combination of medium and source dimensions. In most cases, however, campaign will serve as a more specific *de facto* key as described in the figure caption.
- You must import one of the following three metrics: impressions, clicks, and cost. In many cases, such as Bing Ads, it makes sense to import all three. You can use this schema, however, even if the data you're importing does not contain all three values.

3. Export a `.csv` file from the ad platform as shown for Bing in Figure 17.11.
   - Although the date does not appear in the schema, you'll need to make sure that `ga:date` appears as the first column in the .csv before import. Each date must appear in YYYYMMDD format.
   - You can manually add the `ga:medium` and `ga:source` columns to the export, with respective values `cpc` and `bing` for each row.

- The Search Term column in the AdWords export corresponds to the Matched Search Query dimension in GA.

4. Import the `.csv` file as in the previous examples.

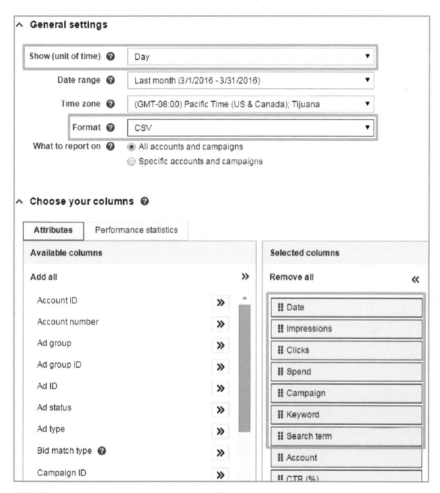

FIGURE 17.11 Campaign cost data export from Bing Ads.

Campaign as *De Facto* Key for Cost Data Import

Since best practice has already dictated that you include the `utm_campaign` parameter in your inbound links (or that you import `ga:campaign` against a single `utm_id` value as described in the campaign data import above), you'll want to be sure that the imported campaign values exactly match the campaign values that you've already recorded with each campaign clickthrough. In this way, campaign serves as the key more than just medium and source, which are the default but are not sufficiently specific in most cases.

Comparing Campaign Cost and Performance

Once you import campaign cost data, you'll be able to access the Campaigns > Cost Analysis report, as shown in Figure 17.12.

Campaign ?	Source / Medium ?	Sessions ↓	Cost	Cost per Conversion
1. dining room sale	bing / cpc	20,769 (21.50%)	$2,998.64 (37.86%)	$0.40 (140.21%)
2. carpet liquidation	bing / cpc	7,065 (7.32%)	$1,067.48 (13.38%)	$0.65 (233.20%)
3. upholstered chairs	bing / cpc	5,160 (5.34%)	$748.18 (9.38%)	$0.54 (195.22%)
4. no-stain guarantee	facebook / social-paid	3,804 (3.94%)	$501.00 (6.28%)	$0.42 (145.09%)
5. bamboo coffee table	bing / cpc	2,589 (2.68%)	$412.00 (5.17%)	$0.64 (229.92%)

FIGURE 17.12 Cost Analysis report for imported paid campaign cost data.

Notice, however, two types of data that the Cost Analysis report does not include:

- Postclick performance data, such as bounces and conversions, does not appear.
- While AdWords campaign data does also appear in the general All Campaigns report, AdWords cost data does not appear in the Cost Analysis report.

To incorporate cost and performance data for AdWords and non-AdWords campaigns into a single report, we can easily configure a custom report as shown in Figure 17.13.

Note

Automated Cost Data Import

To automate cost data import from Facebook and Bing or custom data import from other sources, you can use `analyze.ly` (as a paid solution).

Importing Product Data into Google Analytics

Product data import is quite straightforward and allows you to add or overwrite many Ecommerce and Enhanced Ecommerce dimensions, as well as the price metric, using product SKU as the key.

Product SKU or name is, in fact, the only product detail that you are required to provide when you're coding your actual Enhanced Ecommerce interactions on your website; you could potentially provide SKU only at transaction time and match to imported Ecommerce dimensions.

In addition to the dedicated Ecommerce dimensions, you can import custom dimensions—such as size, color, warranty level, or any other product or service

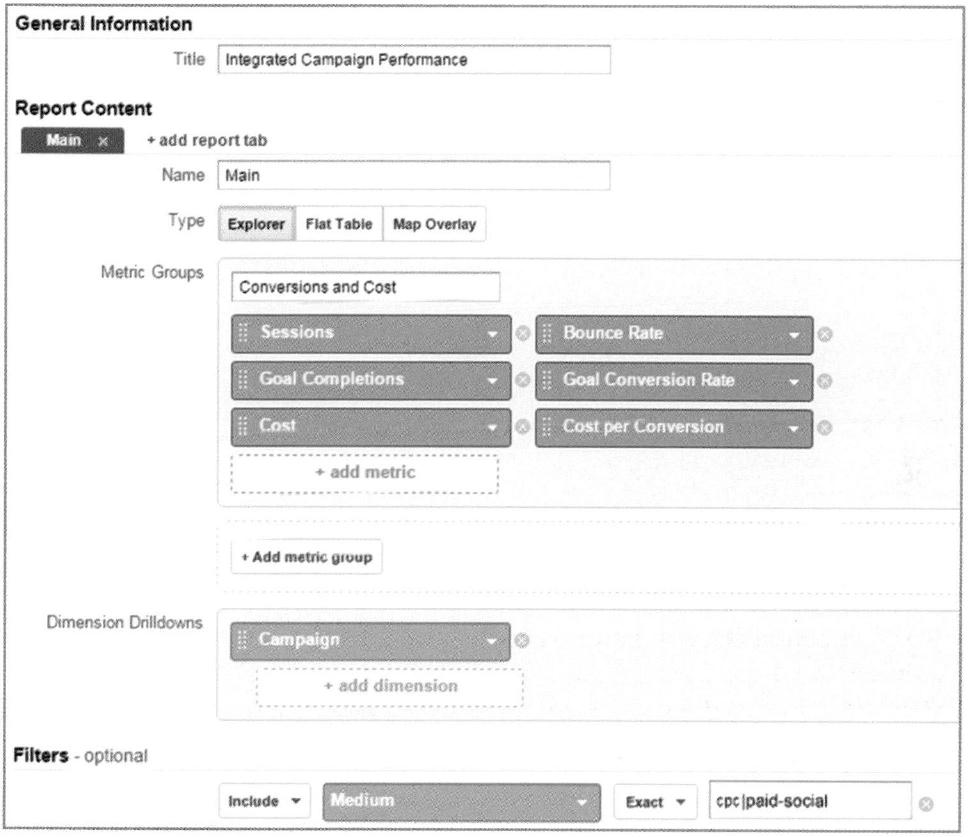

FIGURE 17.13 This custom report configuration integrates performance and cost data for AdWords and non-AdWords campaigns.

descriptor—per SKU, as the custom report in Figure 17.14 illustrates. Keep in mind that you could also populate any of these built-in or custom dimensions while the user is interacting with your Web pages or mobile app; the product data import is a different option for associating this extra data with each SKU.

	Product ⑦	Color ⑦	Transactions ↓	Product Revenue
1.	sweatshirt	grey	1,024 (0.49%)	$20,469.75
2.	sweatshirt	blue	989 (0.47%)	$19,770.11
3.	ski hat	red	801 (0.38%)	$10,404.99
4.	scarf	blue	750 (0.34%)	$7,492.95
5.	ski hat	blue	699 (0.30%)	$9,080.08

FIGURE 17.14 This custom report breaks down performance by the built-in Product dimension and the imported Color dimension.

Importing Geo Data into Google Analytics

In addition to the geographic hierarchy GA offers by default, you can create your own geographic divisions by importing against city, region (which usually corresponds to province or state), country, or subcontinent.

For instance, you could create a custom dimension named US Regional and import a value such as Northeast, Southeast, and so on against the built-in Region ID dimension value for each U.S. state and then report performance by these imported dimension values, as in Figure 17.15.

	US Regional ?	Sessions ? ↓	Bounce Rate ?	Lead Submit (Goal 1 Completions) ?
		7,197 % of Total: 100.00% (7,197)	**53.86%** Avg for View: 53.86% (0.00%)	**898** % of Total: 100.00% (898)
☐	1. Mountain	**2,579** (35.83%)	56.57%	273 (30.40%)
☐	2. West Coast	**2,193** (30.47%)	51.76%	302 (33.63%)
☐	3. Midwest	**2,084** (28.96%)	50.77%	300 (33.41%)
☐	4. Southeast	**189** (2.63%)	58.73%	11 (1.22%)
☐	5. Northeast	**127** (1.76%)	74.02%	6 (0.67%)

FIGURE 17.15 Custom report showing goal conversion by imported US Regional custom dimension.

MEASUREMENT PROTOCOL

When Google Universal Analytics was first released and began to be adopted, we as GA users observed that most of GAs functionality remained the same. There were a few additional admin settings, and the syntax for native tracking had changed to a simpler format, but not too much else had changed in terms day-to-day reporting.

Several of the new capabilities are what makes Universal universal: cross-device tracking, custom metrics and additional custom dimensions, and, perhaps more than any other feature, the MP. The MP is arguably the most universal part of Universal Analytics in that it allows you to send Hypertext Transfer Protocol (HTTP) requests from any programmed, networked device or environment to record data into GA.

Measurement Protocol is a much more specialized usage of GA, but it's important to know that this option exists. Scenarios for MP usage include mobile apps designed for Windows, Blackberry, or other mobile operating systems for which GA SDKs are not available. In the following sections, Hazem Mahsoub provides key insights on MP, and Matt Stannard walks us through two innovative and outcomes-focused examples of the MP in action.

Hazem Mahsoub

Hazem Mahsoub is an Analytics Solutions Engineer at E-Nor.

Measurement Protocol is not a different technology to send hits to GA servers. It's more like the underlying low-level language used by analytics. js, as well as SDKs for Android and iOS, to communicate with GA servers.
 You would use MP most typically in the two following cases:

➤ In case your platform can't run JavaScript, Android, or iOS. A device running Windows Mobile or a point-of-sale device would be good examples for using MP.

➤ In case you need to send hits server-to-server. A good example for this is when the web application is integrated with another system through an API. That is, this integration happens server-to-server and there's no browser involved. However, we would like GA to track when this API is called and send the relevant information to GA. Using MP, a hit can be sent by the web application with the necessary data.

Developers should remember this: analytics.js and the mobile SDKs provide a more user-friendly interface to configure the hits and automate a lot of work behind the scenes, to make the practitioner's or developer's life easier. Using MP, the developer has to write code to do all of the automated work.

When sending hits from a web server to the GA server, GA automatically assumes the server IP as the client IP. Luckily, MP provides several parameters to override the values automatically detected by the GA server. It's very important to write code that reads the user's IP, and user agent, and resend them using the proper parameters. Otherwise, all hits will appear to be coming from the server IP and no OS, browser or device information will appear in the reports. Geographic information, as well as carrier/ISP, is derived from the IP. Sending the server IP, instead of the client's IP, will corrupt this data in the reports.

In some cases, the tracking solution will rely in part on analytics.js, running on the client's browser, and in part on MP to send hits from the server. It differs from case to case, but if it is desired for a hit sent from the server to be included in the same session the user has started on the Web, code must be written to read the client ID from the cookie and send it with the hits sent from the server. The same may apply to the user ID, which may be available from the server app and not the client.

The "Google Analytics Measurement Protocol Overview" documentation (https:// developers.google.com/analytics/devguides/collection/protocol/ v1/?hl=en) lists the mandatory parameters for each hit type. However, it's best practice to include more information than that. For example, in the Top Events report, it's very common to add the page as a secondary dimension. This won't be possible if the developer forgot to include page information with the event hit. GA won't reject the hit since it has all the mandatory parameters. However, the missing information will hinder meaningful reports.

Measurement Protocol: Two Case Studies

Matt Stannard

Matt Stannard is CTO of 4Ps Marketing.

Offline Tracking Using the Measurement Protocol

The problem for the CEO of a storage facility—let's say that its name is Space Manager—was the lack of visibility of the quoting and booking process. While he could see the number of quotes and booking inquiries, he could not easily see how these converted, nor whether the facilities followed up on them: while the initial leads are generated online, the follow-up and conversion happen offline.

One of the most exciting features of Universal Analytics is the ability to track interactions that happen offline. This is particularly helpful where a website serves as a lead generation tool, with the conversion happening offline.

In this example, the GA Measurement Protocol was used to track offline conversions for the Storage Facility, providing the CEO with insight and visibility into the true user journey.

Overview

The diagram in Figure 17.16 shows the process of a potential customer's interactions with the Storage Facility. The initial interactions all happen onsite through the point of quote and booking inquiry, after which the customer interactions switch to offline.

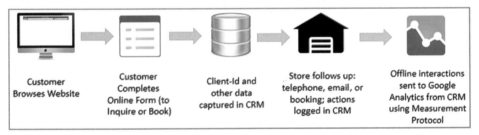

| Customer Browses Website | Customer Completes Online Form (to Inquire or Book) | Client-Id and other data captured in CRM | Store follows up: telephone, email, or booking; actions logged in CRM | Offline interactions sent to Google Analytics from CRM using Measurement Protocol |

FIGURE 17.16 User journey, including online and offline interactions.

As discussed in Chapter 15, "Integrating Google Analytics with CRM Data," GA you can record a unique but anonymous visitor identifier as a custom dimension in GA that corresponds with the same visitor identifier in your CRM. For the Storage Facility, the client ID (read from the _ga) is suitable to store as a visitor identifier, as outlined in the following steps:

1. When a user submits a storage quote, we're recording the client ID in GA as a custom dimension. We're also recording the location of the storage facility, storage size, and storage duration as additional GA custom dimensions.
2. When the storage quote form is submitted, we're including that same client ID as a hidden form field to be stored as a custom field in Space Manager's CRM with the customer record, along with the customer details (but without PII).
3. We configured the CRM as in Figure 17.17 so that whenever a member of staff within the Storage Facility makes a call or sends an email, the CRM sends data to GA using the Measurement Protocol. The client ID stored in the CRM (in the previous step) is now sent as part of the M request, as is the custom dimension for the storage facility location.

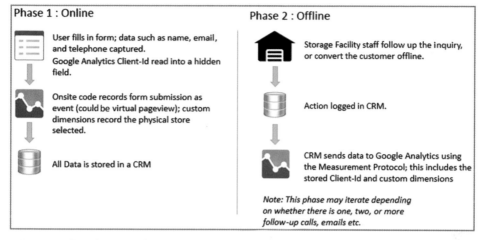

Phase 1 : Online

User fills in form; data such as name, email, and telephone captured.
Google Analytics Client-Id read into a hidden field.

Onsite code records form submission as event (could be virtual pageview); custom dimensions record the physical store selected.

All Data is stored in a CRM

Phase 2 : Offline

Storage Facility staff follow up the inquiry, or convert the customer offline.

Action logged in CRM.

CRM sends data to Google Analytics using the Measurement Protocol; this includes the stored Client-Id and custom dimensions

Note: This phase may iterate depending on whether there is one, two, or more follow-up calls, emails etc.

FIGURE 17.17 The online and offline process.

4. When a customer visits the storage facility to check in, staff at the facility record this completed transaction in the CRM, which again triggers the CRM to record a hit—including the client ID and storage location—in GA through the MP.

Invoking Measurement Protocol Requests from the Space Manager's CRM

As our CRM now included the client ID, we were able to use the Measurement Protocol to track interactions. The CRM allowed for custom scripts to be created and attached to be triggered when specific events occurred such as call, email, visit, or booking. The scripting language was XML based and allowed for a HTTP POST to be created; this could read data from the CRM to construct the necessary MP Hit and trigger a pageview in GA. Although we used pageviews, events could also be used.

> **LISTING 17.5:** XML-based script that we configured in the CRM to construct the Measurement Protocol request when storage facility staff records an offline transaction in the CRM.

```
<Job xml:space="preserve" breakpoint="No">
  <Message text="(V31032014) - Google Analytics - Contact Event,
Please Wait..."/>
  <Parameters>
    <Parameter name="ContactEventID"/>
    <Parameter name="ClassCode"/>
    <Parameter name="CustomerID"/>
    <Parameter name="ContractID"/>
  </Parameters>
  <SQLQuery xml:space="preserve">
      <SQLSelect>select ClientID, REPLACE(ClassDescrip,' ','%20')
AS ClassDescripNew, REPLACE(Site.SiteName,' ','%20') as TheStore
from Site join Customer join ContactEvent join ContactClass where
contacteventid='{ContactEventID}'</SQLSelect>
```

continues

continued

```
        <IfAnyRows>
          <ForEachRow>
           <HTTPRequest operation="post" url="http://www.google-
analytics.com:80/collect" dumpfolder="c:\temp\t.html">
          <HTTPRequestData><![CDATA[v=1&cm1=1&cd11={ClientID}&cd
3={TheStore}&cid={ClientID}&tid=UA-21639967-4&t=pageview&dp=/
offline/{ClassDescripNew}&dt={ClassDescripNew}&cs=Space%20
Manager&cm=Offline]]></HTTPRequestData>
          </HTTPRequest>
          </ForEachRow>
        </IfAnyRows>
      </SQLQuery>
    </Job>
```

LISTING 17.6: Measurement Protocol request generated from the CRM script shown in Listing 17.5.

```
http://www.google-analytics.com:80/collect?v=1&cm1=1&cd11=5000.12
34&cd3=Cambridge&cid=5000.1234&tid=UA-21639967-4&t=pageview&dp=/
offline/Telephone%20Call&dt=Telephone%20Call&cs=Space%20
Manager&cm=Offline
```

Results

As an offline interaction is sent to GA, we are able to use real-time reporting, dashboards, and the standard GA reports to give visibility to the CEO. We created a dashboard like the one shown in Figure 17.18, which shows the performance filtered by the Storage Facility location (using the custom dimension).

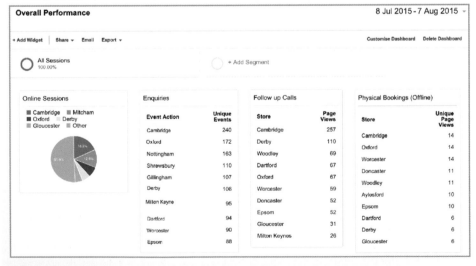

FIGURE 17.18 GA dashboard showing offline activity, including completed storage facility bookings and conversion paths.

The Multi-Channel Funnel reports (Figure 17.19) can then be used to show which online channels were involved in an offline conversion—in this instance, we may choose to weight First Touch interactions.

FIGURE 17.19 Multi-Channel Funnel reports indicate which channels drove traffic that eventually converted offline.

Real-Time Twitter Measurement in GA

Overview

This may sound strange, but Real-Time reporting in GA actually provides a very good way of measuring interactions with Twitter as well as being able to report on Hashtags, Shared URLs, or the Handles that interact the most. In the example below, we use the MP to display live tweet data in GA.

Step 1: Pull from the Twitter Phirehose

The first part is to register as a Twitter Developer and use the excellent 140dev (`http://140dev.com/`) library to connect to the Twitter Phirehose. This allows you to attach a piece of PHP script to mentions of a specific user or hash tag and have them stored in a MySql database.

As well as the configuration files, which tell the library what database to use and contain information about your Twitter credentials, there are two core parts:

➤ `get_tweets.php`: This retrieves tweets and stores them in a local MySql database. In this script you can define what should be tracked, for example a specific hash tag or user. This "caches" tweets for processing later.
➤ `parse_tweets.php`: This reads the stored tweets and extracts information, storing it in the local MySql database.

Step 2: Update Script to Write Tweet Data to GA through the Measurement Protocol

You can amend *parse_tweets.php* to do whatever you like. In this case, we're using the php *file_get_contents* function to read the Twitter data that we send to GA using the MP and an HTTP Get Request.

The code extract in Listing 17.7 shows the *parse_tweets.php* file, which reads a tweet and extracts the twitter username mentioned in a tweet. By adding the highlighted lines we can push data into GA via the MP.

continues

continued

LISTING 17.7: We've revised *parse_tweets.php* to read our Twitter data using the *file_get_contents* function and to record a pageview hit in GA using a Measurement Protocol request.

```
// The mentions, tags, and URLs from the entities object are also
// parsed into separate tables so they can be data mined later
foreach ($entities->user_mentions as $user_mention) {
$where = 'tweet_id=' . $tweet_id . ' ' .
'AND source_user_id=' . $user_id . ' ' .
'AND target_user_id=' . $user_mention->id;
if(! $oDB->in_table('tweet_mentions',$where)) {
$field_values = 'tweet_id=' . $tweet_id . ', ' .
'source_user_id=' . $user_id . ', ' .
'target_user_id=' . $user_mention->id;
$oDB->insert('tweet_mentions',$field_values);
}
$strUA = "http://www.google-analytics.com/collect?v=1&tid=UA-
43297900-1&cid=" . $user_id . "&t=pageview&dp=/mentions/" .
$user_mention->screen_name;
$strData = file_get_contents($strUA);
}
```

The code creates an HTTP Measurement Protocol request for a pageview. The Twitter Username is read from the MySql database (as the `parse_tweets.php` file extracts it) and appended to the `dp` parameter; this will then record a pageview `/mentions/[Twitter Username]` in GA.

You could use a similar approach to record instances of keywords or hashtags.

Step 3: Launch Scripts from the Command Line

As the scripts are PHP, you must invoke them from the Command Prompt (Figure 17.20). Two prompts are needed: one to run the `get_tweets.php` script, and one to run the `parse_tweets.php` script.

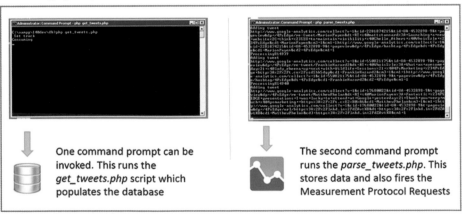

One command prompt can be invoked. This runs the *get_tweets.php* script which populates the database

The second command prompt runs the *parse_tweets.php*. This stores data and also fires the Measurement Protocol Requests

FIGURE 17.20 Running the PHP scripts from the command prompt.

Once these two scripts are running, you should then be able to see tweets (containing the Twitter handle or hashtag you used in `parse_tweets.php`) appearing in Real-Time Analytics as pageviews, as shown in Figure 17.21.

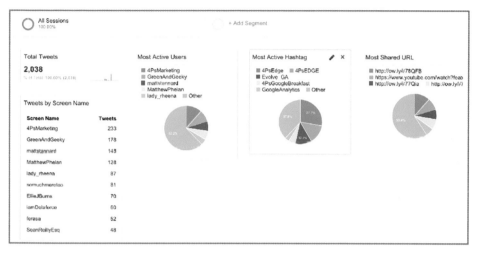

FIGURE 17.21   Real-time tweet reporting in Google Analytics.

Next Steps

The concept of measuring Twitter could be further expanded. If you stored a user's screen name in a CRM, you could in theory look up Twitter activity by either a client ID or user ID also stored in a CRM and GA and then pass the Twitter data to GA to track pre- or post-sale Twitter interactions.

One use case of this could be competition where a user has to tweet a certain hash tag to receive a voucher which they then redeem. Ideally, our customer record in the CRM would store both my email and Twitter handle:

ID (User-Id): 123456
Name: Matt Stannard
Email: `matt.stannard@4psmarketing.com`
Twitter: mattstannard

When I tweet with the `#competition` hash tag, my User ID is retrieved from the CRM and a Measurement Protocol request is sent to GA with my User ID of 123456. If I then go onsite and purchase, when I login with my email address `matt.stannard@4psmarketing.com`, then the same User ID 123456 can be retrieved and captured by the onsite GA code as shown in Figure 17.22.

continues

continued

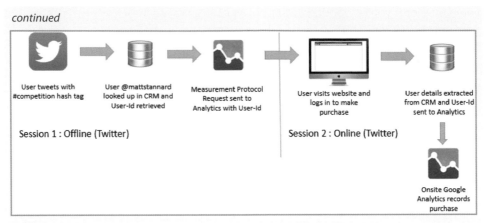

User tweets with   User @mattstannard   Measurement Protocol   User visits website and   User details extracted
#competition hash tag   looked up in CRM and   Request sent to   logs in to make   from CRM and User-Id
                                User-Id retrieved   Analytics with User-Id   purchase   sent to Analytics

Session 1 : Offline (Twitter)   Session 2 : Online (Twitter)

Onsite Google
Analytics records
purchase

FIGURE 17.22 Twitter integration.

This allows us to measure the impact of Twitter competitions or other offsite activity and again I can see whether certain campaigns drive pre- or postsale interactions.

 **KEY TAKEAWAYS**

Data import is based on keys and targets.   You import based on a common key in GA and the uploaded `.csv`, and populate dimensions and metrics in GA based on the key match.

Import custom dimensions (and metrics).   In addition to importing built-in dimensions (such as product category), you can import custom dimensions (such as product size or article author). The import of custom dimensions was formerly referred to as *dimension widening*, since the process adds dimensions to user, hit, and product data that has already been recorded.

Data import retroactivity. If you're using Analytics 360, you have the option of query-time import for retroactivity. In GA Standard, data import is performed at processing time, that is, on a go-forward basis only. Cost-data import does apply retroactively, even in GA Standard.

Key refinements for content imports.   The Page dimension usually serves as the key for content imports, but in many cases, the key value in the `.csv` file matches only a portion of the Page dimension value. In this case, you can apply a regex or query refinement to extract only a part of the Page value as a match against the key value in the import file.

Import campaign parameters based on campaign ID. If you prefer not to display the `utm_medium`, `utm_source`, and `utm_campaign` parameters directly in your URLs, or if you're working with an advertising platform that allows only a single parameter, you could add a single, discreet `utm_id` parameter, which will populate the `ga:campaignCode` dimension that you can use as a key for importing medium, source, and campaign.

Import cost data from advertising channels.   You can import cost data from other advertising channels such as Bing or Facebook and compare metrics such as cost per conversion or Ecommerce transaction for each of the channels, and for AdWords, whose cost data you can import instead using the autotagging automation without any manual importing.

While the combination of metric and source values serve as the key in the schema for cost data import, the campaign value acts as the *de facto* key in many cases, so you must ensure that any campaign value that you're importing from the .csv exactly matches a campaign value that you've already populated in GA.

Measurement Protocol.   You can use the Measurement Protocol to send data through HTTP requests from an environment where the GA tracking code or SDKs cannot run, such as a Windows or Android app or a kiosk.

 ## ACTIONS AND EXERCISES

1. **Review the data import scenarios in this chapter.** Make a plan for any of the imports that would help your analysis. Because it's immediately relevant for many people working with GA, cost data import may be the first import to perform.

2. **Review the custom dimensions that you identified in Chapter 12, "Implementation Customizations."** Some of the custom dimensions that you might need (such as author and category) may be easier for you to populate into GA through an import rather than going through your development team to populate data layer variables that you read into a GA tag in Google Tag Manager. If the import would, in fact, offer a simpler and faster option, even in just the near term, plan accordingly.

Analytics 360

Google is a unique company and does things in a unique and often revolutionary way. In 2005, when Google purchased a relatively unknown company called Urchin, rebranded the product to Google Analytics (GA), and offered it for free, what used to belong to the elite was made available to all. Fast-forward to today and millions of sites and apps—start-ups, the Fortune 500, and the entire spectrum of businesses and organizations—are running GA.

Following the wide adoption of the free tool, Google made a strategic decision to enter the enterprise Web and mobile analytics market and offer an enterprise edition of GA. Google Analytics Premium was thus born in 2011. In March 2016, the product was rebranded to Analytics 360, one of six integrated products of the Google Analytics 360 Suite.

WHY ANALYTICS 360?

Although GA Standard (the non-paid version of GA) is feature-rich and has powerful capabilities, it does, expectedly, have some limitations. For instance, according to the published GA's Terms of Service, GA Standard is offered at no charge for up to *10 million hits per month per account,* and "Google may change its fees and payment policies for the Service from time to time including the addition of costs for geographic data, the importing of cost data from search engines, or other fees charged to Google or its wholly owned subsidiaries by third-party vendors for the inclusion of data in the Service reports. The changes to the fees or payment policies are effective upon your acceptance of those changes, which will be posted at www.google.com/analytics."

Historically, Google been very generous in allowing GA Standard accounts to exceed the 10 million hits per month. But organizations shouldn't take this leniency for granted but should instead assess their measurement and data needs and decide if it's time to upgrade to Analytics 360.

Google has made it easy for you to monitor how many hits you are sending to their servers and how close you are (or over) the 10 million hits. Go to Admin > Property Settings and you'll find a section called "Property Hit Volume" that lists your hits for yesterday, last 7 days, and last 30 days. If your organization has multiple properties, you'll want to add up all the hits from all the properties since the 10 million hit limit is calculated on a per-account basis and not on a per-property basis.

For additional details on hit volume, you can refer to 'Hit Count in Google Analytics' (`https://www.e-nor.com/blog/google-analytics/hit-count-in-google-analytics`) by our colleague Tracy Rabold.

In the next few sections, we cover the main three benefits of acquiring Analytics 360, namely:

- Increased capacity
- Service-level agreements
- Analytics 360-only capabilities

INCREASED CAPACITY

Large organizations as well as any organization with a high volume of data might find the GA Standard thresholds limiting and prevent them from seeing a full picture of the user journey. With Analytics 360 these thresholds are vastly expanded: we've seen some of the most aggressive data-collection and reporting requirements met by Analytics 360.

10 Times More Custom Dimensions and Custom Metrics

With Analytics 360 you have access to 200 custom dimensions and 200 custom metrics, while GA Standard accounts have 20 custom dimensions and 20 custom metrics. 200 dimensions and 200 metrics might seem like a lot of custom fields, but the customizations required for enterprise-level analysis, data context, and data mining can easily exceed the limit of 20 custom dimensions and metrics available in GA Standard.

12 Times Fresher Data

With GA Standard, it might take up to 24 hours or longer to see your data in the reports, nor will sites or apps with high hit volumes (tens of millions of hits/month) get intraday updates. For many businesses, including media, publishers, and Ecommerce retailers, this is not fresh enough. Analytics 360 solves this issue by offering a four-hour guarantee.

Increased Data Limits

Depending on your site or app hit volume and the type of report you're looking at, in GA Standard, sampling can render the data unreliable (and at times unusable). Analytics 360 solves this issue by providing its users with the entire dataset.

As discussed in Chapter 10 data, sampling occurs in GA Standard when:

- The reporting time period includes 500,000 sessions or more.
- A segment or secondary dimension is applied or a custom report is accessed.

Analytics 360 offers the following advantages for accessing unsampled data.

Unsampled Export

If you do run a report and it returns sampled data, you have the option to export the report as comma- or tab-separated values. By accessing the menu option shown in Figure 18.1, you can perform an unsampled export one time only, or set up a recurring email for daily, weekly, monthly, or quarterly distribution.

FIGURE 18.1 Analytics 360 allows you to export an Unsampled version of the report.

Scheduled exports will be accessible under Customization > Unsampled Reports, as shown in Figure 18.2, as will once-only exports, approximately one hour after you configure them.

Recent Reports

	Title	Date Created ↓	Date Range	Status	Download	
1.	Source/Medium by Country	Apr 17, 2016	Apr 10, 2016 - Apr 16, 2016	Completed	CSV	Actions ▾
2.	Device Categories - South Korea Segment	Apr 15, 2016	Apr 8, 2016 - Apr 14, 2016	Completed	CSV	Actions ▾
3.	Custom Report - Partner Performance	Apr 10, 2016	Apr 3, 2016 - Apr 9, 2016	Completed	CSV	Actions ▾

FIGURE 18.2 Scheduled and once-only exports appear under Customization > Unsampled Exports.

Higher Sampling Threshold in the User Interface

Instead of the 500,000-session threshold for GA Standard, Analytics 360 reports sampled data only if the date range includes 50 million sessions or more.

Higher Row Count in Export

If you see "(other)" in your Standard reports, say in your Site Content > All Pages report, then you're exceeding the daily maximum allowable rows. Data for all these rows is aggregated into on row called "other." In GA Standard, the maximum allowable row limit in the User Interface is 50,000, and in Analytics 360 it's 75,000. With Analytics 360 you have access to 3 million rows via the unsampled report export. Google continues to improve the Analytics 360 product; for the latest on increased thresholds, see "Unsampled Reports" in the GA help docs:

```
https://support.google.com/analytics/answer/
2601061?hl=en&ref_topic=2601030&vid=1-
635783051712655749-3523100256
```

Custom Tables

If you find yourself frequently reporting on a set of metrics and dimensions with various filters and segments that cause sampling, you can leverage an Analytics 360 capability called Custom Tables to request a daily unsampled process of this combination.

The GA help pages provide the following description of Custom Tables:

With Custom Tables, you specify a combination of metrics, dimensions, segments, and filters that you want Analytics to process unsampled on a daily basis. Any report that matches a subset of the configuration of your Custom Table will then access that table by default, giving you fast, unsampled data.

https://support.google.com/analytics/answer/2774517

This means that if a custom report, a standard report with a secondary dimension applied, or a standard report with a segment applied falls within the definition of the custom table, you can access that report unsampled, as illustrated in Figure 18.3. In this way, Custom Tables are an extremely convenient time saver.

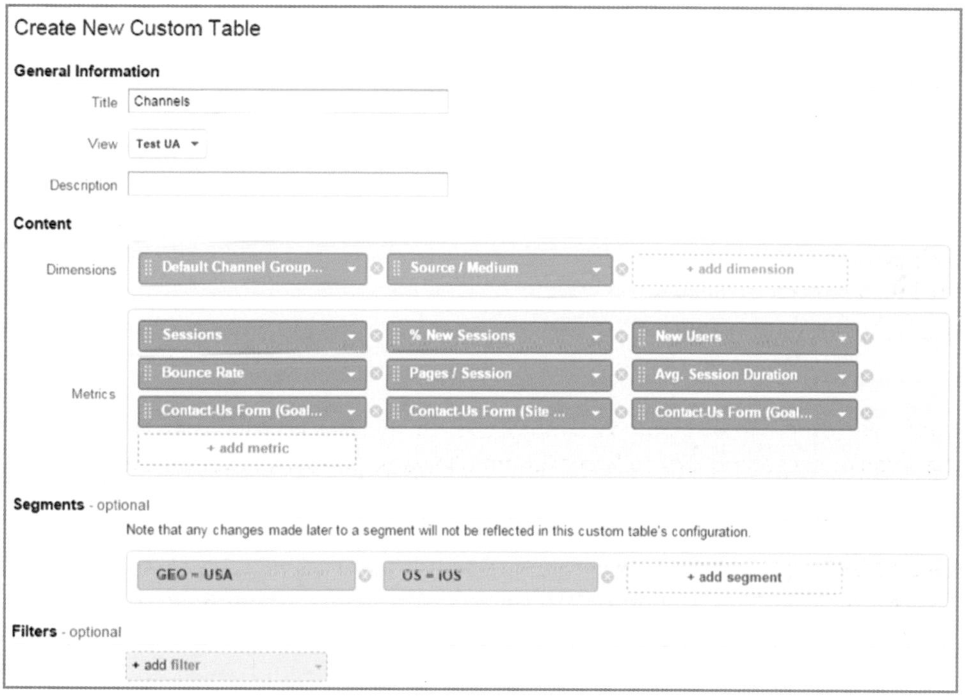

Create New Custom Table

General Information

Title	Channels
View	Test UA
Description	

Content

Dimensions: Default Channel Group... | Source / Medium | + add dimension

Metrics: Sessions | % New Sessions | New Users
Bounce Rate | Pages / Session | Avg. Session Duration
Contact-Us Form (Goal... | Contact-Us Form (Site ... | Contact-Us Form (Goal...
+ add metric

Segments - optional

Note that any changes made later to a segment will not be reflected in this custom table's configuration.

GEO – USA | OS = iOS | + add segment

Filters - optional

+ add filter

FIGURE 18.3   With this Custom Table in place, you'll be able to apply Source/Medium as a secondary dimension or add either segment, or access a Custom Table that contains a subset of the Custom Table configuration, all without sampling.

Note that it could take up to two days for the unsampled data to appear after you requested a custom table, and you'll have access to data 30 days prior to the date of the creation of the Custom Table. Also, reports such as Flow Visualization, Search Engine Optimization, Multi-Channel Funnels (MCFs), and Attribution are not available in Custom Tables.

SERVICE-LEVEL AGREEMENTS (SLAS)

While you are more or less on your own for GA Standard, Analytics 360 provides Service Level Agreements (SLAs), guarantees, and support, as you would expect when investing in an enterprise-level software.

Data-Collection SLA   Analytics 360 guarantees at least 99.9% data collection, calculated on a calendar-month basis.

Reporting SLA   The Analytics 360 reporting interface is available for at least 99% of the time, calculated on a calendar-month basis.

Data Processing/Freshness SLA   For properties and roll-up properties that receive two billion or fewer hits per month, Analytics 360 processes collected data 98% of the time within four hours of receipt. For properties and roll-up properties that receive more than two billion hits per month, the service processes collected customer data 98% of the time within 24 hours of midnight (Pacific Time). In each case, the calculations are done on a calendar-month basis.

Tag Management Container Delivery SLA   Tag containers will be served 99.99% of the time to properties enabled under Analytics 360, calculated on a calendar-month basis.

Tag Management Configuration SLA   Tag container configuration interface provided as part of the Google Tag Manager is available 99% of the time, calculated on a calendar-month basis.

Support, Escalation, and Terms

In addition to the SLAs, Analytics 360 contracts include a customer support and issue escalation mechanism. From time to time, these terms are updated by Google; check with your Analytics 360 contact or your Analytics 360 reseller for the latest SLA terms and ensure the support terms meet your analytics and reporting needs.

Custom Funnels

GA Standard has offered goal funnels since its introduction. While these funnels are useful, they do require you to proactively think of your funnel steps ahead of time, since funnel data will be displayed only from the date of the funnel creation; the Funnel Visualization for goals does not populate retroactively. In Analytics 360, custom funnels, as illustrated in Figure 18.4, allow for on-the-fly pathing and funnel creation that is somewhat comparable to the on-the-fly custom segment creation examined in Chapter 10.

Custom Funnel configuration is accessible through Customization > New Custom Report.

Five Stages   You can define up to five stages in any funnel.

Pageviews or Events   Each stage consists of one or more filters based usually on a page or an event, but you can also filter on other dimensions (e.g., traffic source).

The option to create a stage based on an event is particularly helpful, as GA Standard allows you to define funnel steps for physical or virtual pageviews only, not for events.

Single or Multiple Sessions   You have the option to restrict the Custom Funnel to a single session or allow the stages to span multiple sessions. The multiple-session option is extremely useful for transcending session scope and achieving user-centric analysis to a much greater degree (also similarly to user-scope custom segments).

Entry   You can allow entry into the Funnel at any of the five stages or only record entries at the first stage.

Sequence   You can configure the Custom Funnel to record stages only completed in direct succession, or you can allow interceding stages.

Remarketing Audiences   As can be seen in Figure 18.5, you can configure any drop-off or continuation point in a Custom Funnel as an audience for remarketing and RLSA (for AdWords or DoubleClick) as described in Chapter 14.

Retroactive   Unlike traditional GA goal funnels, Custom Funnels are retroactive.

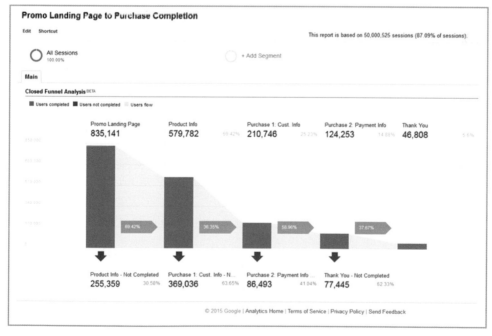

FIGURE 18.4 The Custom Funnel report displays continuation and drop-off between the stages that you define.

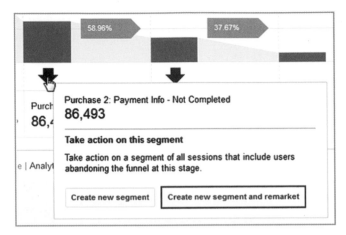

FIGURE 18.5 You can define a remarketing audience based on any continuation or drop-off point.

BigQuery Export

For marketers and Business Intelligence (BI) professionals who are not afraid of deep dives and data mining, granular hit-level data can be exported out Analytics 360 and directly into BigQuery. BigQuery is Google's Big Data analytics platform, and a component of Google Cloud Platform (GCP). It's a fully managed, no-infrastructure, pay-as-you-go platform (see more details on BigQuery integration in Chapter 16).

Roll-Up Reporting

Roll-up reporting is a common reporting request for organizations with multiple sites and mobile apps. You might have different sites for different countries, or for different brands and product lines, that you might want to report on as an integrated GA property. On GA Standard, it's a common practice to "manually" create a roll-up GA property by adding a common GA tracker across all your sites or all of your apps, as discussed in Chapter 12. Analytics 360 introduces an easier mechanism to provide this executive-level view of the data without code-level changes. The Analytics 360 rollup option provides key benefits:

- **Common tracking ID not required:** you set up your roll-up property for any combination or all of the GA properties (aka Source Properties) under one GA account.
- **Session de-duplication:** in the Analytics 360 roll-up property, sessions merge when users navigate across Source Properties. Note that sessions are not merged if session timeouts are exceeded. (Default session timeout is 30 minutes.)
- **Cost savings:** in your roll-up property, hits are counted at 50%. So if you received 100 million hits in the roll-up property, it will count as 50M hits (toward your Analytics 360 tier).

If you want to import data or link other Google products such as AdWords, you must set up the import and the linking for the roll-up property regardless whether you have them set up for the Source Properties or not.

DoubleClick Integrations

If you're using GA Standard, you're likely to be familiar with a number of integrations between GA and other Google products such Google AdWords, Google Search Console and Google AdSense. In the following sections, we cover integrations with Google's DoubleClick family of products; these integrations are available only for Analytics 360 accounts.

DoubleClick Campaign Manager Integration

DoubleClick Campaign Manager (DCM) (formerly called DoubleClick for Advertisers or DFA) is part of Google's DoubleClick Digital Marketing platform. It allows advertisers to manage display campaigns across sites and mobile apps.

While DCM offers robust built-in reporting capabilities, DCM integration with Analytics 360 allows Analytics 360 users to view and analyze campaign data within the GA interface, as shown in Figure 18.6. If you are familiar with AdWords integration into GA, DCM integration similarly provides marketers with visibility into the customer journey starting with impressions (when the user sees a display banner), all the way through conversion.

FIGURE 18.6 You can access all the integrated DCM reports in Analytics 360 under the Acquisition reports.

As illustrated in Figure 18.7, DCM reports in Analytics 360 display metrics for visitors who have visited your website by clicking directly on an ad ("Click-through") and visitors who received an ad impression but visited your site through another channel ("View-through").

DFA Site (DFA Model)	DFA Attribution Type (DFA Model)	Sessions ? ↓	Pages / Session ?	Avg. Session Duration ?	% New Sessions ?	Bounce Rate ?	Goal Completions ?	Revenue ?
	View-through	182,802 % of Total: 47.08% (388,320)	5.77 Avg for View: 5.67 (1.69%)	00:04:54 Avg for View: 00:04:53 (0.19%)	2.36% Avg for View: 2.92% (-18.98%)	46.18% Avg for View: 46.70% (-1.12%)	64,691 % of Total: 47.22% (136,990)	$4,483,414.02 % of Total: 39.26% ($11,420,532.89)
	Click-through	130,716 % of Total: 89.26% (146,445)	5.66 Avg for View: 5.66 (0.00%)	00:04:29 Avg for View: 00:04:28 (0.38%)	2.17% Avg for View: 4.73% (-54.19%)	45.70% Avg for View: 45.03% (1.48%)	79,627 % of Total: 91.93% (86,619)	$1,695,295.62 % of Total: 86.11% ($1,968,835.94)
1. Criteo	View-through	155,149	5.81	00:04:55	2.05%	46.72%	54,189	$3,936,296.61
	Click-through	128,998	5.66	00:04:30	1.92%	45.67%	78,707	$1,600,186.80
2. Adroll	View-through	27,653	5.52	00:04:50	4.12%	43.13%	10,502	$547,117.41
	Click-through	1,718	5.85	00:03:59	21.01%	48.08%	920	$95,108.82

FIGURE 18.7 In this example, 89.26% of the total sessions came from people who viewed and clicked (click-through) the DCM ads and 47.08% from people who visited the site after being exposed (but didn't click) to the DCM ad (view-through).

Note

DCM Auto-tagging

To complete the integration, you must enable auto-tagging in the DCM admin; this is similar to the AdWords Autotagging process. For AdWords, your destination URLs will be tagged with a "gclid" parameter that GA interprets, and for DCM, your URLs will be tagged with a "dclid" parameter. If more than one URL tagging schema are used, the following rules apply:

➤ DCM auto-tagging overrides any manual tagging.
➤ AdWords auto-tagging overrides DCM auto-tagging.

As shown in Figure 18.8, DCM has its own conversion attribution model (DFA model) similar to how AdWords has its own conversion model. The DFA Model considers DCM traffic only and doesn't take into account other channels. As discussed in Chapter 14 in reference to AdWords versus GA conversions for your AdWords campaigns, you can refer to both DFA and GA conversions for your DCM campaigns, focusing more on trends and less on the offset between the two conversion models.

For more on configuring DoubleClick tags in GTM, see www.e-nor.com/gabook.

DFA Advertiser (DFA Model)	DFA Attribution Type (DFA Model)	DFA Conversions	DFA Revenue
	View-through	**2,932** % of Total: 100.00% (2,932)	**$1.00** % of Total: 100.00% ($1.00)
	Click-through	**119,571** % of Total: 373,659.38% (32)	**$62.00** % of Total: ∞% ($0.00)
1. Google Store US	View-through	2,932	$1.00
	Click-through	119,571	$62.00

FIGURE 18.8 According to the DFA Model, for all DCM Campaigns for the Google Store, there were 2,932 view-through conversions and 119,571 click-through conversions.

Another great benefit of the DCM integration is that you can see the DCM data in the MCF reports as a Source/Medium of `dfa/cpm`, providing additional visibility into campaign performance across channels and campaigns, as illustrated in Figure 18.9.

Primary Dimension: MCF Channel Grouping Path **Source/Medium Path** Source Path Medium Path Other Channel Groupings

Secondary dimension advanced

Source/Medium Path	Conversions	Conversion Value
1. dfa / cpm > google / organic	**96,206** (44.37%)	**$225,202.81** (36.77%)
2. google / organic > dfa / cpm	**17,155** (7.91%)	**$49,095.78** (8.02%)
3. (direct) / (none) × 2	**7,070** (3.26%)	**$19,075.93** (3.11%)
4. dfa / cpm > google / organic > (direct) / (none)	**5,702** (2.63%)	**$13,024.60** (2.13%)
5. google / organic > (direct) / (none)	**3,768** (1.74%)	**$15,691.46** (2.56%)
6. dfa / cpm × 2 > google / organic	**3,103** (1.43%)	**$6,424.00** (1.05%)

FIGURE 18.9 As can be seen here, the *dfa/cpm* Source/Medium is present in a number of conversion paths.

Occasionally, Google updates its privacy policy requirements. We recommend you review the "Policy Requirements for GA Advertising Features" in the GA help docs and ensure that your privacy policy is in compliance with the Google terms:

`https://support.google.com/analytics/answer/2700409?hl=en`

DoubleClick Bid Manager Remarketing Integration

While the DCM integration with Analytics 360 allows you to view and segment on the DCM data within the GA User Interface, the DoubleClick Bid Manager (DBM) integration allows you to create Remarketing Audiences in Analytics 360 and use those audiences in DBM. See the DBM menu in GA in Figure 18.10.

DBM is a sophisticated demand-side platform (DSP) that's designed to deliver precise and powerful display buying. The platform allows for Real-Time Bidding (RTB), and according to Google: "Our algorithm evaluates up to 40 variables in less than 40 milliseconds to calculate each bid" and enables advertisers to connect to audiences they target, across channels (mobile, video, display, etc.).

Conceptually, the DBM integration with Analytics 360 is very similar to how advertisers can programmatically leverage AdWords and GA Standard integration in using Segments to create remarketing lists in AdWords as detailed in Chapter 14.

> **Note**
>
> ### DBM Configuration
> Contact your Analytics 360 account manager or Analytics 360 reseller and they'll manage the enablement of DBM after you agree to the terms and an email agreement.

FIGURE 18.10   You can access all the integrated DBM reports in Analytics 360 under the Acquisition reports.

As stated previously for the DCM integration, we recommend that you review the "Privacy Policy Requirements for GA Advertising Features" in the GA help docs to ensure compliance.

DoubleClick for Search

Another DoubleClick integration we will cover is DoubleClick for Search (DS).

DS is a unified interface to manage your Search Campaigns across multiple engines such as Google AdWords, Microsoft adCenter/Yahoo Search Marketing. DS streamlines the search campaign management and provides integrated reporting and automated bidding and attribution (without DS, you'd have to manage your ads and keywords on each engine separately).

The DS reports in Analytics 360 are available in the Acquisition reports, as illustrated in Figure 18.11.

FIGURE 18.11 You can access all the integrated DS reports in Analytics 360 under the Acquisition reports.

To track conversions from DS campaigns, you add DoubleClick's Floodlight tag to your conversion page (e.g., Purchase Confirmation Page). Since DS is a member of the DoubleClick Digital Marketing family, you can leverage the same tags used for DCM.

To view the GA metrics, including GA-defined goal conversions and Ecommerce transactions associated with the DC campaigns, click on the Campaigns link in the DS reports and evaluate how your campaigns from various search engines are performing, as illustrated in Figure 18.12. Again, you can refer to both Floodlight and GA conversions for your DS campaigns, focusing more on trends and less on the offset between the two models.

DS Campaign	Acquisition			Behavior			Conversions eCommerce ▾		
	Sessions ↓	% New Sessions	New Users	Bounce Rate	Pages / Session	Avg. Session Duration	Ecommerce Conversion Rate	Transactions	Revenue
	2,014 % of Total: 0.76% (266,362)	78.75% Avg for View: 79.04% (-0.37%)	1,586 % of Total: 0.75% (210,540)	56.85% Avg for View: 50.55% (12.46%)	5.49 Avg for View: 6.30 (-12.78%)	00:01:50 Avg for View: 00:02:19 (-20.93%)	0.45% Avg for View: 0.69% (-35.69%)	9 % of Total: 0.49% (1,851)	$327.07 % of Total: 0.13% ($248,462.12)
1. AW - Accessories	968 (48.06%)	69.32%	671 (42.31%)	44.83%	8.25	00:02:53	0.52%	5 (55.56%)	$180.12 (55.07%)
2. AW - Wearables	440 (21.85%)	86.36%	380 (23.96%)	63.64%	3.83	00:01:08	0.91%	4 (44.44%)	$146.95 (44.93%)
3. BA - Wearables	180 (8.94%)	91.67%	165 (10.40%)	68.89%	2.37	00:00:40	0.00%	0 (0.00%)	$0.00 (0.00%)
4. BA - Accessories	125 (6.21%)	75.20%	94 (5.93%)	67.20%	3.87	00:01:28	0.00%	0 (0.00%)	$0.00 (0.00%)

FIGURE 18.12 All conversions/transactions in the report are coming from the AdWords campaigns (the first two rows), while the Bing campaigns (the last two rows) could use some optimization.

DoubleClick for Publishers

While the DoubleClick integrations discussed so far are focused on Advertisers, publishers (those who have inventory and serve display ads) can also take advantage of GA reporting. Analytics 360 integrates with DoubleClick for Publishers (DFP) as shown in Figure 18.13.

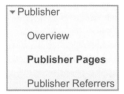

FIGURE 18.13 DFP reports for Publisher Pages and Referrers can be found under the Publish reports in the Behavior section.

DFP is the DoubleClick platform that enables ad and revenue management across all demand sources, formats, and channels.

DFP Integration with Analytics 360 allows publishers to create targeted audiences and make these audiences available to advertisers. Examples of segments include:

- Visitors viewing specific content category.
- Visitors who are engaged (based on time on site, number of pages visited, etc.).
- Visitors who responded to a specific campaign.

The DFP reports in Analytics 360 are available Behavior > Publisher Reports. A sample report is shown in Figure 18.14.

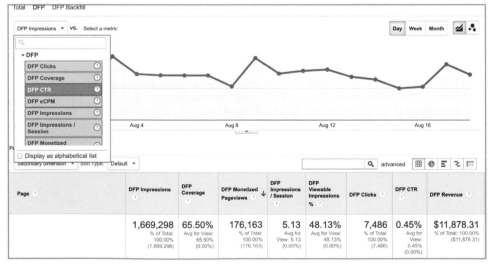

FIGURE 18.14 DFP Publisher Pages provide detailed reporting on a number of DFP metrics including DFP Impressions, Clicks, CTR, and Revenue.

Note

DFP Configuration

Contact your Analytics 360 account manager or reseller to enable DFP reporting in GA.

Data-Driven Attribution

Google defines Data-Driven Attribution as a model that "uses actual data from your Analytics account to generate a custom model for assigning conversion credit to marketing touch points throughout the entire customer journey."

GA does all the heavy lifting for you and incorporates in the model all the data from your various traffic sources, including data you have linked from AdWords and DoubleClick Campaign Manager and data you have imported in Analytics 360. GA then crunches the numbers based on probability models and algorithmically assigns conversion credit to the various channels in the conversion path.

Note

Configuration for Data-Driven Attribution

When you enable the Data-Driven Attribution Modeling in the Admin Tab > View Settings, you'll see data in your reports within seven days.

You can access the Data-Driven Attribution Model Explorer shown in Figure 18.15 from the Conversions > Attribution section of GA.

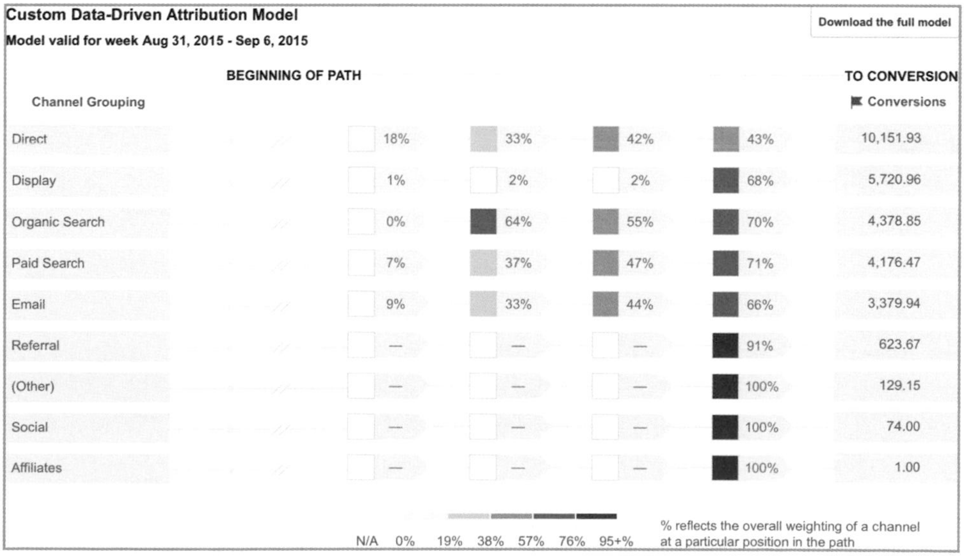

Custom Data-Driven Attribution Model
Model valid for week Aug 31, 2015 - Sep 6, 2015

Download the full model

Channel Grouping	BEGINNING OF PATH				TO CONVERSION Conversions
Direct	18%	33%	42%	43%	10,151.93
Display	1%	2%	2%	68%	5,720.96
Organic Search	0%	64%	55%	70%	4,378.85
Paid Search	7%	37%	47%	71%	4,176.47
Email	9%	33%	44%	66%	3,379.94
Referral	—	—	—	91%	623.67
(Other)	—	—	—	100%	129.15
Social	—	—	—	100%	74.00
Affiliates	—	—	—	100%	1.00

N/A   0%   19%   38%   57%   76%   95+%

% reflects the overall weighting of a channel at a particular position in the path

FIGURE 18.15 Attribution Model Explorer shows the weighted average credit for the path positions prior to conversion for each marketing channel.

Use this report to validate your assumptions about channel performance. In our specific example in Figure 18.15, this business is running Display retargeting campaigns. You see that overall weighting of Display, in the last touch position in the conversion path, is 68%. Display is assisting in the very last touch and not helping upper funnel performance. (As discussed in Chapter 7, we have the option of breaking out retargeting/ remarketing traffic into a separate channel within the Default Channel Grouping used in the Attribution reports.)

Attribution beyond the Google Ecosystem

If your marketing mix is primarily comprised of Google products, be it AdWords or DoubleClick, the MCF reports and Analytics 360 attribution reports will most likely provide a good basis for your multi-channel analysis.

However, if you use ad serving platforms or programmatic buying outside of the Google ecosystem, data from these systems is not available natively in GA or Analytics 360. You might consider a cross-channel marketing attribution solution (such as Google Attribution 360, Visual IQ, or Convertro, etc.) that brings in all data from offline (e.g., TV) and online sources to optimize the marketing spend, user acquisition, and engagement.

If you're contemplating advanced attribution, guest contributor June Dershewitz identifies four fundamental questions that you should answer and helps sort out some the complexity.

GUEST SPOT   **Four Questions to Ask Before You Tackle Advanced Attribution**

June Dershewitz

June Dershewitz is head of Data Governance & Analytics at Twitch (an Amazon subsidiary).

You may be wondering whether it's finally time to move your company away from the standard "last-click" approach (or the Google-centric Multi-Channel Funnel reports) to marketing attribution in favor of more advanced techniques. Before you go too deep, though, ask yourself these four questions and make sure it's a problem that your business truly needs to solve.

1. **Is your marketing strategy sufficiently complex?**
   If you're working with only a couple of paid marketing channels, advanced attribution is probably overkill. However, if you believe that some of your most important marketing initiatives are underrepresented in the "last-click" model, advanced attribution might be worthwhile. Considerations include the length of your sales cycle, the significance of offline investment (like TV spend), and the overall size of your marketing budget.

2. **Can you describe the added value you'll get from advanced attribution?**
   If you manage to get advanced attribution afloat and all you do is make reports, you have failed. A successful attribution program should drive strategic and tactical changes in

your marketing practices. If you knew the true value of every single marketing tactic, what would you do differently? This is also a good discussion topic to cover with attribution platform vendors—ask them to explain what actionability looks like.

3. **Are you willing to dedicate the resources needed to launch and maintain this program?**
   It takes real effort—you'll need data fluency, marketing subject matter expertise, communication skills, and a boatload of patience. And once you get past the initial setup phase, you have to be ready to honor a long-term commitment to acting on insights. If you don't have this kind of dedication in place, your program is at risk from the start.

4. **Do your executives agree that it's important?**
   Marketing channel managers may own specific tactics, but it's the executives who oversee the big picture. Attribution should have holistic benefit, and as such requires coordination across multiple channels. It won't work as a grassroots initiative. In order for advanced attribution to succeed, the executives who own your entire marketing program—and budget—need to view it as a priority.

If you're able to answer "yes" to all of these questions, you should definitely explore advanced attribution solutions. When done well, it should fuel ongoing improvements across all of marketing.

ANALYTICS 360 RESOURCES

With Analytics 360 you're not on your own. Between Google and your Analytics 360 reseller, you should have what you need to start taking advantage of your analytics investment right away. The MCF reports to marketing resources include:

The Portal

For large organizations with tens (if not hundreds) of sites and apps, managing the Analytics 360 account(s) can be an onerous job.

Google provides (as part of the Google Analytics 360 suite) an Analytics 360 portal, designed as an administrative interface for Analytics 360 resellers and clients.

The portal allows you to view your billing information and enable Analytics 360 on your GA properties. While Analytics 360 is a company-wide license, you have full control over adding GA properties to Analytics 360; this is easily done through the Analytics 360 portal.

In addition, and as a portal admin, you can add users to the portal and view hit volumes and usage.

The portal will be enabled as soon as Analytics 360 is activated for your organization.

Training Resources

If you are an Analytics 360 customer, you'll have access to the Analytics 360 help articles and a number of training videos on the "About Analytics 360" help page:

```
https://support.google.com/analytics/answer/3437434?hl=en
```

To access this page in your browser, you'll have to be logged in as an Analytics 360 user.

Releases and Beta Features

Google introduces new features very frequently. Follow up with your reseller or Google to ensure that you are receiving the Analytics 360 updates as well as access to early betas.

Billing and Tiers

Analytics 360 is typically sold on a flat-fee basis, with a tiered fee structure for higher hit volume. Prior to the introduction of Analytics 360 (in March 2016), the retail annual price for *Analytics 360* was $150,000 USD, €105k euros, or £90k GBP. This price covered 0 to one billion hits per month. If your monthly total hit count exceeded one billion hits, you were charged an additional monthly amount.

New Analytics 360 clients will select one of two options:

- Less than or equal to 500 million hits per month. Monthly hits exceeding 500 million will be billed in 100-million-hit increments.
- Less than or equal to 1.5 billion hits per month. Monthly hits exceeding 1.5 billion will be billed in 500-million-hit increments.

When your hit volume fluctuates, as it does for seasonal businesses, and your monthly volume exceeds the respective 500 million or 1.5 billion hits for two months, you're billed for the two months of overage.

Please refer to www.e-nor.com/gabook for the updates as the new pricing is rolled out.

If you are an existing Analytics 360 client, a nonprofit, an educational institution, or a governmental agency, speak with your reseller or Google for any applicable or grandfathered discounts. In addition to the investment in the Analytics 360 platform itself, organizations should allocate resources for customization, integration, consulting, and training as warranted.

WHERE TO BUY—RESELLERS OR GOOGLE DIRECT?

Analytics 360 can be purchased directly from Google or from one of the Analytics 360 Authorized Resellers listed here:

```
https://www.google.com/analytics/partners/search/services
```

A question we hear frequently from Analytics 360 prospects is whether to buy the license from Google Direct or from a reseller. Analytics 360 features and SLAs are identical, independent of how you buy Analytics 360, so this need not be a consideration, but following are some factors that can vary significantly, depending on your vendor choice.

Analytics 360 requires a large investment, so it's recommended to question the vendor quite thoroughly. Be a prudent buyer: examine the technical, process, and interpersonal aspects.

(Disclaimer: E-Nor is an Analytics 360 Authorized Reseller.)

The Technical Aspect

- Level of on boarding and migration support (from GA Standard or from another Analytics platform).
- Level of customization support for Analytics 360 and the numbers of properties and/ or apps for which implementation support is included.
- Ongoing consulting beyond the initial implementation.
- Integration expertise with other Google products such as DCM, DBM, DFP, AdWords, and BigQuery.
- Integration expertise with non-Google products such CRM (e.g., SalesForce), email platforms, marketing automation platforms, etc.
- Data integration and report automation.
- Data visualization support.

The Process Aspect

- Campaign tagging support.
- Development and QA support.
- Road map and assessment.
- Tools for automatic reporting, tagging, QA and validation.
- Support for different time zones.

The People Aspect

- Level of expertise of the Analytics 360 account team you'll be working with.
- Will you be assigned a dedicated Account Manager?
- Knowledge transfer and training:
  - Do you require and will you receive onsite training?
  - Will you receive virtual training?
  - What other educational resources are available to you?
- Access to Analytics 360 conferences and early betas.

Google adheres to a thorough and rigorous process for accepting analytics agencies into the Analytics 360 Authorized Reseller program, but all resellers are not identical. Below are some additional considerations for evaluating Analytics 360 resellers.

Additional Considerations for Reseller Evaluation

- Some resellers specialize in a specific vertical (e.g., Ecommerce).
- Some might be more focused on media, SEM, and other areas rather than analytics.

- Some are purely focused on analytics and provide strategy, implementation, training and integration.
- Some charge hourly and some charge a fixed price.
- Some work with other analytics vendors (e.g., it might be useful to have an agency with expertise in Adobe Analytics if you are migrating from Adobe to Analytics 360).
- Analytics is getting more complex—it's not just about tracking visits and pages. Some implementations require advanced tagging techniques including but not limited to mobile apps and (as discussed in Chapter 17) Measurement Protocol integration with CRMs, BigQuery, Data Visualization, and so on.
- Geography and physical proximity don't seem to be of a concern in vendor selection, giving today's prevalent virtual work environment. But at least ensure the vendor can support you in your time zone.

 KEY TAKEAWAYS

Monitor your Total Hit Volume.   If you are a GA Standard user, and the data you're collecting is approaching the 10 million hits/month mark, it's time to review your needs and analytics requirements and assess a Analytics 360 upgrade.

Take advantage of all the Google product integrations.   We discussed a number of DoubleClick integrations to allow you a quicker access to insights about your users. Take the time to set up these integrations, contact your Analytics 360 account manager and they'll guide you through the process.

Attribution is here to stay.   Get comfortable with attribution concepts and attribution modeling. Use the capabilities offered by GA Standard and Analytics 360 to begin assessing your visitors' journeys.

Be a smart buyer.   Document your requirements, share them with your vendor, and do your overall due diligence before you commit to long-term contracts.

ACTIONS AND EXERCISES

1. **Run a Total Hits custom report.** If you are a GA Standard user, build a custom report with the "Total Hits" metrics and have it sent to your inbox on a weekly basis.

2. **Review all your UTM tagging for all your campaigns.** Make sure your campaign and channel tracking foundation is solid before you enter the big league of attribution.

3. **Develop an analytics road map.** Technology won't solve all your optimization challenges. Sit down with your analytics team and/or consulting agency and develop a 12-month road map on how to best leverage all of the Analytics 360 capabilities to become a more data-driven organization.

Appendix A: Broadening Your Optimization Program

Google Analytics Breakthrough has covered the strategy, implementation, reporting, and analysis phases of the optimization pyramid that we saw all the way back in Figure 3.1. Throughout our discussions, we have suggested specific optimization steps that you can take based on the data that Google Analytics provides, but there are aspects of optimization that we have not yet discussed directly.

As essential as quantitative Web and mobile analytics data is for achieving insight and action, it's important to remember that your overall optimization program should also comprise qualitative inputs, overlay visualizations, and testing strategies. As the next level of optimization, personalization goes beyond analytics to present different experiences to specific user segments.

In this appendix, experts share key insights and strategies for these components of your optimization program.

QUALITATIVE INPUTS

In our optimization context, *quantitative* refers to numbers-based Web and mobile app analytics data that users generate but do not provide directly and *qualitative* refers to any inputs or evaluations that end users or testers do provide directly.

Qualitative inputs can sometimes identify conversion issues that analytics could not. As an example, what if your users are expecting to see a money-back guarantee on your payment page? If you have set up a goal funnel or Enhanced Ecommerce in Google Analytics for your checkout process, you'll be able to identify a high drop-off on the payment page, but a single comment in a customer evaluation or a usability test could readily reveal the specific problem.

In this section, Duff Anderson of iPerceptions discusses the power of surveys (as well as iPerceptions integration with GA), and Hannah Alvarez of UserTesting provides key insights on usability testing. Note also that Google Consumer Surveys is available as a tag template in GTM for deploying basic survey functionality.

As you consider qualitative inputs, remember to actively seek out opportunities to speak with your organization's prospects and current customers, as well as the people in your organization who interface most frequently with your customer base, such as the sales team, call center representatives, and customer/technical support specialists. Never underestimate the importance of these conversations.

GUEST SPOT   **Enhancing Google Analytics with Visitor Surveys**

Duff Anderson

Duff Anderson is senior vice president and co-founder at iPerceptions.

You can't get into your Visitors Heads with Google Analytics Alone

The power of clickstream data in understanding what visitors experience is colossal. But for all the insight that can be gleaned from Google Analytics such as "What are your visitors doing?"; "When are they are on your site?"; and "Where are they coming from?" the WHY remains unanswered. Avinash Kaushik, digital marketing evangelist for Google and bestselling Web analytics author, stated that, "It [Web analytics] cannot, no matter how much you torture the data, tell you WHY something happened."[1]

When you're wondering why a landing page has only a 0.5% conversion rate or if 3.34 pages/session indicates a good or bad visitor experience, you need to gather and interpret qualitative inputs in addition to your quantitative data. It is only by getting inside your visitors' heads with qualitative inputs that you can start to complete the visitor experience picture.

How do You Get Into the Heads of Your Visitors?

The only way to understand your visitor behavior is by asking them and collecting qualitative feedback data or what is commonly referred to as Voice of the Customer (VoC) data. There is a variety of ways to engage visitors and collect qualitative data ranging from a passive persistent feedback button to random active solicitation.

PASSIVE PERSISTENT	TRIGGERED	RANDOM ACTIVE
COMMENT CARD	TACTICAL	RESEARCH FRAMEWORKS
Persistent	Targeted	Random
Remediation	Optimization	Strategic Direction

Individual	Target Audience	Representative

FIGURE A.1 Voice of the Customer data.

---

[1] http://www.kaushik.net/avinash/4q-the-best-online-survey-for-a-website-yours-free/.

Passive Persistent Engagement

Passive feedback or comment cards are a persistent button that is available for visitors to click on to leave their feedback. iPerceptions research shows that users who use passive engagement methods are more likely to leave negative feedback. Therefore, passive persistent approaches are more of a remediation tool that can help fix broken links and give visitors an outlet to vent.

Targeted Engagement

Targeted engagement collects qualitative data by showing a survey to a specific audience based on target criteria such as number of pages viewed or time on site. It is typically used to optimize sections of a website or a particular site feature. As an example, by triggering a survey to collect feedback from visitors who visited only the support section of your site, you can understand how effectively your online support tools are meeting visitors' needs and how you can optimize those resources.

Pre/Post Random Active Engagement

The other type of qualitative data is representative and leverages a random pre/post sampling methodology. This method collects qualitative data by inviting a portion of your website visitors early in their visit to take a survey at the end of their visit. This provides information that is representative of the population being sampled creating internal alignment and helps drive strategic decisions.

It is important to understand that not all qualitative data is created equal. The method you choose will ultimately impact the type of data you collect (representative to individual) and how it can be used (strategic to tactical).

How to Ask for Feedback?

The way you ask will also have a big impact on the quality of the results you collect. Below are some fundamentals that you should always follow:

- ➤ Asking your visitors for feedback is an extension of your brand. This means it is essential to customize your research to match your brand; from survey invitation to thank you page, ensure your brand is front and center.
- ➤ In today's multiscreen world, it's important to collect customer feedback across devices. Whether it is on a desktop, tablet, mobile, or in-app, ensure the survey or comment card is responsive to your customer's device.
- ➤ Keep your research objectives focused. One of the biggest mistakes is to try and answer everything in one survey. Running multiple studies with clear objectives—from improving site usability to increasing marketing effectiveness to increasing conversion—will help increase your responses and the quality of the data you collect.

What Should You Ask?

It's important to collect a variety of qualitative metrics to contextualize your Google Analytics data and get a holistic picture of how well you're meeting visitor needs. As mentioned, it is essential to keep your research focused on your objectives, but there are few metrics that should form the backbone of any qualitative research.

continues

continued

Visitor Satisfaction

Based on today's visit, how would you rate your overall experience on the website today?

Understanding and measuring the overall experience is critical to gauge the end-to-end experience of your visitors. With visitors providing a score of your website's experience on a scale of 0–10 (where 0 represents a very bad experience and 10 is an outstanding experience) you can quickly evaluate your website's performance and then see how your site improves over time.

Visitor Intent

Which of the following best describes the primary purpose of your visit?

Why are people visiting your website? What are they trying to do during their visit? Visitor intent, also known as purpose of visit, is essential to understand the needs of your visitors. Once you know why people are coming to your site, you can better align your content to what visitors are trying to achieve.

Task Completion

Were you able to accomplish everything you wanted to do on the site today?

Task completion tells you if visitors are able to successfully complete the reason for their visit. If visitors are not able to complete the purpose of their visit, this will impact their satisfaction with your site, their likelihood to return and their likelihood to recommend your site.

The Powerful Combination of Google Analytics and Qualitative Data

With the right data and taking a focused approach to collecting qualitative data you can fill the Web analytics void and better understand your customers to ultimately optimize the visitor experience.

The integration process, depending on the provider, should be a straightforward affair. Typically the data collected is sent to Google Analytics using events, so you can create a segment as shown in Figures A.2 and A.3. (Segments are discussed in detail in Chapter 10.)

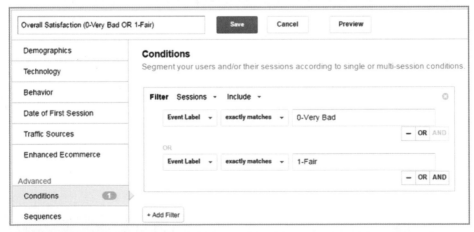

FIGURE A.2 If your qualitative data integrates into Google Analytics as events, you can create a Google Analytics segment based on event data for visitors who responded to a qualitative survey with very low overall satisfaction (0 – Very Bad OR 1 – Fair).

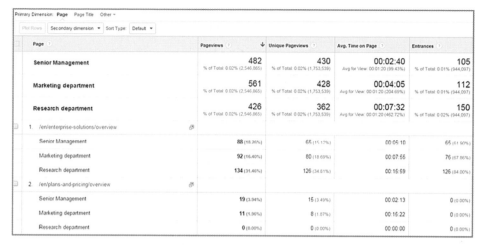

Page	Pageviews	Unique Pageviews	Avg. Time on Page	Entrances
Senior Management	482 % of Total: 0.02% (2,546,865)	430 % of Total: 0.02% (1,753,539)	00:02:40 Avg for View: 00:01:20 (99.43%)	105 % of Total: 0.01% (944,097)
Marketing department	561 % of Total: 0.02% (2,546,865)	428 % of Total: 0.02% (1,753,539)	00:04:05 Avg for View: 00:01:20 (204.69%)	112 % of Total: 0.01% (944,097)
Research department	426 % of Total: 0.02% (2,546,865)	362 % of Total: 0.02% (1,753,539)	00:07:32 Avg for View: 00:01:20 (462.72%)	150 % of Total: 0.02% (944,097)
1. /en/enterprise-solutions/overview				
Senior Management	88 (18.26%)	65 (15.12%)	00:05:10	65 (61.90%)
Marketing department	92 (16.40%)	80 (18.69%)	00:07:55	76 (67.86%)
Research department	134 (31.46%)	126 (34.81%)	00:15:59	126 (84.00%)
2. /en/plans-and-pricing/overview				
Senior Management	19 (3.94%)	15 (3.49%)	00:02:13	0 (0.00%)
Marketing department	11 (1.96%)	8 (1.87%)	00:15:22	0 (0.00%)
Research department	0 (0.00%)	0 (0.00%)	00:00:00	0 (0.00%)

FIGURE A.3 As an example of segmentation based on survey responses that appear in Google Analytics as events. The Pages report above has three segments applied based on job role: Senior Management, Marketing, and Research.

Once you have set up Google Analytics segments based on the qualitative event data, you can:

➤ Better evaluate landing pages, exit pages, keywords, traffic sources, and campaigns by qualitative Visitor Satisfaction rates.

➤ Compare Google Analytics goal conversion rates against your qualitative Task Completion rates (*Did you accomplish your task?*) to gain a better understanding of the conversion cycle.

➤ Compare Visitor Satisfaction rates by time on site, pages visited, sections visited, and geographic region.

➤ Examine time on site by Task Completion rates to distinguish between visitors struggling to find information and those positively engaged on the site.

In order to understand your customers, web analytics is not enough, you need to know what they are thinking. Make sure your optimization strategies focus on understanding the "why" behind the "what." It's only then that your objectives and strategies will align to your visitor needs and expectations. Using the techniques outlined above, you can begin understanding the why behind the what and aligning your design, content, and marketing strategies with visitor needs and expectations.

GUEST SPOT   **User Research and Qualitative Optimization**

Hannah Alvarez

Hannah Alvarez leads the content marketing team at UserTesting.

As you're digging deeper into your analytics, you may find yourself asking a lot of questions.

Why does one product page have a much higher bounce rate than the others? Why has average time on page dropped over the last two months? Why does traffic from Twitter convert at a higher rate than traffic from LinkedIn?

continues

continued

That's where user research—specifically user testing—comes in.

User testing is watching over the shoulder of real people interacting with your site and speaking their thoughts aloud as they go. Listening to users think aloud is great for finding out where and why users become stuck, confused, or frustrated on your site. It's your opportunity to see your site through the fresh eyes of a first-time visitor.

By user testing, you'll uncover the usability issues on your site that cause high bounce rates, low conversion rates, and unusual session durations. Some of the most common usability issues include confusing navigation, unclear forms, and unhelpful search results. These issues can be very difficult to uncover through analytics alone, but analytics are a great place to start. When you've pinpointed specific pages or behavior flows that look problematic in your analytics, you can run user tests on those pages and flows to find out why users are giving up. In your user test, you will choose which tasks you'd like to watch users complete and which questions you want them to answer about their experience.

User testing isn't limited to websites, either! It's equally important to gather user feedback on your mobile apps, if your company has them. You can test mobile apps using the same process outlined below. Make sure to test both your iOS version and Android version, if you have both.

In-Person vs. Remote User Testing

User testing can be in-person or remote, and both styles have their advantages and disadvantages.

In-person user testing usually requires a usability lab and a moderator (though it can happen in an office, a conference room, or even a coffee shop). You can gain very rich and deep insights from in-house research. Researchers can observe the test participants' body language and facial expressions as well as their on-screen actions and verbal feedback—and the moderator can help guide the participants if they become stuck at any point or need to ask a question. In-person sessions tend to run longer than remote sessions, so they can be better for activities that require a very long time to complete (such as applying for health insurance).

On the other hand, it is often expensive and time-consuming to set up for in-person user testing sessions, and it can be challenging to recruit test participants who accurately represent your target market. Plus, first-time test participants may feel nervous or overly eager to please, so it's up to your moderator to press them for open and honest feedback.

Remote user testing tends to be faster and easier than in-person testing. You can recruit participants from anywhere in the world via an online panel of users, or you can recruit your own users and invite them to participate. Because remote user tests don't require participants to be in a certain place at a certain time, it's often much easier to quickly find people to take your test, and you can run larger-scale studies more easily.

In a remote user testing session, test participants record their screen and their voice as they interact with your website, and you watch the video recording when it's complete. Depending on which platform you use and the complexity of your study, you can get results in hours, days, or weeks. Most remote user testing does not involve a moderator, so it's essential to write a clear test plan that will guide participants through the tasks you need them to complete. (However, some remote user testing platforms do allow for moderated testing.) Since you usually do not see the facial expression and body language of the participants, it's critical that test participants continue speaking their thoughts aloud the whole time.

How to Run a Successful User Testing Study

You don't have to be a professional researcher to conduct a study. All you need to do is follow five steps.

1. Identify your testing objective.

What are you trying to learn? If you're simply trying to find the most obvious usability issues on your site, your test plan will be different than it would if you were trying to find out why the bounce rate is high on a particular landing page. This is your opportunity to establish what you're aiming to optimize.

2. Think about the audience for your test.

You will likely want to run your user test with your target market. If you have a niche audience, the recruiting process may be more time-consuming. For in-person testing, you'll need to find those users and make arrangements for them to come in to your lab. For remote testing, you will designate your demographic requirements when you set up your study in the platform.

Make a note of which devices you'll want to include in your test. The user experience on your mobile site is just as important as your desktop site, so don't forget to test with iPhone, Android, and tablet users.

If you're aiming to uncover usability problems, you don't need very many test participants. Five to eight users will reveal most serious issues.

On the other hand, if you're trying to find trends in users' opinions (such as how likely they would be to trust your company), then you'll want a larger dataset. Aim for at least 20 to 30 participants, and make sure to include users from each of your different audience segments.

3. Write the test plan.

Focus on writing tasks and questions that will uncover the insights you need. Make sure to keep your questions neutral so you don't bias your test participants' answers.

When you write tasks, make sure you don't handhold participants too much or lead them to the "right" way of accomplishing the task. For example, if you say, "Find a pair of men's dress shoes in size 10," you'll uncover more insights about how participants would naturally go about finding shoes—and any struggles they encounter—than if you said, "Click on the tab labeled *Men's*, and then scroll down until you see the *Shoes* category. . . ." It's always a good idea to run your test with one participant first to make sure there aren't any confusing instructions that could derail your study.

4. Run the study!

If you are testing in-house, you'll want to make sure your moderator is ready and you have your audio and video recording tools set up beforehand. Your moderator will lead the participant through the test task by task, asking clarifying questions along the way. If you are using a remote testing tool instead, you'll order your tests online and wait for your videos to be completed.

5. Analyze the results.

As you watch the users interact with the website, take note of any places where they become stuck or confused. These insights will help you answer the questions about your data. Using either your remote testing platform or traditional video editing software, you can create clips of interesting moments from your tests to focus on the most important findings.

continues

What to Do with Your Results

Now that you've gotten feedback from your users, you can organize and prioritize the issues you've found. You've likely created a list of problems your users ran into. These are your optimization opportunities! Any one of them could become your next A/B test.

Start by assigning a priority to each issue you've found. How many customers does this affect? How big of an impact could it make if you improved it? How many resources will you need to allocate in order to make a change?

If you find it's always a challenge to get buy-in to make changes, try showing your stakeholders video clips from your user testing sessions. This is a great way to convince your team to make improvements.

The qualitative insights you'll gain from user testing are the perfect way to humanize the data and complete the story of what's happening on your website. A combination of analytics and qualitative feedback can be your secret weapon of optimization. As an added bonus, these real user stories can help you build a customer-centric culture at your company.

How StubHub Used Qualitative Optimization to Boost Revenue by Millions

The team at the online ticket marketplace StubHub noticed that a lot of customers were entering their purchase funnel but never completing it. The analytics showed that there was a significant drop-off on the ticket search results page, which prompted users to "See details" to go to the purchasing page for each available ticket. They ran user tests to find out why this drop-off was happening, and they discovered that users thought "See details" would take them to the fine print, not the purchasing page.

With this insight, the team changed the "See details" link to an orange button with the word "Go." After making the change, they saw a 2.6% increase in conversions, leading to millions of dollars in increased revenue. (See Figure A.4.)

FIGURE A.4 Following user research, a change to the button text and styling on StubHub's ticket search results page drove a significant conversion increase.

OVERLAY REPORTING

As mentioned in Chapter 12, the Enhanced Link Attribution setting in your GA pageview tags can help the GA In-Page Analytics report to display more meaningful data in overlay format, that is, numeric data or data visualizations superimposed onto the page itself. In-Page Analytics, however, is currently limited in functionality (and sometimes does not display at all).

Several tools offer fuller-featured overlay reporting (and session recording), such as CrazyEgg, SessionCam, or HotJar, which Alex Harris uses in conjunction with the GA Landing Pages report to generate quick wins, as he demonstrates next.

GUEST SPOT	Quick Wins for Big Results

Alex Harris

Alex Harris is a conversion rate optimization manager with over 15 years experience with Ecommerce, lead generation, and UX.

Numerous years as a Web designer focused on conversion optimization helped me discover that the biggest opportunities start with understanding how to find quick wins, including identifying your most important landing pages, interactions on those pages, and why or why not visitors are completing the intended actions.

Let's say you're optimizing your site to improve your conversion rates. Here's how you can start finding those quick wins:

➤ Review your top landing pages.

  Locate the Google Analytics "Landing Pages" report under Behavior, then Site Content. Review the top 5–10 landing pages generating the most traffic.

➤ Understand how visitors interact with your landing page.

  Use tools like HotJar, we can create heat maps, scroll maps, form completion tracking, and visitor recordings. These data collection actions give you the ability to fine-tune the user experience. Watching your visitor's sessions, as they go from page to page, will give you valuable insight to form a hypothesis.

➤ Determine why (or why not) visitors are completing a conversion.

  To collect this qualitative insight, we can also use Qualaroo polls and surveys. Say, if people are on your landing pages, and they move their mouse to the back button, you may want to pop open a survey that asks them, "What is missing from this page?"

Conclusion

Through the years, I have applied this same process with all my new projects to effectively help my clients increase their conversion rates, understand their visitors and the interactions on their sites, and make more money off of their websites.

TESTING

Your lead generation form for the Machu Picchu tour on your travel site is showing a 70% exit rate in GA, so you change the main graphic on the form from mountains to hikers, and the exit rate goes down to 50% the next month. The hikers photo made the difference, right?

In a usability evaluation for one of your main landing pages on your health care website, the tester suggests that you include insurance information at the top of the page. In the next week, the conversion rate for your contact-us goal rises from 0.9% to 1.5%. Can we be confident that the insurance information drove the conversion increase?

In both cases, the changes likely had a positive impact, the increase could have been due to any number of external factors that changed at the same time as your page update.

As a more data-driven approach, you can instead test two or more concurrent variations against each other relative to the same performance metric such as bounce, goal conversions, or Ecommerce revenue, thereby ensuring a cleaner comparison.

Following, Chris Goward walks us through hypothesis generation for your testing, Bobby Hewitt shares best practices for test documentation and analysis of test results, and Tara Dunn offers tips for successful testing as well as framework for mobile app testing through Optimizely.

GUEST SPOT   **Creating Powerful Experiment Hypotheses Using the LIFT Model**

Chris Goward

Chris Goward is the founder of optimization agency WiderFunnel and author of You Should Test That!

An A/B testing program can produce some of the greatest returns on investment of any marketing activity. Many companies are lifting their revenue from the insights their optimization experiments deliver. But other companies aren't so fortunate.

What makes the difference between successful and failed programs? Our experience building these programs at WiderFunnel since 2007 shows remarkable consistency. One of the characteristics that separates the best is the company's commitment to using frameworks to answer business questions.

Finding a list of conversion optimization tips is a simple Google search away, but will the tips and tricks you find work for you? More likely, they'll be guesses that ignore your situation. They're nearly useless.

Using frameworks to help you answer your question is more robust. It gives you an answer that doesn't expire when one of the variables changes.

The LIFT Model[2] is just such a framework, which you can use to create powerful experiment hypotheses. First, we'll look at how the LIFT Model works, then show how to use it within a proper hypothesis structure.

Using the LIFT Model

When I developed the LIFT Model as a framework for creating A/B testing hypotheses, I didn't realize it would become as popular as it has. It's now used in hundreds of companies and universities globally. And you too can use the model to improve your marketing.

The LIFT Model shows the six factors that affect your conversion rates right now. By testing hypotheses to improve each of these factors, you can improve the results of all of your marketing touchpoints.

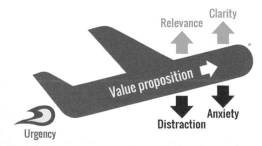

The WiderFunnel LIFT Model

---

[2] LIFT Model is a registered trademark of WiderFunnel Marketing Inc.

Value Proposition

The vehicle that provides the potential for the conversion rate is your Value Proposition, making it the most important of the six conversion factors. You can think of it as an equation that goes on in the mind of your visitors when they're subconsciously considering whether to take action on your page (i.e., to convert).

If the perceived benefits outweigh the perceived costs of taking action, they'll have motivation. If costs outweigh the benefits, they'll bounce immediately.

All the other factors simply enhance or detract from the value proposition.

Relevance

Does the landing page relate to what the visitor thought they were going to see?

The Relevance of the value proposition and context of the source media is critical. Your page must use terms your visitor relates to and be consistent with the incoming link or your visitor will be disoriented and leave the page.

Clarity

Does the landing page clearly articulate the value proposition and call to action?

Clarity is the most common of the six that we find marketers struggling with. The two aspects of Clarity that must be analyzed are Design and Content. Designing for Clarity creates an unimpeded "eye-flow." Content clarity ensures the images and text combine to minimize comprehension time.

Urgency

Is there a motivation for the action to be taken now?

Urgency has two components: Internal (or how the visitor is feeling upon arrival) and External (or influences the marketer can introduce to the visitor). While Internal Urgency is generally preexisting when the visitor arrives on the page, the tone of the presentation, offers, and deadlines can all influence External Urgency.

Anxiety

What are potential misgivings the visitor could have about undertaking the conversion action?

Anxiety is any uncertainty in your prospect's mind about taking action. Are there things on the page or missing from the page that could create that feeling? Anxiety is inversely proportional to the Credibility you have built with the visitor and the Trust you are asking them to have.

Distraction

Are there items on the page that could divert the visitor away from the goal?

The more visual inputs and action options your visitors have to process, the less likely they are to make a conversion decision. Minimizing distractions like unnecessary product options, links, and extraneous information will increase the conversion rate.

Within each of these six factors are the many tips and subfactors that are used by the skilled conversion rate expert to develop hypotheses to be tested.

By evaluating your website, landing pages and conversion funnel from the perspective of your prospective customer, you can identify conversion problems that can be tested and improved.

continues

continued

While there are other fine conversion frameworks available as well, LIFT has gained popularity, I believe, because of its ease-of-use and apparent simplicity that belie its powerful results. The framework itself is a demonstration of how maximizing Clarity and minimizing Distraction can gain acceptance!

A LIFT Analysis Example

The optimization experts at WiderFunnel use the LIFT Model every day to analyze user journeys and create experiment hypotheses. For example, when International Rescue Committee needed to increase donations from their main paid search landing page, they brought in WiderFunnel to run a series of experiments. Our optimization strategists identified dozens of copy and design elements that could increase relevance, clarity and urgency while decreasing anxiety and distraction—and reinforcing the IRC's compelling work.

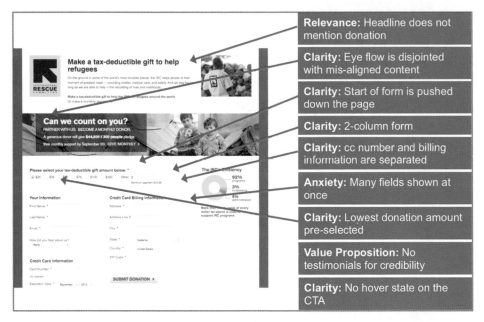

Landing Page LIFT Analysis: this page contained several conversion barriers.

Among other issues, the two-column layout of the form created anxiety, appearing more difficult than it actually was. The form also lay below the page's "fold" and the Call-to-Action (CTA) button didn't include a hover state. On the copy side, there was a lack of clarity around the programs the donation would support, and no positive messaging supporting the decision to donate.

Once the roadblocks to conversion were identified, we were able to create an optimization plan designed to generate the greatest amount of lift and learning for IRC. Early tests showed, surprisingly, that much longer persuasive copywriting and content increased donations.

WiderFunnel's series of experiments using their LIFT Analysis resulted in a 30% conversion rate lift. And the best part? Not only did the number of donors jump, but they were also more generous: Revenue shot up by 94.6%–extending the work the IRC could do around the world!

Landing Page Winner: testing the LIFT-identified hypotheses generated a 30% conversion improvement and a 94.6% donation increase.

continues

continued

Creating a Hypothesis

Once you've identified problems on your touchpoints using the LIFT Model, you can create hypotheses out of them. This is a process of changing your weaknesses into strengths that you can test.

Creating a strong hypothesis is an important part of any scientific experiment. The strength of your hypotheses determines the outcome of your testing.

A hypothesis follows the following structure:

Changing [the thing you want to change] into [what you would change it into] will lift the conversion rate for [your conversion goal].

For example, you may believe your headline doesn't fulfill the internal urgency your shoppers are feeling. Your hypothesis may be:

Changing our current headline...

Quality widgets since 1997

...into...

Next-day widget delivery with free shipping over $50

...will lift our conversion rate for...

Ecommerce sales

A strong hypothesis will clarify the purpose of your experiment.

You can create hypotheses about any of the six conversion factors, but some of the most insightful tests you can run will aim at the core of the LIFT Model—your value proposition.

Testing Your Value Proposition

You need to discover your best value proposition to have the best chance to close the most sales. Emphasizing the most important parts of your value proposition will maximize your conversion rate.

When you run experiments to discover your best value proposition, you gain more than just a conversion rate lift on a single page. You gain a valuable insight that can be leveraged across your other marketing activities.

So, how do you know which features are most important to your customers?

Traditionally, marketers have relied solely on their own thinking to come up with the right features to create and emphasize. They might do some customer research, focus groups, or a survey.

Today, there's a better way.

By testing different value proposition approaches, you can find out what works best with statistical certainty before committing to one assumed positioning.

I like to use a framework adapted from Joel E. Urbany and James H. Davis (`https://hbr.org/2007/11/strategic-insight-in-three-circles`). The following Venn diagram encourages you to think about your Points of Parity (POPs), Points of Difference (PODs) and Points of Irrelevance (POIs):

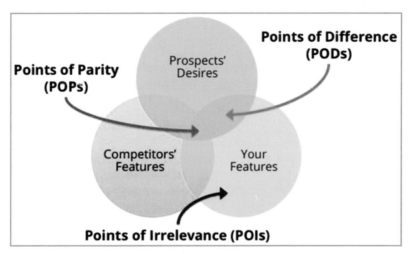

Identifying Points of Difference in your value proposition can give you powerful hypotheses to test.

➤ Points of Parity (POPs)

These are the features you offer that are important to your prospects that you also share with your competitors. Think of them as the basic entry requirements to the game. Your prospects need to know that you offer the POPs, but emphasizing them won't impress anyone.

➤ Points of Difference (PODs)

Here's where you can win the game. These are the features that are important to your prospects and not available from your competitors.

➤ Points of Irrelevance (POIs)

All the other features that you offer, but aren't interesting to your prospects are Points of Irrelevance (POIs).

Your PODs are where you want to focus. These are the features you can emphasize that will move your prospects to action. They're your differentiators.

Once you've discovered what you believe to be your best PODs, your work is not quite done. You have some good ideas. Now, you should test them.

Your landing pages are some of the best areas to test value proposition approaches. Create separate variations of your page, each emphasizing a different POD and run controlled A/B tests to find your winners. Then, use the PODs you discover to destroy your competition.

GUEST SPOT   **Get More Out Of Your Split Testing with Documentation and Post-Test Analysis**

Bobby Hewitt

Bobby Hewitt is the president and founder of Creative Thirst, the conversion rate optimization agency that focuses exclusively on increasing revenue and average order value for companies selling direct-to-consumer health products and natural health supplements.

If we don't understand where we've been, it's very hard to figure out where we're going. Where do we start? With systematic documentation.

Keeping track of your split test data is no easy task, which is why documentation is often overlooked. Yet, it's vital to a successful optimization program. Done correctly, it acts as a resource of past performance and provides a knowledge base of insights across time. Plus you can develop many new hypotheses for future tests from past inspiration.

As a fictitious example, suppose we wanted to A/B test which treatment of testimonials had a bigger impact on sales. For this test, we're going to take our existing customer testimonials that are on the control page and restyle them to have more of a Facebook type of look.

Control and Treatment 1 test examples showing the differences in the visual treatment of the testimonials being tested.

Naming Convention for Your Tests

First we'll give our test a descriptive name that includes what we're testing, the product or page category, as well as a test ID number, as shown in the following figure.

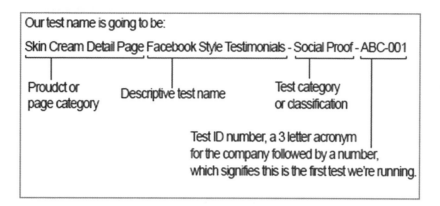

Test Type:

A/B, Multivariate, etc.

Goal:

State the goal in a sentence. For example: *Increase the sales of skin cream xyz.*

Primary Metric:

Metric you will use to measure success: *Conversion Rate, Average Order Value*, etc. If we have two metrics, we'll also document the second metric.

Background:

Any specific information that provides context. Is this a follow-up test? Is this test being launched for a particular reason? Is this test running during a seasonal slump or high period? Include any information that we might want to know when we're looking back on this test a year from now.

For this test it might be why we're testing this particular treatment. For example: *Our audience is somewhat active on social media, but we're not sure how influential it is to purchase intent.*

Primary Question:

States what you're trying to accomplish with this test in the form of a question starting with the word "which" (e.g., *Which testimonial treatment will get more visitors to buy our skin cream product?*).

Hypothesis:

The hypothesis section simply presents what you think will happen: *If social media plays a factor in social proof, then more visitors will buy our skin cream as measured by conversion rate.*

Treatments:

The specific combination of test variables and values.

Variables:

Describe the variables we're testing. A variable is a general element that you intend to test (e.g., *Headline, Image, Price,* etc.).

The variable in this test is the testimonials section.

continues

continued

Values:

Describe the values we're testing. A value is the specific variation you are testing. If your variable is the headline then your values would be the different versions of that headline.

The values of this test are what the different testimonials sections look like: *The control is all text. Variation 1 is presented to mimic the look of a Facebook conversation.*

URLs:

List the URLs of the test pages if this is an A/B Test (e.g., *Control URL*, *Variation 1 URL*, etc.), including the primary goal URL and any secondary goal URLs if you have them.

Traffic Source:

Because different traffic types convert differently, we want to include the primary traffic type that will be driven to the test. For example, *cold traffic, email promo traffic, affiliate traffic*, etc.

Note: Targeting Specific Traffic Sources   Targeting specific traffic sources is available with some split testing vendors. However, you can also segment a traffic source by driving specific traffic to a landing page that you've targeted for a test.

Test Period

Log the date the test started as well as the end date once the test is concluded.

Final Results

Record the number of visits and conversions each treatment received as well as the final conversion rates of each. Also, record the statistical confidence level reached and the percentage of improvement.

TABLE A.1 Final comparison of key metrics for control and treatment.

	Control	Treatment 1
Conversions	235	294
Visits	5,276	5,283
Conversion Rate	4.45%	5.56%

Statistical Confidence: 95%

Total Results: 25% Increase in Conversion Rate

Treatment 1 is the winner!

Insights

The Insights section is reserved for after you've finished your post-test analysis, which we'll unpack in just a minute. You'll use this area to write out what you learned from the test, and about your visitors.

Appendix

Finally, the appendix section is a collection of screenshots of each test treatment, so that you can refer to what the pages actually looked like during the test period.

Once your split test has conclusive results, you'll know if you had a lift or not, but your work is not over, yet. Maximizing the impact of conversion optimization to the bottom line requires more than knowing which treatment won.

Using the Decision Insight Post-Test Analysis Framework you'll be able to maximize your optimization program by answering the question: *"What do the results of this test tell me about my visitors?"*

DECISION INSIGHT FRAMEWORK

The decision insight post-test analysis framework (registered trademark of Creative Thirst, LLC).

When you understand the *why* behind *what* happened, you can get to the root of customer insight, and compound your optimization efforts across your entire organization.

Test Outcome

The first step in the framework is to examine the outcome of your test. Did one of the treatments win or lose?

Hypothesis

Go back to your initial hypothesis and look for evidence that supports that it was proven.

In the case where your hypothesis has been disproven, is there evidence that suggests a different hypothesis?

To find such evidence, the framework takes a multi-step approach.

Evidence

In the first step of analysis we look at click map and scroll reach data with Crazy Egg to see behavior at a broad level.

The click map reveals that visitors are clicking on the Facebook style testimonial treatments, perhaps they are expecting it to link out to Facebook or they expect to comment and or like certain testimonials.

The average scroll reach of the page supports that visitors are scrolling to the area where our testimonial treatments have been presented.

continues

continued

Behavior

In the second step, we go deeper, by viewing individual screen recordings gathered during the test, using a tool like HotJar or Inspectlet. Observing the behaviors of visitors, and noting the mouse movements, pauses, clicks, and scrolls.

Pro Tip: Segment Recordings   Segment recordings into two groups: those that converted and those that did not. You can even further segment based on desktop versus mobile.

Insight

From watching visitor screen replays, we observe that visitors who purchased our skin cream interact more with the Facebook-style testimonials. In most cases the behavior on the top section of the page that has the product offer is virtually identical to both treatments. However, we do see mouse movement pausing on scrolling through both the Facebook-style testimonials.

In each step of analysis we write down the observed behavior for each test treatment in a series of bullet points.

For example our refined list might look like this:

➤ Pauses on scrolling to testimonial section.
➤ Scrolls slower over Facebook treatments.
➤ Moves mouse horizontally over Facebook style testimonials as if reading with their mouse.
➤ Scrolls back up to purchase after reviewing testimonials.

Once we have a refined list, we ask the question, what does this behavior suggest about the action the visitor took? And create yet another list, adding what each behavior suggests.

For example:

Behavior:	This Suggests:
Pauses on scrolling to testimonial section.	Testimonials are acting as a speed bump slowing them down to read.
Scrolls slower over Facebook treatment.	
Moves mouse horizontally over Facebook-style testimonials as if reading with their mouse.	They are consuming the content.
	More evidence point to them reading the testimonials.
Scrolls back up to purchase after reviewing testimonials.	The testimonial treatment is influencing purchase.

By analyzing each behavior this way, we can see inside the prospects mental decision process.

Connecting the dots uncovers the *why* of *what* happened and we can glean insight by mapping our test results to the specific behavior visitors performed during our test. In other words, visitors from the winning converting group behaved this way. And visitors from the losing group behaved this other way. This helps us answer our ultimate insight question: What does this tell us about the visitor?

The insights for this test might be something like: If visitors are more engaged with the Facebook style testimonials than the control, then perhaps this means that they are more influenced by social proof. We would then add this to the insights section of our test document.

What this may tell us about our visitors is that Facebook is influential on purchase decisions.

If this is the case, then some key opportunities that we should pursue as a business might be:

1. Increase our Facebook sponsored post marketing.
2. Create a Facebook specific-campaign funnel.

You never know what gold nuggets you're going to uncover from conducting posttest analysis. But in any case, a deeper insight into the visitors behavior can be used to develop new hypotheses to test, create new product lines, change how you manage customer service, etc. The possibilities are endless and true optimization across your entire organization then becomes possible.

Downloadable Resource

Download the Creative Thirst Test Document template to use on your next split test at `www.e-nor.com/gabook`.

GUEST SPOT **Tips for Success with A/B Testing**

Tara Dunn

Tara Dunn is a Digital Analytics Consultant at E-Nor.

In the ever enriching world of Web optimization, we now have the luxury of choosing between several visual editor/WYSIWYG testing tools. These tools make it easier than ever to plan, implement, and monitor a test. The challenge that marketers are now discovering is that with such a user-friendly interface for testing, it can be easy to get overexcited and quickly create tests that are not optimized for success.

In addition to the strategies for hypothesis generation, test documentation, and test analysis offered by Chris Goward and Bobby Hewitt, these are my tips for you to use, to avoid creating ineffective tests and take advantage of some of the deeper features of most visual editor-based testing tools.

Involve at Least One Designer, One Developer, and One Stakeholder in Your Testing

Often the problem with visual editor based testing tools is hand-in-hand with their key selling point–they enable *anyone* to get involved in testing. This can mean that marketers are responsible for optimizing their own landing pages, or that data analysts are suddenly directly involved in web development.

It's important to remember that when you're testing, you are making changes to the website. Although testing can (and should!) iterate at a separate schedule than normal Web releases, it still needs to be treated as part of the web development process. Involving a designer helps to

continues

ensure the test creative remains on point within your brand, and involving the developer helps to ensure that the test can and will work within the confines of your CMS. The stakeholder is there to make sure that the test is in line with overall business objectives.

When Creating and Editing Your Test, Make Sure to Select Exactly the Element You Want to Change

When you have many elements sharing the same space it can be tricky to select exactly the element you want to edit with your cursor. A fairly common scenario may be that you want to select a link, and you have a div container wrapped around a link wrapped around an image. Your cursor may select the image itself, rather than the link.

Most visual editor based tools offer a way to review and edit the code that is generated by the visual editor. This often requires a basic knowledge of jQuery and/or CSS.

Check Compatibility across All Browsers and Devices

While most tools attempt to prevent cross browser compatibility issues, you should always preview a test in a variety of browsers and devices. A call to action image that you want to test could look great on desktop, but move around the page or disappear completely with a responsive mobile design.

If you do not like the way your test variation appears in mobile, you can either adjust your variation to be responsive with some clever CSS, or you can often opt to exclude the test from mobile devices using your audience targeting settings.

Additionally, most tools offer a way to generate some form of preview link to help you to discuss the A/B test and QA internally before pushing live. This is a great way to involve your teams in testing and get stakeholder sign-off as well.

Always Test at Least Two Variations

I am often tempted to ignore my own rule with this one, but I promise it's a valuable one! Testing one variation will only answer "Does this change have an impact?" So you will only get a yes or no answer. Testing two variations enables you to answer a wider range of questions and develop new hypotheses. "How much of an impact does this change have compared to alternatives? Why does one variation outperform the other? Which of these options is the best way to improve conversion rate?"

Thankfully most tools help you make additional variations quickly, by allowing you to copy existing variations. This way, you are not starting from scratch each time. Once you've copied a variation, you can simply adjust the copy variation as desired.

Communicate, Communicate, Communicate

Consider who may be impacted by this test. I've had it happen several times where an exciting test was completely derailed because of some external factor that could have been avoided with better communication. Say your design team has launched a new test, but the marketing team was not informed. Turns out, an email with a promotional offer was being sent out at that time, but the landing page doesn't reflect that promotion in the test variations. With all of this happening live, either the marketing promotion or the test must come to a screeching halt.

Document and share with your teams:

➤ The objective of the test. Why are we doing this?
➤ Who this test impacts. What audiences will see the test and why?

➤ The run dates of the test. When do we anticipate results? When will we start and stop testing?

➤ What the test looks like so they will know what to expect. Include screenshots or send preview links.

You can utilize some features of your analytics tools and often the test reporting tools to add a little more control to this, as well. You can set up a scheduled email with a custom report and a message to remind internal teams of the test and share progress effortlessly.

When targeting test audiences in your testing tool, you usually have the option to include or exclude certain marketing efforts. For example, you can exclude users who come from email campaigns by excluding the URL query parameters that indicate they are from email. You can also usually block the test from certain IP addresses, such as your internal teams. Consider that it may be beneficial for your internal teams to have visibility to the test, however.

If you follow these tips, your tests may still fail, but you will not fail to get actionable insights from them.

GUEST SPOT   **Testing Mobile Apps with Optimizely**

Tara Dunn

Creating a mobile app is a massive undertaking in and of itself. For each new version release, your team must plan, document, design, code, QA, and finally submit to the Apple or Android store for review. If someone wants to introduce a change at any point in the future, the whole process starts over again. The idea of introducing yet another element, testing, to mobile app development can seem like a step in the way of progress.

So Why Do A/B Testing on a Mobile App?

One of the biggest reasons actually has to do with the way mobile apps have to be released. Unlike a website, where changes can be pushed live within minutes or even seconds, a mobile app is actually downloaded by the user onto their device. Think of it as being similar to installing Microsoft Word onto a Mac or a PC. So rolling out new features or bug fixes can *only* be done by submitting a new version of your app to the app store for review, and hopefully publication.

Testing allows you to try out variations to your app without going through the entire mobile app development process each time. If a test fails, you can roll it back without your developers ever having to build it into a finished release. You can also conduct a phased rollout, with only a small percentage of users seeing the variation when it is first pushed live in your experiment. Most importantly, testing enables you to make data driven decisions. Knowing not only whether a new feature had an impact or not, but also the magnitude of the impact, will help you to make key design and development changes to your app as time goes on.

Optimizely offers A/B testing for both iOS and Android devices. Note that Optimizely does not currently offer support for Unity—we would recommend checking out Splitforce or Leanplum for Unity app testing. Optimizely is well known for their huge testing community, great documentation, and stellar customer support.

I'll use Optimizely for the specific examples below, but note that many of these tips and philosophies work for other mobile app testing tools as well.

continues

continued

Plan Ahead

Although you'll find that tools like Optimizely will likely save some time in the long run, you will need to invest some time towards your initial planning and implementation. Consider these questions:

➤ What are the key aspects of my app's functionality? Examples: add to cart, create an account, subscribe to users, post, share, list products, updates in push notifications.
➤ What are the distinguishing features of my app that separate me from my competitors? Examples: Frequent promotions, simple navigation, easy return policy.
➤ Who are the different types of users I want to target my tests to? Examples: new adopters, frequent users, high revenue, business specific categories.
➤ What are the different stages in the lifecycle of my app?
➤ Will I conduct staged rollouts of my tests? If so, what is my rollout plan?

The answers to these questions will help you to plan out the inclusion of your testing tool in your next app release. For example, you might identify that your percent discount is something you will regularly want to experiment with.

Testing Ideas

A great place to start is the user's first impression. By improving your "forgot my password" prompts, you may be able to increase your successful login rate. You may also be able to drive influence into the app store by experimenting with the notification in your app asking users to submit a review.

For existing users, the goal is to keep them coming back to your app regularly. Testing the frequency and nature of push notifications is a great way to impact your retention rate. You can also test different motivators to create an account, such as access to new content, so that you can reengage from other platforms as well.

To test your conversion process, it is recommended to evaluate any form fill processes to ensure they are easy to understand and short. You can experiment with your discounts and promotions as well, to find a good motivation/profit margin balance.

Create Your Experiments

Optimizely offers three features to help you implement tests on mobile apps. The first one is the visual editor, which is easy to use and intuitive to understand. You can click on elements and select options to modify their position, color, size, and much more.

The second feature is Optimizely's Live Variables. With this feature, you would identify in your app all the elements related to the percent discount. You could then use Optimizely as many times as desired in the future to experiment with different discount levels.

The last feature is Optimizely's Code Blocks. This feature enables you to identify which code to run in your experiment variation. This feature works very well for a variety of uses, such as testing entire new forms or releasing an experiment to your users slowly by using a staged approach.

Note that you can use any of these features in combination. For example, you could use Code Blocks to serve different variations of a form, but then use the visual editor to tweak the form styles.

QA Your Work

There is no escaping QA! Thankfully Optimizely helps to simplify QA by offering a preview mode, which you can share with other developers if needed. Optimizely also offers some developer debugging tools, such as Optimizely's data object.

A nice feature of Optimizely is that the Optimizely datafile is downloaded by the SDK every two minutes by default. So if the user accesses the app and is put into an experiment but then travels somewhere where their phone is out of network, they will continue to see the variation because the data for that variation is now stored on their device.

Launch & Analyze

This is usually my favorite part of any experiment. It's addictive to monitor the data as it pours in, and figure out how your test idea actually performed! If it doesn't happen to perform so well, you can very quickly shift the experiment in Optimizely to show the original to 100% of users.

Optimizely offers a clean and friendly reporting interface, with data backed by their impressive stats engine. Their stats engine is meticulously fine-tuned to provide users performance data that is as accurate and reliable as possible, so that you know if your variation really won or lost in the experiment.

Although I have seen the stats engine evolve to be more and more reliable over the years, I will continue to consistently encourage a culture of questioning data and doing deeper analysis to better understand the depth and breadth of the experiment's impact. Integration with other analytics tools can really help with this deeper dive. Optimizely's mobile app testing solution integrates with Universal Analytics and Mixpanel, as well as Amplitude and Localytics, which are mobile specific analytics platforms. Integration with Universal Analytics offers a wide array of additional dimensions for analysis, such as landing screen and custom events.

Optimizely will likely continue to expand their integration offering in the future, to be more on par with the much more extensive list of integrations offered to Optimizely website experiments.

In Summary

One final benefit of testing that wasn't covered earlier is that it lays a foundation to help you personalize your app. An example of this would be if you found that targeting notifications to new product shoppers boosted your conversion rate, you could use that information or possibly even the testing tool itself to implement that feature for that specific audience in your mobile app.

If you have a mobile app and you aren't testing it, it's time to get started!

MARKETING AUTOMATION AND PERSONALIZATION

One of the primary themes of the book has been segmentation: analyzing your data based on audience subsets rather than aggregates to amplify trends and more quickly gain insight. We also learned how we can use segments, aka audiences, to remarket based on specific visitor characteristics and behaviors.

If we analyze and market to specific audience segments, it's a logical next step to actually offer a customized experience to different types of visitors. Below, Mike Telem introduces an RTP (real-time personalization) platform that allows us to present different images and messaging based on previous behaviors and (anonymous) CRM data. He also discusses the integration of company "firmographics" data for both personalization and analysis.

GUEST SPOT   **Marketing Automation and Google Analytics: Integration and Personalization**

Mike Telem

Mike Telem is vice president of product marketing, real-time personalization at Marketo, the leader in digital marketing software and solutions.

As two of the main pillars in your marketing toolbox, Marketing Automation (MA) and Web analytics can work together to provide valuable and actionable information about the interactions of your prospects and customers in ways that neither platform can do as well on its own. An MA platform, such as Marketo, benefits from the rich interaction reporting and flexible segmentation that Web analytics provides, while a Web analytics platform such as Google Analytics benefits from the broader offsite or offline data that MA can provide, including anonymous, non-PII visitor firmographics, email campaigns, social media campaigns and interactions, trade show and convention attendance, and, to some extent, face-to-face interactions via CRM data.

However, the integration between these two tech assets isn't fully utilized until you have all of the relevant data flowing between them. With MA data available in GA, you can segment your GA reports based on this richer set of data that includes offline interactions and firmographics, which in turn provides tightly focused optimization opportunities. If, for example, you create a segment for the financial services industry and note a high drop-off at a certain point in the Behavior Flow or Goal Flow reports, you can take advantage of the personalization capabilities in the MA platform to display customized content to that segment at the drop-off point instead of the more generic default content, as displayed in Figure A.7.

Real-time Web personalization—the capability to dynamically change the user experience based on his or her attributes—furthers the potential of this integration by not only reporting on interactions but also optimizing them on the fly—not just reporting based on segments, but presenting different messaging and imagery based on these segments.

Modern marketers are leveraging the capabilities and data that exists in MA, especially if it includes real-time personalization capabilities, and GA to achieve the following objectives:

➤ B2B Data enrichment and advanced analytics.
➤ Personalized Web experiences and performance data.
➤ Personalized remarketing ads.

For those MA platforms that provide out-of-the box integration with GA (yes, Marketo does, I must admit) it is literally just flipping on a switch: the same JavaScript tag that sends data to GA is then used to enrich Google Analytics through the Google Analytics API with relevant info that your MAP has on both anonymous and known visitors.

B2B Data Enrichment and Advanced Analytics

B2B marketers care a lot about which companies people work at, how big the companies are, and what industry they belong to. Marketers would rather focus on specific groups of companies in targeted account lists where they can be more successful by driving more revenue or closing deals faster (an approach typically referred to as ABM [Account-Based

Marketing]). Marketers also care very much about people's job title, role, and their stage in the sales cycle or lead score. All of this information exists in select marketing automation platforms but not in GA. Enriching GA with anonymous *firmographics* data such as the visitor's company, industry, size, and revenue (yes, even if that visitor is still anonymous) to provide more precise analytics for the B2B marketer and leveraging GA's extensive reporting capabilities together allow you to understand which ads drove not just the most clicks but which one drove the most clicks and conversions from target accounts or which referring channels were more effective in driving C-level exec's to your site.

By adding lead and firmographics data as a secondary dimension to your Acquisition reports, you could also correlate which channels and campaigns drove more opportunities and deals within different audience segments and place more budget on those traffic channels that eventually impacted more revenue. (See Figures A.5, A.6, and A.7 below.)

	Industry ?	Sessions ↓ ?	Lead Submission (Goal 1 Conversion Rate) ?	Lead Submission (Goal 1 Completions) ?
		24,449 % of Total: 13.00% (18,841)	**0.69%** Avg for View: 0.82% (-15.62%)	**177** % of Total: 10.97% (155)
☐	1. Education	**5,641** (23.03%)	0.53%	30 (17.65%)
☐	2. Telecommunications	**2,888** (11.76%)	0.00%	40 (23.53%)
☐	3. Software & Internet	**2,839** (11.56%)	0.71%	19 (11.76%)
☐	4. Business Services	**2,372** (9.68%)	2.11%	50 (29.41%)
☐	5. Retail	**1,850** (7.55%)	0.54%	11 (5.88%)

FIGURE A.5 This custom report is showing performance by industry, one of the several types of firmographic data that Marketo can provide to Google Analytics as custom dimensions.

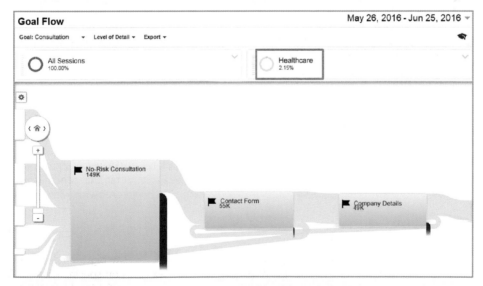

FIGURE A.6 You can apply segments based on lead status and firmographics data to your flow reports to identify where those audience segments are dropping off.

continues

continued

Top 10 Orgs		
Organization	Visits	Pages / Visit
Samsung	10	2.60
Panasonic	8	1.20
Microsoft Corporation	6	1.67
Yale University	5	2.20
HITACHI DATA SYSTEMS	5	4.00
ACADEMY OF ART UNIVERSITY	4	1.25
Amazon.com	4	1.00
Google	4	2.00
Bank of America	4	4.50
SALESFORCE.COM	4	1.50

ABM		
Event Action	Unique Visitors	Pages / Session
ABM | Dream Accounts	1,231	2.90
ABM | Existing Customers	329	1.77
ABM | Lost Opportunities	195	2.17

Job Role / Product from CRM		
Event Action	Unique Visitors	Pages /Session
Software & Internet / Product A	2,785	2.46
CRM | Score 50+	662	2.60
Persona | CTOs	527	2.62
Persona | CIOs	410	2.92
Financial Services / Product B	358	2.49

FIGURE A.7 This Google Analytics dashboard displays lead and firmographic data.

Personalized Web Campaign Performance Data

Personalizing the Web experience based on various attributes such as location, behavior and known lead data is becoming common practice. No need to explain why providing the right message to the right person at the right time works to your benefit, whether you're selling cars, watches, servers or software. Imagine someone visiting your site from an insurance company: shouldn't they see relevant case studies and videos on your home page and across their visit to your site? How about returning visitors to your site or, moreover, people who have already purchased from you before: should they have the same experience and see the same offers as first timers? Of course not.

The reasoning for real-time Web personalization is clear. However, tying the performance of these targeted page variations to your main web analytics platform is essential to see the overall impact on engagement levels (# of visits, pages viewed, time on site, etc.), goals (click-throughs, lead conversions, purchased, etc.) and bottom-line revenue. With the personaliza-tion variations appearing in GA as events, we can create segments based on these variations and measure goal and Ecommerce outcomes for visitors who saw the variation vs. visitors who saw the default, as shown in Figure A.8. (The *Behavioral Segments* section in Chapter 10 discusses segmentation based on events.)

Personalized Remarketing Ads

Remarketing ads have been with us for a few years now and have proven to be very effec-tive compared to regular display ads and other advertising methods. However, these ads are still not too personal as they are based mainly on pages or products viewed on the site, geo-location, and other.

By sharing valuable MA information with GA, you can define your Google remarketing ads based on firmographic and lead/contact data in addition to the other built-in GA dimensions. (Defining a remarketing audience is described in detail in "AdWords Remarketing with Google Analytics Audiences" in Chapter 14.) Imagine being able to show ads only to the audiences you care about the most such as prospects using your competitor's software or individuals from the finance industry or shoppers that previously bought a specific product and are marked as VIPs in your database. Unleashing the power of this data with your ads means much better ROI on a budget that is typically quite large.

FIGURE A.8 An MA platform such as Marketo allow you to personalize a landing page by industry, as in this example, or other firmographics data, and report the performance of personalized variation in Google Analytics.

Benefits of Integration

As part of the ongoing evolution towards a more user-centric approach to marketing, sales, and Web analytics, the integration of Marketing Automation and Google Analytics provides a big leap forward. For more information, see Marketo's "Definitive Guide to Web Personalization" at https://www.marketo.com/software/web-personalization/.

Appendix B: Resources

Checklists and Code

Resources below are available at: www.e-nor.com/gabook.

Google Analytics Implementation Checklist
Includes all of the implementation steps described in this book and is updated as changes to Google Analytics and Google Tag Manager warrant.

Google Analytics Reporting Checklists
Checklists to help focus on important metrics for a variety of sectors, including retail, media, health care, insurance, finance, and government.

Scripts
Event autotracker, YouTube, and scroll tracking scripts discussed in the book.

Google Documentation, Learning Resources, and Tools

Google Analytics Academy
Five courses for the beginning to intermediate level. The *Digital Analytics Fundamentals* course as a useful review for core concepts and techniques in Google Analytics. Other courses on Google Tag Manager, Google Analytics Ecommerce, and Google Analytics for Mobile Apps.

Google Analytics and Google Tag Manager Help Centers
Structured documentation on the range of Google Analytics and Google Tag Manager functionality.

Google Analytics YouTube Channel
Wide range of instructional and informational videos on GA, GTM, and AdWords.

Google Analytics for Android (on Udacity)
Built by Google and hosted on Udacity, this outstanding course examines Google Analytics implementation for Android either through GA native-code SDK for Android or through GTM for Android.

Google Analytics Changelog

RSS feed of Google Analytics changes at https://developers.google.com/analytics/changelogs/xml/analytics.xml

Google Analytics Developer Center

Links to a wide range of documentation and tools.

Google Analytics Dimensions and Metrics Explorer

Lists all dimensions and metrics available through the Core Reporting API (which corresponds to most of the dimensions and metrics visible in the GA Web UI).

Google Analytics Query Explorer

Fun and useful tool for building queries to the Core Reporting API.

Google Analytics Hit Builder

Allows you to construct and validate Measurement Protocol hits.

Google Analytics Spreadsheet Add-on

Easy access of Google Analytics data in Google spreadsheets.

Google PageSpeed Insights

Provides recommendations for page speed optimization on desktop and mobile, which should benefit user experience as well as organic ranking.

Google Search Console

With reports on organic clickthroughs and URL query parameters that you can consolidate in GA, Google Search Console is an extremely useful and highly recommended complement to Google Analytics.

Social

Google Analytics Group on Google Plus

Great variety of new and interesting posts. (Managed directly by the Google Analytics team.)

Google Tag Manager Group on Google Plus

Actively monitored group with a focus on GTM.

Google Analytics LinkedIn Group

Fairly active forum on a range of GA-related topics.

Google Analytics on Twitter

Follow @googleanalytics for updates.

Blogs

analytics.blogspot.com
www.e-nor.com/blog
gademos.com
brianclifton.com/blog
lunametrics.com/blog

cardinalpath.com/blog
analyticspros.com/blog
plus.google.com/+StephaneHamel-immeria
simoahava.com
optimizesmart.com
kaushik.net/avinash
marketingexperiments.com/blog

Podcasts

Digital Analytics Power Hour
Landing Page Optimization
Marketing Optimization
Jeffalytics

Books

Successful Analytics by Brian Clifton

Brian followed up the first three editions of his seminal *Advanced Web Metrics* with this important new volume, written from a higher-level business perspective and expert experience.

Practical Google Analytics and Google Tag Manager for Developers by Jonathan Weber

Very helpful strategies and keen insights for Google Analytics deployment through Google Tag Manager.

Google Analytics Integrations by Daniel Waisberg

Interesting discussions and key tips on a broad range of Google Analytics integrations with other environments such as AdSense, email, and offline data.

Google BigQuery Analytics by Jordan Tigani and Siddharth Naidu

For a very well written and thought out technical dive into BiqQuery, this book is your resource.

Web Analyics 2.0 by Avinash Kaushik

A perpetual classic, and the foundation of the analytics and optimization canon.

Landing Page Optimization by Tim Ash and Laura Ginty

Not to be missed, the book provides a great foundation in optimization principles and techniques for your landing pages (and every page on your website).

Don't Make Me Think by Steve Krug

Steve drives home the point that we must always put our end-users first. A short, entertaining read that will influence your thinking on usability and optimization.

Mobile Usability by Jakob Nielsen and Raluca Budiu

Mobile usability factors from the usability thought leaders at the Nielsen Norman Group.

You Should Test That **by Chris Goward**

Expert perspectives and strategies for your testing program, very well written and very actionable.

Buyer Legends: The Executive Storyteller's Guide **by Bryan Eisenberg and Jeffrey Eisenberg**

As an addition to their major contributions in optimization research and guidance, Bryan and Jeffrey map out a business process that combines the emotional power of storytelling with hard data to open new opportunities.

Building a Digital Analytics Organization: Create Value by Integrating Analytical Processes, Technology, and People into Business Operations *by Judah Phillips*

An enlightening, tool-independent strategy guide to establishing and driving analytics in the enterprise.

Measuring the Digital World: Using Digital Analytics to Drive Better Digital Experiences *by Gary Angel*

Valuable, actionable, thought-provoking work about analytics for measurable improvement across many verticals.

Career

Google Analytics Individual Qualification (GAIQ)

After completing this book, reviewing the GAIQ study guide provided by Google, and practicing everything within a Google Analytics account, you should be very well positioned for passing the GAIQ.

Digital Analytics Association

Take advantage of learning resources, career development guidance, certification, and live events where you can directly connect with your analytics peers.

Index

W

Y